THE GEOGRAPHY OF TOURISM AND RECREATION

The fully updated third edition of this highly successful and acclaimed text continues to offer a comprehensive synthesis of the key issues associated with the area of tourism, leisure and recreation. It provides a cohesive overview of the landmark studies that exist within tourism, leisure and recreation at a time of rapid growth in the subject area. The book offers the reader a series of chapters which not only explain how important tourism and leisure are in modern society, but also outline the key contributions made by geographers in the global growth of tourism and leisure research.

The chapters within the book explore:

- the supply and impacts of, and the demand for recreation and tourism
- recreation and tourism in urban, rural and coastal environments
- recreation and tourism in wilderness areas and national parks
- recreation and tourism policy and planning
- the future of recreation and tourism and the role of geography in applied research.

While this third edition retains the successful format and structure of previous editions with a wide range of maps and plates, it is completely revised and redeveloped to accommodate new case studies, summary points and learning objectives for students. The global focus of the text is retained, with a greater emphasis on North America as outbound and destination areas, as well as the importance of less developed countries and the critical issues of inequality, exploitation, underdevelopment and globalisation as powerful forces affecting tourism and leisure.

C. Michael Hall is Professor and Head of the Department of Tourism, University of Otago, New Zealand; Gästforskare, Department of Social and Economic Geography, Umeå University, Sweden; and Docent, Department of Geography, Oulu University, Finland.

Stephen J. Page is Scottish Enterprise Forth Valley Chair in Tourism, Department of Marketing, University of Stirling, Scotland.

THE GEOGRAPHY OF TOURISM AND RECREATION

Environment, place and space

Third edition

C. Michael Hall and Stephen J. Page

Routledge
Taylor & Francis Group

LONDON AND NEW YORK

First published 1999
by Routledge
2 Park Square, Milton Park, Abingdon, Oxon OX14 4RN

Simultaneously published in the USA and Canada
by Routledge
270 Madison Avenue, New York, NY 10016

Second Edition 2002

Third Edition 2006

Reprinted 2007

Routledge is an imprint of the Taylor & Francis Group, an informa business

© 1999, 2002, 2006 C. Michael Hall and Stephen J. Page

Typeset in Sabon by Keystroke, Jacaranda Lodge, Wolverhampton
Printed and bound in Great Britain by Bell & Bain Ltd, Glasow

British Library Cataloguing in Publication Data
A catalogue record for this book is available from the British Library

Library of Congress Cataloging in Publication Data
Hall, Colin Michael, 1961–
The geography of tourism and recreation : environment, place, and space /
C. Michael Hall and Stephen J. Page.–3rd ed.
p. cm.
Includes bibliographical references and index.
ISBN 0–415–33560–4 (hardcover) – ISBN 0–415–33561–2 (softcover)
1. Tourism. 2. Recreation. 3. Recreation areas. I. Page, Stephen, 1963– II. Title.
G155.A1H343 2005
338.4'791–dcc22   2004028639

ISBN10: 0–415–33560–4   ISBN13: 9–78–0–415–33560–7(hbk)
ISBN10: 0–415–33561–2   ISBN13: 9–78–0–415–33561–4(pbk)

CONTENTS

List of plates   xi
List of figures   xv
List of tables   xvii
Acknowledgements   xix

1 INTRODUCTION: TOURISM MATTERS!   1
   Tourism, Recreation, Leisure and Mobility   3
   The Issue of Scale: Empiricism, Paradigms and Transformations   7
   Development of the Geography of Tourism and Recreation   8
   Status of the Geography of Tourism and Recreation   11
   Knowledge   12
   Action: Development of an Applied Geography of Tourism and Recreation   20
   Culture   24
   *Insight: The Geography of Tourism and Recreation Outside the Anglo-American
   Tradition*   28
   Transforming the Geography of Tourism and Recreation   30
   Questions   32
   Reading   32

2 THE DEMAND FOR RECREATION AND TOURISM   33
   Geographers and Demand: Historical Perspectives   33
   Recreational Demand   35
   Barriers to Recreation   41
   Seasonality   43
   Financial Resources and Access to Recreational Opportunity   44
   Gender and Social Constraints   45
   The Geography of Fear in Recreation and Leisure Spaces: Gender-based Barriers
   to Participation   46

*Case Study: The Geography of Fear and Recreational Participation Implications for
Exclusion*   47
    The Geography of Fear and Urban Park Use in Leicester   48
    Summary Points   50
Social Exclusion: Conditioning Leisure Participation   50
Resources and Fashions   52
Walking as a Leisure Pursuit: A Function of Resources and Fashion   53
Case Study: Myles Dunphy and the Australian Bushwalking Movement   54
Measuring Recreational Demand   57
Problems and Methods of Measuring Recreational Demand   57
Time Budget Survey Techniques   58
National Evaluations of Recreational Demand: International Perspectives   61
Regional Demand for Leisure and Recreation in London   64
Spatial Analysis of Demand at the Micro Level: Site Surveys   65
Tourism Demand   67
What is Tourism Demand?   68
Tourist Motivation   68
Maslow's Hierarchy Model and Tourist Motivation   70
Measurement of Tourism Demand: Tourism Statistics   73
Defining Tourism   75
Technical Definitions of Tourism   76
Domestic Tourism Statistics   79
International Tourism Statistics   81
Methodological Issues   82
Patterns of Tourism: International Perspectives   84
Patterns of Global Tourism   84
Patterns of Domestic Tourism   86
New Zealand Domestic Tourism Survey   87
Conclusions   89
Questions   90
Reading   90

3 THE SUPPLY OF RECREATION AND TOURISM   92
   The Supply Factor in Recreation   92
   How has the Geographer Approached the Analysis of Recreational Supply Issues? 93
   *Insight: Local Authority Expenditure on Leisure and Recreation Provision – Walsall
   Metropolitan Borough Council*   95
   Descriptive Research on Location and Travel   97
   Explanatory Research on Location and Travel   99
   Predictive Research on Location   100
   Normative Research on Location   101
   Supply and Demand in Recreational Contexts: Spatial Interactions   102
   The Green Belt Concept   105
   *Insight: Country Parks as a Spatial Recreational Tool: Intercepting Urban
   Recreationalists Seeking the Countryside*   106
   Multiple Use of Recreational Resources   109

The Supply of Tourism   109
Insight: The Destination Life Cycle   112
Towards a Critical Geography of Tourism Production   114
Insight: Economic Globalisation   118
International Hotel Chains   120
The Leisure Product   123
Role of the Public and Private Sector in Tourism Supply   123
Spatial Analytical Approaches to the Supply of Tourism Facilities   127
Tourist Facilities   132
Insight: Towards Geographical Analyses of Hospitality: Research Agendas   137
Conclusion   142
Questions   142
Reading   143

4   THE IMPACTS OF TOURISM AND RECREATION   144
Impacts: Recreation Resource Management   144
Carrying Capacity   147
Insight: The Recreation Opportunity Spectrum   150
The Limits of Acceptable Change   150
Insight: The Tourism Optimisation Management Model (TOMM)   151
Economic Analysis   154
Insight: The Economic Impact of Events   158
Analysis of Tourism's Social Impacts   159
Insight: Trafficking, Sex Tourism and Slavery   163
Physical Environmental Impacts   165
Conclusion   170
Questions   170
Reading   171

5   URBAN RECREATION AND TOURISM   172
Insight: Stanley Park, Vancouver   173
Geographical Approaches to Urban Recreation   174
Evolution of Urban Recreation in Britain   174
Urban Recreation: A Socio-geographic Perspective   175
The 1800s   177
The 1840s   177
The 1880s   178
The 1920s   178
The 1960s and Beyond   178
Case Study: The Evolution of Parks and Open Space in Victorian Leicester   180
   Park Development in Victorian Leicester   181
   Post-Victorian Park Development   181
   Summary Points   185
Methods of Analysing Urban Recreation   185
Urban Recreational Planning   188
Open Space Planning: Spatial Principles   189

*Case Study: The Management, Planning and Provision of Parks and Open Space
in the London Borough of Newham*   192
    Urban Park and Open Space Provision in London   193
    The London Borough of Newham   194
    Summary Points   196
Urban Tourism   196
Understanding the Neglect of Urban Tourism by Researchers   197
Approaches to Urban Tourism: Geographical Analysis   198
The Tourist Experience of Urban Tourism   201
Insight: Tourism in Capital Cities   203
The Urban Tourism Market: Data Sources   205
Urban Tourism: Behavioural Issues   206
Tourist Perception and Cognition of the Urban Environment   208
Tourism Cognitive Mapping   212
Insight: The Value of Urban Heritage Resources   213
Service Quality Issues in Urban Tourism   216
Significance of Urban Tourism   217
Conclusion   221
Questions   221
Reading   222

6   RURAL RECREATION AND TOURISM   223
In Pursuit of the Concept of 'Rural'   224
Conceptualising the Rural Recreation–Tourism Dichotomy   226
The Geographer's Contribution to Theoretical Debate in Rural Contexts   227
Towards a Concept of Rural Tourism   230
What Makes Rural Tourism Distinctive?   230
Rural Recreation and Tourism in Historical Perspective   232
The Geographer's Approach to Rural Recreation and Tourism   233
Studies of Demand   233
Supply of Rural Recreation   236
Impact of Rural Recreation   237
Insight: Second Homes in the Countryside   238
Rural Tourism: Spatial Analytical Approaches   241
Impact of Rural Tourism   241
Economic Impact   242
Environmental Effects of Rural Tourism   244
Insight: Wine, Food and Tourism   244
Recreation, Tourism and Sustainability   250
Conclusion   251
Questions   252
Reading   252

7   TOURISM AND RECREATION IN THE PLEASURE PERIPHERY:
WILDERNESS AND NATIONAL PARKS   253
The Changing Meaning of Wilderness in Western Society   253

Insight: What is the effect of World Heritage listing?   261
Environmental History of National Parks and Wilderness Areas   262
The Value of Wilderness   263
Insight: National Parks and Indigenous Peoples   267
Identifying Wilderness   269
Case Study: Wilderness Inventory in Australia   269
   Wilderness Inventories   270
   From Identification to Preservation   277
   Summary Points   278
Tourist and Recreational Demand for Wilderness, National Parks and Natural Areas   278
Supplying the Wilderness and Outdoor Recreation Experience   284
Insight: Peripheral Areas, Wilderness and Global Environmental Change   288
Conclusion   290
Questions   290
Reading   290

8   COASTAL AND MARINE RECREATION AND TOURISM   291
Coastline as a Recreation and Tourist Resource: Its Discovery and Recognition as a
Leisure Resource   292
The Geographer's Contribution to the Analysis of Coastal Recreation and Tourism   296
Historical Analysis of Recreation and Tourism in the Coastal Zone   298
Insight: Promotion of the Seaside Resort: Place-Promotion Strategies   298
Models of Coastal Recreation and Tourism   300
Tourist and Recreational Travel to the Coast   302
Tourist and Recreational Behaviour: Use and Activity Patterns in Coastal Environments   303
Environmental Perspectives on Coastal Recreation and Tourism   307
Integrated Coastal Zone Management   309
Insight: Cruise Tourism   311
Conclusion   312
Questions   314
Reading   314

9   TOURISM AND RECREATION PLANNING AND POLICY   315
Recreation Planning Policy   315
The Evolution of Leisure and Recreation Planning   315
Recreation Planning: The Concern with Space and Place   317
Tourism Planning and Policy   320
What is Tourism Planning?   321
Approaches to Tourism Planning   323
Co-operative and Integrated Control Systems   327
Insight: The Changing Role of Government and Sustainability   328
Development of Industry Co-ordination Mechanisms   330
Raising Consumer Awareness   331
Raising Producer Awareness   331
Insight: International Association of Antarctica Tour Operators (IAATO)   332
Strategic Planning to Supersede Conventional Approaches   332

Insight: Singapore: Tourism 21   334
Tourism Policy   335
Conclusion   339
Questions   341
Reading   342

10 THE FUTURE   343
Geography – The Discipline: Direction and Progress   344
Revisiting Applied Geography   345
Contributions   348
The Role of GIS and Tourism: A Tool for Applied Geographic Research   350
The Role of the Geographer in the New Millennium: Whither Tourism and Recreation?   352
Insight: The Future – The Ageing Population   355
Transformations?   356
Questions   357
Reading   358

Bibliography   359
Index   424

PLATES

1.1 Cambridge, England. Which of the people in this High Street scene are tourists or recreationalists? Researchers need to carefully differentiate between recreationalists and tourists.   3

1.2/1.3 Loch Lomond, Scotland. The retail mix can provide a major attraction for visitors, as in the case of the Loch Lomond Shores project, which is underpinned by an anchor tenant and a large visitor attraction.   20

1.4 National Park Gateway Centre, Loch Lomond and the Trossachs National Park, Scotland, provides visitor information and orientation at the southern boundary of and major visitor gateway to the park.   20

2.1 Disneyland, California, is a popular family setting for tourism and recreation. Personal security is a hallmark of its atmosphere.   45

2.2 Largs, west Scotland. Promenading illustrates that the Victorian and Edwardian Sunday constitutional walk is still a key feature in coastal resorts for day visitors and tourists.   70

2.3 Transport to connect peripheral locations such as islands provide a vital element in the supply chain and an attraction and activity in their own right.   70

3.1 San Francisco, California. Unlikely locations can be developed as tourism and recreational resources. This queue is for a visit to Alcatraz Prison.   93

3.2 Alcatraz Prison, San Francisco.   93

3.3 Stirling, Scotland. Events, such as the Highland Games have worldwide repute and are also hosted in other countries with Scottish migration as a form of cultural heritage (copyright: AILLST).   129

3.4 Trossachs, Scotland. Literature and art have popularised wilder areas, such as Sir Walter Scott's 'Lady of the Lake' in the Trossachs, as illustrated by visitors sailing on the SS *Sir Walter Scott* at Loch Katrine (copyright: AILLST).   129

3.5 Historic reconstructions such as a Scottish Medieval Fair provide an enticing experience for visitors in the urban environment (copyright: AILLST).   129

4.1 White Cliffs of Dover, Kent. How much of this footpath erosion is due to recreational versus tourist use?   147

4.2   Athens, Greece. Historic sites such as the Acropolis suffer visitor pressure and erosion
     of the built fabric.   147
4.3   Market scene, Vanuatu, South Pacific. Local communities can benefit from visitors if
     they are encouraged to patronise local facilities rather than being cocooned in the
     environmental bubble of resort hotels.   159
4.4   Tourist saturation in St Mark's Square, Venice, Italy.   164
4.5   Front of St Mark's Square, Venice. The unique marine environment provides
     opportunities for sustainable tourist transport as the water taxis (gondolas) show.   164
5.1/5.2   Margate, Kent. A Regency period seaside resort which has passed through a series
     of stages of development and is now mainly a day trip and low-price holiday
     destination. Once one of the major tourist resorts in England, the town is now trying
     to rejuvenate itself through heritage tourism, such as the development of the Turner
     Gallery.   197
5.3/5.4   London Docklands marketing images.   220
5.5   Entrance to the cathedral precinct, Canterbury, Kent. Crowding may have substantial
     impacts not only on the quality of the visitor experience but also on the attraction
     itself.   220
6.1   Souvenir shop, Leyden, The Netherlands. To what extent does tourism lead to cultural
     stereotyping and changed perceptions of cultural identity by both locals and tourists?   229
6.2   Sissinghurst, Kent. Rural heritage is a significant attraction base for rural tourism and
     recreation. Made famous through the writings and lifestyles of Vita Sackville-West
     and Harold Nicholson, Sissinghurst is an attraction for gardeners and literary-minded
     visitors alike.   234
6.3   Otago, New Zealand. Tourism and the development of new agricultural industries
     may often be interrelated. Vineyard development in Central Otago has not only
     been important for tourism development and amenity migration in the area but also
     benefited from cellar door sales.   234
6.4   Elga, Norway. Hunters, anglers and walkers serve as an important source of income
     for many small villages in Scandinavia.   242
6.5   Telluride, Colorado. Tourism has revitalised many former mining towns in the western
     United States through the development of resort and accommodation facilities.   242
6.6   Helsinki, Finland. The harbourfront producers' market attracts both locals and visitors
     and connects marine and rural producers with the city.   249
6.7   Savonlinna, Finland. Much of the tourist infrastructure of the rural municipality of
     Savonlinna is unused for most of the year because visitation is concentrated in the
     summer months.   249
7.1   Arizona. Some national parks are often under enormous pressure in terms of visitor
     numbers. The Grand Canyon National Park, Arizona, receives over 5 million visitors
     a year.   278
7.2   Waitakere Regional Park, Auckland, New Zealand. In order to minimise erosion
     caused by large visitor numbers in natural areas, substantial site and trail hardening
     may have to be undertaken, as here. However, what effect does such work have on
     the visitor experience and does the increased ease of access actually encourage more
     visitation?   287
7.3   Northern Sweden. Wild rivers may provide options for jetboating, but the noise of
     such river use may disturb other recreationists.   288

8.1   Blackpool Pier, England. The Victorians built piers to enable promenading as well as
      to represent humans dominating and taming nature (i.e. the coast and sea).   301
8.2   Denarau Island, Fiji. Modifying a mangrove swamp to build a resort complex has
      meant that erosion measures are necessary now the ecosystem has been changed.   306
8.3   Sidmouth, England. Beach erosion protection.   309
8.4   Victoria Harbour, British Columbia, Canada, serves as a base for marine tourism
      operations as well as private vessels, ferries, cruise ships and float planes.   312
9.1/9.2   Cairndow/Loch Fyne, Scotland. Community based and owned tourism developments.   327
9.3   Singapore waterfront. The area has been developed into a restaurant district through
      the conscious application of tourism policy and planning measures.   335
9.4   Granville Island, Vancouver, Canada, is one of the best examples in the world of an
      integrated development that meets local and visitor needs in a sustainable fashion.
      The mixed development of the island, including a market, restaurants, shops, ships'
      chandlers, artists' workshops, theatres, a hotel and a concrete works, utilises a port area
      that was left redundant following the onset of container shipping in the early 1970s.   335

FIGURES

1.1	Relationships between leisure, recreation and tourism	5
1.2	The context of tourism studies	12
1.3	Organising framework for the book	31
2.1	The decision-making process in outdoor recreation	36
2.2	Maslow's hierarchy of needs	39
2.3	Crawford and Godbey's three types of leisure constraints	42
2.4	The impact of distance and geographical catchment areas on the provision of leisure facilities	52
2.5	Time budgets for males, females and the total population of adults aged 16 and over in 2000	60
2.6	Holidays of four nights or more by British residents by number taken per year, 1971–2003	62
2.7	Glyptis' model of visitor dispersion at an informal recreation site	67
2.8	Determinants of tourism demand	69
2.9	Plog's psychographic positions of destinations	72
2.10	The leisure ladder for theme park settings (domestic visitors)	73
2.11	A classification of travellers	78
2.12	Growth of international arrivals, 1950–2002	85
2.13	Growth of international visitor expenditure, 1950–2002	85
2.14	New Zealand tourist flow	88
3.1	Leisure services spending by Walsall Borough Council 2003–4	96
3.2	London Borough of Havering's urban fringe countryside management area	108
3.3	Four types of tourism transaction chain	115
3.4	An enclave model of tourism in a peripheral economy	121
3.5	The elements of tourism	122
3.6	The tourism business district	128
3.7	Model of a tourism attraction system	131
3.8	Model of urban hotel location in west European cities	132
3.9	Types of tourism accommodation	133

3.10   Distribution of bedspaces in London in 1989   134
3.11   Distribution of bedspaces in London in 1999   135
3.12   Distribution of public houses of J.D. Wetherspoon in the UK   136
3.13   The domains of hospitality activities   138
5.1   The expansion of Leicester in the nineteenth century   182
5.2   Urban park development in Leicester   183
5.3   Parks in Leicester, c.1996   184
5.4   London Borough of Newham maps   195
5.5   A systems approach to urban tourism   200
5.6a   Tourism, leisure and the postmodern city   201
5.6b   Tourism, leisure and the postmodern city: the inner dimension   202
5.7   Factors to consider in evaluating the urban tourism experience   202
5.8   Functional areas in the tourist city   207
5.9   Perceptions of place   209
5.10   The Lynchean landscape of Armidale, New South Wales   211
6.1   Relationship between national, regional and local strategies   246
6.2   Creating different supply chains and local food systems   248
7.1   The wilderness continuum   276
7.2   National parks and scenic areas in New Zealand frequented by international tourists   286
8.1   Spatial distribution of beaches in California   295
9.1   The Countryside Agency's designated and defined interests   319
9.2   Elements in the tourism policy-making process   336
10.1   The DEEP process for applied geographical analysis   345

TABLES

1.1 Categorisations of main approaches to the geography of tourism and recreation   13
1.2 Approaches to geography and their relationship to the study of tourism and recreation   18
2.1 Crandall's list of motivations   38
2.2 Kabanoff's list of leisure needs   39
2.3 Influences on leisure participation   41
2.4 The world's leading international tourism destinations (by country): 1980 and 2002 compared   86
3.1 The land-use classes of the Canada land inventory   98
3.2 Linton's landscape evaluation scale   99
3.3 A general classification of outdoor recreational uses and resources   103
3.4 Elements of the tourism industry   110
3.5 Key characteristics of low cost carriers which make them more competitive than other carriers   111
3.6 Operating performance of Hilton International by region in 2001   121
3.7 Some reasons for government involvement in tourism   126
3.8 Criteria to be considered in distinguishing between intentional shopping and intentional leisure and tourism   140
4.1 Positive and negative dimensions of the impacts of tourism on host communities   145
4.3 Assessment criteria for selecting indicators for Tourism Optimisation Management Model on Kangaroo Island   153
4.4 Management objectives and potential indicators for assessing the quality of the environment on Kangaroo Island   153
4.5 Resident reaction to tourists in Coffs Harbour   161
4.6 Costs and benefits of tourism development in Broome, Australia   162
4.7 The impact of tourism on the urban physical environment   167
4.8 Environmental and ecological impacts of tourism on the Pacific islands   169
5.1 Hierarchical pattern of public open space   186

5.2 Summary and explanation of key variables deployed within the recreation resource typology   187

5.3 Basic typology of outdoor recreation facilities in urban areas   188

5.4 The evolution of green structure planning in Warsaw in 2001   189

5.5 Categories of green space in Warsaw   190

5.6 Open space standards   191

5.7 Typologies of urban tourists   206

5.8 Applications of visitor management techniques   218

7.1 The development of the wilderness concept in the United States, Canada, New Zealand and Australia   258

7.2 Components of the wilderness experience   265

7.3 The scientific values of wilderness   266

7.4 Interactions between values associated with wilderness and common disruptive activities   266

7.5 Australian wilderness inventories   272

7.6 Responses to variables listed in question 'Indicate whether you feel that the following activities/facilities are acceptable based on your perception of wilderness'   280

7.7 Responses to variables listed in question 'Motivations for coming to this location'   282

8.1 California state beaches   294

8.2 Illustrations of the geographer's contribution to the analysis of coastal recreation and tourism   297

9.1 Approaches to planning for leisure   318

9.2 International tourism policies, 1945 to the present   322

9.3 Tourism planning approaches: assumptions, problem definition, methods and models   324

9.4 Rural tourism development policy instruments   340

10.1 The skills of a geographer   348

10.2 Capabilities of a Geographical Information System   350

10.3 Problems of tourism and the potential of Geographical Information Systems   351

ACKNOWLEDGEMENTS

The purpose of this book is to provide an account of the growth, development and changes that are occurring within the geography of tourism and recreation, a purpose made all the more interesting because it is written by two geographers who, at the time this manuscript was completed, *did not* work in geography departments. While the book covers a lot of material, the authors acknowledge that there are a number of significant areas which have not been fully covered, and could not be unless the book was almost twice its size and more encyclopaedic than some of the reviewers of the first edition noted!

To a great extent this book concentrates on the developed world. However, it is not a discussion solely of Anglo-North American geography, as this would neglect the substantial contribution of geographers from Australia, New Zealand, Singapore, South Africa and the South Pacific; rather it deals with the literature on the geography of tourism and recreation in English. This is not to deny the substantial research base that European and other geographers have in tourism and recreation (see Chapter 1). However, arguably, the majority of English-speaking geographers have developed most of their work in tourism and recreation in isolation from the European and Asian experience, although as tertiary education and research becomes increasingly globalised and English the international language of the academy, such isolation is declining.

This book therefore serves to identify many of the major concerns and interests of geographers in the fields of tourism and recreation. There is clearly a substantial body of work in the subdiscipline. However, as the book also notes, the field is not seen as seriously as perhaps it should be; a conclusion with substantial implications not only for the further development of the subdiscipline but also for the growth of tourism studies as a separate field of academic endeavour. Indeed, the book observes that we are in a time of transformation and change in terms of a better positioning of tourism and recreation issues within the contemporary concerns of social theory and human geography, while simultaneously also having increased demands to be more 'applied' with respect to industry and tourism education. The third edition has been thoroughly revised, updated and expanded within the very tight constraints of space. At a time of rapid growth in tourism- and recreation-related literature by geographers, this was more than a challenge. For that reason, many of the seminal and leading studies which have been incorporated where space permits are reflected in the expanded bibliography. Indeed, one of the things that this book seeks to do is emphasise the substantial legacy of studies in the geography of tourism and recreation before all students of tourism and recreation needed to do was download articles from the web. And as the book demonstrates, tourism and recreation, and the geography of tourism and recreation in particular are *not* new subjects!

Stephen Page would like to acknowledge a number of people who made this book possible. Many people have also contributed ideas and the time to discuss themes and offer hospitality including the late Martin Oppermann, Simon Milne, Charles Johnston, Pip Forer, Doug Pearce, Tom Hinch, and Kevin Woo. Tim Bentley and Michael Barker, both former postdoctoral researchers in tourism at Massey University, provided a welcome source of intellectual stimulation and focus for research-oriented issues. Roy Wood formerly of the Scottish Hotel School provided his usual hospitality and critical perspective on tourism and hospitality research which was invaluable. Also, thanks to Stephen Williams at Staffordshire University for engendering my early interest in the geography of leisure and recreation.

Other people who have had a very formative effect for both authors are Professor Tony Vitalis, Robin Smith and the Department of Management Systems at Massey University at Palmerston North, and the Faculty of Commerce and Administration at Victoria University of Wellington.

Michael Hall would like to thank Bill Bramwell, Peter Burns, Dick Butler, Tim Coles, Arthur Conacher, Dave Crag, Ross Dowling, David Duval, Derek Hall, Cecilia Hegarty, Thor Flognfeldt, Stefan Gössling, Atsuko Hashimoto, James Higham, Tom Hinch, Bruno Jansson, John Jenkins, Alan Lew, Simon McArthur, Madelaine Mattson, Dieter Müeller, Meiko Muramaya, Julie Pitcher, Robert Preston-Whyte, Greg Richards, Chris Ryan, Jarkko Saarinen, Anna-Dora Saetorsdottir, Judit Sulyok, David Telfer, Dallen Timothy, Gustav Visser, Geoff Wall, Jim Walmesley, Brian Wheeler, Allan Williams and Sandra Wall, who have all contributed in various ways to some of the ideas contained within, although the interpretation of their thoughts is, of course, my own. Gavin Bryars, Jeff Buckley, Nick Cave, Bruce Cockburn, Elvis Costello, Stephen Cummings, Hoodoo Gurus, The Sundays, Ed Kuepper, Neil and Tim Finn, Jackson Code, Sarah McLachlan, Vinnie Reilly, David Sylvian, Jennifer Warnes, Chris Wilson and BBC Radio 6 were also essential to the writing process. Monica Gilmour was a huge help getting this book to the publishers, while acknowledgement must also be given to the convivial atmosphere of the Department of Social and Economic Geography, Umeå University, Sweden where the book was completed during sabbatical.

At the personal level Stephen would like to thank Jo and Rosie, while Michael would like to thank Jody. Both of us realise that without the support and incentive that you all give us, particularly as Rosie's excellent proofreading skills continue to improve, our work would be considerably more difficult and our recreation not so much fun.

Finally, the authors would like to express their appreciation to Andrew Mould at Routledge for his continued interest in the project.

C. Michael Hall   Stephen J. Page
City Rise & Umeå   Stirling

PERMISSIONS

A number of organisations and bodies have provided the authors with permission to reproduce material in the book and they wish to express their thanks to them. If any unknowing use of copyright material has been made, please contact the authors via the publishers, since every effort was made to trace copyright owners.

A number of organisations have granted permission to use material and they include: The former London Docklands Development Corporation, The Geographical Association, Taylor and Francis, Pearson Education, Carolyn Harrison, Elsevier, Channel View Publications, The Countryside Agency, The National Recreation Park Association and the Journal of Leisure Research, John Wiley and Sons and the John Hopkins University Press. In addition, the London Borough of Newham and Leicester City Council's Legal Services Department granted permission to re-use various Figures as did James Higham, Centre for Tourism, University of Otago and Simon McArthur. The New Zealand Tourism Research Council permitted use of its wide ranging statistical research and J.D. Wetherspoon's provided the data to construct the changing distribution of its public houses in the UK. The former Argyll, Islands, Loch Lomond, Stirling and Trossachs Tourist Board (now part of the Visit Scotland network) kindly provided a range of images for use in the book with the remaining images provided by the authors.

1

INTRODUCTION
Tourism matters!

Geographical knowledge is more important than ever in an increasingly global and interconnected world. How can a graduate claim to be a learned scholar without any understanding of geography?

(Susan Cutter, President of the Association of American Geographers, 2000: 2)

Who we are is shaped in part by where we are. Human interactions with each other and the environment are rooted in geographical understandings, as well as the opportunities and constraints of geographical circumstance. Geographical approaches and techniques offer critical insights into everything from local land-use decisions to international conflict.

(Alexander Murphy, President of the Association of American Geographers, 2004: 3)

Tourism is widely recognised as the world's largest industry. The figures on the size and significance of tourism are staggering. For example, according to the World Tourism Organisation (WTO 1996), in 1995 world tourist arrivals reached 567 million with estimated international tourism receipts of US$60 billion. By 2000 world tourism arrivals were estimated to have reached 698.3 million with receipts from international tourism climbed to US$476 billion (WTO 2001). Although international arrivals for 2003 were estimated to have fallen by 1.2 per cent in 2003 to 694 million, some 8.5 million less than in 2002 and the biggest drop ever in international tourism arrivals, a substantial rebound was expected in 2004 (WTO 2004a, 2004b).

However, tourism, tourists and their impacts are clearly not evenly distributed. Substantial differentiation occurs at a variety of international, regional and local scales. For example, with respect to 2003 (WTO 2004a):

- There was zero international tourism growth in Europe. International arrivals in Western Europe showed a fall of 3.7 million (–3 per cent) although growth continued in Eastern Europe.
- The Americas recorded an overall decrease in international arrivals (–1 per cent), with the North American region experiencing a decline (–5 per cent) for the third year in a row. However, in contrast substantial growth was experienced in both the Caribbean (8 per cent) and South America (12 per cent).
- Asia and the Pacific experienced a massive drop of 12 million arrivals (–9 per cent) due to the SARS epidemic, with the South East Asia region experiencing a decline of 16 per cent, yet South Asia had 17 per cent growth.
- Despite security concerns, the Middle East and Africa recovered quickly during the year and recorded the best results of all the regions with estimated increases of 10 per cent and 5 per cent respectively.

At a global level the World Travel and Tourism Council (WTTC 2000), using a tourism satellite accounting system, has measured that, directly and indirectly, the travel and tourism industry constitutes 11 per cent of global GDP (US$3575 billion) and supports 200 million jobs worldwide (8 per cent of total employment or 1 in every 12.4 jobs).

By 2010, the travel and tourism economic contribution is estimated to grow to 11.6 per cent (US$6591 billion) of global GDP and will support 250 million jobs (9 per cent of total employment or 1 in every 11 jobs). The WTTC (2001a) estimates that by 2011, the travel and tourism economy will constitute 11.0 per cent of global GDP and support 260,417,000 jobs worldwide (9 per cent of total employment or 1 in 11.2 jobs).

The immediate economic significance of such figures is to be seen not only in tourist destination and tourist generating areas but also in those destinations from which tourists switch their travel in order to take advantage of cheap prices, faster travel times or more favourable perceptions of safety. However, changes in the international tourism market will also be related to domestic holiday travel, as consumers can switch their travel plans not only between international destinations but also between domestic and international destinations. Tourism, as with other forms of economic activity, therefore reflects the increasing interconnectedness of the international economy. Indeed, by its very nature in terms of connections between generating areas, destinations and travel routes or paths, tourism is perhaps a phenomenon which depends more than most not only on transport, service and trading networks but also on social, political and environmental relationships between the consumers and producers of the tourist experience. Such issues are clearly of interest to geographers. For example, according to L.S. Mitchell (1979), in his discussion of the contributions that geography can make to the investigation of tourism:

> The geographer's point-of-view is a trilogy of biases pertaining to place, environment and relationships. . . . In a conceptual vein the geographer has traditionally claimed the spatial and chorographic aspects as his realm. . . . The geographer, therefore, is concerned about earth space in general and about place and places in particular. The description, appreciation, and understanding of places is paramount to his thinking although two other perspectives (i.e. environment and relationships) modify and extend the primary bias of place.
>
> (Mitchell 1979: 237)

Yet despite the global significance of tourism and the potential contribution that geography can make to the analysis and understanding of tourism, the position of tourism and recreation studies within geography is not strong. However, within the fields of tourism and recreation studies outside mainstream academic geography, geographers have made enormous contributions to the understanding of tourism and recreation phenomena (Butler 2004). It is therefore within this somewhat paradoxical situation that this book is being written, while the contribution of geography and geographers is widely acknowledged and represented in tourism and recreation departments and journals, relatively little recognition is given to the significance of tourism and recreation in geography departments, journals, non-tourism and recreation-specific geography texts, and within other geography subdisciplines. Although, as Lew (2001) noted, not only do we have an issue of how we define leisure, recreation and tourism (see below), but also there is the question of what is geographical literature? This book takes an inclusive approach and includes material published by geographers who work in both geography and other academic departments; material published in geography journals; and, where appropriate, includes discussion of literature that has a geographical theme and which has influenced research by geographers in tourism and recreation. In part the categorisation of literature into either 'recreation' and 'tourism' is self-selecting in terms of the various works that we cite. If one was to generalise then recreation research tends to focus on more local behaviour, often has an outdoors focus, and is less commercial. Tourism research tends to look at leisure mobility over greater distances, often international, usually including overnight stay, and is more commercial. However, such categories are not absolutes and arguably, as the book indicates, are increasingly converging over time. This book therefore seeks to explain how the contemporary situation of the geography of tourism and recreation has developed, indicate the breadth and depth of geographical research on tourism and recreation, and suggest ways in which the overall standing of

Plate 1.1: Cambridge, England. Which of the people in this High Street scene are tourists or recreationalists? Researchers need to carefully differentiate between recreationalists and tourists.

research and scholarship by geographers on tourism and recreation may be improved.

This first chapter is divided into several sections. First, it examines the relationship between tourism and recreation. Second, it provides an overview of the development of various approaches to the study of tourism and recreation within geography. Finally, it outlines the approach of this book towards the geography of tourism and recreation.

TOURISM, RECREATION, LEISURE AND MOBILITY

Tourism, recreation and leisure are generally seen as a set of interrelated and overlapping concepts. While there are many important concepts, definitions of leisure, recreation and tourism remain contested in terms of how, where, when and why they are used (Poria et al. 2003; Butler 2004). In a review of the meaning of leisure, Stockdale (1985) identified three main ways in which the concept of leisure is used:

- as a period of time, activity or state of mind in which choice is the dominant feature; in this sense leisure is a form of
- an objective view in which leisure is perceived as the opposite of work and is defined as non-work or residual time
- a subjective view which emphasises leisure as a qualitative concept in which leisure activities take on a meaning only within the context of individual perceptions and belief systems and can therefore occur at any time in any setting.

According to Herbert (1988), leisure is therefore best seen as time over which an individual exercises choice and undertakes activities in a free, voluntary way.

Leisure activities are of considerable interest to geographers (e.g. Lavery 1975; Patmore 1977, 1978, 1979, 1980; Coppock 1982; Herbert 1987). Traditional approaches to the study of leisure by geographers focused on leisure in terms of activities. In contrast, Glyptis (1981a) argued for the adoption of the concept of leisure lifestyles which emphasised the importance of individual perceptions of leisure.

> This allows the totality of an individual's leisure experiences to be considered and is a subjective approach which shifts the emphasis from activity to people, from aggregate to individual and from expressed activities to the functions which these fulfill for the participant and the social and locational circumstances in which he or she undertakes them.
>
> (Herbert 1988: 243)

Such an experiential approach towards leisure has been extremely influential. For example, Featherstone (1987) argued that

> The significance and meaning of a particular set of leisure choices . . . can only be made intelligible by inscribing them on a map of the class-defined social field of leisure and lifestyle practices in which their meaning and significance is relationally defined with reference to structured oppositions and differences.
>
> (Featherston 1987: 115)

Similarly, such an experiential definition of leisure was used by G. Shaw and A.M. Williams (1994) in their critical examination of tourism from a geographical perspective.

However, while such a phenomenological approach to defining leisure, and therefore tourism and recreation, is valuable in highlighting the social context in which leisure is both defined and occurs, such an approach will clearly be at odds with 'objective', technical approaches towards definitions which can be applied in a variety of situations and circumstances (see Chapter 2). Yet it should be emphasised that such definitions are being used for different purposes. A universally accepted definition of leisure, tourism and recreation is an impossibility. Definitions will change according to their purpose and context. They are setting the 'rules of the game' or 'engagement' for discussion, argument and research. By defining terms we give meaning to what we are doing.

Even given the subjective nature of leisure, however, at a larger scale it may still be possible to aggregate individual perceptions and activities to provide a collective or commonly held impression of the relationship between leisure, tourism and recreation. In this sense, tourism and recreation are generally regarded as subsets of the wider concept of leisure (Coppock 1982; P.E. Murphy 1985; Herbert 1988). In the wider context of geography, R.J. Johnston (1985a: 10) argued that 'Academic disciplines exist to maintain, further and promote knowledge', and this is certainly the case in tourism and recreational geography.

Figure 1.1 illustrates the relationship between leisure, recreation and tourism. As Parker (1999) eloquently explained,

> It is through studying leisure as a whole that the most powerful explanations are developed. This is because society is not divided into sports players, television viewers, tourists and so on. It is the same people who do all these things.
>
> (Parker 1999: 21)

This indicates the value of viewing tourism and recreation as part of a wider concept of leisure. Broken lines are used to illustrate that the boundaries between the concepts are 'soft'. Work is differentiated from leisure with there being two main realms of overlap: first, business travel, which is seen as a work-oriented form of tourism in order to differentiate it from leisure-based travel; second, serious leisure, which refers to the breakdown between leisure and work pursuits and the development of leisure career paths with respect to their hobbies and interests (Stebbins 1979). As Stebbins (1982) observed:

> leisure in postindustrial society is no longer seen as chiefly a means of recuperating from the travail of the job. . . . If leisure is to become, for many, an improvement over work as a way of finding personal fulfillment, identity enhancement, self-expression, and the like, then people must be careful to adopt those forms with the greatest payoff. The theme here is that we reach this goal through engaging in serious rather than casual or unserious leisure.
>
> (Stebbins 1982: 253)

Figure 1.1 also indicates the considerable overlap that exists between recreation and tourism. For example, Bodewes (1981) saw tourism as a phenomenon of recreation. Similarly, D.G. Pearce (1987a: 1) observed the 'growing recognition that tourism constitutes one end of a broad leisure spectrum'.

Historically, research in outdoor recreation developed independently of tourism research. As Crompton and Richardson (1986: 38) noted: 'Traditionally, tourism has been regarded as a commercial economic phenomenon rooted in the private domain. In contrast, recreation and parks has been viewed as a social and resource concern rooted in the public domain.' Outdoor recreation studies have focused on public sector (i.e. community and land management agencies) concerns, such

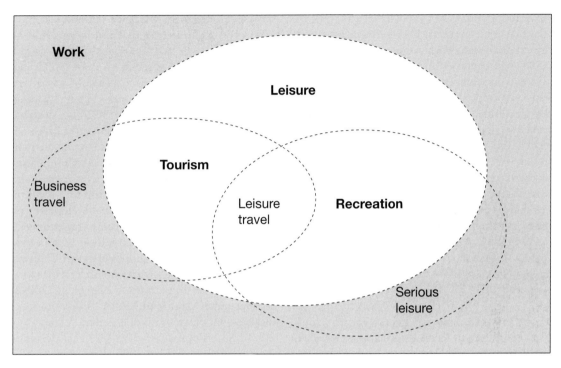

Figure 1.1: Relationships between leisure, recreation and tourism

as wilderness management, social carrying capacity and non-market valuation of recreation experiences. In contrast, tourism has tended to have a more 'applied orientation' which concentrates on traditional private sector (i.e. tourism industry) concerns, such as the economic impacts of travel expenditures, travel patterns and tourist demands, and advertising and marketing (Harris et al. 1987).

Although the division between public and private activities may have held relatively true from the end of the post-war period through to the early 1980s, in more recent years the division between public and private sector activities has been substantially eroded in western countries (Hall and Jenkins 1995). The distinction between tourism and recreation may therefore be regarded as one of degree. Tourism primarily relates to leisure and business travel activities which centre around visitors to a particular destination, which will typically involve an infusion of new money from the visitor into the

regional economy (Hall 1995). According to Helber (1988: 20), 'In this sense, tourism can be viewed as a primary industry which, through visitor spending, increases job opportunities and tax revenues, and enhances the community's overall economic base'. On the other hand, recreation generally refers to leisure activities which are undertaken by the residents of an immediate region, while their spending patterns will involve 'a recycling of money within the community associated with day, overnight and extended-stay recreation trips' (Helber 1988: 20–1).

Natural settings and outdoor recreation opportunities are clearly a major component of tourism, perhaps especially so since the development of interest in nature-based and ecotourism activities (e.g. P. Valentine 1984, 1992; Weiler and Hall 1992; Lindberg and McKercher 1997). Indeed, outdoor recreation and tourist resources should be seen as complementary contexts and resources for leisure experiences (Fedler 1987). Nevertheless, while authors such as Pigram (1985: 184) take the view that 'tourism is carried on within an essentially recreational framework', others such as Murphy (1985) have expressed an opposing view, conceptualising recreation as one component of tourism. However, this argument smacks of something of the 'glass is half-full or half-empty' argument. The reality is that as tourism and recreation studies have grown and borrowed concepts from each other (Ryan 1991), and as society has changed, particularly with respect to the role of government, so the demarcation line between recreation and tourism has rapidly become 'fuzzy and overlap is now the norm' (Crompton and Richardson 1986: 38). As Pigram (1985) argued:

> Little success has been afforded to those attempting to differentiate between recreation and tourism and such distinctions appear founded on the assumption that outdoor recreation appeals to the rugged, self-reliant element in the population, whereas tourism caters more overtly for those seeking diversion without too much discomfort.
>
> (Pigram 1985: 184)

Similarly, in a wider context, Jansen-Verbeke and Dietvorst (1987: 263) argued that 'in the perception of the individual at least, the distinction between recreation and tourism is becoming irrelevant'. As with Shaw and Williams (1994), we would argue that this is not completely the case, particularly with respect to how individuals define their own activities. However, it is readily apparent that there is increasing convergence between the two concepts in terms of theory, activities and impacts, particularly as recreation becomes increasingly commercialised and the boundaries between public and private responsibilities in recreation and leisure change substantially. It is interesting to note the inclusion of a same-day travel, 'excursionist' category in official international guidelines for the collection and definition of tourism statistics, thereby making the division between recreation and tourism even more arbitrary (United Nations (UN) 1994). Tourism may therefore be interpreted as only one of a range of choices or styles of recreation expressed through either travel or a temporary

short-term change of residence. Technical definitions of tourism are examined in more detail in Chapter 2.

A more recent approach to conceptualising tourism is to regard tourism as simply one, albeit highly significant, form of human mobility (Bell and Ward 2000; Coles et al. 2004; Hall 2005a, 2005b), with Coles et al. (2004) arguing that research on tourism must be willing to formulate a coherent approach to understanding the meaning behind the range of mobilities undertaken by *individuals*, not tourists. The notion of tourism as a form of mobility has therefore meant the development of an approach that relates tourism to other dimensions of mobility such as migration (King et al. 2000; Williams and Hall 2000; Hall and Williams 2002; Duval 2003), transnationalism and diaspora (Coles and Timothy 2004; Coles et al. 2004), second homes (Hall and Müller 2004) and long distance mobility (Frändberg and Vilhelmson 2003). Such approaches parallel recent developments in sociology (Urry 2000, 2004) but actually have a far longer lineage dating to the work of geographers such as Hägerstrand (1970, 1984) and Pred (1977) on time geography which itself was a major influence on sociology (Giddens 1984). Indeed considerations of mobility in tourism is nothing new. For example, Wolfe (1966) observed that 'most students of recreation concentrate on the reasons for travel, but few have much to say about the significance of mobility'. Mobility is 'at the very heart of certain aspects of leisure activity today – outdoor recreation in particular and, by definition, recreational travel'. Similarly, Cosgrove and Jackson (1972), in writing on resort development, noted:

> 'Fashion' is therefore capable of analysis, and it can be shown to be motivated by social distinction, which is characterised by geographical segregation. Within the confines of such segregated areas individual initiative may then account for variations in development. The geographic mobility of the different social strata results in continuous changes in the location and extent of these segregated areas. The word 'mobility' is used here deliberately rather than accessibility, since access alone did not create the resorts of the nineteenth century. Only when incomes were sufficiently high and

when free time was readily available could the facilities of access be fully exploited.

(Cosgrove and Jackson 1972: 34)

Cosgrove and Jackson's (1972) identification of time and income level are highly significant for the study of tourism (Hall 2005a, 2005b) For while time budgets have been a major focus of time geography, their role in tourism has been relatively little explored. Arguably, one of the main reasons for this is that tourism is often portrayed as being an escape from the routine (Hall 2005a, 2005b). Yet space–time compression has led to fundamental changes to individual space–time paths in recent years. The routinised space–time paths of those living in 2005 are not the same as those of people in 1984 when Giddens was writing and even more so in the 1960s and 1970s when Hägerstrand (1970) was examining daily space–time trajectories (Hall 2005a, 2005c). Instead, for those with sufficient income and time, particularly in the developed world, extended voluntary leisure or business travel (what we would usually describe as tourism) is part of their routine on a seasonal or annual basis, and for some highly mobile individuals, on a weekly or daily basis. Hall (2005b) has even argued that one possible interpretation of this is that the study of tourism is intrinsically the study of the wealthy, particularly given the relative lack of research in tourism as to those who do not travel and are relatively immobile.

Despite the expansion of spatial mobility for many people time constraints still operate, there is always only a finite amount of time in which people can travel in or take part in touristic activities (Hägerstrand 1970; Pred 1977; Hall 2005a). Through increased access to transport resources and the economic capacity to utilise them it may be possible to increase the geographical space it is possible to visit within a given time. Given that a travel money budget represents the fraction of disposable income devoted to travel, a fixed travel money budget establishes a direct relationship between disposable income and distance travelled, provided average user costs of transport remain constant (see Schafer and Victor 2000). If people

are on a fixed time budget then those who are willing to pay the increased costs will shift from one mode of transport to another so as to increase speed and therefore reduce the amount of time engaged in travelling relative to other activities within the constraints of the overall time budget (Schafer 2000; Hall 2005a), thereby challenging both conceptually and technically the commonly used approaches to defining tourism in time (see Chapter 2).

THE ISSUE OF SCALE: EMPIRICISM, PARADIGMS AND TRANSFORMATIONS

The geographer's preoccupation with place, space and environment, all of which feature in many of the seminal studies of geography (e.g. Haggett 1979), reveals a preoccupation with one fundamental concept – namely scale (Del Casino and Hanna 2000). For the geographer, it is the scale at which phenomena are studied, analysed and explained which differentiates it from many other areas of social science. The ability to recognise phenomena at different geographical scales ranging from global, national, regional through to local scales and the interactions of processes and change at each scale have traditionally been the hallmark of a positivist–empiricist geography (see Johnston 1991 for more detail). In many of the classic studies reviewed in the next section, it is clear that Aitchison's (1999) critique of geographical contributions to leisure and recreation research has been overwhelmingly modelled on the empiricist–positivist mode of analysis, where the route to scientific explanation closely follows the positivist models developed in Anglo-American geography in the period 1945 to 1970. The preoccupation with building and testing models in human geography and their application to tourism and recreation (see D.G. Pearce 1995a for a review) has largely mirrored trends in the main discipline, while new developments in behavioural geography, humanistic geography and, more recently, cultural geography have only belatedly begun to permeate the consciousness of tourism and recreation geographers.

What began to develop during the 1990s and has now gathered momentum in tourism and recreation geography is the evolution of new paradigms (i.e. ways of thinking about and conceptualising research problems). As a result, developments in the 'new cultural geography' have begun to permeate, transform and redefine the way in which geographers approach tourism and recreation. Crouch (1999a) conceptualises leisure and tourism as an encounter, in the anthropological tradition, noting the geographer's contribution to this perspective, where the concern is between people, between people and space and the contexts of leisure/tourism. However, what is a fundamental redefinition of geographers' concern with space is the manner in which space is viewed and contextualised. Crouch (1999a) argued that space may be something material, concrete, metaphorical or imagined questioning the traditional notion of location and space, where activity is located. This new conceptualisation is reflected in that 'The country and the city, the garden, the beach, the desert island, and the street hold powerful metaphorical attention in significant areas of leisure/tourism' (Crouch 1999a: 4).

This concern with conceptions from cultural geography, where space is something metaphorical, whereby it is something that shapes people's enjoyment of leisure/tourism, derives much of its origins from humanistic geography (Relph 1976, 1981) and cultural studies. For example, Squire (1994) argued that leisure and recreation practices are a reflection of the way in which people make maps of meaning of their everyday word. This concern with the individual or group, the human experience and the symbolic meaning of leisure and tourism in space has opened a wide range of geographical avenues for research in tourism and recreation. For example, Cloke and Perkins (1999) examined representations of adventure tourism, exploring many of the issues of meaning and symbols.

D. Williams and Kaltenborn's (1999) analysis of the use and meaning of recreational cottages is significant in this context because it also questioned the traditional notion of geography and tourism, with the focus on tourism as a temporary phenomenon in time and space (see also A.M. Williams and Hall 2000). Indeed, they challenged the conventional way of viewing tourism, arguing that tourism and leisure needs to be viewed as a more dynamic phenomenon, where the circulation and movement of people in space is the rule rather than the exception. They argue that it is the movement to tourism and leisure spaces that adds meaning, by allowing people to establish an identity and to connect with place. In other words, tourism and leisure are deeply embedded in everyday lives and the meaning that people attach to their lives, since changing work practices and less separation of work, leisure and pleasure has made tourism and recreation more important to people's lives. This is intrinsically linked to the rapidly changing nature of time–space compression (see Hall 2005a for more detail), with other mechanisms contributing to people's lives increasingly connected to the concept of a 'global village'. What is clear from the transformation occurring in the new cultural geographies of leisure and tourism is the lack of a specific frame of reference or guiding research agenda to incorporate these perspectives into mainstream tourism and recreation geography. There appears to be an emerging social and cultural detachment within the subdiscipline, mirroring other developments in human geography, where two different languages, knowledge bases and modes of analysis are emerging (i.e. the empiricist– positivist and inducture– qualitative culturalists), neither of whom have found a common language to communicate with each other. With these issues in mind, attention now turns to the historical development of the geography of tourism and recreation and a discussion of many of the formative studies.

DEVELOPMENT OF THE GEOGRAPHY OF TOURISM AND RECREATION

Tourism and recreation have been the subject of research and scholarship in Anglo-American geography since the early twentieth century, with an early focus on demographic and economic issues (Cleveland 1910; Wrigley 1919; Whitbeck 1920; Allix 1922; Cornish 1930, 1934; McMurray 1930; S.B. Jones 1933; O'Dell 1935; Selke 1936; Carlson 1938), as well as the role of recreation in the national parks and national forest areas of the United States (e.g. Carhart 1920; Graves 1920; Meinecke 1929; Atwood 1931; Chapman 1938). Brown (1935) offered what he termed 'an invitation to geographers' in the following terms:

> From the geographical point of view the study of tourism offers inviting possibilities for the development of new and ingenious techniques for research, for the discovery of facts of value in their social implications in what is virtually a virgin field.
>
> (Brown 1935: 471)

However, as Campbell (1966: 85) wryly commented, 'it would appear that this invitation was declined'. As Deasy (1949: 240) observed: 'because of the inadequate attention to the tourist industry by geographers, there exists a concomitant dearth of techniques, adaptable to the collection, analysis, interpretation and cartographic representation of geographical data of the subject.' Yet the period from 1945 to the late 1960s is perhaps not as barren as Campbell would have us believe.

Building on the initial research on tourism and recreation in American economic geography in the 1930s, research was primarily undertaken in the post-war period in the United States on the economic impact of tourism in both a regional destination setting (e.g. Crisler and Hunt 1952; Ullman 1954; Ullman and Volk 1961; Deasy and Griess 1966) and on travel routes (Eiselen 1945). Although Cooper's (1947) discussion of issues of seasonality and travel motivations foreshadowed some of the geographical research of the 1980s and 1990s, interest in this area of study lay dormant for many years. Nevertheless, the geography of recreation and tourism was at least of a sufficient profile in the discipline to warrant a chapter in an overview text on the state of geography in the United States in the 1950s (McMurray 1954). (See also Meyer-Arendt's (2000) article on tourism as a subject of North American doctoral dissertations

and master's theses 1951 to 1998, which expands on the earlier studies by Jafari and Aaser (1988) and Meyer-Arendt and Lew (1999) in the United States.)

In Britain, significant research was undertaken by E.W. Gilbert (1939, 1949, 1954) on the development of British seaside resorts, with geographers also contributing to government studies on coastal holiday development (*Observer* 1944). But, little further direct research was undertaken on tourism and recreation in the United Kingdom until the 1960s, although some doctoral work on resorts was undertaken (Butler 2004). There was certainly an interest from the generation of geographers studying patterns of tourism and recreation in postcolonial South Asia, as Robinson (1972) noted the contribution of earlier studies by Spencer and Thomas (1948), Withington (1961) and Sopher (1968) published in *The Geographical Review*. In Canada over the same period substantive geographical research on tourism was primarily focused on one geographer, Roy Wolfe (1964), whose early work on summer cottages in Ontario (Wolfe 1951, 1952), laid the foundation for later research on the geography of second home development (e.g. Coppock 1977a; Hall and Müller 2004) and tourism and migration (Williams and Hall 2000; Hall and Williams 2002).

While significant work was undertaken on tourism and recreation from the 1930s to the 1950s, it was not really until the 1960s that research started to accelerate with a blossoming of publications on tourism and recreation in the 1970s. During the 1960s several influential reviews were undertaken of the geography of tourism and recreation (R.E. Murphy 1963; Wolfe 1964, 1967; Winsberg 1966; L.S. Mitchell 1969a, 1969b; Mercer 1970), while a substantive contribution to the development of the area also came from regional sciences (e.g. Guthrie 1961; Christaller 1963; Piperoglou 1966), with the conceptual developments and research undertaken on carrying capacity in a resource and land management context (R. Lucas 1964; Wagar 1964) still resonating in present-day discussions on sustainability and environmental management (Coccossis 2004).

Nevertheless, even as late as 1970, A. Williams and Zelinsky (1970) were able to comment that 'virtually all the scholarship in the domain of tourism has been confined to intra-national description and analysis'. Indeed, in commenting on the field of tourism research as a whole they observed:

> In view of its great and increasing economic import, the probable significance of tourism in diffusing information and attitudes, and its even greater future potential for modifying patterns of migration, balance of payments, land use, and general socio-economic structure with the introduction of third-generation jet transport and other innovations in travel, it is startling to discover how little attention the circulation of tourists has been accorded by geographers, demographers, and other social scientists.
>
> (Williams and Zelinsky 1970: 549)

Similarly, Mercer (1970: 261) commented: 'Until recently geographers have had surprisingly little to say about the implications of growing leisure time in the affluent countries of the world. Even now, leisure still remains a sadly neglected area of study in geography.' Nevertheless, there were, and to some extent still are, significant regional variations in the focus on leisure, recreation and tourism. For example, Butler (2004: 146) noted that a large body of research on recreation and leisure was undertaken in North America by geographers and non-geographers alike, although 'Until the 1980s it was hard to find much research on tourism conducted in North America by geographers, except for the work of British ex-patriots (Butler, Marsh, Murphy and Wall, for example) and their students'.

During the 1970s and early 1980s, a number of influential texts and monographs appeared in the geography literature (e.g. Lavery 1971c; Cosgrove and Jackson 1972; Coppock and Duffield 1975; Matley 1976; H. Robinson 1976; Coppock 1977a; D.G. Pearce 1981, 1987a; Mathieson and Wall 1982; Patmore 1983; Pigram 1983; S.L.J. Smith 1983a), giving the appearance of a healthy area of research. Indeed, a number of extremely significant concepts in the tourism literature, such as a tourism area life cycle (Butler 1980) and the notion of a tourism system (Board et al. 1978) emerged from geographers during this period. For example,

in their 1972 study of leisure behaviour in the Dartmoor National Park, Board et al. commented:

> The tourism system then consists of concentrations of visitors (nodes) and road networks (links) set within areas of varying character: the relationships between them are expressed in terms of flows of people. Researchers set out to examine a tourist system in inner Dartmoor ... by making observations at all major nodes, several minor nodes and three sets of links in the network, here called circuits.
>
> The information collected related to three basic properties of the system – the characteristics of the visitors, the activities they carry out at these various places and between various places within it.
>
> (Board et al. 1978: 46)

However, despite the growth in publications by geographers on tourism and recreation, concerns were being expressed about the geography of tourism. In the introduction to a special issue of *Annals of Tourism Research* on the geography of tourism, L.S. Mitchell (1979: 235) observed that 'the geography of tourism is limited by a dearth of published research in geographical journals, the relatively few individuals who actively participate in the sub-discipline, and the lack of prestige the subject matter specialty has in geography'. In the same issue, D.G. Pearce (1979: 246), in an excellent historical review of the field, commented, 'even after half a century, it is difficult to speak of the geography of tourism as a subject with any coherence within the wider discipline of geography or in the general field of tourism studies'. S.L.J. Smith (1982), in a discussion of recreation geography, referred to the development of geographies of recreation and leisure in terms of Kuhn's (1969) notion of paradigms:

> One might also argue that recreation geography is in a pre-paradigmatic state – The history of recreation geography is one of growing intellectual diversity with no convergence towards a set of unified theories and methods ... If there is any special challenge that recreation geography is faced with as a field of intellectual activity it is not the lack of a paradigm.
>
> (Smith 1982: 19)

Nevertheless, in a comment as appropriate now as it was then, he went on to note that there was 'a lack of appreciation and knowledge of past accomplishments and of the complexity of the field' (Smith 1982: 19).

More recently, Pearce (1995a: 3) argued that 'the geography of tourism continues to lack a strong conceptual and theoretical base'; even so, models such as Butler's (1980, 2005) cycle of evolution and those reviewed in Pearce (1987a) have assisted to a limited degree in developing a conceptual understanding, while L.S. Mitchell (1991: 10) also expressed concern that 'there is no widely accepted paradigm or frame-of-reference that serves as a guide to tourism research'. Indeed, Butler (2000, 2004) has even argued not only that leisure, recreation and tourism (LRT) research may have a negative image in geography, but also that 'geography pales in terms of its influence in LRT compared to economics, sociology and even anthropology' (Butler 2004: 152). These comments therefore raise questions about the contemporary status of the geography of tourism and recreation, and it is to these concerns that we now turn.

STATUS OF THE GEOGRAPHY OF TOURISM AND RECREATION

The study of the geography of tourism and recreation does not occur in isolation from wider trends in geography and academic discourse, nor of the society of which we are a part. Tourism and recreation geographers are 'a society within a society', academic life 'is not a closed system but rather is open to the influences and commands of the wider society which encompasses it' (R.J. Johnston 1991: 1). The study of the development and history of a discipline 'is not simply a chronology of its successes. It is an investigation of the sociology of a community, of its debates, deliberations and decisions as well as its findings' (Johnston 1991: 11). Indeed, Johnston (1985a) highlighted the prevailing criticisms of applied geography where

Promotion of geography as an applied empirical-analytic science firmly grounds it, according to some, in the political status quo. The problems identified are at the levels of the empirical and the actual and the solutions advanced do not attach the real, the processes that produce the current problems. Symptoms are treated, not causes. Arguments for a more fundamental applied geography, especially applied human geography, seek to distance the discipline from links with governments, public services and commercially oriented enterprises.

(Johnston 1985a: 21)

The problem in tourism and recreation is that the organisation, management and funding of research is primarily a public and private sector activity. In this sense, it raises moral dilemmas for the geographer since it is increasingly difficult to disengage from the public policy framework or economic/decision-making context in which research is commissioned or undertaken. Indeed, detachment can lead to valid criticisms of academic 'ivory towers' and a fundamental failure to engage in critical public and private sector policy making.

Tourism geographers are a subcommunity of the geographic community within the wider community of academics, scientists and intellectuals which is itself a subset of wider society; that society has a culture, including a scientific subculture within which the content of geography and tourism is defined. Action is predicated on the structure of society and its knowledge base: research praxis is part of that programme of action, and includes tourism research. The community of tourism academics is therefore an 'institutionalizing social group' (Grano 1981: 26), a context within which individual tourism academics are socialised and which defines the internal goals of their subdiscipline in the context of the external structures within which they operate (after Johnston 1991). The content of the subdiscipline must be linked to its milieu, 'so that disciplinary changes (revolutionary or not) should be associated with significant events in the milieu' (Johnston 1991: 277). Similarly, Stoddart (1981: 1) in his review of the history of geography stated, 'both the ideas and the structure of the subject have developed in response to complex social, economic, ideological and intellectual stimuli'.

'The contents of a discipline at any one time and place reflect the response of the individuals involved to external circumstances and influences, within the

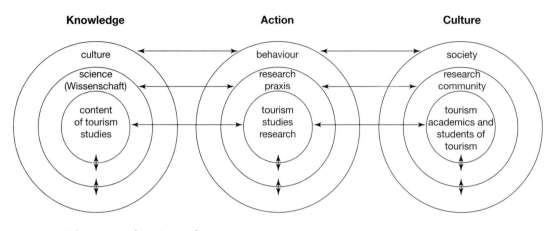

Figure 1.2: The context of tourism studies
Source: after Grano (1981)

context of their intellectual socialization' (Johnston 1983a: 4). See Table 1.1 for categorisations of the main approaches to the geography of tourism and recreation. Grano (1981) developed a model of external influences and internal change in geography that provides a valuable framework within which to examine the geography of tourism and recreation (Figure 1.2). The figure is divided into three interrelated areas:

- *knowledge* the content of the geography of tourism and recreation studies
- *action* tourism and recreation research within the context of research praxis
- *culture* academics and students within the context of the research community and the wider society.

KNOWLEDGE

The Dictionary of Human Geography (Johnston et al. 1986) defines geography as 'The study of the earth's surface as the space within which the human population lives' (Haggett 1986: 175). Such a concise definition is deceptively simple, and conceals the changing and contested nature of academic geography and, consequently, the geography of

tourism and recreation. The development of geography as an academic discipline and its ability to provide specialist educational contributions to knowledge can be dated to the 1870s when geography departments were established in Germany (P.J. Taylor 1985). Similar developments were closely followed in the UK and the USA, although the main growth of the discipline came in the twentieth century. James (1972) argued that the establishment of specialised programmes of training marked the evolution of geography from the classical age as it entered the contemporary period. Freeman's (1961) *A Hundred Years of Geography* identified six principal trends within geography. These were:

- The *encyclopaedic* trend where new information about the world was collated for the rulers, mercantile classes and residents of western Europe and North America.
- The *educational* trend where an academic discipline began to establish its need to generate knowledge, determine relevance and ensure its own reproduction to derive its future. The development of geographical work in schools, colleges and universities characterised this trend.
- The *colonial* tradition in the early decades of the twentieth century characterised by a concern

Table 1.1: Categorisations of main approaches to the geography of tourism and recreation

D.G. Pearce (1979)	R.V. Smith and Mitchell (1990)	Mitchell and Murphy (1991)	Pearce (1995a)	Hall and Lew (1998)
Spatial patterns of supply considerations	Spatial patterns	Environmental considerations	Tourism models	Environmental considerations
Spatial patterns of demand	Tourism in developing countries	Regional considerations	Demand for tourist travel	Regional considerations
Geography of resorts	Evolution of tourism	Spatial considerations	International tourism patterns	Spatial considerations
Tourist movements and flows	Impacts of tourism	Evolutionary considerations	Intra-national travel patterns	Evolutionary considerations
Impact of tourism	Tourism research methods		Domestic tourist flows	Tourism planning
Models of tourist space	Planning and development		Spatial variations in tourism	Urban tourism
	Coastal tourism		National and regional structures of tourism	Modernisation and development
	Tourism accommodation		Spatial structure of tourism on islands	Gender and identity
	Resort cycles		Coastal resorts	Place marketing and promotion
	Tourism concepts		Urban areas	Globalisation and economic and cultural change
	Tourism destinations			Sustainable development

with the environment. In the UK, the focus on empire, and its spatial and political organisation from a metropolitan hub, made extensive use of geographical skills.

- The *generalising* trend describes the use to which data are put generated through the encyclopaedic and colonial tradition. The methods used to interpret these data formed the basis of the early paradigms of the discipline's development.
- The *political* trend was indicative of the way in which contemporary uses of geographical expertise were used for political purposes (e.g. the redrawing of the map of Europe after the First World War).
- The *specialisation* trend was the natural corollary of the expansion of knowledge in geography and the inability of one person to be an expert in every field. The expansion of more rigorous research training required geographers to specialise.

Following on from these trends, Johnston (1991: 38) argued that 'some of these trends represent philosophies, some methodologies, and some ideologies with regard to the purpose of academic geography'. However, Johnston regarded three particular paradigms as being especially important in the development of human geography: exploration, environmental determinism and possibilism, and the region.

Exploration

Exploration refers to the situation where unknown areas of the world (to those who live outside of them) are explored to collect and classify information. Many of these activities were financed by geographical societies as well as by philanthropists. The Royal Geographical Society of London (RGS) was one such example, and even nowadays the RGS is a major sponsor of expeditions which are reported in its publication – *The Geographical Journal*. The theme of exploration remains significant in tourism geography, particularly as the images of places conveyed by explorers in the

metropolitan regions has served to create destination images that remain to the present day. For example, the 'discovery' of the Pacific by Europeans was the crucial point for the imaging of the Pacific as a romantic paradise (Douglas and Douglas 1996).

Environmental determinism and possibilism

Environmental determinism and possibilism were two competing approaches which, according to Johnston (1991), were early attempts at generalisation in the modern period. These approaches sought explanations rather than just descriptions of patterns of human occupation on the earth. The underlying assumption was that human activity was controlled by the elements in the physical environment within which it was located. Environmental determinism can be dated to the research by Darwin and *On the Origin of Species* (published in 1859), where ideas on evolution were used by an American geographer William Morris Davies to develop the model of land form development. The nineteenth century also saw a number of geographers become protagonists of environmental determinism, especially the German geographer Friedrich Ratzel (1844–1904), and the American geographer Ellen Churchill Semple (1863–1932), whose book *Influences of Geographic Environment* (1891) stated that 'man is the product of the earth's surface'.

The response to determinism was the counter-thesis possibilism. French geographers presented arguments to show that people perceive a range of alternative uses to which the environment could be put. This was, in part, determined by their own cultural traditions and predispositions. The debate on possibilism and determinism continued into the 1960s and has had some influence on tourism geography because of the extent to which concepts such as place, cultural landscape and heritage underlie much debate about tourism's impacts. Arguably some elements of environmental determinism are to be found in some of the discussions on the role of climate on tourism behaviour (Paul

1972; Adams 1973; Mieczkowski 1985; de Freitas 1990, 2003) and the potential impact of climate change (Wall et al. 1986; Wall and Badke 1994; Agnew and Viner 2001; Hall and Higham 2005).

The region

Ideas of the region and regional geography dominated British and American geography until the 1950s, based on the principle that generalisations and explanations were best derived from an areal approach. Johnston (1991) points to the role of Herbertson (1905) in dividing the earth into natural regions and the attempt to examine areas at a smaller scale to identify particular characteristics. In North America, the influence of Richard Hartshorne's ongoing research established the focus of geography as a concern for areal differentiation so that the principal purpose of geographical scholarship is synthesis, an integration of relevant characteristics to provide a total description of a place as a powerful focus for the discipline which remained a feature of many school, college and university programmes even in the 1990s. In the new millennium the region has become integrated into what L. Murphy and Le Heron (1999: 15) describe as the '"new regional geography" which incorporates elements of the earlier regional geography and new elements from political economy, geography, feminist geography and geographic information systems'. The development of regional synthesis required topical specialisms in geography to contribute to the regional paradigm.

Regional concepts continue to play a major role in the geography of tourism and recreation and underlie five main areas of research and scholarship:

• *Regional tourism geographies* A number of collections of regional material have been developed by geographers since the late 1980s, in part influenced by the development of regional economic and political blocs, which serve as frameworks for the development of baseline studies of contemporary tourism processes. Major regional reviews of tourism have been undertaken by geographers on western Europe (A.M. Williams and Shaw 1988), Canada (Wall 1989), eastern Europe (D.R. Hall 1991), Europe (Montanari and Williams 1995), polar regions (C.M. Hall and Johnston 1995), Australia (C.M. Hall 1995, 2003a), China (Lew and Wu 1995), South Africa (Rogerson and Visser 2004; Visser and Rogerson 2004), the South Pacific (Hall and Page 1996), the Pacific Rim (Hall et al. 1997) and South and South-East Asia (Hall and Page 2000).

• *Destination regions* Given the importance of the destination as an analytical concept in tourism, significant effort has been given to the ways in which destination regions can be identified, managed, and marketed (see S.L.J. Smith and Brown 1981; Mitchell 1984; S.L.J. Smith 1983a, 1987, 1995; Heath and Wall 1992).

• *Regional planning and development* The delineation of political and administrative regions provides a focus for administrative and planning research as well as a focus for the encouragement of development efforts through tourism and recreation. There is a significant body of research in this area, particularly with reference to Europe and the overall focus by government on tourism as a tool for economic development (see e.g. D.G. Pearce 1988a, 1992a, 1995a, 1995b; A.M. Williams and Shaw 1988; D.R. Hall 1991; Heath and Wall 1992; C.M. Hall et al. 1997; Hall 1999; Hall and Boyd 2005).

• *Synthesis and integration* The importance of synthesis and integration within regions has proven to be an important component in the development of approaches to integrated resource management within a regional context (see e.g. Lang 1988; Wight 1993, 1995; Pearce 1995b; Hall 1999).

• *Reviews of progress* In the development of the subdiscipline (e.g. Pearce 1979; Butler 2004) and specific progress reports for individual countries such as the UK (Duffield 1984), Spain (Bote Gomez 1996), Germany (Kreisel 2004), Australasia (D.G. Pearce and Mings 1984; Pearce 1999a), China (Bao 2002), Japan (Takeuchi 1984), France (Barbier and Pearce

1984; Iazzarotti 2002), South Africa (Rogerson and Visser 2004; Visser and Rogerson 2004) and the USA (L.S. Mitchell 1969a, 1979, 1984; R.V. Smith and Mitchell 1990; Mitchell and Murphy 1991).

Johnston (1991) also charts the development of geography as a discipline, focusing on a number of other trends which provided a direction for development. These are as follows:

- The growth of systematic studies and adoption of a scientific method, where methods of investigation are developed.
- The development of a new focus around the spatial variable and the analysis of spatial systems in the 1960s and 1970s where spatial analytical techniques were developed and systems theory was introduced.
- The development of behavioural geography as a response to the spatial science approaches, recognising that human behaviour cannot easily be explained using logical positivist models. Behavioural geography focuses on the processes which underlie human decision-making and spatial behaviour rather than the outcomes which are the focus of much conventional spatial analysis (J. Gold 1980).
- The rise of humanistic geography with its emphasis on the individual as a decision-maker. The behavioural approach tended to view people as responses to stimuli to show how individuals do not correspond to models built to predict possible human outcomes. In contrast, humanistic geography treats the individual as someone constantly interacting with the environment that changes both self and milieu (R.J. Johnston 1991). It does not use any scientifically defined model of behaviour, with each paradigm recognising appropriate contexts where the respective approaches are valid.
- Applied geography, which refers to 'the application of geographical knowledge and skills to the solution of economic and social problems' (Johnston 1986: 17).
- Radical approaches to geography, often with a

neo-Marxist base (Peet 1977a, 1977b), but which have broadened in the 1980s and 1990s to consider issues of gender, globalisation, localisation, identity, postcolonialism, post-modernism and the role of space in critical social theory (e.g. Harvey 1987, 1988, 1989a, 1989b, 1990, 1993; Soja 1989; Benko and Strohmmayer 1997; Crouch 1999b; Blom 2000).

All of the above approaches to geography have relevance to the study of tourism and recreation. However, their application has been highly variable with the greatest degree of research being conducted in the areas of spatial analysis and applied geography (Table 1.2). It is useful to note that two of the most influential books on the geography of tourism and recreation – Pearce (1987a, 1995a) on tourism and S.L.J. Smith (1983a) on recreation – primarily approach their subjects from a spatial perspective although both give an acknowledgement to the role of behavioural research. In contrast, the text on geographical perspectives on tourism by Shaw and Williams (1994) provides a far more critical approach to the study of tourism with acknowledgement of the crucial role that political economy, production, consumption, globalisation and commodification play in the changing nature of tourism. In one sense, Pearce (1995a) and Shaw and Williams (1994, 2002, 2004) are representative of the two most significant strands in present-day tourism and recreation geography. The former, dominant approach represents a more 'traditional' form of spatial analysis and 'applied' geography (in the sense that it may be immediately useful to some public sector and commercial interests). The latter, emerging approach represents more discursive and reflexive forms of analysis with a broader perspective on what the appropriate focus for the study of tourism and recreation should be. Although arguably Crouch (1999b) represents another reflexive form of analysis that has taken a different direction through its focus on identities, encounters and people as socialised and embodied subjects, but which may act as a bridge for greater communication between tourism and cultural geography. Undoubtedly, leisure and tourism are 'beginning to be rendered visible, situated and placed within the rapidly evolving discourses of post-positivist or post-structuralist geographies' (Aitcheson et al. 2000: 1). The recent 'cultural turn' in human geography has substantially influenced tourism research (Debbage and Ioannides 2004), particularly with respect to issues of performance, the body, gender, postcolonialism (Hall and Tucker 2004) and power. Indeed, the terrain of human geography has shifted so much that it is rather debatable whether the 'radical' geography of Johnston (1991) can really be described as radical any more.

In many ways Shaw and Williams (1994, 2002, 2004) represent an explicit response to Britton's (1991) call for a theorisation of geography of tourism and leisure that explicitly recognises, and unveils, tourism as a predominantly capitalistically organised activity driven by the inherent and defining social dynamics of that system, with its attendant production, social and ideological relations. An analysis of how the tourism production system markets and packages people is a lesson in the political economy of the social construction of 'reality' and social construction of place, whether from the point of view of visitors and host communities, tourism capital (and the 'culture industry'), or the state – with its diverse involvement in the system (Britton 1991: 475).

To many students of the geography of tourism and recreation, such a call would not seem appropriate, as it would be seen to be taking geography too far from its spatial core interpreting the mapping of decision-making outcomes in space. This should be no surprise though, as the subdiscipline reflects the wider turmoil in the discipline as a whole in terms of competition between various frameworks of analysis regarding how space is conceived. Nevertheless, while conventional spatial science may yield useful information, it does little to promote an understanding of the processes by which outcomes at given points of time are actually reached, nor does it do much to connect the geography of tourism and recreation to wider debates and issues in the social sciences.

One of the great stresses in the geography of tourism and recreation is the extent to which it connects with other components of the discipline. While it is quite easy to agree with Matley's (1976: 5) observation that 'There is scarcely an aspect of tourism which does not have some geographical implications and there are few branches of geography which do not have some contribution to make to the study of the phenomenon of tourism' (see also Mercer 1970), one must also note that the relative influence of these branches has proven to be highly variable since the late 1920s.

One of the great difficulties has been that while tourism and recreation geographers have seen the significance of relationships to other geographical subdisciplines and, indeed, other disciplines, such relationships are not reciprocal. For example, while Mercer (1970) recognised the significance of recreation, tourism and leisure for social geography (see also W.M. Williams 1979), textbooks, such as that by Jackson and Smith (1984), do not examine such concepts. Similarly, a text such as Whitehead (1993) on *The Making of the Urban Landscape* failed to note the role of tourism and recreation activities in urban environments. Tourism is also a notable absentee from textbooks on economic geography (Debbage and Ioannides 1998). Perhaps the most significant indicator of the way the geography of tourism and recreation is seen by the wider discipline can be found in Johnston's (1991) standard work on post-war Anglo-American geography. Here the terms leisure, recreation and tourism are absent from the index, while the only comment on the subject is three lines in the environmentalism section of the chapter on applied geography: 'A topic of special interest was the study of leisure, of the growing demand for recreation activities on the environment' followed by reference to the work of Patmore (1970, 1983) and Owens (1984). This is not to denigrate Johnston's magnificent work of scholarship. It is probably an appropriate comment on the perception of the standing of tourism and recreation geography in Anglo-American geography, that the only area where tourism and recreation are considered significant is in rural areas where, perhaps, tourists

Table 1.2: Approaches to geography and their relationship to the study of tourism and recreation

Approach	Key concepts	Exemplar publications
Spatial analysis	Positivism, locational analysis, maps, systems, networks, morphology	• spatial structure: Fesenmaier and Lieber 1987 • spatial analysis: S.L.J. Smith 1983b; Wall et al. 1985; Hinch 1990; Ashworth and Dietvorst 1995 • tourist flows and travel patterns: A. Williams and Zelinsky 1970; Corsi and Harvey 1979; Forer and Pearce 1984; D.G. Pearce 1987a, 1990a, 1993b, 1995a; Murphy and Keller 1990; Oppermann 1992 • gravity models: Malamud 1973; Bell 1977 • morphology: Pigram 1977 • regional analysis: S.L.J. Smith 1987
Behavioural geography	Behaviouralism, behaviourism, environmental perception, diffusion, mental maps, decision-making, action spaces, spatial preference	• mental maps: Walmesley and Jenkins 1992; Jenkins and Walmesley 1993 • environmental cognition: Aldskogius 1977 • tourist spatial behaviour: Carlson 1978; Cooper 1981; Debbage 1991 • tourist behaviour: Murphy and Rosenblood 1974; Arbel and Pizam 1977; Pearce 1988a • environmental perception: Wolfe 1970 • recreational displacement: Anderson and Brown 1984
Humanistic geography	Human agency, subjectivity of analysis, hermeneutics, place, landscape, existentialism, phenomenology, ethnography, lifeworld	• placelessness of tourism: Relph 1976 • historical geography: Wall and Marsh 1982; Marsh 1985; Towner 1996
Applied geography	Planning, remote sensing, Geographic Information Systems (GIS), public policy, cartography, regional development, carrying capacity	• planning: Murphy 1985; Getz 1986a; Dowling 1993, 1997; C.M. Hall et al. 1997; C.M. Hall 2000a • regional development: Coppock 1977a, 1977b; D.G. Pearce 1988b, 1990a, 1992a • tourism development: D.G. Pearce 1981, 1989; Cooke 1982; Lew 1985; P.E. Murphy 1985; Cater 1987 • indigenous peoples: Mercer 1994; Butler and Hinch 1996; Lew and van Otten 1997 • rural tourism and recreation: Coppock and Duffield 1975; Getz 1981; Glyptis 1991; Page and Getz 1997; Butler et al. 1998 • urban tourism and recreation: Ashworth 1989, 1992b; Law 1993, 1996; Page 1995a; Hinch 1996; Murphy 1997; Page and Hall 2003; Connell and Page 2005 • health: Clift and Page 1996; Wilks and Page 2003 • destination marketing: Dilley 1986; Heath and Wall 1992 • place marketing: Ashworth and Voogd 1988; Madsden 1992; Fretter 1993 • public policy and administration: Cooper 1987; D.G. Pearce 1992b; J. Jenkins 1993; C.M. Hall 1994; Hall and Jenkins 1995; Bramwell and Lane 2000 • tourism impacts (micro-level): Pigram 1980; Mathieson and Wall 1982; Edington and Edington 1986; Edwards 1987

- tourism life cycle: Butler 1980, 2005; Cooper and Jackson 1989; Debbage 1990;
- transport: Wall 1971, 1972; Page 1994b, 1999, 2005
- attractions: Lew 1987
- second homes: Aldskogius 1968; Coppock 1977a; Gartner 1987; Hall and Müller 2004
- GIS: Kliskey and Kearsley 1993; Elliott-White and Finn 1998
- national parks: Nelson 1973; Olwig and Olwig 1979; Marsh 1983; Calais and Kirkpatrick 1986; Cole et al. 1987; Davies 1987; Hall 1992a; McKercher 1993c
- heritage management: Gale and Jacobs 1987; Lew 1989; Ashworth and Tunbridge 1990, 1996; Hall and McArthur 1996, 1998; Graham et al. 2000
- outdoor recreation management: Pigram and Jenkins 1999
- sustainable development: Butler 1990, 1991, 1992, 1998; Pigram 1990; Ashworth 1992b; Bramwell and Lane 1993; Cater 1993; Dearden 1993; McKercher 1993a, 1993b; Cater and Lowman 1994; Ding and Pigram 1994; Murphy 1994; Mowforth and Munt 1997; Hall and Lew 1998; Aronsson 2000; Page and Thorn 1997, 2002
- ecotourism: Weiler 1991; Eagles 1992; Cater 1993; Cater and Lowman 1994; Blamey 1995; Weaver 1998; Fennel 1999; Page and Dowling 2001
- security: C.M. Hall 2002; Hall et al. 2003b
- global environmental change and climate change: K. Smith 1990; Wall and Badke 1994; Gössling 2002; Gössling et al. 2002; de Freitas 2003; Hall and Higham 2005
- small business and entrepreneurship: Buhalis and Cooper 1998; Page et al. 1999; Ateljevic and Doorne 2000; Getz and Carlsen 2000; Getz et al. 2004

'Radical' approaches

Neo-Marxist analysis, role of the state, gender, globalisation, localisation, identity, postcolonialism, postmodernism role of space

- political economy: Britton 1982; Ley and Olds 1988; A. Williams 2004
- social theory: Britton 1991; Shaw and Williams 1994, 2002, 2004
- semiotic analysis: Waitt 1997
- place promotion and commodification: Ashworth and Voogd 1990a, 1990b, 1994; Kearns and Philo 1993; Chang et al. 1996; Tunbridge and Ashworth 1996; Waitt and McGuirk 1997
- cultural identity: Byrne et al. 1993; D. Crouch 1994; Squire 1994
- gender: Adler and Brenner 1992; Kinnaird and Hall 1994; Aitchison 1997, 1999; Aitchison et al. 2000; Crouch 1999b
- 'new cultural studies': Aitchison 1999; Aitchison et al. 2000; Crouch 1999b
- postcolonialism: C.M. Hall and Tucker 2004

Plate 1.2/1.3: Loch Lomond, Scotland. The retail mix can provide a major attraction for visitors, as in the case of the Loch Lomond Shores project, which is underpinned by an anchor tenant and a large visitor attraction.

Plate 1.4: National Park Gateway Centre, Loch Lomond and the Trossachs National Park, Scotland, provides visitor information and orientation at the southern boundary of and major visitor gateway to the park.

and recreationists are seen as a nuisance! The reasons for this situation are manifold but perhaps lie in the cultural and action dimensions of geographical research.

ACTION: DEVELOPMENT OF AN APPLIED GEOGRAPHY OF TOURISM AND RECREATION

Within the literature on geographical research, there was a growing concern for relevance in the 1950s (see Johnston 1991). Part of that concern may have been a function of trying to improve the marketability of the discipline. At the same time, this call for relevance was accompanied by the development of scientific methods in geography that highlighted the growing systematic focus and concern with applying geographical principles and concepts to real-world problems. One possible interpretation of the post-1945 concern with relevancy and, more belatedly, an applied focus, may be related to the expansion of undergraduate student enrolments in geography departments and the need to secure employment opportunities beyond teaching. The 1960s also saw the development of notable studies (e.g. Stamp 1960) extolling the virtues of the geographer's art and tools in relation to their contribution to society. Yet recreation and tourism received only a passing mention in that seminal study, as geography remained preoccupied with the move towards 'scientific method', 'logical positivism', quantification and a move away from regional description to more systematic forms of spatial analysis. Such developments were crucial, since they provided the training and foundations for the next generation of geographers who were to begin to nurture the recreation–tourism continuum as a legitimate research focus. But one consequence of geography's development in the 1950s and 1960s and the rise of a more 'applied' focus was the increasing move towards narrow specialisation which appears to have reached its natural peak in the 1990s. Johnston (1991) outlines an increasing tension within geography in the 1960s and 1970s over the focus of the discipline, which in part transcended the debate over radical approaches (see Harvey 1974). The basic tension related to how geographers should contribute their skills to the solution of societal problems. This questioned the philosophical basis of geography – who should the geographer benefit with an applied focus?

Both British and American geography conferences in the 1970s saw an increasing debate and awareness of the value of geographers contributing to public policy. Coppock (1974) felt that policy-makers were unaware of the contribution geographers could make to policy-making. But critics questioned the value of advising governments which were the paymasters and already constrained in what geographers could undertake research on. Harvey (1974) raised the vital issue of 'what kind of geography for what kind of public policy?', arguing that individuals involved in policy-making were motivated by

> personal ambition, disciplinary imperialism, social necessity and moral obligation at the level of the whole discipline, on the other hand, geography had been co-opted, through the Universities, by the growing corporate state, and geographers had been given some illusion of power within a decision-making process designed to maintain the status quo.
>
> (Johnston 1991: 198)

Indeed, Pacione's (1999a) defence of applied geography reiterates many of the inherent conflicts and problems which the 'purists' in human geography raise, in that

> Applied geography is concerned with the application of geographical knowledge and skills to the resolution of real-world social, economic and environmental problems. The underlying philosophy of relevance of usefulness and problem-orientated goals of applied geography have generated critical opposition from other 'non-applied' members of the geographical community. Particular criticism of the applied geography approach has emanated from Marxist and, more recently, postmodern theorists who reflect the potential of applied geography to address the major problems confronting people and places in the contemporary world.
>
> (Pacione 1999a: 1)

The emergence of the 'new cultural geography' highlights the increasing tensions within the discipline where 'the idea of applied geography or useful research is a chaotic concept which does not fit with the recent "cultural turn" in social geography or the postmodern theorising of recent years' (Pacione 1999a: 3). In fact, Pacione claimed that it was a matter of individual conscience as to what individual geographers study. What is clear is that some research is more 'useful' than other forms, and the application to tourism and recreation phenomenon is certainly a case in point. Although the 'concept of "useful research" poses the basic questions of useful for whom? Who decides what is useful' (Pacione 1999a: 4) is part of the wider relevance debate which continues in human geography as paradigm shifts, and new ways of theorising and interpreting information question the central role of the discipline. In P.J. Taylor's (1985) provocative and thoughtful analysis of 'The value of a geographical perspective', a cyclical function emerged in the development of eras of pure and applied research. What Taylor (1985) observed was that when external pressures are greatest, problem-solving approaches are pursued within the discipline. Conversely, in times of comparative economic prosperity, more pure academic activity is nurtured. Taylor (1985) related these trends to longer-term trends in the world economy, identifying three distinct periods when applied geography was in its ascendance: the late nineteenth century, the inter-war period and the mid-1980s.

However, Johnston (1991) also points to a liberal contribution to an applied geography which can be dated to Stamp's land use survey of Britain in the 1930s and his involvement in post-war land use planning (Stamp 1948). While much of this early 'applied geography' was set in an empiricalist tradition, Sant's (1982) survey of applied geography traces the use of the term back to the late nineteenth century with the early conferences of the International Geographical Union (IGU). While the title lapsed until the 1960s, the principal interest in applied geography has been promulgated by that organisation and a number of publications have resulted (e.g. Ackerman 1963). Sant's (1982) study concurs with Johnston's (1991) analysis, in that geographers' interest in applied geography between the 1930s and 1950s was based on:

- administrative regionalisation (E.W. Gilbert 1951)
- land use surveys (Stamp 1948)
- terrain analysis and air-photointerpretation (G. Taylor 1951)
- urban and regional planning.

Stamp's (1960) influential book on *Applied Geography* documents his own research activities in geography, and the spirit of the book highlights how a spatial focus could offer so many potential areas for study. Sant (1982) assesses Stamp's contribution as follows:

> There is a deceptive innocence about Stamp's book which stems not from naivety but from confidence in his own judgement and experience. He had achieved much and his credentials commanded attention. Today we live in a less confident age. Perhaps this is because we have a greater propensity to invent complexities. . . . At any rate, the scope and methods of applied geography are more elaborate than they were a generation ago.
>
> (Sant 1982: 8)

Sant (1982) argued that applied geography was not a subdiscipline but had a dependent relationship with academic geography. It has a different *modus operandi*. It is intended to offer prescription, has to engage in dialogue with 'outsiders' not familiar

with the discipline, its traditions, problems and internal conservatism, and an ability to overtly criticise developments which are not central to the prevailing paradigm. While the discipline has published a range of journals with an applied focus (e.g. *Applied Geography*) and offers a number of applied courses in universities, the term is used loosely. As Sant (1982: 136) argued, 'the crux of applied geography is (at the risk of tautology) fundamentally that it is about geography. That is, it deals with human and physical landscapes'. What is interesting to note in Sant's text is the inclusion of recreation and the contribution of geographers to this area of applied geography, a feature reierated in the study edited by Kenzer (1989) and the brief mention by Johnston (1991) noted above.

Some commentators, however, feel that the rise of an 'applied focus' has meant the discipline has lost touch with its roots, and thereby compromised the ability of 'explicating the relationship between people, places, cultures and the global/ regional mix of each' (Kenzer 1989: 2). One indication of this, according to critics, is the greater emphasis on techniques and their application to geographical concerns among human geographers and a subsequent decline in real-world, fieldwork-oriented studies. For example, the application of Geographical Information Systems (GIS) in research has meant a move away from traditional fieldwork and more laboratory-based analysis (Van der Knaap 1999), which may be distant from the real world. As Forer (1999: 96) argued, 'New geographic information technology is becoming ubiquitous, and is revolutionising what we measure and how we measure it'. In fact, as Tarrant and Cordell (1999) noted in their examination of outdoor recreation in US national forest areas, the use of GIS can be an extremely valuable tool in the analysis of environmental justice and equity. The natural corollary of the development of more techniques-based geographical courses, some critics suggest, is the potential loss of the 'core' in human geography if applied studies become dominant, and traditional concepts and the roots of the discipline are no longer taught. It is ironic, therefore, that in many undergraduate geography degrees where the development of geographical thought is taught, the broader context of applied geography often receives limited or poor treatment in contrast to the emphasis now placed on quantification, computer-based analysis and skills-based training.

In contrast, supporters of a more applied focus have argued that despite the apparent splintering and fragmentation of geography in the late 1980s and 1990s as a function of specialisation, it has made a valid contribution to society. Many able geographers have recognised the need to move away from academia in order to make their skills, knowledge and perspective of use to society through a range of contributions while still being capable of reflexive analysis of their actions.

In the case of recreation and tourism, many geographers involved in these areas may no longer be based in geography departments in universities. However, they maintain and extend the value of a geographical analysis and understanding for the training and research in the wider field of recreation and tourism studies. The discipline of geography, in the UK at least, paid very little attention to the growing role of geographers in the educational and research environment of tourism. Only in the 1990s have organisations such as the Institute of British Geographers acknowledged the significance of recreation and tourism as a serious area of academic study. In contrast, the Association of American Geographers and the Canadian Association of Geographers have been much more active, with their study groups being established since the 1970s. International organisations such as the International Geographical Union (IGU) Study Group on the Geography of Tourism, Leisure and Global Change (lifespan: 2000 to 2008) (formerly the IGU Geography of Sustainable Tourism, 1994 to 2000, and IGU Commission on Tourism and Leisure, 1984 to 1992) provided another forum for research developments and interaction by geographers and non-geographers with similar research interests. Nevertheless, despite such initiatives, the relationship of the geography of tourism and recreation to the broader discipline of geography has suffered two major problems:

- the rise of applied geography within the discipline, and tourism and recreation geography within it, has seen critics view it as rather ephemeral and lacking in substance and rigour
- in some countries (e.g. the UK and Australia), national geographical organisations and geography departments have often failed to recognise the significance of recreation and tourism as a legitimate research area capable of strengthening and supporting the discipline.

One consequence is that many geographers who developed recreational and tourism research interests in the 1980s and 1990s have left the inherent conservatism and ongoing criticism of their research activity to move to fresh pastures where autonomous tourism research centres or departments have eventuated. This does not, however, denigrate the excellent contribution that leading geographers such as Patmore, Coppock, Mercer, Glyptis and Pearce have made to establishing recreation and tourism as serious areas of academic study within the discipline. Nevertheless, a significant number of geographers are now based in business schools or tourism, recreation or leisure departments where their research interests are aligned within a multidisciplinary environment that can cross-fertilise their research and support an applied focus. Indeed, in some respects, history is perhaps repeating itself all over again, where planning emerged as a discipline and split from some of its geographical roots and where the development of environmental studies departments has also led to a departure of geographers to such centres.

Since the mid-1980s many geographers unwilling to have the progress of their careers impeded by views held by peers who did not see tourism and recreation as mainstream spatial research have similarly split from the discipline. For example, in New Zealand, with one or two exceptions, all the geographers with a tourism or recreation focus are now located in business schools, departments of tourism and recreation or other non-geographical departments. This situation is not dramatically different from the situation in Australia, where educational expansion in this area has made extensive use of professional geographers to develop and lead such developments (Weiler and Hall 1991). As Janiskee and Mitchell (1989) concluded:

> This is certainly an interesting and exciting time to be a recreation geographer. After a slow start, the sub-discipline has achieved a critical mass and seems destined to enjoy a bright future. . . . There is no question that the application of recreation geography knowledge and expertise to problem solving contexts outside academia offers potential rewards of considerable worth to the sub-discipline: more jobs for recreation geographers, a stimulus to academic research with implications for problem solving, a more clearly defined sense of purpose or social worth, and greater visibility, both within and outside academic circles.
>
> (Janiskee and Mitchell 1989: 159)

It is interesting to note that Janiskee and Mitchell (1989) also perceive that

> since there is no clear distinction between 'basic' and 'applied' research, nor any appreciable threat to quality scholarship, there is no simmering argument on the issue of whether applied research is good for recreation geography. Rather, the real question is whether recreation geographers will have the resources and the zeal to move into the problem-solving domain on a much more widespread and consistent basis.
>
> (Janiskee and Mitchell 1989: 159)

While this may be true in a North American context, it is certainly not the case in the UK in 2005, and a number of other countries where applied geographical research in recreation and tourism has been viewed as dissipating the value and skills of the geographer for pecuniary reward, or without contributing to the development of the discipline. Ironically, however, the proliferation of 'dabblers' (i.e. people who do not consider themselves recreation geographers, but contribute articles to journals using simplistic notions of tourism and recreation) has grown and still abounds in the geography and, to a lesser extent, in the recreation and tourism journals. Indeed, tourism and recreation have been 'discovered' by geographers and other social scientists in the late 1980s and 1990s as tourism is utilised by governments to respond to the effects of global economic restructuring and increasing concerns over conserving the environment (Hall and Lew 1998). Such contributions, according to Janiskee and Mitchell (1989: 157), 'although welcome, are not a satisfactory substitute for output of a substantial number of specialists doing scientific–theoretical–nomothetic research which is needed for the area to progress'. Calls for a 'heightened awareness and appreciation of problem solving needs and opportunities outside the traditional bounds of scholarly research' (Janiskee and Mitchell 1989: 159) are vital if academics are to connect with the broad range of stakeholders and interests that impinge upon geography and academia. Geographers with knowledge and skills in the area of tourism and recreation research need to develop a distinctive niche by undertaking basic and applied research to address public and private sector problems, which illustrates the usefulness of a spatial, synthesising and holistic education. Even so,

> the list of research undertaken by applied geographers is impressive, but there are no grounds for complacency [as] the influence of applied geography has been mixed, and arguably less than hoped for. . . . Several reasons may account for this [including] the eclectic and poorly focused nature of the discipline of geography and the fact that 'geographical work' is being undertaken by 'non-geographers' in other disciplines. This undermines the identity of geography as a subject with something particular to offer.
>
> (Pacione 1999a: 10–11)

Even so, in Pearce's (1999a) review of tourism geography in New Zealand, many of the geographers' applied contributions appear to have been overlooked in favour of geographical journal publications on tourism. For this reason, it is worth considering the skills and techniques that geographers can harness in tourism and recreation research.

CULTURE

The cultural dimensions of the geography of tourism and recreation – the sociology of knowledge of the subdiscipline – as with that of tourism and recreation studies as a whole, have been little studied. This is extremely unfortunate as it means there is a very incomplete comprehension of where the subdiscipline has been, which must also clearly affect our understanding of where it might go. As Barnes (1982) commented:

> Social, technical and economic determinants routinely affect the rate and direction of scientific growth. . . . It is true that much scientific change occurs despite, rather than because of, external direction or financial control. . . . Progress in the disinterested study [of certain] . . . areas has probably occurred just that bit more rapidly because of their relevance to other matters.
>
> (Barnes 1982: 102–3)

Similarly, Johnston (1991) observed that

> the study of a discipline must be set in its societal context. It must not necessarily be assumed, however, that members of academic communities fully accept the social context and the directives and impulses that it issues. They may wish to counter it, and use their academic base as a focus for their discontent. But the (potential) limits to that discontent are substantial. Most academic communities are located in universities, many of which are dependent for their existence on public funds disbursed by governments which may use their financial power to influence, if not direct, what is taught and researched. And some universities are dependent on private sources of finance, so they must convince their sponsors that their work is relevant to current societal concerns.
>
> (Johnston 1991: 24–5)

As noted above, research into the geographical dimensions of tourism has received relatively little attention in the wider fields of academic geography. Several related factors can be recognised as accounting for this situation:

- There is only a narrow set of official interest in conducting research into the geography of tourism.
- Tourism is not regarded as a serious scholarly subject.
- Not only are there substantial unresolved theoretical issues in conducting geographical studies of tourism and recreation but also much theorisation is relatively weak.
- Tourism and recreation geographers have had little success in promoting their subdiscipine in the broader geographical context.
- Many tourism and recreation geographers are now operating in non-geography departments or in the private sector.

Unlike some areas of tourism research, such as politics and public policy, for example (Hall 1994; Hall and Jenkins 1995), there is some government support for research and consulting on the geography of tourism and recreation. However, such research support tends to be given to the analysis of spatial patterns of tourist flows and issues of infrastructure location rather than areas of applied geographical research in gender and social impacts that may produce unwanted political results. Indeed, even support for research on the environmental impacts on tourism has the potential to produce politically contestable results, particularly if the results are not seen as supportive of industry interests. Therefore, funding for tourism and recreation research will tend to reinforce the more conservative spatial science aspects of the geography of tourism and recreation at the expense of more fundamental analysis which would have a greater capacity to extend the theoretical contributions of the subdiscipline. Despite the apparent lack of interest in studies of the broader dimensions of tourism by government and industry, and the community conflicts that occur in relation to tourism development, it is important to recognise that such research may be of an extremely practical nature. The results of such research may help facilitate and improve tourism planning through an increased understanding of decision-making processes (e.g. P.E. Murphy 1985), and help maintain the long-term viability of tourist destinations.

Despite the extensive growth of research on tourism and recreation in the 1980s and 1990s, many people still do not regard tourism as a serious subject of study, often equating it with booking a holiday at a travel agency or learning how to pour a beer. Indeed, research on tourism is often seen as frivolous. The observation of Matthews (1983: 304) that 'at a typical American university, a political scientist with a scholarly interest in tourism might be looked upon as dabbling in frivolity – not as a serious scholar but as an opportunist looking for a tax-deductible holiday', holds almost universal applicability. Similar to V.L. Smith's (1977: 1) observations on the anthropology of tourism in the 1970s, it is a topic that still appears to be thought by many in the discipline as unworthy of consideration by the serious geography scholar. Indeed, L.S. Mitchell (1997), a noted scholar within tourism and recreation geography, in a personal communication following a discussion on RTSnet (the interest newsgroup of the recreation, tourism and sport speciality group of the Association of American Geographers) regarding the position of recreation and tourism in American geography, argued that

> Recreation geography, has never been a valued member of the establishment, because, it is believed, it is impossible to be serious about individuals and groups having fun. Note the subtitle of the feminist oriented tourism conference being held in California this month ('Tourism is not about having fun'). In spite of the fact that tourism is the number one economic activity in the world, that recreation (especially passive recreation) takes up a large portion of the population's time, and that sport is almost a religion for many in this country, geographers who study these phenomena are not highly regarded.

There are also substantial methodological, theoretical and spatial problems in conducting geographical research. Problems have arisen because of the multiplicity of potential frameworks for analysis as well as relatively weak theorisation in some quarters. As Ioannides (1996: 221) notes, 'Although tourism geography has long been an established specialization, the weak theoretical grounding associated with this research area relegates it to the discipline's periphery'.

The lack of a clearly articulated or agreed-upon methodological or philosophical approach to geography per se, let alone the geography of tourism and recreation, may create an intellectual and perceptual minefield for the researcher, particularly

as the value position of the author will have an enormous bearing on the results of any research. Burton (1982: 323–4), for example, argued that leisure and tourism research is plagued by problems of 'lack of intellectual co-ordination and insufficient cross-fertilization of ideas among researchers; an inadequacy of research methodologies and techniques; and a lack of any generally agreed concepts and codes in the field'. However, in contrast, Hall (1994: 7) argued that 'In fact, the debate which marks such concepts should probably be seen as a sign of health and youthful vigour in an emerging area of serious academic study and should be welcomed and encouraged rather than be regarded as a source of embarrassment'.

Another factor which may have influenced the standing of the geography of tourism and recreation is the extent to which the subdiscipline is being promoted to the discipline as a whole. For example, in the American context, Mitchell (1997) argued:

> There is no one individual superstar in the US who has popularized the subject matter through publications and/or personality. From my perspective a lot of good geographic research has been published and the research frontier has been advanced, however, little of this research has appeared in the geographic literature; rather it tends to be found in specialty or multi-disciplinary journals. . . . Lots of publications are produced but they do not engender the kind of interest or reputation that leads to widespread recognition.

In the British context, the publication of *Critical Issues in Tourism* by Shaw and Williams (1994) as part of the Institute of British Geography Studies in Geography Series helped raise the profile of the area. Nevertheless, the situation remains that the key academic audience of the majority of research and publications by tourism and recreation geographers are people within tourism and recreation departments rather than geography. However, there are some signs that this situation may be changing. First, there is the publication of the journal *Tourism Geographies* in 1999 (edited by Alan Lew and published by Routledge) which seeks to promote the subdiscipline both within its immediate audience and beyond. To some extent the emergence of this specialised journal may be regarded as a sign of maturity of the field akin to other specialist geography journals (e.g. *Applied Geography*, *Journal of Transport Geography*). Second, there are activities of the IGU Study Group on the Geography of Tourism, Leisure and Global Change and its forerunner, the Study Group on the Geography of Sustainable Tourism which has co-hosted a number of conferences and special sessions with other IGU Commissions, such as Sustainable Rural Systems, and with national associations, such as the Association of American Geographers. Third, the increased significance of tourism and recreation in urban and rural environments in contemporary society has led to a greater appreciation of the potential significance of the field. In other words, tourism is now such a significant activity in the cultural landscape that it would be difficult for other geographies to ignore it for much longer. Finally, tourism and recreation geographies are now arguing that they have something to contribute to the wider discipline, particularly in such areas as understanding the service economy, industrial-isation and regional development (e.g. Ioannides 1995, 1996; d'Hauteserre 1996), as well as more traditional resource management concerns and sus-tainability (e.g. Zurick 1992; Hall and Lew 1998).

The final factor influencing the standing of the subdiscipline is the extent to which geographers in the field are increasingly undertaking employment outside geography departments and in tourism, recreation and leisure studies departments, business schools, and environmental studies and planning departments. Across most of the western world, tourism has become recognised as a major employer which, in turn, has placed demands on educational institutions to produce graduates with qualifica-tions relevant to the area. Therefore, there has been a substantial growth in the number of universities and colleges that offer undergraduate and graduate qualifications in tourism, recreation and hospitality which provide potential employment for tourism and recreation geographers. The opportunity to develop a career path in tourism and recreation departments which are undergoing substantial student growth, or in a new department, will clearly

be attractive to individuals whose career path may be slower within long-established geography departments and who carry the burden of being interested in a subdiscipline often on the outer edge of mainstream geographic endeavour. As Johnston (1991: 281) recognised, 'this reaction to environ-mental shifts is undertaken by individual scholars, who are seeking not only to defend and promote their own status and careers within it'.

The massive growth of tourism and recreation studies outside geography also means that increas-ingly many geographers publish in tourism and recreation journals rather than in geography jour-nals. Such publications may be extremely significant for tourism studies but may carry little weight within geography beyond the subdiscipline (e.g. Butler's (1980) hugely influential article on the destination life cycle). This has therefore meant that geographers who work in non-geography departments may find themselves being drawn into interdisciplinary studies with only weak linkages to geography. The question that of course arises is: does this really matter? Disciplines change over time, areas of specialisation come and go depending on intrinsic and extrinsic factors. As Johnston (1991) observes:

> The continuing goal of an academic discipline is the advancement of knowledge. Each discipline pursues that goal with regard to particular areas of study.
>
> Its individual members contribute by conducting research and reporting their findings, by integrating material into the disciplinary corpus, and by peda-gogical activities aimed at informing about, promoting and reproducing the discipline: in addition, they may argue the discipline's 'relevance' to society at large. But there is no fixed set of disciplines, nor any one correct division of academic according to subject matter. Those disciplines currently in existence are contained within boundaries established by earlier communities of scholars. The boundaries are porous so that dis-ciplines interact. Occasionally the boundaries are changed, usually through the establishment of a new discipline that occupies an enclave within the pre-existing division of academic space.
>
> (Johnston 1991: 9)

However, to borrow the title of a leading geogra-phy textbook of the 1980s, *Geography Matters!*

(Massey and Allen 1984), it matters because concepts at the heart of geography such as spatiality, place, identity, landscape and region are critical, not only to the geography of tourism and recreation but also to tourism and recreation studies as a whole. Indeed, the growing interest in the concept of mobility among the social sciences (e.g. Bell and Ward 2000; Urry 2000) is testimony to the long focus that tourism and recreation geographers have had on leisure mobility (Hall 2005a). In commenting on work undertaken by geographers in the tourism field, Britton (1991) noted that they have

> been reluctant to recognise explicitly the capitalistic nature of the phenomenon they are researching. . . . This problem is of fundamental importance as it has meant an absence of an adequate theoretical foundation for our understanding of the dynamics of the industry and the social activities it involves.
> (Britton 1991: 451)

However, such a criticism may be made of tourism and recreation studies overall (Hall 1994).

INSIGHT: The geography of tourism and recreation outside the Anglo-American tradition

While this book concentrates on the geography of tourism and recreation within the English-speaking world, it is important to note that the growing interest of geographers in tourism and recreation is also occurring within other geographical traditions. The internationalisation of the tourism and recreation academic community through such organisations as the IGU Study Group on Tourism, the growth of student and academic exchanges within the European Union and the use of English as the international language of scholarship has also meant a growing interchange between native English-speaking and English as a second language scholars. Academic journals in English are now increasingly being produced in countries where English is not the native tongue, for example, *Anatolia* in Turkey and *Tourism Today* in Cyprus. In addition, several tourism geographers, most notably Doug Pearce, who undertook his doctoral studies in France, have had the capacity to bring non-English literature to the attention of English-speaking geographers (most significantly his books *Tourism Development* (1981, 1989) and *Tourism Today* (1995a)).

In examining the tourism and recreation literature of a number of languages and countries, it may be noted that the growth of publishing on tourism and recreation in English is mirrored in these other traditions along with some of the disciplinary differences and issues noted above. For example, a review of *German Geographical Research 1996–1999* edited by the Committee of the Federal Republic of Germany for the IGU (2000) reveals that tourism is now a major subject for publication. A review of German geographical research in East and South-East Asia also reveals a substantial growth in research on tourism in the region (Kraas and Taubmann 2000). Kreisel (2004) provides an excellent review of the geography of tourism and leisure in the German-speaking world and highlights particular themes and issues including the focus of the so-called Munich School on leisure behaviour.

The excellent review of Spanish tourism geography by Rubio (1998–9) also reveals the very significant expansion in publications on the geography of Spanish tourism, particularly in terms of rural areas, which has gone hand-in-hand with the growth of international visitor arrivals. Similarly, Wayens and Grimmeau (2003) also reported a substantial growth in Belgian geographic research on tourism.

French geography also has a strong tradition of research on tourism and recreation (Iazzarotti 2002) that was, arguably, much further advanced in the 1960s and 1970s in terms of both theoretical development and extent of publication than the Anglo-American tradition. One reason for this advanced interest possibly lay in the long recognition of tourism as a factor in the economic development of French alpine regions and its impact on the cultural and physical landscape (e.g. Knafou 1978). In addition, the growth of tourism on the Mediterranean coast provided a basis for research on coastal resort development (e.g. Burnet 1963; Barbaza 1966) while the significance of second homes for tourism and leisure also has a strong research tradition. More recently, French geographers have written substantive works regarding the impacts of tourism (e.g. Michaud 1983, 1992; Escourrou 1993; Debarbieux 1995), urban tourism (e.g. Iazzarotti 1995; Potier and Cazes 1996, 1998), as well as the social construction of tourism (e.g. Boyer 1996; Deprest 1997). In a review of the geography of tourism and leisure in France, Knafou (2000) notes the diversity of approaches and topics that exist. Indeed, an examination of several French texts and readings (e.g. Lozato 1985; Clary 1993; Dewailly and Flament 1993; Deprest 1997; Baron-Yellés 1999) suggests that, as in Anglo-American human geography, traditional spatial approaches to studying tourism geography are increasingly under challenge from perspectives strongly influenced by postmodernism (Knafou et al. 1997).

Dutch and Nordic geographies have been much more influenced by Anglo-American tourism and recreation geography than their French and German counterparts to a great extent because of the role of English as a second language and the publication of much of their research in English. Coastal tourism, rural tourism and regional development are particularly strong themes in Dutch tourism geography (Ashworth and Dietvorst 1995; Dietz and Kwaad 2000), while the work of Greg Ashworth has had a major influence on the fields of urban and heritage tourism (see e.g. Ashworth 1989, 1999; Ashworth and Tunbridge 1996; Ashworth and Ennen 1998) (see also Chapter 5). Nordic tourism and recreation geography has had considerable influence in the areas of tourism in peripheral regions and second home development (e.g. Finnveden 1960;

Aldskogius 1968; Jaakson 1986; Halseth and Rosenberg 1995; Kaltenborn 1997a, 1997b, 1998; Müller 1999; Aronsson 2000; Saarinen 2001, 2003; Hall and Müller 2004; Saarinen and Hall 2004; Hall and Boyd 2005), global environmental change and contemporary mobility (Gössling 2002; Frändberg and Vilhelmson 2003; Gössling and Hall 2005). Nevertheless, as with Anglo-American tourism geography, a number of significant geographers are not based in departments of geography and are instead located in business schools (e.g. Ettema and Timmermans 1997; Timmermans and Morgansky 1999) or departments of tourism (e.g. Flognfeldt 1998). Asian tourism geographers have also been substantially influenced by Anglo-American publications and research, although unfortunately there is much of the Asian research which is yet to be published in English. For example, reviews of Korean human geography (Kim 2000) and applied geography (Lee 2000) indicate a large body of literature in Korean on event tourism, rural tourism, coastal tourism and resort development. There is also evidence of a growing interest in the geography of tourism in China (e.g. Lew and Wu 1995; Guo et al. 2000; Bao 2002).

One area which has shown a massive growth in tourism research by geographers is South Africa. Although some areas of South African geography were undoubtedly substantially influenced by developments in Anglo-American geography, relationships also existed with Dutch and German geographical traditions, while the apartheid years also contributed to a reduced contact with the international academic community. The removal of apartheid reconnected South African geography with the wider field (perhaps best indicated in the hosting of an IGU regional conference in South Africa in 2002 with tourism being one of the largest stream of papers at the conference) as well as reinforced the importance that South African tourism and recreation geographers would be able to connect with specific development issues in the new South Africa in manner that responded with local issues as much as international concerns (Rogerson and Visser 2004; Visser and Rogerson 2004).

The above discussion is by no means a comprehensive review of the enormous body of literature of tourism and recreation which exists outside of English. Nevertheless, it does indicate that there appears to be almost universal growth in research on tourism and recreation by geographers regardless of language, and that several of the tensions existing in Anglo-American tourism and recreation geography exist elsewhere. Moreover, there is also increasing cross-over between the different literatures as English continues to expand its academic influence, as indicated by both the growing literature by non-native English speakers in journals published in English and the continued growth in attendance at IGU conferences in which papers are primarily presented in English.

TRANSFORMING THE GEOGRAPHY OF TOURISM AND RECREATION

The situation described in this chapter is that of an area of academic endeavour which is at a critical point in its evolution. Tourism and recreation geography is an applied area of study that is at the periphery of its own discipline but with strong connections to academic research and scholarship outside the area. Dominated by systematic spatial analysis it has a relatively weak theoretical base that has exacerbated its inability to influence wider disciplinary endeavours. Nevertheless, since the early 1990s there appear to be signs of a transformation in its character and fortunes. First, there has been a major growth in the number and quality of publications by tourism and recreation geographers which, although not influencing geography outside the subdiscipline, has had a major impact on the direction of tourism and recreation studies. Second, there is clearly a conscious attempt to provide a stronger theoretical base to tourism and recreation geography which would both be informed by and contribute to contemporary social theory, particularly with respect to such issues as globalisation, localisation, commodification, restructuring and sustainability (e.g. Britton 1991; Hall 1994; Shaw and Williams 1994; Hall and Jenkins 1995; Ioannides 1995, 1996; Montanari and Williams 1995; Hall and Lew 1998). Finally, tourism and recreation geographers are seeking to promote their work more actively in academic and non-academic spheres.

This book reinforces several of the above themes. At one level it seeks to highlight the scope, nature and contribution of geography and geographers to the study of tourism and recreation. However, at another it also aims to provide some insights into the nature of the theoretical transformations which are occurring in the field. Figure 1.3 provides an overall framework for many of the key issues discussed in the book. The figure attempts to illustrate the relationships between some of the foci of the geography of tourism and recreation, including the opportunity spectrum that exists in relation to home-based leisure, recreation and tourism, and corresponding factors of demand and supply. These are themselves influenced and mediated by regulatory structures and the institutional arrangements that govern tourism. The impacts that occur through the intersection of supply and demand, consumption and production are located in a range of different environments which each provide separate experiences of place and constructed leisure/tourism spaces.

The following two chapters examine the demand and supply elements of tourism and recreation. Chapter 2 examines how the demand for tourism and recreation is conceptualised and analysed, the concepts developed to derive a focus for research and the implications for a geographical analysis. In Chapter 3, the main techniques and methods of evaluating tourist and recreational resources are discussed as a basis for Chapter 4, and looks at the interactions of demand and supply variables in relation to the impacts of tourism and recreation.

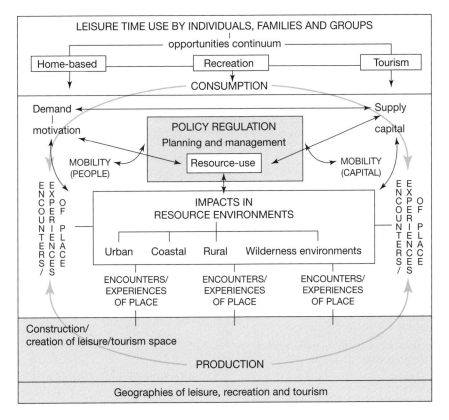

Figure 1.3: Organising framework for the book

The role of the state and government policy as a determinant of tourist and recreational opportunities is examined, as are issues of access to public and private space for tourists and recreationists.

Chapter 4 examines the differing types of impacts generated by tourist and recreational activities and the way in which different methodologies have been devised to analyse the environmental, socio-cultural and economic impacts. The following four chapters (5–8) consider the distinctive nature of tourist and recreational activities in a variety of contexts (urban, rural, wilderness, coastal and ocean areas), emphasising their role in shaping and influencing people's tourist and recreational opportunities, and the effects of such activities on the places in which they occur.

One of the strongest contributions of geography in the tourism and recreation field is in terms of

the development of planning and policy analysis. Chapter 9 reviews the need for developing a planning and policy framework at different geographical scales with particular concern for the different traditions of tourism planning which exist. Chapter 10, the final chapter, examines the future prospects of the field and the potential contributions which geography and geographers may make to understanding tourism and recreation phenomena. Tourism and recreation have been the direct subject of geographical analysis since the late 1920s and have developed into a significant area of applied geography. In that time methodologies and philosophies have changed as has the subject matter. Tourism is now regarded as the world's largest industry. Tourism and recreation are complex phenomena with substantial economic, socio-cultural, environmental and political impacts at scales from the global through to the individual. It is now time for geographers not only to develop a deeper understanding of the processes which lead to the spatial outcomes of tourism and recreation, but also to convey this understanding to other geographers, students of tourism and recreation, the public and private sectors and the wider community which is affected by these phenomena.

QUESTIONS

- Is geographical knowledge more important than ever? What is its relevance to understanding the contemporary world?
- 'This is an interesting time to be a recreational geographer.' Discuss.

READING

Useful introductions to some of the main approaches to the field of the geography of tourism and recreation include

Crouch, D. (ed.) (1999) *Leisure/Tourism Geographies: Practices and Geographical Knowledge*, London: Routledge (a fascinating range of readings from a 'new' cultural studies perspective).

Lew, A.A., Hall, C.M. and Williams, A.M. (eds) (2004) *Companion to Tourism*, Oxford: Blackwell (a large collection of essays on various major research themes and traditions in the geography of tourism as well as the wider tourism literature).

Pearce, D.G. (1995) *Tourism Today: A Geographical Analysis*, 2nd edn, Harlow: Longman (from a traditional spatial perspective).

Shaw, G. and Williams, A.M. (2002) *Critical Issues in Tourism: A Geographical Perspective*, 2nd edn, Oxford: Blackwell (from more of a critical perspective).

Shaw, G. and Williams, A. (2004) *Tourism and Tourism Spaces*, London: Sage (from a more theoretical perspective).

With respect to recreation see

Pigram, J.J. and Jenkins, J. (1999) *Outdoor Recreation Management*, London: Routledge

(also provides a good introduction to the contemporary literature).

See also

World Travel and Tourism Council website: http://www.wttc.org

World Tourism Organisation website: http://www.world-tourism.org

2

THE DEMAND FOR RECREATION AND TOURISM

Understanding why human beings engage in recreational and tourism activities is an increasingly important and complex area of research for social scientists. Historically, geographers have played only a limited part in developing the literature on the behavioural aspects of recreational and tourists' use of free time (Jackson 1988), tending to have a predisposition towards the analysis of aggregate patterns of demand using quantitative measures and statistical sources. In only a few cases have theoretical and qualitative approaches been used (e.g. Stokowski 2002) which embody notions of leisure and place. This almost rigid demarcation of research activity has, with a few exceptions (e.g. Goodall 1990; Mansfeld 1992), meant that behavioural research in recreation and tourism has only since the early 1990s made any impact on the wider research community (see e.g. Walmesley and Lewis 1993 on the geographer's approach to behavioural research), with notable studies (e.g. Walmesley and Jenkins 1992; Jenkins and Walmesley 1993) applying spatial principles to the analysis of recreational and tourism behaviour. Since the early 1990s, geographers have begun to identify how the demand for leisure and tourism has resulted in *geographies* of leisure and tourism specific to certain social, ethnic, gendered and marginalised groups (e.g. disabled people) and the meanings they attach to the spaces they consume in their leisure time, or are unable to consume due to barriers and constraints. As McAvoy's (2002) work demonstrates, there are distinct place meanings attached to the ways that Native American Indians and white Americans value and use leisure resources. The results are a series of leisure and tourism landscapes, socially, culturally and politically constructed for different groups of people (Aitchison et al. 2000).

GEOGRAPHERS AND DEMAND: HISTORICAL PERSPECTIVES

Even historians of tourism and recreation, such as Durie (2003: 1), note: 'There has been in the last few years a major sea change in the literature on tourism'. Quite a number of substantial studies have been published on the history of tourism, many of which have described the evolution of tourism and recreation in different eras, typically as monographs (e.g. Walton 1983; Gold and Gold 1995) among new texts such as Durie's (2003) *Scotland for the Holidays: Tourism in Scotland 1780–1939*. These types of historical studies have been apparent in the tourism and recreation literature in the English-speaking and French literature (e.g. McGibbon 2000; Tissot 2000). Yet geographers have not played a major role in developing the historical analyses of tourism and recreation demand, with some notable exceptions (e.g. Towner 1996) which are based upon two important processes of development: continuity in the patterns and nature of demand through time, and contextual changes as the continuity in tourism and leisure phenomena is shaped by evolving social, political, cultural and economic forces within society (Page 2003a). Even where these approaches to the geography of demand exist, they are not a prominent element of geographical analysis or the interpretations of tourism and leisure with some notable exceptions (Towner 1996). But as with any form of historical analysis, it provides the underlying basis, context and explanations of how tourism and recreation has evolved spatially and through time. As a result, the interconnection between historical geography and history and the methodologies used to analyse tourism and recreation phenomena remain undervalued but frequently referred to, to contextualise the complexity of modern day leisure phenomena. This is reinforced by the arguments that the past is the key to the present. Such an approach can also question current assumptions on prevailing interpretations of modern day leisure. For example, Bayliss' (2003) study of leisure on two Unwin-designed quasi-rural council estates in outer London in the inter-war period use oral histories and documentary evidence to reconstruct the leisure lives of residents. It illustrates the complexity of generalising about inter-war council estates which provided over 1 million homes in the period 1919–39. These estates were often seen by researchers as social failures in the post-war period, being desolate areas devoid of community feelings and spirit. Bayliss (2003) showed the diversity of leisure pursuits in the two contrasting estates studied, the importance of organisations and social groups in promoting formal and informal leisure, and the ideology and rhetoric of attempts at social control in the physical planning of such estates to create leisure spaces designed to promote the enrichment of life, to educate and promote physical recreation as well as the provision of gardens and allotments. The results were far from indicative of such estates as social failures as oral histories suggest. Bayliss (2003) also illustrated how the inter-war years saw the evolution of home-based forms of leisure demand, as the radio became a commonplace item of mass consumed media, shaping leisure behaviour and social interaction. Therefore, the role of the historical geographer and historical analysis of recreation and tourism is a theme which will emerge throughout this book in seeking to understand and explain the geography of leisure-based phenomenon in time and space.

The geographers' contribution to demand-based research: an overview

Within the recreational literature, the geographers' contributions have often been subsumed into social science perspectives, such as sociology, psychology and planning, so that the spatiality and placefulness of their contribution has been implicit rather than explicit. This chapter discusses some of the key behavioural issues associated with recreation and tourism demand and some of the new concepts being used to understand why certain social groups are not able to participate in leisure (i.e. social exclusion) and how this shapes leisure patterns. The spatiality of leisure has been implicit in much of the research on leisure spaces (e.g. Shields 1991; Urry 1995). This discussion is followed by an analysis of the major data sources which researchers use, emphasising how the geographer has used and manipulated them to identify the patterns, processes and implications of such activity.

Within the literature on recreation and tourism, there is a growing unease over the physical separation of the theoretical and conceptual research that isolates behavioural processes and spatial outcomes, and fails to derive generalisations applicable to understanding tourism in totality (see Chapter 1). According to Moore et al. (1995: 74) there are common strands in the 'relationships between the various motivating factors applicable to both leisure and tourism'; as Leiper (1990) argued, tourism represents a valued category of leisure, where there is a degree of commonality between the factors motivating both tourist and recreational activities and many of the needs, such as relaxation or being with friends, can equally be fulfilled in a recreational or tourism context. Although there is some merit in Leiper's (1990) approach, grouping leisure into one amorphous category assumes that there are no undifferentiated attributes which distinguish tourism from leisure. As Pigram and Jenkins (1999: 19) confirm, 'the term recreation demand is generally equated with an individual(s) preferences or desires, whether or not the individual has the economic and other resources necessary for their satisfaction'. In this respect, it is the preference–aspiration–desire level, reflected in behaviour or participation in activities. It is interesting to note that Leiper's (1990) approach has a great deal of validity if one recognises that some tourism motivations may in fact differentiate tourism from leisure experiences, just as the reverse may be true, and that ultimately the particular range of motives associated with a tourism or recreational activity will be unique in each case despite a range of similarities. For this reason, the following discussion examines recreational demand, emphasising many of the explanations commonly advanced in the recreational literature followed by a discussion of the tourism context and the issues raised, bearing in mind the need to compare and contrast each literature base in the light of the arguments advanced by Moore et al. (1995) and Leiper (1990).

RECREATIONAL DEMAND

Human activity related to recreation and tourism is a function of an individual's or group's willingness or desire to engage in such pursuits. Yet understanding this dimension in recreation and tourism requires a conceptual approach which can rationalise the complex interaction between the desire to undertake leisure activities, however defined, and the opportunities to partake of them. As Coppock and Duffield (1975) argued:

> the success of any study of outdoor recreation depends on the synthesis of two contrasting elements: the sociological phenomenon of leisure or . . . that part of leisure time which an individual spends on outdoor recreation [and tourism] and . . . the physical resources that are necessary for the particular recreational activities.
>
> (Coppock and Duffield 1975: 2)

In other words, Coppock and Duffield (1975) acknowledged the need to recognise the interrelationship between human demand as participation or a desire to engage in recreation and tourism, and the supply of resources, facilities and opportunities

which enable such demand to be fulfilled. The concepts of demand and supply have largely been developed and applied to conventional market economies, where the individual has a choice related to the consumption of recreation and tourism (for a discussion of these issues in the former Soviet Union, see Vendenin 1978; D.J. Shaw 1979; Riordan 1982). As Roberts et al. (2001) show, since the 1980s the former Soviet Union (now Russian Federation) has gone from one of the most equal societies to one of the most unequal, but leisure does make a significant contribution to the Russian quality of life, despite inequalities in leisure provision. In numerous reviews of Soviet geography in the post-war period, the impact and influence of Russian research has been deemed to have had little impact on the development of geography internationally (excluding theoretical debates on Soviet ideology and Marxism). Yet within the field of leisure and recreation, there has been a strong tradition of the study of leisure demand and an ongoing interest in leisure phenomenon as various studies attest (Nefedova and Zemlianoi 1997; Tchistiakova and Pabanne 1997; Ioffe and Nefedova 2001; Kruzhalin 2002) as well as wider social science contributions such as Gvozdeva's (1999) study exploring the expansion of women's leisure time in post-communist Russia.

According to Smith (1989):

> Recreation geographers use the work [demand] in at least four different ways. The most traditional sense is a neoclassical definition: demand is a schedule of the quantities of some commodity that will be consumed at various prices. . . . A second definition of demand is that of current consumption [which] is of limited utility to recreation planners because it tells nothing about trends in participation or about current levels of unmet need. Demand is also used to refer to unmet need. This is sometimes referred to as latent demand. . . . Finally, demand is used to describe the desire for a psychological experience.
>
> (S.L.J. Smith 1989: 45)

In contrast, Patmore (1983: 54) acknowledges, 'leisure is far more easily recognised than objectively analysed . . . the difficulties are only in part conceptual: equally important are the nature and limitations of available data', which this section will seek to explain in a recreation context.

According to Pigram (1983) there is a general lack of clarity in the use of the term *demand* in the recreational literature. One can distinguish between demand at a generic level, where it refers to an 'individual's preferences or desires, whether or not the individual has the economic or other resources necessary for their satisfaction' (Pigram 1983: 16) reflecting behavioural traits and preference for certain activities. At another level, there are the specific activities or participation in activities often expressed as visitation rates and measured to reflect the actual observed behaviour. One factor that prevents observed demand equating with participation is the concept of latent demand (the element which is unsatisfied due to a lack of recreational opportunities). Knetsch (1969) identified the mismatch and confusion between participation and demand, arguing that one cannot simply look at what people do and associate it with what people want to do, so ideally any analysis of demand should also consider why people do not participate, and examine ways of overcoming such obstacles by the provision of new resources as well as under-

standing social and cultural barriers. As Pigram and Jenkins (1999) argued,

> In the real world, recreation demand rarely equals participation. The difference between aggregate demand and actual participation (or expressed, effective, observed, revealed demand) is referred to as latent demand or latent participation – the unsatisfied component of demand that would be converted to participation if conditions of supply of recreation opportunities were brought to ideal levels.
>
> (Pigram and Jenkins 1999: 20)

Attempting to summarise the factors which influence the decision to participate in recreation led Pigram (1983) to construct Figure 2.1, which highlights the complex range of variables that affect the process.

Most research has examined effective demand which is actual participation rather than latent demand, and the geographers' contribution has largely been related to the spatial and temporal expression of demand in relation to supply (i.e. demand at specific sites). This is very much resource specific, and dates back to the geographical tradition of resource identification, use and analysis which can be traced to at least the 1930s. However,

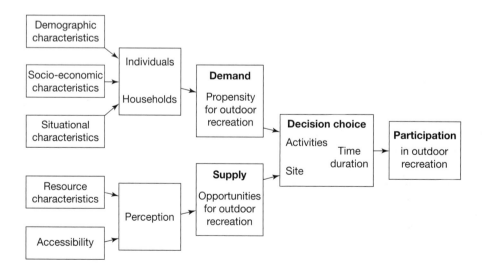

Figure 2.1: The decision-making process in outdoor recreation
Source: Pigram (1983)

Coppock and Duffield (1975) also distinguish between passive recreation and active recreation, thereby beginning to differentiate between different forms of demand. While passive recreation is by far the most important type numerically, it is difficult to study due to its diffuse and often unorganised nature. Coppock and Duffield (1975) argued that

> Active recreation in the countryside differs from passive recreation in a number of ways. Not only are participants a minority of those visiting the countryside for outdoor recreation, but they are generally younger and differ in respect of a number of socio-economic characteristics: they often depend on particular (and sometimes scarce) recreational resources in the countryside . . . yet as with passive recreation, information about such activities is scanty.
> (Coppock and Duffield 1975: 40)

This illustrates the necessity of trying to measure recreational demand together with gauging the types of factors which can facilitate and constrain recreational demand. But what motivates people to engage in recreational activities?

Argyle (1996) argues that part of the reason why people undertake leisure and recreational activities can be found in the process of socialisation and personality traits, where childhood influences such as parents and peers are forms of social influence and learning that affect future activity choice. In fact, nearly half of adult leisure interests are acquired after childhood, and personality factors influence preferences towards specific forms of recreation. However, understanding the broader psychological factors which motivate individuals to undertake forms of recreation is largely the remit of psychologists, being an intrinsic form of motivation (i.e. something one is not paid to undertake).

A simplistic approach to recreational motivation is to ask recreationalists what actually motivates them. Crandall (1980) outlined seventeen factors from leisure motivation research (Table 2.1), derived from a synthesis of previous studies in this field, while Kabanoff (1982) identified a similar list of factors (Table 2.2). From Tables 2.1 and 2.2 it is apparent that relaxation, the need for excitement and self-satisfaction are apparent, though Argyle

(1996) argues that specific motivations are evident in particular forms of recreation. Torkildsen (1992: 79), however, posits that homeostasis is a fundamental concept associated with human motivation where people have an underlying desire to maintain a state of internal stability. Human needs, which are 'any lack or deficit within the individual either acquired or physiological' (C. Morgan and King 1966: 776), disturb the state of homeostasis. At a basic level, human needs have to be met where physiological theory maintained that all human behaviour is motivated. This leads to one of the most commonly cited studies in relation to recreation and tourism motivation – Maslow's hierarchy of human needs.

Maslow's hierarchy model of human needs and recreational and tourist motivation

Within the social psychology literature on recreation and tourism, Maslow's (1954) needs hierarchy remains one of the most frequently cited theories of motivation. It follows the principle of a ranking or hierarchy of individual needs (Figure 2.2), based on the premise that self-actualisation is a level to which people should aspire. Maslow argued that if the lower needs in the hierarchy were not fulfilled then these would dominate human behaviour. Once these were satisfied, the individual would be motivated by the needs of the next level of the hierarchy. In the motivation sequence, Maslow identified 'deficiency or tension-reducing motives' and 'inductive or arousal-seeking motives' (Cooper et al. 1993: 21), arguing that the model could be applied to work and non-work contexts. Despite Maslow's research shaping much of the recreation and tourism demand work, how and why he selected five basic needs remains unclear, though its universal application in recreation and tourism appears to have a relevance with regard to understanding how human action is related to understandable and predictable aspects of action compared to research which argues that human behaviour is essentially irrational and unpredictable.

Table 2.1: Crandall's list of motivations

1 *Enjoying nature, escaping from civilisation* To get away from civilisation for a while To be close to nature	10 *Recognition, status* To show others I could do it So others would think highly of me for doing it
2 *Escape from routine and responsibility* Change from my daily routine To get away from the responsibilities of my everyday life	11 *Social power* To have control over others To be in a position of authority
	12 *Altruism* To help others
3 *Physical exercise* For the exercise To keep in shape	13 *Stimulus seeking* For the excitement Because of the risks involved
4 *Creativity* To be creative	14 *Self-actualisation (feedback, self-improvement, ability utilisation)* Seeing the results of your efforts Using a variety of skills and talents
5 *Relaxation* To relax physically So my mind can slow down for a while	15 *Achievement, challenge, competition* To develop my skills and ability Because of the competition To learn what I am capable of
6 *Social contact* So I could do things with my companions To get away from other people	
7 *Meeting new people* To talk to new and varied people To build friendships with new people	16 *Killing time, avoiding boredom* To keep busy To avoid boredom
8 *Heterosexual contact* To be with people of the opposite sex To meet people of the opposite sex	17 *Intellectual aestheticism* To use my mind To think about my personal values
9 *Family contact* To be away from the family for a while To help bring the family together more	

Source: Crandall (1980)

While Maslow's model is not necessarily ideal, since needs are not hierarchical in reality because some needs may occur simultaneously, it does emphasise the development needs of humans, with individuals striving towards personal growth. Therefore, Maslow assists in a recreational (and tourism context) in identifying and classifying the types of needs people have. Tillman (1974) summarised some of the broader leisure needs of individuals within which recreational needs occur, and these may include the pursuit of

- new experiences (i.e. having an adventure)
- relaxation, escape and fantasy
- recognition and identity
- security (being free from thirst, hunger or pain)
- dominance (controlling one's environment)
- response and social interaction (relating and interacting with others)
- mental activity (perceiving and understanding)
- creativity
- a need to be needed
- physical activity and fitness.

Table 2.2: Kabanoff's list of leisure needs

Leisure needs scale	Items comprising scales	Item means
1 Autonomy	Organise own projects and activities	2.78
	Do things you find personally meaningful	3.39
2 Relaxation	Relax and take it easy	3.20
	Give mind and body a rest	2.94
3 Family activity	Bring family closer together	2.81
	Enjoy family life	3.30
4 Escape from routine	Get away from responsibilities of everyday life	2.85
	Have a change from daily routine	3.12
5 Interaction	Make new friends	2.35
	Enjoy people's company	2.55
6 Stimulation	To have new and different experiences	2.66
	For excitement and stimulation	2.89
7 Skill utilisation	Use skills and abilities	2.89
	Develop new skills and abilities	2.61
8 Health	Keep physically fit	2.47
	For health reasons	2.46
9 Esteem	Gain respect or admiration of others	2.11
	Show others what you're capable of	2.15
10 Challenge/competition	Be involved in a competition	1.87
	Test yourself in difficult or demanding situations	2.31
11 Leadership/social power	Organise activities of teams, groups, organisations	1.79
	To gain positions of leadership	1.48

Source: Kabanoff (1982)

Figure 2.2: Maslow's hierarchy of needs

A different perspective is offered by Bradshaw (1972), who argued that social need is a powerful force, explaining need by classifying it as normative, felt, expressed and comparative need. Mercer (1973), Godbey (1976) and McAlvoy (1977) extended Bradshaw's argument within a recreational context, modifying the four categories of need by adding created, changing and false needs. Normative needs are based on value judgements, often made by professionals who establish that what they feel is appropriate to the wider population. Felt needs, which individuals may have but not necessarily express, are based on what someone wants to do and is a perceived need. Expressed needs relate to those needs and preferences for existing recreational activities which are often measured but can only be a partial view of demand, since new recreational opportunities may release latent demand. Comparative needs are apparent where existing provision for the general population is compared with special groups (e.g. disabled or elderly people, or ethnic minorities) to establish if existing provision is not fulfilling the needs of the special group. Created needs may result from policy-makers and planners introducing new services or activities which are then taken up by the population. A false need is one that may be created by individuals or society, and which is not essential and may be marginal to wider recreational needs. Changing needs, however, are a recognition of the dynamic nature of human needs which change through time as individuals develop and their position in the life cycle changes. Thus what is important at one point in the life cycle may change through time as an individual passes through four key stages (Ken and Rapoport 1975):

- youth (school years)
- young adulthood
- establishment (extended middle age)
- final phase (between the end of work and of life).

Other researchers (e.g. Iso-Ahola 1980; Neulinger 1981) prefer to emphasise the importance of perceived freedom from constraints as a major source of motivation. Argyle (1996) synthesises such studies to argue that intrinsic motivation in leisure relates to three underlying principles:

- social motivation
- basic bodily pleasures (e.g. eating, drinking, sex and sport)
- social learning (how past learning explains a predisposition towards certain activities).

One useful concept which Csikszentmihalyi (1975) introduced to the explanation of motivation was that of *flow*. Individuals tend to find a sense of intense absorption in recreational activities, when self-awareness declines, and it is their peak experience – a sense of flow – which is the main internal motivation. The flow is explained as a balance resulting from being challenged and skill which can occur in four combinations:

- where challenge and skill are high and flow results
- where the challenge is too great, anxiety results
- if the challenge is too easy, boredom may occur
- where the challenge and skill level is too low, apathy may result.

But this does not mean that everyone always seeks recreational activities which provide forms of high arousal. Some recreational activities may just fulfil a need to relax, being undemanding and of low arousal. As Ewert and Hollenhurst (1989) reported, those who engaged in outdoor recreational sports with a high-risk factor (e.g. white-water rafting) viewed the sport as providing a flow experience, and the study predicted that as their skill level improved they would increase the level of participation and risk. Yet even though this occurred the internal motivation of the group remained unchanged, where low and high arousal seem to be juxtaposed. Thus levels of arousal vary from time to time, a factor which can be used by adventure tourism operators to manage the adventure experience and increase the level of satisfaction of participants (Hall and McArthur 1994; Egner 2002; Page et al. 2005).

Recreation may also lead to an enhanced self-image, where the identity becomes a basis for motivation because recreational activities can lead to a sense of belonging to a particular and identifiable group. Some activities may also require the development of special skills and enhanced self-esteem. Where recreational activities require a degree of competency, Bandura (1977) proposed that perception of one's ability to perform the skill is a motivator and may result in self-efficacy, a form of self-confidence and judgement of one's ability.

In spite of the significance of motivation, it is apparent that no single theory or even a clear consensus exists in relation to recreation. Instead, 'in theories of motivation need is seen as a force within the individual to gain satisfactions and completeness. There appear to be many levels and types of need, including the important needs of self-actualisation and psychological growth'

Table 2.3: Influences on leisure participation

Personal	Social and circumstantial	Opportunity factors
Age	Occupation	Resources available
Stage in life cycle	Income	Facilities – type and quality
Gender	Disposable income	Awareness
Marital status	Material wealth and goods	Perception of opportunities
Dependants and ages	Car ownership and mobility	Recreation services
Will and purpose in life	Time available	Distribution of facilities
Personal obligations	Duties and obligations	Access and location
Resourcefulness	Home and social environment	Choice of activities
Leisure perceptions	Friends and peer groups	Transport
Attitudes and motivation	Social roles and contacts	Costs: before, during, after
Interests and preoccupations	Environment factors	Management: policy and support
Skill and ability – physical, social	Mass leisure factors	Marketing
and intellectual		
Personality and confidence	Education and attainment	Programming
Culture born into	Population factors	Organisation and leadership
Upbringing and background	Cultural factors	Social accessibility
		Political policies

Source: Torkildsen (1992)

(Torkildsen 1992: 86). An understanding of needs and intrinsic motivation and some of the ideas implicit in studies of recreational motivation may offer a range of insights into why people engage in recreational activities. But not only is it necessary to understand why people engage in recreation, but also what factors or barriers may inhibit them from participating. Torkildsen (1992) outlines the influences on leisure participation in terms of three categories: personal, social and circumstantial, and opportunity factors. These influences (Table 2.3) are also of value in understanding some of the constraints on recreation.

BARRIERS TO RECREATION

Within the wider literature on recreation and leisure, a specialist research area has developed, focused on constraints, namely those factors, elements or processes which inhibit people from participating in leisure activities. From the diverse range of studies published, two forms of constraint have been identified: intervening constraints, namely those which intervene between a preference and participation, and antecedent constraints, which influence a person's decision not to undertake an activity.

Although the constraints on recreation and leisure literature can be dated to the 1960s, the 1980s saw a range of studies published, a number of which (e.g. Crawford and Godbey 1987; Crawford et al. 1991) have set the research agenda in recent years. In the initial formulation, Crawford and Godbey (1987) proposed that constraints were associated with intrapersonal, interpersonal and structural constraints. In the subsequent reformulation of their thinking, Crawford et al. (1991) proposed a hierarchical process model, with their three types of constraint integrated. As a consequence of their model, they proposed Figure 2.3, which indicates that:

- participation in leisure is a negotiation process, where a series of factors became aligned in a sequence
- the order in which constraints occur leads to a 'hierarchy of importance', where intrapersonal constraints are the most powerful in sequence ending with no structural constraints

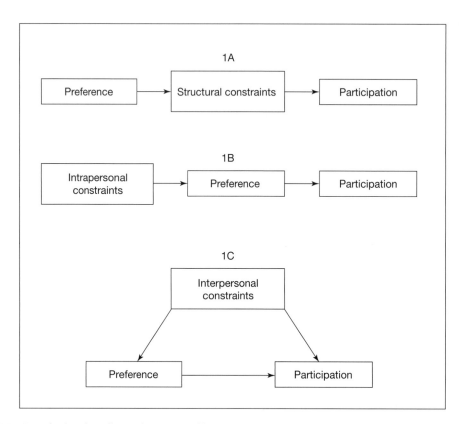

Figure 2.3: Crawford and Godbey's three types of leisure constraints
Source: Crawford et al. (1991)

- social class has a strong influence on participation and non-participation leading to a
  hierarchy of social privilege, i.e. social stratifica-
  tion is a powerful conditioning factor and may
  act as a constraint.

This research has provided a framework for
further evaluations of constraints (e.g. Samdahl
and Jekubovich 1997, and subsequent criticisms
by Henderson 1997). In fact, research by Jackson
et al. (1993) suggested that the real key to understanding leisure constraints was embedded in the
negotiation process, namely how an individual
will proceed with experiencing an activity even
when constraints are apparent. Ultimately, Pigram's
(1983) model helped to frame the context in which
participation may occur, and the way that process

may be affected by underlying constraints on one's
participation. It is against this background that
one can appreciate the use of leisure time and leisure
space in different cultures (see e.g. Horne's 1998
review of Japanese society) and among groups
where leisure time in a western conception is
inappropriate. For example, in a fascinating review
of poor rural women's leisure experiences in
Bangladesh by Khan (1997), it is evident that 'the
conventional approach to leisure studies which has
a myopic view of leisure as free or non-obligatory
time' (Khan 1997: 18) is meaningless due to blurring of boundaries between free or non-work time
and obligatory activities which are often cumber-
some and all-encompassing in everyday life. At
an empirical level, a range of notable studies have
highlighted the prevailing constraints to recreation.

For example, Kay and Jackson's (1991) notable study of 366 British adults' recreational constraints identified:

- 53 per cent who cited money as the main constraint
- 36 per cent who felt lack of time was the main limitation
- conflicts with family or work, transportation problems and health concerns as other contributory factors.

A study in Alberta which surveyed 1891 people asked respondents to rate fifteen possible barriers to a desired activity; the results highlighted social isolation, accessibility, personal reasons (lack of confidence or skill), costs, time and facilities as the main constraints. It has been proposed that such constraints have a specific ordering in terms of importance, with the most significant constraints being interpersonal ones, followed by structural ones (e.g. lack of time or money). Yet such arguments have been queried by S. Shaw et al. (1991), who found that in a survey of 14,674 Canadians, of eleven constraints, only lack of energy and ill-health were associated with a lower rate of participation. Therefore, barriers may be negotiable or solvable, as Kay and Jackson (1991) suggest. Patmore (1983) summarises the main physical barriers to recreation in terms of

- seasonality
- biological and social constraints
- money and mobility
- resources and fashions

with the availability of time also being a major constraint.

Coppock and Duffield (1975: 8) recognised the principal variations which exist in terms of demand due to variable uses of leisure time budgets by individuals and groups in relation to the day, week and year. Both Coppock and Duffield (1975) and Patmore (1983) use similar data sources, for example the UK's Pilot National Recreation Survey (British Travel Association and University of Keele

1967 and 1969) and sociological studies of family behaviour in the pioneering study by Young and Wilmott (1973), to examine time budgets, variations in demand and constraining factors. One of the most important distinctions to make is that 'the weekend thus represents a large increase in the time that can be committed to leisure pursuits, which in turn affects the weekend time budget' (Coppock and Duffield 1975: 14). Yet when one looks beyond the day and week to the individuals and groups concerned, a wider range of influences emerge which are important in explaining recreation patterns.

Argyle (1996) highlights the fact that one of the main reasons for examining constraining and facilitating factors is to understand 'how many people engage in different kinds of leisure, how much time they spend on it, and how this varies between men and women, young and old, and other groups' (Argyle 1996). This is because some groups such as

> women, the elderly and unemployed face particular constraints which may affect their ability to engage in leisure and recreational activities which people do because they want to, for their own sake, for fun, entertainment or self-improvement, or for goals of their own choosing, but not for material gain.
>
> (Argyle 1996: 33)

SEASONALITY

Patmore (1983) argued that

> one of the most unyielding of constraints is that imposed by climate, most obviously where outdoor activities are concerned. The rhythms of the seasons affect both the hours of daylight available and the extent to which temperatures are conducive to participant comfort outdoors.
>
> (Patmore 1983: 70)

This is reflected in the seasonality of recreational activity which inevitably leads to peaks in popular seasons and a lull in less favourable conditions. Patmore (1983) identified a continuum in recreational activities from those which exhibit a high degree of seasonality to those with a limited degree of variation in participation by season. The first type, which is the most seasonal, include outdoor activities (often of an informal nature) which are weather dependent. The second, an intermediate group, is transitional in the sense that temperature is not necessarily a deterrent since a degree of discomfort may be experienced by the more hardened participants (e.g. when walking and playing sport). The final group is indoor activities which can be formal or informal, and have virtually no seasonality. In addition, the physical constraints of season, climate and weather inhibit demand by curtailing the periods of time over which a particular resource can be used for the activity concerned (Patmore 1983: 72), although resource substitution (e.g. using a human-made ski slope instead of a snow-clad one) may assist in some contexts, but often the human-made resource cannot offer the same degree of excitement or enjoyment.

FINANCIAL RESOURCES AND ACCESS TO RECREATIONAL OPPORTUNITY

Argyle (1996) observed that while many studies emphasised lack of money as a barrier to engaging in recreational activities, Coalter (1993) found that it had little impact on participation in sports. In fact, Kay and Jackson (1991) also acknowledged that money or disposable income was a barrier to undertaking activities which were major consumers of money (drinking and eating socially) whereas it had little impact on sport, which was comparatively cheap. Bittman (2002) noted in Australia that the results of a Time Use Survey highlighted that time to participate in leisure was determined by hours of employment, family responsibilities and gender. The research found that household income had no significant impact on available leisure time. Income, occupation and access to a car combined have a significant impact on participation, and as Patmore (1983) succinctly summarised,

> those with more skilled and responsive occupations, with higher incomes, with ready access to private transport and with a longer period spent in full-time

education tend to lead a more active and varied leisure life, with less emphasis on passive recreations both within and beyond the home.
>
> (Patmore 1983: 78)

It is the car which has provided the greatest degree of personal mobility and access to a wider range of recreational opportunities in time and space since the 1960s in many developed countries (and earlier in some cases such as the USA and Canada). For example, most car-owning households in UK studies have twice the propensity to participate in sport and recreation than non-car-owning households (Hillman and Whalley 1977). Even so, Martin and Mason (1979) observe that

> one of the paradoxes of leisure is that while time and money are complementary in the production of leisure activities, they are competitive in terms of the resources available to the individual. Some leisure time and some money to buy leisure goods and services are both needed before most leisure activities can be pursued.
>
> (Martin and Mason 1979: 62)

The issue of accessibility and financial resources also raises issues of social inclusion, which are dealt with more fully later in the book. However, as Mather (2003) observed, participation in outdoor recreation (as opposed to leisure per se) is closely correlated with socio-economic status and affluence, which posits that lower socio-economic groups have a lower participation rate, due to constraints such as a lack of supply and limitations from financial resources. In a rural context, Slee (2002) noted that in a survey of visits to the countryside in 1998, among the 17 per cent of the sample respondents who did not visit, no interest or no appeal were key reasons for not visiting rather than financial reasons. Therefore, arguments that increasing supply to meet perceived demand due to constraints may not necessarily be a valid argument. Indeed, Curry (2001) found in England and Wales between 1990 and 1997 a net growth in access to land of 450,000 ha. Even so, Mather (2003) debates the implications of the new legislation in England and Wales (The Countryside and Rights of Way Act 2000) and Scotland (The Land Reform (Scotland) Act 2003) which extend the legal

Plate 2.1: Disneyland, California, is a popular family setting for tourism and recreation. Personal security is a hallmark of its atmosphere.

basis and public access to land more widely. Some of the complex arguments associated with these new approaches to making recreational access to land more widely available relate to health goals, for promoting exercise, reflected in the growth of footpaths and walking. For example, as Mather (2003) suggests, it is estimated that in the 1990s, 300 million walks a year took place in the Scottish countryside (which generated £300 million and supported 20,000 full-time equivalent jobs). Even so, Mather (2003) suggests that the opening of land for recreation will not lead to massive increase in recreational activity.

GENDER AND SOCIAL CONSTRAINTS

The influence of gender on recreation remains a powerful factor influencing participation, a feature consistently emphasised in national surveys of recreational demand. As Argyle (1996) argues,

> there is an influential theory about this topic, due to a number of feminist writers, that women have very little or no leisure, because of the demands of domestic work and the barriers due to husbands who want them at home . . . [and] that leisure is a concept which applies to men, if it is regarded as a reaction to or contrast with paid work.
>
> (Argyle 1996: 44; see also Deem 1986)

Thus women with children appear to have less time for recreation, while those in full- and part-time employment have less time available than their male counterparts (see Argyle 1996 for more discussion of this topic). These general statements find a high degree of support within the recreational literature, with gender differences in part explained by the male free time occurring in larger blocks and in prime time (e.g. evenings and weekends) (Pigram 1983). Even so, studies by Talbot (1979) explore this theme in more detail. Rodgers (1977) documents the wide discrepancy in male versus female participation in sport as a form of recreation within a European context where for every 100 females engaging in sport, there were 188 male participants in Britain, 176 in Spain, 159 in France, 127 in Belgian Flanders, 127 in Norway, 116 in the Netherlands and 111 in former West Germany. While definitions and the variations in data sources may in part explain the variability, the presence of a gender gap is prominent. More recent analyses informed by cultural geography have suggested that different types of body with gendered, classed, aged and sexed meanings may encourage or discourage an individual's participation in specific forms of leisure. In other words, it illustrates the importance of theorising the setting for leisure as spaces which individuals engage in through both body and mind. The examples of geographical research on leisure from this cultural and gendered perspective is admirably demonstrated by the research of Scraton and Watson (1998) and Mowl and Towner (1995). In terms of sexed meanings, Pritchard et al. (2002) examined the example of Manchester's gay village as one such setting.

Age also exerts a strong influence on participation in recreation, with Hendry et al. (1993) describing adolescence as the peak time of leisure needs. Therein lie two key explanations of participation and constraints. Stages in the life course present a useful concept to explain why women with young children appear to have fewer opportunities for recreation than adolescents. Likewise, physical vigour and social energy are traditionally explained in terms of a decline in the later stages of adulthood resulting in a decline in active recreation throughout later life. The Greater London Recreation Survey of 1972 (Greater London Council 1976) identified some of these traits in that

- activities exist where participation markedly declined by age (e.g. energetic sports like football)
- activities occur with sustained participation through the life cycle (e.g. tennis and indoor swimming)
- some activities exist where participation increased as a person got older (e.g. golf and walking).

In fact these results illustrate not only the importance of age (and to a degree gender), but also the need to consider the significance of the life cycle in relation to changes or 'triggers' (Patmore 1983). One such trigger is retirement, and while it is sometimes interpreted as a stressful life event, J.A. Long (1987) found that for 58 per cent of male retirees there was no change in their leisure activities, while 8 per cent undertook education, 3 per cent developed an interest in photography and 3 per cent partook of sport. What Argyle (1996: 63) emphasises from studies of retirement are that 'people carry on with the same leisure as before, though they are more passive and more house-bound, and do not take up much new leisure'.

THE GEOGRAPHY OF FEAR IN RECREATION AND LEISURE SPACES: GENDER-BASED BARRIERS TO PARTICIPATION

Since the 1980s, there has been a growing interest in the role of fear, personal safety and the spatial implications in the urban environment (e.g. Fyfe and Banister 1996; Koskela and Pain 2000). There has also been an accompanying interest in the gender dimensions of personal safety (S.J. Smith 1987; G. Valentine 1989), which has important implications within an urban environment in relation to the use of public leisure resources such as open space and urban parks. In fact, the concern with such issues may be traced to the changes in the discipline of geography 'and transformative developments both resulting from, and contributing to, a number of new and competing philosophies with the social sciences' (Aitchison 1999: 20). In relation to leisure and recreation geography, this transformation effect can be related to the concern with gender relations and theoretical perspectives associated with the new cultural geography as a mechanism to conceptualise and theorise leisure space. One of the central tenets of this approach is embodied in Green et al.'s (1990: 311) comment where 'A significant aspect of the social control of women's leisure is the regulation of their access to public places, and their behaviour in such places'. These critical perspectives have only recently begun to emerge in tourism geography (see Crouch 2000), where empirical, logical-positivist approaches to personal safety have paid little attention to gender and public places.

In conceptual terms, the analysis of the geography of fear, particularly the implications for gender, is a good illustration of the participation issues for particular groups of women. The application of this perspective to recreational and leisure spaces in the city reveals the male domination of public leisure space (Aitchison 1999). The new cultural geographies have seen leisure and recreational geographers move away, albeit slowly, from a positivist paradigm and the model building era as new perspectives were conceptualised and theorised. The rise of feminist perspectives in leisure studies by geographers is a notable development, with the impetus provided by landmark studies by feminist leisure studies (e.g. Talbot 1979; Deem 1986; Green et al. 1987).

One of the principal problems with the emergence of a new cultural geography is epitomised in Shurmer-Smith and Hannam's (1994: 13) comments: 'Place is a deceptively simple concept in geographical thought. We want to make it difficult, uneasy'. Herein lies many of the criticisms of the new cultural geography: one must have a sound grounding in social theory, cultural studies and a knowledge of the new terms underpinning the debates. One consequence is that

> the new cultural geography as it has been referred to since the early 1990s demonstrates that space, place and landscape – including landscapes of leisure and tourism – are not fixed but are in a constant state of transition as a result of continuous, dialectical struggles of power and resistance among and between the diversity of landscape providers, users and mediators.
> (Aitchison 1999: 29)

This means that the focus is on agency rather than structure, criticising earlier geographical studies of leisure and recreation which did not problematise space or recognise the human element in the landscape. This perspective, and one has to recognise it is only one perspective in geographical research, emphasises the diversity, differences and nuances in cultural phenomena which is the antithesis of logical positivist geographical thought which

searches for certainty, coherence and generalisations in relation to patterns, forms and processes of spatial phenomena. As a consequence the new interest in leisure and tourism as cultural phenomena in the

> post-positivist geography [is such] that the new cultural geography has emerged and become merged with sociological and cultural studies analyses which are now combining to investigate the multiplicity of behaviours, meanings, consumption trends and identities constructed in and through leisure and tourism.
> (Aitchison 1999: 30)

The case study below focuses on the sexuality dimension. Given the growing interest in feminism within the leisure constraints literature (e.g. Henderson 1997) and the concern with constraints to participation (e.g. Jackson 1994), it is timely to focus on the issue of fear, derived from Madge's (1997) survey of Leicester's urban park system.

CASE STUDY: The geography of fear and recreational participation implications for exclusion

Urban parks are estimated to be used by 40 per cent of the British population (Garner 1996) on a regular basis, but critics argue that urban parks as a recreational resource are being avoided by the general public (Vidal 1994). This is particularly acute for certain groups of the population (e.g. women, children and ethnic groups), where fear acts as a constraint on use. As Ravenscroft and Markwell (2000) point out, the accessible nature of parks to ethnic young people is notable, if they are properly maintained and managed. This is reiterated by Gobster (2002) in the USA, while notions of environmental justice and leisure resources emerges from such discussions (Floyd and Johnson 2002), where certain groups are able to or prohibited from using such resources. In fact Woolley and Noor-Ul-Amin's (1999) study of Pakistani teenagers' use of public open space in Sheffield considered the diverse passive and active uses made of these spaces. This adds a new dimension to the recreational constraints literature.

Explanations of the growing neglect of urban parks within the UK have been related to a decline in public spending, from 54 per cent of leisure budgets in 1981–82 to 44 per cent in 1991–92 and lower in recent years, although these statistics need to recognise greater financial efficiencies derived from contracting out park services.

In the 1990s there was the growing evidence that urban parks were not perceived as peaceful sanctuaries for recreational and leisure pursuits among the wider population. Burgess et al.'s (1998a) innovative Greenwich Open Space Project documented the dimensions of fear. Dimensions included antisocial behaviour among teenagers and vandalism that reduced local enjoyment and participation. Similar concerns of insecurity, fear and use of parks and open spaces have also been recorded in Australia (Melbourne Parks 1983) and North America (R. Taylor et al. 1985; Westover 1985; Solecki and Welch 1995). Additional research shows how women, black people, elderly people and the gay community may be excluded from using urban space as freely as other subgroups of the population (Adler and Brenner 1992; Maitland 1992). As Burgess et al. (1988a: 472) remarked in the Greenwich context: 'many people expressed feelings of insecurity and vulnerability in open spaces, reflecting fears of personal attack and injury. Among the Asian community, these feelings are exacerbated by the growing incidence of racially motivated attacks in public open spaces'. The outcome as Madge (1997: 238) recognised was that 'This fear, which reflects structural inequalities in society, is translated into spatial behaviour which usually involves a reluctance to occupy certain public spaces at certain times of the day'. For the geographer, it is the spatial manifestation of that fear and its implications for recreational resource use (Page et al 1994). Although the evolution and development of Leicester's urban parks are reviewed later in this book in Chapter 5, it is worth observing the socio-demographic context of Madge's study prior to outlining the principal findings.

THE GEOGRAPHY OF FEAR AND URBAN PARK USE IN LEICESTER

Leicester, located in the English East Midlands, is a medium-sized city of 272,000 people, which is 73.09 square kilometres in spatial extent. What is notable, is its diverse ethnic mix: 72 per cent of the population are white, 24 per cent are Asian, 2 per cent African Caribbean, 2 per cent Chinese and other 'ethnic groups'. Despite the city's urban-industrial development (see Pritchard 1976; Page 1988), it is widely acknowledged that the city has an enviable distribution of open space. By 1994, Leicester City Council was responsible for over 1200 ha of open space, which comprised 20 per cent of the total city area. This is a significant level of provision within an international context, and certainly enhances the city's green and open feel. Most parks are currently having

management plans developed for each park and open space, which were due to be implemented by 2005 (see http://www.leicester.gov.uk).

In this context, Madge's (1997) analysis of the geography of fear was timely. The sampling framework, namely face-to-face interviews with Leicester residents at on-street locations, sought to derive a sample of city-wide park and open space use, with some 535 respondents interviewed. From the survey, ten main constraints emerged which influenced park use. In order of importance they were

- fear
- weather
- lack of time due to work
- family constraints
- lack of transport
- lack of interest
- limited awareness of facilities available
- housework
- distance of parks/too far away
- physically unable to get to the parks.

Some 43 per cent of respondents attributed fear as a 'very important' factor constraining their use of parks. The gender difference was striking with 75 per cent of women compared to 50 per cent of men stating fear was a major constraint on park use. This is in line with Westover's (1985) finding in North America, where 90 per cent of female respondents felt unsafe if alone in parks. Studies of victimisation in Leicester (e.g. Willis 1992) recognise that women have a greater sense of insecurity due to their vulnerability to crime.

When ethnicity was examined, Asian groups expressed higher levels of fear compared with white and African Caribbean groups reflecting victimisation statistics, racial abuse and attacks in the urban environment. In terms of age, those aged over 45 years of age expressed the greatest levels of fear. As Madge (1997: 241) rightly acknowledged: 'The result of fear of crime is, however, concrete: the elderly are less likely to use public parks for recreation'.

In terms of causes of fear, Madge (1997) observed that the main causes of fear of park use were anxieties related to actual or potential bodily harm (e.g. mugging, sexual attack, loitering people, gangs of youths, dogs and racial attack). Women's fears were greatest in relation to fear of sexual attack by men. These findings reflected the prevailing levels of fear of sexual violence, which women in Leicester harbour, particularly the high level of sexual harassment, which was rarely reported (Women's Equality Unit 1993). In fact 77 per cent of female respondents were fearful of sexual attacks in parks, a much higher figure than in similar surveys in Edinburgh (Anderson et al. 1990) and Seattle (Warr 1985). Fear of racial attack was also much higher for African Caribbean and Asian groups than for white groups.

The implications of these findings are reflected in the behaviour and use of parks. Women tended to avoid large open spaces, unlit areas and those areas with dense undergrowth and trees. The onset of nightfall also elevated fear of using such places, especially if they were alone. As Madge (1997) suggested:

> Fear is a significant factor structuring the use of public parks in Leicester. The intensity and cause of fear varied with social traits of gender, ethnicity and age and affected spatial behaviour regarding use of parks. The geography of fear is mediated through a set of overlapping social, ideological and structural power relations which become translated into spatial behaviour.
>
> (Madge 1997: 245)

The findings of Madge's (1997) study highlight how a new constraint on leisure behaviour has specific gender, ethnic and social ramifications for recreational resource use. Although Madge (1997) criticises the existing recreational literature for neglecting this issue, fear is a more profound issue in urban environments than has hitherto been the case in recreational research. While Hoyles (1994) argued for a greater feminisation of public space and Madge (1997) argued for increased informal surveillance to encourage public participation and use of parks and open spaces, creating safer parks is deeply embedded in more complex notions of creating safe cities. Koskela and Pain (2000) point to the problems and failures of designing out fear from the urban environment, given the extent to which fear of crime pervades city spaces. In a review of urban public space in Tokyo and New York, Cybriwsky (1999) recognised the growth in the surveillance of public spaces to improve security which could lead to a return to private spaces and attempts to modify social behaviour in recreational spaces. This is a feature which Giddens (1990: 20) recognised whereby 'surveillance is a means of levering the modern social world away from traditional modes of social activity'. In a wider context, Button (2003: 227) noted that 'during the post-war period there has been a growth in what has been termed 'mass private property' encompassing large shopping malls, leisure facilities, gated communities, airports. . . . These facilities, which are usually private but freely open to the public, have created new debates concerning . . . what is termed 'quasi-public' or 'hybrid' space. The result is that public access to these spaces is at the discretion of the landowner'. Critiques of such spaces for leisure (e.g. Uzzell 1995) illustrate that even private spaces, such as malls, provide social places and spaces which meet many psychological needs and preferences, particularly in terms of leisure consumption. This space is controlled, replacing a former communal culture and public spaces which met many informal needs for leisure like parks and open spaces. These mall spaces have been seen as leading to a sense of placelessness (Relph 1976), where they do not develop a relationship with the place/space for leisure. Therefore, highly managed and secure areas like malls may reduce the perception of fear, but conversely these privately managed spaces will detract from people developing a positive relationship with the space, that people do with urban open spaces.

Indeed, Koskela and Pain (2000: 279) argued that 'Geographers and planners should take greater account of the complexity of fear ... Places have some influence on fear, but perhaps of equal or greater significance is the ways in which fear shapes our understanding, perception and use of space and place'. This is certainly a truism in the case of recreational use of urban parks in Madge's (1997) findings which have a wider application to urban recreational resource use in the developed world. A great deal of progress will need to be made in addressing fear of crime and recreational and leisure spaces in urbanised societies until Koskela and Pain's (2000: 274) analysis that 'Green urban spaces and woodlands are commonly perceived as dangerous places and feelings of insecurity often have a deterrent effect on women's use of them' is no longer a valid assessment. Yet simply providing synthetic and artificially created leisure spaces such as malls as a substitute will not meet such informal leisure needs, since many private leisure spaces within cities are highly designed environments connected with and motivated by consumption, which by their very nature may also exclude some groups who are unable to access the resources to be consumers.

SUMMARY POINTS

- The geography of fear is an important factor shaping participation by certain social groups in recreational activities.
- The problem of fear affects certain groups participation patterns (e.g. elderly people and women) more than others.
- The creation of safer recreational open spaces is more problematic since it will involve greater surveillance, monitoring and control of informal leisure spaces.
- The new cultural geography, particularly the geography of gender, provides invaluable insights to explain how women's leisure space is embedded in notions of fear, constraints on the use of urban space and the resultant inequalities.
- Purpose-built and artificially created urban spaces, like malls, are not a substitute for urban open space
- A more detailed discussion of the development and use of urban parks can be found in Chapter 5.

SOCIAL EXCLUSION: CONDITIONING LEISURE PARTICIPATION

In the previous case study, the constraints on participation derived from fear, concerns for personal safety and the use of public spaces highlight a relatively new concept which many social science researchers have begun using to explain societal constraints on participation – social exclusion. Byrne (1999) traces the emergence of this new phrase in political terms, which is used to explain how changes in the whole of society affect particular people and groups. This is indicative of systematic problems in the structure of society, which determines the lives of certain groups. This has superseded earlier arguments and explanations of poverty related to an underclass (see Page 1988),

replacing simpler notions of poverty. Poverty has been viewed as an absence of resources, notably income as a factor conditioning participation in society. Exclusion, in contrast, is a more dynamic concept which implies that people are shut out (fully or partially) from the systems in society that allow full integration and participation in society. In political terms, exclusion may also be seen as denying the rights of individuals as citizens. In a post-industrial society, theoretical explanations of exclusion are attributed to the changing nature of work in society, increased insecurity in employment, a growing service sector and reconstructed welfare state systems to reduce public expenditure, where ethnic origin may also be a further factor contributing to exclusion and access to goods and services.

Consequently, social exclusion is a multifaceted

process, like poverty, but embodies exclusion from participation in decision-making that allows access to the means of being a citizen, employment, and engagement in the social and cultural processes which the majority of citizens have access to. In geographical terms, such exclusion has been characterised by its concentration in particular neighbourhoods (e.g. areas of multiple deprivation). Multiple deprivation has been mapped by geographers to identify the intersection of poverty and other social conditions (e.g. poverty, unemployment, poor housing conditions and education, high levels of crime and poor health), thereby creating a distinct geography of exclusion. One of the most significant contributory factors to the size and nature of demand is clearly related to socio-economic contrasts. Social well-being (see D.M. Smith 1977 for a discussion of the concept of social well-being and welfare geography) is, according to Rodgers (1993: 126), 'a strong influence on both the volume and structure of leisure demand and on the relative roles of public and commercial provision in meeting it'. Using the Department of the Environment (DoE) Social Deprivation Index (for a discussion of deprivation indices, see Townsend 1979; Page 1988), which derives negative indices based on unemployment, overcrowding, single-parent and pension households, housing quality and ethnic origin, Rodgers (1993) ranked the districts in the north-west of England on this composite measure of social stress and also included levels of car ownership. The results were used to identify a range of geographically based leisure markets which were strong or weak in terms of demand, particularly in relation to their capacity to pay for recreational activities in a market-driven local leisure economy. Similarly, patterns of multiple deprivation in London mapped by ward in 2000 (Office for National Statistics (ONS) 2003) are indicative of the inner city and other 'sink' areas, often associated with large council housing estates which concentrate deprivation into distinct areas of deprivation at a micro scale. For example, the London Boroughs of Tower Hamlets, Hackney and Newham in East London feature prominently in the most deprived areas together with Southwark

and a number of smaller concentrations in particular wards. Similarly, a report by the New Policy Institute (Harrop and Palmer 2002) examined poverty and social exclusion in rural England, noting that in rural areas, 18 per cent of the population were in low income households compared with 24 per cent in urban areas. This creates particular challenges for policy-makers in seeking to address exclusion, particularly in terms of leisure participation.

Not surprisingly, government agencies concerned with leisure (e.g. the Department for Culture, Media and Sport) have developed strategies to target groups at risk of social exclusion in terms of tourism, leisure and sport. Many of these initiatives have been targeted at increasing participation in, for example, the arts and sport through free museum entry and urban regeneration strategies (i.e. neighbourhood renewal) to address physical and social deprivation in some of the worst areas focused on health, crime, employment and education. For example, in Sheffield, a fifteen-year programme of cultural development has helped to stimulate inner city regeneration based on the cultural industries and projects to target marginalised groups (Department for Culture, Media and Sport 1999). The *Count Me In* report (J.A. Long 2002) identified the contribution which leisure could make to social inclusion through sports, arts, media, heritage and outdoor activities by increased involvement of social at risk of exclusion (e.g. unemployed, people, older people and women) through personal development (e.g. self-esteem, interpersonal skills and relationship building), social cohesion (civic pride, celebrating one's own culture and relationship building with other cultural and social groups) and in promoting active citizenship, through taking greater responsibility and in exercising one's rights as well as promoting human potential

These policy initiatives and evaluative research show that while the spatial dynamics of deprivation are the result of a complex process, impacted upon by government policy, local economic conditions, globalisation and the spatial segregation of social group, it is possible to break the cycle of exclusion.

In fact the UK's Disability Discrimination Act 1995 (to have rights of access to premises and services implemented by October 2004 in the UK – see G. Miller and Kirk 2002), which was prompted by EU legislation on social inclusion, will force many tourism and leisure service providers to make all services and facilities accessible to the disabled, improving accessibility at a micro scale.

RESOURCES AND FASHIONS

While models of participation and obstacles to recreation have attempted to predict the probability of people participating in activities, using variables such as age, sex, marital status and social variables (e.g. housing tenure, income and car ownership), predictions decline in accuracy when attempting to identify individual activities (e.g. golf). What such recreational models often fail to acknowledge is the role of choice and preference given a range of options. In this respect, geographical proximity to recreational resources and access to them is a major determinant. This is demonstrated by Burton (1971), who found that in Britain, people were three times as likely to use a recreational resource if they lived between half and three-quarters of a mile away, a feature emphasised by Patmore (1983) and Page et al. (1994) in research on urban parks. Veal (1987) expressed this using classic distance–decay theory reproduced in Figure 2.4 (see also Baxter 1979; Greer and Wall 1979; Chavas et al. 1989). This shows that the proximity to a recreational resource increased the propensity for use at a swimming pool, yet for leisure centres where people attending them used cars to visit them, the distance–decay function had a less rapid decline in attendance in relation to distance. Outside urban areas, the occurrence of recreational resources are more varied in their spatial distribution, and recreational opportunities need to be closely examined in relation to demand and supply. More recently, Colwell et al. (2002) examined the influence of recreation demand on residential location. Their research argued that consumers may live in areas according to their preference for recreational activities, and the trade-offs in terms of wages, location to live and recreation. What they also point to is the significance of second home ownership in areas of recreation preference. However, even here distance plays a major factor in recreational decision-making (Hall and Müller 2004).

In the Swedish case Jansson and Müller (2003) demonstrated that 25 per cent of all second home owners have their property within 14 km from their primary residence, 50 per cent have less than 37 km to their property, and 75 per cent have less than 98 km. Amenity-rich areas disturb the otherwise very regularly declining second home patterns. The time sensitivity of leisure travel means that the location of overnight stays from a generating region tends to cluster at a location related to time/distance from a point of origin (Hall 2005a, 2005b). This means that second home ownership outside the weekend leisure zone is relatively independent of

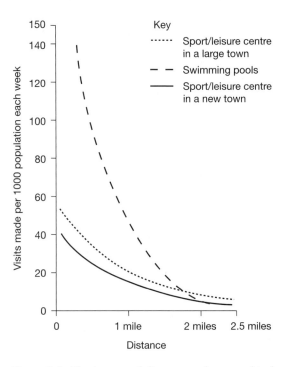

Figure 2.4: The impact of distance and geographical catchment areas on the provision of leisure facilities
Source: Based on Veal (1987)

the location of the primary residence; the second home is visited once or twice annually. However, second home location is not dependent solely on travel times. Instead, second home locations are also influenced by the geography of amenity rich landscapes that concentrates the geographical patterns of at least purpose-built second home to coastal and mountain areas. Furthermore, fashions and tastes can act as a powerful influence on demand as the following example of walking suggests.

WALKING AS A LEISURE PURSUIT: A FUNCTION OF RESOURCES AND FASHION

Walking is a human necessity for able-bodied people to achieve mobility, to engage in work, social activities and non-work functions. Although the industrial and post-industrial period has seen a move towards more mechanised forms of transport such as the car, giving people a greater spatial reach and flexibility in travel patterns, walking remains a key activity in everyday life and as a leisure activity. As Short (2001: 4) noted, 'Walking has created roads, trade routes; generated local and cross-continental senses of place; shaped cities; parks; generated maps. . . . This history of walking is an amateur history, just as walking is an amateur act'. The desire to walk as a leisure pursuit is the result of history over the last 300 years and according to Short (2001) is based on specific beliefs, tastes and values. Prior to the eighteenth century, the desire to walk for pleasure was the pastime of a leisured elite, many of whom resided in mansions, castles and palaces and who walked within the confines of corridors or enclosed garden spaces, many of which were formally designed. The eighteenth and nineteenth centuries saw the rise of romantic notions of nature through the writing of Wordsworth in the Lake District (such as the 1807 *Poems in Two Volumes*) and other romantic poets, where the taste for the natural, long-distance walks, admiring natural features and the associated landscaping of country house estates in the natural style of landscape designers such as Capability Brown, created environments with opportunities for views, solitude, natural surroundings and the removal of traditional designs with geometric layouts. In the case of Wordsworth, de Botton (2003: 138) argues that his poetry led to 'regular travel through nature as a necessary antidote to the evils of the city'. The significance of such surroundings for pleasure walking was extolled in Jane Austen's novels, where escapism from house-based social groups and gatherings could allow leisurely strolls. Such virtues gradually permeated the evolving middle classes in the urban industrial cities of the western world in the nineteenth century (see Chapter 5) and eventually the working classes, as more leisure time was made available after the 1850s. The provision of urban parks and other spaces for walking allowed for formal walks or promenading on Sunday afternoons, which was governed by social rules and norms. This also manifests itself in the day trips to the coast, with formal areas provided for promenading for the Victorians and Edwardians at leisure. Gradually, walking clubs and organised groups emerged which saw the spatial extent and dispersion of leisure walking as rambling (British term), bushwalking (Australia) and tramping (New Zealand) evolved into popular culture and an important factor in gaining increased access to the countryside and the creation of parks, reserves and walkways (see the case study below on the New South Wales bushwalking movement and the creation of national parks in Australia).

The pursuit of walking as a leisure activity in the urban environment in the twentieth century has seen a significant transformation, as Short (2001) argues:

> Walking is about being outside, in public space, and public space is also being abandoned and eroded in older cities, eclipsed by technologies and services that don't require leaving home, and shadowed by fear in many places. . . . In many new places, public space isn't even in the design: what was once public space is designed to accommodate the privacy of automobiles; malls replace main streets, streets have no sidewalks; buildings are entered through their garages. . . . Fear has created a whole style of architecture and urban

design, notably in Southern California, where to be a pedestrian is to be under suspicion in many of the subdivisions and gated communities.

(Short 2001: 10)

Consequently walking in many urban industrial societies has seen it move into rural settings and become embodied as a recreational activity, where the rural environment is encountered both physically and mentally, rather than just as a visual contemplation (Edensor 2000).

CASE STUDY Myles Dunphy and the Australian Bushwalking Movement

Myles Dunphy has been described as the 'father of conservation in New South Wales' (Barnes and Wells 1985: 7). Dunphy was born in Melbourne in 1891, the eldest child of an Irish father and a Tasmanian mother. The family moved to Sydney in 1907 but because of the economic pressures in a large family, Dunphy left school early to join the workforce as a draughtsman, a career that would stand him in good stead to influence the public's appreciation of wilderness through high-quality maps and drawings (Thompson 1986). Although not a follower of organised religion Dunphy did appreciate the spiritual significance of wilderness. Thompson (1985: 26–7), on studying an old notebook of Dunphy, observed that Dunphy had scribbled, 'For a knowledge of God, study nature', lines reminiscent of the romantic ecological writings of John Muir (C.M. Hall 1992a).

Dunphy's central importance in any account of the development of parks in Australia lies in his contribution to the development of the bushwalking movement. Along with friends Herbert Gallop and Roy Rudder, Dunphy formed the Mountain Trails Club in October 1914 (Dunphy 1979b: 55). As revised in 1924, the objects of the club combined an aim 'to reach and enjoy the canyons, ranges and tops of the wildest parts of this country', with an intention to 'establish a definite regard for the welfare and preservation of the wildlife and natural beauties' (Prineas and Gold 1983: 29). According to Dunphy (1979a), the Mountain Trails Club

had become a kind of bush brotherhood. . . . They liked to travel quietly and see wildlife. It was good

to boil the billy in the welcome shade of river-oaks harping in the breeze, to watch wood-smoke drift down the reach, and the bars where the stream purled over the lapstones.

(Dunphy 1979a: 30)

The 'Trailers', as they were known, eschewed 'the roads of the crowd' and practised 'a kind of religion [of] mateship, self-reliance, endurance, protection of wildlife and bushland . . . a way of life close to the manifestations, beauties and outstanding miracles of nature' (Dunphy 1973, in Bardwell 1979: 16). The fervent espousal of the Australian tradition of mateship was well reflected in the club's refusal to admit women to its ranks and in membership being by invitation only; this strategy was recognised as being flawed in assisting the club to be open to wider conservation and bushwalking interests (Dunphy 1973: 3). Nevertheless, the Mountain Trails Club played a major regional role in developing an ethic of nature appreciation and walking experiences in New South Wales comparable to that of the Appalachian Mountain Club in the eastern United States (Manning 1985) and the Sierra Club in the west (C.M. Hall 1988).

The romantic notion of wilderness and the belief that contact with nature was beneficial was not isolated to the Mountain Trails Club. In response to letters from Mr J. Debbit in *The Sun* newspaper advocating the formation of a 'hikers' club', a Miss Jess Scott wrote that, 'with the approach of spring the beauties of the countryside seem to lift their voices appealingly to the "hiker", calling him to view their unadorned splendour'. However, pressures on the Mountain Trails Club to provide information on walking tours helped lead to the formation of a new bushwalking club (Dunphy 1973: 3). Although 'its members would not damage their bush brotherhood' and decided to 'render a public service by forming a new walking club with an easy constitution and easy conditions of membership, with the definite object of being a recreational walkers' club, purely and simply, and open to members of both sexes' (Dunphy 1973: 4).

Initially called 'The Waratah Walking Club', the new club changed its name to 'The Sydney Bush Walkers' at their second meeting on 8 December 1927 (Dunphy 1973: 5). The new walking club had an important part to play in the evolution of an appreciation of wild country as it enabled many people, both men and women, to become involved in an organisation which consciously supported the idea of nature conservation.

The establishment of the Sydney Bush Walkers served as the catalyst for the creation of several other clubs, notably the Bush Tracks Club and the Coast and Mountain Walkers. In 1932 the walking clubs combined to form the New South Wales Federation of Bushwalking Clubs. However, also of significance was the bush-walkers' contribution to the establishment of the National Parks and Primitive Areas Council (NPPAC) in the same year, with Myles Dunphy as secretary.

Among its objectives the NPPAC was concerned with the advocacy of 'the protection of existing tracks, paths and trails in use, particularly those having scenic and historical interests and values' (Dunphy 1973: 7–8, in Bardwell 1979: 17). Although the council viewed wilderness from a recreational perspective, the NPPAC were extremely concerned with preserving wilderness in a similar fashion to the United States. Indeed, the NPPAC along with Myles Dunphy were strongly influenced by American conservation initiatives (C.M. Hall 1992a). In 1932 Dunphy obtained a supply of booklets on American national parks which served as 'propaganda' for

the national park idea in Australia (Thompson 1985: 26), and doubtless helped create the basis for the way in which the bushwalking movement and the NPPAC lobbied for the establishment of parks and natural walking areas.

Upon its creation the NPPAC focused upon the preservation of two primitive areas – the Blue Mountains and the Snowy-Indi area – both regions being of major personal concern to Myles Dunphy. Dunphy had first put forward the idea of a national park to protect the Blue Mountains' wilderness areas as early as 1922 when a park proposal was discussed and adopted by the Mountain Trails Club (Prineas 1976–7; Dunphy 1979b). However, even at this stage Dunphy (quoted in Colley 1984: 29) recalled it had taken '10 years or so to appreciate all the damaging forces at work in this country and to become aware of the need to protect it'. In 1927 the proposal was adopted by the Sydney Bush Walkers (Dunphy 1979b), yet it was not until the 1930s that a major campaign for a Blue Mountains park got underway.

In 1931 the Mountain Trails Club, the Sydney Bush Walkers and the Wildlife Preservation Society joined forces to prevent the ringbarking of a Blue Gum forest on the Grose River. However, the 40-acre lease was not initially protected through state government reservation but through the buying of the lease by the conservation organisations (Dunphy 1979a). The romantic nature of the bushwalkers who helped save the Blue Gums is indicated in the reflections of the poet Roland Robinson (1973) on the Grose River area:

> No Greek temple, no Gothic cathedral could have been so bountiful. Here we set up our tents, and here the possums came down out of the trees with their babies on their backs to be fed by us. Because today the vulgar and ignorant 'Yankee Australians' will destroy anything in order to make a fast buck, this is one place that, thanks to the bushwalkers, is preserved in its primal Aboriginal state.
>
> (Robinson 1973: 163)

The preservation of the Grose River Blue Gums served as an example of the ability of conservation groups to get land reserved in its natural state and provided a basis for the NPPAC on which to campaign for further reservations in the Blue Mountains. The NPPAC's Greater Blue Mountains National Park Scheme probably represented the first major attempt of an Australian conservation group to mobilise mass support for the preservation of wilderness. On 24 August 1934, the NPPAC paid for a four-page supplement, complete with maps and photographs, to be included in the *Katoomba Daily*. The supplement was highlighted by Myles Dunphy's map of a proposed Blue Mountains National Park with 'primitive areas':

The Blue Mountains of Australia are justly famous for their grand scenery of stupendous canyons and gorges, mountain parks and plateaux up to 4400 feet altitude, uncounted thousands of ferny, forested dells and gauzy waterfalls, diversified forest and river beauty, much aloof wilderness – and towns and tourist resorts replete with every convenience for the comfort and entertainment of both Australian and overseas visitors.

That the supplement attempted to link the scenic attractions of the area with tourism is hardly surprising. Australia was then in the grips of a depression and linking preservation with positive economic benefits was a logical ploy. However, it is also interesting to note that in 1934 the NPPAC argued that the sandstone country of the Blue Mountains 'is potentially desert land', thereby reinforcing the 'worthless' lands concept of wilderness (see Chapter 7). Dunphy (1979a: 30) himself noted that 'the great Blue Mountains barrier region providentially was rugged and unproductive in general'. Yet the NPPAC also put forward in 1934 some positive values of wilderness, noting the necessity of providing for wilderness within regional planning in order to prevent stream erosion and land degradation. Otherwise, 'a rocky, useless and repulsive region unsuitable for either forestry, water conservation, residential, recreation, stock-raising, or other useful purposes will be created'. Despite the appeal

to the values of 'progressive' conservation the main thrust of the supplement undoubtedly relied on the aesthetic, spiritual and healing aspects of recreational experiences with nature and the outdoors.

Some 6000 of the NPPAC supplements were produced in 1934, half being distributed in the Blue Mountains region and half in Sydney (Dunphy 1979b: 60). However, despite the high quality of the supplement no action was taken on the park proposal until 25 September 1959, when the Blue Mountains National Park of 62,000 ha. in the central Blue Mountains was gazetted. The area is now part of the Blue Mountains World Heritage area.

Despite some success for Dunphy and the NPPAC in having primitive areas reserved for wilderness recreation, the outlook of the New South Wales state government towards land use was still dominated by utilitarian need. Perhaps this is not surprising given the demands of the depression and the Second World War. Nevertheless, it was in the interwar period when walking clubs flourished that the first tentative steps towards nature conservation in Australia were made. However, the greatest demands for nature conservation and the preservation of wilderness were isolated to the more populous states of Victoria and New South Wales (Bardwell 1974). Perhaps serving as an indication of the importance of urbanisation for the development of outdoor recreation.

National parks during this period were generally perceived by state governments as 'revenue-producing tourist resorts in scenic surroundings' (Bardwell 1982: 5) rather than as areas of scientific importance or wilderness recreation. For instance, in 1926 a request for the protection of flora as well as fauna within national parks was rejected by the West Australian Department of Lands and Survey, 'for the primary inducement for people to go to the reserves . . . is to gather the wildflowers with the object of adorning their homes and taking part in the wildflower shows' (Under Secretary to Minister of Lands and

THE DEMAND FOR RECREATION AND TOURISM

Surveys, Lands and Surveys Department (Western Australia), File No. 13479/98, 19 October 1926, in C.M. Hall 1992a). A far cry from the motto of the Sydney Bush Walkers: 'The bushland was here before you; leave it after you' (Dunphy 1979b: 60).

Therefore, to understand how specific activities are shaped by fashions, culture, societal changes, economic transformations and the rise of new technology (e.g. the multimedia home-based entertainment systems associated with television), and the role of factors constraining, facilitating and the trends associated with leisure, attention now turns to: how demand is measured, the problems it raises for geographers and the ways it can be analysed at different geographical scales from the national and regional down to the local level or micro scale.

MEASURING RECREATIONAL DEMAND

Most geographers acknowledge the continued lack of suitable data on recreational demand, as Patmore (1983) explains:

> Prior to the 1960s sources were scattered and fragmentary, and lacked any coherent basis. The studies undertaken for the American Outdoor Recreation Resources Review Commission and published in 1962 gave the impetus for work in Britain. Two wide-ranging national surveys were carried out later in the latter part of that decade: the Pilot National Recreation Survey . . . and the Government social survey's Planning for Leisure. . . . These surveys remain unique at national level.
>
> (Patmore 1983: 55)

Although such surveys also have a number of limitations – they were 'one-off' studies, the methods of data collection did not allow comparability of the data for each survey, and the results are often dated on publication due to the time required to analyse the results – they were a starting point for analysing demand. Yet since 1972 no major survey specifically focusing on leisure has been undertaken in the UK, although the General Household Survey (GHS), which normally occurs every four years (see

Parker 1999), has included a number of questions on leisure.

PROBLEMS AND METHODS OF MEASURING RECREATIONAL DEMAND

When seeking to understand their recreational habits, asking individuals questions about their recreational habits using social survey techniques remains the most widely used approach. A landmark study by Rowntree and Lavers (1951) of *English Life and Leisure* provides a good illustration of the early use of a diverse range of research methods and sources to construct patterns of participation in leisure and recreation in post-war Britain. Even so, researchers recognise that precision is needed to identify participation, non-participation and the frequency of each. For this reason, questions on surveys need to follow the type of format used on the GHS, to provide both a temporal and quantitative measure of demand. Patmore (1983: 57) cites the GHS, which begins by asking respondents: 'What . . . things have you done in your leisure time . . . in the four weeks ending last Sunday?'

Survey data rarely record all the information a researcher seeks (e.g. respondents' recall ability may not accurately record the full pattern), or respondents have a different understanding of a term from that intended by the researcher. As a result, a variety of survey techniques are necessary to derive a range of complementary and yet unique insights into recreation demand.

Within the recreation literature, three techniques have primarily been used:

• A continuous record of recreation activities of a sample population for a given time period which involves respondents keeping a diary of activities (the time budget approach) (Zuzanek et al.'s (1998) cross-national survey of Dutch and Canadian use of time is a good source to consult).

- Questionnaire surveys which require respondents to recall activities either in the form of an individual case study, which are detailed and sometimes contain both qualitative and quantitative questions and which are inevitably small-scale due to the time involved in in-depth qualitative interviews.
- Questionnaire surveys which are large scale, enabling subsamples to be drawn which are statistically significant. Such surveys may be derived using simple and unambiguous questions which focus on a specific recreation activity or one that covers the entire spectrum of leisure activities (e.g. the GHS surveyed 17,574 people in 1993 in Great Britain aged 16 and over). To illustrate how these techniques have been used and the way such data have been analysed, the time budget approach and national surveys of recreational activities are now examined.

TIME BUDGET SURVEY TECHNIQUES

Leisure time budgets

According to Coppock and Duffield (1975):

> recreation takes place in that portion of people's lives in which they are free (within constraints) to choose their activities, that is, their leisure time, [and] how they spend their time (time-budgets) is of paramount importance in any attempt to establish recreational demand, since it determines where recreational activities are possible.
>
> (Coppock and Duffield 1975: 5)

Therefore, time budget analysis is a vital tool in analysing demand (Anderson 1971; Fukaz 1989). Time budgets provide a systematic record of a person's use of time. They describe the duration, sequence and timing of a person's activities for a given period, usually of between a day and a week.

When combined with the recording of the location at which activities occur, the record is referred to as a space time budget. Time budget studies provide for the understanding of spatial and temporal behaviour patterns which may not be directly observable by other research techniques either because of their practicality or their intrusion into individual privacy. Such studies are often undertaken through the use of detailed diaries which are filled in by participants (see Pearce 1988a; Debbage 1991). However, this method has not been widely used in comparison with more traditional survey techniques due to the difficulty for individuals of accurately keeping records. For example, in 1966 and 1974 to 1975 the British Broadcasting Corporation used its Audience Research Department to recruit people to keep a diary for a full week with half-hour entries. Yet even in such a short time span, diarists' willingness to record information accurately declined towards the end of the week (Patmore 1983). However, pioneering research by Glyptis (1981a) used a diary technique which examined a sample of 595 visitors to the countryside. Respondents kept a diary record spanning three days and five evenings, recording the dominant pursuit in half-hour periods. While respondents identified up to 129 different leisure activities, each cited an average of 11. The value of the study was that through the use of cluster analysis to statistically analyse the sample and to group the population, it identified the leisure lifestyles of respondents with distinct groupings, where people of different social classes engaged in similar activities.

Tourism time budgets

In tourism studies, this technique has been used to provide a systematic record of a person's use of time over a given period, typically for a short period ranging from a single day to a week (D.G. Pearce 1988a; Debbage 1991). One of the fundamental assumptions in using this research method is that tourist behaviour and activities are the result of choices, a point illustrated by Floor (1990). Pearce (1987c) argues that there has been a comparative neglect of tourist activities by tourist researchers, compounded by the lack of available data. Where questionnaire surveys have addressed such issues, the results have often failed to provide a comprehensive assessment of tourist activities, both formal/informal and the relative importance of each. Thrift (1977) provides an assessment of three principal constraints on tourists' daily activity patterns, which are:

- *comparability constraints* (e.g. the biologically based need for food and sleep)
- *coupling constraints* (e.g. the need to interact and undertake activities with other people)
- *authority constraints* (e.g. where activities are controlled, not allowed or permitted at a certain point in time).

Thus both Chapin (1974) and Thrift (1977) identify choices and constraints which will influence the specific activities and context of tourist daily activities, which has similarities with the leisure constraints literature discussed earlier. The use of time budgets via diaries to record tourists activity patterns has been used in a number of contexts as research by Gaviria (1975), Cooper (1981), P.L. Pearce (1981), D.G. Pearce (1986) and Debbage (1991) indicates. Methodological issues raised by these studies highlight the problem of selecting appropriate temporal measures to record tourists' activities. P.L. Pearce (1981) used three main time periods (morning, afternoon and evening) with Gaviria (1975) selecting quarter-hour periods and Cooper (1981) using five time sequences. While the recording of activities by time is a demanding activity for tourists, D.G. Pearce (1986) argues that the main methodological concerns for such surveys are the type of technique to be used, the period to be covered and the type of sample selected. In addition, Chapin (1974) argues that such studies can choose to use three main survey techniques as follows:

- *a checklist technique*, where respondents select the list of activities they engage in from a pre-categorised list

- *the yesterday technique*, where subjects are asked to list things they did the previous day, where and when they did them
- *the tomorrow technique*, where participants keep a diary on what they do, where and when they undertake them.

Although time budget studies may still be viewed as experimental in tourism research, they do offer great potential to gain a detailed insight into tourist use of time and their activity patterns (Woo 1996).

UK 2000 Time Use Survey

The most substantive study to date is the UK 2000 Time Use Survey (ONS 2002), which set out to measure how people spent their time. It comprised a representative sample of households and individuals within households, based on a household questionnaire survey and diaries, a one week work and education time sheet. It was undertaken in 2000–1 (see http://www.statistics.gov.uk for more details). What is interesting is the aggregated results which were used to produce time spent on main and secondary activities, by category of time use. The profile of time use based on the main activities over a day are shown in Figure 2.5. This shows that almost 44 per cent of male and just over 44 per cent of female time is spent on personal care and sleeping each day, followed by employment as the next major time use. This varied between almost 15 per cent of male and almost 9 per cent of female time being devoted to employment-related activities, while family and household care accounts for almost 17 per cent of female time and less than 10 per cent of male time. In terms of time spent on leisure activities (e.g. sport, hobbies, games, social life, entertainment and mass media), 20 per cent of male and 20.33 per cent of female time is devoted to such pursuits, with marginally more male time given over to mass media (e.g. watching the television). Almost 65 per cent of male leisure time is devoted to watching television, compared to 55 per cent of female time. What is also notable is the dominance of passive leisure pursuits.

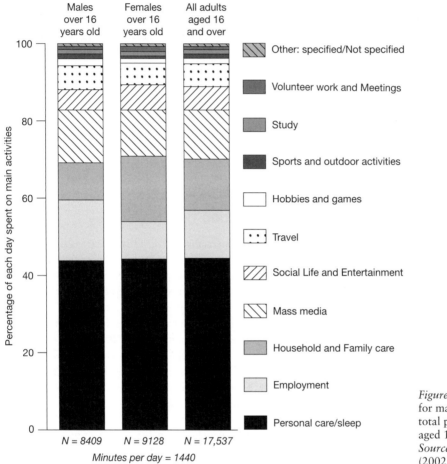

Figure 2.5: Time budgets for males, females and the total population of adults aged 16 and over in 2000
Source: based on ONS (2002) data

In terms of the timing of leisure activities for all adults, at 8 a.m., 7 per cent were engaged in leisure which increased to 14 per cent at 12 noon; this increased to 23 per cent at 4 p.m. and to 57 per cent at 8 p.m. dropping to 13 per cent at midnight, when 79 per cent were sleeping. This, however, varied between weekdays (Monday to Thursday), with 17 per cent of adults in leisure at midnight on a Friday. At weekends, rest and recuperation were principal leisure activities. Weekend evenings were the most popular for leisure, activities, with two-thirds of adults engaged in leisure especially socialising on Saturday evenings at 9 p.m.

The results of a diary analysis of young people aged between 8 and 15 found that young people

- spend more time than adults sleeping, an average of 10 hours a day (compared to 8 hours and 30 minutes for all adults)
- spent half an hour a day on sport.

The value of such research is in the identification of factors beyond simplistic analogies of demand determined by biological, social and economic factors, where the relationship between different time-consuming activities are examined in a holistic manner. Indeed, at a EU level, the July 2003 Time Use at Different Stages of Life survey of time use in thirteen different EU countries provides some comparable transnational data (http://www.europa.eu.int).

NATIONAL EVALUATIONS OF RECREATIONAL DEMAND: INTERNATIONAL PERSPECTIVES

The most useful survey of national surveys of leisure time and the recreational activities undertaken may be found in Cushman et al. (1996a) which reviews international data on leisure and the existence of cross-national comparative research. It is also useful since the origins and role of participation surveys are reviewed, a feature subsequently updated by Parker (1999) in the UK context.

United Kingdom

Since the publication of Patmore's (1983) detailed review of data sources for analysing leisure and recreation patterns in the UK, Veal (1992) updated the situation pointing to the GHS and the role of the Australian Commonwealth government in commissioning the first National Recreation Participation Survey in Australia in 1985 to 1986.

The most authoritative source is *Social Trends 33* (ONS 2003). This uses the UK 2000 Time Use Survey to identify the amount of time spent on leisure. The most popular sport that people particcipated in was walking/hiking. Almost a quarter of women engaged in this activity in the month before the survey. Only 19 per cent of men had undertaken this activity. Keep fit and swimming were the most common activities for women to participate in, with nearly half surveyed not participating in any form of sport. For men, snooker, swimming and cycling were the activities most frequently undertaken.

In terms of passive leisure pursuits, attending a 'cultural event' (i.e. an art gallery or museum) comprised 22 per cent of attendances in 2001–2. In contrast, 57 per cent of respondents had been to the cinema, 24 per cent had attended plays, 12 per cent attended a performance of classical music, 6 per cent the ballet, 6 per cent the opera and 5 per cent contemporary dance. What is notable is that cinema attendance had nearly doubled while attendance at other cultural events had been stable. However, attendance varies by socio-economic group and age group. For example, the rise in

cinema attendance was highest in the 15–24 age group, with 50 per cent who reported that they had been to cinema once a month compared with 15 per cent of those aged 35 and over. Also, children aged 7–14 have been a major growth market in 2000 and 2001, particularly at multiplex complexes.

In terms of day trips as a pursuit, the 1998 UK Day Visits Survey provides data on round trips from home to locations in the UK and the 2002–2003 report provides the most accessible data.

In 2002–2003, the UK Day Trips Survey found that 80 per cent of adults in Great Britain had made a leisure day visit in the past two weeks, with 50 per cent visiting a town or city, 21 per cent the countryside, 10 per cent to the seaside and coast and 8 per cent to a forest or woodland area. A further 6 per cent had visited water with a boat and 5 per cent had visited the water without boats (TNS 2004).

In terms of tourism, domestic holiday trips grew 20 per cent between 1995 and 1999, with an estimated 102 million trips in 2001, down on 106 million trips in 2000. The most popular type of accommodation used in 2001 was staying in the home of friends or relatives (41 per cent) with 24 per cent staying in a hotel, motel or guesthouse. This was followed by static caravans (8 per cent) and rented accommodation (house, flat or chalet) (8 per cent). The most popular destinations for domestic tourism were south-west England, the Heart of England (the Midlands), Scotland and London. Within these destination areas, towns, cities, rural areas and coastal areas continue to act as major attractors. Within the UK, an estimated 6400 visitor attractions exist, and free and paying attractions received 452 million visits in 2001.

In terms of the overseas holiday habits of UK residents, 2003 saw 41.2 million holidays taken overseas. The growth of UK outbound tourism has grown from 4.2 million trips of four nights or more by British residents in 1971 to 13.1 million in 1981 to 20.8 million in 1991 and 32 million in 1998 and 38.7 million in 2001 and 41.2 million in 2003.

Figure 2.6 illustrates the changing tastes of British holidaymakers in overseas holidays

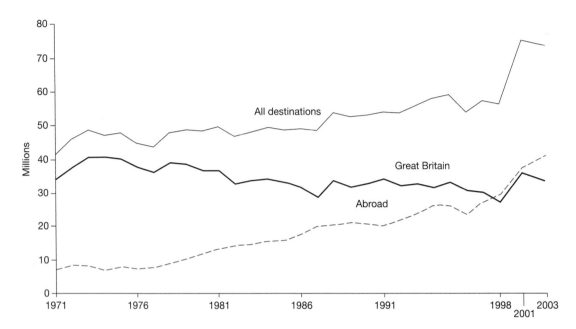

Figure 2.6: Holidays of four nights or more by British residents by number taken per year, 1971–2003
Source: based on *Social Trends 33*, Office for National Statistics (2003); http://www.staruk.org

where many destinations have seen significant fluctuations in arrivals. In 2001, the countries with the greatest growth in numbers of visits were in the Mediterranean while the greatest falls were in visits to Germany, Canada and Israel.

What is problematic, as researchers observe, is that many data sources such as *Social Trends* do not consistently record time series of data. As a result, the data in 2003 was derived from the 2000 Time Use Survey compared to the General Household Survey that previously derived more data on participation in home-based leisure.

United States

In the USA, one of the most useful studies of leisure is the National Survey on Recreation and the Environment, which is an ongoing national, federal survey. Its origins can be dated to the Outdoor Recreation Resources Review Commission of 1960, which was the first nationwide outdoor recreation survey, repeated in 1965, 1970, 1972, 1977,

1982–3, 1994–5 and 2000–1, renamed the National Survey on Recreation and the Environment (NSRE) in 1994. The 2001 study conducted interview with 50,000 individuals across all ethnic groups and locations in the USA examining themes such as outdoor recreation participation, demographic profiles, household characteristics, lifestyle issues, constraints to participation and environmental issues in recreation. As Cordell et al. (2002) report, this was the most detailed survey of its kind to date in the USA.

The USA has a population of over 284 million, which is forecast to grow to 325 million by 2020, 404 million by 2050 and 481 million by 2075. One notable change will be the greater ethnic diversity of the population, as the proportion of Anglo-Americans declines to 2050 from 76 per cent to 50 per cent. Conversely, by 2050 the proportion of African Americans will rise from 12 per cent to 15 per cent; the proportion of Hispanic origin will rise from 9 per cent to 21 per cent and other ethnic groups from 4 per cent to 11 per cent. This will have major implications for the demand and type of leisure that these groups consume. Cordell et al. (2002: 22) summarised the results of the 2001–2 NSRE as follows:

- Nearly all respondents (97 per cent) had participated in at least one outdoor recreation activity in the previous 12 months prior to interview (which yields 206 million people aged over 15 undertaking one or more of 77 outdoor activities examine in the survey.
- Walking remains the most important activity, with 83.8 per cent participating.
- Other activities include attending an outdoor gathering with family/relatives/friends (73.5 per cent); picnicking (53.5 per cent); visits to outdoor centres/attractions/nature trails/zoos (57.2 per cent); scenic viewing/photography (54 per cent).
- Least popular activities were migrating bird hunting (2.3 per cent); scuba diving (1.9 per cent); surfing (1.5 per cent) and wind surfing (0.8 per cent).
- The fastest growing activity was birding, in line with the 1995 NSRE which has seen a 236 per cent growth rate 1983–2000. Other growth sectors over the same period were: hiking (19.6 per cent growth); snow-mobiling (107.5 per cent growth); swimming in natural waters (64 per cent growth); back-packing (165.9 per cent growth) and walking (97.2 per cent growth).
- The percentage of the population participating in the top five fastest growing activities were: bird watching (33.4 per cent); hiking (34.3 per cent); back-packing (10.9 per cent) and snow-mobiling (31.4 per cent).

As Cordell et al. (2002: 39) conclude, if 'real incomes (inflation adjusted) continue to rise in this country, as it did between 1960 and 2000 . . . we can expect upward pressure for participation in all outdoor activities', particularly high-cost activities (e.g. off-road driving) while inexpensive activities such as walking will be less affected. The growing ethnic diversity will also affect the demand for leisure as different groups have social and culturally

determined views of the outdoors, and for that matter, indoor forms of leisure (Virden and Walker 1999).

Poland

Poland is an interesting example, given the new roles for recreation in the post-communist state (Jung 1994, 1996), since market reforms and ideological change have led to new roles for leisure post-1989 (see Kwiatkowska 1999 for a discussion of contemporary leisure in Poland as a cultural form and the change from mass consumption of communist forms of leisure to more westernised individually consumed forms of leisure). Although one consequence of austerity programmes to deal with budget deficits, a number of pre- and post-communist data sources exist to reconstruct leisure participation, while individual researchers have also tracked changes such as the gender differences in leisure time (Tarkowska 2002) and the impact on disability on leisure (Siwiński 1998). The government Central Statistical Office (GUS) collects the majority of data, published in its Polish language study, the Statistical Yearbook of the Republic of Poland, on an annual basis, with tourism data compiled by the Institute of Tourism (http://www.intur.com.pl). Jung (1996) noted that over the period between 1972 and 1990, participation trends showed the following:

- Listening to the radio and watching television remained the dominant activities in terms of participation.
- Former communist culture activities, such as going to the cinema, theatre and opera, declined in importance from over half of the population in 1972 to under one-third by 1990.
- Economic and political reforms in the 1980s may account for a sharp decline in participation of consumption of high forms of culture (e.g. visiting museums, exhibitions and concert halls).

More detailed time budget studies have been examined by Olszewska (1989) and Jung (1996) highlighted a number of key global influences upon leisure participation: a growing media influence on mass culture, outbound travel by the Polish population (and inbound tourism), despite the withdrawal of state social subsidies for holiday travel. The electronic mass media also had an impact on leisure consumption. In the post-communist era, problems associated with the commercialisation of leisure and a growing polarisation of wealth, less economic security, rising unemployment and increasing rates of crime provide a new context for leisure participation.

These three examples of recreational demand show that the patterns of leisure activities for each population exhibit a common range of characteristics, in terms of the predominance of passive activities, and the constraints of urban living which largely structure the time budgets of those in employment due to weekday work commitments. In other words, the patterns of demand highlighted in the three national surveys point to the existence of factors which facilitate and constrain recreational activities in each particular context. Even so, it is important to recognise the current criticisms and concerns with national participation surveys observed by Cushman et al. (1996b: 12): 'Recently surveys have had a "bad press" from academics, particularly in light of the growing popularity – and indeed orthodoxy – of qualitative research methods in the field'. As a result, qualitative researchers point to the shortcomings, limitations and somewhat outmoded approach of quantitative 'positivist' research methods (see Johnston 1991 for a discussion of philosophical perspectives on geography, geographers and research methodologies). However, so far the discussion of demand has focused on national patterns, and therefore attention now turns to the regional level to examine the contribution the geographer can make to the analysis of demand within a regional geographic framework.

REGIONAL DEMAND FOR LEISURE AND RECREATION IN LONDON

Within the studies of national recreational demand reviewed in the previous section, it is clear that the analyses of geographical patterns of demand were relatively scant, given the tendency for national studies to lack a regional dimension. It is the spatial variations in demand which are of interest to the geographer, and a number of studies have been undertaken which utilise the geographer's spatial analytical approach to examine demand patterns. North-west England is one such area which has seen a significant contribution made to understanding the scale and nature of regional recreational demand including evidence in Rodgers' (1969) insights from the *Pilot National Recreation Survey*, Rodgers' (1977) contribution to leisure in the north-west and Rodgers and Patmore's (1972) *Leisure in the North-West*. A similar study can be achieved through the series of reports by ONS (2003) entitled *Focus on London*.

London is a world city with a population of around 7 million; in 2002, its residents took 11.5 million trips abroad, comprising 19 per cent of the total number of trips made by UK residents. This reflects the economic, political and cultural importance of the city as a place to live and work, even though Londoners account for only 12 per cent of the total population of the UK. Many of these trips, undertaken in leisure time and for business purposes, were to western Europe (7.9 million), with 900,000 trips to the USA and Canada. This specific use of leisure time for travel overseas is also underscored by a use of leisure time for many of the purposes discussed above in the UK 2000 Time Use Survey. In London, watching television, video or DVDs in 2000 varied by age group, with those aged 8 to 15 years watching 16.9 hours a week, and those aged 16 to 34 years 17.1 hours, to 16.7 hours for those aged 35 to 64 and rising to 25.7 hours a week for those aged 65 or over. An average of 18 hours a week emerged for all those aged 8 years or over. These figures are marginally lower than the figures for the UK population, probably as a result of a more diverse range of attractions and cultural facilities available to them than the average population. In terms of participation in sport and physical activities, the majority of sports halls and swimming pools (66 per cent) are in Outer London where 60 per cent of the population reside. Watching football is a major pastime: London is the home of twelve football teams with between 19,000 and 39,000 attending home matches, depending on the football club involved and its spectator audience. Cinemas are also a major pastime too, with London accounting for 176 million cinema admissions in 2002. Almost 60 per cent of Londoners attended a cinema showing twice a year in 2002. In fact almost one-third attended the cinema once a month, a much higher attendance rate than the population as a whole. Similarly, access to other cultural facilities like the theatre was reflected in higher theatre attendances by Londoners than the UK population. At cultural events, the theatre, art galleries, pop/rock concerts, classical music performances, jazz performances, contemporary dance and ballet in that order of significance generated 1 billion attendances in 2002 in London.

In terms of expenditure on leisure, the ONS statistics from the Family Expenditure Survey in 2001–2 found that:

- London households spent an average of £75 a week on recreation and leisure in 2001–2. This was 10 per cent higher than the UK population as a whole.
- The London population, reflecting their lifestyle, higher earnings and habits, spent £364 more per year than the UK population on eating out, reflecting access to the 19 per cent of the UK's cafe and restaurants located within the London area.
- They also spent £93 a year more on cultural activities and £31 a year more on audio-visual equipment than their UK counterparts.

Interestingly, Londoners spent £156 less per year on package holidays (although up to 25% of the population are unable to afford a holiday). In terms

of leisure-related sites (restaurants, cafes, public houses, bars, clubs, hotels, camping sites, libraries, museums and sport and recreation sites), London has 13 per cent of the total. Not surprisingly, London employed 16 per cent of all leisure-related industry jobs in the UK in 2001, with the largest proportion (32 per cent) in theatres and cinemas.

Therefore, it is evident that through regional analysis, which epitomises the geographer's interest in places, and differences and similarities in both time and space, regional differences exist in the demand for leisure in the UK, a feature often replicated in many other countries. These differences highlight the importance of geographical research in understanding demand at different levels. However, one of the most important contributions has been made through site-specific studies of demand, notably site surveys. For this reason, the remaining focus of this section on recreation examines recreation site surveys.

SPATIAL ANALYSIS OF DEMAND AT THE MICRO LEVEL: SITE SURVEYS

Within the growing literature on geographical studies of recreation in the 1960s and 1970s (see e.g. Rodgers (1973) on demand), site surveys have become the most documented (a feature reiterated in Chapter 6). As Glyptis (1981b: 277) indicated, 'numerous site surveys – mostly set in the format devised by Burton (1966) . . . established the characteristics of visitors and their trips. Social profiles, trip distances, modes of transport and the duration, purpose and frequency of visits are well documented (Elson 1977)'. Glyptis (1981b) also noted that the 1980s were ripe for behavioural analysis which had been neglected in relation to site surveys. While reviews of site surveys are too numerous to list (see Harrison 1991), novel research methods which examine the behaviour rather than the socio-economic characteristics of recreationalists have remained less common in the published literature, although some reports have probed this area (e.g. Locke 1985). Glyptis' (1981b) analysis of one 242 ha site – Westwood Common, Beverley near

Hull (UK) – is one such example. By employing participant observation methods to examine an undulating grassland area of common pasture land 13 km from the urban area of Hull, the spatial distribution of site use by recreationalists was observed and analysed. The main recreational activities observed at the site were sitting, sunbathing, walking, picnicking, informal games and staying inside one's car. On a busy Sunday in summer, up to 2000 visitors came to the site. Using dispersion maps, observational mapping permitted the visitor distributions to be located in time and space while length of stay (using car registration data) and maps of use for different days and times complemented traditional social survey methods to analyse visitor behaviour. The site features, access points, availability of parking and location of landscape features and facilities permit a more detailed understanding of site use. Glyptis (1981b) used observations on five days in August and September between 11 a.m. and 6 p.m. to collate data. Visitor arrivals at the site during the weekend occurred between 12 noon and 2 p.m., and peak use occurred at 4.30 p.m., with the majority of visitors spending one to two hours on site. The gradual increase in intensity of use by time of day varied by activity, with informal games and picnicking declining after Sunday lunch and walking increasing throughout the afternoon. Local users also displayed a preference to use the site at off-peak times, with increased patterns of dispersion and clumping through time. This reflects access roads, with visitors parking close to (within 15 yards) the site they visited. Visitors were also recorded going to landmarks and facilities (e.g. viewpoints) as well as buying refreshments (e.g. from mobile vans), with the density of use increasing through the day rather than the distribution.

Glyptis (1981c) devised a simple model to explain the dynamics of visitor dispersion (Figure 2.7). Figure 2.7 shows that initial visitors to a site choose a favoured location linked to parking areas, with further inflows of visitors during the early afternoon marking an 'invasion phase' which extends the initial cluster. Thereafter, as the pace of arrivals slows, a degree of infilling and

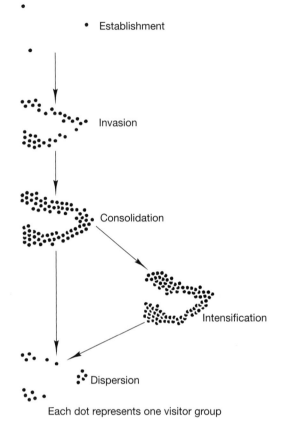

Each dot represents one visitor group

Figure 2.7: Glyptis' model of visitor dispersion at an informal recreation site
Source: redrawn from Glyptis (1981c)

consolidation occurs. Then as people depart, dispersion occurs, with a more irregular pattern of distribution arising, although it may be affected by new arrivals in the afternoon who intensify the pattern. What Glyptis (1991: 119) recognised was that even though 'sites clearly experience an increase in visitor density, visitor dispersion in a spatial sense remains fairly constant, even with space to spare and no restrictions on public access'. Using nearest neighbour analysis, Glyptis (1981c) was able to measure the distances between groups of visitors, and that comfortable levels of tolerance exist for visitors in terms of proximity to other people, although the amount of personal space which recreationalists require may vary between different cultures. In fact, Glyptis (1991: 119) remarked that 'as levels of use increase on a given day, the percentage occupancy of space actually decreases: visitors only ever use about a fifth of the space available to them, and at times of heaviest use they choose to occupy even less. In other words, site carrying capacity changes continually'. This study also highlighted the significance of recreation sites with multiple uses, where a variety of recreational needs are capable of being met and, as Burton's (1974) survey of Cannock Chase, Staffordshire (UK) found, individual sites cannot be viewed in isolation: there are relationships between them and understanding them is vital to site management. Glyptis (1981c) highlighted a certain degree of consistency in visitor use of a site, explaining the patterns as a function of the resource base, visitor use and behavioural factors. It may be possible to accommodate or reduce capacity through simple modifications as 'the geographer is well placed to examine fundamental aspects of . . . recreation, to diagnose issues in site management, and to propose solutions' (Glyptis 1981b: 285). In fact one study by Brainaird et al. (2003) identified the value of a Geographical Information Systems approach to understanding forestry sites and the demand for open access sites to construct site based models of arrivals, incorporating travel time data, being a function of surrounding population (i.e. catchment), accessibility and two measures of site facilities (car parking facilities and length of woodland walks provided). Therefore, having outlined many of the factors and dimensions of recreational demand at a variety of spatial scales from the national, regional and local level, the discussion now turns to tourism demand.

TOURISM DEMAND

One of the fundamental questions that tourism researchers consistently seek to answer is: why do tourists travel? This seemingly simple proposition remains one of the principal challenges for tourism research. D.G. Pearce (1995a: 18) expands this proposition by asking 'What induces them to leave their home area to visit other areas? What factors condition their travel behaviour, influencing their choice of destination, itineraries followed and activities undertaken?' Such questions not only underpin issues of spatial interaction, but also lead the geographer to question:

- why tourists seek to travel
- where they go
- when they go and how they get there.

These basic issues have spatial implications in terms of the patterns of tourism, where tourism impacts will occur and the nature of management challenges for destinations which may attract a 'mass market' or be seeking to develop tourism from a low base. In other words, an understanding of tourism demand is a starting point for the analysis of why tourism develops, who patronises specific destinations and what appeals to the client market. As de Botton (2003: 9) argues in his treatise, *The Art of Travel*, 'we are inundated with advice on *where* to travel to; we hear little of *why* and *how* we should go'. However, geographers are at a comparative disadvantage in answering some of the principal questions associated with tourism demand since 'geographers have not been at the forefront of this research which has been led by psychologists, sociologists, marketers and economists. Some of these researchers have touched on such issues as the potential significance of variations in motivation on destination choice' (D.G. Pearce 1995a: 18). However, tourist behaviour and the analysis of motivation has not traditionally been the logical positivist and empirical approach of traditional forms of spatial analysis on tourism with some exceptions (e.g. Walmsley and Jenkins 1992). The area of tourist behaviour has a more developed literature within the field of social psychology than geography, and the emphasis in this section is on the way such approaches assist in understanding how tourist behaviour may result in the spatial implications for tourism.

WHAT IS TOURISM DEMAND?

The precise approach one adopts to the analysis of tourism demand is largely dependent upon the disciplinary perspective of the researcher (see G. Crouch 1994). Geographers view demand in a uniquely spatial manner as 'the total number of persons who travel, or wish to travel, to use tourist facilities and services at places away from their places of work and residence' (Mathieson and Wall 1982: 1), whereas in this context demand 'is seen in terms of the relationship between individuals' motivation [to travel] and their ability to do so' (D.G. Pearce 1995a: 18) with an attendant emphasis on the implications for the spatial impact on the development of domestic and international tourism. In comparison, the economist emphasises 'the schedule of the amount of any product or service which people are willing and able to buy at each specific price in a set of possible prices during a specified period of time. Psychologists view demand from the perspective of motivation and behaviour' (Cooper et al. 1993: 15), while Uysal (1998) reviewed the wider context of tourism demand.

In conceptual terms, there are three principal elements to tourism demand:

- *Effective or actual demand* comprises the number of people participating in tourism, usually expressed as the number of travellers. This is most commonly measured by tourism statistics which means that most official sources of data are measures of effective demand.
- *Suppressed demand* is the population who are unable to travel because of circumstances (e.g. lack of purchasing power or limited holiday entitlement) which is called potential demand. Potential demand can be converted to effective demand if the circumstances change. There is also deferred demand where constraints (e.g. lack of tourism supply such as a shortage of bedspaces) can also be converted to effective demand if a destination or locality can accommodate the demand.
- *No demand* is a distinct category for the population who have no desire to travel.

According to Cooper et al. (1993: 16) the demand for tourism may be viewed in other ways using a number of other concepts:

- *substitution of demand* where the demand for a specific activity is substituted by another activity
- *redirection of demand* where the geographical distribution of tourism is altered due to pricing policies of competing destinations, special events or changing trends and tastes.

Therefore, it is apparent that the analysis of tourism demand as an abstract concept remains firmly within the remit of tourism economics (Witt and Martin 1989, 1992; Bull 1991). Figure 2.8 based on Uysal's (1998) overview of tourism demand summarises the main determinants of demand within a multidisciplinary context. There has, however, been comparatively little discussion of the significance of what might be termed 'background' factors which act as geographical constraints on travel, such as the role of travel epidemiology (Steffen et al. 2003). It can be argued that exposure to pathogens in high risk countries with poor endemic hygiene standards can pose major risk factors to tourist health which are not given sufficient credence in many debates on demand, as Wilks and Page (2003) show. For example, the UK Foreign and Commonwealth Office (FCO) advice to travellers and risk notices do illustrate the scale of risk which tourists face along with some of the dangers of travelling to high risk areas such as assault, attacks, robberies, mild stomach bugs from drinking local tap water and lost/stolen passports. However, the factors which shape the tourist decision-making process to select and participate in specific forms of tourism is largely within the field of consumer behaviour and motivation.

TOURIST MOTIVATION

According to Moutinho (1987: 16), motivation is 'a state of need, a condition that exerts a push on the individual towards certain types of action that are

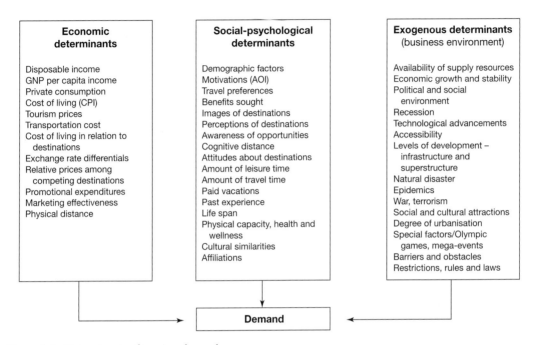

Figure 2.8: Determinants of tourism demand
Source: Uysal (1998)

seen as likely to bring satisfaction'. In this respect Cooper et al. (1993: 20) rightly acknowledge that 'demand for tourists at the individual level can be treated as a consumption process which is influenced by a number of factors. These may be a combination of needs and desires, availability of time and money, or images, perceptions and attitudes'. Not surprisingly, this is an incredibly complex area of research and it is impossible within a chapter such as this to overview the area in depth. Nevertheless, P.L. Pearce's (1993) influential work in this field outlined a 'blueprint for tourist motivation', arguing that in an attempt to theorise tourist motivation one must consider the following issues:

- the conceptual place of tourism motivation
- its task in the specialism of tourism
- its ownership and users
- its ease of communication
- pragmatic measurement concerns
- adopting a dynamic approach
- the development of multi-motive perspectives

- resolving and clarifying intrinsic and extrinsic motivation approaches.

To date no all-embracing theory of tourist motivation has been developed which has been adapted and legitimised by researchers in other contexts. This is largely due to the multidisciplinary nature of the research issues identified above and the problem of simplifying complex psychological factors and behaviour into a set of constructs and ultimately a universally acceptable theory that can be tested and proved in various tourism contexts. As a result, Cooper et al. (1993: 20) prefer to view the individual as a central component of tourism demand to understand what motivates the tourist to travel. Their research rightly acknowledges that:

No two individuals are alike, and differences in attitudes, perceptions and motivation have an important influence on travel decisions [where] attitudes depend on an individual's perception of the world. Perceptions are mental impressions of . . . a place or travel company and are determined by many factors which include childhood, family and work experiences. However, attitudes and perceptions in themselves do not explain why people want to travel. The inner urges which initiate travel demand are called travel motivators.

If one views the tourist as a consumer, then tourism demand is formulated through a consumer decision-making process, and therefore one can discern four elements which initiate demand:

- *energisers of demand* factors that promote an individual to decide on a holiday
- *filterers of demand* which means that even though motivation may prevail, constraints on demand may exist in economic, sociological or psychological terms
- *affecters* which are factors that may heighten or suppress the energisers that promote consumer interest or choice in tourism
- *roles* where the family member involved in the purchase of holiday products and the arbiter of group decision-making on choice of destination, product, and the where, when and how of consumption.

These factors underpin the tourist's process of travel decision-making although it does not explain why people choose to travel.

MASLOW'S HIERARCHY MODEL AND TOURIST MOTIVATION

Within the social psychology of tourism there is a growing literature which has built upon Maslow's work (discussed earlier in relation to recreation) to identify specific motivations beyond the concept of needing 'to get away from it all' pioneered by Grinstein (1955), while push factors motivating individuals to seek a holiday exist, and pull factors (e.g. promotion by tourist resorts and tour operators) encourage as attractors. Ryan's (1991: 25–9) analysis of tourist travel motivators (excluding business travel) identifies the following reasons commonly cited to explain why people travel to tourist destinations for holidays, which include

- a desire to escape from a mundane environment
- the pursuit of relaxation and recuperation functions
- an opportunity for play
- the strengthening of family bonds
- prestige, since different destinations can enable one to gain social enhancement among peers
- social interaction
- educational opportunities
- wish fulfilment
- shopping.

Plate 2.2: Largs, west Scotland. Promenading illustrates that the Victorian and Edwardian Sunday constitutional walk is still a key feature in coastal resorts for day visitors and tourists.

Plate 2.3: Transport to connect peripheral locations such as islands provide a vital element in the supply chain and an attraction and activity in their own right.

From this list, it is evident that while all leisure involves a temporary escape of some kind,

> tourism is unique in that it involves real physical escape reflected in travelling to one or more destination regions where the leisure experience transpires . . . [thus] a holiday trip allows changes that are multi-dimensional: place, pace, faces, lifestyle, behaviour, attitude. It allows a person temporary withdrawal from many of the environments affecting day to day existence.
> (Leiper 1984, cited in D.G. Pearce 1995a: 19)

Within most studies of tourist motivations these factors emerge in one form or another, while researchers such as Crompton (1979) emphasise that socio-psychological motives can be located along a continuum, Iso-Ahola (1980) theorised tourist motivation in terms of an escape element complemented by a search component, where the tourist is seeking something. However, Dann's (1981) conceptualisation is probably one of the most useful attempts to simplify the principal elements of tourist motivation into

- travel as a response to what is lacking yet desired
- destination pull in response to motivational push
- motivation as fancy
- motivation as classified purpose
- motivation typologies
- motivation and tourist experiences
- motivation as definition and meaning.

This was simplified a stage further by McIntosh and Goeldner (1990) into

- physical motivators
- cultural motivators
- interpersonal motivators
- status and prestige motivators.

On the basis of motivation and using the type of experiences tourists seek, Cohen (1972) distinguished between four types of travellers:

- The organised mass tourist, on a package holiday, who is highly organised. Their contact

with the host community in a destination is minimal.
- The individual mass tourist, who uses similar facilities to the organised mass tourist but also desires to visit other sights not covered on organised tours in the destination.
- The explorers, who arrange their travel independently and who wish to experience the social and cultural lifestyle of the destination.
- The drifter, who does not seek any contact with other tourists or their accommodation, preferring to live with the host community (see V.L. Smith 1992).

Clearly, such a classification is fraught with problems, since it does not take into account the increasing diversity of holidays undertaken and inconsistencies in tourist behaviour (P.L. Pearce 1982). Other researchers suggest that one way of overcoming this difficulty is to consider the different destinations that tourists choose to visit, and then establish a sliding scale similar to Cohen's (1972) typology, but which does not have such an absolute classification.

In contrast, Plog (1974) devised a classification of the US population into psychographic types, with travellers distributed along a continuum (see Figure 2.9) from psychocentrism to allocentrism. The psychocentrics are the anxious, inhibited and less adventurous travellers while at the other extreme the allocentrics are adventurous, outgoing, seeking new experiences due to their inquisitive personalities and interest in travel and adventure (also see Plog 2001; S.L.J. Smith 1990a, 1990b).

D.G. Pearce (1995a) highlights the spatial implications of such conceptualisations, that each tourist type will seek different destinations which will change through time. However, criticisms by P.L. Pearce (1993) indicate that Plog's model is difficult to use because it fails to distinguish between extrinsic and intrinsic motivations without incorporating a dynamic element to encompass the changing nature of individual tourists. P.L. Pearce discounts such models, suggesting that individuals have a 'career' in their travel behaviour where people 'start at different levels, they are likely to change levels

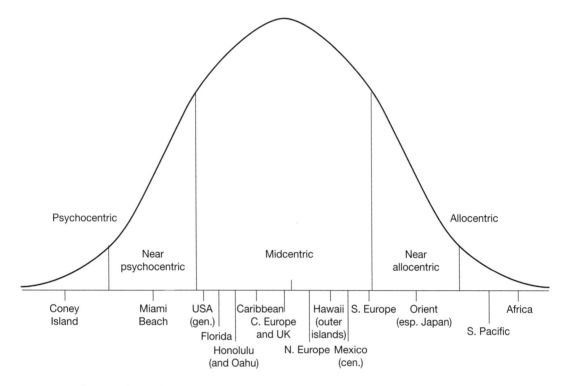

Figure 2.9: Plog's psychographic positions of destinations
Source: redrawn from Plog (1977)

during their life-cycle and they can be prevented from moving by money, health and other people. They may also retire from their travel career or not take holidays at all and therefore not be part of the system' (P.L. Pearce 1993: 125).

Figure 2.10 outlines Pearce's model based on a leisure ladder, which builds on Maslow's hierarchical system, where there are five motivational levels. These are

1 a concern with biological needs
2 safety and security needs
3 relationship development and extension needs
4 special interest and self-development needs
5 fulfilment or self-actualisation needs.

Cooper et al. (1993: 23) argue that 'the literature on tourism motivation is still in an immature phase of development, it has been shown that motivation is an essential concept behind the different patterns of tourism demand'. From the existing literature on tourist motivation, the problems of determining tourist motivation may be summarised as follows:

• Tourism is not one specific product, it is a combination of products and experiences which meet a diverse range of needs.
• Tourists are not always conscious of their deep psychological needs and ideas. Even when they do know what they are, they may not reveal them.
• Tourism motives may be multiple and contradictory (push and pull factors).
• Motives may change over time and be inextricably linked together (e.g. perception, learning, personality and culture are often separated out but they are all bound up together) and dynamic conceptualisations such as P.L. Pearce's (1993) leisure ladder are crucial to advancing knowledge and understanding in this area.

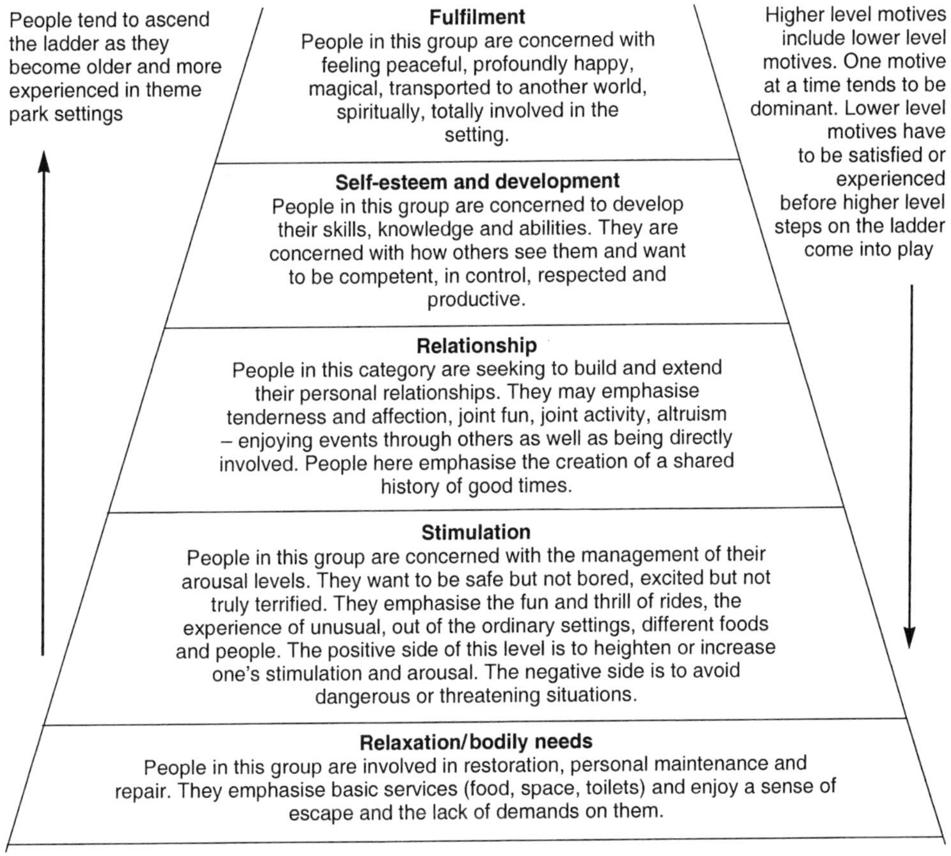

People tend to ascend the ladder as they become older and more experienced in theme park settings

Fulfilment
People in this group are concerned with feeling peaceful, profoundly happy, magical, transported to another world, spiritually, totally involved in the setting.

Higher level motives include lower level motives. One motive at a time tends to be dominant. Lower level motives have to be satisfied or experienced before higher level steps on the ladder come into play

Self-esteem and development
People in this group are concerned to develop their skills, knowledge and abilities. They are concerned with how others see them and want to be competent, in control, respected and productive.

Relationship
People in this category are seeking to build and extend their personal relationships. They may emphasise tenderness and affection, joint fun, joint activity, altruism – enjoying events through others as well as being directly involved. People here emphasise the creation of a shared history of good times.

Stimulation
People in this group are concerned with the management of their arousal levels. They want to be safe but not bored, excited but not truly terrified. They emphasise the fun and thrill of rides, the experience of unusual, out of the ordinary settings, different foods and people. The positive side of this level is to heighten or increase one's stimulation and arousal. The negative side is to avoid dangerous or threatening situations.

Relaxation/bodily needs
People in this group are involved in restoration, personal maintenance and repair. They emphasise basic services (food, space, toilets) and enjoy a sense of escape and the lack of demands on them.

Figure 2.10: The leisure ladder for theme park settings (domestic visitors)
Source: Pearce (1993a)

Having examined some of the issues associated with what motivates tourists to travel, attention now turns to the process of measurement and recording tourist demand using statistical measures.

MEASUREMENT OF TOURISM DEMAND: TOURISM STATISTICS

Ritchie (1975, cited in Latham and Edwards 2003: 55) argued that 'an important part of the maturing process for any science is the development or adaptation of consistent and well-tested measurement techniques and methodologies which are well-suited to the types of problems encountered in practice'. In this context, the measurement of tourists, tourism activity and the effects on the economy and society in different environments is crucial to the development of tourism as an established area of study within the confines of social science (Lennon 2003). Burkart and Medlik (1981) provide an insight into the development of measurements of tourism phenomena by governments during the 1960s and their development through to the late 1970s. While it is readily acknowledged by most tourism researchers that statistics are a necessary feature to provide data to enable researchers, managers, planners, decision-makers and public and private sector bodies to gauge the significance and impact of tourism on destination areas, Burkart and Medlik (1981: 74) identify four principal reasons for statistical measurement in tourism:

- to evaluate the magnitude and significance of tourism to a destination area or region
- to quantify the contribution to the economy or society, especially the effect on the balance of payments
- to assist in the planning and development of tourism infrastructure and the effect of different volumes of tourists with specific needs
- to assist in the evaluation and implementation of marketing and promotion activities where the tourism marketer requires information on the actual and potential markets and their characteristics.

Consequently, tourism statistics are essential to the measurement of the volume, scale, impact and value of tourism at different geographical scales from the global to the country level down to the individual destination. A more recent development has been the evolution of Tourism Satellite Accounts (TSAs) for individual countries to establish a set methodology for assessing the tourism economy in each country (see Frechtling 1996 for more detail on how this technique has been developed and applied). Yet an information gap still exists between the types of statistics provided by organisations for and the needs of users. The compilation of tourism statistics provided by organisations associated with the measurement of tourism has established methods and processes to collect, collate and analyse tourism statistics (World Tourism Organisation 1995), yet these have been understood by only a small number of researchers and practitioners. Thus this section attempts to demystify the apparent sophistication and complexity associated with the presentation of statistical indicators of tourism and their value to spatial analysis, since geographers have a strong quantified methods tradition (Johnston 1991), which is reflected in the use and reliance upon such indicators to understand spatial variations and patterns of tourism activity. All too often, under-

graduate and many postgraduate texts assume a prior knowledge of tourism statistics and they are dealt with only in a limited way by most tourism texts; where such issues are raised they are usually discussed in over-technical texts aimed at a limited audience (e.g. Frechtling 1996).

A commonly misunderstood feature which is associated with tourism statistics is that they are a complete and authoritative source of information (i.e. they answer all the questions posed by the researcher) (Lennon 2003). Other associated problems are that statistics are recent and relate to the previous year or season, implying that there is no time lag in their generation, analysis, presentation and dissemination to interested parties. In fact, most tourism statistics are 'typically measurements of arrivals, trips, tourist nights and expenditure, and these often appear in total or split into categories such as business or leisure travel' (Latham 1989: 55–6). Furthermore, the majority of published tourism statistics are derived from sample surveys, with the results being weighted or statistically manipulated to derive a measure which is supposedly representative of the real-world situation. In reality, this often means that tourism statistics are subject to significant errors depending on the size of the sample.

The statistical measurement of tourists is far from straightforward; Latham and Edwards (1989, 2003) identifies a number of distinctive and peculiar problems associated with the tourist population:

- Tourists are a transient and highly mobile population, making statistical sampling procedures difficult when trying to ensure statistical accuracy and rigour in methodological terms.
- Interviewing mobile populations such as tourists is often undertaken in a strange environment, typically at ports or points of departure or arrival where there is background noise which may influence responses.
- Other variables, such as the weather, may affect the responses.

Even where sampling and survey-related problems can be minimised, one has to treat tourism statistics with a degree of caution because of additional methodological issues that can affect the results. For example, tourism research typically comprises:

- pre-travel studies of tourists' intended travel habits and likely choice of destination (intentional studies)
- studies of tourists in transit to provide information on their actual behaviour and plans for the remainder of their holiday or journey (actual and intended studies)
- studies of tourists at the destination or at specific tourist attractions and sites, to provide information on their actual behaviour, levels of satisfaction, impacts and future intentions (actual and intended studies)
- post-travel studies of tourists on their return journey from their destination or on-site experience or once they have returned to their place of residence (post-travel measures).

In an ideal world, where resource constraints are not a limiting factor on the generation of statistics, each of the aforementioned approaches should be used to provide a broad spectrum of research information on tourism and tourist behaviour. In reality, organisations and government agencies select a form of research which meets their own particular needs. In practice, most tourism statistics are generated with practical uses in mind and they may usually, though not exclusively, be categorised as follows:

- measurement of tourist volume, enumerating arrivals, departures and the number of visits and stays
- expenditure-based surveys which quantify the value of tourist spending at the destination and during the journey
- the characteristics and features of tourists to construct a profile of the different markets and segments visiting a destination.

However, before any tourism statistics can be derived, it is important to deal with the complex and thorny issue of defining the population – the tourist. Therefore, how does one define and differentiate between the terms *tourism* and *tourist*?

DEFINING TOURISM

The terms *travel* and *tourism* are often interchanged within the published literature on tourism, though they are normally meant to encompass 'the field of research on human and business activities associated with one or more aspects of the temporary movement of persons away from their immediate home communities and daily work environments for business, pleasure and personal reasons' (R. Chadwick 1994: 65). These two terms tend to be used in differing contexts to mean similar things, although there is a tendency for researchers in the United States to continue to use the term 'travel' when in fact they mean tourism. Despite this inherent problem, which may be little more than an exercise in semantics, it is widely acknowledged that the two terms are used in isolation or in unison to 'describe' three concepts:

- the movement of people
- a sector of the economy or an industry
- a broad system of interacting relationships of people (including their need to travel outside their communities and services that attempt to respond to these needs by supplying products) (Chadwick 1994).

From this initial starting point, one can begin to explore some of the complex issues in arriving at a working definition of the terms *tourism* and *tourist*.

In an historical context, Burkart and Medlik (1981: 41) identify the historical development of the term *tourism*, noting the distinction between the endeavours of researchers to differentiate between the concept and technical definitions of tourism. The concept of tourism refers to the 'broad notional framework, which identifies the essential characteristics, and which distinguishes tourism from the similar, often related, but different phenomena'. In contrast, technical definitions have evolved through time as researchers modify and develop appropriate measures for statistical, legislative and operational reasons implying that there may be various technical definitions to meet particular purposes. However, the concept of tourism, and its identification for research purposes, is an important consideration in this instance for tourism statistics so that users are familiar with the context of their derivation.

While most tourism books, articles and monographs now assume either a standard definition or interpretation of the concept of tourism, which is usually influenced by the social scientists' perspective (i.e. a geographical, economic, political, sociological approach or other disciplines), Burkart and Medlik's (1981) approach to the concept of tourism continues to offer a valid assessment of the situation where five main characteristics are associated with the concept.

- Tourism arises from the movement of people to, and their stay in, various destinations.
- There are two elements in all tourism: the journey to the destination and the stay including activities at the destination.
- The journey and the stay take place outside the normal place of residence and work, so that tourism gives rise to activities which are distinct from those of the resident and working populations of the places, through which tourists travel and in which they stay.
- The movement to tourist destinations is of a temporary, short-term character, with the intention of returning home within a few days, weeks or months.
- Destinations are visited for purposes other than taking up permanent residence or employment remunerated from within the places visited (Burkart and Medlik 1981: 42).

Furthermore, Burkart and Medlik's (1981) definition of tourism as a concept is invaluable because it rightly recognises that much tourism is a leisure activity which involves a discretionary use of time and money, and recreation is often the main purpose for participation in tourism. But this is no

reason for restricting the total concept in this way and the essential characteristics of tourism can best be interpreted to embrace a wider concept. All tourism includes some travel but not all travel is tourism, while the temporary and short-term nature of most tourist trips distinguishes it from migration. Therefore, from the broad interpretation of tourism, it is possible to consider the technical definitions of tourism (also see Leiper (1990) for a further discussion, together with Medlik (1993) and Hall (1995) for a concise set of definitions).

TECHNICAL DEFINITIONS OF TOURISM

Technical definitions of tourism are commonly used by organisations seeking to define the population to be measured, and there are three principal features which normally have to be defined (see BarOn 1984 for a detailed discussion):

- Purpose of travel (e.g. the type of traveller, be it business travel, holidaymakers, visits to friends and relatives or for other reasons).
- The time dimension involved in the tourism visit, which requires a minimum and a maximum period of time spent away from the home area and the time spent at the destination. In most cases, this would involve a minimum stay of more than 24 hours away from home and less than a year as a maximum.
- Those situations where tourists may or may not be included as tourists, such as cruise passengers, those tourists in transit at a particular point of embarkation/departure and excursionists who stay less than 24 hours at a destination (e.g. the European duty-free cross-channel day-trip market).

Among the most recent attempts to recommend appropriate definitions of tourism was the World Tourism Organisation International Conference of Travel and Tourism in Ottawa in 1991, which reviewed, expanded and developed technical definitions, where tourism comprises 'the activities of a person travelling outside his or her usual environment for less than a specified period of time and whose main purpose of travel is other than exercise of an activity remunerated from the place visited', where 'usual environment' is intended to exclude trips within the areas of usual residence and also frequent and regular trips between the domicile and the workplace and other community trips of a routine character, where 'less than a specified period of time' is intended to exclude long-term migration, and 'exercise of an activity remunerated from the place visited' is intended to exclude only migration for temporary work. The following definitions were developed by the WTO:

- International tourism: consists of inbound tourism.
- Visits to a country by non-residents and outbound tourism residents of a country visiting another country.
- Internal tourism: residents of a country visiting their own country.
- Domestic tourism: internal tourism plus inbound tourism (the tourism market of accommodation facilities and attractions within a country).
- National tourism: internal tourism plus outbound tourism (the resident tourism market for travel agents and airlines) (WTO, cited in R. Chadwick 1994: 66).

In order to improve statistical collection and improve understanding of tourism, the United Nations (1994) and the WTO (1991a) also recommended differentiating between visitors, tourists and excursionists (day trippers). The WTO (1991a) recommended that an international tourist be defined as 'a visitor who travels to a country other than that in which he/she has his/her usual residence for at least one night but not more than one year, and whose main purpose of visit is other than the exercise of an activity remunerated from within the country visited' and that an international excursionist (e.g. cruise ship visitors) be defined as 'a visitor residing in a country who travels the same day to a country other than which he/she has his/her

usual environment for less than 24 hours without spending the night in the country visited and whose main purpose of visit is other than the exercise of an activity remunerated from within the country visited'. Similar definitions were also developed for domestic tourists, with domestic tourists having a time limit of 'not more than six months' (WTO 1991a; UN 1994).

Interestingly, the inclusion of a same-day travel, 'excursionist' category in UN/WTO technical definitions of tourism makes the division between recreation and tourism even more arbitrary, and there is increasing international agreement that 'tourism' refers to all activities of visitors, including both overnight and same-day visitors (UN 1994: 5). Given improvements in transport technology, same-day travel is becoming increasingly important to some countries, with the UN (1994: 9) observing that 'day visits are important to consumers and to many providers, especially tourist attractions, transport operators and caterers'.

R. Chadwick (1994) moves the definition of tourists a stage further by offering a typology of travellers (tourists) which highlights the distinction between tourists (travellers) and non-travellers (non-tourists) which is summarised in Figure 2.11. Figure 2.11 is distinctive because it highlights all sections of society which are involved in travel of some kind, but it also looks at the motivation to travel. It is also useful because it illustrates where technical problems may occur in deciding which groups to include in tourism and which to exclude. From this classification of travellers, the distinction between international and domestic tourism needs to be made. Domestic tourism normally refers to tourists who travel from their normal domicile to other areas within a country. In contrast, international tourism normally involves tourists leaving their country of origin to cross into another country which involves documentation, administrative formalities and movement to a foreign environment.

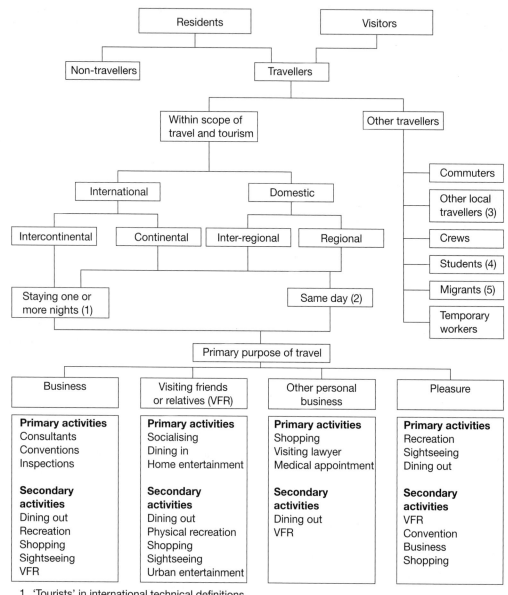

1 'Tourists' in international technical definitions
2 'Excursionists' in international technical definitions
3 Travellers whose trips are shorter than those which qualify for travel and tourism, e.g. under 50 miles (80 km) from home
4 Students travelling between home and school only – other travel of students is within scope of travel and tourism
5 All persons moving to a new place of residence including all one-way travellers such as emigrants, immigrants, refugees, domestic migrants and nomads

Figure 2.11: A classification of travellers
Source: Chadwick (1987)

DOMESTIC TOURISM STATISTICS

D.G. Pearce (1995a) acknowledges that the scale and volume of domestic tourism worldwide exceeds that of international tourism, though it is often viewed as the poorer partner in the compilation of statistics. For example, most domestic tourism statistics tend to underestimate the scale and volume of flows since certain aspects of domestic tourist movements are sometimes ignored in official sources. Latham (1998) estimated that the scale of domestic tourism globally may be ten times the volume of international tourism. But in contrast to international tourism, domestic tourism statistics remain poor in quantity and quality (Latham and Edwards 2003). This is compounded by the fact that domestic tourism has no direct impact on a government's foreign exchange earnings or balance of payments. The 'visits to friends and relatives, the use of forms of accommodation other than hotels (for example, second homes, camp and caravan sites) and travel by large segments of a population from towns to the countryside are not for the most part included' (Latham and Edwards 2003: 64). This is supported by the WTO, which argues that 'there are relatively few countries that collect domestic travel and tourism statistics. Moreover some countries rely exclusively on the traditional hotel sector, thereby leaving out of account the many travellers staying in supplementary accommodation establishments or with friends and relatives' (WTO 1984, cited in Latham 1989: 65). Therefore, the collection of domestic tourism statistics requires the use of different data sources aside from the more traditional sources such as hotel records which identify the origin and duration of a visitor's stay. The development of TSA's has partly overcome the reliance on single data sources, including a wider range of data which is available on domestic tourism.

To assist in the identification of who to include as a domestic tourist, the WTO (1983) suggests the following working definition:

> any person, regardless of nationality, resident in a country and who travels to a place in the same country for not more than one year and whose main purpose of visit is other than following an occupation remunerated from within the place visited.

Such a definition includes domestic tourists where an overnight stay is involved and domestic excursionists who visit an area for less than 24 hours and do not stay overnight. In fact, Latham and Edwards (2003: 65) points to the variety of definitions which exist aside from those formulated by WTO and the following issues complicate matters further:

- *Purpose of visit* all countries using this concept define a domestic tourist as one who travels for a purpose other than to perform a remunerated activity.
- *The length of trip and/or distance travelled* certain definitions state that travellers should, for example, be involved in an overnight stay and/or travel a prescribed minimum distance.
- *Type of accommodation* for practical reasons, some countries restrict the concept of domestic tourism to cover only those persons using commercial accommodation facilities (after Latham and Edwards 2003: 65–6).

Problems in applying WTO definitions may also reflect an individual country's reasons for generating such statistics, which may not necessarily be to contribute to a better understanding of statistics per se. For example, WTO (1981) identified four uses of domestic tourism statistics:

- To calculate the contribution of tourism to the country's economy, whereby estimates of tourism's value to the Gross Domestic Product is estimated due to the complexity of identifying the scope of tourism's contribution.
- To assist in the marketing and promotion of tourism, where government-sponsored tourism organisations seek to encourage its population to take domestic holidays rather than to travel overseas (see Hall 1997a) for a discussion of this activity among Pacific Rim countries).
- To aid the regional development policies of governments which harness tourism as a tool

for area development where domestic tourists in congested environments are encouraged to travel to less developed areas and to improve the quality of tourism in different environments.

- To achieve social objectives, where socially oriented tourism policies may be developed for the underprivileged which requires a detailed understanding of the holiday-taking habits of a country's nationals.

Regional and local tourist organisations also make use of such data to develop and market destinations and different businesses within the tourism sector. But how is domestic tourism measured?

Burkart and Medlik (1981) argue that two principal features need to be measured: first, the volume, value and characteristics of tourism among the population of the country; second, the same data relating to individual destinations within the country. The WTO (1981, cited in Latham 1989) considers the minimum data requirements for the collection of domestic tourism statistics in terms of arrivals and tourist nights in accommodation classified by

- month
- type of grade of accommodation establishment
- location of the accommodation establishment and overall expenditure on domestic tourism.

Latham and Edwards (2003) argue that it is possible to generate additional data from such variables including length of stay, occupancy rate and average expenditure. Many countries also collate supplementary information beyond the minimum standards identified by WTO, where the socio-economic characteristics of tourists are identified, together with their use of tourist transport and purpose of visit, though the cost of such data collection does mean that the statistical basis of domestic tourism in many less developed countries remains poor.

The methods used to generate domestic tourism statistics are normally based on the estimates of volume, value and scale derived from sample surveys due to the cost of undertaking large-scale surveys of tourist activities. The immediate problem facing the user of such material is the type of errors and degree of accuracy which can be attached to such data. For example, Latham (1989) identifies the following sample surveys which are now used to supplement data derived from hotel records:

- *Household surveys*, where the residents of a country are interviewed in their own home to ascertain information of tourist trips for the purpose of pleasure. A useful example of a pan-European study is the EC Omnibus study. Even so, little progress has been made internationally to collate common data on household surveys since the attempt by the Organisation for Economic Cooperation and Development (OECD) in 1967 to outline the types of data which national travel surveys should collect. In Canada, Statistics Canada runs a monthly household survey which has carried questions on tourism for the Canadian Travel Survey (see http://www.statcan.ca). In the USA, the National Travel Survey is one additional example of a household-based survey.
- *Destination surveys*, where high levels of tourist activity occur in a region or resort. Such studies frequently compile statistics on accommodation usage, sample surveys of visitors and may be linked to existing knowledge derived from household surveys.
- *En route surveys*, where tourists are surveyed en route to examine the characteristics and features of tourists. Although it is a convenient way to interview a captive audience depending upon the mode of transport used (see Page 1994a, 1994b), the results may not necessarily be as representative without a complete knowledge of the transport flows for the mode of tourist transport being surveyed.

The problem of incomplete questionnaires or non-response may occur where such surveys require a respondent to post the form back to the surveyor (see Hurst 1987 for a review on the use of this survey type).

INTERNATIONAL TOURISM STATISTICS

The two principal organisations which collate data on international tourism are the World Tourism Organisation and the OECD. In addition, international regional tourism organisations such as the Pacific Asia Travel Association and the ASEAN Tourism Working Group also collect international tourism statistics (Hall 1997a). Page (1994b) reviews the major publications of the first two organisations in relation to international tourism, noting the detailed contents of each. In the case of the WTO, the main source is the *Yearbook of Tourism Statistics*, which contains a summary of the most salient tourism statistics for almost 150 countries and territories. In the case of the OECD, its *Tourism Policy and International Tourism* (referred to as the 'Blue Book') is less comprehensive, covering only 25 countries, but it does contain most of the main generating and receiving areas. While the main thrust of the publication is government policy and the obstacles to international tourism, it does expand on certain areas not covered in the WTO publication (for a more detailed discussion of data sources, see Withyman 1985).

In contrast to domestic tourism, statistics on international tourism are normally collected to assess the impact of tourism on a country's balance of payments, though as Withyman (1985) argued:

> Outward visitors seem to attract less attention from the pollsters and the enumerators. Of course, one country's outward visitor is another country's (perhaps several countries) inward visitor, and a much more welcome sort of visitor, too, being both a source of revenue and an emblem of the destination country's appeal in the international market. This has meant that governments have tended to be generally more keen to measure inward than outward tourism, or at any rate, having done so, to publish the results.
>
> (Withyman 1985: 69)

This statement indicates that governments are more concerned with the direct effect of tourism on their balance of payments. Yet such statistics are also utilised by marketing arms of national tourism organisations to base their decisions on who to target in international campaigns. The wider tourism industry also makes use of such data as part of their strategic planning and for more immediate purposes where niche markets exist. Even so, Shackleford (1980) argued that the collection of tourism statistics should be a responsibility of the state to meet international standards for data collection (WTO 1996). However, it is increasingly the case that only when the economic benefits of data collection can be justified will national governments continue to compile tourism statistics. Where resource constraints exist, the collection and compilation of tourism statistics may be impeded. This also raises important methodological issues related to what exactly is being measured. As Withyman (1985) argued:

> In the jungle of international travel and tourism statistics, it behoves the explorer to step warily; on all sides there is luxuriant growth. Not all data sources are what they appear to be – after close scrutiny some show themselves to be inconsistent and often unsuitable for the industry researcher and planner.
>
> (Withyman 1985: 61)

The key point Withyman (1985) recognises is the lack of comparability in tourism data in relation to what is measured (e.g. is it visitor days or visitor nights?) and the procedures and methodology used to measure international tourism.

Frechtling (1976a) concluded that the approaches taken by national and international agencies associated with international tourism statistics were converging towards common definitions of trip, travel and traveller (see Chadwick 1994 for a fuller discussion). Yet the principal difficulty which continues to be associated with this is whether business travel should be considered as a discrete activity in relation to tourism. Chadwick (1994: 75) notes that 'the consensus of North American opinion seems to be that, despite certain arguments to the contrary . . . business travel should be considered part of travel and tourism'. While BarOn (1984) examines the standard definitions and terminology of international tourism as used by the UN and WTO, research by Ngoh (1985) is useful in that it considers the practical problems posed by such definitions when attempting to measure international tourism and find solutions to the difficulties.

Latham (1989) suggests that the main types of international tourism statistics collated relate to

- volume of tourists
- expenditure by tourists
- the profile of the tourist and their trip characteristics.

As is true of domestic tourism, estimates form the basis for most statistics on international tourism since the method of data collection does not generate exact data. For example, volume statistics are often generated from counts of tourists at entry/exit points (i.e. gateways such as airports and ports) or at accommodation. But such data relate to numbers of trips rather than individual tourists since one tourist may make more than one trip a year and each trip is counted separately. In the case of expenditure statistics, tourist expenditure normally refers to tourist spending within a country and excludes payments to operators of tourist transport. Yet deriving such statistics is often an indirect measure based on foreign currency estimates derived from bank records, from data provided by tourism service providers or more commonly from social surveys undertaken directly with tourists. Research by White and Walker (1982) and Baretje (1982) directly questions the validity and accuracy of such methods of data collection, examining the main causes of bias and error in such studies.

According to Edwards (1991: 68–9), 'expenditure and receipts data apart, tourist statistics are usually collected in one of the five following ways':

- Counts of all individuals entering or leaving the country at all recognised frontier crossings, often using arrival/departure cards where high-volume arrivals/departures are the norm. Where particularly large volumes of tourist traffic exist, a 10 per cent sampling framework is normally used (i.e. every tenth arrival/departure card). Countries such as New Zealand actually match

the arrival/departure cards, or a sample, to examine the length of stay.

- Interviews carried out at frontiers with a sample of arriving and/or departing passengers to obtain a more detailed profile of visitors and their activities within the country. This will often require a careful sample design to gain a sufficiently large enough sample with the detail required from visitors on a wide range of tourism data including places visited, expenditure, accommodation usage and related items.
- Selecting a sample of arrivals and providing them with a self-completion questionnaire to be handed in or posted. This method is used in Canada but it fails to incorporate those visitors travelling via the United States by road.
- Sample surveys of the entire population of a country including travellers and non-travellers, though the cost of obtaining a representative sample is often prohibitive.
- Accommodation arrivals and nights spent are recorded by hoteliers and owners of the accommodation types covered. The difficulty with this type of data collection is that accommodation owners have no incentive to record accurate details, particularly where the tax regime is based on the turnover of bed-nights (see Page 1989 for a discussion of this problem in the context of London).

The final area of data collection is profile statistics, which examine the characteristics and travel habits of visitors. For example, the UK's International Passenger Survey (IPS) is one survey that incorporates volume, expenditure and profile data on international tourism.

METHODOLOGICAL ISSUES

Latham and Edwards (2003) review the major types of data collection used for tourism statistics. They report that among state-sponsored tourism research in the United States, conversion studies are a popular method to examine and evaluate advertising campaigns and visitor surveys, to assess a sample of visitors to individual states. The use of other methods of data collection are also discussed (e.g. diary questionnaires, participant observation and personal interviews – see Mullins and Heywood 1984; Perdue 1985). Yet few studies consider the issue of sampling, sample design and the sources of error which may arise from such surveys (Aaker and Day 1986; Cannon 1987). In fact the lack of research on the reliability of the estimate from a sample survey (the standard error) is rarely discussed in most tourism surveys (for a more technical discussion of this point, see Latham and Edwards 2003: 70–1)). In many cases, large tourism surveys focus on the logistics of drawing the sample and the bias which may be reflected in the results. Therefore, any tourism survey will need to pay careful attention to the statistical and mathematical accuracy of the survey, especially the survey design and the effect it may have on the results, a feature which is discussed in great detail by Ryan (1995).

Ryan (1995) provides an excellent review of survey design, questionnaire design, sampling and also an insight into the statistical techniques to use for different forms of tourism data. As a result it serves as an important reference point for issues of methodology and the technical issues associated with the statistical analysis of tourism data. Without reiterating the excellent features of Ryan's findings, it is appropriate to consider some of the main accuracy problems associated with the collection of domestic and international tourism statistics.

Ryan (1995) argues that errors in data collection can lead to errors in data analysis. Among the most frequently cited problems associated with domestic and international tourism statistics are

- the methods by which the data are collected, which are influenced by administrative, bureaucratic and legislative factors in each country
- sample sizes which are too small and lead to unacceptable sampling errors and in some instances where the sample design is flawed
- the procedures for collecting tourism statistics are not adhered to by the agency collecting the data.

In addition, Edwards (1991: 68) argues that a 'fourth potential reason – arithmetic mistakes and data processing errors – only occasionally produce significant errors'. In fact, Edwards (1991: 68) supports the cause of 'tourist statisticians [who] are both knowledgeable and conscientious, but are having to work with tools which they know could produce inaccurate or misleading data', concluding that for any set of tourist data, potential sources of error obviously depend on the method of collection employed. This, in turn, tends to be largely determined by the legislative and administrative framework and by the financial and manpower resources available.

In the case of tourist expenditure and receipts data, organisations such as the International Monetary Fund (IMF) issue guidelines for the compilation of balance of payments statistics. But errors may occur where leakage results from tourist services paid for in overseas bank accounts and in extreme cases, where a black market exists in currency exchange. Edwards (1991) suggests that a regular programme of interviews with departing tourists and returning residents may assist in estimating levels of expenditure.

Despite the apparent problems which may exist with tourism statistics, Edwards (1991) argues that data on arrivals and nights spent for most destinations outside of Europe appear reasonably reliable.

Within Europe, data for both inbound and outbound travel are fairly satisfactory for the UK. Greece, Portugal, Spain and [the former] Yugoslavia all appear to have usable frontier arrivals data. The most serious problems are in core continental European countries such as France, Germany, Italy and the Netherlands for which there are no adequate volumetric measures of travel in either direction.
Accommodation arrivals and nights data are clearly gross understatements for many European countries . . . often expenditure and receipts data appear better indicators. Outside Europe, the major problems are also in relation to high volume land flows, as between Canada and the USA (in both directions), from the USA to Mexico and from Hong Kong to China.
(Edwards 1991: 72)

Therefore, in view of these potential constraints, Edwards (1991) advocates that researchers should compile a range of data from different sources which will not only highlight the deficiencies in various sources, but also extend the existing baseline data. Although Edwards (1991) provides guidelines for comparative tourism research using a range of data for different countries (see also Dann 1993 for the limitations of using different tourism indicators such as nationality), trends in tourism data remain one of the main requirements for travel industry organisations. Edwards (1991: 73) lists some key issues to consider in examining tourism trends:

- Have arrivals or accommodation data been changed in coverage or definition?
- Have provisional data for earlier years been subsequently revised?
- Has the reliability of the data changed and how are changing tastes in travel products affecting the statistics?

Even so, the analysis of trends remains the fundamental starting point for most research studies in tourism. Having considered the issues associated with how tourism statistics are generated, attention now turns to the ways in which geographers analyse such statistics, and variations in tourism activity at different scales.

PATTERNS OF TOURISM: INTERNATIONAL PERSPECTIVES

D.G. Pearce's (1995a) seminal study on the geographer's analysis of tourism patterns offers an excellent synthesis reflecting his international contribution to the methodological development of spatial analysis of tourism. By using geographical methodologies and concepts, Pearce (1995a) uses statistical sources and primary data on tourist activity patterns to analyse the processes and patterns associated with the dynamics of domestic and international tourist activity. This section can provide only a limited evaluation of the geographer's approach to analysis of the presentation of spatially oriented insights on modern-day tourism

demand (for more detail consult D.G. Pearce 1995a).

PATTERNS OF GLOBAL TOURISM

The WTO provides the main source of data for international tourism, collated from a survey of major government agencies responsible for data collection. While most international tourists are expressed as 'frontier arrivals' (i.e. arrivals determined by means of a frontier check), arrival/departure cards (where used) offer additional detail to the profile of international tourists, and where they are not used periodic tourism surveys are often employed. WTO statistics are mainly confined to all categories of travellers, and in some cases geographical disaggregation of the data may be limited by the collecting agency's use of descriptions and categories for aid of simplicity (e.g. rest of the world) rather than listing all categories of arrivals.

In terms of the growth of international travel, Figure 2.12 documents the expansion of outbound travel with constant growth in the 1960s in an age of discovery of outbound travel for many developed nations. The late 1960s saw international travel expanded by new technology in air travel (e.g. the introduction of the Boeing 747 jumbo jet and the 737 as well as the DC10) which led to rapid growth until the oil crisis in the early 1970s. Growth rates varied in the 1980s, with 'shock waves' to the upward trend being caused by events such as the Gulf Crisis, but international travel has maintained strong growth rates, often in excess of 5 per cent per annum until the late 1990s, where the growth rates have slowed down considerably. However, as Figure 2.13 shows, the growth in international receipts from travel outperformed arrivals up until the late 1990s, with consistent rates of growth (with the exception of the oil crisis and Gulf Crisis) of 10 to 20 per cent which is indicative of the powerful economic effect of tourism for countries. Since 2000, the rate of growth slowed, especially with 9/11 and the terrorist threats that explains the –2.9 per cent drop on 2000 expenditure, which rose by 3.2 per cent in 2002 as confidence spending on

International arrivals

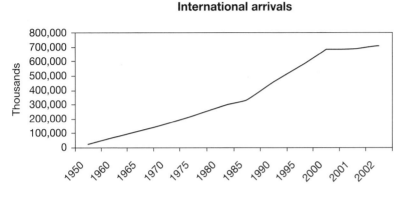

Figure 2.12: Growth of international arrivals, 1950–2002
Source: based on WTO data

Receipts from international tourism

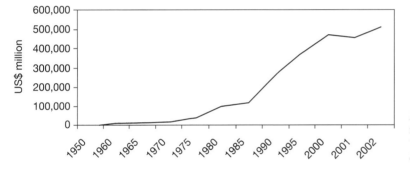

Figure 2.13: Growth of international visitor expenditure, 1950–2002
Source: based on WTO data

international travel increased. Table 2.4 outlines the top tourism destinations for 1980 and 1990, where the ranking of France has remained prominent throughout the 22-year period, with certain developing nations such as China recording major growth and, with the exception of the USA and China, Europe still dominates the pattern of arrivals by country with comparatively little change in the ranking of the first seven destinations. However, China is the notable success story in terms of growth in inbound arrivals and was ranked fifth in terms of receipts from international arrivals in 2002. As the world's largest tourism markets by expenditure, the USA and Spain have retained their prominence in the top two rankings, followed by France, Italy, China, Germany, the UK, Austria,

Hong Kong and Greece as world earners of tourism receipts in 2002.

Future trends in the geography of international tourism to 2020

The WTO also produces future growth scenarios for world tourism, based on existing patterns and past trends in growth, to extrapolate to the future using forecasting methods which economists use from the area known as econometrics (see Frechtling 1996 for more detail). These are interesting to the geographer as they make assumptions and predict where tourist growth is likely to occur in time and space. The WTO reported these findings in its *Tourism 2020* report, which is a long-term

Table 2.4: The world's leading international tourism destinations (by country): 1980 and 2002 compared

Country	Number of arrivals	Rank 2002	Rank 1980
France	77,000,000	1	1
Spain	51,000,000	2	2
USA	41,900,000	3	3
Italy	39,800,000	4	4
China	36,800,000	5	19
UK	24,200,000	6	7
Canada	20,100,000	7	6
Mexico	19,700,000	8	8
Austria	18,600,000	9	5
Germany	18,000,000	10	9

Source: modified and developed from WTO data for 1980 and 2002

forecast assessment using 1995 as the base year and making forecasts for 2010 and 2020. As the period of growth examined is up to 25 years in length, short-term fluctuations such as rapid growth are often followed by short-term downturns and slower growth rates in arrivals, which has tended to compensate and smooth out growth rates over the forecasting periods in the past. As a result, WTO suggests that globally, international tourism will grow from 565 million arrivals in 1995 to 1 billion in 2010 to 1.5 billion in 2020. These growth rates will have spatially distinct implications for where the growth is expected to occur. WTO expects that in 2020 the top three receiving regions will be Europe (717 million arrivals), East Asia Pacific (EAP) (397 million) and the Americas (282 million). This implies that EAP will experience the highest rates of growth in line with previous studies (Hall and Page 2000; Page 2001), achieving rates of 5 per cent growth per annum, in excess of the world average growth rate of 4.1 per cent. It is also expected that Europe's share of international arrivals will drop from 60 per cent in 1995 to 46 per cent in 2020, as world tourism is reconfigured geographically to accommodate new trends in demand for EAP. At the same time, long-haul travel will be expected to grow at 5.4 per cent 1995–2020, while intra-regional travel will only grow at 3.8 per cent per annum.

PATTERNS OF DOMESTIC TOURISM

The growing interest in Tourism Satellite Accounts has seen a growing research focus on domestic tourism in many countries, to try to fill in the missing gaps in research knowledge that prevail in this area of tourism research. What might have been a fair assessment of the situation in the early 1990s by D.G. Pearce (1995a: 67) that 'domestic tourism, which is often more informal and less structured than international tourism, and a consequent tendency by many government agencies, researchers and others to regard it as less significant' has been re-examined in many countries, as slow growth rates in international tourism and crises in arrivals after disasters such as 9/11 led to a major refocusing of attention on domestic travel in the USA and Europe, for example. Certainly government agencies began to realise the significance of domestic tourism. Nevertheless, a paucity of data in some countries is problematic, since it is not a straightforward matter of recording arrivals and departures. It requires an analysis of tourism patterns and flows at different spatial scales to consider spatial interaction of tourists between a multitude of possible origin and destination areas within a country as well as a detailed understanding of inter-regional flows. In some cases, these flows can be identified from well-known tourist circuits, such as the UK's milk run of coach tourism circuits between the popular key destinations (D.G. Pearce 1995a) and more recent analysis of VisitScotland data at a regional level by Page (2003a) to assess the regional distribution of coach tourist visits in Scotland. At the micro level, studies of specific areas such as small islands may yield contained environments where spatial analysis is much easier and the effects of tourist activity can be monitored. For example, in 2003, the former First World War battle site of Ieper in Belgium (Ypres in French) attracted around 350,000 visitors a year, 50 per cent of whom were British and 50 per cent of these were children studying the history of the First World War. At least 20 per cent of the British visitors had a family link to the war and it has generated a tourism boom at the local level among businesses.

At a methodological level, it is evident that where government agencies and other public sector organisations undertake data collection of domestic tourism, 'the results are not often directly comparable, limiting the identification of general patterns and trends' (D.G. Pearce 1995a: 67). For this reason, the innovative research undertaken by D.G. Pearce (1993b) is worthy of attention here since it comprises one of the few systematic analysis of domestic tourism in a country, which in this case is New Zealand. As Pearce (1995a) rightly acknowledges,

> there are still few examples of comprehensive inter-regional studies where the analysis is based on a complete matrix of both original and destination regions . . . [since] few appropriate and reliable sets of tourism statistics exist which might be used to construct such a matrix.
>
> (D.G. Pearce 1995a: 67)

Nationwide surveys are undertaken which are weighted to reflect the population base. One of the few comprehensive studies which yielded an origin–destination matrix is the somewhat dated New Zealand Domestic Travel Survey (NZDTS), established in 1983 (New Zealand Tourism Board 1991a) and later updated.

NEW ZEALAND DOMESTIC TOURISM SURVEY

Domestic tourism data are harder to collect than those for international visitors, simply because no frontiers are crossed or formal registers required. Domestic travel estimates can thus be made only by factoring up from representative surveys of the population. As with all surveys, sample size and representativeness are critical, so that a manageable (and affordable) sample size of a thousand or so will give reasonably accurate figures for national trends but is useless at a regional level.

Scale and significance of New Zealand domestic travel

The domestic travel surveys of the 1980s carried out by the New Zealand Travel and Publicity Department (NZTP) were based on a sample of 12,000 interviews. This gave confidence limits of ± 0.9 per cent at the 95 per cent level and so were extremely reliable for national estimates. Even so, the authors of the research noted that potential error limits increase very quickly as sample sizes reduce and particular care should be taken in interpreting results for small subgroups of the sample. They went on to remind us that when a large proportion is being sampled and the sample result is projected, the sampling error is magnified also, and that a sampling error may run into very large numbers when expressed as a projection, even though, expressed as a percentage, it may appear to be quite small (NZTP 1987). The implication of this is that even regional statistics derived from a national survey may be quite inaccurate (Hall and Kearsley 2001).

In 1999, New Zealanders are estimated to have made 16.6 million trips with at least one night away, comprising a total of 52.9 million nights; they spent NZ$4.1 billion on overnight trips. In addition, they made 44.3 million day trips of more than 40 km each way and spent a further NZ$2.8 billion on them (Forsyte Research 2000). As well as easily equalling the expenditure of international tourists, albeit in local currency, domestic travellers provide the essential base for most tourism infrastructure. These domestic tourism figures were derived from a major 1999 study carried out by Forsyte Research on contract to the former Public Good Science Fund. The primary focus of the research was to determine the direct economic impact of domestic tourism in New Zealand. A secondary objective was to measure domestic travel patterns for both overnight and day trips for 1999, to a level that allowed regional analysis. This was the first study of its scale since the last of the domestic travel survey series, noted above, carried out by AGB McNair in 1989–90 and the first to measure day trips in addition to overnight trips. Prior to this, the only research was a pilot survey carried out by D.G. Simmons (1997). The Forsyte sample was substantial, at 17,037 interviews, and provides high-grade data.

Patterns and spatial economic effects of domestic travel in New Zealand

In all, almost 70 per cent of domestic travel in New Zealand was to the North Island, or within it. Canterbury, and then Otago, were the major destinations in the South Island. Regional flows, in net person nights, show a more interesting picture. The North Island is a net exporter of some 2.5 million person nights to the South. Within the North Island, Auckland and Wellington are the main deficit regions, exporting a total of almost 9 million person nights. The major beneficiaries are Northland, Waikato and the Bay of Plenty. In the South Island, the main beneficiaries are Otago and Nelson, followed by Marlborough and the West Coast. Canterbury is the only deficit region (Figure 2.14).

About half of all travel (46 per cent) is for holidays and leisure, with an average duration of 3.8 nights, and one-third (35 per cent and 2.9 nights) for visiting friends and relatives; a further 12 per cent is business travel, with an average stay of 2.5 nights. Of course, the economic impacts will not fall in direct proportion to the type of travel. Accommodation used is, overwhelmingly, the private home of a friend or relative or a borrowed second home. Motels are the commonest form of commercial accommodation with a total of 14 per cent; hotels attract only 7 per cent, many of whom would be business travellers (Forsyte Research 2000; Hall and Kearsley 2001).

Overall patterns of expenditure are split between the two islands broadly proportionately to visitor numbers, but the average amount spent per night varies considerably by region, with Wellington and Auckland the highest and Northland, Gisborne and Marlborough the lowest. As a result, Auckland has the largest total receipts at over NZ$700 million, followed by Waikato, Wellington and Canterbury. In total, the North Island receives almost NZ$2.8 billion and the South NZ$1.29 billion. Even the least earning region, Gisborne, receives nearly NZ$47 million, although in Gisborne's case there is a small net outflow. In terms of regional flows of income, the North Island is an exporter of money, to the value of NZ$212 million, to the South. Auckland shows the largest net deficit by far (–NZ$453 million). In the South Island, every region is a net beneficiary, so that domestic tourism is a major economic sector and a powerful agent of income redistribution on a regional basis. In aggregate, one-quarter of all expenditure is on accommodation and just over one-quarter is on food. Shopping of all types consumes one-fifth of expenditure, while transport, recreation and alcohol account for about one-tenth each. Business travel is getting on for three times the cost of other trips per night, and is heavily weighted towards travel and accommodation costs when compared with other sectors, both proportionately and in real terms. VFR travel is slightly more demanding of travel expenditure than are holidays, but accommodation costs, not surprisingly, are considerably less (Forsyte Research 2000; Hall and Kearsley 2001).

CONCLUSIONS

The analysis of behavioural issues in recreational and tourism research indicates that 'in behavioural terms then, there seems little necessity to insist on a major distinction between tourism and leisure

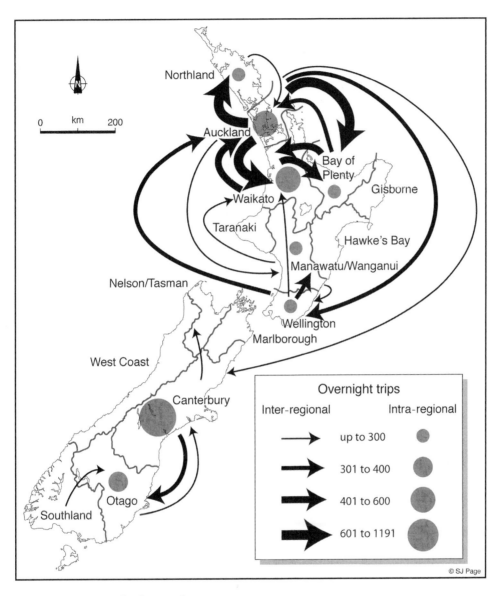

Figure 2.14: New Zealand tourist flow

phenomena. Therefore, it should follow that a greater commonality between the research efforts in the two areas would be of advantage' (Moore et al. 1995: 75) although different social theoretical approaches exist towards the analysis of recreation and tourism phenomena. As a result, Moore et al. (1995: 79) conclude that 'there is little need, if any, to take a dramatically different approach to the

behavioural analysis of tourism and leisure'. One needs to view each activity in the context of the everyday life of the people involved to understand how each is conceived. There is a clear distinction within the literature between what motivates recreationalists and tourists, and comparative studies of similar groups of people and the similarities and differences between these motivations has yet to permeate the research literature. While geographers have focused on recreational and tourist behaviour in relation to demand issues, the analysis has largely been quantitative, site specific, and has not adapted a comparative methodology to examine the recreation–tourism continuum. One notable study by Connell (2005) questions the tendency to overlook the historical context of much tourism and leisure research, which is particularly pertinent to the spatial analysis of tourism and leisure phenomena. As Page (2003a) argued, the patterns of continuity and change in the analysis of tourism and leisure geographies provide a containing context for research, since cultural, social and spatial interactions shape and form the landscapes and forms of leisure and tourism experience through time that are constantly evolving. This historical imperative is essential, as many of the chapters in this book demonstrate, to understand tourism and leisure beyond the research context as a snapshot in time. This is now where more evident than in the analysis of supply issues, which demonstrate their durability to adapt and evolve through time as the demand and markets for their products and services changes.

QUESTIONS

- What is recreational demand and how have geographers attempted to measure it?
- How far does the use of recreational resources conform with models of leisure and recreational demand?
- What is the role of tourism demand in the analysis of tourism patterns in time and space?
- 'The use of psychological constructs and models of tourist behaviour does not explain why people go on holiday to specific locations.' Discuss.

READING

For recreational demand the following studies are very useful introductions:

Pigram, J.J. and Jenkins, J. (1999) *Outdoor Recreation Management*, London: Routledge (by far the best book on recreational research published to date by geographers).

In terms of factors constraining demand see

Crawford, D., Jackson, E. and Godbey, G. (1991) 'A hierarchical model of leisure constraints', *Leisure Sciences*, 13: 309–20.

A good example of the constraints on demand can be found in

Madge, C. (1997) 'Public parks and the geography of fear', *Tijdschrift Voor Economische en Sociale Geografie*, 88: 237–50.

At a general level, the best overviews of studies of tourism demand are:

Crouch, G. (1994) 'The study of tourism demand: A review of findings', *Journal of Travel Research*, 33(1): 2–21.
Shaw, G., Agarwal, S. and Bull, P. (2000) 'Tourism consumption and tourist behaviour: A British perspective', *Tourism Geographies*, 2(3): 264–89.
TNS (2004) Leisure Day Visits 2004, TNS: Edinburgh.
Uysal, M. (1998) 'The determinants of tourism demand: A theoretical perspective', in D. Ioannides and K. Debbage (eds) *The Economic Geography of the Tourist Industry: A Supply-side Analysis*, London: Routledge, pp. 79–95.

For tourism demand the following is a useful introduction to the growth of demand in one country:

Barke, M., Towner, J. and Newton, M. (eds) (1996) *Tourism in Spain: Critical Issues*, Wallingford: CAB International.

This should be read in conjunction with

Shaw, G. and Williams, A. (eds) (1997) *The Rise and Fall of British Coastal Resorts: Cultural and Economic Perspectives*, London: Mansell.

A useful collection of readings with respect to tourism statistics is

Lennon, J. (ed.) (2003) *Tourism Statistics: International Perspectives and Current Issues*, London: Continuum.

and the chapter by:

Latham, J. and Edwards, C. (2003) 'The statistical measurement of tourism' in C. Cooper (ed.) *Classic Reviews in Tourism*, Clevedon: Channel View, 55–76.

3

THE SUPPLY OF RECREATION AND TOURISM

Within the literature on recreation and tourism, there is a paucity of conceptual and theoretical research on the supply component of these activities (Sinclair and Stabler 1992). The geographer has traditionally approached the supply of recreation and tourism from a somewhat traditional spatial analysis perspective reflecting the tendency to apply concepts and models from economic geography and, to a lesser degree, from cognate areas of geography where the underlying concern has been with location and the spatial distribution of recreational and tourism resources which shape the activity patterns and spectrum of opportunity for leisure pursuits. However, since the mid-1990s with the advent of more qualitative research, some geographical research on supply issues has also begun to challenge the positivist approach to spatial analysis with reference to leisure supply (e.g. Aitchison 1999). This has resulted in more sophisticated cultural geographies of leisure (as discussed more fully in Chapter 2) that highlight the importance of more theoretically derived explanations of key geographical questions on leisure and tourism provision (i.e. supply). In particular, such research questions the notion of who gets what, where with more emphasis on why? The result is that the geographer needs to consider more challenging perspectives related to the way in which leisure (and tourism) supply is produced by the state and private sector at different scales. This chapter will review some of these new debates together with the evolution of the geographer's contribution to the analysis of supply issues.

THE SUPPLY FACTOR IN RECREATION

According to Kreutzwiser (1989: 21), 'supply refers to the recreational resources, both natural and man-made, which provide opportunities for recreation. It is a complex concept influenced by numerous factors and subject to changing interpretations'. As Pigram and Jenkins (1999) recognised:

> In a perfect world, demand for outdoor recreation activities would be matched by an ample supply of attractive and accessible recreation resources. . . . In reality, interaction between demand and supply factors is qualified by spatial, social/institutional/political, psychological, economic and personal impediments.
> (Pigram and Jenkins 1999: 57)

Recreational supply is also a concept which has prompted much thought in terms of classification and evaluation, particularly among geographers. Yet Coppock and Duffield (1975: 151) pursue this theme a stage further in a spatial context, claiming that it is the 'spatial interaction between the homes of recreationalists and the resources they use [which] has emerged as a key factor in the demand/supply model' and, arguing for an integrated analysis of such interactions to explain how the activity patterns of recreationalists in terms of their origins and destinations affect the supply variable in terms of where they go, what they do there and how this affects the resource base. For this reason, this section commences with a discussion of the underlying approach used to describe and document the supply of recreational opportunities by geographers, which is followed by an analysis of the spatial interaction of demand and supply to illustrate how the two components are interrelated. This is developed in relation to the three characteristics that geographers have synthesised to analyse recreational activities, namely:

- the locational characteristics associated with the supply of different forms of recreational resource
- the patterns of demand and usage
- the spatial interactions which occur between the demand for and supply of the recreational resource, emphasising journey patterns and the patterns of usage of specific resources.

This gives rise to concentrated, dispersed and combinations of each pattern at the site of the resources, which therefore raises questions as to how to evaluate the capacity of such resources to accommodate users and to reconcile conflicts in use and the identification of management and planning issues.

For the cultural geographer with an interest in leisure, the interest is less about the resulting spatial patterns of supply, but how the cultural dimension conditions, affects and impacts upon the spatial interactions between supply and demand.

HOW HAS THE GEOGRAPHER APPROACHED THE ANALYSIS OF RECREATIONAL SUPPLY ISSUES?

The geographer's approach is epitomised in many of the classic recreational texts (e.g. Patmore 1970; Lavery 1971c; I.G. Simmons 1974; Pigram 1983) where the supply perspective is largely dependent upon the evaluation and assessment of resources for recreation. The concept of a resource may often be taken to include those tangible objects in nature which are of economic value and used for productive purposes. But when looking at leisure and recreation natural resources have an important bearing, particularly those such as water bodies, countryside and open space. The fact that resources have a physical form (i.e. coal and iron ore) does not actually mean they constitute a resource. Such elements become a resource only when society's subjective evaluation of their potential leads to their recognition as a resource to satisfy human wants and needs (O'Riordan 1971).

Yet a resource is far from just a passive element – it has to be used creatively to meet certain socially valued goals. Thus recreational resources are 'an element of the natural or man-modified environment which provides an opportunity to satisfy recreational wants. Implicit is a continuum ranging from biophysical resources to man-made facilities'

Plate 3.1: San Francisco, California. Unlikely locations can be developed as tourism and recreational resources. This queue is for a visit to Alcatraz Prison.

Plate 3.2: Alcatraz Prison, San Francisco.

(Kreutzwiser 1989: 22). However, according to Glyptis (1989a: 135), to 'couple recreational with resources complicates definitions. . . . In a recreational context resources are the natural resources of land, water and landscape, together with man-made resources including sport centres, swimming pools, parks and playing fields', though she also notes that few recreational activities make use of resources solely designed or in existence for recreational purposes.

As Pigram and Jenkins (1999: 59) argued, 'identification and valuation of elements of the environment as recreation resources will depend upon a number of factors (e.g. economics, social attitudes and perceptions, political perspectives and technology'. As a result, Pigram and Jenkins (1999: 59) recognised that outdoor recreational resources may encompass a wide range of settings associated with space, topography and climatic characteristics. This expands upon Hart's (1966) early notion of the 'recreation resource base', which were the natural values of the countryside or respective landscape. Such a notion was clarified in specific terms by Clawson and Knetsch (1966) thus:

> There is nothing in the physical landscape or features of any particular piece of land or body of water that makes it a recreation resource; it is the combination of the natural qualities and the ability and desire of man to use them that makes a resource out of what might otherwise be a more or less meaningless combination of rocks, soil and trees.
> (Clawson and Knetsch 1966: 7)

However, such resources are not static, since new trends or cultural appraisals can lead to new notions of the environment as a recreational resource.

Recreation in rural contexts (Chapter 6) often occurs alongside agriculture, forestry and water supply functions (Goodall and Whittow 1975). In this respect, the identification of recreational resources needs to recognise the management implications of multiple use, a feature discussed below. While Glyptis (1989a) also outlined the demands of many forms of recreation which have few land needs, this analysis is concerned with recreational forms that have a land use component given the geographers' interest in how human activities

and phenomena are interrelated and occur on the earth's surface. Yet even Glyptis' (1989a) review pays little explicit attention to the resource base – the supply dimension – beyond highlighting Patmore's (1983)

> perspective [which] is specifically geographical, but with full recognition of the interplay of social, economic and political factors, and with a wealth of data. . . . The bulk of the text concerns [sic] contemporary patterns of recreational activity and the demands they place on the land and water resources, with myriad references to management issues and solutions.
> (Glyptis 1989a: 137)

But this still does not illuminate the approaches, concepts and specific skills the geographer brings to the analysis of recreational supply issues.

The wanton absence of such studies within the published literature and the tendency for writers to step sideways and develop simplistic descriptions of recreational resources confirms two of the weaknesses which S.L.J. Smith (1983a: 184) argued confronted the study of recreation: 'recreational geography is still at the stage of naive phenomenology and induction in the 1980s.' What this statement means is that as researchers discover more recreational phenomena, they classify it and develop specialist areas of study, where external pressures (e.g. government and business funding of research) combine to generate a situation of naive induction. Naive induction is where the use of relatively unsophisticated concepts are used to study the subject, even though complex analytical techniques may be employed (e.g. multiple regression and factor analysis) to understand recreational phenomena. This is particularly the case in terms of the supply function of recreation. A lack of theoretically derived research has meant that the geographer has failed to develop this area beyond the use of simple spatial analytical tools. Thus the underlying theoretical framework remains inadequate despite the limited degree of theoretically informed research (e.g. Perkins 1993), and novel attempts to integrate the leisure and tourism functions within an urban context using constructs related to power and political decision-making (Doorne 1998). The assessment by S.L.J. Smith

(1983a) remains an important debating point in recreational geography, particularly in relation to supply issues. For this reason, Smith's (1983a) synthesis of the field remains one of the only comprehensive surveys of the research geographers have undertaken on recreation. For this reason, it is worthy of discussion, not necessarily because it is the most up-to-date study of recreational geography but because it illustrates the variety of approaches geographers have developed. S.L.J. Smith (1989: 304) listed the principal research questions geographers pose which outline the particular concerns for supply issues:

- Where are the resources? What is their quality and capacity? What effect will use of those resources have on the resource base and the local environment? What will the effect be on other people who live in the area and on other users?
- How easy is it for people to travel to the resource or facility? What are their travel costs? Are there other constraints, such as problems of physical accessibility, inconvenient scheduling, excessive admission fees, and racial, linguistic and social barriers?
- What new facilities or resources need to be supplied? What areas have priority for the new supply? Who should pay to support those who play? How many people are expected to use a new facility at a given location?
- What are the regional differences in recreation preferences? Why do these exist? Do they represent differences in tastes, culture or historical inequalities?

An interesting illustration of these issues can be seen in the following Insight on Walsall Metropolitan Borough Council's leisure provision based on a 2003 report by the UK Audit Commission on service provision. It also highlights how many spatial issues are intertwined with and embedded in wider socio-economic issues of locality, provision and how scare resources are allocated on a fair and meaningful basis.

INSIGHT: Local authority expenditure on leisure and recreation provision – Walsall Metropolitan Borough Council

In the UK, the government body which audits public sector expenditure, the Audit Commission (http://www.audit-commission.gov.uk), reviews the performance of local authority expenditure in relation to provision as part of the Local Government Act 1999. It produces 'Inspection Reports' which illustrate the scope and extent of a local authority's leisure provision in specific areas. In October 2003 it produced a report on Walsall, a metropolitan borough in the West Midlands, England, with a population of 253,500. Some 13.6 per cent of the population comprises ethnic minorities and its former industrial base and restructuring of the local economy has generated an unemployment rate of 4.9 per cent in March 2003, almost double the national average. About 45 per cent of the population live within the top 10 per cent most deprived wards in England, with Walsall ranked twentieth. The expenditure on leisure services for 2003–4 was £7.03 million, of which almost 50 per cent was on capital intensive leisure centres and almost another £3 million on parks (see Figure 3.1). This illustrates the scope of local authority provision, which has both an indoor and outdoor open spaces range of resources. What is also apparent from Figure 3.1 is the growing interest in programmes to engage the local population in active involvement in sport and recreation as part of the drive to increase the health and well-being of local residents. For example, the council's Active Communities Project in a high unemployment area sought to reduce the percentage of people who are not physically active from 40 per cent to 25 per cent by 2011 along with other specific projects. Many of the local authority's objectives are set out in Council Plans (e.g. improving health and well-being) as well as sector-specific strategies (e.g. the 2003–4 Service Plan for Leisure and Community Services and the Sport and Active Recreation Strategy and Playing Pitches Strategy). Despite such documents, the Audit Commission (2003: 9) report found that 'The current lack of clarity on the strategic direction for leisure in Walsall and for the Council's sport and leisure service within overall provision in the borough means that the Council cannot clearly direct resources on the basis of local need or priorities'. The council's response was to review provision to develop a borough wide framework to link leisure provision to local needs. The Audit Commission also reviews specific aspects of provision (e.g. quality of experience, reaching people, performance compared to other councils and measures to improve performance). As part of the Audit Commission (2003) recommendations, it summarises areas for action, including clear strategic objectives to balance local, regional and national needs, driving decisions on investment planning and design/delivery of services and testing value for money in delivery.

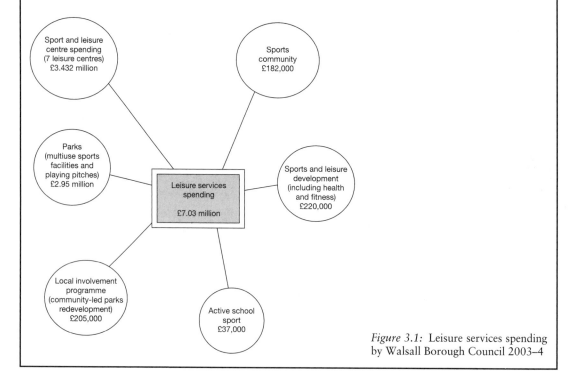

Figure 3.1: Leisure services spending by Walsall Borough Council 2003–4

According to S.L.J. Smith (1983a), geographers have approached the analysis of recreational geography in a number of ways, including

- descriptive research on location
- descriptive research on travel
- explanatory research on location
- explanatory research on travel
- predictive research on location
- predictive research on travel
- normative research on location
- normative research on travel.

For this reason, each of the types of research are briefly discussed to emphasise the geographer's contribution to supply research where relevant. Due to the constraints of space, the principal themes discussed here are descriptive research on location and travel, explanatory research on location and travel, and predictive and normative research on location. More detail on other aspects of the research developed in this context can be found in Smith (1983a).

DESCRIPTIVE RESEARCH ON LOCATION AND TRAVEL

S.L.J. Smith (1983a: 1) argued that the 'description of location is the study of differences' which can be classified in terms of description of facility of recreational resource location, where the distribution of resources pertinent to the specific activity may be enumerated and mapped. Within this context the inventories of recreational resources has attracted a great deal of attention, which arguably underpins much of the preliminary research undertaken to establish recreational supply features in quantity and quality. Resource inventories, such as the Outdoor Recreation Resources Review Commission (Chubb and Chubb 1981; see also Chapter 7), typify this approach, whereby the quantity and number of designated public recreation areas were tabulated and mapped by area along US coastlines. A more complex method is to develop a typology of resource types and uses such as Clawson and Knetsch's (1968) widely cited model of recreational resources which can be classified as urban and rural resource-based, intermediate and user-oriented. Additional variables which might be added to such classifications include human-modified and natural resources; formal and informal; intensive and extensive; fragile and resistant; while public and private ownership may also be included (Wall 1989). The Canada Land Inventory (Department of Regional Economic Expansion 1972) is a useful example of one such inventory that set out to provide an overview of 'the quality, quantity, and distribution of natural recreation resources within the settled points of Canada; to indicate comparative levels of recreation capability for non-urban lands based upon present

preferences; to indicate the types of recreation and land use'. The classification is illustrated in Table 3.1. While there are criticisms of this approach related to the consistency of data collection and interpretation, it provides a valuable synthesis on the potential of Canadian land resources to support recreational activity. S.L.J. Smith (1983a) also explores more advanced methods used to classify recreational resources, including deglomerative methods (where resources are subdivided into distinct groups) and agglomerative methods (where resource types are grouped into general categories). An interesting example of a deglomerative study is Filoppovich's (1979) assessment of recreational development around Moscow. In contrast, Dubaniewicz's (1976) examination of the Lodz Voivodiship in Poland explored aggregate patterns of recreational development, having located, mapped and defined biotic and abiotic resources and human resource patterns at a regional level. Deglomerative studies remain more widely used than the latter. Yet such methods of analyses pay less attention to the importance of human (i.e. subjective) evaluations of resources for recreation (e.g. Coppock and Duffield's 1975 assessment of recreational potential in the countryside).

One of the notable debates in resource studies for recreation in the late 1960s and early 1970s was the evaluation of recreation environments (Duffield and Owen 1970) related to preferential descriptions of recreational resources, namely aesthetic studies which measure human preferences and how they respond to landscape alterations. According to Pigram and Jenkins (1999: 76) the multifaceted nature of landscape, personal preferences and individual perception make evaluation a highly subjective activity. In the assessment of scenic landscape elements, two fundamental elements exist: the character of the landscape (i.e. the components of the landscape which are visual and part of an inventory such as vegetation, water, human occupation) and quality which is a comparative–evaluative concept, in part determined by landscape characteristics. Unwin (1976) identified landscape quality as a three-stage process:

Table 3.1: The land use classes of the Canada land inventory

Classes	
1 Very high capability	These lands have natural capability to engender very high total annual use of one or more intensive activities. These lands should be able to generate and sustain a level of use comparable to that evident at an outstanding and large bathing beach or a nationally known ski slope.
2 High capability	These lands have natural capability to engender and sustain high total annual use based on one or more intensive activity.
3 Moderately high capability	These lands have a natural ability to engender and sustain moderately high total annual use based on moderate to intensive or intensive activities.
4 Moderate capability	These lands have natural capability to engender and sustain moderate total annual use based on dispersed activities.
5 Moderately low capability	These lands have natural capability to engender and sustain moderately low total annual use based on dispersed activities.
6 Low capability	These lands lack the natural quality and significant features to rate higher, but have the natural capability to engender and sustain low total annual use based on dispersed activities.
7 Very low capability	These lands have practically no capability for any popular type of recreation activity, but there may be some opportunity for very specialised activities with recreation aspects, or they may simply provide open space.

- *Landscape description*, which is the objective inventory of landscape characteristics to classify the landscape type.
- *Landscape preference*, where visual preference ratings are allocated to specific landscape characteristics. This is largely dependent upon subjective preferences and value judgements.
- *Landscape evaluation*, where the specific qualities of the landscapes being considered are assessed to examine preferences of specific respondents.

Fines' (1968) influential study in East Sussex epitomises this approach, where a group of people with a background in design work were asked to assign a value to a series of landscape photographs compared to a reference photograph with an indifferent landscape. Once the landscapes were assessed by individuals, a consensus score was assigned and then the people were asked to rank landscapes viewed around East Sussex. While Linton (1968) disagreed with both the nomenclature and scale used by Fines (1968), he concluded that two key elements existed in the landscape: land use and

landforms. These could be mapped and categories established, where a composite score could be devised to reflect the beauty of the landscape (Table 3.2). Linton (1968) developed his study in Scotland, and again, controversy was associated with the almost arbitrary use of a points system, where urban areas were seen as low scoring.

In the 1980s, landscape assessment became used as a tool to separate classification and description of landscape character, as the Countryside Agency (2003) suggest. This has now been superseded by more holistic approaches to landscape, based on the concept of Landscape Character Assessment, with a clearer link to sustainable development and environmental protection. The characterisation of landscape involves the integration of identification, mapping, classification, description and the associated formulation of a character. The significance is that it has a clearer basis for the spatial management of landscapes for recreation and leisure (see http://www.countryside.gov.uk/livinglandscapes).

The importance of the geographer's contribution to landscape evaluation (see Cornish 1934 for an early contribution) was summarised by Penning-

Table 3.2: Linton's landscape evaluation scale

Landforms	Points	Land uses	Points
Mountains	8	Wild landscapes	6
Bold hills	6	Richly varied farming	5
Hill country	5	Varied forest with moors and farms	4
Plateau uplands	3	Moors	3
Low uplands	2	Treeless farms	1
Lowlands	0	Continuous forest	-2
		Urban and industrial land	-5

Source: Linton (1968)

Rowsell (1975) whereby it could assist in landscape management with direct consequences for outdoor recreation. The four areas of significance were as follows:

- *Landscape preservation*, so that landscapes worthy of conservation could be identified.
- *Landscape protection*, where landscapes that are under threat from pressure for development (e.g. economic activity and environmental impacts) can be placed under planning controls.
- *Recreation policy*, where specific policies and forms of outdoor recreation can be facilitated in valued environments within planning constraints.
- *Landscape improvement*, where potential negative landscape features (e.g. eyesores) can be remedied to transform the landscape into more attractive recreational purposes. A good example is the transformation of former extractive sites for gravel within urban fringe locations to provide angling and recreational boating opportunities.

Indeed, the application of such techniques in a wider recreational context is noted by Pigram and Jenkins (1999) in relation to New Zealand. The Resource Management Act 1991 (see Page and Thorn 1997, 1998, 2002; Hall and Kearsley 2001) has seen planning move away from land use zoning methods to ones where the impacts of specific activities are evaluated so that what the environmental outcomes might be are also considered.

Yet urban areas remain important for recreation and tourism (Chapter 5) and it seems naive to dismiss certain resources in such a generalised manner. While a great deal of debate exists in relation to such approaches to landscape evaluation, it does illustrate the importance of human perception, and recognition of what is attractive and valued by different people in relation to recreational time. In terms of descriptive research on travel, it has little immediate relevance to supply unless one is concerned with the impact of demand on the resource base. As a result, the geographer's concern with recreational travel using concepts such as nodes, routes, mode of travel and accessibility of resources for recreationalists has little immediate value.

EXPLANATORY RESEARCH ON LOCATION AND TRAVEL

Moving from purely descriptive to explanatory research illustrates the importance of location as a recreational facility which someone may want to use. S.L.J. Smith (1983a) outlined two concerns regarding the location of such facilities: those factors affecting public and those affecting private location decisions, although the distinction between such issues has blurred where public–private sector involvement, co-operation and management has complicated traditional locational models developed in economic geography, which has separated public and private goods (Hall and Jenkins 1995). For example, L.S. Mitchell (1969b) applied central place theory to the location of urban parks as public recreational resources, establishing that a hierarchy existed, but it rather simplified a number of real-world issues by substituting assumptions, while also ignoring influential variables such as land prices, availability and political influences (see Chapter 5). Other studies (e.g. Mitchell and Lovingwood 1976; Haley 1979) adopted empirical measures to examine correlations between variables which might explain locational patterns, where Haley (1979) observed that present-day patterns often reflect the demands of previous generations. Likewise, where new suburban developments did not require developers to provide park facilities, a dearth of parks exist. Communities in such areas have not sought such provision due to local factors (e.g. private recreation sites and access to the urban fringe). The role of private recreation provision was examined by Mitchell and Lovingwood (1976) and Lovingwood and Mitchell (1978), who mapped 172 public and 112 private recreational facilities, using nearest neighbour analysis to examine the spatial patterns. They concluded that public facilities had a tendency to cluster while private facilities had a regular pattern of distribution for camp sites, country clubs and miscellaneous uses, while water-based facilities and hunting/fishing clubs tended to cluster. The outcome of their analysis was that

- *public facilities* are concentrated in areas of population density to meet the wider good and in accessible locations, having no major resource considerations
- *private facilities* are located on one of two bases: either in or near open space, as in the case of campsites and country clubs and are located throughout the region, or conversely, water-based facilities and hunting clubs are closely tied to a land or water location, clustering around the resource.

In contrast, much of the geographical research on private recreational facility development has been based on the approach developed in retail marketing and location studies, where location is seen as the critical success factor, although Bevins et al. (1974) observed that this was not necessarily

a critical factor for private campsites in north-east USA. Within most studies of recreational location, principal concepts are related to the threshold population, catchment areas or hinterlands and distance to travel to the facility. As Crompton and Van Doren (1976) observed, tram companies in mid-nineteenth-century America built amusement parks at the end of tramlines to attract weekend visitors, illustrating the importance of recreational travel as part of the overall experience.

PREDICTIVE RESEARCH ON LOCATION

The geographer's tradition of model building to predict location of characteristics of private enterprise has been applied to recreational geography in terms of the transfer of location theory and site selection methods. Within the research on location theory, transport cost has played a significant role based on Von Thünen's agricultural land use model, and Vickerman (1975) simplistically applied the model to predict urban recreation businesses. Yet the use of concepts such as locational interdependence, where the potential buyers are not uniformly distributed in space, means that businesses may be able to exercise a degree of control over their clients by their location. Such studies based on the early work of economic geographers such as Reilly (1931), Christaller (1933) and Lösch (1944) developed a number of principles which geographers have used to underpin locational modelling recreational research. While subsequent research by Isard (1956) and Greenhut (1956) can be added to the list, S.L.J. Smith (1983a: 106) summarises the contribution of such studies to the analysis of recreational location choices by business:

- A firm with relatively low transportation costs and a relatively large market area will have a greater chance of success than a firm with high transportation costs and a small market area.
- Some trade-offs are possible between transportation costs, production costs, land rents and market size.

- Transportation costs include both the cost of bringing resources to the site of the firm and the costs of distributing the product to the customer. The relative costs of transporting both resources and products determine, in part, where the firm will locate: high resource transportation costs pull a business close to the resource; high product transportation costs pull a business close to the market.
- Some types of business seek to locate close to each other; some are indifferent to each other; some are repelled by each other.
- Different locations will be attractive to different types of businesses. Attractiveness is based on resources; market location; transportation services; availability of capital, labour and business services; and personal preferences of the decision-maker.
- Firms in any given industry will tend to divide up the available market by selecting different locations to control different spatial segments of the market.
- The size of the market and the number and location of competitors tend to limit the size of the potential development.

These need to be examined in relation to the decision-making of entrepreneurs and individual firms. In terms of site selection methods, feasibility studies have provided a starting point for geographers seeking to assess the most suitable site from a range of alternatives, with the purpose of maximising profit (or wider social benefits in the public sector) though comparatively little research has been published given the scope of such studies (i.e. sources of capital, management issues, design and development issues, market size, population characteristics, economic profile of the potential market and the suitability of the site) and the tendency for such documents to remain commercially sensitive in both the public and private sector. What is evident from the existing research seeking to predict locational characteristics for recreational activities and facilities is the reliance upon economic geography, particularly retail geography with its concomitant concern for marketing.

NORMATIVE RESEARCH ON LOCATION

Within the public sector, the objectives for locational decision-making are distinctly different (or at least traditionally have been different, despite changing political philosophies towards public recreation provision). The characteristics of public sector provision have traditionally been associated with taxes paying for facility provision and its ongoing operation, with a collective use that cannot be withheld, so that access is not knowingly prohibited to anyone. In other words, their contribution to the quality of life and wider social well-being of the affected population underpins public provision that cannot easily be accommodated into conventional locational theory which is market driven. Austin (1974) identifies recreational facilities as 'site preferred' goods, where proximity to their location is often seen as a measure of their use (i.e. its utility function). Thus maximum distances exist as in the case of urban parks (see Chapter 5). The object, therefore, in public facility location for recreation is to balance the 'utility' factor with minimising the distance people have to travel and providing access to as many people as possible; though Cichetti (1971) examined a number of the problems associated with different methods of balancing travel distances, social utility and other approaches to demand maximisation. Smith (1983a) reviews a range of methods of analysis used by geographers to assist in work on public facility. Site selection, namely models, which emphasise mechanical analogues, comparative needs assessment, demand maximisation, heuristic programming and intuitive modelling (for more detail, see Smith 1983a: 156–68).

Howell and McNamee (2003) reviewed the literature on how public sector leisure policy allocates scarce resources, particularly how fiscal retrenchment in the public sector, as a response to a greater managerialism, has placed a greater emphasis on private sector provision as well as Best Value in local authority provision. Erkip's (1997) evaluation of the distribution of urban parks and recreational services in Ankara, Turkey, raised a number of important debates which the geographer, public policy-maker and recreational planner need to address. The normative nature of urban public service provision for recreation as public goods raises distribution issues such as:

- To what extent can the spatial distribution of public goods and services achieve equal versus selective access? Although equal access is a normative concept, in reality goods and services will rarely achieve equality of access, particularly where fixed resources have to be located.
- The extent to which the public versus private sector should be responsible for the provision of services, a feature which is inherently politically determined and has transformed the nature of leisure and recreation provision since 1980 (Coalter 1998).
- The extent to which private sector profit objectives can be balanced with public sector distributional objectives for public goods and services such as leisure and recreation resources.

In the case of Ankara, Erkip (1997) found that the use of the nearest park or recreational facility was a function of users' income and distance from the resource. As a result, for low income groups proximity was more important, with higher income groups enjoying greater distributional justice. This highlights one of the inherent concerns of welfare geographers such as D.M. Smith (1977): concepts of territorial justice obscure the social and economic processes which condition recreational activity, whereby distributional justice by social group is neglected and access to public goods is constrained. In fact, Crouch (2000: 72) questions the value of such rational concepts as territorial justice that were used in the early research on welfare geography, since in a leisure context, 'People behave subjectively rather than rationally. It is easy to apply explanations of rationality to what people do, but very often that provides categories that do not fit subjective practices' – again questioning the empiricist–positivist tradition of model building and testing to understand critical recreational supply issues. As a result of Crouch's (2000) criticisms of the empiricist–positivist paradigm in human geography which have been applied to recreational issues, one might add a new category to the geographical analysis of supply – the interaction between supply and demand. While this results in distinct spatial interactions, research informed by the new cultural geography (Aitchison 1999) departs from a model building tradition, to understand the nuances, unique features and above all, the human experiences of different forms of encounter with recreation and leisure supply. Again, to reiterate some of the comments from Chapter 2, the approach, methodologies used and lines of inquiry pursued in seeking to understand the human geographies of recreation and leisure supply place the people to the fore, affected by agency, structure and the political economy of leisure provision. This places many of the conventional spatially derived explanations of leisure supply in a different context, seeking more theoretically informed answers to conventional place and space-specific forms of leisure consumption. This highlights many of the tensions reviewed in Chapter 10 on the nexus between academic analyses of tourism and recreation which are objective and robust, and the challenge of applied geographical research, often for clients, that does not permit more challenging analyses that are associated with issues of power, control and political economy.

SUPPLY AND DEMAND IN RECREATIONAL CONTEXTS: SPATIAL INTERACTIONS

Given the comparative neglect of recreational supply issues by geographers and the overriding emphasis in demand studies and impact assessment (Owens 1984), it is pertinent to acknowledge the geographer's synthesising role in recognising that 'recreationalists and the resources they use are separated in space, [and] the interaction between demand and supply creates patterns of movement, and the distances between origins and destinations influence not only the scale of demand, but also the available supply of resources' (Coppock and Duffield 1975: 150). Few studies, with the exception of Coppock and Duffield (1975), acknowledge this essential role the geographer has played in contextualising the real-world impact of recreational activities in a spatial framework. While many recreational researchers may view such contributions as passé, they are notable since no other discipline offers such a holistic and integrative assessment of recreation and tourism phenomena. Coppock and Duffield (1975) acknowledge the resource base as a precondition to assessing the 'space needs' of recreationalists in that the amount of land, the activities to be undertaken, length of journey and nature of the resource help to determine the type of interactions which occur. Clawson et al.'s (1960) typology (Table 3.3) and its subsequent application to England and Wales (S. Law 1967) both confirm the importance of distance and the 'zones of influence' of recreational resources

according to whether they had a national, regional, subregional, intermediate or local zone of influence, using actual distance to classify the resource according to the 'pull' or attraction of each. Law (1967) argued that the majority of day trippers would be drawn from no more than 48 km away. What Coppock and Duffield (1975) recognised was that it was not individual but groups of resources which attract active recreation.

At a descriptive level, the relationships outlined in Table 3.3 indicate that the Clawson et al. (1960) model appears to have an application, where, in a

- 0–16 km zone, many resource needs for recreation can be met in terms of golf, urban parks and the urban fringe
- 16–32 km zone, the range of activities is greater, though particular types of resource tend to dominate activity patterns (e.g. horse-riding, hiking and field sports)

Table 3.3: A general classification of outdoor recreational uses and resources

Item	User-oriented	Type of recreation area resource-based	Intermediate
General location	Close to users; on whatever resources are available	Where outstanding resources can be found; may be distant from most users	Must not be too remote from users; on best resources available within distance limitation
Major types of activity	Games, such as golf and tennis; swimming, picnicking, walks, horse riding; zoos, etc.; play by children	Major sightseeing, scientific, historical interest; hiking, mountain climbing, camping, fishing, hunting	Camping, picnicking, hiking, swimming, hunting, fishing
When major use occurs	After hours (school or work)	Vacations	Day outings and weekends
Typical sizes of areas	One to a hundred or at most to a few hundred acres	Usually some thousands of acres, perhaps many thousands	A hundred to several thousand acres
Common types of agency responsibility	City, county or other local government; private	National parks and national forests primarily; state parks in some cases; private, especially for seashore and major lakes	Federal reservoirs; state parks; private

Source: Clawson et al. (1960: 136)

- 32 km or greater, sports and physical pursuits with specific resource requirements (e.g. orienteering, canoeing, skiing and rock-climbing) exist.

Yet despite increased mobility of recreationists, the majority of popular activities are undertaken relatively near to the home. To expand upon these findings, attention now turns to classifying and analysing the supply of recreational resources within the context of the urban fringe.

Classifying recreational resources

In the analysis of recreation patterns, trends and resource use by specific groups, the complexity of the existing recreation stock requires some form of classification to improve our understanding (see Fisher et al. 1974; Doren et al. 1979; Gilg 1985). In other words, the recognition of recreational resources needs to be accompanied by an inventory process to take stock of the quantity, quality and extent of the resource base. For this reason, classification schemes have been derived. In the previous section, the preliminary attempt by Clawson et al. (1960) to derive a classification system distinguished between recreation areas according to location, activity type, major uses, size of the area and who was responsible for recreation resource management (Table 3.3). One of the problems with this classification scheme was that it neglected urban and near-urban sites and developed a narrow conception of outdoor recreation resources. Even so, this classification was a critical turning point in recreational thinking, since it spurned numerous adaptations, stimulating new ways of thinking about classifying recreational resources.

Although no definitive scheme exists for classifying recreational resources, the need to distinguish between human-made and natural resources, different resource environments and resource types provides a useful starting point. In this respect, Chubb and Chubb's (1981) classification is valuable since it incorporates much of the thinking in recreational research, building on Clawson et al. (1960) where the following classes of recreation resources exist:

- *the undeveloped recreation resources*, where the physical attributes of land, water and vegetation are untouched
- *private recreation resources*, such as second homes, resources owned by quasi-public organisations (e.g. conservation groups, farm and industrial sites)
- *commercialised private recreation resources*, such as shopping malls, theme parks, museums, gardens, stadiums and resorts
- *publicly owned recreation resources*, including parks, sports and leisure facilities, national parks, forest and tourist sites
- *cultural resources*, based in both the public and private sector, such as libraries, the Arts and what is increasingly being termed 'the cultural industries' (see Pratt 1998)
- *professional resources*, which may be divided into the administrative functions for recreational provision (organisation, policy-making and financial support systems) and management (e.g. research, planning, development and conservation/programming functions).

Other attempts to classify recreational resources have also recognised that a continuum exists from the home-oriented space through to the neighbourhood (including the street – see S. Williams 1995) with increasing scale through to community and regional space (S. Gold 1980). With these issues in mind, attention now turns to the recreational resources that exist in an urban landscape – the urban fringe.

Recreational resources and the urban fringe

The impact of urbanisation on the development of industrial societies and the effects in terms of recreational resource provision is discussed in detail in Chapter 6. Yet the growing consumption of rural land for urban uses has led to increased concerns for the loss of non-urban land, as observed by Abercrombie (1938). Pigram (1983: 106) observed that 'every year some 1.2 ha of rural land are converted to urban and built-up uses across America' and the greatest competition over the retention of land for recreational uses is in the city periphery or what is termed the 'urban fringe'. Elson (1993) recognised the considerable potential of the urban fringe as a resource able to accommodate recreation and sport for four reasons:

- It comprises an area of recreational supply, accessible with good public transport to large populations, though Fitton (1976) and Ferguson and Munton (1978, 1979) recognised the inaccessibility to the most deprived areas of inner London. As the Countryside Commission (1992) noted, one in five informal recreational day trips to the countryside had a return trip of less than 10 miles.
- It may be an overflow location for recreational and sporting activities displaced from urban areas.
- It can function as an 'interceptor area', reducing pressure on more fragile and vulnerable rural resources.
- It may be an area of opportunity as environmental improvements and landscape regeneration (e.g. the reclamation of former quarry sites or gravel extraction) and may generate new forms of recreation including fishing, sailing and informal use.

As Elson (1993) observes, with active recreation the fastest growing sector of countryside recreation in the UK, the urban fringe has the potential to absorb such uses. Thus by altering supply, it is assumed that demand may be directed to new resources. In this sense, the urban fringe is a useful example in which to examine the nature of spatial interactions between demand and supply.

THE GREEN BELT CONCEPT

Within the UK the urban fringe has been a created landscape. In the 1930s the green belt concept was developed in London, along with many other European cities, based on the influential work of Raymond Unwin and the Green Belt Act 1933.

Unwin helped establish the principle of creating a band of open space on the city's periphery in order to compensate for the lack of open space in the built urban environment. These principles were embodied in post-war planning during the 1950s (Ministry of Housing and Local Government 1955). While such designations were intended to limit urban sprawl, recreational provision was never their intended purpose. Elson (1986) shows that planning authorities in the West Midlands, Manchester and Sheffield identified green belt plans (e.g. green wedges, recreation and amenity areas) in their development plans only to find them downgraded or removed through the ministerial assessment of the plans. In fact, Harrison (1991: 32) argued that

> public authorities adopted a standards approach to provision that was a legacy of the inter-war period with its heavy emphasis on organised sport rather than on a wider range of individual and family pursuits. Moreover, while these standards were based on the number of active members of the population who might be expected to participate . . . even the minimum standard of provision of 2.4 hectares per 1000 head of population could not be met in inner cities.

As a result, the urban fringe and its green belt was seen as the likely location for provision. At a policy level it is interesting to note that in the late 1960s both the Countryside Commission and local authorities used green belts as a mechanism to reduce standards of provision in the inner city (for more discussion of the politics of green belt land and recreational use, see Harrison 1991). Even so, Harrison (1980–1) found that the carrying capacity of many sites could be improved through better resource management, with the Greater London Council (1975) study of London's green belt indicating that organised activities constituted half of the trips to the green belt for recreation. In spatial terms, approved green belts now comprise 3,824,000 acres or 12 per cent of the land of England and it is expected to continue to grow as more cities use this mechanism for urban containment. For example, Elson (1993) reports that the designation of twelve community forests in the UK of between 8000 and 20,000 ha will add environmental improvements and resources for the urban fringe. One notable development which predates much of the early research on the urban fringe is the Countryside Commission's (1974) involvement in the establishment of Country Parks in the urban fringe, following on from a UK government Rural White Paper on *Leisure and the Countryside* in 1966.

INSIGHT: Country parks as a spatial recreational tool: intercepting urban recreationalists seeking the countryside

The Countryside Commission viewed Country Parks as an area of '25 acres in extent, with basic facilities, for the public to enjoy informal open air recreation' (Harrison 1991: 95). Between 1969 and 1993 the Countryside Commission spent £16 million developing these resources, establishing a network of 206 country parks and 239 picnic sites. After 1993, the Countryside Commission capital works grants were cut and this marked the end of the development of these type of capital intensive projects in and around urban areas. However, their significance cannot be underestimated as in 2003, it was estimated that they attracted 57 million visits a year. While a number of studies account for the evolution of Country Park policy (Zetter 1971; Slee 1982; Groome and Tarrant 1984), it is clear that the researchers point to the absence of research which indicates whether park provision provides the experiences recreationalists require. Despite growing provision of Country Parks in the 1970s, disparities existed in their spatial distribution, with large conurbations having only limited provision (Ferguson and Munton 1979).

Thus spatial inequalities in supply simply reinforced existing patterns of provision, though Country Parks have assisted in retaining land for recreation at a time of pressure for development. Fitton (1979), for example, found that while Country Parks comprised 0.13 per cent of the land surface of England and Wales, they accounted for 4.2 per cent of trips, a finding supported by Elson (1979) whose analyses of 31 sites visited in south-east England found that urban fringe sites with a range of facilities were visited more frequently than other recreational destinations, though patterns of use were related to distance–decay functions, distance from individuals' home area, other attractions, individual choice and a range of other factors. As Harrison (1991: 103) suggests, Country Parks 'had not achieved a separate identity but people's experiences of particular sites within [them] . . . contributed to their own separate evaluations of what particular locations offered'. The continual gap between provision and users was evidenced in the Countryside Commission's (1988) study, which concluded that while 58 per cent of people had heard of a Country Park, only 26 per cent could name one correctly, reflecting a lack of promotion and general awareness of their existence.

At a national level, Country Parks appear to have only a minor role to play in diverting demand from the countryside, with some parks having catchments that are extremely localised. This was due to the impact of the car in diverting traffic straight to countryside sites. For example, Harrison (1981, 1983) found that 75 per cent of visitors to south London's green belt were car users. Their study discovered that inner city residents never comprised more than 10 per cent of users. Although sites were also accessible to those not having access to a car over short distances, Groome and Tarrant (1984) found public transport to Country Parks effective over a 5–8 km distance (i.e. short distance) for a local population. At an aggregate level, it is clear that Country Parks (and their forerunner – Regional Parks) in the UK play a vital role in locating recreational resources near to demand. The somewhat dated 1981 National Survey of Countryside

Recreation found that 40 per cent of destinations were within the urban area or within 1 km (Sidaway and Duffield 1984), with a further 22 per cent in the countryside around urban areas. Only 16 per cent of destinations were located 10 km from the urban areas.

In 2003, the Countryside Agency argued that these sites still act as focal points for leisure, acting as honeypots and as gateways to the countryside. The recent interest in redeveloping the resource base of these sites has been apparent in the serious decline that has occurred in open space provision in the UK, especially as many of these Country Parks rely upon local authorities for over 90 per cent of their funding at a time of cuts in leisure spending and new priorities, such as social inclusion and the problems of inner city deprivation. PriceWaterhouseCooper (1999) found that in the UK there were 60,000 parks, gardens and designed landscapes that were competing for funding, 33,000 of which were owned by the local authority. These sites saw expenditure of around £800 million a year, £325 million of which came from the local authority. Yet using economic techniques of contingent valuation, these sites were deemed to be worth £5000 million to the people who used them, comprising around 6 per cent of all recreational visits each year.

The example of Havering in Greater London (Figure 3.2) illustrates how the development of a management plan by a project officer acknowledged the problems of multiple use and the legacy of former derelict land. In the case of Havering, the scale of dereliction and the variety of land agencies involved created problems for the development of recreation provision. The land was a former First World War Royal Flying Corps base defending London from Zeppelin attack and in the Second World War, it was a front line 'Battle of Britain' spitfire squadron base. The land was also used for sand and gravel extraction to the point that by the 1970s a legacy of dereliction remained, as housing development surrounded the site. While the Countryside Commission (1983) reviewed Havering's scheme and found a legacy of poor public provision in public housing areas and inadequate recognition of rights of way, landscaping schemes also remained a neglected feature. Expecting the London Borough of Havering to set a precedent for landowners to follow has taken a long time to reach fruition. Nevertheless, the approach has brought modest success through environmental improvements establishing attractive recreational facilities by effectively tidying up many sites (Harrison 1991). The success of such projects was also followed by a new initiative in 1985 – the Groundwork Trust, based on a scheme in St Helen's urban fringe (Groundwork Foundation 1986). Since the early 1990s, this area been further developed to comprise 250 acres of fields and trees, with 4 miles of parks and horse rides, a lake and picnic sites. The nature reserve (Ingrebourne Marshes) which now forms a key component of the site is classified as a Site of Special Scientific Interest (SSSI). It has also been incorporated as part of the Thames Chase Community Forest Initiative since 1990.

Variability in the usage of Country Parks reflects public knowledge of their existence and the attraction of individual locations. The precise location of recreation sites in the urban fringe appears to directly influence usage, with those located near to residential areas which permit residents to walk to them recording highest usage rates. As Harrison (1991) concludes

> the recreational role played by sites in the urban fringe will differ depending upon their ease of access to local people who walk or cycle to them and not necessarily on the preferences of a wider constituency served by car . . . [and] the recreational role of countryside areas embedded in the urban area or abutting it is likely to be very different from that of more distant countryside sites.
>
> (Harrison 1991: 166)

What is clear is that the supply of recreational resources alone (e.g. Country Parks) is not sufficient in the urban fringe if the needs and recreational preferences of users are not analysed since these factors directly affect recreational behaviour.

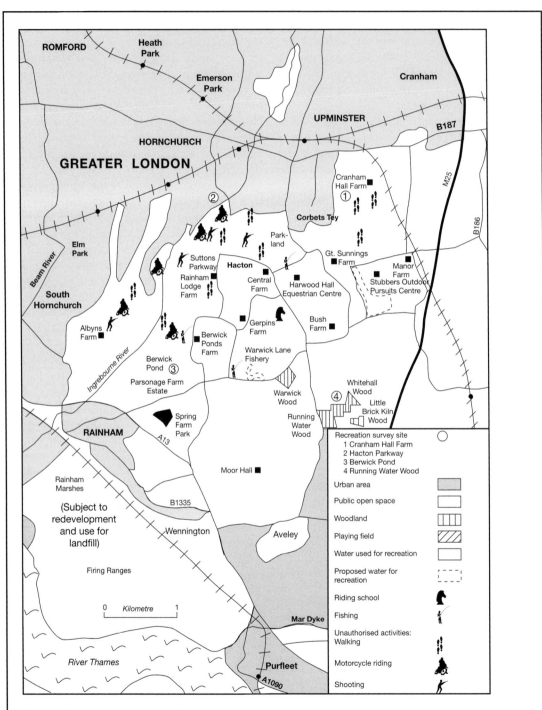

Figure 3.2: London Borough of Havering's urban fringe countryside management area
Source: based on Countryside Commission (1982) in Harrison (1991)

MULTIPLE USE OF RECREATIONAL RESOURCES

The example of the urban fringe highlights the diversities of land uses which may occur in a some-times contested landscape, where a wide range of resource management issues emerge. O'Riordan (1971: 19) described resource management 'as a process of decision-making whereby resources are allocated over space and time according to the needs, aspirations and desires of man'. In this process, it is the ability to accommodate multifunctional resource use in specific recreational spaces that is critical to achieving societal recreation objectives. The key to achieving this lies in the compatibility of specific recreational activities with both the resource base and other users. Although Chapter 9 discusses the role of planning and management in more detail, it is important to recognise at this point that two fundamental concepts need to be explored in managing the supply of recreational resources: *conflict* and *compatibility*.

Many notions of recreational conflict (avoidance of which is one of the goals of planning) are predicated on the concept of the incompatibility of one activity versus another. Jacob and Schreyer (1980: 369) define conflict thus: 'For an individual, conflict is defined as goal interference attributed to another's behaviour.' This definition assumes that people recreate to achieve certain outcome goals. Yet they argue that goal interference does not necessarily lead to incompatibility. In understanding the nature of recreation user conflict, the interactions which occur need to be understood in relation to a range of factors:

- the nature of the activity and personal meaning attached to it
- the significance attached to a specific recreation resource
- the mode of experience, especially how the natural environment is perceived
- lifestyle tolerance, namely an individual's willingness to accept or reject lifestyles different from one's own.

These factors provide an interesting framework in which to evaluate conflict, especially for recreational resources with a high degree of conflict potential. As Jacob and Schreyer (1980: 378) assert, 'In failing to recognise the basic causes of conflict, inappropriate resolution techniques and management strategies are likely to be adopted'. These findings are reflected in the recreational behaviour observed in Illinois by Bristow et al. (1995), where a wide variety of activities were incompatible and led to increased travel times to seek recreational sites able to accommodate personal preferences. Not only does this raise important planning issues for recreation site planning and design (for more technical detail see Ravenscroft 1992; Pigram and Jenkins 1999), it also raises the importance of recreation resource management to monitor sites to ensure the resource base can continue to accommodate the compatibility of uses. For example, Bell's (2000) analysis of the public inquiry into attempts to impose a speed restriction on the use of Lake Windermere to curb power boating serves as a notable example of the conflicting demands often faced in recreational settings between passive and active users, both recreational and tourist together with the arguments levelled by the local community as stakeholders in the process of recreational management (see also C.M. Hall and Härkönen 2006).

THE SUPPLY OF TOURISM

Within most conventional texts on tourism, the issue of supply attracts comparatively little attention. According to Sinclair and Stabler (1992):

> past research on the tourism industry can be classified into three main categories: first, descriptions of the industry and its operation, management and marketing; second, the spatial development and interactions which characterise the industry on a local, national and international scale; and third, the effects which result from the development of the industry.
>
> (Sinclair and Stabler 1992: 2)

In contrast, Shaw and Williams (1994) prefer to view the issue in relation to two other concepts:

production and consumption. Shaw and Williams (1994) acknowledge that the production and consumption of tourism are important approaches to the analysis of tourism since

> production is the method by which a complex array of businesses and industries are involved in the supply of tourism services and products, and how these are delivered to consumers, and consumption is how, where, why and when the tourist actually consumes tourism services and products.
>
> (Shaw and Williams 1994: 16)

Agarwal et al. (2000) argue that:

> There are two main reasons for the lack of research on tourism production. First, the theoretical framework for tourism production studies has been relatively threadbare and isolated from mainstream economic geography . . . Second, tourism geography suffers from an opaque industrial definition, which is related to the composite nature of tourism, being both a consumer (final demand) and producer service (intermediate demand). Furthermore, the fragmentation of the production and delivery of tourism services amongst a number of conventionally defined sectors (such as transport, retailing and catering) results in poor representation in secondary statistics. Moreover, the tourism industry per se tends to be institutionally weak, which also contributes to its poor representation in . . . research and in policy-research.
>
> (Agarwal et al. 2000: 242)

These weaknesses are compounded by a lack of data on the operation and performance of individual tourism enterprises. Sessa (1993: 59), however, considers 'tourism supply is the result of all those productive activities that involve the provision of goods and services required to meet tourism demand and which are expressed in tourism consumption' which comprises resources for tourists, infrastructure, receptive facilities, entertainment, sports venues as well as tourism reception services (Table 3.4). While there is an inevitable degree of overlap in this conceptualisation of tourism supply with leisure and recreational uses, it highlights the scope of productive activities associated with tourism supply.

The feature which makes many of these resources of interest to the geographer is what Urry (1990)

describes as 'spatial fixity'. In other words, tourists are mobile consumers and able to consume at a global level. This contrasts with most forms of supply which are fixed at specific locations. Perhaps the exception here are the transnational corporations that are able to relocate capital at a global level to meet shifts in demand. Underlying the concept of spatial fixity is the nature of tourism entrepreneurs who are largely small scale in their operations and less able to access forms of capital to relocate to new sources of demand. Thus supply is often unable to respond geographically to demand beyond a fixed point, and this means that peaks and troughs in demand at particular locations

Table 3.4: Elements of the tourism industry

Tourism resources

Free
- climate, culture, traditions and 'way of life'

Scarce
- land
- labour (including goodwill)
- capital (public and private provision)

General and tourism infrastructure
- means of communication and travel
- water, power and sewage
- transport infrastructure
- information technology

Receptive facilities
- accommodation for visitors
- accommodation for staff
- food and beverage premises
- second homes

Entertainment and sports facilities
- recreational
- cultural facilities
- sports facilities

Tourism reception services
- travel agencies
- promotional offices
- information offices
- car and transport hire
- guides, interpreters

Sources: after Bull (1991); Sessa (1993)

need to be managed through differential forms of pricing (Seaton and Bennett 1996) and the use of seasonal labour (Ball 1989).

Law (1993) expands upon these simple notions, arguing that

> in many respects tourism is the geography of consumption outside the home area; it is about how and why people travel to consume. . . . [On] the production side it is concerned to understand where tourism activities develop and on what scale. It is concerned with the process or processes whereby some cities are able to create tourism resources and a tourism industry.
>
> (Law 1993: 14)

Law emphasises here the way in which scale is a critical concept in understanding supply issues together with the ways in which the tourism industry is organised and geographically distributed through time and space.

One useful illustration of the effect of a new form of production can alter the landscape of tourism and leisure consumption is the rise of the low cost airline sector. As Page (2003a) has shown, this new form of production has the following features as outlined in Table 3.5. In the USA and Europe, new low cost carriers using secondary airports have generated demand for leisure and to a lesser degree, business travel. This has not only seen entrepreneurial organisations like EasyJet and Ryanair challenge the existing scheduled carriers, but also generated new markets for low-cost air travel and domestic/international travel. As a result, some coastal and urban destination in western and eastern Europe have enjoyed the expansion of new price-sensitive markets, especially short breaks and VFR travel together with new niche markets such as stag parties and hen nights in Prague and Dublin.

Table 3.5: Key characteristics of low cost carriers which make them more competitive than other carriers

- Some carriers have introduced single/one-way fares not requiring stopovers or Saturday night stays to get advanced purchase (APEX) prices
- No complimentary in-flight service (no frills) which often reduce operating costs 6–7 per cent
- One class cabins (in most cases)
- No pre-assigned seating (in most cases)
- Ticketless travel
- High frequency routes to compete with other airlines on popular destinations and up to three flights a day on low density routes
- Short turnarounds (often less than half an hour), with higher aircraft rotations (i.e. the level of utilisation is higher than other airlines) and less time charged on the airport apron and runway
- The use of secondary airports where feasible (including the provision of public transport where none exists)
- Point to point flights
- Lower staffing costs, with fewer cabin crew as no complimentary in-flight service, which also reduces turnaround times due to the lack of cleaning caused by food service
- Flexibility in staff rostering, a lack of overnight stays for staff at non-base locations and streamlined operations (e.g. on some airlines toilets on domestic flights are emptied only at cabin crew requests rather than at each turnaround to reduce costs)
- Many of the aircraft are leased, reducing the level of depreciation and standardising costs
- Many airline functions are outsourced, such as ground staff and check-in, minimising overheads and reducing costs by 11–15 per cent
- Standardised aircraft types (i.e. Boeing 737s) to reduce maintenance costs and the range of spare parts which need to be held for repairs
- Limited office space at the airports
- Heavy emphasis on advertising, especially billboards, to offset the declining use of travel agents as the main source of bookings
- Heavy dependence upon the internet and telephone for bookings
- Small administrative staff, with many sales-related staff on commission to improve performance (as well as pilots in some cases)

Source: Page (2003a)

Low cost airlines have changed the geographical access to leisure consumption by widening the domestic tourist and leisure traveller's search area for new consuming experiences, while radically impacting upon scheduled airline services and standards of provision as competition increases.

INSIGHT: The destination life cycle

The notion of a destination product life cycle has been extremely influential in tourism research and probably ranks as one of the most substantial contributions by geographers to the wider tourism literature. The tourist area life cycle (TALC) also has a wider significance beyond a focus on tourism destination development because it challenges the notion of tourism studies having a simplistic theoretical base. As Oppermann (1998a: 180) noted: 'Butler's model is a brilliant example of how scientific progress could and should work. . . . [having] been scrutinized in many different contexts with modifications suggested to fit specific situations and circumstances.'

Butler's (1980, 2005) concept of a tourist area life cycle of evolution, based on some of the initial observations of Christaller (1963) and Plog (1974, 1977), has been applied in a number of environments and settings representing the development of a destination through time and space (Cooper and Jackson 1989; Cooper 1992, 1994; Ioannides 1992; Butler 2005). Because of its relative simplicity the concept of a tourist area life cycle has emerged as a significant concept for strategic destination marketing and planning and which underpins much of our understanding of urban tourism development. As Lundgren (1984: 22) commented, 'Butler put into the realistic cyclical context a reality that everyone knew about, and clearly recognised, but had never formulated into an overall theory'.

According to Cooper and Jackson (1989) the two most substantial managerial benefits of the life cycle concept are its use as a descriptive guide for strategic decision making and its capacity as a forecasting tool. As a descriptive guide the life cycle idea implies that in the early stages of product development the focus will be on building market share while in the later stages the focus will be on maintaining that share (Rink and Swan 1979). However, the utility of the life cycle concept as a forecasting tool relies heavily on the identification of those forces that influence the flow of tourists to a specific destination. As Haywood (1986) recognised, most models work well in their early stages but then fail in their prediction of the latter stages of the model. Haywood (1986) along with other commentators (e.g. Rink and Swan 1979; Cooper 1992; Ioannides 1992) note that there are a variety of different shaped curves with the shape of the curve depending on both supply and demand side factors. Indeed, Haywood (1986: 154) goes so far as to argue that the life cycle approach 'represents the supply side view of the diffusion model', by which consumers adopt new products.

According to Haywood (1986) there are six operational decisions when using the life cycle concept:

- unit of analysis
- relevant market
- pattern and stages of the tourist area life cycle
- identification of the area's shape in the life cycle
- determination of the unit of measurement
- determination of the relevant time unit.

Using Haywood's insights as a basis for undertaking research on the life cycle, Graber (1997) undertook an analysis of the destination life cycles of 43 European cities using the variables of growth data for domestic and international tourism, first time visitor percentage, length of stay, guest-mix distribution and number of competitors. Only a small number of the variables tested proved to be significant correlates of the life cycle. According to Graber (1997: 69), 'A diminishing rate of first-time visitors is obvious for cities passing through later stages of the cycle'.

In contrast to many of the more product life cycle interpretations of Butler's life cycle model which have come from a marketing orientation, Hall (2005c) has argued that the life cycle of a destination should be assessed in terms of accessibility and spatial interaction modelling. Hall (2005a, 2005c) observed that Butler's (1980) model is an analogue of changed accessibility between generating areas and a destination.

Butler (1980) cited Wolfe's (1952) research on summer cottages in Ontario as an example 'that each improvement in the accessibility to a recreation area results in significantly increased visitation and an expansion of the market area' (Butler 1980: 11). In addition to Wolfe's work, Butler also cited the research of Stansfield (1972, 1978) as highlighting the importance of accessibility as a factor in influencing change in tourism destinations. Stansfield's (1978) discussion of Atlantic City and a cycle of resort change is particularly instructive with respect to transport and accessibility issues with Stansfield noting the influence of transport related time/distance on the development of Atlantic City as a 'surf and sand' (Stansfield 1978) destination:

> Connecting customers with the resort is the basis of all resort development; all recreation and tourism patterns take place within a time and space frame. Atlantic City's time-distance and cost-distance relative to Philadelphia were a successful blend of shortest straight line distance and the efficiency of the railroad,
>
> (Stansfield 1978: 242)

also noting that 'changes in time-space functions can affect the relative attractiveness of destinations' (Stansfield 1978: 242). Atlantic City's dependence on the railroad meant that with the growth of automobile infrastructure and greater individual mobility through increased car ownership levels, the competitiveness of Atlantic City as a destination decreased. A morphology that had developed in relation to the point-to-point mobility of railroad users could not easily adapt to the demands of the car. Changing patterns of accessibility were therefore integral to Stansfield's understanding of the relative competitiveness of destinations and resorts.

Hall (2005a, 2005c) argues that a destination should be primarily conceptualised as a geographical place, e.g. as a point in space which is subject to a range of factors which influence locational advantage and disadvantage. Most significant to these is the movement outward from a tourist generating and trips as a function of distance. Such travel movement cannot be adequately represented in the classic linear form of a distance decay model whereby the location of numbers of trips or people travelling at any given time is highest closer to the generating area and diminishes in relation to distance. Instead, factors which influence travel behaviour, such as decisions relating to overnight stays and time to undertake leisure activities as well as overall amenity values, create a series of peaks and troughs in relation to distance from the generating area (Hall 2005a). However, regardless of what form of transport is used, there will be a different set of distance/time functions at which overnight stays will need to be made because all travellers have the necessity of travellers to stop at some stage to sleep.

> Given the above assumptions then changes in distance (whether time, cost, behavioural, or network) between the tourist generating origin and the surrounding hinterland will then lead to corresponding changes in the number of travellers for any given point in the spatial system. However, locations within the spatial system are spatially fixed, towns and cities do not suddenly get up and move away in order to maximise advantageous distance functions although they do change and adapt over time in relation to new networks and patterns of accessibility. . . . if the numbers of tourist bed-nights (or other measures of tourism related density) at a spatially

> fixed point 'destination' (L) are drawn at ᵗ1, ᵗ2, ᵗ3, . . . in relation to the changed accessibility with respect to a tourist generating region or trip origin then this provides a representation of overnight stay density at a specific location which is analogous to that of the TACE when presented in its standard two dimensional form.
>
> (Hall 2005a: 119)

While production and consumption have been the focus of the more theoretically derived explanations of tourism production (e.g. Mullins 1991), such approaches raise conceptual issues related to how one should view production and consumption in the context of urban tourism. The purpose of this chapter is to address how one can examine the relationship between production and consumption in terms of the supply of products. Both the tourists' consumption (often expressed as the demand – examined in Chapter 2) and the products and services produced for their visit (the supply) form important inputs in the overall system of tourism and the wider development of society. However, prior to examining different facets of production, the geographer's contribution to theoretical analysis in this area is examined.

TOWARDS A CRITICAL GEOGRAPHY OF TOURISM PRODUCTION

According to Britton (1991: 451), the geography of tourism has suffered from weakly developed theory since 'geographers working in the field have been reluctant to recognise explicitly the capitalistic nature of the phenomenon they are researching'. While Shaw and Williams (1994) review the concepts of production and consumption (also see Debbage and Ioannides 2004; A.M. Williams 2004), it is pertinent to examine critically Britton's (1991) innovative research in this area since it provides a theoretical framework in which to interpret tourism production. Within the tourism production systems are

- economic activities designed to produce and sell tourism products
- social groups, cultural and physical elements included in tourism products as attractions

- agencies associated with the regulation of the production system.

In a theoretical context, Britton (1991) argued that the tourism production system was

> simultaneously a mechanism for the accumulation of capital, the private appropriation of wealth, the extraction of surplus value from labour, and the capturing of (often unearned) rents from cultural and physical phenomena (especially public goods) which are deemed to have both a social and scarcity value.
>
> (Britton 1991: 455)

The production system may be viewed as having a division of labour between its various components (transport, accommodation, tour operators, attractions and ancillary services) as well as markets (the demand and supply of tourist products) and regulatory agencies (e.g. industry associations) as well as industry organisations and structures to assist in the production of the final product. Britton (1991: 456) rightly points out that 'the geography texts on tourism offer little more than a cursory and superficial analysis of how the tourism industry is structured and regulated by the classic imperatives and laws governing capitalist accumulation'.

The tourism industry is made up of a range of separate industry suppliers who offer one or more components of the final product which requires intermediaries to co-ordinate and combine the elements which are sold to the consumer as a discrete package. Both tour operators and travel agents have a vital role to play in this context when one recognises the existence of a supply chain (Figure 3.3). What this emphasises is the variety of linkages which exist and the physical separation of roles and responsibilities to the supply chain (see Page 1994b). While information technology may assist in improving communication and co-ordination between different components associated with the production of tourism, other developments (notably horizontal and vertical integration) assist in addressing the fragmentation of elements within the supply system. Likewise, tour operators are able to use economies of scale and their sheer buying power over suppliers to derive a competitive advantage in the assembly of tour components into packages. The tour operators also have the power and ability to shift the product to match demand, and to exercise an extraordinary degree of power over both inter-industry transactions and the spatial distribution of tourist flows. As Agarwal et al. (2000: 244–45) indicate, 'increasing scale, or market concentration, has been achieved through horizontal and vertical integration as airlines expand into tour operations, tour operators acquire airlines and travel agencies and invest in the accommodation sector', a feature also observed by Ioannides (1995). As a result, the process of market concentration can occur through various strategies (or a combination thereof): strategic alliances, mergers, acquisitions and take-overs, franchising agreements and the use of marketing consortia. Such strategies are used by the highly globalised multinational economies of scale, to reduce competition and to seek greater control of the market. Strategic alliances also assist in this regard, since suppliers in one part of the system are dependent on those either upstream or downstream. Therefore, there is pressure on suppliers to exert control over other suppliers through transaction arrangements (i.e. through long-term contracts, vertical and horizontal integration) as well as through commissions, licensing and franchising. The two most powerful organisations in this respect are national airlines and tour wholesalers (also known as tour operators). Through the financial

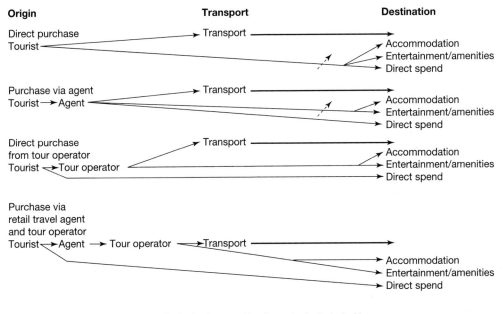

The broken line indicates opportunity for brokerage. Food may be included with accommodation or be in 'direct spend'.

⟶ Transaction chain

⟶ Tourist travel (to a domestic or international destination)

Figure 3.3: Four types of tourism transaction chain
Source: after Witt et al. (1991: 81) and Page (1994b)

resources and industry leverage that these organisations can wield in the tourism business, they are able to exact advantageous business terms and the introduction of computer reservation systems (CRS), now referred to as global distribution systems (GDS), which provide not only integration of the supply chain but also a competitive advantage in revenue generation through bookings made through these systems.

Papatheodorau (2003) examined the oligopolistic behaviour (i.e. bargaining power) of the transnational tour operators in the Mediterranean in relation to their corporate strategies. He observed that in the UK mass package holiday market (see Page 2003a for an analysis of the organisation and licensing of this market), over 54 per cent of overseas holidays by UK residents were to the Mediterranean, with demand concentrated in Spain and Greece. This accounted for a £12 billion tour operator business in the UK in 2000, and it is widely accepted that local producers and specific destinations heavily dependent upon mass tourism may see oligoposonistic behaviour in the way contracts in the supply of services are negotiated. These may seek maximum discounts and long settlement terms on payment of goods/services supplied to tour operators, reinforcing Ioannides' (1998) argument that tour operators are gatekeepers to tourism, applying a similar concept to that developed by P. Williams (1978) with an analysis of housing markets and how agencies such as building societies can 'redline' areas. This means that building societies delineate areas they will not lend in. In a similar vein, tour operators can redline destinations, based on previous experience of tourist problems, particularly terrorism, a feature which affected the Kenyan tourist industry post-2002 with Al Qaeda attacks on resort areas. A combination of tour operators and insurers can effectively redline resorts and destinations.

Britton (1991) also indicates that the state has a fundamental role to play in encouraging industry groups to meet and co-ordinate problem-solving such as reducing critical incidents (Bitner et al. 1990) in the supply chain. In addition, the state makes a major contribution in terms of funding the market-ing of regions and destinations via national and regional tourism organisations (D.G. Pearce 1992b) so that place promotion takes place (Ashworth and Voogd 1990a, 1990b; Page 1995a). The state may also offer inducements to underwrite major supply inputs where territorial competition or development may not otherwise occur. Interventions in the market include the underwriting of national 'flag-carrier' airlines (see Kissling 1989), and public economic and welfare goals are emphasised to justify state intervention.

One of the interesting areas hitherto ignored in geographical research on tourism supply is labour supply and markets (see Shaw and Williams 1994 for a good synthesis of the literature). Since in the tourism business many workers simultaneously provide and are part of the consumed product, service quality assumes a vital role. This is broadened in many research studies to include the 'tourist experience' (Ryan 1997). While Britton (1991) rightly points to the role of capitalist social relations in the production of tourist experiences, such experiences cannot easily be characterised as tangible elements of tourist supply. This poses major difficulties for capital, where quality of service is easily influenced by personal factors, the behaviour and attitude of staff, as well as by the perception of the consumer in relation to their expectations, values and belief system. One result is that much of the demand for labour is not necessarily recognised through formal qualifications but through personal qualities, which leads to an undervaluing of labour. Add to this the fact that the labour willing to supply such skills is often casual and female (and often with a local ethnic component), the tourism labour market is characterised by ethnic and gender divisions, with relatively poor employment conditions existing relative to other sectors (T. Baum 1993). For example, in the Australian context, the Industry Commission (1995: 21) characterised the tourism workforce and its working conditions as follows:

- it is, on average, young
- it is characterised by female, part-time employment

- it has more casual and part-time work than other industries, but the majority of hours are nevertheless worked by full-time employees
- it is poorly unionised
- it is relatively low-skilled work
- the hours of work are sometimes considered unsociable
- the pay is relatively low
- it is a mobile workforce with high turnover rates
- the workforce has low levels of formal educational qualifications.

Tourism employment has particular characteristics stemming from the spatial and temporal fixity of tourism consumption and production (Shaw and Williams 1994). Tourism services have to be experienced *in situ*, and (in most senses) they are not spatially transferable and cannot be deferred (Urry 1987). This implies that the tourism labour force has to be assembled *in situ* at the point of consumption and, moreover, that it is available at particular time periods. The nature of demand is such that a labour force is required with sufficient flexibility to meet daily, weekly and seasonal fluctuations. The extent to which these conditions generate migration flows, rather than reliance on local labour, is contingent on a number of factors, both intrinsic to the tourism development and to the locality. Two prime considerations are the scale of demand and the speed of tourism development, the latter affecting the extent to which labour may be transferred from other sectors of the local economy/society. In addition, the degree of enclavism or spatial polarisation is important, with the dependency on migration likely to be positively correlated with this. Over time the spatial form of tourism consumption and production is in constant flux. In addition, local demographic, social and economic structures will condition the availability of local labour and the requirement for in-migration. Comparative wage differentials, levels of education and training, working conditions and job status in tourism and other sectors all influence the availability of workers, as does the overall level of unemployment. For example, the availability of better paid and higher status jobs in other sectors

has conditioned the requirement for immigrant labour in the Swiss tourist industry (King 1995). Finally, the degree of temporal polarisation is also significant, for the demands for in-migration are likely to be greatest in large-scale, single-peaked season destinations. All else being equal, the lack of alternative jobs outside of the peak time period will mean either seasonal unemployment in the local labour market or reliance on seasonal labour migrants (King 1995).

Tourism labour migration is also highly segmented (A.M. Williams and Hall 2002). King (1995) identified a hierarchy of labour migrants in respect of tourism. In the first rank are skilled managerial posts, typically found in the upper enclaves of major international hotels and local branches of leading airlines. It can be hypothesised that there will be greater reliance on immigrants to fill such posts in less developed economies where there are shortages of such human capital. The second rank consists of intermediate posts such as tour guides and agency representatives, where the ability to speak the language of international tourists, and even to share their nationality (if only for the purpose of consumer reassurance), is considered critical. Finally, the third level of the hierarchy comprises unskilled labour which is relatively common, given low entry thresholds to most tourist jobs. The pay and working conditions of each of these three ranks in the hierarchy is likely to be varied, as are the national origins of each stream of migrants. For example, although research is somewhat limited, there is evidence to suggest that in the Pacific Islands, core positions are often taken by expatriate workers while 'peripheral' positions are taken by indigenous employees (Minerbi 1992).

The significance of migration in tourism labour markets therefore stems from three main features (Williams and Hall 2000). First, it serves to fill absolute shortages of labour, particularly in areas of rapid tourism expansion or where tourism is highly spatially polarised. However, the first two levels of the migration hierarchy may also function to fill particular employment niches, even where there are no generalised labour shortages. Second, the availability of migrant labour will help to reduce labour market pressures, and consequently wage inflation pressures. Third, labour migration can contribute to labour market segmentation, and especially where the divisions are along racial/ethnic or legal/illegal lines, this can serve to reduce the costs of labour to firms. Labour migration therefore serves to ensure that the process of tourism capital accumulation is not undermined. Nevertheless, labour migration also has two other significant functions with respect to tourism. The first of these is the generation of visits to friends and visitors. Second, labour migration experiences do help to define the search spaces of lifestyle and retirement migrants, as King et al. (1998) have shown with respect to retirement from the UK to southern Europe (Williams and Hall 2002).

Thus to understand some of these components of the tourism production system the geographer is required to appreciate concepts related to capital–labour relations, the interweaving of consumption, the business environment associated with the competitive strategies of enterprises, economic concepts (e.g. transaction analysis), product differentiation, international business as a mode of operation and global markets, along with basic business and marketing concepts. Within a capitalist mode of production this is essential so that one may understand how each component in the tourism production system operates (i.e. how it develops products, generates profits and competes with other businesses) and how social groups and places are incorporated into the production system, so that the production system and the spatial relationships which exist may be fully understood (see insight below). To illustrate these ideas, the example of international hotel chains is used to examine relationships between the geography of supply, functions, the industrial structure of the business and the social relations which exist.

INSIGHT: Economic globalisation

Globalisation is a complex, chaotic, multiscalar, multitemporal and multicentric series of processes operating in specific structural and spatial contexts (Jessop 1999; Amin 2002). Globalisation should be seen as an emergent, evolutionary phenomenon which results from economic, political, socio-cultural and technological processes on many scales rather than a distinctive causal mechanism in its own right. It is both a structural and a structuring phenomenon the nature of which depends critically on sub-global processes. According to Jessop (1999: 21) 'structurally, globalisation would exist in so far as co-variation of relevant activities becomes more global in extent and/or the speed of that covariation on a global scale increases'. Therefore, global interdependence typically results from processes which operate at various spatial scales, in different functional subsystems, and involve complex and tangled causal hierarchies rather being a simple, unilinear, bottom-up or top-down movement (Jessop 1999). Such an observation clearly suggests that globalisation is developing unevenly across space and time. Indeed, 'a key element in contemporary processes of globalisation is not the impact of "global" processes upon another clearly defined scale, but instead the relativisation of scale' (Kelly and Olds 1999: 2). Such relativities occur in relation to both 'space–time distantiation' and 'space–time compression'. The former refers to the stretching of social relations over time and space, e.g. through the utilisation of new technology such as the internet, so that they can be co-ordinated or controlled over longer periods of time, greater distances, larger areas, and on more scales of activity. The latter involves the intensification of 'discrete' events in real time and/or increased velocity of material and non-material flows over a given distance; again this is related to technological change, including communication technologies, and social technologies (Jessop 1999).

The discourse of globalisation therefore goes further than the simple description of contemporary social change; it also carries with it the power to shape material reality via the practical politics of policy formulation and implementation (Gibson-Graham 1996; Kelly and Olds 1999). It can also construct a view of geographical space that implies the deferral of political options from the national to the supranational and global scales, and from the local to the national. In effect, globalisation 'itself has become a political force, helping to create the institutional realities it purportedly merely describes' (Piven 1995: 8), as indicated by the growth of structures such as APEC and NAFTA. In addition to the 'structural context' of globalisation noted above, authors such as Ohmae (1995), Jessop (1999) and Higgott (1999) point to a more strategic interpretation of globalisation, which refer to individual and institutional actors' attempts to promote the global co-ordination of activities on a continuing basis within different orders or functional systems. For example, interpersonal networking, inter-firm strategic alliances, the creation of international and supranational regimes to govern particular fields of action, and the broader development of modes of international and supranational systems of governance. Therefore, given the multiscale, multitemporal and multicentric nature of globalisation, we can recognise that globalisation 'rarely, if ever, involves the full structural integration and strategic coordination across the globe' (Jessop 1999: 22). Instead, processes usually considered under the rubric of 'economic globalisation' include the following:

- The formation of regional economic and trading blocs – particularly in the triadic regions of North America (North American Free Trade Area (NAFTA)), Europe (European Union (EU)) and East Asia-Pacific (Asia-Pacific Economic Cooperation) – and the development of formal links between those blocs (e.g. the Asia-Europe Meetings). In all of these regions tourism is a major component of economic and social policy (Hall 2001a).

- The growth of 'local internationalisation', 'virtual regions', through the development of economic ties between contiguous (e.g. 'border regions') or non-contiguous local and regional state authorities (e.g. growth regions and triangles) in different national economies which often bypass the level of the nation state but which still retain support at the national level. For example, the Pacific North West Economic Region (PNWER), consisting of the American states of Alaska, Idaho, Montana, Oregon and Washington plus the Canadian provinces of Alberta, British Columbia and Yukon Territory, as well private sector members, has a tourism working group to promote greater economic development in the region (Hall 2001a).

- The widening and deepening of international and supranational regimes which cover economic and economically relevant issues and which may also provide for regional institutionalised governance.

- The internationalisation of national economic spaces through growing penetration (inward flows) and extraversion (outward flows) as with the increasing mobility of tourists and capital.

- The extension and deepening of multinationalisation by multinational firms including hospitality and tourism firms.

- The 'emergence of globalisation proper through the introduction and acceptance of global norms and standards, the development of globally integrated markets together with globally oriented strategies, and "deracinated" firms with no evident national operational base' (Jessop 1999: 23).

INTERNATIONAL HOTEL CHAINS

The hotel industry is arguably a global industry, since it fulfils some of the criteria which distinguish businesses as truly global, whereby it may be one which can create a competitive advantage from its activities on a worldwide basis. Alternatively it may be one in which the strategic positions of competitors in major geographic or national markets are fundamentally affected by their overall global positions (Porter 1980: 175). Much of the debate on the influence of international hotel chains may be dated to the research by Dunning and McQueen (1982) on what constitutes a multinational, international and transnational firm. Dunning and McQueen's (1982) use of an international hotel company, which has direct investments and other types of contractual agreements in more than one country, remains a simple but effective definition (see also Shaw and Williams 1994: 120–5). One concept which economists and sociologists have embraced to analyse the linkages of transnational companies in local and regional tourism economies is embeddedness. This essentially refers to the links between external capital and local firms' relationships, though it has proved problematic to adequately operationalise in tourism, since the concept is also opaque (Agarwal et al. 2000), as researchers seek to define the most appropriate methodologies to use to measure and understand embeddedness.

Britton (1991: 460) analysed the product which hotel chains offered in terms of their competitive strategies as a package of on-premises services which provide a certain experience (ambience, lifestyle) based on kinds and qualities of accommodation, on-site recreation and shopping facilities, and catering, the offering of off-premises services (airport shuttles, local excursions, booking facilities) and a trademark guarantee which signals to the customer a predictable quality of service.

The competitive strategies which follow from these features are based on an understanding of the customer (i.e. needs and preferences), where the brand name is able to command a premium price in the marketplace. Britton (1991: 460) explains the commercial advantage of international chains in terms of

- the firms' location in the customers' home country
- experience in understanding demand through operating hotels in the domestic markets
- managerial expertise and staff training to ensure the elements of the tourists' experience related to the brand name are met through appropriate training and operating manuals.

The key to successful competition is for the hotel company to internalise its firm-specific intellectual property (i.e. training methods and manuals), while ensuring profit levels for shareholders. Unfortunately this is extremely difficult when staff leave and move to competitors, since the intellectual property is essentially 'know-how'. Yet this is often the basis for horizontal integration into overseas markets, with management contracts a preferred mechanism for operation rather than outright ownership to control design, operation, pricing and staffing, though the same companies (e.g. Holiday Inns) prefer to use franchising as a mechanism to control managerial, organisational and professional input. One notable dimension here is the effect of international hotel and tourism development on less developed countries. For example, in Kenya, 60 per cent of hotel beds were accounted for through equity participation schemes with such hotel groups (Rosemary 1987; Sinclair 1991). The implications are that where international involvement occurs, there is a concomitant loss of central control and leakage of foreign earnings, and where there is concentrated development of enclaves remote from local population this inevitably leads to little benefit for the host country. Despite these problems, attitudes towards such development among a survey of 22 developing countries (WTO 1985) saw the benefits outweighing the cash. This may lead to dependency relationships, as Britton (1980a) indicated in his innovative study of the distribution of ownership and commercial control by metropolitan tourist markets of less developed world destinations. In the context of the UK, the corporate

Table 3.6: Operating performance of Hilton International by region in 2001

	Turnover (£ million)	Profit (£ million)
UK	598.2	126.1
Europe, Middle East and Africa	786.9	72.8
Asia / Australasia	496.6	14.0
Living Well (health and fitness clubs in the UK)	53.8	4.1
New Scandic operation (154 hotels with 132 in Scandinavia)	257.2	33.9
	2,454.5	255.3

Source: modified from Hilton Group plc (2002)

organisation of tourism production also exhibits a core–periphery relationship, defined by the location of corporate headquarters and the higher level posts in the hotel, airline and tour operator sector which are largely located in London. While some lower level order jobs have been located in peripheral regions to take advantage of low labour and premises costs (e.g. call centres), decisions involving capital, the form of production and its spatial distribution are firmly embedded in London and south-east England. Indeed, the transnational nature of some tour operators (e.g. Pressaug, the German conglomerate which controlled Thomson Holidays in the UK) highlights how investment and production decisions also have a transnational and global dimension. An indication of the global operating budgets for one international hotel chain (Hilton International) can be seen in Table 3.6. The

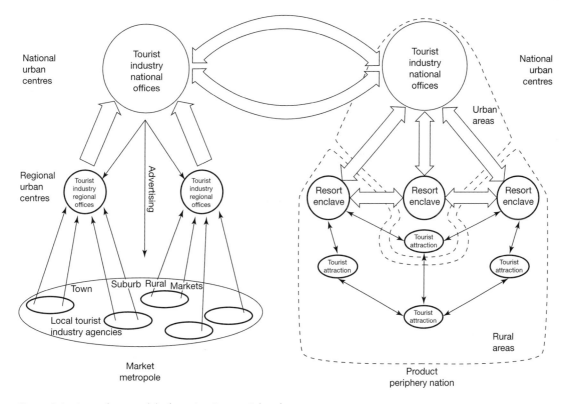

Figure 3.4: An enclave model of tourism in a peripheral economy
Source: redrawn from Britton (1980a)

company also owns and operates the Ladbrokes retail betting businesses in the UK, the eGaming business in fourteen currencies and football pools (the Vernon brand) in the UK, illustrating diversification in the tourism and leisure sector.

Britton's model of tourism development (Figure 3.4) illustrates the nature of tourism dependency, where international tourism organisations (in the absence of strong government control) develop and perpetuate a hierarchical element to tourism development. While dependency theory is useful in explaining how capitalist production leads to the resulting patterns of tourism demand and supply, it is evident that this is only a simplification of the wider geographical dimensions of capital–labour relations in a global context, where political economy perspectives assist in explaining the processes leading to the spatial patterns of tourism development that occur. The economic dynamics of the tourism production system begin to help to develop a more central perspective of tourism which fits into the broader conceptualisation of capitalist accumulation, and the social construction of reality, though marketing and the construction of place may provide new areas for future geographical research. In fact, what one realises from a critical analysis of tourism using political economy perspectives is that it is a constantly changing phenomenon, with an ever-changing spatial organisation. The processes affecting the political economy of production and consumption require a critical awareness of the role and activities of entrepreneurs, the flow of capital and its internationalisation, the impact of industrial and regional restructuring, urban development, changes in the service economy and how the production of tourism results in new landscapes of tourism in a contemporary society (Meethan 2004). Aside from theoretical analysis, geographers have developed other concepts and methods of analysis, and we now turn to these approaches.

Primary elements

Activity place

Cultural facilities
- Concert halls
- Cinemas
- Exhibitions
- Museums and art galleries
- Theatres

Sports facilities
- Indoor and outdoor

Amusement facilities
- Bingo halls
- Casinos
- Festivities
- Night-clubs
- Organised events

Leisure setting

Physical characteristics
- Ancient monuments and statues
- Ecclesiastical buildings
- Harbours
- Historical street pattern
- Interesting buildings
- Parks and green areas
- Water, canals and river fronts

Socio-cultural features
- Folklore
- Friendliness
- Language
- Liveliness and ambience of the place
- Local customs and costumes
- Security

Secondary elements
- Hotels and catering facilities
- Markets
- Shopping facilities

Additional elements
- Accessibility and parking facilities
- Tourist facilities: information offices, signposts, guides, maps and leaflets

Figure 3.5: The elements of tourism
Source: modified from Jansen-Verbeke (1986)

THE LEISURE PRODUCT

Within the context of urban tourism, Jansen-Verbeke (1986) viewed the urban area as a 'leisure product' (Figure 3.5) which comprises primary elements including a variety of facilities that may be grouped into:

- an activity place, thereby defining the overall supply features within the city, particularly the main tourist attractions
- a leisure setting, which includes both the physical elements in the built environment and the socio-cultural characteristics which give a city a distinct image and 'sense of place' (see Walmesley and Jenkins 1992 for a discussion of this concept) for visitors

and secondary elements which consist of

- the supporting facilities and services which tourists consume during their visit (e.g. hotel and catering outlets and shopping facilities) which shape the visitors' experience of the services available in the city
- additional elements which consist of the tourism infrastructure that conditions the visit, such as the availability of car parking, tourist transport provision and accessibility and tourist-specific services (e.g. visitor information centres and tourist signposting).

Shaw and Williams (1994) rightly argue that

while such an approach allows a systematic consideration of the supply side of urban tourism, it is not without its difficulties. For example, in many cities, the so-called secondary elements of shops and restaurants may well be the main attractions for certain groups of visitors.

(Shaw and Williams 1994: 202)

Nevertheless, the supply-side variables within the context of the urban tourism system help in understanding the interrelationships between supply and demand and the interaction between the consumers and the products. In this respect, it is also useful to identify what aspect of the 'leisure product' tourists consume; some may consume only one product (e.g. a visit to an art gallery) while others may consume what Jansen-Verbeke (1988) terms a 'bundle of products' (i.e. several products during their stay such as a visit to a theatre, museum and a meal in a restaurant).

Jansen-Verbeke (1986) examined this concept within the inner-city tourism system to identify the nature of tourists visiting the inner city and the organisations responsible for the promotion of the inner city as an area for tourists to visit. The role of organisations promoting urban areas for tourism is discussed in more detail in Chapter 6, but to explain Jansen-Verbeke's (1986) analysis it is useful to consider the relationship which she believes exists between the product, the tourist and the promoter. Promoters affect the relationship in two ways:

- they build an image of the inner city and its tourists' resources to attract potential tourists, investors and employers
- the promotion of the inner city may also lead to direct product improvement.

Consequently, the model that Jansen-Verbeke (1986) constructs (Figure 3.5) illustrates how different elements of the inner-city tourism system are interrelated and the significance of the inner city as a leisure product. However, the public and private sector have distinct roles to play in this context.

ROLE OF THE PUBLIC AND PRIVATE SECTOR IN TOURISM SUPPLY

D.G. Pearce (1989) observed that the

provision of services and facilities characteristically involves a wide range of agents of development. Some of these will be involved indirectly and primarily with meeting the needs of tourists, a role that has fallen predominantly to the private sector in most countries. . . . Other agents will facilitate, control or limit development . . . through the provision of basic infrastructure, planning or regulation. Such activities have commonly been the responsibility of the public sector with the government at various levels being charged with looking after the public's interest and providing goods and services whose cost cannot be attributed directly to groups or individuals.

(D.G. Pearce 1989: 32)

Pearce's comments illustrate the essential distinction between the role of the private and public sector in the provision of services and facilities for tourists that existed for much of the twentieth century. However, the tendency to privatise and commercialise functions that were once performed by government has been almost universal in western nations since the late 1970s and has affected the nature of many national governments' involvement in the tourism industry (Hall 1994). According to Hall and Jenkins (1995), three principal reasons for this trend may be identified. Governments are interested in

- reducing the dependency of public enterprises on public budgets
- reducing public debt by selling state assets
- raising technical efficiencies by commercialisation.

This has meant that there has been a much greater blurring in the roles of the public and private sectors with the development of enterprise boards, development corporations and similar organisations. In such a political and economic climate the role of government in tourism has undergone a dramatic shift from a traditional public administration model which sought to implement government policy for a perceived public good, to a corporatist model which emphasises efficiency, investment returns, the role of the market, and relations with stakeholders, usually defined as industry. Corporatism, here, is used in the sense of a dominant ideology in western society which claims rationality as its central quality and which emphasises a notion of individualism in terms of self-interest rather than the legitimacy of the individual citizen acting in the democratic interest of the public good. However, in many policy areas including tourism, the changed role

of the state and the individual's relation to the state provides a major policy quandary. On the one hand, there is the demand for less government interference in the market and allowing industries to develop and trade without government subsidy or assistance while, on the other, industry interest groups seek to have government policy developed in their favour, including the maintenance of government funding for promotion as in the case of the tourism industry. This policy issue has generally been resolved through the restructuring of national and regional tourist organisations not only to reduce their planning, policy and development roles and increase their marketing and promotion functions, but also to engage in a greater range of partnerships, network and collaborative relationships with stakeholders. Such a situation has been described by Milward (1996) as the hollowing out of the state in which the role of the state has been transformed from one of hierarchical control to one in which governing is dispersed among a number of separate, non-government entities. This has therefore led to increased emphasis on governance through network structures as a 'new process of governing; or a changed condition of ordered rule; or the new method by which society is governed' (Rhodes 1997: 43).

Awareness of the need of tourist organisations to create links with stakeholders is, of course, not new. The community tourism approach of P.E. Murphy (1985, 1988) emphasised the importance of involving the community in destination management because of their role as key stakeholders, although in actuality this often meant collaboratively working with industry and community-based groups in a destination context rather than through wider public participation mechanisms. The difficulty in implementing community-based tourism strategies is reflective of wider difficulties with respect to effective destination management and tourism planning (Davidson and Maitland 1997), namely the diffuse nature of tourism phenomena within economy and society and the problem this creates with respect to co-ordination and management. Nevertheless, while collaboration clearly has potential to contribute to the development of more sustainable forms of tourism in that they can create social capital, it has to be emphasised that the goal of partnership, as emphasised by a number of western governments which have restructured their involvement in tourism in recent years, need not be the same as an inclusive collaborative approach.

In the case of the United Kingdom, for example, many of the partnerships established between government and business in the 1980s and early 1990s as part of urban and regional development programmes have been heavily criticised for their narrow stakeholder and institutional base. Goodwin (1993: 161) argued that in order to ensure that urban leisure and tourism development projects were carried out, 'local authorities have had planning and development powers removed and handed to an unelected institution. Effectively, an appointed agency is, in each case, replacing the powers of local government in order to carry out a market-led regeneration of each inner city'. Harvey (1989a) recognised that

> the new entrepreneurialism of the smaller state has, as its centrepiece, the notion of a 'public–private partnership' in which a traditional local boosterism is integrated with the use of local government powers to try [to] attract external sources of funding, new direct investments, or new employment sources.
>
> (Harvey 1989a: 7)

In this case, partnership does not include all members of a community: those who do not have enough money, are not from the right lifestyle, or simply do not have sufficient power, are ignored. For example, in referring to Derwentside in the north-east of England, Sadler (1993) argued:

> The kind of policy which had been adopted – and which was proving increasingly ineffective even in terms of its own stated objectives . . . rested not so much on a basis of rational choice, but rather was a simple reflection of the narrow political and intellectual scope for alternatives. This restricted area did not come about purely or simply by chance, but had been deliberately encouraged and fostered.
>
> (Sadler 1993: 190)

The private sector

As Britton (1991) observed earlier, the private sector's involvement in tourism is most likely to be motivated by profit, as tourism entrepreneurs (Shaw and Williams 1994) invest in business opportunities. This gives rise to a complex array of large organisations and operators involved in tourism (e.g. multinational chain hotels – Forte and the Holiday Inn) and an array of smaller businesses and operators, often employing fewer than ten people or working on a self-employed basis (Page et al. 1999). If left unchecked, this sector is likely to give rise to conflicts in the operation of tourism where the state takes a *laissez-faire* role in tourism planning and management.

The public sector

In contrast to the private sector, the public sector involves government at a variety of geographical scales and may become involved in tourism for various economic, political, social and environmental reasons (Table 3.7). The International Union of Tourism Organisations (IUOTO 1974), the forerunner to the WTO, in its discussion of the role of the state in tourism, identified five areas of public sector involvement in tourism: co-ordination, planning, legislation, regulation and entrepreneur stimulation. To this may be added two other functions: a social tourism role, which is very significant in European tourism (Murphy 1985), and a broader role of interest protection (Hall 1994).

Much intervention in tourism is related to market failure, market imperfection and social need. The market method of deciding who gets what and how is not always adequate, and therefore government often changes the distribution of income and wealth by measures that work within the price system. Across the globe almost every industry has been supported at various times by subsidies, the imposition of tariff regulations, taxation concessions, direct grants and other forms of government intervention, all of which serve to affect the price of goods and services and therefore influence the distribution of income, production and wealth. The size or economic importance of

Table 3.7: Some reasons for government involvement
in tourism

Economic reasons
- to improve the balance of payments in a country
- to attract foreign exchange
- to aid regional (or local) economic development
- to diversify the economy
- to increase income levels
- to increase state revenue from taxes
- to generate new employment opportunities

Social and cultural reasons
- to achieve social objectives related to 'social tourism'
  to ensure the well-being and health of families and
  individuals
- to protect cultural mores, traditions, resources and
  heritage
- to promote a greater cultural awareness of an area
  and its people
- to promote international understanding

Environmental reasons
- to undertake the stewardship of the environment and
  tourism resources to ensure that the agents of
  development do not destroy the future basis for
  sustainable tourism development
- to create a natural resource which will serve to attract
  tourists

Political reasons
- to further political objectives by promoting the
  development of tourism in order to broaden the
  political acceptance of a government among visitors
- to control the development process associated with
  tourism
- to protect the public interest and the interests of
  minorities
- to further political ideology

Sources: C. Jenkins and Henry (1982); D.G. Pearce (1989);
Hall (1994); Hall and Jenkins (1995)

the tourism industry, so commonly emphasised by
the public and private sectors, is no justification in
itself for government intervention; within market-
driven economies justification must lie in some
aspect of

- market failure
- market imperfection
- public/social concerns about market outcomes.

Therefore, implicit in each justification for intervention is the view that government offers a corrective
alternative to the market (Hall and Jenkins 1998).

The role of the state as entrepreneur in tourist
development is closely related to the concept of
the 'devalorisation of capital' (Damette 1980).
The 'devalorisation of capital' is the process by
which the state subsidises part of the cost of production, for instance, by assisting in the provision
of infrastructure or by investing in a tourism project
where private venture capital is otherwise unavail-
able. In this process what would have been private
costs are transformed into public or social costs.
The provision of infrastructure, particularly transport networks, is regarded as crucial to the
development of tourist destinations (Page 2005).
There are numerous formal and informal means for
government at all levels to assist in minimising the
costs of production for tourism developers. Indeed,
the offer of government assistance for development
is often used to encourage private investment in a
particular region or tourist project; for instance,
through the provision of cheap land or government-
backed low-interest loans.

As well as acting as entrepreneurs, governments
can also stimulate tourism in several ways: first,
financial incentives such as low-interest loans or a
depreciation allowance on tourist accommodation
or infrastructure, although 'their introduction often
reflected both the scarcity of domestic investment
funds and widespread ambition to undertake economic development programmes' (Bodlender and
Davies 1985, quoted in D.G. Pearce 1992b: 11);
second, sponsoring research for the benefit of the
tourism industry rather than for specific individual
organisations and associations; third, marketing
and promotion generally aimed at generating
tourism demand, although it may also take the form
of investment promotion aimed at encouraging
capital investment for tourism attractions and
facilities (Hall 1995).

One of the more unusual features of tourism
promotion by government tourism organisations is
that they have only limited control over the product
they are marketing, with very few actually owning
the goods, facilities and services that make up the

tourism product (D.G. Pearce 1992b). This lack of control is perhaps testimony to the power of the public good argument used by industry to justify continued maintenance of government funding for destination promotion. However, it may also indicate the political power of the tourism lobby, such as industry organisations, to influence government tourism policies (Hall and Jenkins 1995).

Throughout most of the 1980s and the early 1990s, 'Thatcherism' (named after Conservative Prime Minister Margaret Thatcher) in the United Kingdom and 'Reaganism' (named after Republican President Ronald Reagan) in the United States saw a period of retreat by central government from active intervention. At the national level, policies of deregulation, privatisation, free trade, the elimination of tax incentives and a move away from discretionary forms of macro-economic intervention, were and have been the hallmarks of a push towards 'smaller' government and lower levels of government intervention. Given such demand for smaller government in western society in recent years, there have been increasing demands from government and economic rationalists for greater industry self-sufficiency in tourism marketing and promotion. The political implications of such an approach for the tourism industry are substantial. As H.L. Hughes (1984: 14) noted, 'The advocates of a free enterprise economy would look to consumer freedom of choice and not to governments to promote firms; the consumer ought to be sovereign in decisions relating to the allocation of the nation's resources.' Such an approach means that lobbyists in the tourism industry may do better by shifting their focus on the necessity of government intervention to issues of externalities, public goods and merit wants rather than employment and the balance of payments (Hall 1994). 'Such criteria for government intervention have a sounder economic base and are more consistent with a free-enterprise philosophy than employment and balance of payments effects' (H.L. Hughes 1984: 18). Nevertheless, as D.G. Pearce (1992b) recognised,

> general destination promotion tends to benefit all sectors of the tourist industry in the place concerned;

> it becomes a 'public good'. . . . The question of 'free-loaders' thus arises, for they too will benefit along with those who may have contributed directly to the promotional campaign.
>
> (D.G. Pearce 1992b: 8)

In many cases, the state's involvement is to ensure a policy of intervention so that political objectives associated with employment generation and planning are achieved, although this varies from one country to another and from city to city according to the political persuasion of the organisation involved. D.G. Pearce (1989) rightly acknowledges, however, that

> the public sector then is by no means a single entity with clear cut responsibilities and well-defined policies for tourist development. Rather, the public sector becomes involved in tourism for a wide range of reasons in a variety of ways at different levels and through many agencies and institutions . . . [and] there is often a lack of coordination, unnecessary competition, duplication of effort in some areas and neglect in others.
>
> (D.G. Pearce 1989: 44)

SPATIAL ANALYTICAL APPROACHES TO THE SUPPLY OF TOURISM FACILITIES

Much of the research on tourism supply in relation to facilities and services is descriptive in content, based on inventories and lists of the facilities and where they are located. In view of the wide range of literature that discusses the distribution of specific facilities or services, it is more useful to consider only two specific examples of how such approaches and concepts may be used to derive generalisations of patterns of tourism activity.

The tourism business district

Within the literature on the supply of urban tourism, Ashworth (1989) reviews the 'facility approach' which offers researchers the opportunity to map the location of specific facilities, undertaking inventories of facilities on a city-wide basis. The difficulty with such an approach is that the users of urban services and facilities are not just tourists, since workers and residents as well as recreationists may use the same facilities. Therefore, any inventory will be only a partial view of the full range of facilities and potential services tourists could use. One useful approach is to identify the areas in which the majority of tourist activities occur and to use it as the focus for the analysis of the supply of tourism services in such a multifunctional city which meets a wide range of uses for a wide range of users (see Chapter 5). This avoids the individual assessments of the location and use of specific aspects of tourism services such as accommodation (Page and Sinclair 1989), entertainment facilities such as restaurants (S.L.J. Smith 1983b, 1989) and night-life entertainment facilities (Ashworth et al. 1988) plus other attractions. This approach embraces the ecological approaches developed in human geography to pinpoint regions within cities as a basis to identify the processes shaping the patterns.

The ecological approach towards the analysis of urban tourism dates back to E.W. Gilbert's (1949) assessment of the development of resorts, which was further refined by Barrett (1958). The outcome is a resort model where accommodation, entertainment and commercial zones exist and the central location of tourism facilities were dominant elements. The significance of such research is that it identifies some of the features and relationships which were subsequently developed in urban geography and applied to tourism and recreation. The most notable study is Stansfield and Rickert's (1970) development of the Recreational Business District (RBD). This study rightly identifies the multifunctional land use of the central areas of cities, including tourism and recreational activities, in relation to the central area for business (Central Business District (CBD)). Meyer-Arendt (1990) also expands this notion in the context of the Gulf of Mexico coastal resorts, while D.G. Pearce (1989) offers a useful critique of these studies. The essential ideas in the RBD have subsequently been extended to urban and resort tourism to try to explain where the location and distribution of the range of visitor-oriented functions occur in space.

Burtenshaw et al.'s (1991) seminal study of tourism and recreation in European cities deals with the concept of the Central Tourist District (CTD) where tourism activities in cities are concentrated in certain areas. This has been termed the TBD by Getz (1993a: 583–4), who argues that it is

The concentration of visitor-oriented attractions and services located in conjunction with urban central businesses (CBD) functions. In older cities, especially in Europe, the TBD and CBD often coincide with heritage areas. Owing to their high visibility and economic importance, TBDs can be subjected to intense planning by municipal authorities. . . . The form and evolution of TBDs reveals much about the nature of urban tourism and its impacts, while the analysis of the planning systems influencing TBDs can contribute to concepts and methods for better planning of tourism in urban areas.

Therefore, TBDs are a useful framework in which to understand the supply components of urban tourism and how they fit together. Figure 3.6, based on Getz's (1993a) analysis of the TBD, is a schematic model in which the functions rather than geographical patterns of activities are considered.

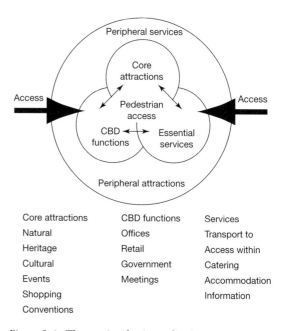

Core attractions	CBD functions	Services
Natural	Offices	Transport to
Heritage	Retail	Access within
Cultural	Government	Catering
Events	Meetings	Accommodation
Shopping		Information
Conventions		

Figure 3.6: The tourism business district
Source: based on Getz (1993a)

Plate 3.3: Stirling, Scotland. Events such as the Highland Games have worldwide repute and are also hosted in other countries with Scottish migration as a form of cultural heritage (copyright: AILLST).

Plate 3.5: Historic reconstructions such as a Scottish Medieval Fair provide an enticing experience for visitors in the urban environment (copyright: AILLST).

Plate 3.4: Trossachs, Scotland. Literature and art have popularised wilder areas, such as Sir Walter Scott's 'Lady of the Lake' in the Trossachs, as illustrated by visitors sailing on the SS *Sir Walter Scott* at Loch Katrine (copyright: AILLST).

This model illustrates the difficulty of separating visitor-oriented services from the CBD and use of services and facilities by residents and workers. Yet as Jansen-Verbeke and Ashworth (1990) argue, while tourism and recreational activities are integrated within the physical, social and economic context of the city, no analytical framework exists to determine the functional or behavioural interactions in these activities. They argue that more research is needed to assess the extent to which the clustering of tourism and recreational activities can occur in cities without leading to incompatible and conflicting uses from such facilities. While the TBD may offer a distinctive blend of activities and attractions for tourist and non-tourist alike, it is important to recognise these issues where tourism clusters in areas such as the TBD. Even so, the use of street entertainment and special events and festivals (Getz 1997) may also add to the ambience and sense of place for both the city worker and visitor. By having a concentration of tourism and non-tourism resources and services in one accessible area within a city, it is possible to encourage visitors to stay there, making it a place tourists will want to visit, as is the case in the West End of London (Page and Sinclair 1989; Page and Hall 2002). However, the attractions in urban areas are an important component in the appeal to potential visitors.

Tourism attractions

Attractions are an integral feature of urban tourism, which offer visitors passive and more active occupations on which to spend their time during a visit. They also comprise a key component of Jansen-Verbeke's (1986) 'primary element' (Figure 3.5). Recent studies have adapted descriptive analyses of specific types of attraction (e.g. Law 1993) rather than exploring their relationship with urban tourists. Lew (1987: 54) acknowledges that 'although the importance of tourist attractions is readily recognised, tourism researchers and theorists have yet to fully come to terms with the nature of attractions as phenomena both in the environment and the mind'. As a result, Lew's (1987) study

and Leiper's (1990) synthesis and conceptual framework of 'Tourist Attraction Systems' remain among the most theoretically informed literature published to date. Lew (1987) identifies three perspectives used to understand the nature of tourist attractions:

- *The ideographic perspective*, where the general characteristics of a place, site, climate, culture and customs are used to develop typologies of tourism attractions, involving inventories or general descriptions. For example, Standard Industrial Classification codes (SICs) are one approach used to group attractions (see S.L.J. Smith 1989). These approaches are the ones most commonly used to examine tourist attractions in the general tourism literature.
- *The organisational perspective*, in contrast, tends to emphasise the geographical, capacity and temporal aspects (the time dimension) of attractions rather than the 'managerial notions of organisation' (Leiper 1990: 175). This approach examines scales ranging from the individual attraction to larger areas and their attractions.
- *The cognitive perspective* is based on 'studies of tourist perceptions and experiences of attractions' (Lew 1987: 560). P.L. Pearce (1982: 98) recognises that any tourist place (or attraction) is one capable of fostering the feeling of being a tourist. Therefore, the cognitive perspective is interested in understanding the tourists' feelings and views of the place or attraction.

The significance of Lew's (1987) framework is that it acknowledges the importance of attractions as a research focus, although Leiper (1990) questions the definition of attractions used by many researchers. He pursues the ideas developed by MacCannell (1976: 41), that an attraction incorporates 'an empirical relationship between a tourist, a sight and a marker, a piece of information about a sight'. A 'marker' is an item of information about any phenomenon which could be used to highlight the tourist's awareness of the potential existence of a tourist attraction.

This implies that an attraction has a number of components, while conventional definitions consider only the sight (Leiper 1990: 177). In this respect, 'the tourist attraction is a system comprising three elements: a tourist, a sight and a marker' (Leiper 1990: 178). Although sightseeing is a common tourist activity, the idea of a sight really refers to the nucleus or central component of the attraction (Gunn 1972). In this context a situation could include a sight where sightseeing occurs, but it may also be an object, person or event. Based on this argument, Leiper (1990: 178) introduces the following definition of a tourist attraction as 'a system comprising three elements: a tourist or human element, a nucleus or central element, and a marker or informative element. A tourist attraction comes into existence when the three elements are interconnected'. On the basis of this alternative approach to attractions, Leiper (1990) identifies the type of information which is likely to give meaning to the tourist experience of urban destinations in relation to their attractions.

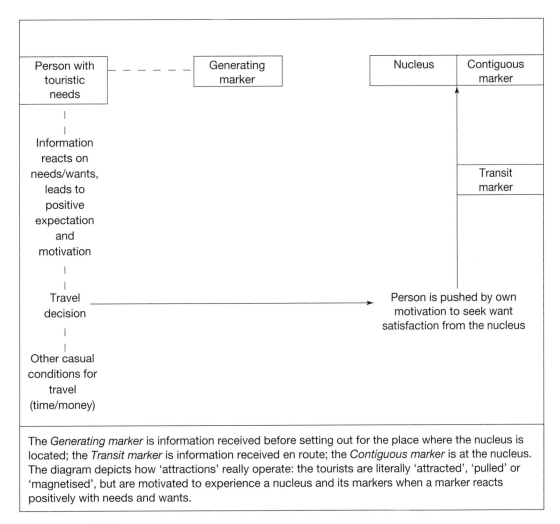

The *Generating marker* is information received before setting out for the place where the nucleus is located; the *Transit marker* is information received en route; the *Contiguous marker* is at the nucleus. The diagram depicts how 'attractions' really operate: the tourists are literally 'attracted', 'pulled' or 'magnetised', but are motivated to experience a nucleus and its markers when a marker reacts positively with needs and wants.

Figure 3.7: Model of a tourism attraction system
Source: based on Leiper (1990)

These ideas were developed further in Leiper's model of a tourist attraction system (Figure 3.7), breaking the established view that tourists are not simply 'attracted' or 'pulled' to areas on the basis of their attractions. Instead, visitors are motivated to experience a nucleus and its markers in a situation where the marker reacts positively with their needs and wants. Figure 3.7 identifies the linkages within the model and how tourist motivation is influenced by the information available and the individual's perception of their needs. Thus, an attraction system may develop only when the following have become connected:

- a person with tourist needs
- a nucleus (a feature or attribute of a place that tourists seek to visit)
- a marker (information about the nucleus).

This theoretical framework has a great deal of value in relation to understanding the supply of urban tourism resources for visitors. First, it views an attraction system as a subsystem of the larger tourism system in an urban area. Second, it acknowledges the integral role for the tourist as consumer: without the tourist (or day tripper) the system would not exist. Third, the systems approach offers a convenient social science framework in which to understand how urban destinations attract visitors, with different markers and nuclei to attract specific groups of visitors. Having examined the significance of different approaches towards the analysis of tourism supply in urban areas, attention turns to the significance of different components of Jansen-Verbeke's leisure product and tourism destinations.

TOURIST FACILITIES

Among the 'secondary elements' of the leisure product in urban areas, four components emerge as central to servicing tourist needs (Jansen-Verbeke 1986). These are

- accommodation

- catering facilities
- tourist shopping
- conditional elements.

Accommodation

Tourist accommodation performs an important function in cities: it provides the opportunity for visitors to stay for a length of time to enjoy the locality and its attractions, while their spending contributes to the local economy. Accommodation forms a base for the tourists' exploration of the urban (and non-urban) environment. The tendency for establishments to locate in urban areas is illustrated in Figure 3.8, which is based on the

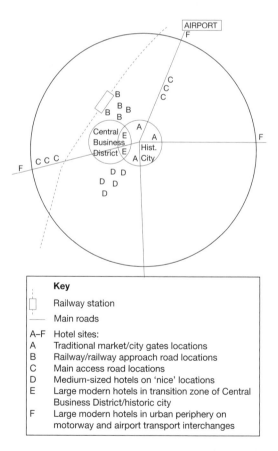

Figure 3.8: Model of urban hotel location in west European cities
Source: after Ashworth (1989)

typical patterns of urban hotel location in west European cities (Ashworth 1989; see also the seminal article on urban hotel location by Arbel and Pizam 1977). Figure 3.8 highlights the importance of infrastructure and accessibility when hotels are built to serve specific markets, i.e. the exhibition and conference market will need hotels adjacent to a major conference and exhibition centre, as Law (1996) emphasised. The accommodation sector within cities can be divided into serviced and non-serviced sectors (Figure 3.9). Each sector has developed in response to the needs of different markets, and a wide variety of organisational structures have emerged among private sector operators to develop this area of economic activity. As D.G. Pearce (1989) notes, many large chains and corporations now dominate the accommodation sector, using vertical and horizontal forms of integration to develop a greater degree of control over their business activities (see McVey 1986 for a more detailed discussion).

In London, the number of bedrooms in hotels and other forms of accommodation has grown from 44,000 bedrooms in 1966 to 80,000 in 1970, 130,000 in 1974, 137,844 in 1989 and 150,419 in 1999. The patterns of accommodation supply remained geographically concentrated in Westminster, Kensington, Chelsea and Camden with one outlier – Hillingdon – with its Heathrow Airport hotel. However, in the mid-1990s a new cluster in Croydon developed to equal and then exceed the number of bedspaces in Hillingdon.

Sector Market segment	Serviced sector		Non-serviced sector (self-catering)	
	Destination	Routes	Destination	Routes
Business and other non-leisure	City/town hotels (Monday–Friday) Resort hotels for conferences, exhibitions Educational establishments Serviced apartments	Motels Inns Airport hotels	Unserviced apartments Urban second homes	Not applicable
Leisure and holiday	Resort hotels Guest house/ pensions Farm houses City/town hotels (Friday–Sunday) Some educational establishments	Motels Bed and breakfast Inns	Hotels Condominia Holiday villages Holiday centres/ camps Caravan/chalet parks Gîtes Cottages Villas Apartments/flats Some motels Second homes (primarily rural)	Touring pitches for caravans, tents, recreation vehicles YHA Some hotels

Figure 3.9: Types of tourism accommodation
Source: after Middleton (1988)

Croydon developed to service Gatwick Airport and routes to London by rail and the M25 orbital motorway. Consequently, from 1989 to 1999, the spatial distribution of bedspaces has expanded from the CTD concentrated on the West End. One immediate beneficiary was the area to the south of the River Thames, as planning constraints in the main CTD area and limited development saw the CTD expand across the river (e.g. in Southwark). Bedspaces have also developed on this overspill principle to the east (i.e. in Tower Hamlets) and to the west (i.e. in Hammersmith) and also at other 'honeypots' or hubs such as Greenwich (see Figures 3.10 and 3.11). These have also been on the

periphery in Outer London where the M25 leisure/ business traveller has seen budget hotels developed by many of the hotel chains (e.g. Travelodge).

At a more global scale, Ivy (2001) examined the development of gay tourism and recreation space, particularly accommodation establishments catering for this niche market. Based on the Spartacus International Gay Guide for 1997, Ivy (2001) found that the Top Ten countries for gay-friendly accommodation were, in order of significance, the USA (35.1 per cent of the total), Germany, France, the UK, the Netherlands, Italy, Spain, Brazil, Japan and Belgium. These ten countries accounted for 74.1 per cent of bedspaces and the location of

Figure 3.10: Distribution of bedspaces in London in 1989
Source: Page and Hall (2002)

% Distribution of
establishments

33.8
10
1.5
0.9
0.01

Total number of establishments – 1154

Figure 3.11: Distribution of bedspaces in London in 1999
Source: Page and Hall (2002)

accommodation within countries was not spatially uniform, with a distinct clustering in certain locations, and even within such locations, a further clustering in districts offering gay travel services. These patterns expand upon a growing literature on the gay community (Weightman 1981; Adler and Brenner 1992) and their geographical activity patterns which have been neglected, overlooked or omitted in many geographical analyses of tourism and leisure.

Catering facilities

Ashworth and Tunbridge (1990) note that catering facilities are among the most frequently used

tourism services after accommodation. For example, of the £15 billion of overseas and domestic tourist spending in the UK in 1990, nearly £2 billion was estimated to be on eating and drinking (Marketpower 1991). What is meant by catering facilities? Bull and Church (1994) suggest that one way of grouping this sector is to use the Standard Industrial Classification which comprises:

• restaurants
• eating places
• public houses
• bars, clubs, canteens and messes
• hotels and other forms of tourist accommodation.

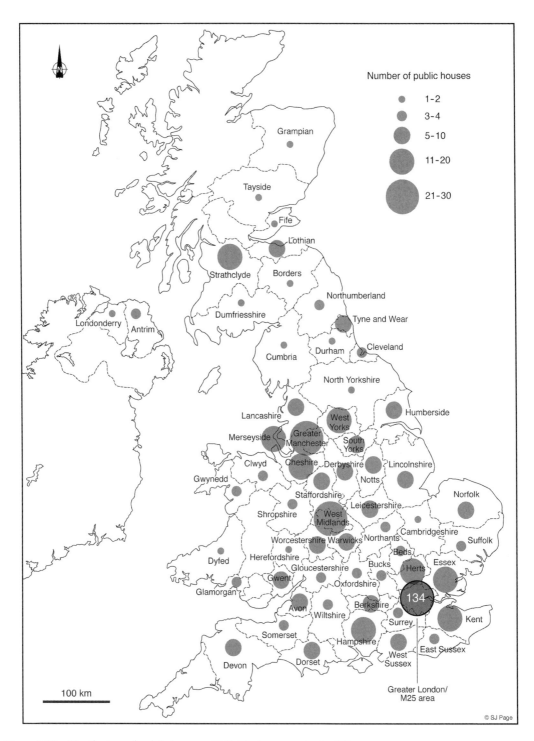

Figure 3.12: Distribution of public houses of J.D. Wetherspoon in the UK

Using the products which this sector produces, they further subdivide the groups into the provision of accommodation and the provision of food for immediate consumption. While there is considerable overlap between the two sectors, there are organisational links between each sector as integration within larger hospitality organisations (e.g. the Forte Group) with their subsidiaries offering various products. One of the immediate difficulties is in identifying specific outlets for tourist use, as many such facilities are also used by residents.

Tourist use of catering facilities varies according to the specific service on offer, and on their being located throughout cities, often in association with other facilities (S.L.J. Smith 1983b). Many catering establishments in cities reflect local community needs, and tourism complements the existing pattern of use. Nevertheless, Ashworth and Tunbridge (1990: 65) do acknowledge that restaurants and establishments combining food and drink with other entertainments, such as night-clubs, discos, casinos and the like, have two important locational characteristics that render them useful in this context: they have a distinct tendency to cluster together into particular streets or districts (what might be termed the 'Latin-quarter effect') and they tend to be associated spatially with other tourism elements including hotels, which probably themselves offer public restaurant facilities. Catering facilities also have a predisposition to cluster within areas where shopping is also a dominant activity, particularly in mall developments where food courts have become a popular concept in the USA and Australasia, while cosmopolitan cities have also developed a distinctive café culture aimed at residents and the visiting market who seek a café ambience. In the UK, deregulation of the brewery-owned (tied) public houses in the 1990s led to the development of new chains which have moved into this leisure market. Figure 3.12 illustrates the distribution of public houses for one of the more dynamic and enterprising chains – J.D. Wetherspoon. The origin of the company's expansion and development in the West Midlands is reflected in Figure 3.12 as is a clear strategy to have a market prominence in most of the key urban centres where the population and demand exist (including London). In 2001, the company operated 530 public houses, offering competitive staff wages and well-priced drinks and food. Company employees have grown from just under 4000 in 1997 to over 14,000 in 2001, as the number of public houses increased from 194 in 1997 to 530 in 2001, with a turnover of £484 million.

INSIGHT: Towards geographical analyses of hospitality: research agendas

While the geographer has predominately focused on the spatial and cultural implications of catering, there is a well-developed hospitality literature which has examined the historical evolution of the hospitality trades (Walton 2000). Critical debates associated with the 'McDonaldization' of society (Ritzer 1993) and linked to globalisation, where the principles of fast food restaurants are dominating society, especially hospitality (e.g. the use of technology in place of people, service standardisation, set rules and procedures and clear division of labour) have introduced predictability into hospitality services globally. For the tourist experience, a global and spatial homogeneity associated with the McDonaldization concept raises important cultural questions related to the type of experience being produced and consumed by tourists. In new conceptualisations of hospitality, Lashley (2000) challenges existing concerns with hospitality as a narrowly defined commercial activity, namely the 'provision of food and/or drink and/or accommodation away from home' (Lashley 2000: 3), preferring new approaches. Lashley (2000: 4) introduces a new

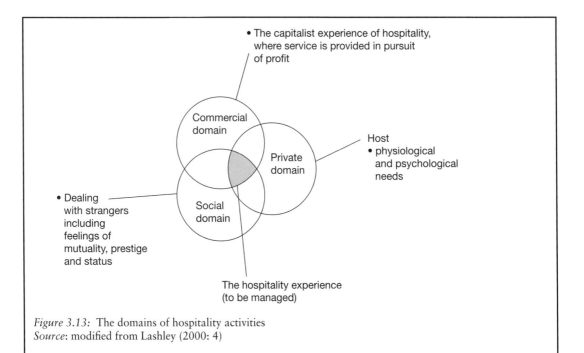

• The capitalist experience of hospitality, where service is provided in pursuit of profit

Commercial domain

Private domain

Host
• physiological and psychological needs

• Dealing with strangers including feelings of mutuality, prestige and status

Social domain

The hospitality experience (to be managed)

Figure 3.13: The domains of hospitality activities
Source: modified from Lashley (2000: 4)

breadth of definition with the use of the social, private and commercial domains of hospitality (Figure 3.13). Each domain represents one aspect of hospitality which is both independent and overlapping. From the social domain, the social setting of hospitality shapes the production and consumption of food/drink/accommodation. In the private domain, the issues of hospitableness and the host: guest encounter and cultural context of these relationships became important. In the commercial domain, the focus is on the production of hospitality services and their consumption as an economic activity.

For the geographer, much of the research has been conceived in the empiricist tradition and primarily concerned with employment in hospitality, its spatial form and processes shaping the supply of hospitality businesses (Getz et al. 2004; Hall and Rusher 2004). Again, this area of research is particularly underdeveloped and certainly is well situated to utilise a wide range of research approaches (Walle 1997) and agendas ranging from an empiricist mode to new cultural geographics. Indeed, the growing interest in the relationships between tourist, food production, regionalisation and wine is certainly opening new domains for the spatially inclined (Hall et al. 2000a, 2000b; Hall and Mitchell 2002). Therefore, with a range of processes operating (e.g. globalisation and McDonaldization) and concerns for the meaning of hospitality in a post-modern society (A. Williams 2000), it is clear that geographers have been ominous by their absence from debates in this area.

Tourist shopping

A number of studies in the tourism and leisure literature have expanded the knowledge base on tourist shopping, providing more detailed insights on this increasingly important market (Hobson 2000; Snepenger et al. 2003; J. Wong and Law 2003). The English Historic Town Forum's (1992) study on retailing and tourism highlights many of the relationships between

THE SUPPLY OF RECREATION AND TOURISM 139

tourism and retail activity [which] are inextricably linked to historic towns with three-quarters of tourists combining shopping with visiting attractions. . . . The expenditure is not only on refreshments and souvenirs, as might be expected, but also on clothing and footwear, stationery and books.

(English Historic Towns Forum 1992: 3)

The study also emphasises the overall significance of the environmental quality in towns which is vital to the success of urban tourism and retailing. In fact the report argues that, 'for towns wishing to maintain or increase leisure visitor levels, the study reveals a number of guide-lines. For example, cleanliness, attractive shop fronts and provision of street entertainment are all important to tourists' (English Historic Towns Forum 1992: 3).

Unfortunately, identifying tourist shopping as a concept in the context of urban tourism is difficult, since it is also an activity undertaken by other users such as residents. Jansen-Verbeke (1990, 1991) considers the motives of tourists and their activities in a range of Dutch towns. She makes a number of interesting observations on this concept. However, the range of motives associated with tourism and leisure shopping are complex: people visit areas due to their appeal, and shopping may be a spontaneous as well as a planned activity. Even so, the quality and range of retail facilities may be a useful determinant of the likely demand for tourism and leisure shopping: the longer the visitor is enticed to stay in a destination, the greater the likely spending in retail outlets.

One important factor which affects the ability of cities to attract tourism and leisure shoppers is the retail mix – namely the variety of goods, shops and presence of specific retailers. For example, the English Historic Towns Forum (1992) notes that over 80 per cent of visitors consider the retailing mix and general environment of the town to be the most important attraction of the destination. Although the priorities of different tourist market segments vary slightly, catering, accessibility (e.g. availability of car parking, location of car parks and public transport), tourist attractions and the availability of visitor information shape the decision to engage in tourism and leisure shopping. The

constant search for the unique shopping experience, especially in conjunction with day trips in border areas and neighbouring countries (e.g. the UK cross-channel tax-free shopping trips from Dover to Calais) are well-established forms of tourism and leisure shopping.

The global standardisation of many consumer products has meant that the search for the unique shopping experience continues to remain important. The growth of the North American shopping malls and tourist-specific projects (Lew 1985, 1989; Getz 1993b) and the development in the UK of out-of-town complexes (e.g. the Metro Centre in Gateshead and Lakeside at Thurrock, adjacent to the M25) have extended this trend. For example, in the case of Edmonton Mall (Canada), Jansen-Verbeke (1991) estimates that 10 per cent of the total floor space is used for leisure facilities with its 800 shops and parking for 27,000 cars. Such developments have been of great concern for many cities as out-of-town shopping has reduced the potential in-town urban tourism in view of the competition they pose for established destinations. The difficulty with most existing studies of leisure shopping is that they fail to disentangle the relationships between the actual activity tourists undertake and their perception of the environment. For this reason, Jansen-Verbeke (1991) distinguishes between intentional shopping and intentional leisure shopping in a preliminary attempt to explain how and why tourists engage in this activity; she also suggests that several criteria need to be considered to distinguish between intentional shopping and intentional leisure and tourism (Table 3.8).

Many successful cities in western Europe have used tourism and leisure shopping to establish their popularity as destinations as a gradual process of evolution. For example, research by Page and Hardyman (1996) examines the concept of town centre management as one attempt to address the impact of out-of-town shopping malls and complexes as a threat to tourism and leisure spending in town centres. Their research found that based on concepts developed in North America, town centres can identify their users more closely and undertake

Table 3.8: Criteria to be considered in distinguishing between intentional shopping and intentional leisure and tourism

---

Behaviour pattern of visitors
- trip length – short, possibly longer
- length of stay – limited or rather unplanned
- time of stay – a few hours during the day, an evening, a full day
- kinds of activity – window shopping, intentional buying, drinking, eating, various leisure activities, cultural activities, sightseeing
- expenditure – goods, possibly some souvenirs, drinks, meals, entrance fees to leisure facilities

Functional characteristics of the environment
- wide range of retail shops, department stores, catering, leisure and other facilities, tourist attractions, spatial clustering of facilities
- parking space and easy access
- street retailing, pedestrian priority in open spaces

Quality of the environment
- image of the place, leisure setting, display of goods on the street, street musicians and artists
- accessibility during leisure time, including weekends and evenings
- aesthetic value, image of maintenance and safety
- architectural design of buildings, streets, shops, windows, sign boards, lighting
- social effective value, liveliness of the open space
- animation, entertainment, amusement and surprise

Hospitableness of the environment
- social, visual, physical
- orientation, information, symbolism, identification

Source: Jansen-Verbeke (1991: 9–10)

in-town improvements to attract the user as a means of developing leisure shopping. In particular, improvements to town centres by city authorities have acted as catalysts to this process by

- establishing pedestrian precincts
- managing parking problems and implementing park-and-ride schemes to improve access and convenience
- marketing the destination based around an identifiable theme, often using the historical and cultural attractions of a city
- investing in new and attractive indoor shopping galleries, improving facades, the layout and

design of the built environment and making the environment more attractive.

The English Historic Towns Forum (1992: 12) identify the following factors which tourism and leisure shoppers deemed important:

- the cleanliness of the town
- pedestrian areas/pavements which are well maintained
- natural features such as rivers and parks
- the architecture and facades/shop fronts
- street furniture (seating and floral displays)
- town centre activities (e.g. outdoor markets and live entertainment).

One can also add issues of urban safety, (Walker and Page 2003), particularly where new shopping environments are now designing out crime in consultation with police. Indeed, the discussion in Chapter 2 regarding social inclusion and the rise of private spaces as shopping malls also raises many accessibility and environmental issues, where many new retail environments are being developed as synthetic, protective and cosseted environments, lacking in character and a sense of place. Many shopping malls are becoming global in their design, retail mix and focus so that attracting the tourist and leisure shopper is more competitive, given that many areas have similar retail offerings in larger cities and in out-of-town locations.

Changes that alter the character of the town, where it becomes more tourist oriented, are sometimes characterised by the development of speciality and gift/souvenir shops and catering facilities in certain areas. However, as Owen (1990) argues, many traditional urban shopping areas are in need of major refurbishment, and tourism may provide the necessary stimulus for regeneration, especially in downtown areas that are competing with out-of-town centres. Developments such as theme shopping (Jones Lang Wooten 1989) and festival marketplaces (Sawicki 1989) are specialised examples of how this regeneration has proceeded in the UK and North America. Other developments such as designer factory shops that sell off surplus designer stock, such as Sterling Mills in central Scotland, have also developed a distinct segment in the market for leisure shopping.

The period from 2005 to 2015, therefore, would seem to be set for tourism and leisure shopping development to further segment markets by seeking new niches and products, such as the development and refinement of airport retailing (Freathy 2004). Jansen-Verbeke (1991) describes the 'total experience' as the future way forward for this activity – retailers will need to attract tourism and leisure spending using newly built, simulated or refurbished retailing environments with a variety of shopping experiences. Keown's (1989) experience is that the opportunity to undertake a diverse range of retail activities in a locality increases the tourist's propensity to spend. However, the growing saturation of retailing provision in many industrialised countries may pose problems for further growth in tourism and leisure shopping due to the intense competition for such spending. Urban tourism destinations are likely to have to compete more aggressively for such spending in the new millennium, as new investment strategies, constant expansion and value adding to the shopping experience are part of this competitive development, with public–private sector partnerships promoting such development.

Conditional elements

The fourth feature which Jansen-Verbeke (1986) views as central to the city's 'leisure product' is the conditional elements, such as transport, physical infrastructure and the provision of signposting. Unless adequate infrastructure is provided, tourists will be reluctant to divert from established patterns of visitor activity and tourism and leisure shopping will fail to materialise. Transport is a vital element in the facilitation of tourism, as it allows people to move from origin to destination (i.e. it permits mobility), and at the destination it provides the mechanism to enjoy sightseeing, touring, and the linking of visitors with their place of accommodation to the attractions/activities they wish to pursue. Good signposting, connectivity in transport systems, inter-modal interchanges and a clear circuit/itinerary are important to link visitors and resources/places. Numerous studies exist which examine the conceptual basis of the transport-tourism interface (Page 1994b, 1999, 2005) with new perspectives on research agendas questioning the significance of transport (Lumsdon and Page 2004). In fact many geographical analyses of tourism have mapped the routes tourists take by car on holiday within cities and regions (Page 1998), the flows by means of air travel (Graham 1998; Page 2003b) as well as by coach (Page 2003c) and rail (Page 2002), and the importance of transport as an attraction in the 'leisure product' (e.g. Melbourne's refurbished tram restaurant) and as icons in destinations like the London Routemaster bus, which is now under threat as fleet replacements have seen these vehicles used more on sightseeing services. This last issue of sightseeing also highlights one new area for geographical research on tourism as part of the conditional elements – tourism and visual culture.

There is a growing body of interdisciplinary research, informed by cultural geography which examines how tourists consume visual culture, which refers to the image-making devices and skills of a particular culture. This has been broadened in context to include fine art, the media, television, video, photography and advertising and the way these forms of media are used to attach meanings to artefacts, objects and places. In a tourism context, Crouch and Lübbren (2003: 5) note that 'visual culture is consumed in spaces. Geographical thought is an important component of understanding the consumption of, or encounter with, visual culture. Tourism has frequently been depicted and theorized, as a journey; a journey to and in places, identities and experiences'. As the physical space and places that tourists visit are consumed, the visual culture is part of the tourist experience of the place, site and way in which it is visually consumed. In other words, tourism is a sensual encounter, based on visual images and Baudrillard (1981) noted the strategies of desire, whereby tourists' interests and needs are met through consumption. The tourism industry is therefore very adept at using visual culture to develop the tourist offering, as well as using advertising, promotion, signs and symbols which the tourist gazes at, observes and consumes. Therefore, visual culture has important links in the conditional elements of tourism, since the consumption of tourism is part of a cultural process.

CONCLUSION

This chapter has examined a range of issues and concepts associated with the analysis of recreation and tourism supply issues. One interesting comparison which appears to hold true is S.L.J. Smith's (1983a) criticisms of recreational research being applicable to tourism due to the simplistic conceptualisation of the subject matter. In fact, Britton's (1980a, 1991) innovative and theoretically derived analyses offer a fresh and welcome attempt to rethink the geography of tourism, particularly the production side which has been notoriously descriptive and somewhat naive in its borrowing of geographical concepts while making no contribution to theory (Debbage and Ioannides 2004). This chapter has achieved two purposes: the first is to show how the geographer approaches the spatial complexity of supply issues in both recreation and tourism, while introducing some of the concepts, methods and ways of thinking about supply. Second, it has detailed the importance of developing a more meaningful assessment of tourism and the production system by situating the supply of tourism and recreation within the contexts of concepts of core and periphery, consumption and production, and tourism as a capitalist activity. It is apparent that in the more theoretically derived analyses of supply issues, there is a need to derive more culturally specific explanations which indicate why certain phenomena exist, have developed and now dominate the tourism and leisure environment (Debbage and Ioannides 2004). Terkenli (2002) offered a number of insights on how space is organised in the postmodern western world based on a number of trends:

- conventional notions of place, particularly our sense of place transcends geographical barriers of distance (i.e. the media and information technology have created globally aware consumers in the west)
- a de-differentiation occurring between public and private spheres of everyday life
- a desegregation of leisure from home and work life, making distinctions such as leisure more tentative
- globalisation processes, where communications media provide images, information and awareness of leisure travel opportunities on a daily basis through television programmes, consumer magazines and a strong dependence upon visual communication.

These trends have led to a cultural economy of space with leisure/tourism interactions shaped by processes simultaneously which are transforming geographical configurations of supply. Such processes, operating at a global scale, also have a local impact as reflected in the many forms of mass consumption in tourism and leisure. The spatial articulation of these forms of consumption are in a constant state of flux, particularly as the blurring of work–home life questions the geographer's conventional supply-side models of leisure, defined in relation to home and patterns of consumption (see Pacione 2001 for more details). As a result, the postmodern society and geographers' understanding of how tourism and leisure is integrated into the everyday lives of people is now a more complex process, in a theoretical and spatial context. Consequently, understanding the impacts of tourism and leisure activity pose in postmodern society and the 'myriad of ways in which local people have responded to, and sometimes resisted, tourism development' (Scheyvens 2002: 37). Chapter 4 now turns to the impact of tourism and recreation.

QUESTIONS

- How have geographers conceptualised recreational supply?

- What techniques and tools have geographers used to examine the supply of recreational facilities?
- What is the role of Britton's (1991) geography of production and consumption in the analysis of tourism?
- Are the majority of studies of tourism supply descriptive and based on empirical data rather than theoretical models?

READING

In terms of recreational supply, the following are useful introductions to the subject:

Countryside Agency (2000) *The State of the Countryside 1999*, Cheltenham: Countryside Agency.

Evans, G. (1998) 'Urban leisure: Edge city and the new leisure periphery', in M. Collins and I. Cooper (eds) *Leisure Management: Issues and Applications*, Wallingford: CAB International, pp. 113–38.

Morgan, R., Jones, T. and Williams, A. (1993) 'Opinions and perceptions of England and Wales Heritage coast beach users: Some management implications from the Glamorgan Heritage Coast, Wales', *Journal of Coastal Research*, 9(4): 1083–93.

For a good review of conceptual issues on the supply of tourism services and facilities see

Agarwal, S., Ball, R., Shaw, G. and Williams, A. (2000) 'The geography of tourism production: Uneven disciplinary development', *Tourism Geographies*, 2(3): 241–63.

Williams, A.M. (2004) 'Toward a political economy of tourism', in A. Lew, C.M. Hall and A.A. Williams (eds) *Companion to Tourism*, Oxford: Blackwell, pp. 61–73.

For studies of specific supply issues in different environments see

Carter, R. (1982) 'Coastal caravan sites in Northern Ireland 1960–1980', *Irish Geography*, 15: 123–6.

Ilbery, B., Bowler, I., Clark, G., Crockett, A. and Shaw, A. (1998) 'Farm-based tourism as an alternative farm enterprise: A case study from the Northern Pennines, England', *Regional Studies*, 32(4): 355–64.

Smith, R.A. (1992) 'Review of integrated beach resort development in South East Asia', *Land Use Policy*, 211–17.

For two useful historical reviews of recreational and tourism/hospitality service provision see

Maver, I. (1998) 'Glasgow's public parks and the community 1850–1914', *Urban History*, 25(3): 323–47.

Walton, J. (2000) 'The hospitality trades: A social history', in C. Lashley and A. Morrison (eds) *In Search of Hospitality: Theoretical Perspectives and Debates*, Oxford: Butterworth-Heinemann, pp. 56–76.

4

THE IMPACTS OF TOURISM AND RECREATION

The growth of international and domestic tourism has been matched by a corresponding increase in the numbers of those who study tourism and its impacts. Indeed, it has even been said that tourism research was one of the academic growth industries of the late twentieth century (Hall 1995). The literature on tourism has expanded enormously with the result that research has become 'highly fragmented, with researchers following separate and often divergent paths' (Mathieson and Wall 1982: 2). Nevertheless, one of the major areas of interest for geographers, as well as other tourism researchers, is the impacts of tourism and recreation.

Tourism and recreation cannot be studied in isolation from the complex economic, environmental, political and social milieux in which they occur (Runyan and Wu 1979; Mason 2003). If geographers are to make a valid contribution to the study of tourism and recreation and their impacts, it is vital that they are aware of the widest possible implications of such events for host communities, particularly as concerns over the sustainability of tourism and recreation grow (Butler 1990, 1991; Hall and Lew 1998; Butler 2000; G. Hughes 2004; Weaver 2004). This has therefore meant that there has been substantial interchange of ideas, frameworks and methodologies between geographers and non-geographers in analysing the impacts of tourism and recreation.

There are a number of ways of categorising the impacts of tourism. One of the most common is that used by Mathieson and Wall (1982), which divided impacts into economic, social and physical (environmental categories). A more detailed breakdown of the impacts of tourism has been used by Getz (1977), Ritchie (1984) and Hall (1992b). An overview of these categories is provided in Table 4.1 where they are categorised in terms of their positive or negative nature for a destination community. However, it should be noted that such a division is not absolute, as whether something is seen as positive or negative will often depend on the goals, ideology and value position of an individual with respect to different types of tourism development. This chapter will provide a broad overview of the development of frameworks to manage recreation and tourism impacts, the impacts of tourism and recreation, and some of the main issues which arise out of the analysis and management of impacts.

IMPACTS: RECREATION RESOURCE MANAGEMENT

Resource management for recreational purposes is a useful tool with which to begin understanding the relationships between recreational and tourist impacts, sites and the action needed to address conflicts, namely planning (Seeley 1983), a theme explored in Chapter 9. In this context, resource management is concerned with the way the geographical approach meshes with the multidisciplinary contributions to understanding how resources need to be managed (Mercer 2004). Glyptis (1989a) made a fundamental assumption which many recreational texts overlook: that few

Table 4.1: Positive and negative dimensions of the impacts of tourism on host communities

Type of impact	Positive	Negative
Economic dimensions Economic	• increased expenditures • creation of employment • increase in labour supply • increase in standard of living • increase in investment	• localised inflation • real estate speculation • failure to attract tourists • better alternative investments • capital outflows • inadequate estimation of costs of tourism development • undesirable opportunity costs including transfer of funds from health and education
Tourism/commercial	• increased awareness of the region as a travel/tourism destination • increased knowledge concerning the potential for investment and commercial activity in the region • creation of new facilities, attractions and infrastructure • increase in accessibility	• acquisition of a poor reputation as a result of inadequate facilities, improper practices or inflated prices • negative reactions from existing enterprises due to the possibility of new competition for local personnel and government assistance
Socio-cultural impacts Social/cultural	• increase in permanent level of local interest and participation in types of activity associated with event • strengthening of regional values and traditions	• commercialisation of activities which may be of a personal or private nature • modification of nature of event or activity to accommodate tourism • potential increase in crime • changes in community structure • social dislocation
Psychological	• increased local pride and community spirit • increased awareness of non-local perceptions	• tendency toward defensive attitudes concerning host regions • high possibility of misunderstandings leading to varying degrees of host/visitor hostility
Political/administrative	• enhanced international recognition of region and values • development of skills among planners	• economic exploitation of local population to satisfy ambitions of political elite • distortion of true nature of event to reflect values of political system • failure to cope • inability to achieve aims • increase in administrative costs • use of tourism to legitimise unpopular decisions • legitimation of ideology of local elite
Environmental impacts Physical/environmental	• development of new facilities • improvement of local infrastructure • conservation of heritage • visitor management strategies	• environmental damage • changes in natural processes • architectural pollution • destruction of heritage • overcrowding • changed feeding and breeding habits of wildlife

Sources: after Getz (1977); Mathieson and Wall (1982); Ritchie (1984); Hall (1992b)

recreational activities make use of resources that are solely recreational. Indeed, recreation is often juxtaposed in relation to forestry, agriculture, water supply, conservation and a host of competing activities that each make use of socially constructed leisure spaces. Consequently, the issue of multiple use of resources (as discussed in Chapter 3) is an underlying principle which recreation resource management seeks to accommodate.

Glyptis (1989a) examined the contemporary context of recreation resource management, observing that four major influences could be discerned:

- the belief that recreation is the right of every citizen
- social change, particularly an ageing population and the changing demand for specific forms of recreation
- changing economic and political doctrines which have seen debates associated with the demise of post-war notions of full employment and leisure as non-work or of less significance than work
- strategic planning by public sector recreation agencies in relation to the previous three influences.

Within a UK context, the added changes in the 1980s under the Thatcher government saw the privatisation of many forms of recreation and leisure provision, a theme discussed later in Chapter 5 in terms of urban parks. What was critical here was the changing public policy framework within public service provision in leisure in the UK and other countries. Aitchison (1997) reviewed the impact of such changes, acknowledging the effect on access for women and other target groups.

Research has examined the introduction of compulsory competitive tendering (CCT) which has been seen as naive and ill thought out. Coalter (1998) pointed to the emphasis on economy and financial efficiency while neglecting non-financial performance measures such as the contribution of recreational outputs to a community's quality of life. Even simple notions of recreational supply (reviewed in Chapter 3) related to equity of access,

and community needs do not appear to be met in many cases of CCT contracts. Simplistic measures of expressed demand have also not been evaluated systematically. Thus political and ideological changes in government can have a major bearing on the nature and approach to recreation resource management.

Both Chubb and Chubb (1981) and Patmore (1983) provided excellent appraisals of recreational behaviour, the resource requirements and the complex interplay of forces shaping recreational resource management from a geographical standpoint (Masser 1966–7). What emerged from the wide range of geographical contributions to recreational resource analysis during the 1960s, 1970s and 1980s was that the fundamental starting point for any discussion is demand. Reiterating the discussion in Chapter 2, data from site surveys and overall levels of participation in time and space as a dynamic process provide the baseline information for resource management. It is then a question of establishing the impact of specific activities.

Understanding the extent of impacts such as the effect on natural resources, social and psychological impacts arising from overcrowding, traffic congestion, aesthetic intrusions and conflict between recreational activities illustrate how the resource is being impacted upon (Spink 1994). Even at the present time, over three decades since Burton's (1974) innovative study of carrying capacity of Cannock Chase, Staffordshire, UK, its methodological and conceptual value remains high despite innovations in mapping and analysis with GIS. Indeed, the interest in pursuing critical spatial concepts such as overcrowding and tolerance to visitor numbers has seen only a growing interest by geographers since the 1970s, especially in the context of rural recreation. In fact G.M. Robinson (1999: 270) argued that 'During the last three decades, work by geographers on the management of rural recreation and tourism has grown from a trickle to form a highly varied and substantial literature'. One notable example is O'Riordan and Paget's (1978) analysis of anglers and boaters where spatial tools were devised to achieve multiple use of the resource.

Probably one of the greatest challenges facing recreational resource planners in a non-urban context is the impact of the motor car in the post-war period. Many novel studies in the 1960s and 1970s (e.g. J.M. Hall 1972; Wall 1971, 1972) highlighted both the greater spatial reach and flexibility of access to recreational sites afforded by the car. Even so, the car is not a surrogate for individual mobility and recreational resource use, although as Page (1998, 1999) highlighted, the car is one of the major issues facing the recreational planner, especially in national parks (Eaton and Holding 1996). Within an urban context, Glyptis (1989a) also observed that the car was highly correlated with the use of sports facilities in the 1970s by middle-class males contributing to inequalities in access. Mobility and access to transport does limit certain social groups from enjoying the wider continuum of outdoor recreation opportunities, particularly those living in deprived inner-city environments, a feature constantly reiterated in urban recreation and summarised by S. Williams (1995: 35) thus: 'The net effect of car ownership is that participation rates in sports and outdoor recreations are significantly higher in households with access to a car.'

In the case of Loch Lomond, the pressure has come from another form of transport: recreational boating (see Bisset et al. 2000; Dickinson 2000). Recreational boat pressure, as in the case of The Broads in East Anglia (see Page 1999), has also posed concerns in terms of environmental pollution (Bannan et al. 2000). This concern has been heightened by the designation of the area as part of Scotland's first national park – the Loch Lomond and Trossachs National Park (see Page and Dowling 2001). For resource managers, much of the concern is with the use and management of individual sites, where specific tools such as site closure, rejuvenation, reconfiguring visitor flows on sites and discriminatory measures such as placing obstacles are used. In this respect, vehicles such as the private car have been prohibited or closely controlled to minimise impacts. At a practical level, recreation resource management involves maintaining and enhancing sites and the geographer has a valid role to play in understanding visitor behaviour, usage patterns, potential conflicts and spatial measures which can harmonise multiple use. This provides fundamental information to feed into the management and planning process.

CARRYING CAPACITY

Carrying capacity is one of the most complex and confusing concepts which faces the geographer in seeking to understand recreation sites and their ability to support a certain level of usage (Coccossis

Plate 4.1: White Cliffs of Dover, Kent. How much of this footpath erosion is due to recreational versus tourist use?

Plate 4.2: Athens, Greece. Historic sites such as the Acropolis suffer visitor pressure and erosion of the built fabric.

2004). In many early applications of the concept, it was viewed as a management tool to protect sites and resources from excessive use, while also seeking to balance usage with recreational enjoyment for participants (Wagar 1964; Stankey 1973; Graefe et al. 1984a, 1984b; Shelby and Heberlein 1984, 1986; Stankey and McCool 1984). In many respects, it is a precursor of the much wider concept of 'sustainability' which has now embraced both recreation and tourism (see Hall and Lew 1998; Page et al. 2001). One early definition of carrying capacity by the Countryside Commission (1970: 2), with its central precept of the long-term capacity of resources and human activity, embodied the dual characteristics of protection and use: the level of recreation use an area can sustain without an unacceptable degree of deterioration of the character and quality of the resource or recreation experience. This was followed by an identification of four types of recreational carrying capacity: physical, economic, ecological and social carrying capacity.

The notion of physical carrying is primarily concerned with quantitative measures of the number of people or usage a site can support, primarily being a design concept. This may also act as a constraint on visitor use by deliberately limiting access to sites. The notion of economic carrying capacity is primarily concerned with multiple use of resources (Pigram and Jenkins 1999; Coccossis 2004), particularly its compatibility with the site and wider management objectives for the site. The notion of ecological (or what Lavery 1971a terms 'environmental capacity') is primarily 'concerned with the maximum level of recreational use, in terms of numbers and activities, that can be accommodated by an area or ecosystem before an unacceptable or irreversible decline in ecological values occur' (Pigram and Jenkins 1999: 91). The chief problem here lies in what individuals and groups construe as acceptable change. In an early study by Dower and McCarthy (1967) of Donegal, Ireland, they estimated the environmental capacity which recreational and tourism resources could support at any point in time. Lavery (1971a) developed these ideas, based on subsequent work by Furmidge (1969) and Houghton Evans and Miles

(1970) to produce a series of suggested space standards for environmental capacity. Although this table may be criticised for using such absolute values of capacity, it is notable that it provides a starting point for discussing how many visitors can support a site and how many might be too many. While critics have questioned the notion of fixed capacity for individual sites, it should be stressed that carrying capacity will only ever be one element of a management strategy for outdoor recreation. This shows is the need to move beyond environmental capacity to recognise the significance of users, visitor satisfaction and the role of perception – embodied in the last notion – of social carrying capacity.

Social carrying capacity, often referred to as perceptual, psychological or behavioural carrying capacity, was defined by Pigram and Jenkins (1999: 93) as 'the maximum level of recreational use, in terms of numbers and activities, above which there is a decline in the quality of the recreation experience, from the point of view of the recreation participant'. The basic principles inherent in this approach relate to the ability of individuals and groups to tolerate others, their activities and the level of acceptability. Patmore (1973: 241) summed this up as 'the number of people [a site] can absorb before the latest arrivals perceive the area to be full and seek satisfaction elsewhere'. This has both a spatial and temporal dimension, embodied in the study by Glyptis (1981b). One of the fundamental concepts here is the extent to which crowding impacts upon visitor satisfaction.

Developing a carrying capacity for a site involves at least eight steps (Hall and McArthur 1998):

1   Specify management objectives or standards for the state of the heritage resource to be maintained or attained and the type of experience to be provided.
2   Identify current levels of use for a defined period (e.g. hour, day, week, month, year).
3   Identify indicators for the biophysical, sociocultural, psychological and managerial components.
4   Measure the current state of each indicator.

5   Identify apparent relationships between the state of the indicator and the level of use.

6   Make value judgements about the acceptability of the various impacts.

7   Determine a carrying capacity that is more, the same or less than current visitation.

8   Implement management strategies to ensure carrying capacity is not breached.

An example of the establishment of a carrying capacity is the Angkor World Heritage Site in Cambodia. A capacity of 300 to 500 visitors at any one time has been established, with an annual capacity set at 500,000, which assumes visitors will make two visits to the site during their stay (Wager 1995).

The most defendable carrying capacity is an estimate representing a compromise between individual capacities for each component. For example, suppose there was a biophysical carrying capacity set at 50 visits per day, a socio-cultural capacity set at 100 visits per day, a psychological capacity set at 80 visits a day and a managerial capacity set at 90 visits a day. If each component was valued equally, then an overall carrying capacity may be set at 80 visits per day. However, the typical scenario is one where the overall figure is influenced by the most sensitive or threatened factor, so in this example the capacity may be set at 50 visits per day (Hall and McArthur 1998).

Despite the concept of carrying capacity having originated in the early 1960s, it remains in practice, although highly elusive to successfully implement although it remains an extremely significant and influential management concept.

It is commonly recognised that there are no fixed or standard tourism carrying capacity values. Rather, carrying capacity varies, depending upon place, season and time, user behaviour, facility design, patterns and levels of management, and the dynamic character of the environments themselves. Moreover, it is not always possible to practice to separate tourism activity from other human activities.

(Ceballos-Lacuarain 1996: 131)

Indeed, it is relatively easy to argue that there is no such thing as a single carrying capacity for any given site and that any capacity put forward is highly subjective and thus difficult to defend. A good example of the judgemental limitation is Green Island in far North Queensland. Concern over current crowding resulted in a carrying capacity being set at 1900 visitors per day or no more than 800 at any one time (Queensland Department of Environment and Heritage 1993). Green Island currently receives some 300,000 visits per year. If the maximum daily level was reached every day, Green Island would receive 693,500 visitors in a year, over twice the current level (Hall and McArthur 1998). Nevertheless, the notion of carrying capacity has made a methodological and practical contribution to recreational and tourism resource management and has been at the heart of a number of visitor management tools in natural areas (Page and Connell 2006). Yet management ideas are changing as new debates within the recreational literature emerge, particularly regarding the limits of acceptable change framework (Newsome et al. 2002).

INSIGHT: The Recreation Opportunity Spectrum

The Recreation Opportunity Spectrum (ROS) is a conceptual framework to clarify the relationship between recreational settings, activities and experiences (R.N. Clark and Stankey 1979). It is premised on the assumption that quality is best assured through the provision of a diverse array of opportunities. The ROS provided a conceptual framework for thinking about how to create a diversity of recreation experiences, rather than just provide standard recreational facilities (Driver 1989).

A ROS is developed by identifying a spectrum

of settings, activities and opportunities that a given region may contain. For example, a national park may contain a spectrum of settings that range from easily accessible, highly developed areas and facilities, to remote, undeveloped areas with no facilities. The information relating to each setting is entered into a tabular format to present the characteristics of the site, the type of activities undertaken and the opportunities available alongside each other. Comparisons can then be made across sites to determine what sort of core opportunities appear to provided and the under or over supply to specific activities and opportunities. The ROS can therefore be very useful at reviewing then repositioning the type of visitor experiences most appropriate to a recreation or natural heritage site (Hall and McArthur 1998).

Management factors considered when determining which recreational class a setting should be categorised as include the following:

- access (e.g. difficulty, access system (roads and trails) and means of conveyance)
- the non-recreational resource
- on-site management (e.g. extent, apparentness, complexity and facilities)
- social interaction
- acceptability of visitor impact (e.g. magnitude and prevalence)
- regimentation.

The standard range of recreational classes established by ROS are developed, semi-developed, semi-natural and natural.

Perhaps the key limitation to the use of the ROS is its emphasis on the setting at the expense of the type of visitor. Part of the reason for this is the influence of earlier cultures from the landscape planning and architecture professions that suggested visitor management could be largely addressed through site and facility design. Although the ROS was extensively used in the early 1980s, its adoption by recreation resource managers was starting to wane by the early 1990s (Lipscome 1993; Hall and McArthur 1998).

THE LIMITS OF ACCEPTABLE CHANGE

The Limits of Acceptable Change (LAC) system began with the fundamentals of the Recreation Opportunity Spectrum and initial principles of carrying capacity. Its designers then shifted the focus from a relationship between levels of use and impact to identifying desirable conditions for visitor activity to occur in the first place, as well as management actions required to protect or achieve the conditions (Clark and Stankey 1979; Stankey and McCool 1984). The LAC implies an emphasis on establishing how much change is acceptable, then actively managing accordingly. The LAC model avoids the use/impact conundrum by focusing on the management of the impacts of use (Stankey et al. 1985). The model informs management whether the conditions are within acceptable standards; that is, that current levels and patterns of use are within the capacity of the host environment. When conditions reach the limits of acceptable change they have also reached the area's capacity under current management practices. Management is then equipped with a logical and defensible case to implement strategic actions before any more use can be accommodated. One action may be to limit use.

The LAC system is based on a nine-stage process:

1 Identification of area concerns and issues.
2 Definition and description of opportunity classes.
3 Selection of indicators for conditions.
4 Inventory of resource and social conditions.
5 Specification of standards for indicators.
6 Identification of alternative opportunity class allocations.
7 Identification of management actions for each alternative.
8 Evaluation and selection of the preferred option.

9 Implementation of actions and monitoring of conditions.

Prosser (1986a) identified a number of key strengths of the LAC system as being:

- emphasis on explicit, measurable objectives
- promotion of a diversity of visitor experiences
- reliance on quantitative field-based standards
- flexibility and responsiveness to local situations
- opportunity for public involvement
- minimisation of regulatory approaches
- a framework for managing conditions.

Unfortunately, only a few LAC systems have been generated and successfully implemented, mostly in wilderness areas of North America and, to a small extent, in one or two natural areas in Australia (Hall and McArthur 1998). The most critical aspect of the development of the LAC system has been establishing stakeholder endorsement and support (Prosser 1986b). Stakeholders from the local tourism sector and community can provide valuable input into desired conditions and acceptable standards, and are usually essential in providing the economic and political support necessary to maintain monitoring programmes and implement management decisions. The failure to establish suf-ficient stakeholder support has largely occurred because the LAC was created by natural area managers, for natural area managers (Stankey et al. 1985).

According to Hall and McArthur (1998), the culture of the LAC is not attuned to attracting wider stakeholder involvement, and provides three examples of problems in its implementation. First, the use of the term 'limits' within the title, which the tourism industry has interpreted as being dis-couraging to growth and thus business. Second, the conventional narrow focus on the condition of the physical environment and, to some extent, the nature of the visitor experience. Other critical dimensions such as characteristics of the visitor market, socio-cultural aspects of the local com-munity and economic activity associated with the tourism industry are not included. Third, the lack of co-operative involvement of the tourism sector in identifying indicators and standards that are acceptable to the industry. Without this involve-ment the monitoring results become prone to conjecture, particularly if they reveal surprising or controversial implications. However, if the cul-ture of the LAC system was diversified and its components broadened it may be better able to deliver the significant opportunities it was originally designed to generate (McCool and Cole 1997).

INSIGHT: The Tourism Optimisation Management Model (TOMM)

The Tourism Optimisation Management Model (TOMM) is one of the most recent and relatively untried models to monitor and manage visitors (McArthur 1996, 2000b; Hall and McArthur 1998). The conceptual emphasis of the TOMM is on achieving optimum performance rather than limiting activity. The TOMM positions a range of influences in the heritage–visitor relationship to focus on sustainability of the heritage, viability of the tourism industry, and empowerment of stakeholders. The TOMM has borrowed the key strengths of the Visitor Impact Management Model (VIMM) developed by the United States

National Parks and Conservation Association (Graefe 1989, 1991) and LAC, then broadened their focus into fields linked with the tourism industry and local community. Besides environ-mental and experiential elements, the TOMM addresses characteristics of the tourist market, economic conditions of the tourism industry and socio-cultural conditions of the local com-munity. The expansion recognises the complex interrelationships between heritage management, the tourism industry and supporting local pop-ulations. In this respect the TOMM is more politically sensitive to the forces which shape visitation and subsequent impacts (McArthur 2000a, 2000b).

The TOMM contains three main components – context analysis, a monitoring programme and a management response system (Manidis Roberts Consultants 1996; McArthur 2000b). The context analysis identifies the current nature of community values, tourism product, tourism growth, market trends and opportunities, positioning and branding. This information is collected through literature reviews, face-to-face interviews with relevant expertise, and a community workshop. The context analysis also identifies alternative scenarios for the future of tourism, used later to test the validity of the model.

The second stage of the development of a TOMM is the development of a monitoring programme. The basis for the monitoring programme is a set of optimal conditions which tourism and visitor activity should create (rather than impacts they should avoid). In this way the model avoids setting limits, maximum levels or carrying capacities, and can offer the tourism industry opportunities to develop optimal sustainable performance. The monitoring programme is essentially designed to measure how close the current situation is to the optimal conditions. The measurement yardstick is a set of indicators (one for each optimal condition). Table 4.3 provides a list of assessment criteria for selecting the most appropriate indicators for a TOMM. Each indicator has a benchmark and an acceptable range for it to be expected to operate within. Table 4.4 provides an example of the desired outcomes and their supporting indicators and acceptable ranges; in this instance they are environmentally orientated. The data generated from the monitoring programme is then plotted to determine whether the status is within the acceptable range or not. Annual performance is presented via report charts already displaying benchmarks, and a relatively simple table that is principally designed to quickly reflect whether each indicator is within its acceptable range or not. The presentation of data is therefore designed to provide a 'quick and dirty

look' that all stakeholders can utilise (Hall and McArthur 1998).

The third stage of development is a management response system. This system involves the identification of poor performing indicators, the exploration of cause-and-effect relationships, the identification of results requiring a response and the development of management response options. The first part of the response system is to annually identify which indicators are not performing within their acceptable range. This involves reviewing the report charts to identify and list each indicator whose annual performance data are outside its acceptable range. It also involves identifying the degree of the discrepancy and whether the discrepancy is part of a longer term trend. The trend is determined by reviewing previous annual data that have been entered onto the report charts. A qualitative statement is then entered under the degree of discrepancy. The second part in the response mechanism is to explore cause and effect relationships. The essential question relating to cause and effect is whether the discrepancy was principally induced by tourism activity or other effects such as the actions of local residents, initiatives by other industries, and regional, national or even global influences. The third part in the system simply involves nominating whether a response is required. Specific choices for the response could include a tourism-oriented response, a response from another sector, or identification that the situation is beyond anyone's control.

The fourth and final part involves developing response options, dependent upon whether they

- require a response from a non-tourism sector (this involves identifying the appropriate body responsible, providing them with the results and suggesting a response on the matter)
- were out of anyone's control (in this instance no response is required)
- require a response from the tourism sector (this involves generating a series of management options for consideration, such as

Table 4.3: Assessment criteria for selecting indicators for Tourism Optimisation Management Model on Kangaroo Island

Criterion	Explanation	Example
Degree of relationship with actual tourism activity	The indicator needs to have a clear relationship with tourism activity to be relevant to the model	The number of fur seals at Seal Bay is more relevant than the number of possums at Stokes Bay
Accuracy	The indicator needs to represent the desired condition accurately	The number of traffic accidents is more accurate than the perception of parking difficulties
Utility	The indicator is more worthwhile if it generates additional insights	Visitation (number of visitors) has greater utility than perception of crowding
Availability of data	The indicator is more worthwhile if data already exist and are accessible, rather than needing to be collected from scratch	Data on the level of expenditure are more available than operator profit
Cost to collect and analyse	The indicator is more worthwhile if it requires minimal additional human resources to collect and analyse	The level of direct tourism employment is cheaper to monitor than the number of tourism products developed by local suppliers in response to tourist demand

Source: McArthur (2000a)

Table 4.4: Management objectives and potential indicators for assessing the quality of the environment on Kangaroo Island

Optimal conditions	Indicators	Acceptable range
The majority of the number of visits to the island's natural areas occur in visitor service zones	• The proportion of visitors to the island's natural areas who visit areas zoned specially for managing visitors	65 to 100% of visitors
Ecological processes are maintained or enhanced in areas where tourism activity occurs	• Net overall cover of native vegetation at specific sites	0 to 5% increase in native vegetation from base case
Major wildlife populations attracting visitors are maintained and/or enhanced in areas where tourism activity occurs	• Number of seals at designated tourist site • Number of hooded plover at designated tourist site • Number of osprey at designated tourist site	0 to 5% annual increase in number sighted
The majority of tourism accommodation operations have implemented some form of energy and water conservation practice	• Energy consumption/visitor night/visitor • Water consumption/visitor night/visitor	3 to 7 kilowatts 20 to 40 litres of water

Source: McArthur (2000a)

additional research to understand the issue, modification to existing practices, site-based development, marketing and lobbying).

After the tourism-related options are developed, the preferred option is tested by brainstorming how the option might influence the various indicators. This requires the reuse of the predicted performance and management response sections of the model. Once several years of data are collected, the model can be transferred to a simple computer program to streamline the reporting, predicting and testing of options.

The final application of the model is to test potential options or management responses to a range of alternative scenarios. The first form of testing for application is the performance of a sample of individual indicators. The second form of testing the model's performance is against several potential future scenarios that have already been developed and presented in the contextual analysis. The testing helps ensure that the model has some degree of predictive capability.

The first TOMM was produced in late 1996 and implemented during 1997 (Hall and McArthur 1998; McArthur 2000a). It spanned public and private land in South Australia's Kangaroo Island, and was co-funded by the Federal and South Australian Tourism Departments, and the South Australian Department of Environment and Natural Resources. The TOMM has attracted support not only from its three public sector funders, but also from local government, the local tourism association, the tourism industry, conservation groups and members of the local community (Hall and McArthur 1998; McArthur 2000a). This has been achieved because of several key characteristics, including

- the TOMM covers a range of dimensions to the heritage–visitor relationship
- a wide range of stakeholders collect data and therefore 'own' part of the intellectual property
- the results of the monitoring are produced in easy-to-follow formats so that any untrained eye can pass over them and broadly deduce the health of the heritage–visitor relationship
- management strategies can be jointly determined through shared understandings of the current situation and emerging trends.

ECONOMIC ANALYSIS

Within tourism and recreation research, 'until recently, attention has concentrated on the more obvious economic impacts with comparatively little consideration being given to the environmental and social consequences of tourism' (Mathieson and Wall 1982: 3–4). However, considerable debate has arisen over methodological problems in the economic analysis of tourism, including the hosting of events (see below), particularly in the measurement of tourism as an economic activity, through the use of satellite accounts, economic multipliers and cost–benefit analysis (Archer 1976, 1977a, 1977b, 1984; Murphy 1985; D.G. Pearce 1989; S.L.J. Smith 1994, 2000; S.L.J. Smith and Wilton 1997; World Tourism Organization 1999; Sinclair

et al. 2003), the evaluation of opportunity cost (Vaughan 1977) and the relationship of tourism and recreation to regional development and employment (Royer et al. 1974; Doering 1976; Frechtling 1976b; Hudman 1978; Ellerbrook and Hite 1980; Williams and Shaw 1988; Sinclair 1998).

Many economic impact studies focus on what is known as the 'multiplier effect'. This effect is concerned with 'the way in which expenditure on tourism filters throughout the economy, stimulating other sectors as it does so' (D.G. Pearce 1989: 205). Several different types of multiplier are in use, each with their own emphasis (Archer 1977a, 1977b, 1982). However, the multiplier may best be regarded as 'a coefficient which expresses the amount of income generated in an area by an additional unit of tourist spending' (Archer 1982: 236). It is the ratio of direct and secondary changes within an economic region to the direct initial change itself. In this context geographers have not played a major role, although multiplier analysis is not devoid of a spatial component with its linkage to regional science and its spatial concerns for quantitative analysis of areas and locations. In some cases, geographers have not pursued the regional analytical approaches of the economists in measuring and analysing tourist activity in a spatial context due to the prevailing geographic paradigms in human geography, with such approaches instead being located more in the bounds of regional science research. Although economic geography has overlapped with economics in some cases, tourism and recreation is not an area where this occurred on a wide scale (Ioannides 1995; Ioannides and Debbage 1998) although the publication of the journal *Tourism Economics* has arguably led to greater cross-disciplinary engagement. Likewise, collaborative research between geographers and economists has not emerged as a theme in research until the mid-1990s (Martin 1999; G. Clark et al. 2000). This is often because each subject area has its own concepts, language, approach and few obvious intersections in the research field because tourism and recreation remained a fringe area for research in the 1960s and 1970s for both geographers and economists.

The economic impacts of tourism and recreation are usually classified as being either primary or secondary in nature (Archer 1982). Primary or direct impacts are those economic impacts which are a direct consequence of visitor spending (e.g. the purchase of food and beverages by a tourist in a hotel). Secondary impacts may be described as being either indirect or induced. Indirect impacts are those arising from the response of money in the form of local business transactions (e.g. the new investment of hotel owners in equipment and supplies). Induced impacts are those arising from the additional income generated by further consumer spending (e.g. the purchase of goods and services by hotel employees). For each round of spending per unit of initial visitor expenditure leak-age will occur from the regional economy until little or no further re-spending is possible. Therefore, the recreation or tourism multiplier is a measure of the total effects (direct plus secondary effects) which result from the additional tourist or recreational expenditure. However, despite their extensive use, it should be noted that 'multipliers are difficult to calculate precisely under the best circumstances. They require substantial amounts of very detailed data. The methods used are also difficult and require a high degree level of statistical and/or macro-economic expertise' (S.L.J. Smith 1995: 16; see also Saeter 1998).

The size of the visitor multiplier will vary from region to region and will depend on a number of factors, including

- the size of area of analysis
- the proportion of goods and services imported into the region for consumption by visitors
- the rate of circulation
- the nature of visitor spending
- the availability of suitable local products and services
- the patterns of economic behaviour for visitor and local alike.

As a measure of economic benefit from recreation and tourism, the multiplier technique has been increasingly subject to question, particularly as its use has often produced exaggerated results (Archer 1977a, 1982; Cooper and Pigram 1984; Frechtling 1987; D.G. Pearce 1989; S.L.J. Smith 1995; Sinclair et al. 2003). Nevertheless, despite doubts about the accuracy of the multiplier technique, substantial attention is still paid to the results of economic impact studies by government and the private sector as a measure of the success of tourism development or as a way of estimating the potential contribution of a proposed development in order to justify policy or planning decisions. As S.L.J. Smith (1995: 16) noted: 'Regrettably, the abuses of multipliers often seem to be as frequent as legitimate uses – thus contributing further to the industry's lack of credibility.'

The size of the tourist multiplier is regarded as a significant measure of the economic benefit of visitor expenditure because it will be a reflection of the circulation of the visitor dollar through an economic system. In general, the larger the size of the tourist multiplier, the greater the self-sufficiency of that economy in the provision of tourist facilities and services. Therefore, a tourist multiplier will generally be larger at a national level than at a regional level, because at a regional level leakage will occur in the form of taxes to the national government and importation of goods and services from regions. Similarly, at the local level, multipliers will reflect the high importation level of small communities and tax payments to regional and national governments (Hall 1995).

According to Murphy (1985: 95), 'for practical purposes it is crucial to appreciate that local multiplier studies are just case studies of local gains and no more' and several questions remain unanswered about the real costs and benefits of tourism on local and regional development. Indeed, a major question should be: Who are the winners and losers in tourism development? As Coppock (1977b) argued in relation to the use of tourism as a tool for economic development:

> Not only is it inevitable that the residents of an area will gain unequally from tourism (if indeed they gain at all) and probable that the interests of some will actually be harmed, but it may well be that a substantial proportion does not wish to see any development of tourism.
>
> (Coppock 1977b: 1)

One of the primary justifications used by government in the encouragement of tourism development is that of tourism's potential employment benefits (D.G. Pearce 1992a; Hall 1994; Jenkins et al. 1998; R. Hudson 2000). However, as Hudson and Townsend (1992) observed, there is

> a growing involvement of local authorities in policies to sustain existing tourist developments and encourage new ones, although often the actual impacts of tourism on local employment and the economy are imperfectly understood. The direction of causality between growing employment and increasing policy involvement is often obscure and in any case variable.
>
> (Hudson and Townsend 1992: 64)

One of the ironies of the perceived employment benefits of tourism and recreation is that areas which have tourism as a mainstay of the local economy tend to have high levels of unemployment where there is substantial flexibility in the regulation of the labour market (Hall 2003a). For example, two of Australia's major destination areas, the Gold Coast and the Sunshine Coast in Queensland, have had unemployment rates significantly above the national average (Mullins 1984, 1990). Such a situation is often regarded by local politicians as an 'imported problem', by which

> the unemployed flock into these cities for the 'good life'. Yet data . . . on interstate transferees on unemployment benefits shows that the net number remaining in the Gold Coast and Sunshine Coast over any 12 month period barely makes 1 per cent of these cities unemployed.
>
> (Mullins 1990: 39)

Instead of 'dole-bludger' (an Australian term which refers to people who deliberately seek unemployment benefits rather than paid employment) and surfer migration, the answer to the unemployment situation rests on the nature of the two regions' economies. The economies of both areas are founded on two unstable industries: tourism, which is seasonal, and construction, which is cyclical and is itself related to actual or predicted tourist flows. Therefore, as Mullins (1990: 39) reported, 'high rates of unemployment seem inevitable', although as the economic base of the regions diversifies, unemployment levels should fall.

Another major consideration in the potential contribution of tourism to the national economy is the organisation and spatial allocation of capital and, in particular, the penetration of foreign or international capital (R. Hudson 2000; Shaw and Williams 2004). The distribution and organisation of capital and tourists is also spread unevenly between and within regions; indeed, D.G. Pearce (1990a, 1992a) has even argued that tourism is often seen as a mechanism for redistributing wealth between regions. However, the extent to which this actually occurs once all capital flows are taken into account may be highly problematic. Geographers have long noted the manner in which tourism tends to distribute development away from urban areas towards those regions in a country which have not been developed (e.g. Christaller 1963), with the core–periphery nature of tourism being an important component of political-economy approaches towards tourism (Britton 1980a, 1980b, 1982; Shaw and Williams 2004; Hall 2005a), particularly with respect to tourism in island microstates (Connell 1988; Lea 1988; Weaver 1998; Gössling 2003; Duval 2004).

More recently, geographers have begun to critically analyse tourism with reference to issues of economic restructuring, processes of globalisation and the development of post-Fordist modes of production, including recognition of 'the cultural turn' in economic geography (e.g. Britton 1991; Hall 1994; Debbage and Ioannides 1998; Milne 1998; Williams and Shaw 1998; Debbage and Ioannides 2004; Shaw and Williams 2004). Tourism is a significant component of these shifts which may be described as 'post-industrial' or 'post-Fordist', which refers to the shift from an industrial to an information technology/service base. In addition, tourism is part of the globalisation of the international economy, in which economic production is transnational, interdependent and multipolar, with less and less dependence on the nation state as the primary unit of international economic organisation. As Williams and Shaw (1998) recognise:

> The essence of tourism is the way in which the global interacts with the local. For example, mass tourism emphasises a global scan for destinations for global (or at least macro-regional) markets, while some forms of new tourism seek to exploit the individuality of places. These global–local relationships are not static but are subject to a variety of restructuring processes.
>
> (Williams and Shaw 1998: 59)

The notion of the 'globalisation' of tourism implies its increasing commodification. The tourist production system simultaneously 'sells' places in order to attract tourists, the means to the end (travel and accommodation) and the end itself (the tourist experience). Therefore, tourism finds itself at the forefront of an important recent dynamic within capitalist accumulation in terms of the creation and marketing of experiences. Tourists 'are purchasing the intangible qualities of restoration, status, life-style signifier, release from the constraints of everyday life, or conveniently packaged novelty' (Britton 1991: 465). Within this setting, place is therefore commodified and reduced to an experience and images for consumption. However, while place promotion is recognised as increasingly important for tourism and recreation (see Chapter 5), there have been insufficient attempts, with the exception of some of the authors noted above, to locate such issues within the context of mainstream tourism studies or tourism geography.

Related to the economic analysis of tourism has been the study of the forecasting of visitor demand (e.g. Blake and Sinclair 2003; Durbarry and Sinclair 2003) and the marketing of the tourist product. Several studies of hallmark events, for example, have attempted to deal with the problem of forecasting visitor demand (see Ritchie and Aitken 1984; Hall 1992b). Nevertheless, substantial methodological problems still remain, and 'although relatively sophisticated statistical measures have been used, forecasts of tourism demand can produce only approximations' (Uysal and Crompton 1985: 13). Many of the early studies of the effects of tourism were restricted to economic analyses and enumerated the financial and employment benefits which accrued to destination areas as a result of tourism development. However, since the late 1970s a number of studies have emerged that examine the socio-cultural impacts of tourism which cast a more negative light on tourism's development capacities (Mathieson and Wall 1982).

INSIGHT: The economic impact of events

An area which has seen considerable attention by geographers (e.g. B.J. Shaw 1985; Getz 1991a, 1991b; Hall 1992b; Hall and Hodges 1996) is the impact of hosting staged, short-term attractions, usually referred to as hallmark, special or mega events (Ritchie 1984; Ritchie and Yangzhou 1987; Hall 1989) and particularly the impact of sports teams and events (Hall 2001b; Hinch and Higham 2003; Owen 2003). The hallmark event is different in its appeal from the attractions normally promoted by the tourist industry as it is not a continuous or seasonal phenomenon. Indeed, in many cases the hallmark event is a strategic response to the problems that seasonal variations in demand pose for the tourist industry (Ritchie and Beliveau 1974). Although, the ability of an event 'to achieve this objective depends on the uniqueness of the event, the status of the event, and the extent to which it is successfully marketed within tourism generated regions' (Ritchie 1984: 2). As with other areas of research on the economic impacts of tourism, the analysis of hallmark events has been characterised by overstated large benefit–cost ratios (Hall 1989, 1992b; Getz 1991b). Several reasons can be cited for this:

• There has been a failure to account for the economic impact that would have occurred anyway but has switched from one industry to another.
• There has been an 'unfortunately common mistake' of attributing all the benefits received from the event to government expenditure, instead of establishing the marginal impact of that contribution' (Burns and Mules 1986: 8, 10).
• The taxation benefits of expenditure generation has been counted as additional to the multiplier 'flow-ons' when they have already been included.
• 'Output' rather than 'value-added' multipliers, which can result in major overestimates of the economic impact of events, are frequently uncritically used.
• There has been a general failure to delimit the size of the regional economy that is to be studied. The smaller the area to be analysed, the greater will be the number of 'visitors' and hence the greater would be the estimate of economic impact.

As Long and Perdne (1990: 10) observe 'attracting non-residents to the community with the expectation that their spending will contribute significantly to the local economy' has been a key argument used to justify public sector investment to develop, underwrite and promote event-based tourism development (Connell and Page 2005). Yet there are also significant economic costs which can arise when adverse weather conditions prevail, as in the case of Edinburgh's Hogmany celebrations in 2003 when losses of £1.5 million arose from cancelling the event. In this respect, risk assessment needs to accompany any public sector (and private sector) investment in staging hallmark, special or mega events.

ANALYSIS OF TOURISM'S SOCIAL IMPACTS

The social impact of tourism refers to the manner in which tourism and travel effects changes in collective and individual value systems, behaviour patterns, community structures, lifestyle and the quality of life (Hall 1995; Mason 2003). The major focus of research on the social impacts of tourism is on the population of the tourist destination rather than on the tourist generating area and the tourists themselves, although significant work is also done in this area particularly with respect to outdoor recreationists. The variables which contribute

Plate 4.3: Market scene, Vanuatu, South Pacific. Local communities can benefit from visitors if they are encouraged to patronise local facilities rather than being cocooned in the environmental bubble of resort hotels.

to resident perceptions of tourism may be categorised as either extrinsic or intrinsic (Faulkner and Tideswell 1996). Extrinsic variables refer to factors which affect a community at a macro level (e.g. stage of tourism development, the ratio between tourists and residents, cultural differences between tourists and residents, and seasonality). Intrinsic variables are those factors which may vary in association with variations in the characteristics of individuals in a given population (e.g. demographic characteristics, involvement in tourism and proximity to tourist activity) (Hall 1998).

Researchers from a number of disciplinary backgrounds have conducted work on the social impacts of tourism. For example, interest in tourism marketing strategies and increased concern for the social consequences of tourism led to the social psychology of tourism becoming a major area of research (e.g. P.L. Pearce 1982, 2005; Stringer 1984; Stringer and Pearce 1984). Research has focused on aspects of the tourist experience as diverse as tourism and culture shock (Furnham 1984), and tourist–guide interaction (P.L. Pearce 1984). Research in the marketing of the tourist product sees attention being paid to the demand, motivations and preferences of the potential tourist (e.g. R.L. Jenkins 1978; Van Raaij and Francken 1984; Kent et al. 1987; D.G. Pearce 1989; S.L.J.

Smith 1995; P.L. Pearce 2005), the evaluation of the tourist product and potential tourist resources (e.g. Ferrario 1979a, 1979b; Gartner 1986; S.L.J. Smith 1995), the intended and unintended use of tourist brochures (e.g. Dilley 1986), the utility of market segmentation for specific targeting of potential consumers (e.g. Murphy and Staples 1979; S.L.J. Smith 1995) and tourist and recreationist satisfaction. In the latter area, geographers have done a substantial amount of work in the outdoor recreation and back-country use field, particularly with respect to the effects of crowding on visitor satisfaction (e.g. Shelby et al. 1989; see also Chapter 7).

Marketing research acts as a link between economic and psychological analysis of tourism (Van Raaij 1986) and gives notice of the need for a wider understanding of the social impact of tourism on visitor and host populations. Research on the social psychology of tourism has run parallel with the research of behavioural geographers in the area, with there being increased interchange between the two fields in recent years (e.g. Jenkins and Walmesley 1993; see also Walmesley and Lewis 1993).

Interestingly, the development of a more radical critique of behaviour in geography also has parallels in the social psychology of tourism as well (P.L. Pearce 2005). For example, the research of Uzzell (1984) on the psychology of tourism marketing from a structuralist perspective offered a major departure from traditional social psychology. Uzzell's (1984) alternative formulation of the role of social psychology in the study of tourism has been reflected in much of the research conducted in anthropological, geographical (e.g. Britton 1991) and sociological approaches to the social impacts of tourism (e.g. Urry 1990, 1991).

The early work of Forster (1964), Cohen (1972, 1974, 1979a, 1979b), M. Smith and Turner (1973) and MacCannell (1973, 1976) along with the more recent contribution by Urry (1990) have provided the basis for formulating a sociology of tourism, while V.L. Smith (1977) and Graburn (1983) have provided a useful overview of anthropology's contributions to the study of tourism. The research of geographers such as G. Young (1973), Butler (1974, 1975, 1980), D.G. Pearce (1979, 1981), Mathieson and Wall (1982) and Murphy (1985) has also yielded significant early insights into tourism's social impacts.

Many studies of the social impacts of tourism have focused on the impact of tourism on developing countries (Unesco 1976). This research is no doubt necessary, yet caution must be used in applying research findings from one culture to another. Nevertheless, problems of cultural change and anxiety, social stress in the host community, and social dislocation resulting from changes to the pattern of economic production, may be identified in a wide number of studies undertaken in a variety of cultures and social settings (e.g. Farrell 1978; Mathieson and Wall 1982; Clary 1984b; Oglethorpe 1984; Meleghy et al. 1985; Lea 1988; Getz 1993c; Shaw and Williams 1994; Hall and Page 1996; D. Nash 1996; Mowforth and Munt 1997, 2003; Weaver 1998; Mason 2003; Reid 2003).

The social costs of tourism to the host community will vary according to the characteristics of both visitor and host (Pizam 1978). However, tourism does undoubtedly cause changes in the social character of the destination (J.A. Long 1984; Mason 2003). These changes may be related to the seasonality of tourism (Hartmann 1984), the nature of the tourist (Harmston 1980), the influence of a foreign culture (Mathieson and Wall 1982) and/or to the disruption of community leisure space (O'Leary 1976). An appreciation by planners of the social costs of tourism is essential for both financial and social reasons (Reid 2003). Rejection of visitors by segments of the host community may well result in a decline in the attractiveness of the tourist destination, in addition to the creation of disharmony within the host community (Murphy 1985; Getz 1994b; Page and Lawton 1997). Nevertheless, it is also important to recognise that it may be difficult at times to distinguish between tourism as a factor in social change from other dimensions of change, such as globalisation of communication technology.

Tourism development may initiate changes in government and private organisations (Baldridge and Burnham 1975; Hall and Jenkins 1995; Mason 2003; Reid 2003) in order to cater for the impact of tourism. For instance, additional law enforcement officers may be required (Rothman et al. 1979), while special measures may be needed to restrict dislocation created by increased rents and land values (Cowie 1985) where such regulation is possible. Geographers have long emphasised the importance of meaningful community participation in the decision-making process that surrounds the formulation of tourism policy and development (e.g. Butler 1974, 1975; Brougham and Butler 1981; D.G. Pearce 1981; Getz 1984; Murphy 1985; Mason 2003; Reid 2003; Murphy and Murphy 2004). Furthermore, studies such as those of Keller (1984) and B.J. Shaw (1985, 1986) indicate that the social impacts of tourism are complex and need to be examined within the context of the various economic, environmental, political and social factors that contribute to tourism development in a destination (Mings 1978; Runyan and Wu 1979; Wu 1982; D.G. Pearce 1989; Mason 2003; Murphy and Murphy 2004; Hall 2005a).

Community attitudes towards tourism invariably simultaneously reveal both positive and negative attitudes towards tourism (Butler 1975). For example, various positive and negative attitudes towards tourism were indicated in several studies of resident attitudes towards tourism in northern New South Wales, Australia, in the 1980s (Hall 1990). Pigram (1987) utilised Doxey's (1975) irridex scale of euphoria, apathy, annoyance and antagonism to investigate resident attitudes in the resort town of Coffs Harbour (Table 4.5). According to Pigram, 'the overwhelming majority felt that the economic and otherwise benefits of tourism outweighed the disadvantages' (Pigram 1987: 67). Despite the overall favourable or apathetic response of residents, several negative reactions towards tourism did emerge from the study. According to Pigram (1987), the greatest impact of tourism on the local community was the perceived increase in the cost of goods and services because of the presence of tourists. The respondents also indicated that they believed that petty crime was also worse during the tourist season, an observation supported by

Table 4.5: Resident reaction to tourists in Coffs Harbour

Irridex scale	Survey scale	(% response)
Euphoria	Friendly	29
Apathy	No worry	58
Annoyance	Nuisance	10
Antagonism	Rude/unbearable	3

Source: after Pigram (1987: 68)

Walmesley et al.'s (1981, 1983) study of crime in the region during the late 1970s. Furthermore, the natural environment of the Coffs Harbour area was perceived as slightly worse as a result of tourism with the greatest impact being on the beaches. However, opportunities for public recreation were perceived as the attribute of community life registering the most significant improvement as a result of tourism (Pigram 1987).

Resident attitudes are undoubtedly a key component in the identification, measurement and analysis of tourism impacts. However, investigation of community attitudes towards tourism is not just an academic exercise. Such attitudes are also important in terms of the determination of local policy, planning and management responses to tourism development and in establishing the extent to which public support exists for tourism (D.G. Pearce 1989; Page and Lawton 1997). For example,

Getz (1994b) argued that resident perceptions of tourism may be one factor in shaping the attractiveness of a destination, where negative attitudes may be an indicator of an area's ability to absorb tourism. Although Getz suggests that 'identification of causal mechanisms is a major theoretical challenge, and residents can provide the local knowledge necessary to link developments with their consequences' (1994b: 247), it assumes that residents are sufficiently aware, perceptive and able to articulate such views to decision-makers and planners. Nevertheless, negative resident perceptions may lead to adverse reactions towards tourism and create substantial difficulties for the development of further facilities and infrastructure (Page and Lawton 1997). For example, although communities with a history of exposure to tourism may adapt and change to accommodate its effects (Rothman 1978), active or passive support or opposition may exist at any given time, as interest groups take political action to achieve specific objectives in relation to tourism (Murphy 1985; Hall and Jenkins 1995; Murphy and Murphy 2004).

In locations where the original community is 'swamped' by large-scale tourism development in a relatively short space of time, disruption to the community values of the original inhabitants is more likely to occur (P. Hudson 1990a, 1990b). Table 4.6 details the costs and benefits of such tourism development in Broome, Western Australia.

Table 4.6: Costs and benefits of tourism development in Broome, Australia

Costs	Benefits
Marginalisation of the Aboriginal and coloured people	Expansion of new services and businesses
Too much power in vested interests	More infrastructure and community facilities
Destruction of multicultural flavour of the town and the original form of Shinju Matsuri	More sealed roads and kerbing and guttering
Increased racism	Increased variety of restaurants/entertainment
High accommodation costs/shortage	Restoration of Broome architecture
High local prices	Better health system
Less friendly/more local conflicts	Tidier town
Environmental impacts (e.g. dune destruction)	
Loss of historical character of town and imposition of artificially created atmosphere	
More crime/domestic violence	

Source: P. Hudson (1990b: 10)

However, it must be emphasised that resident attitudes to tourism development will be influenced by where they fit into the existing social and economic order, their personal gains from the development process, and/or their response to the changing environment in light of their pre-existing values and attitudes (Hudson 1990b). In addition, it should be noted that while individuals may perceive there to be negative tourism impacts, they may still be favourable towards tourism's overall benefits to the community. Faulkner and Tideswell (1996) referred to this phenomenon as the 'altruistic surplus' and suggested that this could be the result of a mature stage of tourism development in a destination region whereby residents have adapted to tourism through experience and migration.

In addition to attitudinal studies, a number of other approaches and issues are of interest to the geographer. For example, historical studies of tourism may indicate the role tourism has in affecting attitudes and values with a destination community (e.g. Wall 1983a; Butler and Wall 1985). Studies of tourism policy may assist in an understanding of the way governments develop strategies to manage the negative impacts of tourism and in the overall manner that tourism is used in regional development (e.g. Papson 1981; Kosters 1984; Oglethorpe 1984; Hall and Jenkins 1995; Reid 2003). Another area of tourism's social impact which has received more attention in recent years is that of health (Clift and Page 1996). Researchers have examined the spatial misinformation provided by travel agents when advising clients of the potential health risks they may face when travelling to Pacific Island destinations (Lawton et al. 1996; Lawton and Page 1997a and b). What such research shows is the vital role of understanding place, space and the geography of risk in relation to the epidemiology of disease. While geographers have studied disease for many years, making the link between travel and disease is a comparatively new development (Clift and Page 1996). For example, tourism may assist in the spread of disease, while tourists themselves are vulnerable to illness while travelling. Indeed, one of the major focal points for geographers' research on tourist health in recent years has been the spread of AIDS and its association with sex tourism. There is growing evidence that the geographer will continue to develop expertise in this area and a major contribution could be made at a public policy level in the rapid dissemination of disease alerts to medical practitioners and health professionals through the use of GIS technology. Important collaborations have been forged between geographers, tourism and health researchers to ensure this area expands the frontiers of knowledge (Clift and Page 1996; Wilks and Page 2003).

Prostitution has also been related to tourism in both historical and contemporary settings, with research being focused on tourism in the less developed countries (D.R.W. Jones 1986), issues of gender (Kinnaird and Hall 1994) and sex tourism in particular (Ryan and Hall 2001). Yet prostitution and sex tourism's significant connection to western tourism should also be noted. For example, tourist promotion may highlight the more licentious attributes of a tourist destination. As Bailie (1980) commented:

> Tourism promotion in magazines and newspapers promises would-be vacationers more than sun, sea, and sand; they are also offered the fourth 's' – sex. Resorts are advertized under the labels of 'hedonism', 'ecstacism', and 'edenism'. . . . One of the most successful advertizing campaigns actually failed to mention the location of the resort: the selling of the holiday experience itself and not the destination was the important factor.
>
> (Bailie 1980: 19–20)

The extent of the relationship between crime and tourism has also been examined by several geographers (e.g. L.L. Nichols 1976; Walmesley et al. 1981, 1983), with research on Australian hallmark events also examining the relationship between increased visitor numbers and crime rates (Hall et al. 1995).

Another area to which geographers have been paying increasing attention is the relationship between tourism and indigenous peoples in both developed and less developed nations. While anthropology has focused considerable attention on the impacts and effects of tourism on indigenous peoples (e.g. V.L. Smith 1977, 1992), geographers have assisted greatly in broadening the research agenda to include greater consideration of the way in which indigenous peoples interact with wildlife, the relationship between indigenous peoples and ecotourism and national parks, tourism and land rights, and indigenous business development (e.g. Nelson 1986; Nickels et al. 1991; Mercer 1994; Butler and Hinch 1996; Lew and van Otten 1997).

One of the most important concepts in humanistic geography is that of a 'sense of place'. A sense of place arises where people feel a particular attachment or personal relationship to an area in which local knowledge and human contacts are meaningfully maintained. 'People demonstrate their sense of place when they apply their moral or aesthetic discernment to sites and locations' (Tuan 1974: 235). However, people may only consciously notice the unique qualities of their place when they are away from it or when it is being rapidly altered.

The sense of place concept is of significance to tourism development for a number of reasons. The redevelopment and re-imaging of communities for tourism purposes (see Chapter 5) may force long-term residents to leave and may change the character of the community (Ley and Olds 1988). In these instances, the identification of residents with the physical and social structure of the neighbourhood may be deeply disturbed, leading to a condition of 'placelessness' (Relph 1976). Residents of destinations which find themselves faced with rapid tourism development may therefore attempt to preserve components of the townscape including buildings and parks in order to retain elements of their identity.

The conservation of heritage is often a reaction to the rate of physical and social change within a community. Generally, when people feel they are in control of their own destiny they have little call for nostalgia. However, the strength of environment and heritage conservation organisations in developed nations is perhaps a reflection of the desire to retain a sense of continuity with the past (Lowenthal 1975, 1985). In addition, the protection of historic buildings and the establishment of heritage precincts can also effect a significant economic return to destinations because of the desire of many visitors to experience what they perceive as authentic forms of tourism (Konrad 1982; Hall and McArthur 1996).

INSIGHT: Trafficking, sex tourism and slavery

Mobility is an integral part of the process of globalisation. However, one of the more unsavoury aspects of mobility is the extent to which there has been an increase in the extent of trafficking in women and children, often as sex workers. According to Human Rights Watch (1999), a United States based non-government organisation, 'Trafficking, the illegal and highly profitable transport and sale of human beings across or within international borders for the purpose of exploiting their labor, is a human rights abuse with global dimensions', with many thousands of women and girls around the world being lured, abducted or sold into forced prostitution, forced labour, domestic service, or involuntary marriage. Trafficking is therefore closely related to the wider issue of sexual slavery (Matsui 1999). Indeed, K. Barry (1984: 40) argues that 'female sexual slavery is present in ALL situations where women or girls cannot change the immediate conditions of their existence; where regardless of how they got into those conditions they cannot get out; and where they are subject to sexual violence and exploitation'. Nevertheless, Barry does point to the significance of the exploitation that the loss of individual control brings in many situations where prostitution exists.

Many well-publicised media accounts of sex tourism in Thailand in particular have noted the extent to which women and girls have been bonded into prostitution, often through agents and brothel owners making loans or payments to relatives (e.g.

see Bishop and Robinson 1998; Matsui 1999). However, the selling of women into prostitution is not isolated to Thailand: it is a global phenomenon in which the female body is objectified into a commodity to be bought and sold. It is the (ill)logical extent of the objectification of labour in which not only are humans seen purely as a unit of sexual labour which is under the control of their 'owner', but also it represents the denial of self of one human by another (Ryan and Hall 2001). Indeed, in South East Asia much of the demand for sex tourism is through intra-regional travel or from domestic travellers, with many of the border regions being areas in which brothels and other illegal activities are concentrated.

The Executive Director of the Women's Rights Division of Human Rights Watch argues that the number of persons trafficked each year is impossible to determine, but it is clearly a large-scale problem, with estimates ranging from hundreds of thousands to millions of victims worldwide (Ralph 2000). The International Organization for Migration has reported on cases of trafficking in South East Asia, East Asia, South Asia, the Middle East, Europe, South America, Central America and North America. For example, the US State Department estimates that each year, 50,000–100,000 women and children are trafficked into the United States. Many women are trafficked to work in brothels, about half are trafficked into bonded sweatshop labour or domestic servitude. Once in the United States, the women who work in brothels typically are rotated from city to city to evade law enforcement, keep the women disoriented and give clients fresh faces (Rosenfried 1997). In her testimony before the Senate Committee on Foreign Relations, Ralph (2000) reported that, 'in August 1999, a trafficking ring was broken up in Atlanta, Georgia that authorities believe was responsible for transporting up to 1000 women from several Asian countries into the United States and forcing them to work in brothels across the country'.

Plate 4.4: Tourist saturation in St Mark's Square, Venice, Italy.

Plate 4.5: Front of St Mark's Square, Venice. The unique marine environment provides opportunities for sustainable tourist transport as the water taxis (gondolas) show.

PHYSICAL ENVIRONMENTAL IMPACTS

One of the areas of major interest for geographers is the impacts of tourists and recreationists on the physical environment (Butler 2000). The reason for this lies in part in the nature of geography, which has a strong tradition of study of the interactions of humans with their environment (Mitchell and Murphy 1991; Wong 2004). Indeed, the impacts of tourism and recreation on the physical environment and the subsequent resource analysis is one area where human and physical geographers find common ground in studying visitor issues (Johnston 1983b; Butler 2000; Mason 2003). However, another reason is the sheer significance of the physical environment for the recreation and tourism industry. As Mathieson and Wall (1982: 97) commented: 'In the absence of an attractive environment, there would be little tourism. Ranging from the basic attractions of sun, sea and sand to the undoubted appeal of historic sites and structures, the environment is the foundation of the tourist industry.'

The relationship between tourism and the environment is site and culture dependent and will likely change through time and in relation to broader economic, environmental and social concerns. As noted in Chapter 3, the recognition of something as a resource is the result of human perception, so it is also with the recognition that there are undesirable impacts on a environmental resource.

Increasing attention has been given to the impacts that tourism and recreation may have on the environmental and physical characteristics of a host community since the early 1970s (Walter 1975; Organisation for Economic Cooperation and Development 1980; Murphy 1985; S.L.J. Smith 1995). Interest in this area of applied geography is partly a response to the growth of tourism and the sheer impact that increased numbers of visitors will have on specific sites. However, concern has also developed because of the activities of environmental interest groups which have often provided an advocacy role for geographers in terms of arguing the results of the research and scholarship in direct involvement in the planning and policy process (Hall 1992a; Mercer 2000, 2004). The rise of the environmental movement has not only led to improvements in conservation practices but also encouraged public interest in natural areas. However, 'environmentalism' and 'environmentalist' are oft-used terms that are frustratingly vague. According to O'Riordan and Turner (1984):

Although environmentalists are not the only people who object to much of what they interpret as modern-

day values, aspirations and ways of life, it is probably fair to say that one of the two things which unite their disparate perceptions is a wish to alter many of the unjust and foolhardy features they associate with modern capitalism of both a state and private variety. The other common interest is a commitment to cut waste and reduce profligacy by consuming resources more frugally. Environmentalists do not agree, however, about how the transition should be achieved.
(O'Riordan and Turner 1984: 1)

Nevertheless, despite confusion about what is meant by an environmentally 'responsible' approach to tourism development, it is apparent that the protection of the natural and cultural resources upon which tourism is based is essential for the sustainable development of a location (Hall and Lew 1998).

There is no fundamental difference in conducting research on the effects of tourism on the natural environment and research on the environmental impacts of recreation. The footprints of a recreationalist are the same as those of the tourist. The majority of research has been undertaken on the effects of tourism and recreation on wildlife and the trampling of vegetation, with relatively little attention being given to impacts on soils and air and water quality (Wall and Wright 1977; Mathieson and Wall 1982; Edington and Edington 1986; Meyer-Arendt 1993; Parliamentary Commissioner for the Environment 1997).

The majority of studies have examined the impacts of tourism and recreation on a particular environment or component of the environment rather than over a range of environments. According to Mathieson and Wall (1982: 94), 'there has been little attempt to present an integrated approach to the assessment of the impacts of tourism'. However, there is clearly a need to detect the effects of tourism on all aspects of an ecosystem. For example, the ecology of an area may be dramatically changed through the removal of a key species in the food chain or through the introduction of new species, such as trout, for enhanced benefits for recreational fishing or game for hunters (Hall 1995). In addition, it is important to distinguish between perceptions and actual impacts of tourism (Orams 2002). For example, many visitors believe an environment is healthy as long as it looks 'clean and green'. The ecological reality may instead be vastly different; an environment may be full of invasive introduced species which, although contributing to a positive aesthetic perception, may have extremely negative ecological implications (Newsome et al. 2002). For example, while New Zealand promotes its tourism very strongly on the basis of its 'clean, green' image, the reality is quite different with respect to many tourist locations which may have very few indigenous species present and may have very low biodiversity (Parliamentary Commissioner for the Environment 1997).

Research on impacts has focused on particular regions or environments which has limited the ability to generalise the findings from one area to another. In addition, research on visitor impacts is comparatively recent and is generally of a reactionary nature to site-specific problems. We therefore rarely know what conditions were like before tourists and recreationalists arrived. Few longitudinal studies exist by which the long-term impacts of visitation can be assessed. Therefore, there are a number of significant methodological problems which need to be addresssed in undertaking research on the environmental affects of tourism (Mathieson and Wall 1982: 94):

- the difficulty of distinguishing between changes induced by tourism and those induced by other activities
- the lack of information concerning conditions prior to the advent of tourism and, hence, the lack of a baseline against which change may be measured
- the paucity of information on the numbers, types and tolerance levels of different species of flora and fauna
- the concentration of researchers upon particular primary resources, such as beaches and mountains, which are ecologically sensitive.

Nevertheless, despite the difficulties that have emerged in studying the relationship between tourism and the natural environment, it is apparent that 'a proper understanding of biological, or more specifically, ecological factors can significantly reduce the scale of environmental damage associated with recreational and tourist development' (Edington and Edington 1986: 2).

Tourism and recreation can have an adverse impact on the physical environment in numerous ways; for example, the construction of facilities that are aesthetically unsympathetic to the landscape in which they are situated, what D.G. Pearce (1978: 152) has described as 'architectural pollution', and through the release of air-borne and water-borne pollutants. Tourist or special-event facilities may change the character of the urban setting. Indeed, the location of a facility or attraction may be deliberately exploited in an attempt to rejuvenate an urban area through the construction of new infrastructure, as with the 1987 America's Cup in Fremantle (Hall 1992b) or other hallmark events such as the Olympic Games or World Fairs (see Chapter 5). The promotion of tourism without the provision of an adequate infrastructure to cope with increased visitor numbers may well cause a decline in urban environmental quality, for instance, in the impacts of increased traffic flows (Schaer 1978). However, there are a wide range of tourism and recreation impacts on the urban physical environment (Table 4.7) that may have substantial implications for the longer term sustainability of a destination which are only now being addressed in the tourism literature (Page 1995a; Hinch 1996).

Many of the ecological effects of tourist facilities may well take a long time to become apparent because of the nature of the environment, as in the case of the siting of marinas or resorts (Hall and Selwood 1987). The impact of outdoor recreation on the natural environment has been well documented (Wall and Wright 1977; Mathieson and Wall 1982; Liddle 1997; Hammitt and Cole 1998; Mason 2003) and is discussed further in Chapter 7. However, research on the physical impacts of tourism and tourism development on the environment is still at a relatively early stage of development and presents an important area of future research, particularly with respect to sustainable tourism development (Farrell and McLellan 1987; Farrell and Runyan 1991; Hunter and Green 1995; German Federal Agency for Nature Conservation

Table 4.7: The impact of tourism on the urban physical environment

---

The urban physical environment
- land lost through tourism development which might have been used for other purposes
- changes to urban hydrology

Visual impact
- development of tourism/leisure districts
- introduction of new architectural styles
- potential reinforcement of vernacular architectural forms
- potential contribution to population growth

Infrastructure
- potential overloading of existing urban infrastructure with the following utilities and developments:
  - roads
  - railways
  - car parking
  - electricity and gas
  - sewage and water supply
- provision of new infrastructure
- additional environmental management measures to accommodate tourists and adapt areas for tourist use

Urban form
- changes to land use as residential areas are replaced by accommodation developments
- alterations to the urban fabric from pedestrianisation and traffic management schemes which have been constructed to accommodate visitation

Restoration
- the restoration and conservation of historic sites and buildings
- reuse of the facades of heritage buildings

Source: after Page (1995a: 147)

1997; Hall and Lew 1998; Briassoulis and van der Straaten 1999; Gössling 2003; Mason 2003; Gössling and Hall 2005). Where the geographer has employed techniques from environmental science such as Environmental Assessment (EA), the spatial consequences of tourism and recreation activity have not always been fully appreciated. For example, Page (1992) reviewed the impact of the Channel Tunnel project on the natural and built environment and yet the generative effects of new tourist trips had been weakly articulated in the mountains of documents describing the effects to be mitigated, failing to recognise how this might

impact on destination areas. Again, planners and researchers had failed to recognise how recreational and tourist behaviour cannot easily be incorporated into spatially specific plans for individual infrastructure projects which will have knock-on effects for other parts of the tourism system. Page (1999) also reviews the role of geographers in developing more meaningful appraisals of environmental impacts resulting from tourist transport and the need to scrutinise private sector claims of minimising environmental impacts. Nevertheless, tourism's impacts on the natural environment have often been exaggerated. This is because the impacts of tourism have often failed to be distinguished from other forms of development impact or even such factors as overpopulation, poor agricultural practice or poor resource management (Mercer 2000). This is not to say that tourism has not affected the environment. Yet, what is often at issue are aesthetic or cumulative impacts rather than effects that can be related solely to tourism development, such an observation may apply both with respect to individual species, such as sharks (Pollard et al. 1996), albatross (Higham 1998) and dolphins and whales (Orams 2005), specific environments, such as caves (Baker and Genty 1998), and locations, for example the Great Barrier Reef (Lawrence et al. 2002). Indeed, to focus on tourism as a form of negative impact on the natural environment is to miss the far greater environmental problems which arise from other forms of economic development, such as depletion of fisheries and forest resources and the loss of biodiversity, and the overall lack of monitoring and management of many environments (Farrell and Marion 2001).

For example, in the South Pacific, a region threatened by major environmental problems (Hall and Page 1996), there has been no systematic study of the environmental impacts of tourism over the region as a whole. Data and information are highly fragmented (Milne 1990). Baseline data, i.e. information regarding the condition of the natural environment prior to tourism development, are invariably lacking. Even in Australia, one of the most economically developed nations in the region, information about the environmental impacts of tourism is relatively poor (Warnken and Buckley 2000) and, where it does exist, it tends to be available for areas, such as national parks or reserves, which are under government control, rather than for private lands (Hall 1995; Sun and Walsh 1998). In addition, development specific reports, such as environmental impact statements on resort or tourism developments, required by law in many western countries, are often not required in the countries of the South Pacific because environmental planning legislation is still being developed (Minerbi 1992; Hall and Page 1996).

Minerbi (1992) recorded a number of environmental and ecological impacts associated with tourism development on Pacific islands (Table 4.8). The range of tourism-related impacts is similar to that for many other environments (Mathieson and Wall 1982; Edington and Edington 1986). However, in the case of Pacific islands, tourism impacts may be more problematic because tourism is concentrated on or near the ecologically and geomorphologically dynamic coastal environment. Due to the highly dynamic nature of the coastal environment and the significance of mangroves and the limited coral sand supply for island beaches in particular, any development which interferes with the natural system may have severe consequences for the long-term stability of the environment. The impact of poorly developed tourism projects on the sand cays (coral sand islands) of the Pacific, for example, has been well documented:

- near-shore vegetation clearing exposes the island to sea storm erosion and decreases plant material decomposition on the beach, thereby reducing nutrient availability for flora and fauna
- manoeuvring by bulldozer (instead of hand clearing) results in scarring and soil disturbance and makes sand deposits loose and vulnerable to erosion
- excessive tapping of the fresh ground-water lens induces salt-water intrusion which then impairs vegetation growth and human water use and renders the cay susceptible to storm damage and further erosion

- sewage outfall in shallow water and reef flats may lead to an excessive build-up of nutrients, thereby causing algal growth which may eventually kill coral
- sea-walls built to trap sand in the short term impair the natural seasonal distribution of sand resulting, in the long run, in a net beach loss and a reduction of the island land mass
- boat channels blasted in the reef act as a sand trap; in time they fill with sand which is no longer circulating around the island; in turn this sand is replaced by other sand eroded from the vegetated edges, changing the size and shape of the island and in time threatening the island's integrity (Baines 1987).

Another component of the coastal environment in the Pacific and in other tropical and subtropical areas which are substantially affected by tourism is the clearing and dredging of mangroves and estuaries for resorts. Mangroves and estuarine environments are extremely significant nursery areas for a variety of fish species. The loss of natural habitat due to dredging or infilling may therefore have a dramatic impact on fish catches. In addition, there may be substantial impacts on the whole of the estuarine food chain with a subsequent loss of ecological diversity. A further consequence of mangrove loss is reduced protection against erosion of the shoreline thereby increasing vulnerability to storm surge. Therefore, removal of mangroves will not only have an adverse impact on the immediate area of clearance, but also affect other coastal areas through the transport of greater amounts of marine sediment (Clarke 1991).

In concluding his examination of the impacts of tourism development on Pacific islands, Minerbi (1992) was scathing in his criticism of the environmental impacts of tourism:

Resorts and golf courses increase environmental degradation and pollution. Littering has taken place on beaches and scenic lookouts and parks. Marine sanctuaries have been overrun and exploited by too many tourists. Resorts have interfered with the hydrological cycle by changing groundwater patterns, altering stream life, and engaging in excessive ground-

Table 4.8: Environmental and ecological impacts of tourism on the Pacific islands

---

Environmental degradation and pollution
- degradation and pollution of the environment due to golf courses
- pollution by littering

Destruction of habitats and damage to ecosystems
- poorly managed tourism may result in destruction of high-quality natural environments
- unmanaged human interference of specific species of fauna and flora
- dynamite blasting and overfishing

Loss of coastal and marine resources
- interference with inland and coastal natural processes
  - excessive ground-water extraction by large resorts induces salt-water intrusion and deterioration of water quality and recharge of the aquifer
- coastal ecosystem damage and destruction through tourism development
- terrestrial runoff and dredging on coastal areas
  - damage to coral reef and marine resources caused by the construction of tourist infrastructure such as runways, marinas, harbours, parking areas and roads, and use of coral limestone in hotels and resort developments
- destruction by tourist activities
  - destruction of coral reefs, lagoons, mangroves, salt-water marshes and wetlands due to excessive visitation and/or unmanaged exploitation of those resources
  - disturbance to near shore aquatic life due to thrill crafts and boat tours
- introduced exotic species
  - increased sea and air inter-island traffic creates the danger of accidental importation of exotic species, which can be very destructive to indigenous flora and fauna
  - tourism enterprises alter the integrity of the environment and encroach on local lifestyles with imported exotic species for safari hunting
- damage to sand cay ecosystems
- damage to mangrove ecosystems
- damage to coastal rainforest ecosystems
- loss of sandy beaches and shoreline erosion
  - loss of sandy beaches due to onshore development and construction of sea-walls

Coastal pollution
- waste-water discharge and sewage pollution
- coastal water pollution and siltation due to near shore resort construction and runoff from resort areas results in the destruction of natural habitat, coral and feeding grounds for fish
- marine and harbour pollution
  - coastal oil pollution due to motorised vehicles and ships

Surface water and ground-water diversion
- diversion of streams and water sources from local use to resort use, with resulting decline in water availability for domestic and other productive uses and farming, particularly taro cultivation

---

Sources: after Minerbi (1992); see also Milne (1990) and Weiler and Hall (1992)

water extraction. Coastal reefs, lagoons, anchialine ponds, wastewater marshes, mangroves, have been destroyed by resort construction and by excessive visitations and activities with the consequent loss of marine life and destruction of ecosystems. Beach walking, snorkeling, recreational fishing, boat tours and anchoring have damaged coral reefs and grasses and have disturbed near shore aquatic life. . . .

Tourism has presented itself as a clean and not polluting industry but its claims have not come true.

(Minerbi 1992: 69)

Such expressions of concern clearly give rise to questions regarding how sustainable tourism can really be and the need to provide limits on the expansion of tourism and corresponding human impact. Indeed, observation of the potential combined pressures of the social and environmental impacts of tourism has long led researchers to speculate as to whether there exists a carrying capacity for tourist destinations (e.g. J.M. Hall 1974; McCool 1978; Getz 1983; Mason 2003; Coccossis 2004) (see Chapters 7 and 8). Yet regardless of the empirical validity of the notion of carrying capacity (Wall 1983b; Coccossis 2004), attention must clearly be paid by planners to the ability of an area to absorb tourism in relation to the possibilities of environmental and social degradation (see Chapter 9).

CONCLUSION

The purpose of this chapter has been to give a brief account of some of the potential economic, social and environmental impacts of tourism and recreation. This provides a framework for the discussion of specific forms of tourism and recreation in Chapters 5–8. Tourism and recreation needs to be well managed in order to reduce possible adverse impacts (Murphy 1982; Mason 2003; Reid 2003; Murphy and Murphy 2004). In turn, good management is likely to be related to the level of understanding of tourism and recreation phenomena. There is clearly a need to go beyond the image of tourism and recreation, and develop rigorous integrated economic, environmental, social and political analyses.

Geographers have contributed much to the understanding of the impacts of tourism and recreation, particularly with respect to the impacts on the physical environment and the spatial fixity of such effects. What the geographer has contributed is a better understanding of the wider consequences of individual impacts and their cumulative effect on the natural environment. However, there has been considerable exchange of approaches and methodologies through the various social sciences, which means that the demarcation line between geographical and other approaches has become increasingly fuzzy. This is clearly the case

when using multidisciplinary techniques such as EA which has been enhanced by the use of GIS to improve the precision and location of the spatial awareness of impacts. One notable example during the 1980s and 1990s was the planning for the UK's high-speed rail link between London and the Channel Tunnel where GIS was used to model the optimum route for a tourist-transport infrastructure project, and where political changes and lobbying directly altered the geographical routing and distribution of its impacts (Goodenough and Page 1994). Nevertheless, no one discipline will have all the answers. Given the complex nature of tourism phenomena, particularly with respect to 'solving' environmental problems, the development of multidisciplinary approaches towards recreation and tourism may provide an appropriate starting point for the development of more sustainable forms of tourism.

QUESTIONS

- What are the key factors in determining the accuracy of the assessment of the economic impacts of tourism?
- What may determine the acceptability of a recreation resource management model to stakeholders?
- Why are the impacts of tourism on the natural environment poorly assessed?
- Is tourism necessarily a negative impact on a destination?

READING

Although now somewhat dated, one of the most influential books on understanding the impacts of tourism is

Mathesion, A. and Wall, G. (1982) *Tourism: Economic, Physical and Social Impacts*, London: Longman.

Most general textbooks on recreation and tourism will include overview chapters on the impacts of tourism (e.g. Davidson and Maitland 1997; S. Williams 1998; Mason 2003; Mowforth and Munt 2003; Reid 2003). Interesting regional perspectives on the impacts of tourism are to be found in

Duval, D.T. (ed.) (2004) *Tourism in the Caribbean*, London: Routledge.

Gössling, S. (2003) *Tourism and Development in Tropical Islands: Political Ecology Perspectives*, Aldershot: Edward Elgar.

Hall, C.M. and Page, S.J. (eds) (1996) *Tourism in the Pacific: Cases and Issues*, London: International Thomson Business Press.

Hall, C.M. and Page, S.J. (eds) (2000) *Tourism in South and South-East Asia: Cases and Issues*, Oxford: Butterworth-Heinemann.

Excellent books which deal with the environmental dimensions of tourism and recreation and their management include

Fennell, D. (1999) *Ecotourism: An Introduction*, London: Routledge.

Holden, A. (2000) *Environment and Tourism*, London: Routledge.

Newsome, D., Moore, S. and Dowling, R. (2002) *Natural Area Tourism: Ecology, Impacts and Management*, Clevedon: Channel View.

5

URBAN RECREATION
AND TOURISM

Towns and cities hold a special fascination for the geographer, since their evolution as places where people live, work, shop and engage in leisure has resulted from the process of urbanisation (see Johnston et al. 1994 and Pacione 2001 for more detail). Since classical times, towns and cities have performed tourism and leisure functions (Page 2003a) and therefore, such places have a long history as places where tourism and leisure experiences have been produced and consumed. In recreational terms, town and city dwellers traditionally consumed their leisure time in the areas where they lived, with the exception of the wealthy elites who were able to afford properties in the country, and up to the mid-nineteenth century mass forms of urban leisure and recreation were undertaken in close proximity to the home and local family and kinship networks and local pastimes and holidays. In the case of nineteenth century Warsaw, Olkusnik (2001) documents the process of change in urban recreation. Therefore, urbanisation is a major force contributing to the development of towns and cities, where people live, work and shop (see Johnston et al. 1994 for a definition of the term 'urbanisation'). Towns and cities function as places where the population is concentrated in a defined area, and economic activities locate in the same area or nearby, to provide the opportunity for the production and consumption of goods and services in capitalist societies. Consequently, towns and cities provide the context for a diverse range of social, cultural and economic activities which the population engage in, and where tourism, leisure and entertainment form major service activities. These environments also function as meeting places, major tourist gateways, accommodation and transportation hubs, and as central places to service the needs of visitors. Most tourist trips will contain some experience of an urban area; for example, when an urban dweller departs from a major gateway in a city, arrives at a gateway in another city-region and stays in accommodation in an urban area. Within cities, however, the line between tourism and recreation blurs to the extent that at times one is indistinguishable from the other, with tourists and recreationalists using the same facilities, resources and environments although some notable differences exist. Therefore, many tourists and recreationalists will intermingle in many urban contexts. While most tourists will experience urban tourism in some form during their holiday, visits to friends and relatives, business trips or visits for other reasons (e.g. a pilgrimage to a religious shrine such as Lourdes in an urban area), recreationalists will not use the accommodation but frequent many similar places as tourists. This chapter seeks to examine some of the ways geographers conceptualise, analyse and research urban recreation and tourism, emphasising their contribution to understanding the wider context in which such activities take place. One key feature of the chapter is the emphasis on five specific aspects of geographical inquiry:

- description
- classification
- analysis
- explanation

- application of theoretical and conceptual issues to practical problem-solving contexts.

According to Coppock (1982), the geographer's principal interest in the geographical analysis of leisure provides a useful starting point in understanding the areas of research which have also been developed in urban recreation and tourism research in that they examine

> the way in which . . . pursuits are linked to the whole complex of human activities and physical features that determine the distinctive characters of places and region, and the interactions between such pursuits and the natural and man-made environments in which they occur . . . [and] the study of the spatial interactions between participants and resources probably represents the most significant contribution the geographer can make.
>
> (Coppock 1982: 2–3)

The focus on the behavioural aspects of recreational and tourism behaviour together with the planning, and more recently, the management implications of such activities in the urban environment have become fruitful areas for geographical research.

INSIGHT: Stanley Park, Vancouver

In 1886 1000 acres (404 hectares) of Federal Government land on a largely logged peninsula was leased to the Vancouver City Council for park and recreation purposes. The area, which was named Stanley Park, after Lord Stanley, Governor General of Canada in 1888 when the park was officially opened, now lies at the heart of Vancouver's park system and attracts an estimated 8 million visitors a year to North America's third largest urban park. As well as providing a significant secondary growth forest ecosystem and wetland, the park also contains a number of built attractions and recreation opportunities. Although the former zoo in the park has been closed, the park still contains such attractions as the Vancouver Aquarium Marine Science centre, a miniature railway and children's farmyard, summer theatre and Brockton Point Visitor's centre that features a number of First Nations totem poles. Recreational sites include swimming areas, golf course and putting green, tennis courts and, probably most significantly in terms of use, numerous bicycling, rollerblade, jogging and walking paths. Stanley Park therefore continues many of the traditions of a multiple-use large urban park or commons of the Victorian Period, comparable with similar large areas of urban greenspace elsewhere in the world such as Kings Park in Perth, Western Australia, Centennial Park in Sydney, New South Wales, or the Domain, in Auckland, New Zealand.

Significantly, Stanley Park also has considerable ecological importance and constitutes a contemporary urban ecotourism resource. Great blue herons, the largest in the heron family with a wing span of up to 2 metres and a bird species considered vulnerable because of the loss of its natural habitat, has recently staged a revival in the park with about 80 adult herons nesting in the park in 2004. The species was first identified in the park in the 1920s, but they had deserted the park by 1998. The return of the birds has turned them into something of a tourist attraction. However, as well as being noisy the colony is also quite smelly during springtime because of the waste of nesting chicks and adults and the regurgitation of crab and fish by parents in the feeding of chicks. Indeed, park officials have received a number of complaints from people living in apartments near the colony (Hutchinson 2004) that illustrates the potential conflicts that may arise between different users of urban space. See http://www.parks.vancouver.bc.ca.

GEOGRAPHICAL APPROACHES TO URBAN RECREATION

Despite the growth in geographical research on leisure and recreation (Coppock 1982), the focus on urban issues remained neglected, as Patmore (1983: 87) noted, in that 'in the past geographers, with their inherently spatial interest, have tended to concentrate on outdoor recreation in rural areas, where spatial demands, and spatial conflicts have been the greatest'. This is a strange paradox according to Patmore (1983) since

> the greatest changes in recreation habits [since the early 1930s] have taken place in two opposing directions. High personal mobility has extended opportunities away from the home and brought a growing complexity to the scale and direction of leisure patterns. Conversely, the home has come to provide for a greater range of leisure opportunities, and home-centred leisure has acquired a greater significance. The family has become socially more self-sufficient, its links with the immediate community and with its own extended kinship network weaker. Social independence has been underpinned by greater physical independence of homes in the expanding suburban communities, by the weakening need for communal space that comes with lower housing densities and the command of greater private space.
>
> (Patmore 1983: 87)

For the geographer, understanding the spatial implications of such processes and the geographical manifestation of the urban recreational demand for and the supply of resources requires the use of concepts and methodologies to understand the complexity and simplify the reality of recreational activities to a more meaningful series of concepts and constructs. However, one area that has been largely neglected in reviews of urban recreational activities is the historical dimension. Although Towner (1996) provides an all-embracing review of tourism and leisure in an historical context, it is important to acknowledge the significance of social, political, economic and geographical factors which shaped the evolution of modern-day urban recreation. For this reason, no analysis of urban recreation can commence without an understanding of the historical and geographical processes associated with its development (see Bailey 1989 for a review of the historical leisure research in the UK). By focusing on the development of modern-day recreation in cities since their rapid expansion in the early nineteenth century, it is possible to examine many changes to the form, function and format of urban recreation and its spatial occurrence in the nascent urban–industrial cities and conurbations in England and Wales.

EVOLUTION OF URBAN RECREATION IN BRITAIN

Within the context of towns and cities, S. Williams (1995) argues that

> urban populations engage in most of their leisure activities within the same urban area in which they live. The geographical patterns of residence are translated very readily into a pattern of recreation that is focused upon the urban environment, purely by the fact that most people spend the majority of their leisure time in, or close to the home.
>
> (S. Williams 1995: 8)

This indicates that the patterns of residence and recreation are closely related. The current-day patterns of recreation and the ways in which they developed in Britain are fundamental to any understanding of the development of recreational opportunities in urban areas. According to S. Williams (1995), these passed through three district phases: foundation, consolidation and expansion.

Phase 1: foundation

During the nineteenth century, public provision for urban recreational activities emerged through legislative provision (e.g. the number of urban parks in Britain increased from 19 between 1820 and 1850, to 111 between 1850 and 1880: Conway 1991), while innovations in town planning and urban design led to improved quality of streets and housing areas, expanding the space for recreation. In addition, the nineteenth century saw the social geography of towns and cities in England and Wales (R. Lawton 1978) develop with social patterns of segregation and suburbanisation fuelled by urban growth. This also affected the development of recreational opportunities as cities expanded during the late nineteenth and early twentieth centuries. In the case of Liverpool, Marne (2001) examined the class, gender and ethnicity issues associated with the growth of urban park provision in Liverpool, highlighting many of the socio-geographic inequalities which exist at the present time.

Phase 2: consolidation

The period 1918 to 1939 saw a growth in more specialised forms of urban recreational land uses stimulated by legislation such as the rise of the Small Holdings and Allotments Act 1908, which expanded the range and type of amenity space in towns and cities, while other gaps in provision (e.g. the National Playing Fields Association formed in 1925) recognised the need for space in urban areas to support the role of sport. Likewise, the Physical Training and Recreational Act 1937 effectively signalled the emergence of public sector aid from central government for local authority provision of playing fields, gymnasia and swimming baths.

Phase 3: expansion

During the post-war period several key trends emerged including 'greater levels and diversity of provision in which traditional resources established in earlier phases have been augmented by new forms of provision designed to reflect the diversity and flexibility of contemporary recreational tastes' (S. Williams 1995: 20). In fact, one common theme is the recognition of recreation as an element in statutory planning procedures as the range and consumption of land for recreational purposes increased. However, according to Williams (1995: 21), in the absence of theoretical approaches to describing and explaining the pattern of recreation resources in urban areas, the approach to the task must inevitably become empirical, outlining the typical patterns of provision where older parks and recreation grounds are concentrated towards the

core of the settlement (see the case of Leicester, below), while newer parks and grounds associated with inter-war and post-1945 housing produce further significant zones of provision to the periphery of the city. The outer edges of the built area are important for provision of extensive facilities such as sports grounds and golf courses.

While these conclusions are typical of recreational land use patterns in many towns and cities in England and Wales, one must question the extent to which a purely empirical analysis truly explains the spatial development of recreational resources in Britain's urban areas. For this reason it is valuable to consider the social, economic and political processes which contributed to the spatial organisation and occurrence of urban recreation in such areas in the period after 1800, because traditional empirical analyses are devoid of the diversity of people and users of such resources. For this reason, a series of historical snapshots taken in 1800, the 1840s, 1880s, 1920s, 1960s and post-1960s help to explain how present-day patterns were shaped.

URBAN RECREATION: A SOCIO-GEOGRAPHIC PERSPECTIVE

According to J. Clark and Crichter (1985), during the evolution of a capitalist society such as Britain, the analysis of leisure and recreation has traditionally emphasised institutional forms of provision, while each social class has its own history of organised and informal leisure and recreation. The predominant urban histories are those of male leisure, with female leisure and recreation structured around the family with free-time activities associated with the family, the street and neighbourhood in working-class society. Within historical analyses of urban recreation during the evolution of mass urban society in Victorian and Edwardian Britain, the emergence of distinctive forms of urban recreation and leisure and their spatial occurrence within different social areas of cities has been associated with a number of concepts, the most notable being 'popular culture' (see

R. Williams 1976 for a discussion of popular culture). As Clark and Crichter (1985: 55) argue, 'the early nineteenth century was to bring a dramatic transformation to the form . . . and context of popular culture, imposing very different parameters of time and space, rhythms and routines, behaviour and attitude, control and commerce'. However, the resulting changes cannot simply be conceptualised as a straightforward linear progression since different influences and cross-currents meant that this transformation affected different people and areas at different rates and in varying degrees.

Clark and Crichter (1985) provide a useful historical analysis of leisure and recreational forms in Britain during the nineteenth and twentieth centuries, with the emphasis on the urban forms and political factors, forms of social control (Donajgrodski 1978) and the underlying development and functioning of an urban capitalist society; leisure and recreational forms emerged as a civilising and diversionary process to maintain the productive capacity of the working classes as central to the continued development of capitalism. Therefore, the geographical patterns and manifestation of urban recreation and leisure for all social classes in the British city in the nineteenth and twentieth centuries has to be viewed against the background of social, economic and political processes which conditioned the demand and supply of leisure and recreation for each social class, and in Montreal, Dagenais (2002) highlighted the role of local government in park provision. However, Huggins (2000) questioned conventional stereotypes of the respectable urban middle class in different leisure contexts during the Victorian period. Huggins (2000) highlights the spatial differentiation between highly respectable behaviour in cities where work, home and respectability were interconnected. Yet in more liminal locations away from the home (e.g. the seaside and the racecourse), less respectable and 'sinful' pleasures were consumed by the same middle class, where less respectable behaviour occurred.

According to Billinge (1996: 450), 'Perhaps the single newest element in the townscape after the general regulation of the street, was the park, and more specifically the recreation ground . . . [since] the urban park, as distinct from the garden square, was essentially a nineteenth century phenomenon' and a symbol of civic pride. As Maver (1998: 346) argued, 'the development of Glasgow's public parks . . . sparked municipal interest during the 1850s, given the recognised impact of parks in improving the amenity value of middle-class residential areas'. The acknowledged role of parks as the 'lungs of the city', as a haven from industrialisation, was an attempt to recreate notions of community well-being. In T. Young's (1996) analysis of the development of San Francisco's city parks between 1850 and 1920, the main proponents of park development were a middle- to upper-class elite who embodied notions of parks contributing to well-being, reflecting elements of nature which were balanced and inherently good.

Billinge (1996: 444) recognised the way in which the Victorians engineered the term 'recreation' 'to perfection, they gave it a role and a geography. Confined by time, defined by place and regulated by content, recreation and the time it occupied ceased to be possessions freely enjoyed and became instead, obligations dutifully discharged'. The Victorians established a system of approved urban leisure and recreation activities and, as Billinge (1996) recognised, these were allocated to appropriate times and places. In spatial terms, this led to a reconfiguration of the Victorian and Edwardian town and its hinterland to accommodate new, organised and, later, informal recreational and leisure pursuits in specific spaces and at nominated places. In fact, the natural corollary of this in the late nineteenth century was the rise of the English seaside resort (E.W. Gilbert 1939, 1949, 1954; Walton 1983; Towner 1996). As Billinge (1996: 447) argued, it was 'the provision of set aside resorts for the masses at the scale of the whole township: the seaside resort where behaviour inappropriate in any other occasion could be loosed to burn itself out'. This can be viewed as a further example of the way in which Victorian society sought to exercise both a degree of social and spatial control of recreational spaces and activities among its populace. This created a social necessity for recreation as freedom from work: a non-work activity to recreate body and soul, to be refreshed for the capitalist economic system, with its regulated time discipline of a place for everything, and everything in its place.

For this reason, it is pertinent to consider the key features of J. Clark and Crichter's (1985) historical synthesis of urban leisure and recreation in Britain, since it helps to explain how changes in society shaped the modern-day patterns of urban recreation. Clark and Crichter (1985) adopt a cross-section approach to analyse key periods in nineteenth- and twentieth-century British urban society to emphasise the nature of the changes and type of urban recreation and leisure pursuits. It also helps to explain how the evolution of urban places and recreational activities emerged.

THE 1800s

As emphasised earlier in this chapter, Britain was in the process of emerging from a pre-industrial state. While cities were not a new phenomenon (P. Clark 1981), the movement of the rural population to nascent cities meant that the traditional boundary between work and non-work among the labouring classes was increasingly dictated by the needs of factory or mechanised production. Therefore, pre-industrial flexibility in the work–non-work relationship associated with cottage industries and labouring on the land changed. This led to a clearer distinction between work and non-work time, as time discipline emerged as a portent force during the industrial revolution (Pred 1981). In the pre-industrial, non-urbanised society, leisure and recreational forms were associated with market days, fairs, wakes, holidays, religious and pagan festivals which provided opportunities for sport. While the 1800s are often characterised by brutish behaviour and ribaldry, civilising influences emerged in the form of Puritanism to engender moral sobriety and spatial changes associated with the enclosure movement, which removed many strategic sites of customary activity.

In contrast, the geographical patterns of recreation of the ruling classes

> eschewed contact with lower orders. Its forms were as yet disparate. Shooting, hunting and horse racing . . . the major flat race classics date from the 1770s onwards. . . . For the increasingly influential urban bourgeoisie, the theatre, literature, seaside holidays and music hall denoted more rational forms of leisure which depended for their decorum on the exclusion of the mass of the population.
>
> (J. Clark and Crichter 1985: 55)

THE 1840s

In historical analysis, this period is often characterised as a period of deprivation for the urban working classes. Endemic poverty, associated with rapid urbanisation and inadequate housing, poor living standards and limited infrastructure culminated in high rates of mortality, disease and exploitation of the labouring classes through long hours of work (twelve-hour, six-day weeks) (Page 1988). In terms of urban leisure and recreation, the pre-industrial opportunities for pursuits decreased as did the legal outlets, with many customary pastimes suppressed so that popular culture was conditioned through legislative changes. For example, the New Poor Law Act 1834 (Rose 1985) aimed to control the movement of 'travelling balladeers', 'entertainers' and 'itinerant salesmen' all of whom were deemed as vagabonds and returned to their parish of origin. Similarly, the Highways Act 1835 was intended to remove street nuisances such as street entertainers and traders while the Cruelty to Animals Act 1835 sought to suppress working-class pastimes involving animals, thereby driving many activities underground and leading to the emergence of a hybrid range of recreational activities including popular theatre, pantomime and circuses. In the late 1840s, railway excursions pioneered by Thomas Cook also developed. In addition, a range of rational recreation pursuits emerged in purpose-built facilities made possible by Parliamentary Acts including the Museums Act 1845, the Baths and Wash Houses Act 1846 and the Libraries Act 1850. Social theorists argue that such legislation may have acted as a form of social control (Donajgrodski 1978), to tame a new industrial workforce while demarcating recreation and work. Furthermore, the 1840s saw the emergence of the Victorian concept of domesticity and a bourgeois culture, with the use of a gender separation of male and female work.

THE 1880s

While the early Victorian period saw the establishment of urban recreational facilities, improved working conditions and living standards in the mid- to late Victorian period were accompanied by greater municipal provision (Briggs 1969). Yet as Clark and Crichter (1985) argue, four processes were at work in the 1850s and 1860s which led to significant changes in the 1880s:

- a rise of middle-class urban recreation which excluded the working classes
- the expansion of local government's role in leisure and recreational provision
- an increasing commercialisation and greater capitalisation of urban recreation, relying upon mass audiences and licensing (e.g. the rise of football), which also required large areas of land
- attempts by the working classes to organise urban recreation according to their own aspirations.

By the 1880s, the pattern of urban conurbations had emerged in England which focused on London, the West Midlands, West Yorkshire, Merseyside and Tyneside (R. Lawton 1978). In addition to these trends in urban recreation, the rise of urban middle-class recreational pursuits centred on religion, reading, music and annual holidays reflected a more rational form of recreational activity. Nevertheless, the 1870s saw the growth in public parks and by 1885, nearly 25 per cent of the urban population had access to public libraries. At the same time, informal urban recreation based on the street- and neighbourhood-based activities largely remains invisible in documentary sources and official records, although limited evidence exists in the form of autobiographies and oral history. For example, R. Roberts' (1971, 1976) *The Classic Slum* observed that the pub played a major role in informal recreation in Victorian and Edwardian Salford where a community of 3000 people had 15 beer houses. Through sexual segregation it was possible to observe the rise of male-only urban recreational pursuits in the 1880s. Yet the street life and neighbourhood forms of recreation remained unorganised and informal despite the institutionalisation, segmentation and emergence of a customer–provider relationship in Victorian urban recreational pursuits.

THE 1920s

In Britain, the 1920s are frequently viewed as the era of mass unemployment with social class more spatially defined in the urban environment. While the 1900s saw the rising patronage of the cinema, with 3000 cinemas operating in Britain by 1926 and audiences of 20 million, with many people visiting the cinemas once or twice a week, this pursuit increasingly met the recreational needs of women as it displaced the Victorian music-hall, being more heavily capitalised and more accessible in terms of price and social acceptability. The ideological separation of work and home was firmly enshrined in the 1920s, with a greater physical separation and the rise of annual holidays and day trips using charabancs and cars. Spectator sports also retained large audiences although the social segregation of urban recreation based on social class, mass markets and institutional provision characterised this era.

THE 1960s AND BEYOND

Clark and Crichter (1985) identified six distinct trends occurring from the 1960s on:

- rising standards of domestic consumption
- family-centred leisure

- the decline of public forms of urban leisure and recreation
- emergence of a youth culture
- the establishment of ethnic leisure and recreation culture
- increased state activity in prescribed spheres of urban recreation and a growing commercial domination of leisure institutions and services.

This has been well reviewed in the sociological literature (see Pahl 1975).

In terms of urban recreation, various debates exist in relation to the changes induced by a post-industrial society and the implications for urban recreation. Social theorists point to the concomitant changes induced by economic, occupational and technological change, associated with the demise of manufacturing and the rise of the service sector in towns and cities, affecting the pattern of life and recreational activities of urban populations associated with a growing polarisation of wealth and opportunity. S. Williams (1995: 213) outlines the impact of such changes for post-industrial towns and cities, as older central areas of towns decayed as they lost their economic rationale. In some cases this has led to the creation of space for recreation, as high-density housing and industry has been removed and urban regeneration results.

Williams (1995) also points to the effect of the rise of environmentalism since the 1960s, reflected in the concept of the 'green city' where redundant space is 'greened' to enhance the quality of the city environment while adding recreational opportunities (e.g. greenways, linear parks, green wedges and natural corridors). The greening of cities also has a wider concern with the sustainability of urban life. Williams (1995) also argues that a range of factors militate against the continued well-being of urban recreation provision, many of which are associated with political change outlined in detail by Page et al. (1994). A greater concern with financial costs of publicly provided services, more efficient service delivery and the introduction of compulsory competitive tendering (Benington and White 1988; Page et al. 1994) has characterised public and private sector recreational provision in

urban areas in the 1980s and 1990s. Henry (1988) argued that the outcome will be determined by the political climate and philosophy prevailing in public sector environments, fluctuating between a limited role for the state characterised by right-wing ideology, to one based on principles of social equity and significant levels of public intervention influenced by principles of equality.

In the UK in the new millennium, New Labour has sought to critically analyse the quality of the urban environment, given the previous twenty years of changing policies to towns and cities to improve their liveability. A number of notable developments emanating from the Office of the Deputy Prime Minister (ODPM) include the *Cleaner, Safer, Greener Public Space* (ODPM 2002) report which identified a typology of open space in cities that could be divided into green space, comprising parks, gardens, amenity green space, children's play areas, sports facilities, green corridors, natural/semi-natural green space and other functional green space, and civic space, comprising civic squares, marketplaces, pedestrian streets, promenades and seafronts.

Improving these environments has been achieved, via a Liveability Fund in England, with £89 million allocated for 2003–6 supported by other specific green space initiatives such as the establishment of the Commission for Architecture and the Built Environment (CABE), to champion parks and green space in cities to stimulate an urban renaissance in their planning, management and redevelopment after neglect over previous years. (CABE's rationale and focus for action can be found in its various position statements at http://www.cabespace.org.uk.) CABE recognised the importance of cities having green space strategies, since those which possessed them had better quality green space. Other bodies such as the Urban Parks Forum have also been an effective lobby to improve the green space in cities as a basis for social improvements to the liveability of city environments and the residents' quality of life. In fact Toronto has just launched a Green Tourism Map which extends the concept of green recreational activities to visitors who are not aware of the adventures and experiencees available in the city (see http://www.greentourism.ca).

Curry (2000) examined one area of activity, the growth of community participation in outdoor recreation opportunities in urban areas resulted from threats posed by the freeing up of the planning system in the 1980s and 1990s, with the progressive loss of less formal open space. One of the main pressures on local authorities to sell vacant land for development saw a similar neglect of existing open spaces (Open Spaces Society 1992). The rise of partnerships with community groups in an era of declining municipal provision was reflected in the former Countryside Commission (now the Countryside Agency) initiative in 1996 to create 1000 millennium greens by the year 2000. Although this ambitious target was subsequently modified to 250 greens, a stimulus was the competitively funded 50 per cent grant towards site acquisition and creation works (with 50 per cent to be generated from the local community). A Millennium Green (MG) could be located in or on the edge of a city, town, suburb, village or hamlet, and be up to 30 acres in size. The Countryside Agency received £10 million of Lottery Funding from the Millennium Commission and each green had to meet the following basic criteria:

- The site is to be held on trust as a permanent resource for the local community, normally through purchase or donation of the freehold.
- There is public support for the proposal, which also demonstrates that the Millennium Green is needed and that it will make a substantial contribution to the life of the community.
- Anyone may use any part of the land on foot, for informal enjoyment and play.

- Local people will be able to reach the Millennium Green safely and conveniently from their home.
- The community has viable and convincing proposals for the long-term management of the site.
- The Millennium Green could not happen without Millennium Commission funding and convincing proposals from the community (Countryside Agency 2000).

Priority was granted to proposals creating new areas of green space, and by late 1998 252 Site Preparation Grants had been awarded, of which 120 received full funding from partnerships. By 1999, 843 groups had made an initial application (Curry 2000). A comparison of the spatial distribution of Country Parks and MGs, both of which are the main post-war state initiatives to create national recreation sites, revealed an interesting pattern. The Country Parks were haphazard and sporadic in their distribution and the pattern of MGs is not dissimilar.

Many of the initiators of MGs were from the more affluent sections of society, and beneficiaries may be returning to politics of Victorian park founding observed by Maver (1998) in Glasgow. Here the politics of voluntary involvement and activity may simply reinforce patterns of inequality in recreational provision, reflecting political processes and other factors (e.g. human agency) shaping the landscape and pattern of leisure spaces.

Having briefly examined the evolution of urban recreational opportunities in Britain since the 1880s, it is pertinent to focus on one example which typifies the development processes in time and space, notably the evolution of parks and open space. This is considered in relation to one particular city in Britain: Leicester.

CASE STUDY: The evolution of parks and open space in Victorian Leicester

The development of open space in towns and cities in Britain traditionally developed through the emergence of commons and walks prior to the nineteenth century, followed by private squares and greens for the wealthy classes. While towns and cities remained small in scale, the populations were able to enjoy recreation in the surrounding rural areas (Clarke 1981). Urban industrial growth in the industrial revolution transformed the spatial form of towns and cities, as open land was consumed for economic and residential development. Two specific legislative changes during Victorian Britain contributed to the development of large parks, namely the Select Committee on Public Walks (1833) and the Health of Towns (1840), in a period of concern for the health and social well-being of the labouring classes. As Strachan and Bowler (1976) acknowledged, early park development was prompted by donations from industrialists and landowners, and four pieces of legislation enabled local authorities to purchase land for park development, notably:

• Towns Improvement Act 1847
• Public Health Act 1848
• Public Parks, Schools and Museums Act 1871
• Public Improvements Act 1860

While Edwardian and subsequent legislation enhanced park development, including the Housing and Town Planning Act 1909 and Town and Country Planning Acts of 1932 and 1947, the Victorian era was important in terms of the development of large scale parks and open space.

PARK DEVELOPMENT IN VICTORIAN LEICESTER

Leicester expanded as a Victorian city: its population grew from 18,445 in 1801 to 64,829 in 1851, 174,624 in 1891 and 211,579 in 1901. While Pritchard (1976) and Page (1988) examine the spatial development of the city (Figure 5.1), and constraints and opportunities for urban development, the city retained a medieval pattern of land development up until the 1800s. The poorly drained River Soar constrained development to the west of the river and also by owners of estates who refused to sell land for development. Most early urban growth in the 1800s

occurred to the east and north-east. Prior to 1850, two open spaces existed: St Margaret's Pasture, a 13-acre (5.2 ha) meadow to the north of the urban area and at Southfield race course established in 1806 (Figure 5.2). In 1838, the city council provided 40 acres (16 ha) of land at Southfield at Welford to form the first public recreation ground, although only 8 acres (3.2 ha) now remain. This was complimented by a series of private gardens and squares laid out from 1785 at the town council's request along New Walk, which forms the sole surviving urban pedestrian way in England (Strachan and Bowler 1976: 279).

With the growth in population by 1851 urban development occurred to the west of the Soar and the city council developed four parks and recreation grounds (Figure 5.2) in the period 1880–1900. Victoria Park (27.6 ha), established in 1882 on city-owned land, was made possible by the relocation of the city's race course from Southfield to Oadby. Abbey Meadows (22.8 ha) purchased in 1877, which fulfilled the purpose of draining a marsh area unsuitable for building, resulted in an ornamental park. The third park, aimed at providing open space access for the fast growing suburb of Highfields, led to the development of 13.6 ha at Spinney Hill with a formal park in 1885. The fourth major park, established in the western suburbs, saw the establishment of the new parks estate (71.2 ha) in 1899. Each park developed in the tradition of Victorian formal use with fountains, band-stands, gardens and open stretches of grass. In the case of Abbey Park, boating, river views, greenhouses and formal flower beds attracted users from across the city. To complement formal park provision, recreation grounds were also established in 1892 at Belgrave (4.8 ha) and Fosse Road (4.4 ha) in 1897.

POST-VICTORIAN PARK DEVELOPMENT

In 1902, the Aylestone site (8 ha) was purchased as a recreation ground which was followed by

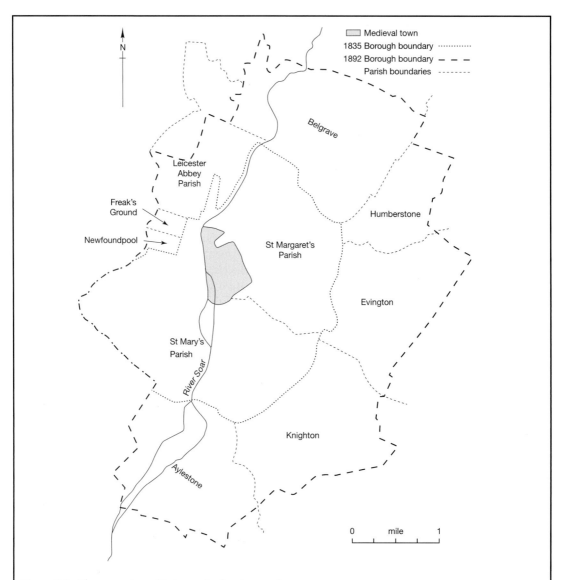

Figure 5.1: The expansion of Leicester in the nineteenth century

a lull up until the 1920s. During the period 1900–20, small open spaces in the town centre led to the establishment of three ornamental gardens (Castle, Westcotes and St George's Church), two playgrounds and a small park at Westcotes. After 1920, further urban expansion led to the establishment of six multipurpose parks with sports facilities, the largest at Braunstone (66.8 ha) in 1925 on the periphery of the city as a focal point of a large inter-war council estate. In contrast, other parks developed in the inter-war period were located in private housing areas such as Humberstone (8 ha) in 1928, Knighton (32.9 ha) in 1937, Evington (17.6 ha) in 1949 in eastern and southern suburbs. To balance the geographical distribution of provision, two large

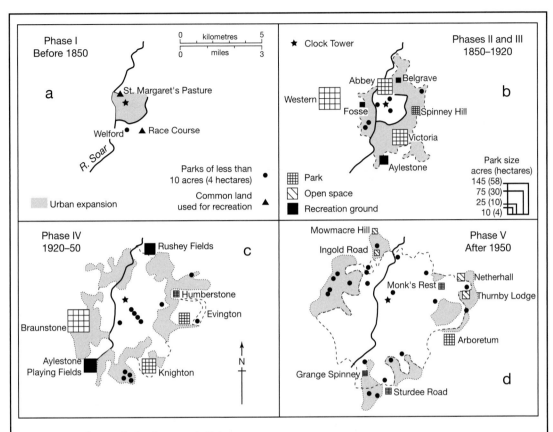

Figure 5.2: Urban park development in Leicester
Source: redrawn from Strachan and Bowler (1976) and with permission from Leicester City Council's Legal Services Department

recreation grounds were opened at Rusley Fields (1 1.4 ha) in 1921 and Aylestone Playing Fields (33.2 ha) in 1946 a number of smaller open spaces were also developed on new council estates at Braunceston Park and Humberstane and a number of amenity open spaces amounting to 40.8 ha. In the post-war period, attention in Leicester City Council shifted towards provision of small neighbourhood and local facilities as key features of new council estates. Only a limited number of larger open spaces were created on land unsuitable for residential development (e.g. Netherhall's 12.8 ha site in 1958 and Ingeld's 5.6 ha site in 1970). Amenity open space was also incorporated into 13 council estates providing 105.6 ha of open

space. A number of small village parks and playgrounds in old villages (e.g. Old Humbestone) contributed to the 27 parks and recreation grounds opened between 1950 and 1975. Since 1975, Leicester City Council has maintained an active role in enhancing open space and park provision to the point where in 1994, it maintained 1200 ha of parkland and open space. This represented one-fifth of the total area of the city, an extremely high level of provision by European and North American standards.

Figure 5.3 shows the current distribution of urban parks in Leicester. By 2000, this had risen to 3000 ha of public open space, comprising country parks, formal parks, gardens, wetlands,

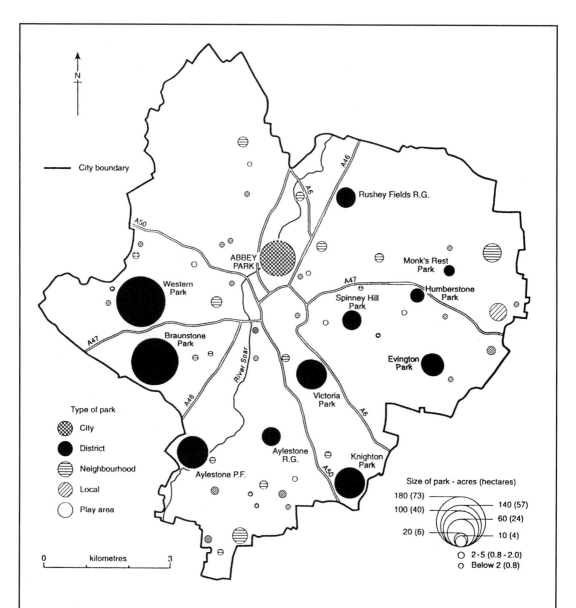

Figure 5.3: Parks in Leicester, *c*.1996
Source: redrawn from Madge (1997: 239)

allotments (for a discussion of allotments as a form of recreation, see Thorpe 1970; Crouch 1989a, 1989b) and woodlands. This is complemented by the provision of gardens with houses which perform an important recreational function (Halkett 1978) in the wider leisure context of the home (Glyptis and Chambers 1982). However, the dominant element is parkland. The City of Leicester Local Plan aim is to have public open space within 500 metres of every home. Within new residential developments, the City Council require developers to provide 1.6 ha of open space per 1000 people housed. As a result Leicester recreation space is an average of only 2.9 km from the city centre for parks/gardens, 3.6 km for recreation grounds, 3.5 km for playing fields, 3.7 km for sports grounds and 4.6 km for golf courses illustrating the role of low cost land for such facilities. Thus, as S. Williams (1995) argues the level of recreational opportunity in modern-day Leicester increases with distance from the city. The result of such patterns of park development and other recreational resources in the case of Leicester is the rationalisation of provision into a geographical planning framework whereby an open space hierarchy results with different parks fulfilling different functions according to their size, characteristics and resource base.

SUMMARY POINTS

The historical evolution of the urban parks was inextricably linked to wider processes of urban industrial change in the Victorian period. Politics, paternalism and a desire to provide formal con-

texts for recreation and leisure are a starting point to understand the philosophy and ideology associated with park development. The evolution of parks and open space passed through a series of philosophical changes, from the formal park and recreation grounds in the Victorian and Edwardian periods to multipurpose parks in the inter-war years and open space provision as part of post-war housing reconstruction with council house estates. The political motivation for open space provision and the role of different social groups in developing investment and development in local neighbourhood is an under-explored area. Leicester City Council has developed an enviable open space provision for a western city, with a well-developed network of leisure spaces. Outdoor recreation, open space provision and the hierarchy of leisure spaces has a distinct geographical pattern. As one moves further away from the city centre, the level of open space provision increases, reflecting the Victorian, Edwardian and inter-war pattern of provision which has strongly influenced the current day patterns.

METHODS OF ANALYSING URBAN RECREATION

Within the limited literature on urban recreation, the geographer has developed a number of concepts used within human geography and applied them in a recreational context to understand how the supply of recreational resources fits within the broader recreational context. For example, the use of the concept of a 'hierarchy of facilities' (Patmore 1983) highlights the catchment relating to the users' willingness, ability and knowledge of the facility or resource (S.L.J. Smith 1983a). What the hierarchy concept does is allow one to ascertain what type of catchment a recreational resource has at different spatial scales, taking into account users' willingness to travel to use them. Constraints of time and distance act as a friction on the potential use of resources. The outcome is an ordered

pattern of resources which serve specific catchments depending on their characteristics, whereby the typical levels of provision may include

- the neighbourhood level (e.g. a community centre)
- local areas (e.g. a recreation ground)
- regions within cities
- a city-wide level (e.g. an art gallery).

An illustration of such a hierarchy for urban open space is illustrated in Table 5.1. The result is an ordered provision, each with its own set of users meeting the needs and aspirations of users which will vary in time and space. Within any urban context the challenge for recreational planning is to match the supply and demand for such resources. One further technique which Patmore (1983) advocated for urban recreation is the resource inventory, whereby the range of existing resources is surveyed and mapped in relation to the catchment population. This population may then be compared to existing recommended levels of provision set by organisations for recreational provision. For example, the National Playing Fields Association in the UK recommended 2.4 ha of space per 1000 population, 'excluding school playing fields except where available for general use, woodlands and commons, ornamental gardens, full-length golf courses and open spaces where the playing of games by the general public is either discouraged or not permitted' (Patmore 1983: 118). In the UK, such playing fields were under increased pressure for housing development to the point that new guidelines were issued to prevent schools and local authorities from selling such leisure assets for short-term development gains.

Patmore (1983) outlined the range of urban recreational resources and facilities and provides a detailed spatial analysis of their occurrence and level of provision within the UK in terms of

- capital intensive facilities (those with modest land requirements but a high capital cost – and those with a high capital cost where the land requirement is extensive)
- parks and open spaces
- golf courses.

S. Williams (1995) adds an interesting array of other contexts including:

- the home
- the street
- gardens and allotments

Table 5.1: Hierarchical pattern of public open space

Type and main function	Approximate size and distance from home	Characteristics
Regional park Weekend and occasional visits by car or public transport	400 hectares 3.2–8 km	Large areas of natural heathland, common woodland and parkland, primarily providing for informal recreation with some non-intensive active recreations. Car parking at strategic locations.
Metropolitan park Weekend and occasional visits by car or public transport	60 hectares 3.2 km but more when park is larger than 60 hectares	Natural heath, common, woods or formal parks providing for active and passive recreation which may contain playing fields, provided at least 40 hectares remain for other pursuits. Adequate car parking.
District parks Weekend and occasional visits on foot, by cycle, car or short bus trip	20 hectares 1.2 km	Landscaped settings with a variety of natural features providing for a range of activities, including outdoor sports, children's play and informal pursuits. Some car parking.
Local parks For pedestrian visitors	2 hectares 0.4 km	Providing for court games, children's play, sitting out, etc. in a landscaped environment. Playing fields if the park is large enough.
Small local parks Pedestrian visits especially by old people and children, particularly valuable in high-density areas	2 hectares 0.4 km	Gardens, sitting-out areas and children's playgrounds.
Linear open space Pedestrian visits	Variable Where feasible	Canal towpaths, footpaths, disused rail lines, etc., providing opportunities for informal recreation.

Source: S. Williams (1995)

adequately considered. The increased use of attitude surveys and monitoring of urban park planning and management by local authorities is a direct response to the new ethos pervading public service provision, a a feature evaluated by the Audit Commission in the UK when examining leisure service provision. Yet research monitoring has a significant resource implication at a time of public sector restrictions on local government expenditure. The growing interest in urban park management is reflected in Welch's (1991) survey which documents many of the issues facing local authorities in the 1990s including park safety, CCT, park-related legislation, recreation management and risk management which are still very real issues, as the case study of fear and leisure provision in Chapter 2 confirmed. Against this background, attention now turns to London in terms of open space provision and the London Borough of Newham as a context in which to understand the role of spatial analysis.

URBAN PARK AND OPEN SPACE PROVISION IN LONDON

Research on recreation and leisure in London has hitherto attracted little interest at a city-wide level following the abolition of the Greater London Council (GLC) in 1986, which had included leisure and recreation in its strategic planning function. Since 1986 each London Borough's Unitary Development Plan is the framework for the formulation of policies to guide the provision of parks and open spaces. Planning advice from the London Planning Advisory Committee (LPAC) has continued with many of the former GLC leisure planning principles, although the draft London Plan (http://www.london.gov.uk) launched in June 2002 is a spatial development strategy for London and seeks to maintain strategic open spaces in the capital – particularly London's green belt, Metropolitan Open Land and green corridors or chains. These designations have been incorporated into most London

Boroughs' leisure and recreation plans with the UDPs. Leisure and recreation still remain a neglected aspect of London's diverse economic, social and cultural activities. Major studies of London's urban geography and expanding service sector (e.g., Hoggart and Green 1991) fail to acknowledge the significance of leisure service provision, although R. Bennett (1991: 212–13) did examine the London Boroughs' statutory responsibility for leisure and recreation provision. The scale and nature of open space provision in London was set out in the Greater London Development Plan (Greater London Council 1969). Table 5.1 outlined the hierarchy of parks and open space provision envisaged in the late 1980s within the revised Greater London Development Plan (see Nicholls 2001 for a North American illustration of this hierarchy). This is still very much a space standard driven approach. Provision was based on a hierarchical principle, with different parks fulfilling various functions according to their size and distance from the users' home. The concept of variety in park supply was to be achieved by the diversity of functions offered by parks in the capital, emphasising the social principle that parks of equal status were to be accessible to all sections of London's population. According to Burgess et al. (1988a), research in Greenwich questioned the suitability of a hierarchical system of park provision at the local area level, arguing that local communities did not recognise parks in terms of the differing functions that the GLC park hierarchy assigned to them. They claimed that most people in their survey felt that open spaces closest to their home failed to meet their leisure needs. This is a considerable problem for local authority leisure service departments, when the scale of public expenditure on open space and parks provision is examined at a London-wide scale. The extent to which financial resources are meeting local recreational needs is an important issue in view of the prioritisation of open space and park budgets of different local authorities across the capital.

THE LONDON BOROUGH OF NEWHAM

Newham is an east London borough (http://www.newham.gov.uk) created in the 1960s from the amalgamation of two former town councils – West Ham and East Ham. The area developed in the Victorian and Edwardian periods, with the extension of the London Underground, the creation of the Royal Docks and other service/utilities (e.g. the Beckton Gas Works, Beckton Sewage Works and Railway Yards at West Ham and Stratford) and manufacturing activities (e.g. Tate and Lyle in Silvertown). The population reached a peak of 249,000 in 1949, declining in the 1980s due to outmigration with the closure of the docks and other employers. In 1991, the population was 212,170 and in 2001 it had risen to 236,000. Newham is one of London's largest boroughs, with a very diverse ethnic population. In 2001, 43 per cent of the population was from ethnic groups (Asian, African and Caribbean) and by 2006 this population was expected to reach 60 per cent of the total. Despite gentrification in pockets of London Docklands and around Stratford, the London Borough of Newham's (LBN) Unitary Development Plan of 2001 states that the area is one of the most deprived areas in the UK, using the government's own deprivation indices, a feature apparent in geographies of London (Hoggart and Green 1991). Although Newham is an outer London borough, it has many inner city characteristics which has led it to consider being classified as part of inner London (see http://www.newham.gov.uk). The borough's main open spaces and parks were created in the Victorian and Edwardian periods, with notable additions in the inter-war and post-war period. In 1991, the proportion of the borough deemed to be parks/open space was 180 ha, or 4.9 per cent of the total area of the borough. By 2001, this had increased to 253 ha (6.95 per cent of the borough), reflecting the creation of new sites/improvements to existing sites as development has occurred in the south and north of the borough, often as a condition of planning consent for development.

Newham Council undertakes a number of roles in leisure service provision (e.g. sports centres, libraries, arts and cultural services, parks and open space provision and tourism), where the UDP is guided by the borough's Leisure Development strategy and London-wide strategies that have to be accommodated at a local level. In planning terms, the LBN establishes policies in its UDP to guide open space provision. Two of its key objectives for increasing open space provision is to incorporate its needs into larger urban regeneration plans for the Stratford railyards area adjacent to the new Channel Tunnel rail terminal and the redevelopment of the Beckton Gas Works site.

The council has a number of open space designations: green belt land to the north of the borough (for example, Wanstead Flats and the City of London Cemetery); Metropolitan Open Land; sites of borough-wide importance; sites of local importance and green corridors, complemented by urban parks (Archer and Yarman 1991). These policies are now incorporated in the Unitary Development Plan for Newham, with urban parks forming one of the most widely available forms of open space either as large multipurpose parks or smaller community based recreation grounds.

What is notable in the LBN 1993 and 2001 UDP is the lack of open and green space among the lowest of London borough's for green space and park provision. The LBN, utilising the National Playing Fields Association Standard of 2.43 ha of playing space per 1000 population. In 2001, this provision was only 1.1 ha per 1000 population. The spatial distribution of similar deficiencies in park provision are shown in Figure 5.4c, which shows that in 2001, large areas of the borough fall short of accessibility to local parks (i.e. where the population is more than 400 metres from any park area over 2 ha). Similarly, the absence of children's play space which is more than 200 metres from an equipped children's play

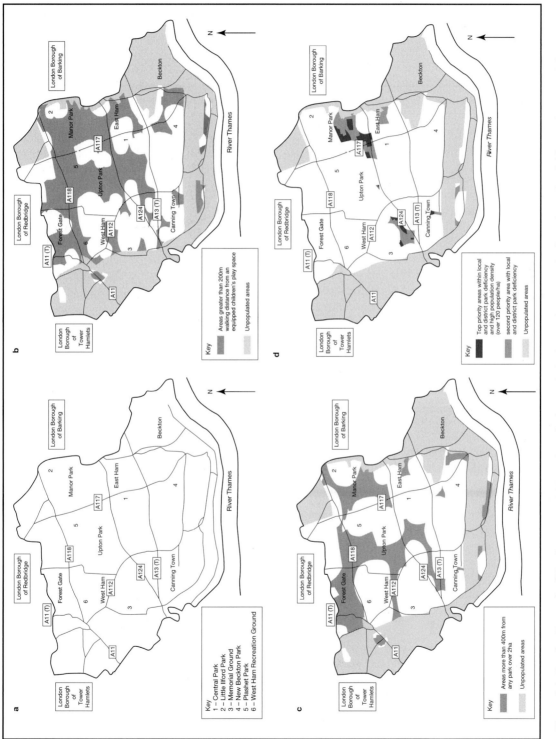

Key (a)
1 – Central Park
2 – Little Ilford Park
3 – Memorial Ground
4 – New Beckton Park
5 – Plashet Park
6 – West Ham Recreation Ground

Key (b)
Areas greater than 200m walking distance from an equipped children's play space
Unpopulated areas

Key (c)
Areas more than 400m from any park over 2ha
Unpopulated areas

Key (d)
Top priority areas within local and district park deficiency and high population density (over 120 people/ha)
second priority area with local and district park deficiency
Unpopulated areas

Figure 5.4: London Borough of Newham maps: (a) Location of urban parks in the London Borough of Newham; (b) Children's play space deficiency; (c) Areas of local park deficiency; (d) Priority areas for tackling open space deficiency

space is also notable (Figure 5.4b). But the 2001 UDP does acknowledge that by 2006, a further 12 ha of play space will be provided. This under-provision is reflected in areas needing additional space, but the UDP recognises the absence of sites may make this difficult. A study by Page et al. (1994) examined the user groups within the hierarchy of open spaces in Newham and confirmed many of the assumptions on park use, namely

- the overwhelming pattern of use was local in relation to the catchment area
- parks perform an important social role, being an accessible leisure resource regardless of gender, race, age and disability
- CCT procedures had reduced the quality of perceived maintenance of parks
- many concerns related to conflicts between dog owners and non-dog owners emerged in the management of park areas
- passive leisure pursuits dominated park use
- local park plans were seen as an innovative way of matching user needs to the management of parks and open spaces.

Therefore, while parks and open spaces may not be as fashionable as capital intensive leisure facilities, they are operated on a non-commercial basis and offer access to the entire population. Their value within the urban environment should be given greater recognition as they contribute to the wider public good of metropolitan populations compared with more specialised and targeted sport and leisure facilities. It is clear that further research is needed to establish how local leisure needs can be met in terms of park provision, so that park management plans focus attention on local areas and communities. Urban parks and open spaces are an important sustainable leisure resource which can accommodate multiple uses, being accessible to local communities who may not have access to countryside areas. They are an integral feature of the urban landscape and assume an important part of the daily lives of local communities.

SUMMARY POINTS

- The provision of open space and recreational opportunities in Newham are severely constrained by the availability of open space.
- The London Borough of Newham has practised open space provision as a priority in areas that are under-supplied.
- Political changes in the philosophy of urban space management have led to new ideologies in the planning, evaluation and development of parts for local people.
- Surveys of user needs provide invaluable data for planners to match park and open space provision to local needs.
- Similar issues of safety, usage by specific groups and the reasons for visiting parks emerge that compare with other national and international studies of urban parks.

This case study of urban parks integrates many of the concepts and ideas already developed in this chapter, concluding with a discussion on management and planning philosophy and the implementation of geographical principles.

URBAN TOURISM

The second half of this chapter examines the concept of urban tourism, reviewing the principal contributions towards its recognition as a tourism phenomenon worthy of study, and it also emphasises the scope and range of environments classified as urban destinations together with some of the approaches towards its analysis. It then considers a framework for the analysis of the tourist's experience of urban tourism which is followed by a discussion of key aspects of urban tourist behaviour: where do urban tourists go in urban areas, what activities do they undertake, how do they

Plate 5.1/5.2: Margate, Kent. A Regency period seaside resort which has passed through a series of stages of development and is now mainly a day trip and low-price holiday destination. Once one of the major tourist resorts in England, the town is now trying to rejuvenate itself through heritage tourism, such as the development of the Turner Gallery.

perceive these places and learn about the spatial attributes of the locality, and how is this reflected in their patterns of behaviour? Having reviewed these features, the chapter concludes with a discussion of service quality issues for urban tourism.

UNDERSTANDING THE NEGLECT OF URBAN TOURISM BY RESEARCHERS

Ashworth's (1989) seminal study of urban tourism acknowledges that a double neglect has occurred. Those interested in the study of tourism 'have tended to neglect the urban context in which much of it is set, while those interested in urban studies . . . have been equally neglectful of the importance of the tourist function of cities' (Ashworth 1989: 33). While some tourism textbooks (e.g. Shaw and Williams 1994) have expanded upon earlier syntheses of urban tourism research in a spatial context (e.g. D.G. Pearce 1987a), it still remains a comparatively unresearched area despite the growing interest in the relationship between urban regeneration and tourism (for a detailed review of the relationship of tourism and urban regeneration, see Page 2000; Page and Hall 2002). The problem is also reiterated in a number of studies as one

explanation of the neglect of urban tourism (see Vetter 1985; Page and Sinclair 1989). Despite this problem, which is more a function of perceived rather than real difficulties in understanding urban tourism phenomena, a range of studies now provide evidence of a growing body of literature on the topic (see Vetter 1985; Ashworth 1989, 1992a, 1992b; Ashworth and Tunbridge 1990; Page 1995a, 1995b, 2000; Law 1996; P.E. Murphy 1997; D.G. Pearce 1998, 1999b). However, even though more publications are now appearing in the academic literature, it does not imply that urban tourism is recognised as a distinct and notable area of research in tourism studies. This is due to the tendency for urban tourism research to be based on descriptive and empirical case studies which do not contribute to a greater theoretical or methodological understanding of urban tourism. In fact, such an approach is perpetuated by certain disciplines which contribute to the study of tourism, where the case study method of approach does little more than describe the situation in each instance and fails to relate the case to wider issues to derive generalisations and to test hypotheses and assumptions within the academic literature. In this respect, the limited understanding is a function of the lack of methodological sophistication in tourism research noted in some critiques of the subject (e.g. D.G. Pearce and Butler 1993). Indeed, Ashworth's (2003) 'Urban tourism: Still an imbalance in attention?' revisiting of his seminal 1989 study concludes that

> the imbalance does still exist. However, previously I found this difficult to understand and felt it should be remedied by a more balanced approach within tourism through the development of the study of urban tourism. Now I accept that the imbalance is quite intrinsic to the nature of tourism studies and the nature of cities.
>
> (Ashworth 2003: 158)

According to Ashworth (1992a), urban tourism has not emerged as a distinct research focus: research is focused on tourism in cities and embodies Law's (1996) argument that urban tourism exists in a recognisable form only in large cities. This strange paradox may be explained by the failure by planners, commercial interest and residents to recognise tourism as one of the main economic rationales for cities. Tourism is often seen as an adjunct or necessary evil to generate additional revenue, while the main economic activities of the locality are not perceived as tourism related. Such negative views of urban tourism have meant that the public and private sectors have used the temporary, seasonal and ephemeral nature of tourism to neglect serious research on this theme. Consequently, a vicious circle exists: the absence of public and private sector research makes access to research data difficult, and the large-scale funding for primary data collection using social survey techniques, necessary to break the vicious circle, is rarely available. The absence of large-scale funding for urban tourism research reflects the prevailing consensus in the 1980s that such studies were unnecessary. However, with the pressure posed by tourists in many European tourist cities in the 1990s (e.g. Canterbury, London, York, Venice and Florence), this perception is changing now that the public and private sectors are belatedly acknowledging the necessity of visitor management (for a discussion of this issue, see English Tourist Board/Employment Department 1991; D. Gilbert and Clark 1997; Meethan 1997; Snaith and Haley 1999) as a mechanism to enhance, manage and improve the tourist's experience of towns and places to visit. Nevertheless, as Ashworth (1992a) argues:

> Urban tourism requires the development of a coherent body of theories, concepts, techniques and methods of analysis which allow comparable studies to contribute towards some common goal of understanding of either the particular role of cities within tourism or the place of tourism within the form and function of cities.
>
> (Ashworth 1992a: 5)

One way of assessing progress towards these objectives is to review the main approaches developed within the tourism literature.

APPROACHES TO URBAN TOURISM: GEOGRAPHICAL ANALYSIS

To understand how research on urban tourism has developed distinctive approaches and methodologies, one needs to recognise why tourists seek urban tourism experiences. Shaw and Williams (1994) argue that urban areas offer geographical concentration of facilities and attractions that are conveniently located to meet both visitor and resident needs alike. But the diversity and variety among urban tourist destinations has led researchers to examine the extent to which they display unique and similar features. Shaw and Williams (1994) identify three approaches:

- the diversity of urban areas means that their size, function, location and history contribute to their uniqueness
- towns and cities are multifunctional areas, meaning that they simultaneously provide various functions for different groups of users
- the tourist functions of towns and cities are rarely produced or consumed solely by tourists, given the variety of user groups in urban areas.

Ashworth (1992a) conceptualises urban tourism by identifying three approaches towards its analysis, where researchers have focused on

- the supply of tourism facilities in urban areas, involving inventories (e.g. the spatial distribution of accommodation, entertainment complexes and tourist-related services), where urban ecological models have been used; the facility approach has also been used to identify the tourism product offered by destinations
- the demand generated by urban tourists, to examine how many people visit urban areas, why they choose to visit and their patterns of behaviour, perception and expectations in relation to their visit
- perspectives of urban tourism policy, where the public sector (e.g. planners) and private sector agencies have undertaken or commissioned research to investigate specific issues related to their own interests in urban tourism.

Further attempts to interpret urban tourism theoretically have been developed by Mullins (1991) and Roche (1992). While these studies do not have a direct bearing on attempts to influence or affect the tourist experience of towns and cities, their importance should not be neglected in wider reviews of urban tourism: they offer explanations of the sudden desire of many towns and cities with a declining industrial base to look towards service sector activities such as tourism. Both studies examine urban tourism in the context of changes in post-industrial society and the relationship with structural changes in the mode of capitalist production. In other words, both studies question the types of process now shaping the operation and development of tourism in post-industrial cities, and the implications for public sector tourism and leisure policy. One outcome of such research is that it highlights the role of the state, especially local government, in seeking to develop service industries based on tourism and leisure production and consumption in urban areas, as a response to the restructuring of capitalism which has often led to employment loss in the locality. It also illustrates the significance of place-marketing in urban tourism promotion (Ashworth and Voogd 1990a, 1990b; Gold and Ward 1994; Gold and Gold 1995; Hall 1997b) as destinations seek to reinvent and redefine themselves in the market for cultural and heritage tourism (Houinen 1995; Judd 1995; Bramwell and Rawding 1996; Chang et al. 1996; Schofield 1996; Dahles 1998; Hall and McArthur 1998).

Mullins' (1991) concept of tourism urbanisation is also useful as it assists in developing the following typology of urban tourist destinations:

- capital cities
- metropolitan centres, walled historic cities and small fortress cities
- large historic cities
- inner-city areas
- revitalised waterfront areas
- industrial cities
- seaside resorts and winter sport resorts
- purpose-built integrated tourist resorts
- tourist-entertainment complexes
- specialised tourist service centres
- cultural/art cities.

(After Page 1995b: 17)

This typology illustrates the diversity of destinations which provide an urban context for tourist visits, and highlights the problem of deriving generalisations from individual case studies without a suitable conceptual framework. Page and Hall (2002) provide a framework for understanding the complexity of urban tourism as shown in Figure 5.5, which identifies many of the interrelationships between the supply, demand and external factors.

Interpreting urban tourism: from concepts to theoretically informed analysis

Page and Hall (2002) point to the growing geographical research on postmodernism (e.g. Dear 1994, 1999; Dear and Flusty 1999) to identify the defining characteristics of the postmodern city. These characteristics have highlighted the significance of sociological literature in the arising urban places and spaces used to produce and consume urban tourism. The postmodern era has been characterised by cultural transformations which have

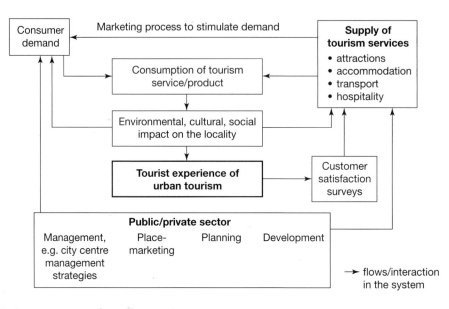

Figure 5.5: A systems approach to urban tourism
Source: Page (1995a)

a spatiality, where the cultural industries that embody the arts, leisure and tourism. Dear and Flusty (1998) coined a number of buzz words to describe the postmodern urbanscape including:

- *privatopia*, an edge city residential form and housing development on the periphery
- *cultures of heteropolis*, where cultural diversity and social polarity arise from the combined processes of racism, structural inequality, homelessness and social unrest
- *the city as a theme park*, embodied in Hannigan's (1998) *Fantasy City*
- *the fortified city*, where residents' concerns with safety, fear and crime have created 'fortified cells of affluence' juxtaposed with 'places of terror', where police seek to try and control crime
- *interdictory space*, where spaces within cities exclude people through their activities and design (i.e. shopping malls as private spaces that have replaced high streets as public spaces).

In the postmodern city, Dear and Flusty (1998) argued that

The concentric ring structure of the Chicago School [eg. Burgess 1925] was essentially a concept of the city as an organic accretion around a central, organising cove. Instead, we have identified a postmodern urban process in which the urban periphery organises the centre within the context of a globalising capitalium.
(Dear and Flusty 1998: 65)

The urban core is no longer the defining and controlling influence upon development. Instead, Dear and Flusty (1998) argued that a Keno capitalism had developed where a collage of non-contiguous consumption-oriented spaces develop. The process of urbanisation and development is far more complex in shaping tourism and leisure spaces. As a result, Page and Hall (2002) produce a model of tourism in the postmodern city where capital defines the nature, form and extent of consumption experiences. The tourism and leisure landscapes that emerge are part of a mosaic of social and cultural layers that add diversity to the urban fabric. The visitor may not easily recognise the tourist city as a distinct entity, since the patchwork of consumption experiences are often grouped into zones. Figure 5.6a identifies a series of processes at work, including gentrification, interconnected zones of tourism and leisure where the conventional downtown area is rivalled by more space-extensive out-of-town areas, such as Garreau's (1991) *Edge City* and Hannigan's (1998) *Fantasy City* (e.g. a theme park/entertainment zone). These develop- ments further accentuate social exclusion and social polarity as Figure 5.6b suggests, as neighbourhoods are cleared by gentrification and marginalised by the emergence of consumption-oriented activities in former housing areas. This contributes to the development of what Roche (2000) called the 'new

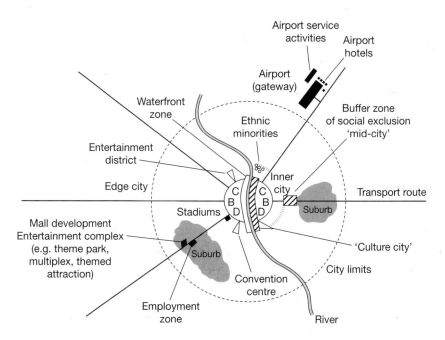

Figure 5.6a: Tourism, leisure and the postmodern city

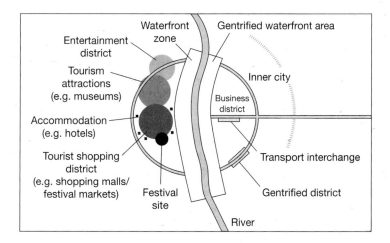

Figure 5.6b: Tourism, leisure and the postmodern city: the inner city dimension

urban tourism', based on the consumption of places in a post-industrial society, which Meethan (1996) points to as

> Tourism involves the visual consumption of signs and increasingly, simulacra and staged events in which urban townscapes are transformed into aestheticised spaces of entertainment and pleasure . . . within these places of consumption . . . a variety of activities can be pursued, such as promenading, eating, drinking, watching staged events and street entertainment and visually appreciating heritage and culture of place.
> (Meethan 1996: 324)

For this reason, it is pertinent to focus on the concept of the 'tourist experience of urban tourism' as a framework to assess some of the experiential aspects of this phenomenon.

THE TOURIST EXPERIENCE OF URBAN TOURISM

There is a growing literature on tourist satisfaction (e.g. Ryan 1995), and what constitutes the experiential aspects of a tourist visit to a locality. In the context of urban tourism, the innovative research by Graefe and Vaske (1987) offers a number of important insights as well as a useful framework. Graefe and Vaske (1987) acknowledge that the 'tourist experience' is a useful term to identify the experience of an individual which may be affected 'by individual, environmental, situational and personality-related factors as well as the degree of communication with other people. It is the outcome which researchers and the tourism industry constantly evaluate to establish if the actual experience met the tourist's expectations' (Page 1995a: 24). Operationalising such a concept may prove difficult in view of the complex array of factors which may affect the visitor experience (Figure 5.7). For example, where levels of overcrowding occur at major tourist sites (e.g. Canterbury, Venice, St Paul's Cathedral, London and the Tower of London), this can have a negative effect on visitors who have a low tolerance threshold for overcrowding at major tourist sites. Yet conversely, other visitors may be less affected

- Weather conditions at the time of visit
- Standard and quality of accommodation available
- The cleanliness and upkeep of the city
- The city's aesthetic value (i.e. its setting and beauty)
- Tourists' personal safety from crime
- Accessibility of attractions and points of interest in the city
- Extent to which local people welcome visitors in a warm manner
- Ability of tourism employees to speak foreign languages
- Range of cultural and artistic amenities
- Ambience of the city environment as a place to walk around
- Level of crowding and congestion
- Range of night-life and entertainment available
- Range of restaurants and eating establishments in the city
- Pleasurability of leisure shopping
- Price levels of goods and services in the city
- Level of helpfulness among local people
- Adequacy of emergency medical care

Figure 5.7: Factors to consider in evaluating the urban tourism experience
Source: modified from Haywood and Muller (1988)

by use levels thereby illustrating the problem within tourism motivation research – predicting tourists' behaviour and their responses to particular situations. In fact Graefe and Vaske (1987: 394) argue that 'the effects of increasing use levels on the recreation/tourist experience can be explained only partially . . . as a function of use level'. Therefore, the individual tourist's ability to tolerate the behaviour of other people, level of use, the social situation and the context of the activity are all important determinants of the actual outcome. Thus, evaluating the quality of the tourist experience is a complex process which may require careful consideration of the factors motivating a visit (i.e. how tourists' perception of urban areas makes them predisposed to visit particular places), their actual patterns of activity and the extent to which their expectations associated with their perceptions are matched in reality (Page 1995a: 25). For this reason, attention now turns to some of the experiential aspects of urban tourists' visits and the significance of behavioural issues influencing visitor satisfaction. In view of the diversity of tourists visiting urban areas, it is useful to define the market for urban tourism.

INSIGHT: Tourism in capital cities

Capital cities represent a special case of urban tourism. As Canada's National Capital Commission (NCC) (2000b: 9) observed, 'The combination of political, cultural, symbolic and administrative functions is unique to national capitals'. The capital functions as 'the political centre and symbolic heart of the country. It is the site of crucial political decision-making, yet it is also a setting for the nation's culture and history, where the past is highlighted, the present displayed and the future imagined'. Although such statements are obviously significant in political and cultural terms the wider significance of capital city status for tourism has been grossly under-researched and, perhaps, under-appreciated (J. Taylor et al. 1993; C.M. Hall 2000a, 2002b). Nevertheless, capital status is important. As capitals provide an administrative and political base of government operations there will therefore be spin-off effects for business travel in terms of both those who work in the capital and those who are seeking to lobby government or influence decisions. In addition to business related travel capital cities are also significant for tourism because of their cultural, heritage and symbolic roles. They are frequently home to some of the major national cultural institutions while also tending to have a significant wider role in the portrayal, preservation and promotion of national heritage and which showcase national culture (Therborn 1996). Such a concentration of arts and cultural institutions will therefore have implications for the travel and activity behaviour of culturally interested tourists as well as contributing to the image of a city as a whole. If capital status is lost it can have a significant affect on visitor numbers, as in the case of the transfer of the German national capital from Bonn to Berlin after the reunification of Germany where Berlin has witnessed a dramatic increase in overnight stays and Bonn a decline.

The use of the notion of a capital in terms of branding and culture is significant for tourism not only regarding place promotion but also attracting high-yielding cultural tourists. Indeed, given the growth of place marketing in an increasingly competitive global economic environment such a development is logical in terms of branding places and place competition. However, for the purpose of this discussion the notion of a capital is related primarily to political, administrative and symbolic functions which operate at a national or provincial level. Indeed, as Dubé and Gordon (2000: 6) observed, 'Planning for cities that include a seat of government often involves political and symbolic concerns that are different from those of other urban areas'. The historical development of capital cities may also provide them with a significant transport gateway or hub function, e.g. London and Paris.

A good example of the relationship between capital city status and tourism is Ottawa in Canada, which was declared the capital of the new Canadian Confederation in 1867. Tourism now contributes well over a billion Canadian dollars to the Ottawa region economy and makes a substantial contribution to employment as well as government taxes. Ottawa is an excellent example of Gottmann's (1983) observation that 'capital cities often act as hinges between different regions of a country'. Ottawa lies at the border between French and English speaking Canada, a history of interaction between labour and capital, as well as being at a location where different ecological regions also coincide (NCC 1999). There are a number of primary benefits of visiting Ottawa that are unique to a capital city. In a survey conducted in 1991 85 per cent of respondents agreed that it was a good way for young people to learn about their country, while the opportunity to learn about Canada was cited as important by 57 per cent of respondents (NCC 1991). Indeed, a unique characteristic that is shared among all visitors to Ottawa-Hull is 'the desire to visit national cultural institutions and physical landmarks that symbolize and reflect all of Canada' (NCC 1991: v).

> The function of a national cultural institution (e.g., museum) is to display, protect and explain past, present and future national phenomena and human achievements. National cultural institutions are also used to communicate social, cultural, political, scientific, technical, or other knowledge through various media.
>
> (NCC 1999: 63)

The main avenue for Canadian government actions to reinforce the role of Ottawa's capital city status is the National Capital Commission, which has the mission 'To create pride and unity through Canada's Capital Region' (NCC 2000a: 5). Established in 1959 the NCC is a Crown corporation governed by a national board of directors (the Commission) and reports to the Canadian Parliament through the Minister of Canadian Heritage.

Clearly the NCC is not primarily a tourist organisation, but its actions and policies over the years have created both substantial tourism resources for the region in the form of attractions as well as imaging the city through its promotional and marketing campaigns. The significance of the NCC for tourism cannot be overstated. As Tunbridge (1998) observed,

> In an unmanaged state Ottawa's tourism resource would be modest: a physical environment recreationally attractive, but unexceptional in Canada; a historic ambience with distinctive elements, but weal

by international standards; and an overall cultural environment which was in the 1960s the butt of jests . . . and a non-place to most further afield.

> (Tunbridge 1998: 95)

According to the NCC, it 'exists to promote national pride through the creation of a great capital for an increasingly diverse body of Canadians' (2000a: 8). A key focus of achieving its strategic goals since the early 1990s has been the theme of renewal and the development of core area vision for the National Capital Region (NCR). In order to achieve its goals it has 'fostered the re-development of the By Ward Market, where a mix of commercial and residential uses has restored life and preserved the character of a unique heritage neighbourhood' and is looking to regenerate the Sparks Street mall area

> only a block from Parliament Hill. . . . It forms the interface of the 'civic' and 'capital' realms. It is an expression of Ottawa and, as such, of Canada. The revitalization of Sparks Street is therefore an important symbol of Canada's commitment to a vibrant future that is solidly rooted in the past.
>
> (NCC 2000a: 3)

(See also Tunbridge 2000 for an excellent discussion of the redevelopment of the market area.) Significantly, a future tourism focus is the development of the NCR 'as an ecodestination. . . . However, to respond successfully to the needs of future travellers – not just eco-tourists, but also increasing numbers of business people, convention-goers and seniors – the NCC must support the development of new Capital services and infrastructure' (NCC 2000a: 9). In addition, the NCC has developed a series of parkways in the Ottawa region that have an historic role as recreational and leisure corridors for motorists and cyclists. The parkways also link into the transitway system and act as 'gateways' to the NCR which remain 'influencing the perception of visitors and to communicating the image and landscape of the Capital' (NCC 1998: 52).

THE URBAN TOURISM MARKET: DATA SOURCES

Identifying the scale, volume and different markets for urban tourism remains a perennial problem for researchers. Urban tourism is a major economic activity in many of Europe's capital cities but identifying the tourism markets in each area is problematic. Page (1995a) provides a detailed assessment of the principal international data sources on urban tourism, reviewing published statistics by the World Tourism Organisation and the OECD. Such data sources commonly employ the domestic and international tourist use of accommodation as one measure of the scale of tourism activity. In the context of urban tourism, it requires researchers to have an understanding of spatial distribution of tourist accommodation in each country to identify the scale and distribution of tourist visits. In countries where the majority of accommodation is urban based, such statistics may provide preliminary sources of data for research. While this may be relevant for certain categories of tourist (e.g. business travellers and holiday-makers), those visitors staying with friends and relatives within an urban environment would not be included in the statistics. Among the most useful studies which examines the availability of data on urban tourism is Cockerell's (1997) analysis of the situation in Europe. Cockerell (1997) recognised that data on urban-based business travel was notoriously difficult to monitor, since it was often associated with a range of non-tourism functions and more specific activities located in towns and cities due to their central place functions in regions and countries, notably the meetings, incentives, conferences and exhibitions (MICE) market. The specialist nature of the facilities and infrastructure required for such business are frequently located in urban areas to make use of complementary facilities such as accommodation, transport hubs (i.e. airports) and the wider range of tourist attractions to provide the wider context for MICE venues.

Within a European context, Cockerell (1997) indicated that comparative data on urban tourism rarely exist due to the different survey method-ologies, sampling techniques and inconsistency in the use of terminology or agreement on what an urban tourist is. For example, many European surveys do not consider the day trip or excursion market as a pure form of urban tourism, and therefore exclude them from surveys. Cockerell (1997) pointed to the only pan-European data source – *The European Travel Monitor* (ETM). The section on city trips refers only to the holiday sector, ignoring business and VFR travel, and including only those international trips involving a minimum stay of one night. A number of other data sources, including academic studies (e.g. Mazanec 1997) and research institutes in Paris, namely the Instit National de la Recherche sur les Transports et leur Sécurité (INRETS) and the Venice based Centro Internazionale di Studi sull'Economica Turistica (CISET) have generated research data on urban tourism demand. In fact Mazanec (2002) provides some of the state of the art research, of which geographers are well represented although many of the studies remain case study in focus.

Even where statistics can be used, they provide only a preliminary assessment of scale and volume and more detailed sources are needed to assess specific markets for urban tourism. For example, Page (1995a) reviews the different market segmentation techniques used by marketing researchers to analyse the tourism market for urban areas, which helps one to understand the types of visitors and motives for visiting urban destinations. Table 5.7 highlights two typologies developed within the tourism literature to acknowledge the significance of individual motives for visiting urban destinations. However, Jansen-Verbeke (1986) does point to the methodological problem of distinguishing between the different users of the tourist city. For example, Burtenshaw et al. (1991) discuss the concept of functional areas (Figure 5.8) within the city, where different visitors seek certain attributes for their city visit (e.g. the historic city, the culture city, the night-life city, the shopping city and the tourist city) where no one group has a monopoly over its use. In other words, residents of the city and its hinterland, visitors and workers all use the resources within the tourist city, but some user

Table 5.7: Typologies of urban tourists

According to Blank and Petkovitch (1980) the motives for visiting urban areas can be classified thus:

- visiting friends and relatives
- business/convention visitation
- outdoor recreation activities
- entertainment and sightseeing activities
- personal reasons
- shopping
- other factors

Page (1995a: 48) identified a broader range of motivations for visiting urban areas:

- visiting friends and relatives
- business travel
- conference and exhibition attendance
- educational reasons
- cultural and heritage tourism
- religious travel (e.g. pilgrimages)
- hallmark events attendance
- leisure shopping
- day trips

groups identify with certain areas more than others. Thus, the tourist city is a multifunctional area which complicates attempts to identify a definitive classification of users and the areas/facilities they visit.

Ashworth and Tunbridge (1990) prefer to approach the market for urban tourism from the perspective of the consumers' motives, focusing on the purchasing intent of users, their attitudes, opinions and interests for specific urban tourism products. The most important distinction they make is between use/non-use of tourism resources, leading them to identify international users (who are motivated by the character of the city) and incidental users (who view the character of the city as irrelevant to their use). This two-fold typology is used by Ashworth and Tunbridge (1990) to identify four specific types of users:

- intentional users from outside the city-region (e.g. holidaymakers and heritage tourists)
- intentional users from inside the city-region (e.g. those using recreational and entertainment facilities – recreating residents)

- incidental users from outside the city-region (e.g. business and conference/exhibition tourists and those on family visits – non-recreating visitors)
- incidental users from inside the city-region (e.g. residents going about their daily activities – non-recreating residents).

Such an approach recognises the significance of attitudes and the use made of the city and services rather than the geographical origin of the visitor as the starting point for analysis. Although the practical problem with such an approach is that tourists tend to cite one main motive for visiting a city, any destination is likely to have a variety of user groups in line with Ashworth and de Haan's (1986) examination of users of the tourist-historic city of Norwich. Their methodology involved tourists self-allocating the most important motives for visiting Norwich. While 50 per cent of holiday-makers were intentional users of the historic city, significant variations occurred in the remaining markets using the historic city. But this does confirm the multiuse hypothesis advanced by Ashworth and Tunbridge (1990) which was subsequently developed in a geographical context by Getz (1993a). Having outlined some of the methodological issues associated with assessing the market for urban tourism, attention now turns to the behavioural issues associated with the analysis of tourist visits to urban areas.

URBAN TOURISM: BEHAVIOURAL ISSUES

Any assessment of urban tourist activities, patterns and perceptions of urban locations will be influenced by the supply of services, attractions and facilities in each location. It is necessary to understand the operation and organisation of tourism in terms of the production of tourism services and the ways in which tourists consume the products in relation to the locality, their reasons for consumption, what they consume and possible explanations for the consumption outcome as visitor behaviour.

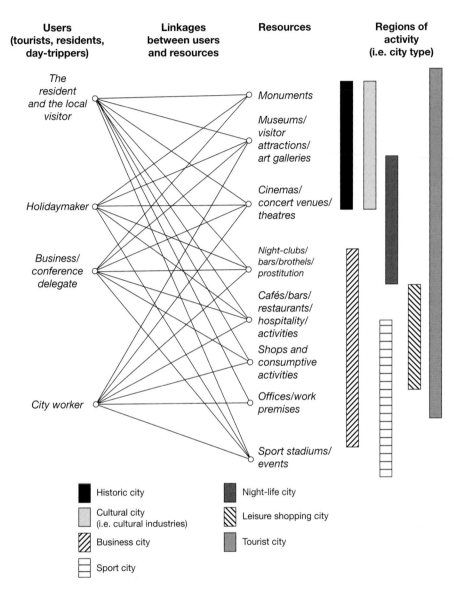

Figure 5.8: Functional areas in the tourist city
Source: modified and developed from Burtenshaw et al. (1991)

As Law (1993) argues:

tourism is the geography of consumption outside the home area; it is about how and why people travel to consume . . . on the production side it is concerned to understand where tourism activities develop and on what scale. It is concerned with the process or processes whereby some cities are able to create tourism resources and a tourism industry.

(Law 1993: 14)

One framework developed in the Netherlands by Jansen-Verbeke (1986) to accommodate the analysis of tourism consumption and production in urban areas is that of the 'leisure product'. The facilities in an urban environment may be divided into the 'primary elements', 'secondary elements' and 'additional elements' (see Jansen-Verbeke 1986 for a more detailed discussion of this approach). To distinguish between user groups, Jansen-Verbeke (1986) identified tourists' and recreationalists' first and second reasons for visiting three Dutch towns (Deneter, Kampen and Zwolle). The inner-city environment provides a leisure function for various visitors regardless of the prime motivation for visiting. As Jansen-Verbeke (1986) suggests:

> On an average day, the proportion of visitors coming from beyond the city-region (tourists) is about one-third of all visitors. A distinction that needs to be made is between week days, market days and Sundays. Weather conditions proved to be important . . . the hypothesis that inner cities have a role to play as a leisure substitute on a rainy day could not be supported.
>
> (Jansen-Verbeke 1986: 88–9)

Among the different user groups, tourists tend to stay longer, with a strong correlation between 'taking a day out', sightseeing and 'visiting a museum' as the main motivations to visit. Nevertheless, leisure shopping was also a major 'pull factor' for recreationalists and tourists, though it is of greater significance for the recreationalists. Using a scaling technique, Jansen-Verbeke (1986) asked visitors to evaluate how important different elements of the leisure product were to their visit. The results indicate that there is not a great degree of difference between tourists' and recreationalists' rating of elements and characteristics of the city's leisure product. While recreationalists attach more importance to shopping facilities than to events and museums, the historical characteristics of the environment and decorative elements combined with other elements, such as markets, restaurants and the compact nature of the inner city, to attract visitors. Thus 'the conceptual approach to the system of inner-city tourism is inspired by common features of the inner-city environment, tourists' behaviour and appreciation and promotion activities' (Jansen-Verbeke 1986: 97). Such findings illustrate the value of relating empirical results to a conceptual framework for the analysis of urban tourism and the necessity of replicating similar studies in other urban environments to test the validity of the hypothesis, framework and interpretation of urban tourists' visitor behaviour. But how do tourists and other visitors to urban areas learn about, find their way around and perceive the tourism environment?

TOURIST PERCEPTION AND COGNITION OF THE URBAN ENVIRONMENT

How individual tourists interact and acquire information about the urban environment remains a relatively poorly researched area in tourism studies, particularly in relation to towns and cities. This area of research is traditionally seen as the forte of social psychologists with an interest in tourism, though much of the research by social psychologists has focused on motivation (e.g. Guy and Curtis 1986 on the development of perceptual maps).

Reviews of the social psychology of tourism indicate that there has been a paucity of studies of tourist behaviour and adaptation to new environments they visit. This is somewhat surprising since 'tourists are people who temporarily visit areas less familiar to them than their home area' (Walmesley and Jenkins 1992: 269). Therefore, one needs to consider a number of fundamental questions related to:

- How will the tourists get to know the areas they visit?
- How do they find their way around unfamiliar environments?
- What features in the urban environment are used to structure their learning experience in unfamiliar environments?
- What type of mental maps and images do they develop?

These issues are important in a tourism planning context since the facilities which tourists use and the opportunities they seek will be conditioned by their environmental awareness. This may also affect the commercial operation of attractions and facilities, since a lack of awareness of the urban environment and the attractions within it may mean tourists fail to visit them. Understanding how tourists interact with the environment to create an image of the real world has been the focus of research into social psychology and behavioural geography (see Walmesley and Lewis 1993: 95–126). Geographers have developed a growing interest in the geographic space perception of all types of individuals (Downs 1970), without explicitly considering tourists in most instances. Behavioural geographers emphasise the need to examine how people store spatial information and 'their choice of different activities and locations within the environment' (Walmesley and Lewis 1993: 95). The process through which individuals perceive the urban environment is shown in Figure 5.9. While this is a simplification, Haynes (1980) notes that no two individuals will have an identical image of the urban environment because the information they receive is subject to mental processing. This is conditioned by the information signals they receive through their senses (e.g. sight, hearing, smell, taste and touch) and this part of the process is known as *perception*. As our senses may comprehend only a small proportion of the total information received, the human brain sorts the information and relates it to the knowledge, values and attitudes of the individual through the

process of *cognition* (Page 1995a: 222). The final outcome of the perception and cognition process is the formation of a mental image of a place. These images are an individual's own view of reality, but they are important to the individual and group when making decisions about their experience of a destination, whether to visit again, and their feelings in relation to the tourist experience of place. As Downs and Stea (1977: 2) observed, 'a cognitive map is a cross section representing the world at one instant in time', a feature explored by Crang and Travelou (2001) in relation to the historic sites of Athens. In the psychology literature, Curiel and Radvansky (2002) note that one way to examine this issue is to understand how people memorise a map to recognise how their resulting mental representation of that map influences their use of that map.

As Walmesley and Lewis (1993) suggested,

> the distinction between perception and cognition is, however, a heuristic device rather than a fundamental dichotomy because in many senses, the latter subsumes the former and both are mediated by experience, beliefs, values, attitudes, and personality such that, in interacting with their environment, humans only see what they want to see.
>
> (Walmesley and Lewis 1993: 96)

Consequently, an individual tourist's knowledge of the environment is created in their mind as they interact with the unfamiliar environment they are

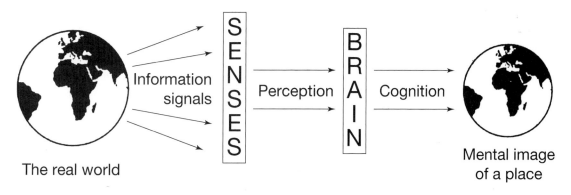

Figure 5.9: Perceptions of place

visiting (or a familiar environment on a return visit). Pacione (2001: 353) observed that 'Certain places are regarded as distinctive or memorable through their unique characteristics or imageability' and so have a strong *sense of place*. This may be explained in terms of the attachments people have to a specific place, gained through experience, memory and intention, a condition described by Tuan (1974) as topophilia. While this may have more relevance to leisure and recreation, as people's daily lives are deeply rooted in their locality, such issues also have a relevance for urban tourism as visitors become more confident and at home in a place they visit to develop some degree of a sense of place.

According to Powell (1978: 17–18) an image of the environment comprises ten key features which include

- a spatial component accounting for an individual's location in the world
- a personal component relating the individual to other people and organisations
- a temporal component concerned with the flow of time
- a relational component concerned with the individual's picture of the universe as a system of regularities
- conscious, subconscious and unconscious elements
- a blend of certainty and uncertainty
- a mixture of reality and unreality
- a public and private component expressing the degree to which an image is shared
- a value component that orders parts of the image according to whether they are good or bad
- an affectional component whereby the image is imbued with feeling.

Among geographers, the spatial component to behavioural research has attracted most interest, and they derive much of their inspiration from the pioneering research by Lynch (1960). Lynch's research asked respondents in North American cities to sketch maps of their individual cities, and by simplifying the sketches, derived images of

the city. Lynch developed a specific technique to measure people's urban images in which respondents drew a map of the centre of the city from memory, marking on it the streets, parks, buildings, districts and features they considered important. 'Lynch found many common elements in these mental maps that appeared to be of fundamental importance to the way people collect information about the city' (Hollis and Burgess 1977: 155). Lynch (1960) found five elements in the resulting maps after simplifying them. These were

- *paths* which are the channels along which individuals move
- *edges* which are barriers (e.g. rivers) or lines separating one region from another
- *districts* which are medium to large sections of the city with an identifiable character
- *nodes* which are the strategic points in a city which the individual can enter and which serve as foci for travel
- *landmarks* which are points of reference used in navigation and way finding, into which an individual cannot enter.

(See Figure 5.10 for a schematic diagram of Lynchean landscape elements.)

The significance of such research for the tourist and visitor to the urban environment is that the information they collect during a visit will shape their image of the place, influencing their feelings and impressions of that place. Furthermore, this imageability of a place is closely related to the legibility, by which is meant the extent to which parts of the city may be recognised and interpreted by an individual as belonging to a coherent pattern. Thus a legible city would be one where the paths, edges, districts, nodes and landmarks are both clearly identifiable and clearly positioned relative to each other (Walmesley and Lewis 1993: 98). Indeed, Lynch argued that a successful urban landscape would possess two desirable urban qualities of *imageability* (the value of objects in the landscape to provoke a strong emotional response in observers) and *legibility* (the extent to which the elements of a city can be seen as a coherent whole).

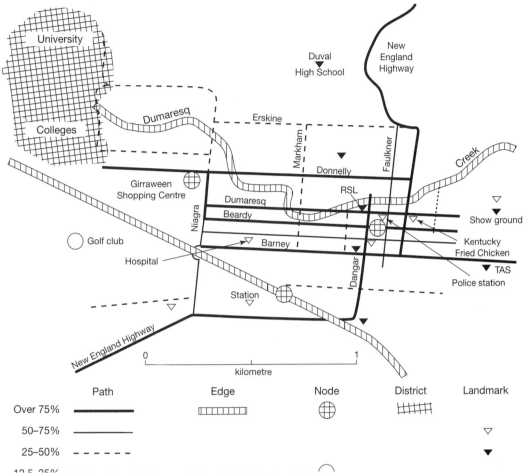

Figure 5.10: The Lynchean landscape of Armidale, New South Wales
Source: after Walmesley and Lewis (1993: 127)

Although there may sometimes be confusion among individuals regarding recognition of Lynchean urban landscape elements, it does help researchers to understand how individuals perceive the environment. Although researchers have criticised Lynch for the small sample sizes of his work based on the cities of Boston, Los Angeles and Jersey City with 60 responses, the real value is in the subsequent interest and research activity which his work stimulated. In fact Lynch (1984) in a review of his work noted the problems of implementing his findings in a public policy context, since many cities are quite idiosyncratic in character

and development. Even so, Walmesley and Lewis (1993) review many of the issues associated with the methodology of imagery research and raise a range of concerns about deriving generalisations from such results. Such studies do have a role to play in understanding how people view, understand and synthesise the complexity of urban landscapes into images of the environment. Nevertheless, criticisms of spatial research of individual imagery of the environment are that it uses a 'borrowed methodology, a potpourri of concepts, and liberal doses of borrowed theory' (Downs and Stea 1977: 3, cited in Walmesley and Lewis 1993). In a tourism context, Walmesley and Jenkins (1992) observed that tourism cognitive mapping may offer a number of useful insights into how tourists learn about new environments and, for this reason, it is pertinent to consider how visitor behaviour may be influenced by the ability to acquire spatial knowledge and synthesise it into meaningful images of the destination to assist them in finding their way around the area or region.

TOURISM COGNITIVE MAPPING

Walmesley and Lewis (1993: 214) review the factors that affect visitor behaviour in terms of five interrelated factors which may initially shape the decision to visit an urban environment. These are

- antecedent conditions
- user aspirations
- intervening variables
- user satisfaction
- real benefits.

These factors will, with experience, raise or reduce the individual's desire for recreational (and tourism) activity. The opportunities and constraints on visitors' behaviour are affected by income, disposable time available and a host of other socio-economic factors. Research by Stabler (1990) introduces the concept of 'opportunity sets' where the individual or family's knowledge of tourism opportunities is conditioned by their experience and the constraints on available time to partake in leisure and tourism activities.

Thus, once the decision is taken to visit an urban environment, the tourist faces the problem of familiarity/unfamiliarity of the location. It is the latter which tends to characterise most urban tourist trips, though visitors are often less hesitant about visiting urban destinations if they live in a town or city environment.

P.L. Pearce (1977) produced one of the pioneering studies of cognitive maps of tourists. Using data from sketch maps from first-time visitors to Oxford, England, the role of landmarks, paths and districts was examined. The conclusion drawn indicated that visitors were quick to develop cognitive maps, often by the second day of their visit. The interesting feature of the study is that there is evidence of an environmental learning process at work. Walmesley and Jenkins' (1992: 272) critique of P.L. Pearce's (1977) findings note that:

- the number of landmarks, paths and districts increased over time
- the number of landmarks identified increased over a period of two to six days, while recognition of the number of districts increased from two to three days
- the resulting sketch maps were complex with no one element dominating them.

A further study by P.L. Pearce (1981) examined how tourists came to know a route in Northern Queensland (a 340-km strip from Townsville to Cairns). The study indicated that experiential variables are a major influence upon cognitive maps. For example, drivers had a better knowledge than passengers, while age and prior use of the route were important conditioning factors. But as Walmesley and Jenkins (1992: 273) argue, 'very little concern has been shown for the cognitive maps of tourists' except for the work by Aldskogius (1977) in Sweden and Mercer (1971a) in Australia. However, as Pacione (2005: 355) notes: 'Although cognitive mapping can identify sub-areas in a city, it does not capture the sense of place. . . . To achieve this goal we need to move from cognitive mapping to the "mapping of meaning" based on a humanistic approach, where the world of experience to understand what the places mean to those people'. This is more phenomenological in approach and has a strong synergy with ethnography (see Jackson 1985) and the early work of the Chicago School of urban research (Park et al. 1925; Wirth 1938). What is clear for tourists in an urban setting is that human needs should be met, particularly in terms of urban design including the innate need for security, clarity (such as the need for being able to move easily and freely in what Lynch 1960 called a *legible* city), environments where social interaction can occur (e.g. public spaces and places), conveniently located facilities and districts for visiting the urban leisure product and an opportunity to gain a sense of place during the visit from a memorable and easily assimilated urban form and structure. In the latter context, not only have urban regeneration strategies for cities (see Page and Hall 2002) pursued physical regeneration but also massive investment has gone into the re-imaging of places that hitherto have not been high on tourists' consciousness as places to visit with a strong imagery and sense of place even when one visits. This has become part of what Pacione (2005) describes as the pursuit of the liveable city, so that planning and redesign of the city environment seeks to accommodate a better living environment for residents and short-term visitors in pursuit of gaining a better sense of place rather than becoming part of what have been described in the UK as *Crap Towns: The 50 Worse Places to Live in the UK* (Jordison and Kieran 2003) which also have quite limited tourism potential. Many of the government strategies within western countries seeking to improve the living environment as a basis for also attracting tourism, a feature noted in post-event reports on hosting the Commonwealth Games in Manchester, which improved the city's image and visitor numbers post-event. However, in the context of developing countries such as Africa, Hoyle (2001) observed the potential for urban redevelopment of water-front sites such as Lamu which may have beneficial effects for tourism and urban conservation, but the juxtaposition of rich visitors with poor local residents could have potential for conflict and crime.

INSIGHT: The value of urban heritage resources

Heritage does not just refer to old buildings. At its most basic, heritage represents the things we want to keep. Nevertheless, as Glasson et al. (1995) described the situation:

> Public definitions of heritage are still largely dominated by highly educated professionals with expertise in fine art, architecture, engineering, literature, music or design whose professional future is underpinned by generating an academic, problem-based, literature on the subject. This often places the professional at considerable remove from the visitor's need.
>
> (Glasson et al. 1995: 20)

Tunbridge and Ashworth (1996) have identified five different aspects of the expanded meaning of heritage:

- a synonym for any relict physical survival of the past
- the idea of individual and collective memories in terms of non-physical aspects of the past when viewed from the present
- all accumulated cultural and artistic productivity
- the natural environment
- a major commercial activity, e.g. the 'heritage industry'.

Undoubtedly, there is significant overlap between these various conceptions of heritage. However, according to Tunbridge and Ashworth (1996):

> there are intrinsic dangers in the rapidly extending uses of the word and in the resulting stretching of the concept to cover so much. Inevitably precision is lost, but more important is that this, in turn, conceals issues and magnifies problems intrinsic to the creation and management of heritage.
>
> (Tunbridge and Ashworth 1996: 3)

Ironically, the uncertainty about what constitutes heritage is occurring at a time when heritage has assumed greater importance *because* of its relationship to identity in a constantly changing world. As Glasson et al. (1995: 12–13) recognised, 'One reason why the heritage city is proving such a visitor attraction is that, in easily consumable form, it establishes assurance in a world which is changing rapidly'.

The formulation of what constitutes heritage is intimately related to wider political, social, economic and technological changes which appear to reflect postmodern concerns over the end of certainty and the convergence between cultural forms which were once seen as separate aspects of everyday life, e.g. education and tourism or, in even more of a heritage context, marketing and conservation. Much discussion in heritage studies has focused on the recognition of multiple meanings of heritage, particularly with respect to the recognition of other voices in heritage, such as those of indigenous peoples. Yet, while the cultural construction and complexity of heritage is now readily acknowledged (e.g., K. Hudson 1987; Corner and Harvey 1991; Hooper-Greenhill 1992; Tunbridge and Ashworth 1996; Hall and McArthur 1998), what has not been readily forthcoming is the translation of this understanding into practical approaches for heritage managers who are faced with the day-to-day reality of multiple demands on heritage and the quality of the heritage product.

In many urban areas, particularly those which have a substantial migrant and/or labour heritage, other histories are also finding their voice and recognition through the work of heritage managers. For example, the comments of Norkunas (1993) with reference to the heritage of Monterey, California, apply to many other communities:

> Ethnic and class groups have not forgotten the totality of their own pasts. They have certainly preserved a sense of themselves through orally transmitted family stories, and through celebrations and rituals performed inside the group. But their systematic exclusion from official history fragments the community so that feelings of alienation and 'loss of soul' are experienced most deeply by minorities.
> (Norkunas 1993: 99)

The recognition of other approaches, attitudes and interests in heritage is not just isolated to external stakeholders. One of the most important aspects of a stakeholder approach to heritage management is that heritage managers also need to explicitly recognise their own values and the way in which this affects the manner in which they define, interpret and manage heritage.

Economic values are but one set of values surrounding the conservation of 'the things we want to keep'. Historically, the attention of public sector heritage managers has been focused on environmental and cultural values and have only a poorly developed understanding of the significance of economic values. Possibly, this is a consequence of their training and education in which physical conservation and concentration on heritage itself has ignored the broader context within which heritage occurs. It is possibly also a reflection of the organisation cultures within which heritage management occurs. However, in recent years a substantial set of new pressures has begun to affect the manner in which heritage management and conservation operates:

- demands for smaller government concentrating on 'core' activities
- the development of a user-pays philosophy
- recognition of the significance of the tourism dollar for business and regional development
- the emergence of public–private partnership
- greater limitations on government expenditure.

From the new context within which heritage conservation occurs several significant principles can be identified which McMillan (1997) has labelled somewhat provocatively as the 'undeniable truths' regarding heritage conservation. Several principles can be identified.

- *That the choice for heritage conservation has both a value and a cost.*

 While much heritage literature and the activities of heritage groups have focused on the values of heritage, relatively little attention has been given to the costs. As McMillan (1997: 4) recognised, 'there is a financial cost in pursuing heritage conservation. Someone has to pay that cost'.

The community exercises choices regarding the quality and nature of heritage conservation. These decisions however, are not without cost. Heritage regulations, rightly, provide the opportunity to introduce a range of controls over public and private properties. These stem from 'freezing' a property, through inclusion on the National estate, to permitting substantial alteration and change while conserving identified important elements.

(McMillan 1997: 3)

- *In the longer term viability means commercial rates of return.*

If capital cannot be applied to achieve a return on equivalent applications – the opportunity cost of heritage conservation, then in the long term, support for conservation of a particular site by the public and/or private sectors will dwindle. In the current political climate there is clearly a threshold on how much government, whether local or national, will continue to subsidise heritage conservation activities or restrict private sector activities without there being an adequate return to either directly the government stakeholders or indirectly to the wider region.

- *Facilitation is productive while confrontation leads to little real progress in conservation.*

Creative outcomes can now be achieved through cooperation and understanding of the mutual needs of stakeholders. Indeed, one of the basic needs for many heritage management agencies is to recognise the range of stakeholders that may exist for a particular site. As Strong (1997) recognised:

I think we must remind ourselves frequently that heritage only has legitimacy if it represents the values of the community. The whole community, not just the heritage mafia or the local historical

society, but all those ordinary people who appreciate these reminders of the past as they go about their daily business.

(Strong 1997: 1)

Indeed, Strong went on to note that 'Heritage identification and assessment is too important to be given to a group of experts. it should involve the whole community' (1997: 4).

- *Reducing uncertainty, reduces time and costs and increases viability.*

This fourth principle is extremely important for heritage conservation, particularly where the private sector is involved. Unfortunately, many heritage management agencies do not have a clear understanding of the economics of conservation, they do not have well-structured strategic plans which are open for evaluation, neither do they have an appreciation of the effectiveness of their expenditure in relation to their conservation objectives, if they have such objectives at all. Moreover, public heritage organisations typically do not have good estimates of forecasting expenditures and costs to meet objectives for given timelines. Indeed, their timeline often appears to be 'infinite'. They do not have good visitor records or details of expenditure patterns. They also fail to factor in costs of annual upkeep and maintenance. If they were operating on a commercial basis many of them would be bankrupt. From the private sector's perspective time is money, even a casual observer of the economic behaviour of investors and commercial operators realise that certainty is vital. However, heritage agencies trying to develop partnerships often seem to have no understanding of the needs of business.

SERVICE QUALITY ISSUES IN URBAN TOURISM

The competitive nature of urban tourism is increasingly being reflected in the growth in marketing and promotion efforts by towns and cities as they compete for a share of international and domestic tourism markets. Such competition has led to tourists' demands for higher standards of service provision and improved quality in the tourist experience. As Clewer et al. (1992) note, certain urban tourists (e.g. the German market) have higher expectations of service quality than do others. But developing an appropriate definition or concept of urban tourism quality is difficult due to the intangible nature of services as products which are purchased and consumed.

In the context of urban tourism, three key issues need to be addressed. First, place-marketing generates an image of a destination that may not be met in reality due to the problems of promoting places as tourist products. The image promoted through place-marketing may not necessarily be matched in reality through the services and goods which the tourism industry delivers. As a result, the gap between customers' perception of a destination and the bundle of products they consume is reflected in their actual tourist experience, which has important implications for their assessment of quality in their experience. Second, the urban tourism product is largely produced by the private sector either as a package or as a series of elements which are not easily controlled or influenced by the place-marketer. Third, there is a wide range of associated factors which affect a tourist's image of a destination, including less tangible elements like the environment and the ambience of the city which may shape the outcome of a tourist's experience. As a result, the customer's evaluation of the quality of the services and products provided is a function of the difference (gap) between expected and perceived service. It is in this context that the concept of service quality is important for urban tourism. D. Gilbert and Joshi (1992) present an excellent review of the literature, including many of the concepts associated with service quality. In the

case of urban tourism, it is the practical management of the 'gap' between the expected and the perceived service that requires attention by urban managers and the tourism industry. In reviewing Parasuraman et al.'s (1985) service quality model, Gilbert and Joshi (1992: 155) identify five gaps which exist between

- the expected service and the management's perceptions of the consumer experience (i.e. what they think the tourist wants) (Gap 1)
- the management's perception of the tourist needs and the translation of those needs into service quality specifications (Gap 2)
- the quality specifications and the actual delivery of the service (Gap 3)
- the service delivery stage and the organisation/provider's communication with the consumer (Gap 4)
- the consumers' perception of the service they received and experienced, and their initial expectations of the service (Gap 5).

Gilbert and Joshi (1992) argue that the effective utilisation of market research techniques could help to bridge some of the gaps. For

- Gap 1 by encouraging providers to elicit detailed information from consumers on what they require
- Gap 2 by the management providing realistic specifications for the services to be provided which are guided by clear quality standards
- Gap 3 by the employees being able to deliver the service according to the specifications; these need to be closely monitored, and staff training and development is essential: a service is only as good as the staff it employs
- Gap 4 by the promises made by service providers in their marketing and promotional messages being reflected in the actual quality offered; therefore, if a city's promotional literature promises a warm welcome, human resource managers responsible for employees in front-line establishments need to ensure that this message is conveyed to its customers

- Gap 5 by the major gap between the perceived service and delivered service being reduced through progressive improvements in the appropriate image which is marketed to visitors, and the private sector's ability to deliver the expected service in an efficient and professional manner.

Such an approach to service quality can be applied to urban tourism, as it emphasises the importance of the marketing process in communicating and dealing with tourists. To obtain a better understanding of the service quality issues associated with the urban tourist's experience of urban tourism, Haywood and Muller (1988) identify a methodology for evaluating the quality of the urban tourism experience. This involves collecting data on visitors' expectations prior to and after their city-visit by examining a range of variables (see Page 1995a for a fuller discussion). Such an approach may be costly to operate, but it does provide a better appreciation of the visiting process, and they argue that cameras may also provide the day-to-day monitoring of city experiences. At a city-wide level, North American and European cities have responded to the problem of large visitor numbers and the consequences of mass tourism for the tourist experience by introducing Town Centre Management Schemes (see Page 1994a for further details of this issue) and Visitor Management Schemes (see Page and Hardyman 1996 for more detail on the developments and application of such schemes).

While there is insufficient space here to review these new management tools to combat the unwieldy and damaging effect of mass tourism on key tourist centres in developed and developing countries, it is notable that many small historic cities in Europe are taking steps to manage, modify and in some cases deter tourist activities. A range of potential visitor management strategies utilised in urban destinations is outlined in Table 5.8. Yet before such measures can be taken to improve the tourist experience of urban tourism in different localities, Graefe and Vaske (1987) argue that the development of a management strategy is necessary to

- deal with problem conditions which may impact on the tourist experience
- identify the causes of such problems
- select appropriate management strategies to deal with these problems.

(See Graefe and Vaske (1987) for more detail on the use of this approach to improve the tourist experience.)

SIGNIFICANCE OF URBAN TOURISM

Tourism's development in urban areas is not a new phenomenon. But its recognition as a significant activity to study in its own right is only belatedly gaining the recognition it deserves within tourism studies. The reasons why tourists visit urban environments, to consume a bundle of tourism products, continues to be overlooked by the private sector, which often neglects the fundamental issue – cities are multifunctional places. Despite the growing interest in urban tourism research, the failure of many large and small cities which promote tourism to understand the reasons why people visit, the links between the various motivations, and the deeper reasons why people are attracted to cities, remains a fertile area for theoretically informed and methodologically sound research. Many cities are beginning to recognise the importance of monitoring visitor perceptions and satisfaction (e.g. Brocx 1994) and the activity patterns and behaviour of tourists (Survey Research Associates 1991). While such studies may have provided rich pickings for market research companies, all too often the surveys have been superficial, naive and devoid of any real understanding of urban tourism. For the public and private sector planners and managers with an interest, involvement or stake in urban tourism, the main concern continues to be the potential for harnessing the all-year-round appeal of urban tourism activity, despite the often short-stay nature of such visitors. Ensuring that such stays are part of a high-quality experience, where visitor expectations are realistically met through well-researched, targeted and

Table 5.8: Applications of visitor management techniques

Visitor management technique	Application
Regulating access – by area	• All visitors are prohibited from visiting highly sensitive sites. • Different types and levels of use are regulated through zoning.
Regulating access – by transport	• Access is regulated to pedestrians only. • Access is regulated to pedestrians or by bicycle. • Public transport is the only allowable form of transport. • Centennial Park, Sydney, Australia has several 'car-free days' each year in which alternative ways to enter and move about the park must be found.
Regulating visitation – numbers and group size	• Regulations on total visitation per year, day or at any moment may be generated for a specific site. • Group size restrictions have been implemented in some European cathedrals.
Regulating visitation – type of visitor	• Some sites and attractions have a limit on visitation and the type of visitor. • Some urban attractions target older high and middle income groups and actively discourage other segments using strict controls on all accommodation and services, keeping prices high and scrutinising all marketing to maintain consistency.
Regulating behaviour	• Zoning in some cities and towns allocates different types of use to specified areas. • Restrictions on length of stay may be imposed. • Tour operators may be required to operate under a detailed set of guidelines of conduct for visitors. • Visitors must visit with a guide.
Regulating equipment	• Vehicular access may be restricted. • Loudspeakers may be restricted because of noise disturbance.
Implementing entry or user fees	• Most heritage managers responsible for highly visited heritage sites now charge fees to access the site or use facilities at the site; influencing some visitors to choose whether to visit or find an alternative destination. • Some heritage sites offer days during low season when residents are offered free entry. • Cities may require tourism operators to pay for a permit or licence to access the heritage site, and operators must also collect entrance fees from each of their clients. • A portion of user fees collected is returned to local stakeholders as a means of demonstrating the value of tourism.
Modifying the site	• Some urban heritage sites may have specially designed walkways so as to reduce visitor impact. • Castlemaine Jail, Victoria, Australia is privately run as a heritage tourism venture, with the prison workshops providing a conference venue, the dungeon kitchen providing a wine bar, the mess hall providing an à la carte restaurant, refurbished cells providing accommodation, and remaining cells being presented as they were originally used for guided tours to access.
Undertaking market research	• A study of the domestic and international visitor market may be conducted in order to identify the market segments most likely to visit urban tourism attractions.
Undertaking visitor monitoring and research	• Visitors may be asked to complete special 'day diary' forms to identify their motivations for visiting and the activities they undertook. • Visitors may be asked for their attitudes towards their experience and the performance of the respective heritage manager as a means of improving visitor management strategies. • Visitor impact monitoring and research is widely undertaken in sensitive urban heritage attractions.

Table 5.8: (continued)

Visitor management technique	Application
Undertaking marketing – promotional	• Visitation pressure may be relieved through the development, marketing and promotion of value-added alternative attractions. • Different urban tourism organisations may undertake common promotional activities in order to reinforce the profile of the destination.
Undertaking marketing – strategic information	• Tour guides can avoid sensitive areas by using a map and pictorial guide that identifies the best vantage points for attractions. • A walking 'trail selector' (brochure and map) may be developed to provide information on lightly used walking trails in order to redistribute use away from heavily used areas.
Implementing interpretation programmes and facilities	• Some urban tourism destinations may generate greater levels of visitor respect for the local culture through the provision of opportunities such as learning to cook with a local family or spending a night with a local family in a homestay. • Visitors may be taken on guided tours by local people who then convey their personal experiences and knowledge of the area to the visitor. This level of authenticity can greatly enhance the quality of the visitor experience.
Implementing education programmes and facilities	• Theme trails may be created to educate visitors about specific aspects of local history and culture. • Many urban heritage attractions have interpretation and signage encouraging appropriate behaviour.
Modifying the presence of heritage management	• Most museums strategically position security staff in corners and corridors to create a high profile when visitors are moving between exhibits and a low profile when they are studying an individual exhibit.
Encouraging and assisting alternative providers – tourism industry	• Some urban destination management organisations encourage the development of small-scale homestay accommodation and tours by local guides who are highly trained in heritage and interpretation, with profits therefore being reinvested in the local community.
Encouraging and assisting alternative providers – volunteers	• Many urban heritage attractions, such as museums and historic sites, have volunteer and friends' associations which assist in various aspects of management as well as providing a source of financial support. For example, the Karori Wildlife Sanctuary in Wellington, New Zealand is a private trust with a membership of several thousand people. A sizeable proportion of members volunteer to help build trails and act as guides, allowing the trust to reinvest funds into activities such as pest control and building a strong community base.
Concentrating on accredited organisations bringing visitors to a site	• National and regional accreditation programmes may be used to check on the appropriateness of tourism operator practices and the quality of facilities. For example, the Austrian Association of Green Villages requires accommodation providers to meet criteria and market co-operatively with others.

Source: after Hall and McArthur (1998)

innovative products, continues to stimulate interest among tour operators and other stakeholders in urban tourism provision. Yet the urban tourism industry, which is so often fragmented and poorly co-ordinated, rarely understands many of the complex issues of visitor behaviour, the spatial learning process which tourists experience and the implications for making their visit as stress free as possible.

Plate 5.3/5.4: London Docklands marketing images.
Source: LDDC

Plate 5.5: Entrance to the cathedral precinct, Canterbury, Kent. Crowding may have substantial impacts not only on the quality of the visitor experience but also on the attraction itself.

These concerns should force cities seeking to develop an urban tourism economy to reconsider the feasibility of pursuing a strategy to revitalise the city-region through tourism-led regeneration. All too often both the private and public sectors have moved headlong into economic regeneration strategies for urban areas, seeking a tourism component as a likely back-up for property and commercial redevelopment (see e.g. Lutz and Ryan 1997). The implications here are that tourism issues are not given the serious treatment they deserve. Where the visitors' needs and spatial behaviour are poorly understood and neglected in the decision-making process, it affects the planning, development and eventual outcome of the urban tourism environment. The experience of waterfront areas in large cities is such that research which reviews the ambitious schemes to market tourism in London Docklands, to pull the centre of gravity and development in London to the east from the central tourism district in the west, resulted in developers underestimating the role of tourist behaviour (e.g. the inertia of tourists who would not travel east from St Katherine's Dock to areas en route to Greenwich). The result was a series of missed business opportunities and a range of business failures. Therefore, tourist behaviour, the tourism system and its constituent components need to be evaluated in the context of future growth in urban tourism to understand the visitor as a central component in the visitor experience. Managing the different elements of this experience in a realistic manner requires more attention among those towns and cities competing aggressively for visitors, using the quality experience approach as a new-found marketing tool. Future research needs to focus on the behaviour, attitudes and needs of existing and prospective urban tourists to reduce the gap between their expectations and the service delivered. But ensuring that the tourism system within cities can deliver the service and experience marketed through promotional literature in a sensitive and meaningful way is now one of the major challenges for urban tourism managers. The approach adopted by the tourism industry needs to be more proactive in its pursuit of high-quality visitor experiences rather than reactive towards individual problems that arise as a result of tourist dissatisfaction after a visit. Research has a vital role to play in understanding the increasingly complex reasons why tourists continue to visit urban environments and the factors which influence their behaviour and spatial activity patterns. While urban tourism continues to be a recognised and established form of tourism activity, research by the academic community and private sector has really paid only lip-service to what is a central feature of the tourism system in most developed and developing countries.

CONCLUSION

This chapter has reviewed the role of recreation and tourism within the context of an urban environment, where recreationalists and tourists inevitably use some of the same resources, a feature recognised in Toronto's launch of a Green Tourism Map which also includes many recreational sites. This feature of multiple use is best summarised by Burtenshaw et al.'s (1991) conceptualisation of different users and functional areas of the city, where no one group has a monopoly over its use, a feature now being recognised in more integrated recreational planning that begins to recognise that residents and visitors use similar resources. The urban environment is still a neglected field of research in relation to the geographer's analysis of tourism and recreation as

Ashworth (2003) reiterated in revisiting his seminal study published in 1989. It is ironic, therefore, that many of the methodologies, techniques and skills which the geographer can harness and utilise with new technology, such as the use of GIS, can help both the public and private sector to understand how a range of research issues affect the functioning of the recreational and tourism system. For the more applied geographical researcher, this is a straightforward process in many instances of utilising a synthesising role to adopt the holistic view to the city, to provide what Lynch (1960) described as *legibility*. It is this absence of legibility that seems to affect the management of urban tourism and recreation even in the new millennium. For example, in recreational planning, issues of access, equality, need and social justice can easily be integrated into spatial analysis using secondary data but the spatially informed planning framework is often only portrayed as a static one point in time analysis produced for structure plans and development plans as this chapter has shown. Few attempts have been made to build and maintain urban models of recreation and tourism that accommodate the dynamic and changing needs of the users of such services. Where data do not exist, spatially orientated social surveys have proved to be extremely valuable in understanding the processes shaping and underpinning existing patterns of use and activity, provision and future development. However, applied geographical research (Sant 1982) can be used to pose questions and address problem-solving tasks for managerial solutions as well as providing a basis for raising more fundamental questions about the nature of tourism and recreation in contemporary capitalist society.

QUESTIONS

- What are the key geographical approaches to the geography of urban recreation?
- What difficulties might exist in measuring the significance of urban tourism?
- Is it possible to reconcile social and economic values in conserving urban heritage?

- To what extent might urban recreation resources also act as resources for tourism?

READING

Useful texts on urban tourism include

Page, S.J. and Hall, C.M. (2003) *Managing Urban Tourism*, Harlow: Pearson Education.
Judd, D. and Fainstein, S. (1999) *The Tourist City*, New Haven, CT: Yale University Press.

An excellent synthesis of the state of urban tourism research since the 1980s can be found in the two 'state of the art reviews' by Ashworth:

Ashworth, G. (1989) 'Urban tourism: An imbalance in attention' in C. Cooper (ed.) Progress in Tourism, Recreation and Hospitality Management, Volume One, London: Belhaven, pp; 35–55.
Ashworth, G. (2003) 'Urban tourism: Still an imbalance in attention' in C. Cooper (ed.) Classic Reviews in Tourism, Clevedon: Channel View, pp. 143–63.

Two articles by Doug Pearce provide a useful overview of tourism in Paris:

Pearce, D.G. (1998) 'Tourism development in Paris: Public intervention', *Annals of Tourism Research*, 25(2): 457–76.
Pearce, D.G. (1999) 'Tourism districts in Paris: Structure and functions', *Tourism Management*, 19(1): 49–65.

A useful case study to complement the London Borough of Newham example on equality of access is

Nicholls, S. (2001) 'Measuring the accessibility and equity of public parks: A case study using GIS', *Managing Leisure*, 6(4): 201–19.

An interesting in-depth case study of the impact of urban events and relationships to processes of gentrification and restructuring is

Olds, K. (1998) 'Urban mega-events, evictions and housing rights: The Canadian case', *Current Issues in Tourism*, 1(1): 2–46.

6

RURAL RECREATION AND TOURISM

As a focal point for geographical research, the recreational and tourism potential of rural areas is not a new theme for geographers to consider. The interest in rural areas has a long tradition (Owens 1984) but the problem remains that much of the research conducted, with a few exceptions (Page and Getz 1997; Sharpley and Sharpley 1997; Butler et al. 1998; D. R. Hall and O'Hanlon 1998), is now dated, fragmented and continues to view rural areas as either a recreational or a tourism resource. It fails to adopt a holistic view of the rural resource base as a multifaceted environment capable of accommodating a wide range of uses (e.g. agriculture, industrialisation, recreation and tourism) and values. As Patmore (1983: 124) recognised, 'recreation use must compete with agriculture, forestry, water abstraction, mineral extraction and military training' within the rural environment which has both spatial implications for competing and complementary land uses as well as for the identification of the ways in which recreation and tourism may be accommodated in an ever-changing rural environment.

According to Coppock (1982):

the contribution to research that geographers have made has been focused primarily on outdoor recreation in the countryside. No clear distinction has been made between tourism and recreation which is not surprising in a small, densely settled country [Britain] where there is considerable overlap between the two; in any case, geographical studies in tourism have been much less numerous than those in outdoor recreation.

(Coppock 1982: 8)

This is an assertion that, to a certain extent, still holds true for present-day rural areas. Butler et al. (1998) argued that:

In many cases, however, the specific activities which are engaged in during leisure, recreation and tourism are identical, the key differences being the setting or location of the activities, the duration of time involved, and, in some cases, the attitudes, motivations and perceptions of the participants. In recent years the differences between recreation and tourism in particular, except at a philosophical level, have become of decreasing significance and distinctions increasingly blurred.

(Butler et al. 1998: 2)

In fact, Pigram (1983) observed that it is

where [such] space consumption and spatial competition and conflict are most likely to occur . . . that spatial organisation and spatial concerns become paramount, and so the geographer has a valuable role to play in considering rural recreation and tourism as a process and phenomenon which has spatial implications.

(Pigram 1983: 15)

Pigram (1983: 15) further argued that the geographer cannot focus only on the spatial organisation and interaction which occurs, but also the 'imbalance or discordance between population related demand and environmentally related supply of recreation [and tourism] opportunities and facilities'. This point is reiterated by Hall (1995), who felt that the rural areas now host a wide range of activities undertaken in people's leisure time and to determine whether the activity is tourism or recreation may seem irrelevant. In contrast, Patmore (1983: 123) argued that 'outdoor recreation in rural areas rapidly achieves a distinctive character of its own and needs separate consideration for more than convention'. Either way, recreation and tourism are increasingly important activities in rural areas throughout the western world.

This chapter examines the growing interest from geographers in the way in which the rural environment is examined as a recreational and tourism resource together with some of the ways in which it has been conceptualised and researched. The chapter commences with a review of the concept of 'rural' and the ways in which geographers have debated its meaning and definition. This is followed by a discussion of the geographer's contribution to theoretical debate in relation to rural recreation and tourism. The contribution made by historical geography to the analysis of continuity and change in the rural environment and its consumption for leisure and tourism is briefly examined. The other contributions made by geographers to the analysis of recreation and tourism in rural environments is examined and a case study of tourism in Ireland is developed as a way of synthesising the geographer's interest in rural tourism.

IN PURSUIT OF THE CONCEPT OF 'RURAL'

G. M. Robinson's (1990) invaluable synthesis of rural change illustrates that the term 'rural' has remained an elusive one to define in academic research, even though popular conceptions of rural areas are based on images of rusticity and the idyllic village life. However, Robinson (1990) argued that:

> defining rural . . . in the past has tended to ignore common economic, social and political structures in both urban and rural areas. . . . In simple terms . . . 'rural' areas define themselves with respect to the presence of particular types of problems. A selective list of examples could include depopulation and deprivation in areas remote from major metropolitan centres; a reliance upon primary activity; conflicts

between presentation of certain landscapes and development of a variety of economic activities; and conflicts between local needs and legislation emanating from urban-based legislators. Key characteristics of 'rural' are taken to be extensive land uses, including large open spaces of underdeveloped land, and small settlements at the base of the settlement hierarchy, but including settlements thought of as rural.

(Robinson 1990: xxi–xxii)

Therefore, research on rural recreation and tourism needs to recognise the essential qualities of what is 'rural'. While national governments use specific criteria to define 'rural', often based on the population density of settlements, there is no universal agreement on the critical population threshold which distinguishes between urban and rural populations. For the developed world, Robinson (1990) summarises the principal approaches used by sociologists, economists and other groups in establishing the basis of what is rural and this need not be reiterated here. What is important is the diversity of approaches used by many researchers who emphasise the concept of an urban–rural continuum as a means of establishing differing degrees of rurality and the essential characteristics of ruralness. Shaw and Williams (1994: 224) advocate the use of the concept of a rural opportunity spectrum, where the countryside is viewed as the location of a 'wide range of outdoor leisure and tourist activities, although over time the composition of these has changed'. Harrison (1991) highlighted the speed of change in rural areas, with the settings and activities undertaken in such areas changing rapidly in the 1970s and 1980s. Even so, such studies do little to establish a meaningful concept of what is meant by a rural setting.

In contrast, Hoggart's (1990) provocative article 'Let's do away with rural' argues that 'there is too much laxity in the treatment of areas in empirical analysis . . . [and] that the undifferentiated use of "rural" in a research context is detrimental to the advancement of social theory' (Hoggart 1990: 245), since the term 'rural' is unsatisfactory due to inter-rural differences and urban–rural similarities. Hoggart (1990) argued that general classifications of urban and rural areas are of limited value. For this reason, recent advances in social theory may offer a number of important insights into conceptualising the rural environment and tourism-related activities.

According to Cloke (1992), rural places have been traditionally associated with specific rural functions: agriculture, sparsely populated areas, geographically dispersed settlement patterns, and rurality has been conceptualised in terms of peripherality (for a discussion of tourism and peripherality, see Page 1994c; Hall and Boyd 2005), remoteness and dependence on rural economic activity. However, new approaches in social theory have argued that rural areas are inextricably linked to the national and international political economy. As Cloke (1992) rightly argues, changes in the way society and non-urban places are organised and function have rendered traditional definitions of rurality less meaningful due to the following changes:

- increased mobility of people, goods and messages have eroded the autonomy of local communities
- delocalisation of economic activity makes it impossible to define homogeneous economic regions
- new specialised uses of rural spaces (as tourist sites, parks and development zones) have created new specialised networks of relationships in the areas concerned, many of which are no longer localised
- people who 'inhabit' a given rural area include a diversity of temporary visitors as well as residents
- rural spaces increasingly perform functions for non-rural users and in these cases may be characterised by the fact that they exist independently of the action of rural populations
  (Mormont 1990: 31, cited in Cloke 1992)

Consequently, Mormont (1987) conceptualises rural areas as a set of overlapping social spaces, each with their own logic, institutions and network of actors (e.g. users and administrators). This reiterates many of the early ideas from behavioural scientists – that a rural space needs to be defined

in terms of how the occupants perceive it, as a social construct where the occupiers of rural spaces interact and participate in activities such as recreation and tourism. In this context, developments in social theory imply that the nature and use of rural areas for activities such as recreation and tourism is best explained by examining the processes by which their meaning of 'rural' is 'constructed, negotiated and experienced' (Cloke 1992: 55). One approach favoured by Cloke (1992) is the analysis of the way in which the commodification of the countryside has occurred, leading to the rise of markets for rural products where:

> the countryside . . . [is] an exclusive place to be lived in; rural communities [are considered] as a context to be bought and sold; rural lifestyle [is something] which can be colonized; icons of rural culture [are commodities which] can be crafted, packed and marketed; rural landscapes [are imbued] with a new range of potential from 'pay-as-you-enter' national parks, to sites for the theme park explosion; rural production [ranges] from newly commodified food to the output of industrial plants whose potential or actual pollutive externalities have driven them from more urban localities.
>
> (Cloke 1992: 55)

In this respect, rural areas are places to be consumed and where production is based on establishing new commodities or in re-imaging and rediscovering places for recreation and tourism. Cloke (1992) cites privatisation in the UK as a major process stimulating this form of rural production focused on rural recreation and tourism. The new political economy influencing agriculture in the EU has also facilitated farm diversification into new forms of tourism accommodation (e.g. farm-stays) and attractions. Yet the critical processes stimulating the demand for the mass consumption of rural products have been essential in effecting such changes. Urry (1988) points to changes in taste following the emergence of a new service class which have led to greater emphasis on consumption in rural environments. These tastes have also influenced other social groups who have adopted similar values in the consumption of rural areas including:

- the pursuit of a pastoral idyll
- acceptance of cultural symbols related to the rural idyll
- a greater emphasis on outdoor pursuits in such environments.

While the detailed social and cultural interpretations of such trends are dealt with in detail by Urry (1988), Poon (1989) illustrates the practical implications of such changes for the tourism industry. Poon (1989) interprets these changes in terms of a 'shift from an "old tourism" (e.g. the regimented and standardized holiday package) to a "new tourism" which is segmented, customized and flexible in both time and space'. In fact some research on services has analysed the change in society from a 'Fordist' to 'post-Fordist' stage which has involved a shift in the form of demand for tourist services from a former pattern of mass consumption 'to more individual patterns, with greater differentiation and volatility of consumer preferences and a heightened need for producers to be consumer-driven and to segment markets more systematically' (Urry 1991: 52). While recreational use of the countryside may not exhibit such a high degree of marketing and reinterpretation to develop novel and profitable experiences, Butler et al. (1998) do point to the increasing use of rural areas for such purposes which are juxtaposed with more traditional recreational and tourist uses. Nevertheless, Hummelbrunner and Miglbauer (1994) support both Poon's (1989) and Urry's (1991) assessments, arguing that these changes to the demand and supply of tourism services have contributed to the emergence of a 'new rural tourism'. From a supply perspective, this has manifested itself in terms of 'an increasing interest in rural tourism among a better-off clientele, and also among some holidaymakers as a growing environmental awareness and a desire to be integrated with the residents in the areas they visit' (Bramwell 1994: 3). This not only questions the need to move beyond existing concepts such as core and periphery with rural tourism as a simplistic consumption of the countryside, but also raises the question of how rural areas are being used to provide tourism and recreational experiences and how businesses are pursuing market-oriented approaches to the new era of commodification in rural environments. If the 1990s was a 'new era of commodifying rural space, characterised by a speed and scale of development which far outstrip farm-based tourism and recreation of previous eras' (Cloke 1992: 59), then a critical review of this process at an international and national scale is timely, to assess the extent and significance of rural tourism and recreation in the 1990s and into the new millennium.

CONCEPTUALISING THE RURAL RECREATION–TOURISM DICHOTOMY

One of the problems within the literature in recreation and tourism is that the absence of a holistic and integrated view of each area has continued to encourage researchers to draw a distinction between recreation and tourism as complementary and yet semantically different activities, without providing a conceptual framework within which to view such issues. Cloke (1992) overcomes this difficulty by observing that the relationship between rural areas and tourism and leisure activities has changed, with the activities being the dominant elements in many rural landscapes which control and affect local communities to a much greater degree than in the past. Therefore, while a critical debate has occurred in the tourism and recreational literature in terms of the similarity and differences between tourists and recreationists, it is the social, economic and spatial outcomes that are probably the most significant feature to focus on in the rural environment. However, there is still a need to recognise the magnitude and effect of recreational and tourist use because of the timing, scale, resource impact and implication of each use. But ultimately each use is a consumption of resources and space in relation to the user's discretionary leisure time and income. According to Shaw and Williams (1994), there are a range of issues to consider in relation to this debate. For example, in many countries, use of the countryside is a popular pastime (e.g. in 1990 the Countryside Commission found that 75 per cent of the population of England visited the countryside) and in such studies there is a clear attempt to avoid simplistic classifications of what constitutes tourist and recreationalist use. Shaw and Williams (1994) prefer to use a more culturally determined definition to show that the use of rural landscapes for tourist and recreational purposes is conditioned by a wide range of social, economic and cultural meanings which affect the host area. Cultural definitions of urban and rural areas highlight not only the intrinsic qualities of the countryside which is significantly different from urban areas, but also the interpretation that 'there is nothing that is inherent in any part of the countryside that makes it a recreational resource' (Shaw and Williams 1994: 223). This recognises that there is a search for new meaning in a research context. In fact Butler et al. (1998) would concur with this since:

> One of the major elements of change in rural areas has been the changes within recreation and tourism. Until the last two decades or so, recreational and tourist activities in rural areas were mostly related closely to the rural character of the setting.
> They were primarily activities which were different to those engaged in urban centers. . . . They could be characterised, at the risk of generalisation, by the following terms: relaxing, passive, nostalgic, traditional, low technological, and mostly non-competitive.
> (Butler et al. 1998: 8)

But in recent years this has been affected by changes to the meaning and use of rural environments, where the setting is no longer a passive component. Yet there is some support for not focusing on the rural setting; as Patmore (1983: 122) argued, 'there is no sharp discontinuity between urban and rural resources for recreation but rather a complete continuum from local park to remote mountain park'. If one maintains such an argument, to a certain extent, it makes the geographer's role in classifying tourism and recreational environments and their uses for specific reasons and purposes rather meaningless if they are part of no more than a simple continuum of recreational and tourism resources, thereby denying new attempts to understand what motivates users to seek and consume such resources

in a cultural context. To overcome this difficulty, Shaw and Williams (1994: 224) prefer to view 'rural areas as highly esteemed as locales for leisure and tourism' and their use is heavily contingent upon particular factors, especially social access, and the politics of countryside ownership. Yet these contingencies may only really be fully understood in the context of the developed world, according to Shaw and Williams (1994), by considering three critical concepts used by geographers: the rural opportunity spectrum, accessibility and time–space budgets. However, prior to any discussion of such key concepts, it is pertinent to consider the historical dimension to tourism and recreational pursuits in rural environments, since historical geographers emphasise continuity, change and the role of spatial separation of social classes in past periods as factors which affected the past use of rural locales.

THE GEOGRAPHER'S CONTRIBUTION TO THEORETICAL DEBATE IN RURAL CONTEXTS

Within any research area, progress is often gauged in terms of the extent to which the subject contributes to the development of theory. As Perkins (1993) argued, a

> social scientist's primary role is to develop theories about society. Theories are sets of logically inter-related statements about phenomena, such as recreation and leisure. The reason for developing such theories is to help us understand the world humans make for themselves. It is on the basis of the understanding reached in the development of these theories that we plan and manage particular social phenomena.
> (Perkins 1993: 116)

As Owens (1984: 174) argued, 'during the mid-1970s there was a hiatus in leisure and recreation research which marked a profound change from the enthusiastic promotion of agency dependent ad hoc applied research to an evaluative phase characterised by introspection and self-criticism' since, prior to 1975, the generation of empirical case studies dominated the literature. After 1975 calls from North American researchers for a greater consideration of leisure behaviour and its contribution to theory was advocated. For example, critical reviews by researchers (e.g. Patmore 1977, 1978, 1979, 1980; Coppock 1980; Mercer 1979a; Patmore and Collins 1981), to name but a few, reiterated these criticisms, and Patmore (1977: 115) poignantly summarised the position where 'this review reveals continuing and glaring gaps in British research, not least in a better understanding of the nature and motivation of recreation demand and in the development of an effective body of integrative theory'.

A series of new texts in the 1980s (e.g. Kelly 1982; S.L.J. Smith 1983a; Torkildsen 1983) and the appearance of two journals, *Leisure Studies* and *Leisure Sciences*, raised the need for more theoretically determined research, but only a limited range of studies by geographers focused on theoretical and conceptual issues (e.g. Owens 1984) while other disciplines contributed to the debate in a more vigorous and central manner (e.g. Graefe et al. 1984a). Despite large-scale research funding by government research agencies (e.g. the Social Science Research Council in the UK) in the 1970s and 1980s, a lack of concern for theory has meant that geographers have made little impact on the problem that

> the large body of rural outdoor recreation research has not been consolidated in more theoretical work but one wonders whether researchers have set themselves an intellectual challenge which they are unable to meet. Certainly, there is now a steady flow of publication, albeit mainly directed to traditional ends, and because of this the argument that lack of progress towards a theory of leisure and recreation simply reflects poor funding is now much less plausible.
> (Owens 1984: 176)

As a consequence, Perkins (1993: 116–17) suggests that 'there are four reasons for this neglect of theoretical geographical leisure research. The first is that within the discipline, leisure research is considered' to be unimportant when compared to the central concerns of economic, social and urban geography. The second reason is that very little research funding has been made available to geographers to pursue theoretical leisure research (see Perkins

and Gidlow 1991). Third, much research has been British or North American in origin, 'where pressures between recreational uses of particular sites are very great . . . geographers have worked closely with recreational site managers to develop short to medium term management strategies for these areas'. Finally, recreation geographers 'have hardly participated in the theoretical debates which have thrived in their discipline since the 1970s' (Perkins 1993: 117).

In fact, Perkins (1993) offers one of the few attempts by geographers to rise to this challenge, using social theory, particularly structuration theory (Giddens 1984), and his research is valuable in relation to the understanding of locales for the analysis of human and spatial interaction. Locales comprise a range of settings which are different and yet connected through interactions. The interactions result from

> the life path of individuals . . . in ways that reflect patterns of production and consumption. These interactions result in a particular pattern of locales which have social and physical forms. Each life path is essentially an allocation of time between these different locales. A particular mode of production will emphasise dominant locales to which time must be allocated.
> (Perkins 1993: 126)

Within the theoretical literature on structuration, in a capitalist society, structure and human interaction are brought together through the concept of the locale. The dominant locales are

- home
- work
- school

and they are settings in which consumption occurs. Thus a leisure locale is a setting for interaction whereby 'people pursue leisure within the context of their life commitments and access to resources. Leisure interactions, of course, occur in and are influenced by places, and to this extent the leisure locale includes a spatial component' (Perkins 1993: 126). In such theoretically determined analyses, Perkins (1993) calls for the geographers of recreation to consider the position and internal organisation of the leisure locale in a rural setting, in relation to the dominant locales (i.e. the home, work and school) and other institutional locales such as religion and the arts. One possible mechanism for pursuing such theoretically determined research may be to employ new conceptualisations of geography using the new regional geography informed by structuration theory. Structuration theory and the new regional geography have emerged, emphasising producers of the interpenetration of structure and agency. Structure 'both constrains and enables people to take particular life paths, the collective effect of which is to produce and enable new members of society in their life paths . . . [where] geographical behaviour' (Perkins 1993: 117) affects people's specific situations. Therefore, the geographer in a rural setting would need to consider both structure and human interaction and how it is all brought together in the context of the locale (for more detail, see Thrift 1977; Giddens 1984; Perkins 1993).

In the context of rural tourism, the theoretical analysis advocated by Perkins (1993) for rural recreation also has a relevance, particularly when one considers the debate engendered by Bramwell (1994):

> does the physical existence of tourism in rural areas create a rural tourism that has a significance beyond the self-evident combination of particular activities in a specific place? In other words, do the special characteristics of rural areas help shape the pattern of tourism so that there is a particular rural tourism?
> (Bramwell 1994: 2)

While the comments by Bramwell (1994) certainly highlight the need for more attention to the concept of the locale, Cloke (1992) indicates that structuration theory does have a role to play, although, as Perkins (1993) indicates, geographers may need to consider the value of humanistic research to ask questions that can address the issues raised by Bramwell (1994): how do people value rural areas and the relationships between locales? Unfortunately, much of the research published to date remains theoretically uninformed and empirically driven. As a result, much of the research on

rural tourism by geographers has, with a number of exceptions, failed to contribute to a growing awareness of its role, value and significance in the wider development of tourism studies and its importance as a mainstay of many rural economies. In this context, Butler and Clark's (1992) comments are relevant in that:

> The literature on rural tourism is sparse and . . . conceptual models and theories are lacking. . . . Many of the references in tourism are case studies with little theoretical foundation . . . or they focus on specific problems. . . . Some take a broader perspective focusing on issues and process. . . . There is, therefore a lack of theory and models placing rural tourism in a conceptual framework.
> (Butler and Clark 1992: 167)

Plate 6.1: Souvenir shop, Leyden, The Netherlands. To what extent does tourism lead to cultural stereotyping and changed perceptions of cultural identity by both locals and tourists?

Much of the research on rural tourism has been published in a diverse range of social science journals (e.g. *Sociologia Ruralis, Rural Studies, Tourism Recreation Research*), reports and edited collections of essays which have been poorly disseminated as well as one or two specific texts (e.g. Sharpley 1993; Butler et al. 1998). Consequently, rural tourism has continued to be peripheral to the focus of tourism research while remaining poorly defined. It continues to be a general term which encapsulates a wide range of interest groups not only from tourism studies, but also from economics, planning, anthropology, geography, sociology and business studies. There has also been a lack of integration between these interest groups, each cultivating its own view and approach to rural tourism. As a result few researchers have attempted to define the concept of rural tourism.

TOWARDS A CONCEPT OF RURAL TOURISM

Keane et al.'s (1992) innovative but little known study on rural tourism offers a number of insights into the definition of rural tourism acknowledging that there are a variety of terms used to describe tourism activity in rural areas: agritourism, farm tourism, rural tourism, soft tourism, alternative tourism and many others which have different meanings from one country to another. Keane also points out that it is difficult to avoid some of this confusion in relation to labels and definitions because the term 'rural tourism' has been adopted by the European Union to refer to the entire tourism activity in a rural area (Keane et al. 1992). One way of addressing this seemingly tautological proposition, that tourism in rural areas is not necessarily rural tourism when so many typologies exist for types of tourism that may or may not be deemed rural tourism, is to examine what makes rural tourism distinctive.

WHAT MAKES RURAL TOURISM DISTINCTIVE?

Lane (1994) discusses the historical continuity in the development of rural tourism and examines some of the key issues which combine to make rural tourism distinctive. Bramwell (1994: 3) suggests that despite the problems of defining the concept of 'rural', 'it may be a mistake to deny our common-sense thoughts that rural areas can have distinctive characteristics or that these can have consequences for social and economic interactions in the country-side'. The views and perceptions that people hold of the countryside are different from those of urban areas, which is an important starting point for establishing the distinctiveness of rural tourism. Lane (1994) actually lists the subtle differences between urban and rural tourism, in which individual social representations of the countryside are a critical component of how people interact with rural areas. In fact, Squire (1994) acknowledges that both the social representations and personal images of the countryside condition whether people wish to visit rural areas for tourism, and what they see and do during their visit.

Lane (1994) also highlights the impact of changes in rural tourism since the 1970s, with far greater numbers of recreationalists and tourists now visiting rural areas. As Patmore's (1983) seminal study on recreation and leisure acknowledges, the impact of car ownership has led to a geographical dispersion of recreationalists and tourists beyond existing fixed modes of transport (e.g. railways). Consequently, tourism has moved away from a traditional emphasis on resorts, small towns and villages to become truly rural, with all but the most inaccessible wilderness areas awaiting the impact of the more mobile tourist. Despite this strong growth in the demand for rural tourism, Lane (1994) acknowledges the absence of any systematic sources of data on rural tourism, since neither the World Tourism Organisation nor OECD have appropriate measures. In addition, there is no agreement among member countries on how to measure this phenomenon. One way of establishing the distinctive characteristics of rural tourism is to derive a working definition of rural tourism. Here the work by Lane (1994) is invaluable since it dismisses simplistic notions of rural tourism as tourism which occurs in the countryside. Lane (1994: 9) cites the following seven reasons why it is difficult to produce a complex definition of rural tourism to apply in all contexts:

- Urban or resort-based tourism is not confined to urban areas, but spills out into rural areas.
- Rural areas themselves are difficult to define, and the criteria used by different nations vary considerably.
- Not all tourism which takes place in rural areas is strictly 'rural' – it can be 'urban' in form, and merely be located in a rural area. Many so-called holiday villages are of this type; in recent years, numerous large holiday complexes have been completed in the countryside. They may be 'theme parks', time shares or leisure hotel developments. Their degree of rurality can be both an emotive and a technical question.
- Historically, tourism has been an urban concept; the great majority of tourists live in urban areas. Tourism can be an urbanising influence on rural areas, encouraging cultural and economic change, and new construction.
- Different forms of rural tourism have developed in different regions. Farm-based holidays are important in many parts of rural Germany and Austria. Farm-based holidays are much rarer in rural USA and Canada. In France, the self-catering cottage or gîte is an important component of the rural tourism product.
- Rural areas themselves are in a complex process of change. The impact of global markets, communications and telecommunication has changed market conditions and orientations for traditional products. The rise of environmentalism has led to increasing control by 'outsiders' over land use and resource development. Although some rural areas still experience depopulation, others are experiencing an inflow of people to retire or to develop new 'non-traditional' businesses. The once clear

distinction between urban and rural is now blurred by suburbanisation, long-distance commuting and second home development.
- Rural tourism is a complex multifaceted activity: it is not just farm-based tourism. It not only includes farm-based holidays but also comprises special-interest nature holidays and ecotourism, walking, climbing and riding holidays, adventure, sport and health tourism, hunting and angling, educational travel, arts and heritage tourism and, in some areas, ethnic tourism. There is also a large general-interest market for less specialised forms of rural tourism. This area is highlighted by studies of the German tourism market, where a major requirement of the main holiday is the ability to provide peace, quiet and relaxation in rural surroundings.

Consequently, rural tourism in its purest form should be

- located in rural areas
- functionally rural – built upon the rural world's special features of small-scale enterprise, open space, contact with nature and the natural world, heritage, 'traditional' societies and 'traditional' practices
- rural in scale – both in terms of buildings and settlements – and, therefore, usually small scale
- traditional in character, growing slowly and organically, and connected with local families. It will often be very largely controlled locally and developed for the long-term good of the area; and of many different kinds, representing the complex pattern of rural environment, economy, history and location (after Lane 1994).

Lane (1994: 16) argues that the following factors also have to be considered in defining rural tourism:

- holiday type
- intensity of use
- location
- style of management
- degree of integration with the community.

Using the continuum concept allows for the distinction to be made between those tourist visits which are specifically rural, and those which are urban, and those which fall in an intermediate category. Thus, any workable definition of rural tourism needs to establish the parameters of the demand for, and supply of, the tourism experience and the extent to which it is undertaken in the continuum of rural to urban environments. With these issues in mind, it is pertinent to examine the most influential studies published to date by historical geographers to illustrate how continuity and change in spatial patterns and processes of tourism and recreation activity contribute to the landscapes of rural leisure use in the present day.

RURAL RECREATION AND TOURISM IN HISTORICAL PERSPECTIVE

Rural environments, often referred to as the countryside or non-urban areas, have a long history of being used for tourism and recreational activities in both the developed and developing world, a feature frequently neglected in many reviews of rural areas. Towner (1996) documents many of the historical changes and factors which shaped tourism and leisure in the rural environment in Europe since 1540, observing how the rural landscape has been fashionable and developed for the use of social elites at certain times in history (e.g. the landed estates of the seventeenth and eighteenth centuries). Such a review provides an invaluable synthesis and point of reference on the history of tourism and recreation. Towner (1996) reconstructs past geographies to show how the growth of towns and cities during the industrialisation of Europe led to an urbanised countryside around those nascent industrial centres (i.e. the construction of an urban fringe). Such patterns of recreational and tourism activity all combine to produce a wide variety of leisure and, more belatedly, tourism environments which exhibit elements of continuity in use, but also have been in a constant state of change. For example, Towner (1996) characterises the pre-industrial period:

where popular recreation in the countryside throughout much of Europe was rooted in the daily and seasonal rhythms of agricultural life . . . and took place in the setting of home, street, village green or surrounding fields and woods and throughout the year, a distinction can be made between ordinary everyday leisure and the major annual holiday events, and between activities that were centred around home and immediate locality and those which caused people to move.

(Towner 1996: 45–6)

The gradual transition towards more 'private rural landscapes for the more affluent and higher social classes' began a process of restricting access to the countryside which has remained a source of contention ever since. At the same time, the rise of rural retreats and landed estates, a feature of earlier leisure history, is complemented by the 'movement of the upper and middle classes into the countryside. . . . During the nineteenth century, however, the scale of movement in Britain, Europe and North America increased considerably' (Towner 1996: 232–3).

While there is a debate as to whether such changes led to a rejection of urban environments and values in some cities (e.g. Paris), Green (1990) argues that a distinct cultural attitude developed whereby the town and country were viewed as a continuum rather than as two distinct resources juxtaposed to each other. Thus the rural environment was more than a simple playground for elites. In England, not only did the urban middle classes begin to visit the countryside in growing numbers in the nineteenth and early twentieth centuries as recreationists and tourists, visiting scenic areas (e.g. the Lake District) and more remote areas (e.g. the Highlands of Scotland: see Butler and Wall 1985), but also it raised spatial issues of access for increasing numbers of urbanites that were celebrated by the mass trespass of Kinder Scout in the Derbyshire Peak District in 1932, which anticipated the controversy over access to the countryside and continues in Britain to the present day. Such pressures certainly contributed to the establishment of the principle of access in the National Parks and Access to the Countryside Act 1949 in the UK, while similar legislative changes in other countries led to further measures to improve access to such resources (Jenkins and Prin 1998).

The 'Grand Tour' in Europe by the British landed classes in the mid-sixteenth to eighteenth centuries and thereafter by the middle classes incorporated a specific interest in rural environments which contained elements of romanticism and scenery (Towner 1985), while innovations in transport technology facilitated a move away from a focus on urban centres to rural environments. Arguably, the advent of mass domestic tourism in the nineteenth century in England and Wales (Walton 1983) with the rise of the seaside resort, and in Europe (Towner 1996), was followed by the development of the rise of second homes in the early twentieth century, which all contributed to a greater use of rural landscapes for tourist consumption.

Rural areas have emerged as a new focus for recreational and tourism activities in the post-war period within most developed countries as their accessibility and attraction for the domestic population, and to a lesser degree, the international visitor, has earned them the reputation as the 'playground of the urban population'. For example, Ward and Hardy (1986) document the development of the English holiday camp with its origins in the late nineteenth century and the rise of entrepreneurs such as Butlins, Warner and Pontins in the 1930s that led to an increasing consumption of rural and coastal locales for lower middle-class and skilled working-class tourism.

THE GEOGRAPHER'S APPROACH TO RURAL RECREATION AND TOURISM

Coppock (1982: 2) argues that 'much of the literature in the leisure field has been produced by multidisciplinary teams' of which geographers have been a part. According to Owens (1984):

> until very recently at least, leisure and recreation have been overwhelmingly viewed as synonymous with the rural outdoors. Participation in rural leisure and recreation grew rapidly during the 1950s and 1960s and was accompanied by a surge of interest in applied research. . . . In the 1950s and 1960s two types of study became particularly important, national and regional demand surveys, and site studies which tackled a wide range of applied problems.
>
> (Owens 1984: 157)

There was a tendency towards such studies being published quite rapidly in Europe and North America, though as Coppock (1982: 9) observed, 'little attention has been paid to geographical aspects of leisure in developing countries', an area which still remains relatively poorly researched.

In documenting the development of geographical research on rural recreation, Coppock (1980) points to books on leisure and recreation which appeared in five years from 1970, which were Patmore (1970, later updated in 1983), Lavery (1971c), Cosgrove and Jackson (1972), I.G. Simmons (1974), Coppock and Duffield (1975), H. Robinson (1976) and Appleton (1974). These books highlight the breadth of focus in recreation and policy management with the spatial dimension being discussed within each text. Yet, according to Owens (1984), in the period 1975 to 1984 few major contributions were published by geographers in the UK due to the lessening of government research funds for this area. At the same time overlapping areas of research emerged in terms of a behavioural focus and perception studies. The research by R. Lucas (1964) marks the early origins and development of work in recreational behaviour in human geography and it reflects a concern over the logical positivist tradition (R.J. Johnston 1991), and its inherent shortcomings, particularly the focus on management-oriented and site-based empirical studies at the expense of conceptual and theoretical studies.

STUDIES OF DEMAND

Demand for rural recreation grew at 10 per cent per annum in the period 1945 to 1958 in the USA (Clawson 1958) and in the UK at a compound rate of 10 to 15 per cent per annum up to 1973 (Coppock 1980) and for researchers this heralded an era of rapid growth. As G.M. Robinson (1990) observes, the demand for rural recreation is strongly

Plate 6.2: Sissinghurst, Kent. Rural heritage is a significant attraction base for rural tourism and recreation. Made famous through the writings and lifestyles of Vita Sackville-West and Harold Nicholson, Sissinghurst is an attraction for gardeners and literary-minded visitors alike.

Plate 6.3: Otago, New Zealand. Tourism and the development of new agricultural industries may often be interrelated. Vineyard development in Central Otago has not only been important for tourism development and amenity migration in the area but also benefited from cellar door sales.

affected by social class, and participation rates consistently show that the more affluent, better educated and more mobile people visit the countryside, while women have much lower rates. As long ago as the mid-1960s, Dower (1965) recognised leisure as the 'fourth wave' which compared the leisure phenomenon with three previous events in history that changed human activity and behaviour: the advent of industrialisation, the railway age, and urban sprawl, with leisure being the fourth wave. Patmore (1983) commented that

> countryside recreation is no new phenomenon, but [since the early 1960s] consequent pressure on fragile environments, has fully justified Dower's vision of a great surge in townspeople breaking across the countryside, the fourth wave. By any measure, the phenomenon is of immense significance.
>
> (Patmore 1983: 124)

Patmore (1983) outlined the geographer's principal concerns with the demand for rural recreation in terms of research on the increasing participation among different socio-economic groups using rural areas for recreational activities coupled with the impact of car ownership, and the resulting development of, and impact on, destinations. As a means of assessing the patterns and processes shaping

recreational use in rural areas, Patmore examined the routes and range and impact of trips by users within the countryside and, at the micro level, the assessment of site patterns and activities yielded detailed insights into rural recreational behaviour. The interest in second homes was also developed, though arguably this is one clear area of overlap between rural tourism and recreation as it attracted extensive research in the 1970s (e.g. Coppock 1977a, 1982). In fact G.M. Robinson (1990) summarises the main concerns for rural areas and how the geographer's interest in spatial concerns have largely remained unchanged since the 1960s and 1970s:

> various studies have shown that, increasingly, people's leisure time is being used in a space-extensive way: a move from passive recreation to participation. Growth has been fastest in informal pursuits taking the form of day or half-day trips to the countryside with the rise in the ownership of private cars, the urban population has discovered the recreational potential of both the countryside on its doorstep and also more remote and less occupied areas.
>
> (Robinson 1990: 260)

For managers, the challenge is in equating demand with supply. As Owens (1984: 159) rightly observed, 'research in terms of people's leisure behaviour [saw] . . . a need to emphasise social science perspectives as a means to providing a more explicit task of managing use with supply'. The development of participation studies (e.g. the Outdoor Recreation Resources Review Commission in the USA and the General Household Survey in Britain) provided a new direction. Here the argument developed was that specific factors such as socio-demographic variables like age, sex, income and education shaped the spatial patterns of participation. Yet many early surveys proved to be only snapshots of recreational use and were not replicated on a regular basis, making comparisons difficult, while demand changed at such a rapid rate that forecasting exercises from such results was difficult to sustain. Such studies also failed to acknowledge the role of latent demand where such opportunities do not currently exist.

Site studies

In terms of studies of demand for rural recreation, these appear to have been the most numerous among geographers, with the site a spatial entity and the source of supply and ultimate object of demand. Such micro scale studies of demand and supply proliferated due to the tendency for research agencies to fund individual site studies, and the publication of results in research articles offered researchers convenient research programmes. Such studies may be classified in terms of studies of demand, in relation to economic evaluation, carrying capacity and user perception. In terms of demand such studies used a range of innovative techniques, including participant observation (e.g. Glyptis 1979), while the geographer's preoccupation with patterns of usage together with a concern for methodological issues such as sampling and respondent bias (e.g. Mercer 1979a) also dominated the literature. The studies of economic evaluation have seen some geographers move into the realms of economics, with cost–benefit models developed and reviewed (e.g. Mansfield 1969), where demand is often conceptualised in terms of sensitivity to distance travelled, cost of travel and entrance fees to derive a simulated demand curve.

Yet research has questioned the rationality of recreational users in spatial patterns of behaviour and activity in models which assume distance minimisation is the sole pursuit for satisfaction (see S.L.J. Smith 1983a, 1995 for more detail).

Carrying capacity

According to Owens (1984):

> the picture to emerge in the wake of the catalytic effect of demand-orientated site surveys is of a range of related but ill-coordinated empirical case studies. It is none the less possible to pick out several broad and important themes in the accumulated body of research. Two of the most important are seen in the burgeoning literature on carrying capacity and user perception studies.
>
> (Owens 1984: 166)

Carrying capacity studies developed from the geographer's interest in the recreationist's impact on resources, as increased participation and the need among managers for greater resource protection provided a ready-made focus for applied geographical research. Yet carrying capacity is among one of the most difficult concepts to put into practice (Patmore 1983; Graefe et al. 1984a). Often one rarely knows what the true carrying capacity is until it has been exceeded. Mercer (1979a) acknowledges that any search for the concept of carrying capacity is futile, implying that a simple concept of carrying capacity may be developed which might be defined thus: 'recreation resources/facilities will only be suitable for use by a certain number of people beyond which figure carrying capacity will be exceeded to the detriment of the resources and/or the users' experience' (Owens 1984: 167). In trying to put the concept into practice, a range of studies were developed to measure capacity (e.g. Dower and McCarthy 1967; Stankey 1973), with the attempt to differentiate between ecological, physical, social and psychological (or perceptual) capacity (see Chapter 4).

The other area of study noted by Owens (1984) was user perception studies. The greatest impetus for such studies emerged in the USA, particularly in relation to perception of wilderness areas (Stone and Taves 1957) with a specific management objective – the extent to which policies could be developed which would not adversely affect users' perceptions. Lucas' (1964) landmark study of Boundary Waters Canoe area saw users' opinions being canvassed which showed that some respondents had a more restricted view of wilderness than others and this assisted managers in developing land use zoning measures.

The key perception studies undertaken have focused on the following range of themes, although in practice a number of the studies have often been dealt with under more than one theme:

- perception of scenery and evaluation of landscape quality
- perception of wilderness, wilderness management, and the psychology of wilderness experience
- social and psychological carrying capacity
- comparison of managers' and users' perceptions
- social benefits of recreation, socialisation into leisure, quality of life elements in leisure experience
- behaviour at sites and social meaning of recreation in relation to particular activities
- perceived similarities between recreation activities and substitutability
- psychological structure of leisure, leisure activity types, typology of recreation activity preferences (see Owen 1984 for more detail of these studies).

Robinson (1990) also documented the behavioural differences between recreationalists in different countries, where there are cultural differences in the perception of rural aesthetics.

SUPPLY OF RURAL RECREATION

The types of studies developed and published reflect the geographer's interest in rural land use and the geographer's concern with the spatial distribution of resources which led to a range of studies of resource inventories and rural recreation. According to Pigram (1983), for many people, the concept of resources is commonly taken to refer only to tangible objects in nature. An alternative way is to see resources not so much as material substances but as functions. In this sense resource functions are created by man through the selection and manipulation of certain attributes of the environment.

Resources are therefore constituted by society's subjective evaluation of their value and potential so that they satisfy recreational needs and wants. Earlier research by O'Riordan (1971: 4) still remains the most quoted definition of a resource: 'an attribute of the environment appraised by man to be of value over time within constraints imposed by his social, political, economic and institutional framework'. The recreational research by Clawson et al. (1960) still remains the popular conceptualisation of recreational resources, particularly in a rural context. Clawson et al. (1960) identified one of the standard approaches to recreational resources which has been developed and modified by geographers since the early 1960s: what constitutes a recreational resource, and how can you classify them so that effective planning and management can be developed? Clawson et al. (1960) distinguished between recreation areas and opportunity using a range of factors: location, size, characteristics, degree of use and extent of artificial development of the recreation resource. The result was the development of a continuum of recreational opportunities from user-orientated to resource-based with rural areas falling into resource-based and intermediate areas (i.e. the urban fringe). While geographers have reworked and refined such ideas, the resource use remains one of the underlying tenets of the analysis of recreational resources (I.G. Simmons 1975). For example, Hockin et al. (1978) classified land-based recreational activities into:

- overnight activities (e.g. camping and caravanning)
- activities involving shooting
- activities involving a significant element of organised competition (e.g. golf)

- activities involving little or no organised competition (e.g. angling, cycling, rambling, picnicking and wildlife observation).

This has moved on a stage from the continuum zoning concept of Clawson et al. (1960) to recognise the diversity of demand and how it did not necessarily fit into any one particular zone.

Coppock and Duffield (1975) outlined their principal contribution in terms of understanding what resources were used and consumed by recreationalists, the levels and volume of use, the capacity of resources to absorb recreationalists, the range of potential resources available, the role of resource evaluation and the techniques of resource evaluation developed by geographers, though their own experience was largely confined to major studies undertaken in Lanarkshire and Greater Edinburgh. By comparing Coppock and Duffield's (1975) synthesis with Patmore (1983), assessment of the geographer's principal concern with recreational resources may be seen to concentrate around three themes.

First, there is the visual character of the resource itself, the very quality that gives stimulus and satisfaction. So much of the quality is intertwined with the theme of conservation and the composition of the rural landscape as a whole: for all its importance, however, that aspect is marginal to our purpose and will receive comparatively scant attention. The second theme is recreational opportunity, the direct use of the rural environment for recreational pursuits, both on sites with a uniquely recreational purpose and on those pursuits which recreation must compete directly and indirectly with other uses. The third theme is recreational variety, the variety of rural landscapes and the variety of recreational opportunity that each affords. It is this variety that is the geographer's concern; the frequent imbalance of recreational demand with resource supply, and the consequent compromises and patterns that such imbalance engenders (Patmore 1983: 164).

It is evident that the range of issues which have guided research exhibit a large degree of commonality. Patmore (1983) outlined the main themes associated with the spatial analysis of rural recreational resources in terms of lost resources (to development and progress), preservation of resources, the active use and enjoyment of resources, the role of balancing conservation and use, and preservation and profit-recreation attractions. In addition, Patmore (1983) outlined the range of resources designed for rural recreation (e.g. forests, parks and the urban fringe), the use of linear resources (e.g. roads and footpaths), water resources and the coastal fringe, each of which have a significant rural dimension. Among the early research on some of these themes was Coppock's (1966) landmark study which sought to summarise information on recreational land and water in Britain, while Duffield and Owen (1970) and Goodall and Whittow (1975) examined forest resources, and Tanner (1973, 1977) researched water resources.

A debate on the perception of scenery and its recreational value also emerged in the controversy over landscape evaluation (Penning-Rowsell 1973; Appleton 1974) which has an explicit recreational dimension and focused on the way people value the aesthetics of the landscape and different methodologies to understand the value and meaning of landscapes. The compilation of resource inventories by geographers focused on the supply of rural recreation resources, though there was little continuity in such research in the 1980s, with Pigram (1983) being critical of such studies where they had only a limited practical application.

IMPACT OF RURAL RECREATION

G.M. Robinson (1990: 270) observed that 'awareness and concern has grown over the environmental impact of recreational activity. In fact the growing severity of this impact reflects the concentrated form of rural recreation with distinctive foci upon a few "honey-pot" sites' where concentrated use may lead to adverse environmental impacts. In addition to direct impacts, the issue of conflict remains a consistent problem associated with recreational resources in the countryside. Many conflicts occur between recreation and agriculture (Robinson 1999) which Shoard (1976) attributed to the ad-hoc manner in which recreational use of agricultural land has developed. For example, farmers are frequently dissatisfied with recreationalists' use of rights of way across their land due to the damage and problems caused by a minority of recreationalists (e.g. litter, harassment of stock and pollution). One problem which has emerged in New Zealand is the rise in the prevalence of giardia, a water-borne disease spread by recreationalists and tourists defecating and urinating in streams and water sources. By contrast, in Wales the Countryside Commission estimate that 16 million people use paths covering a wide scale and there is great potential for adverse environmental impacts and conflict, aside from physical erosion and the subsequent need for ongoing protection

from this erosion and, in some cases, the use of non-natural products (e.g. tarmac) to control it. However, as Owens (1984) summarised:

> In general, research has been problem-orientated to meet specific managerial requirements, with the consequence that ad hoc site studies proliferated without there being any particular intention of making a contribution to the development of testable theory. Interest has tended to focus on concepts (e.g. social carrying capacity) and the intricacies of methodology (e.g. attitude scales and factor analysis). Of course conceptual and methodological development is a vital part of research, but the main criticism here relates to the degree to which there has been introspection.
> (Owen 1984: 173)

In view of these comments, attention is now turned to the geographer's contribution to the analysis of rural tourism.

INSIGHT: Second homes in the countryside

The utilisation of second homes represents a significant portion of the leisure activities of many tourists and day trippers in a number of countries around the world, and as such they are an integral, though often ignored component of both domestic and international tourism (Jaakson 1986; Hall and Müller 2004). Second homes are defined by Shucksmith (1983) as

> a permanent building which is the occasional residence of a household that usually lives elsewhere and which is primarily used for recreation purposes. This definition excludes caravans, boats, holiday cottages (rented for a holiday) and properties in major cities and industrial towns.
> (Shucksmith 1983: 174)

Shucksmith's definition is comparable to a number of approaches to second home research such as in Scandinavia and Canada, where the primary focus is the summer cottage. However, it should be noted that mobile second homes, such as caravans and camper trailers, are also a very significant form of holidaying that has had very little research undertaken on it.

The size of the second home market can be substantial. For example, in Finland it is estimated that in 2003 there were 465,000 second homes meaning that every sixth family owned a second home, while every other family had access to a second home through friends or extended family relations (Hitunen and Pitkänen 2004). In 1999, 7 per cent (823,000) of Canadian households owned second homes or cottages, with 77 per cent of these households owning second homes in Canada (Svenson 2004). In Denmark second homes are the most important category of recreational accommodation, with approximately 220,000 second homes available to the 5.2 million people living in Denmark (Tress 2002). In Sweden there are between 500,000 and 700,000 second homes, with second homes accounting for 23 per cent of all overnight stays (Lundmark and Marjavaara 2004). In the case of New Zealand no accurate census or housing information exists on second homes, however approximately 8 per cent of domestic overnight stays occurs in second homes; while for holiday and leisure purposes, holiday homes or baches account for an even greater proportion (13.9 per cent) of the accommodation used (Keen and Hall 2004).

Historically, the research into second homes has focused on motivational, planning, regional development and impact-related issues. Second homes development has emerged as a major issue in a number of countries, including Canada, Denmark, Sweden and Wales where, in some cases, local communities have perceived second home purchase by 'outsiders' as being socially and economically invasive. However, despite their economic, social and cultural significance, geographical research on second homes has been highly variable in terms of regional studies and the maintenance of continued interest in second homes as a research issue. Two reasons may be put forward for this. First, the degree of research interest they generate may vary in relation to their value or impact, whether it be economic, social or environmental. Second, second home research may well have fallen out of fashion due to the development of other research interests, for example, the rise of interest in ecotourism. Regardless of these points there exists a large body of international research focusing specifically on, or around, second homes (Hall and Müller 2004).

The first major period for research on second homes was in the 1970s. Prior to this time research was undertaken primarily in North America (especially Canada) and Scandinavia where there is a strong tradition of second home ownership (Coppock 1977a) (see also the discussion of French geography in Chapter 1). During the 1970s an increase in the research undertaken from the United Kingdom culminated in Coppock's (1977a) benchmark publication *Second Homes: Curse or Blessing?* Since the mid-1990s, there has been renewed interest in second home development as indicated by work in Australia (Selwood et al. 1995; Selwood and May 2001), Canada (Halseth and Rosenberg 1995; Halseth 1998), Denmark (Tress 2002), New Zealand (Fountain and Hall 2002); Norway (Kaltenborn 1997a, 1997b, 1998; Flognfeldt 2002), Sweden (Müller 1999, 2002a, 2002b,

2002c, 2002d; Gustafson 2002b; Müller and Hall 2003) and the United Kingdom (Gallent 1997; Gallent and Tewdwr-Jones 2000), as well as the development of new comprehensive international overviews of the topic (Hall and Müller 2004; Müller 2004).

Regional economic development is often advocated by local governments as one of the major benefits of second homes. Second homes provide a means for regional development through

- increasing direct visitor expenditure to the region (Tombaugh 1970; Ragatz 1977)
- the provision of infrastructure used for both home owners and other tourists (Jaakson 1986)
- the support of service and construction industries (Ragatz 1977; Shucksmith 1983)
- the opportunity for further regional development through owners retiring to their second home (Deller et al. 1997).

However, despite the opportunities second homes may provide for regional development, the actual contribution varies from location to location, with no consistent benchmark available from which to judge the effect that they will have, particularly in the long term (Fritz 1982). Though the benefits to a region of second home development are potentially high, they may not always exceed the costs created for government in relation to increases in waste, health care and other services (Teisl and Reiling 1992), as well as the social and environmental impacts that may also occur. For example, Deller et al. (1997) estimated that for the United States, second homes generate revenues that just cover the increased expenses for public services. However, in other locations second home tourism is considered an important cornerstone for many rural economies. Second home owners tend to favour small rural shops and therefore contribute to the maintenance of service levels in the countryside (Müller 1999: Hall and Müller 2004). For example, Müller (1999) established that four German second home owners in Sweden spent as much as a permanent Swedish household. In another study in the Nordic countries it was shown that the consumption of between three and thirty-two second home households equalled the consumption of a permanent household. The differences depended primarily on the quality of the housing stock and the owners' intention to actually use the second home (Jansson and Müller 2003). Similarly, in a study of recreational homes in Wisconsin and Minnesota in the United States, Marcouiller et al. (1998) demonstrated that second home owners played an important role in generating local business activity in great part because they use their properties throughout the year (albeit with greater use in summer). 'On average, recreational homeowners spent about [US]$6,000 per year on items directly used or attributed to their recreational homes. Purchases made locally ranged from 20–70 per cent of this amount, including remodelling and meals' (1998: i). Interestingly, Marcouiller et al. (1998) also found that at the county level, the expenditure patterns of the residents and recreational home owners were generally similar with respect to how much money was spent outside the county.

As with all tourism development, second homes invariably bring a range of impacts to an area. Undesirable physical impacts may occur due to a lack of adequate infrastructure and planning; this includes lack of sewage systems, inappropriate site choice, excessive development and a failure to consider the excessive burden upon areas at peak holiday times (Mathieson and Wall 1982; Gartner 1987). The responsibility for these impacts usually lies with regional and local government which must put effective regulatory controls into place (Dower 1977; Shucksmith 1983). Local government may also have a significant role in relation to social impacts, as they can regulate development so as not to incur conflict between second home owners and various groups. Examples of social conflict have included disagreement between locals and second home residents regarding levels of development (Jordan

1980; Gartner 1986; Green et al. 1996; D.G. Pearce 1998; Visser 2004), conflict due to perceived social inequality (Gallent 1997), and competition for the use of land (Gallent 1997; Visser 2004). Second homes, and the related issues of 'homes for locals' and the maintenance of services, are probably (more than most forms of tourism migration/settlement) the focus of contested space issues (Jordan 1980; Girard and Gartner 1993; Fountain and Hall 2002; Hall and Müller 2004).

To understand the impacts of second homes, one must discover the motivations behind the decisions to have a second home. Second home owners are motivated by a number of reasons, many of which have to do with the specific amenity characteristics of a location including distance from primary residence, physical and social characteristics of the area and availability of recreational opportunities (Tombaugh 1970; Boschken 1975; Coppock 1977a; Ragatz 1977; D.G. Pearce 1998). However, one of the most significant aspects of second home ownership is the extent to which it is related to broader travel and lifestyle behaviour and the overall personal, spatial and temporal mobilities on individuals and families. The identification of a desirable second home environment tends to be related to an environmental search process of which travel is a key component. Holidaymaking provides the opportunities to identify potential second home locations, while second homes may also be part of a wider lifestyle strategy that utilises second home purchase as a precursor to more permanent retirement or lifestyle migration. Indeed, recent renewed interest by geographers in second homes and their relationship to domestic and international migration suggests that second home tourism needs to be increasingly seen within a broader framework of human mobility over the human lifecourse (A.M. Warnes 1992; T. Warnes 1994; King et al. 1998, 2000; A.M. Williams and Hall 2000; A.M. Warnes 2001; Hall and Williams 2002; Hall and Müller 2004; Hall 2005a).

RURAL TOURISM: SPATIAL ANALYTICAL APPROACHES

In the literature on rural tourism (e.g. Sharpley 1993; Page and Getz 1997; Sharpley and Sharpley 1997; Butler et al. 1998), there are few comparatively explicit spatial analytical approaches which make the geographer's perspective stand out above other social science contributions. Probably the nearest synthesis one finds is the occasional section on tourism in rural geography texts (e.g. G.M. Robinson 1990) and a limited number of geography of tourism texts (e.g. Shaw and Williams 1994).

IMPACT OF RURAL TOURISM

The literature on tourism impacts has long since assumed a central position within the emergence of tourism research, as early reviews by geographers confirm (e.g. Mathieson and Wall 1982). However, in a rural context, impact research has not been at the forefront of methodological and theoretical developments. One particular problem, as already noted, is the tendency for researchers to adopt well-established theoretical constructs and concepts from their own disciplinary perspective and apply them to the analysis of rural tourism issues. Within the social and cultural dimensions of rural tourism, the influence of rural sociology in the 1960s and 1970s (e.g. Bracey 1970) dominated sociological research while V.L. Smith's (1977) influential collection of anthropological studies of tourism highlighted the approaches adopted by anthropologists. Probably the most influential statement on the social and cultural impacts is Bouquet and Winter's (1987a) diverse anthology of studies of the conflict and political debates associated with rural tourism. For example, Bouquet and Winter (1987b) consider the relationship between tourism, politics and the issue of policies to control and direct tourism (and recreation) in the countryside in the post-war period. Geographers have largely remained absent from this area of study as Hall and Jenkins (1998) and Jenkins et al. (1998) indicate. Even so, non-spatial studies, such as Winter's

(1987) study of farming and tourism in the English and Welsh uplands, argue for circumspection in advocating farm tourism as a solution to the socio-economic development problems of 'less favoured areas', a conclusion which is widely endorsed by subsequent studies (e.g. Jenkins et al. 1998). Sociological studies offer an insight into the social implications of the spatially determined activities of tourists and recreationalists in remote areas, where they may contribute to farm incomes.

A number of researchers have sought to diversify the focus of social and cultural impact research to include concerns about the way in which tourism development may change rural cultures (e.g. Byrne et al. 1993) and the consumption of rural environments and cultures in relation to late modernity or the postmodern society which has a specific relevance for studies in geography. The role of women in rural tourism has also belatedly attracted interest as a highly seasonal and unstable economic activity, since tourism offers one of the few employment opportunities to be taken up by women, which further contributes to the marginal status of women in the rural workforce. Similar arguments are also advanced by gender studies with a tourism component such as Redclift and Sinclair (1991), though few geographers have examined these issues. Other studies by Edwards (1991) and Keane et al. (1992) also indicate the importance of community participation in tourism planning so that the local population, and women in particular, are not excluded from the benefits of rural tourism development. A particularly sensitive issue is that of indigenous people and traditional cultures, including land/resource rights and their roles as performers and entrepreneurs (Butler and Hinch 1996). Increasingly native people are becoming involved in tourism to help meet their own goals of independence and cultural survival, yet tourism development carries special risks for them (C.M. Hall 1996a).

Considerable attention has been paid in the literature to residents' perceptions and attitudes towards tourism (in common with recreation research), including studies of small towns and rural areas (e.g. Allen et al. 1988; P.T. Long et al. 1990;

Getz 1994a; Johnson et al. 1994) but few geographers have undertaken longitudinal studies of rural tourism's impact on the way communities view, interact, accept or deny tourism, though examples in urban areas are also limited (see Page 1997a). However, as Butler and Clark (1992) conclude, an

> area where some research is needed is in the changing relationship between tourism and its host community. Rarely is tourism the sole rural economic activity. Over the last few decades the countryside has witnessed major changes in its social composition, the main symptoms being gentrification, new forms of social polarisation, and a domination by the service class. More research is needed on the relationship between the uneven social composition of the countryside, the spatially variable development of tourism, and the problematic relationship between the two.
>
> (Butler and Clark 1992: 180)

It is somewhat ironic that with rural geographers making such a major contribution to rural studies, only a limited number have examined the implications in terms of social theory as well as the empirical dimensions of tourism development.

Plate 6.4: Elga, Norway. Hunters, anglers and walkers serve as an important source of income for many small villages in Scandinavia.

Plate 6.5: Telluride, Colorado. Tourism has revitalised many former mining towns in the western United States through the development of resort and accommodation facilities.

ECONOMIC IMPACT

The economic impact of rural tourism has been a fruitful area for research among a range of social scientists, often emphasising or challenging the role of tourism as a panacea for solving all the economic and social ills of the countryside although the major contribution of geographers has largely been in relation to the study of farm tourism. But as Butler and Clark (1992) rightly acknowledge, tourism in rural areas is not necessarily the magical solution to rural development, given its

> income leakages, volatility, declining multipliers, low pay, imported labour and the conservatism of investors. The least favoured circumstance in which to promote tourism is when the rural economy is already weak, since tourism will create highly unbalanced income and employment distributions. It is a better supplement for a thriving and diverse economy than as a mainstay of rural development.
>
> (Butler and Clark 1992: 175)

In a longitudinal study of the Spey Valley, Scotland, Getz (1981, 1986b, 1993c, 1994a, 1994b) documents a rural area in which tourism has remained the economic mainstay. In this respect, Butler and Clark's (1992) research is useful in that it identifies the principal concerns in rural economic research and the role of tourism in development in relation to

- income leakage
- multipliers
- labour issues (local versus imported and low pay)
- the limited number of entrepreneurs in rural areas
- the proposition that tourism should be a supplement rather than the mainstay of rural economies.

The principal research in this area has been undertaken by economists such as Archer (1973, 1982) whose pioneering studies of multipliers have been used to establish the economic benefits of tourist expenditure in rural areas. While these studies have remained the baseline for subsequent research on rural tourism, few studies embrace a broad economic analysis to encompass the wide range of issues raised by Butler and Clark (1992). One possible explanation for this paucity of detailed economic studies of rural tourism may be related to the persistence of a 'farm tourism' focus.

Farm tourism

Farm tourism may offer one way of facilitating agricultural diversification. According to N.J. Evans (1992a), research on farm tourism can be divided into two categories. The first is an expanding literature concerned with 'differing types of farm diversification as a major option adapted by farm families to aid business restructuring, necessitated by falling farm incomes' (Evans 1992a: 140). The second is 'one devoted specifically to farm tourism and though these studies remain the most detailed, they are becoming increasingly dated' (Evans 1992a: 140). Evans (1992a) cited those by Davies (1971), C. Jacobs (1973), DART (1974), Bull and Wibberley (1976), Denman (1978) and Frater (1982) which all use 1970s data.

Evans (1992a) is critical of the second group of studies for their lack of definitional clarity, since they fail to distinguish between the accommodation and recreational components of farm tourism (Evans and Ilbery 1989). Evans (1992a: 140) rightly considers the analytical components of the studies

to be too simplistic, focusing on expected economic costs and benefits of these enterprises, and the characteristics and attitudes of farm families to such development. Despite these problems with the farm tourism literature and concerns with its marketing, a major impediment to developing a more sophisticated understanding of farm tourism remains the absence of accurate national studies of the growth and development of farm tourism. However, Dernoi (1983) and Frater (1983) review the situation in Europe, Wrathall (1980) examines the development of France's *gîtes ruraux*, while Oppermann (1995) considers farm tourism in southern Germany, mapping and analysing the spatial distribution of the accommodation base. Vogeler (1977) discussed the situation in the United States, while Oppermann (1998b) provided a valuable baseline survey of the New Zealand scene (see also Hall and Kearsley 2001).

A survey of England and Wales identified almost 6000 farm businesses with accommodation. It also undertook a geographical analysis of the distribution of such accommodation, with south-west England, Cumbria, the Welsh border counties, North Yorkshire and the south-east coast of England popular locations for this activity. The upland areas and south-west England were the dominant locations, with a diversity of modes of operation (bed and breakfast, self-catering, camping and caravanning) and niche marketing used to satisfy particular forms of tourism demand (e.g. weekend breaks, week-long breaks and traditional two-week holidays). N.J. Evans (1992b) acknowledged the absence of national studies of why farm businesses have pursued this activity and the range of factors influencing their decision to undertake it. The survey also points to inherent contradictions in the existing literature, since its findings illustrate that larger farm businesses have also diversified into farm tourism (Ilbery 1991). While this is at odds with Frater's (1982) research, it illustrates that family labour is widely used to service farm-based accommodation. Such research also highlights the capital requirements of farm tourism ventures and the role of marketing, financial advice and the need for external agents in establishing networks to develop their business. Even so, Maude and van Rest (1985) argue that due to the limited returns for small farmers and the constraints of existing planning legislation, it is not a significant means of tackling the serious problem of low farm incomes in upland areas (see also Jenkins et al. 1998). Thus it is unlikely to improve the low-income problem of upland farmers in their Cumbria case study since they argue that farm tourism has been wrongly regarded as the main pillar in a diversified agricultural policy (Maude and van Rest 1985). Consequently, the continued debate and focus on farm tourism has detracted from a more critical debate on the wider significance of rural tourism within an economic context and the way it may be integrated into structuration theory and other contemporary theoretically informed analyses.

ENVIRONMENTAL EFFECTS OF RURAL TOURISM

The environmental impact of tourism has been extensively reviewed in the tourism literature and rural tourism has emerged as a prominent element, with the usual caveat that tourism is destructive in different degrees of the actual qualities which attract tourists. In a rural context, the growing pressure emerging from the development-intensive nature of tourism, and the expansion of mass tourism, has introduced many new pressures as 'new tourism' discovers the qualities of rural environments. In fact, the construction of theme parks in rural environments, second homes (Gartner 1987), timeshares, conference centres, holiday villages and designation of environments as special places to visit (e.g. national parks) have all contributed to the insatiable tourism appetite for rural environments (also see Insight below). Bramwell (1991) highlights the concern for more responsible and environmental forms of rural tourism in the 1990s with the sustainability debate firmly focused on the rural environment. Bramwell (1991) examines the extent to which rural tourism policy in Britain has been integrated with concepts of sustainability, outlining the role of the English Tourist Board and Countryside Commission policy formulation process. The Countryside Commission points to the need for improving the public's understanding and care of the rural environment as outlined in its consultation paper 'Visitors to the Countryside'. A number of special issues of journals have also focused on sustainability and rural tourism (e.g. *Tourism Recreation Research* 1991; *Trends* 1994; *Journal of Sustainable Tourism* 1994) with geographers contributing to the debate (e.g. Butler and Hall 1998; Hall and Lew 1998). However, it is apparent that tourism in a rural context displays many of the features of the symbiotic relationship that exist between tourism and the environment and is a key component of its very attraction to tourists.

INSIGHT: Wine, food and tourism

Wine, food and tourism are all products that are differentiated on the basis of regional identity (Hall et al. 2003a). Wine is often identified by its geographical origin (e.g. Burgundy, Champagne, Rioja) which, in many cases, has been formalised through a series of appellation controls in turn founded on certain geographical characteristics of a place (Moran 1993, 2000, 2001). Foods (e.g. cheese) are also identified by their place of origin. Similarly, tourism is promoted by the attraction of regional or local destinations. It should therefore be of little surprise that the relationship between wine, food and tourism is extremely significant at a regional level through the contribution that regionality provides for product branding, place promotion and, through these mechanisms, economic development (Ilbery and Kneafsey 2000a, 2000b). Ilbery and Kneafsey (2000b) appropriately described this process within the context of globalisation as 'cultural relocalization'. As Moran (1993) observed:

> Burgundy gives its name to one of the best known wines in the world but at the same time the region of Burgundy becomes known because of its wine. Moreover, the little bits of it, often only a few hectares, also derive their prestige from the wines that are produced there. In Burgundy, the process has developed to the extent that in order to capitalize on the reputation of their most famous wines many of the communes . . . have taken the name of their most famous vineyard. Corton was added to make Aloxe-Corton, Montrachet to make both Puligny-Montrachet and Chassagne-Montrachet, Romanee to make Vosne-Romanee, St Georges to make Nuits-St Georges and so on.
>
> (Moran 1993: 266)

The wine, food and tourism industries all rely on regional branding for market leverage and promotion (Hall et al. 1997–8; Hall and Macionis 1998). Indeed, the geographic origins of food are increasingly being protected under intellectual property regulation (Hall et al. 2003). Hall (1996b: 114) describes the importance of tourism place and wine appellation or region thus: 'there is a direct impact on tourism in the identification of wine regions because of the inter-relationships that may exist in the overlap of wine and destination region promotion and the accompanying set of economic and social linkages.' In addition, relationships between food and tourism are also created through the purchasing patterns of tourists which may have a significant impact on local production and the maintenance or expansion of the local farming economy (Reynolds 1993; Telfer and Wall 1996; Bell and Valentine 1997; Van Westering 1999; R. Mitchell and Hall 2001, 2003; A. Smith and Hall 2003).

Tourism has long been regarded as having the potential to contribute to regional development. However, ongoing economic restructuring and change in rural areas has increased the focus on tourism and how agricultural production may be enhanced through tourism demand. Moreover, these changes have been accompanied by the perceived need to retain or attract people in rural areas, maintain aspects of 'traditional' rural lifestyles and agricultural production, and conserve aspects of the rural landscape (Van Westering 1999). Many wine regions around the world have been affected by changed patterns of demand for wine and levels of tariff protection that has led to the planting of new grape varieties or, in some cases, loss of vineyards to other forms of production. Yet demand has also meant that some areas, particularly in New World wine regions such as Australia, Canada, New Zealand and the United States, have now been planted which had previously not been seriously considered for commercial wine production (Telfer 2000a, 2000b; Moran 2001). Within this context food and wine tourism is therefore emerging as an increasingly important component of rural diversification and development (Hall et al. 2000a, 2000b).

Strategies to integrate tourism and cuisine in order to promote economic development and the creation of sustainable food systems occur at national, regional and local levels (Hall and Mitchell 2002). Ideally, these levels should be integrated in order to maximise the likelihood of policy success (Thorsen and Hall 2001; A. Smith and Hall 2003). However, often the reality is that different levels of government and industry will undertake their own initiatives without consulting or co-operating with other levels. As Figure 6.1 indicates, there are a number of mechanisms for promoting sustainable food systems utilising the relationship between wine and food, each of which operates most effectively at particular levels. Although intervention by the national and local state will occur at all levels it is very common for the policy activities at the higher level to be implemented at the lower level in order to achieve targeted regional and local development goals. This approach has been particularly common within the European Union and in federal states, such as Australia, Canada and the United States (Hall et al. 2000a; Telfer 2000a, 2000b).

At the national and regional level promotion

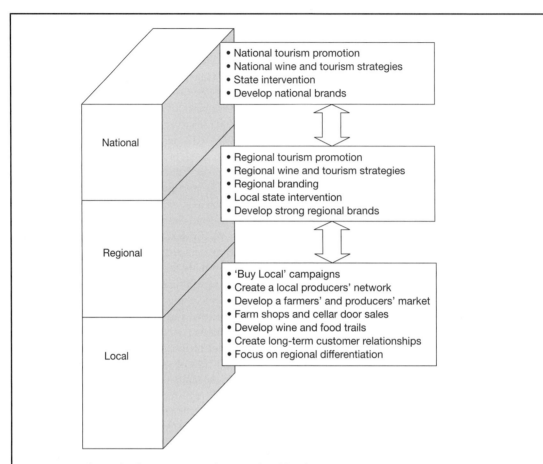

National
- National tourism promotion
- National wine and tourism strategies
- State intervention
- Develop national brands

Regional
- Regional tourism promotion
- Regional wine and tourism strategies
- Regional branding
- Local state intervention
- Develop strong regional brands

Local
- 'Buy Local' campaigns
- Create a local producers' network
- Develop a farmers' and producers' market
- Farm shops and cellar door sales
- Develop wine and food trails
- Create long-term customer relationships
- Focus on regional differentiation

Figure 6.1: Relationship between national, regional and local strategies

and branding are extremely common strategies to link food with tourism. For example, in an effort to capitalise on and maximise the tourism potential of the wine industry, several Australian states have instituted specific wine and food tourism bodies to facilitate and co-ordinate the development of wine tourism (Hall and Macionis 1998). However, despite the ability of regions to brand themselves in terms of wine and food tourism, the establishment of other forms of network relationships between food and wine producers and the tourism industry may be more problematic (A. Smith and Hall 2003; Hall 2004a, 2004b). Hall et al. (1997–8) noted several barriers to creating effective links between wine

producers and the tourism industry which can be extended to the majority of primary producers in Australia and New Zealand, including

- the often secondary or tertiary nature of tourism as an activity in the wine industry
- a dominant product focus of wine-makers and wine marketers
- a general lack of experience and understanding within the wine industry of tourism, and a subsequent lack of entrepreneurial skills and abilities with respect to marketing and product development
- the absence of effective intersectoral linkages, which leads to a lack of inter- and intra-

organisational cohesion within the wine industry, and between the wine industry and the tourism industry.

In Australia, the Bureau of Industry Economics (BIE) (1991a, 1991b) identified four potential roles for government in the development of networks:

- disseminating information on the opportunities created by networks
- encouraging co-operation within industries through industry associations
- improving existing networks between the private sector and public sector agencies involved in research and development, education and training
- examining the effects of the existing legislative and regulatory framework on the formation, maintenance and breakup of networks relative to other forms of organisation, such as markets and firms.

In the case of wine and food tourism in Australia, the federal government directly utilised the first three roles in the creation of specific organisations and/or the provision of funding for research, education, co-operative strategies and mechanisms, and information provision. The BIE (1991a, 1991b) considered information gaps to be a major factor in the impairment of network formation. Indeed, there are substantial negative attitudes towards tourism by wineries and some food producers, whereas tourism organisations tend to be far more positive towards the wine and food industry. This situation is reflective of Leiper's (1989, 1990) concept of tourism's partial industrialisation which suggests that businesses need to perceive they are part of the tourism industry before they will formally interact with tourism suppliers.

Several models of local network development are utilised in food systems (Figure 6.2). The classic industrial model of the food supply chain of producer–wholesaler–retailer–consumer all linked through transport networks has provided for a relatively efficient means of distributing food but it has substantially affected the returns producers get as well as placing numerous intermediaries between consumers and producers. The industrial model has allowed for the development of larger farm properties, reduced labour costs and supported export industry but it has done little to promote sustainable economic development and food systems. In tourism terms this relationship has been utilised in national branding and promotion when multiple supply chains are bundled together to attract the foreign customer. One alternative is to create a direct relationship between producers and consumers. This may be done by direct marketing and 'box deliveries' (e.g. the delivery of a box of seasonal produce direct to the consumer). In relation to tourism an important direct relationship is the opportunity for the consumer to purchase at the farm or cellar door, allowing the consumer to experience where the produce is from and the people who grow or make it, thereby creating the potential for the development of long-term relationship marketing. Such direct sales are extremely popular with small wineries and horticultural producers and are often utilised by peri-urban and rural producers who are located close to urban centres where they can take advantage of the day-trip market. Nevertheless, such individual developments while useful at the business level and adding to the overall attractiveness and diversity of a location do not constitute a network relationship that can promote a region more effectively.

Co-operative relationships between producers provide the basis for the creation of producer networks that can pool resources to engage in local promotion and branding and undertaking research (Hall et al. 1997–8). In addition, the pooling of resources can also lead to the development of new products such as produce markets. According to Hamilton (2002: 77) in the USA, 'By 1994 there were 1,755 farmers' markets nationwide, by 2000 there were 2,863.' In the UK the growth of farmers' markets has been no less

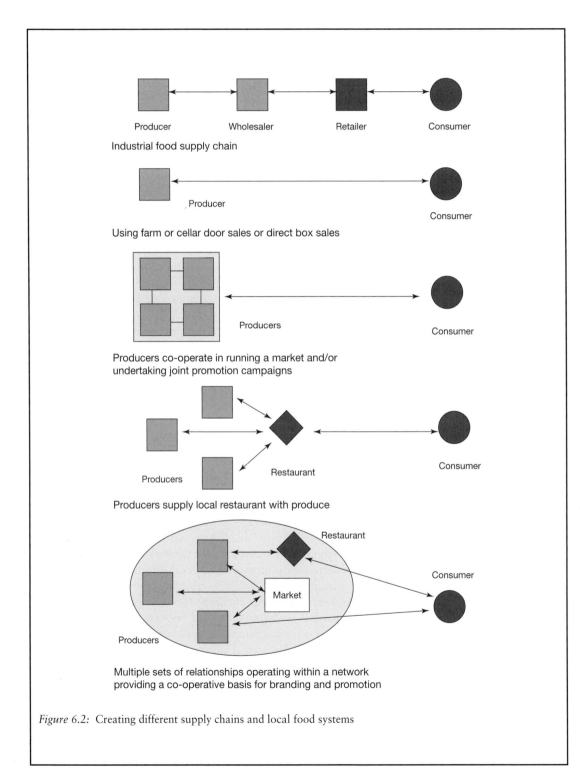

Figure 6.2: Creating different supply chains and local food systems

dramatic. In 1997 the first farmers' market was (re)established at Bath in the UK, by 2002 there were 240 (Purvis 2002). The impacts of farmers' markets on the regional economy and in generating employment may be substantial. For example, Farmers Markets Ontario (2001) estimate that in 1999 farmers' markets in the province attracted about a million shoppers a year, 90 per cent of whom came for the fresh produce. Over 25,000 people work in the markets sector with annual sales at all farmers' markets across Ontario exceeding Can$500 million and with an overall impact on the province's economy of over Can$1.5 billion. Another model of generating local food production is the use of a restaurant to act as the conduit by which local produce is presented to tourists. The development of local purchasing relationships by restaurants can have a substantial impact on local produce as it can assist in developing quality produce, allow producers to gain a clearer understanding of how their produce is being used, as well as providing a guaranteed sales outlet for their produce (A. Smith and Hall 2003). In the case of the latter the knowledge of a guaranteed minimum income may allow producers the opportunity to expand production and find other markets for their produce. Finally, we arrive at the ideal model of multiple sets of producer and consumer relationships operating within a formal network structure which provides for branding and promotion as well as economic networking and resource sharing. A good example of this type of development is Tastes of Niagara in Ontario which is a Quality Food Alliance of Niagara food producers, wine-makers, chefs, restaurateurs and retailers (http://www.tourismniagara.com/tastesofniagara/index.html). Established in 1993, members have joined together to promote the uniqueness of the region's agricultural products to consumers through the development and maintenance of high-quality regional produce, cuisine, events and service (Telfer 2000a, 2000b, 2001).

Plate 6.6: Helsinki, Finland. The harbourfront producers' market attracts both locals and visitors and connects marine and rural producers with the city.

Plate 6.7: Savonlinna, Finland. Much of the tourist infrastructure of the rural municipality of Savonlinna is unused for most of the year because visitation is concentrated in the summer months.

RECREATION, TOURISM AND SUSTAINABILITY

Ideas of sustainable development have been as influential in the area of rural policy as they have elsewhere (Murdoch 1993; Whatmore 1993). However, much of the discussion on applications of sustainability has been about individual components of rurality (e.g. attempts at developing sustainable agriculture), rather than a comprehensive approach to integrate the socio-cultural, economic and environmental components of both sustainability and rurality. For example, the Rural White Paper entitled *Rural England: A Nation Committed to a Living Countryside* (Department of the Environment and Ministry of Agriculture, Fisheries and Food (DoE/MAFF) 1995) was the first specifically rural policy from a British government for fifty years (Blake 1996).

According to Butler and Hall (1998), in many western regions and countries the structure of the relative homogeneous and distinct rural systems of the post-Second World War period has been either destroyed or weakened. They argue that such weakness is a result of at least three types of restructuring, namely, the collapse of peripheral areas unable to shift to a more capital-intensive economy; the selective and reductionist process of industrialisation of the remaining agricultural sector; and the pressures of urban and ex-urban development. Butler and Hall (1998) concluded that the result is a rural system

> suffering absolute decline along its extensive margins and the rural–urban interface, with the intervening core area weakened by decoupling of farm and non-farm sectors and the shift of decision making to urban based corporations and governments. Restructuring has created a fragmented and reduced rural system which seems to lack most of the criteria for sustainability in either economic or community terms.
> (Butler and Hall 1998: 252)

Despite images to the contrary, rurality is no longer dominated by concepts of food production, and new uses of the countryside, particularly related to recreational and tourism activities, are redefining the idea of what constitutes the rural landscape.

In Britain, as in many other industrialised countries, these uses are placing extreme pressures and creating new conflicts not only in terms of rural policy-making and their relationship to agriculture but also between themselves (Curry 1992). For example, Blake (1996) reports that, according to a Countryside Commission survey, 76 per cent of the English population visited the countryside in 1990. Such a high level of visitation inevitably leads to the transformation of villages, and the creation of tourist facilities and infrastructure. However, at the same time, 89 per cent of people believe that the English countryside should be protected at all costs (presumably as long as this cost would not result in the exclusion of those who wanted it saved). In the case of the United Kingdom the outbreak of foot and mouth disease in February 2001 probably focused more attention on what is really happening in the countryside than ever before. As the story unfolded in the media, it quickly became apparent that tourism was a far greater economic contributor to rural areas than was farming. Nevertheless, policy measures were still being primarily developed in relation to the agricultural sector rather than the needs of the tourism sector to recover from the impacts of the measures to control the disease on tourist and recreational mobility and access to the countryside (Coles 2003; G.A. Miller and Ritchie 2003). In terms of issues of sustainability it will be extremely interesting what new management, policy and planning structures are put in place by the central and local governments in Britain in response to the economic and social crisis in the countryside that the disease has revealed to the wider public. Indeed, issues of biosecurity may be regarded as integral to tourism development in agricultural areas because of the possibilities of diseases and pests being spread through human mobility (Hall 2003c, 2005a, 2005e). Indeed, one of the major errors which policy-makers and academics have often made with respect to tourism and recreation in rural areas is to treat them in isolation from the other factors which contribute to the social, environmental and economic fabric of rural regions. Tourism needs to be appropriately embedded within the particular set of linkages and relationships which comprise the essence of rurality with tourism being recognised as but one component of the policy mix which government and the private sector formulate with respect to rural development. Butler and Hall (1998) argue that many regional authorities fail to recognise that it is the visual complexity of the rural landscape which generates amenity values for locals and visitors alike. In the attempt to generate economic development, a wider tax base and employment, inappropriate policies and strategies may be followed. Furthermore,

> Policy measures in one sector, such as the attraction of agribusinesses or large foreign investments to a region, may lead to a decline of the industrial value of the region to other industries, such as tourism and businesses which are based on adding-value to local primary production.
>
> (Hall and Butler 1998: 255)

An integrated approach to rural resource development is therefore essential for sustainable rural development. As J. Jenkins (1997) observed with respect to rural Australia, government can best assist rural areas to meet the challenges of economic restructuring and change by supporting the development of 'soft infrastructure', such as education and entrepreneurial skills, and by attaching greater importance to the provision of relevant research to improve decision-making, rather than specifically supporting programmes which encourage the production of brochures, walking trails and other small-scale local tourism initiatives, such as visitor centres. Such an integrated approach to rural policy is essential given the extent to which tourism and recreation and second home development is embedded in broader processes of counter-urbanisation (Buller and Hoggart 1994; Swaffield and Fairweather 1998; C.J.A. Mitchell 2004a, 2004b) and amenity and lifestyle migration (Hall 2005a). According to Champion (1998):

> A key theme in the debate is the extent to which those moving into rural areas are motivated by a desire for 'rurality' in terms of rural living environment and lifestyle – in essence making a 'new start' that represents a 'clean break' from their past – as opposed

to choosing (or even being forced) to move because of a geographical redistribution of elements that have always been important to their quality of life such as jobs, housing, services and safety.

> (Champion 1998: 22)

Nevertheless, such movements are not new and are part of processes that have been occurring in the developed world since the late 1960s. As Law and Warnes (1973: 377) observed in the early 1970s, 'evidence from both North America and north-west Europe is that rural areas, preferably in either waterside or hilly areas are the preferred setting for vacation and retirement homes'.

CONCLUSION

This chapter has emphasised the development of geographical research in rural recreation and tourism and the major philosophical changes in emphasis from empirically derived analyses through to more socially derived analyses. The geographer has sometimes found it hard to distinguish between the context of recreation and tourism, as users consume the same resources in the rural environment (Jenkins and Pigram 1994). The 1960s and 1970s saw the development of a strong recreational geography of the rural environment emerge from the leading research of noteworthy authors such as Coppock, Duffield, Lavery and Glyptis within the UK and in North America, followed by the influential work of S.L.J. Smith (1983a). The disappointing feature is the lack of continuity and theoretical development after the 1970s. One possible explanation may be derived from Chapter 1 with the denial of mainstream geography and its reluctance to embrace such research as critical to the conceptual and theoretical development of the discipline. This is certainly true in tourism up until the 1990s when research by mainstream human geographers such as Cloke began to cultivate critical social geographies of recreation and tourism in the countryside. Even so, one would expect that research assessment exercises in countries such as the UK would do little to foster a spirit of mainstream incorporation of tourism and recreation into the discipline as it may be assessed under business and management rather than as a subgroup of geography. The nearest inroad is through the study groups of professional bodies such as the Institute of British Geographers (IBG) and Association of American Geographers (AAG) where these developments have not been discouraged. Human geography in particular has been less accepting of such fringe subject areas and a consequence is that even when notable researchers have emerged in these areas they have not fostered the same stature or influence of the human geographers of the 1960s and 1970s who cultivated and really established rural recreation and tourism as a rich area of spatially contingent research. The scope of the studies reviewed and discussed in this chapter have a common theme associated with some of the problems associated with rural areas in general, namely peripherality. Yet, ironically, this can also be a major feature associated with place marketing of rural areas where the peaceful rural idyll is marketed and commodified around the concept of space and peripherality. The rural geographer has made some forays into this area of research but, more often than not, many of the texts on rural geography pay only limited attention to tourism and recreation despite its growing significance in economic, social and political terms. Indeed, the outbreak of foot and mouth disease in the United Kingdom in February 2001 served only to highlight both the critical importance of tourism for the countryside and the absence of appropriate policy and intellectual frameworks that understand how tourism is embedded in the production and consumption of rural areas.

QUESTIONS

- How did the outbreak of foot and mouth disease in the United Kingdom in 2001 affect tourism?

- Is rural tourism distinctive?
- To what extent should second homes be regarded as part of the geography of tourism and recreation in rural areas?
- To what extent is rural recreation and tourism dependent on amenity values?

READING

Useful collections of readings on rural tourism include

Butler, R.W., Hall, C.M. and Jenkins, J. (eds) (1998) *Tourism and Recreation in Rural Areas*, Chichester: Wiley.

Mitchell, M. and Hall, D. (eds) (2005) *Rural Tourism and Sustainable Business*, Clevedon: Channel View.

The chapter by Jenkins et al. in Butler et al. (1998) provides a valuable overview of rural restructuring issues.

On second homes see

Hall, C.M. and Müller, D. (2004) *Tourism, Mobility or Second Homes: Elite Landscapes or Common Ground?* Clevedon: Channel View.

On tourism in more peripheral rural areas see

Hall, C.M. and Boyd, S. (eds) (2005) *Nature-based Tourism in Peripheral Areas: Development or Disaster*, Clevedon: Channel View.

For an overview of rural recreation issues see

Pigram, J.J. and Jenkins, J. (1999) *Outdoor Recreation Management*, London: Routledge.

7

TOURISM AND RECREATION IN THE PLEASURE PERIPHERY
Wilderness and National Parks

There are few really wild areas left in Britain today, and yet the lure of a 'wilderness' experience acts as a strong attraction to outdoor purists. The danger of overuse and degradation by outdoor recreationalists creates an urgent need to comprehensively identify, map and manage these wilder areas. It is possible to map both wild land quality and recreational use, and use the resulting overlays to identify spatial patterns and possible conflict areas. This is essential to developing an understanding of the conflicting needs of different stakeholders in landscape character and/in wilder areas. Only from such an understanding can we then hope to develop appropriate and well-founded policies on protected areas and wild land that are required to protect these unique parts of our natural heritage for future generations.

(Carver 2000)

Historically, wilderness has been one of the main sources of 'the other' in western society. Wilderness was what lay beyond the boundaries of a 'civilised', ordered landscape. Since the beginning of the nineteenth century, however, wilderness and wild areas began to assume a more favourable impression under the influence of the romantic and transcendentalist movements which favoured wild nature as an antidote to an increasingly industrialised and technocratic society. More recently, the conservation and commodification of wilderness has become entwined with the growth of recreation and tourism which has seen national parks established not only for outdoor and adventure recreation enthusiasts but also as one of the main sites in which eco-tourism occurs.

Geographers have long played a significant role in understanding and contributing to the conservation of natural resources and natural areas and their relationship with recreation and tourist activities (e.g. Graves 1920; Marsh and Wall 1982; Sewell and Dearden 1989). Indeed, recreation and tourism has long been used as an economic and political justification for the conservation and legal protection of such areas. Geographers have contributed to an understanding of a number of different dimensions of the relationship between wilderness and national park concepts and recreation and tourism:

- the changing meaning of wilderness in western society
- the environmental history of national parks and wilderness areas
- the value of wilderness
- the identification and inventory of wilderness
- the demand for wilderness and natural areas, including visitor profiles, activities and behaviours
- the development of wilderness and national park policy and the supply of wilderness and natural areas for recreation and tourist activities.

THE CHANGING MEANING OF WILDERNESS IN WESTERN SOCIETY

Definition presents a major problem in the identification of wilderness areas. Definition is important 'because it is the basis for common understanding and communication' and it 'provides a basis for putting a concept into action through creating and preserving a referent' (Gardner 1978: 7). However, wilderness is an elusive concept with many layers of meaning (Gardner 1978; Graber 1978). Tuan (1974: 112) has gone so far as to claim that 'wilderness cannot be defined objectively: it is as much a state of mind as a description of nature'. Wilderness has now become 'a symbol of the orderly progress of nature. As a state of mind, true wilderness exists only in the great sprawling cities'.

The problem of defining wilderness was well summarised by R. Nash (1967), who emphasised that the notion of wilderness was loaded with personal symbolic meaning:

'Wilderness' has a deceptive concreteness at first glance. The difficulty is that while the word is a noun it acts like an adjective. There is no specific material object that is wilderness. The term designates a quality (as the '-ness' suggests) that produces a certain mood or feeling in a given individual and, as a consequence, may be assigned by that person to a specific place. Because of this subjectivity a universally acceptable definition of wilderness is elusive.

(Nash 1967: 1)

The notion of wilderness is substantially culturally determined and is derived in the main from the northern European experience of nature (Oelschlaeger 1991). Although the meaning of wilderness has changed over time, several themes may be distinguished. The word 'wilderness' is derived from the old English word *wilddeoren* meaning 'of wild beasts', which in turn is derived from the Teutonic languages of northern Europe. In German, for example, *Wildnis* is a cognate verb, and *Wildor* signifies wild game (Nash 1967: 2).

The Romance languages have no single word which expresses the idea of wilderness but rely instead on its attributes. In French the equivalent terms are *lieu desert* (deserted place) and *solitude inculte*, while in Spanish wilderness is *la naturaleza, immensidad* or *falts da cultura* (lack of cultivation). 'Italian uses the vivid *scene di disordine o confusione*' (Nash 1967: 2). The Latin root of desert, *de* and *serere* (to break apart, becoming solitary) connotes not only the loneliness and fear associated with separation but also an arid, barren tract lacking cultivation (Mark 1984: 3). Both the northern

European and the Mediterranean traditions define and portray wilderness as a landscape of fear, which is outside the safer bounds of human settlement (Tuan 1971, 1979). This image was taken up by Nash (1967: 2) who noted that the image of wilderness 'is that of a man [*sic*] in an alien environment where the civilization that normally orders and controls life is absent'.

The landscape of fear that dominated early European attitudes towards wilderness was noted in the eighth-century classic *Beowulf* (Wright 1957), 'where *wildeor* appeared in reference to savage and fantastic beasts inhabiting a dismal region of forests, crags, and cliffs' (Nash 1967: 1). The translation of the Scriptures into English from Greek and Hebrew led to the use of wilderness as a description of 'the uninhabited, arid land of the Near East' (Nash 1967: 2–3). It was at this point that wilderness came to be associated with spiritual values. Wilderness was seen as both a testing ground for humans and an area in which humans could draw closer to God.

The biblical attitude towards nature was an essential ingredient of the Judaeo-Christian or western attitude towards wilderness (Glacken 1967; Passmore 1974; Graber 1978; Attfield 1983; Pepper 1984; Short 1991). According to the dominant tradition within Judaeo-Christianity concerning humankind's relationship with nature, it was 'God's intention that mankind multiply itself, spread out over the earth, make its domain over the creation secure' (Glacken 1967: 151). This relationship is best indicated in Genesis 1:28 where God said to man, 'Be fruitful and multiply, and fill the earth and subdue it; and have dominion over the fish of the sea and over the birds of the air and over every living thing that moves upon the earth.'

To the authors of the Bible, wilderness had a central position in their accounts as both a descriptive and as a symbolic concept. To the ancient Hebrews, wilderness was 'the environment of evil, a kind of hell' in which the wasteland was identified with God's curse (Nash 1967: 14–15). Paradise, or Eden, was the antithesis of wilderness. The story of Adam and Eve's dismissal from the Garden of Eden, from a watered, lush paradise to a 'cursed' land of 'thorns and thistles' (Genesis 2:4), reinforced in western thought the notion that wilderness and paradise were both physical and spiritual opposites (G.H. Williams 1962). Isaiah (51:3), for instance, contains the promise that God will comfort Zion and 'make her wilderness like Eden, her desert like the garden of the Lord', while Joel (2:3) stated that 'the land is like the garden of Eden before them, but after them a desolate wilderness'.

The experience of the Israelites during the Exodus added another dimension to the Judaeo-Christian attitude towards wilderness. For forty years the Jews, led by Moses, wandered in the 'howling waste of the wilderness' (Deuteronomy 32:10) that was the Sinai peninsula (Funk 1959). The wilderness, in this instance, was not only a place where they were punished by God for their sins but also a place where they could prove themselves worthy of the Lord and make ready for the promised land. Indeed, it was precisely because it was unoccupied that it 'could be a refuge as well as a disciplinary force' (Nash 1967: 16).

The experience of the Exodus helped to establish a tradition of going to the wilderness 'for freedom and purification of faith' (Nash 1967: 16). Elijah spent forty days in the wilderness in order to draw guidance and inspiration from God (1 Kings 19:4–18). John the Baptist was the voice crying in the wilderness to prepare for the coming of the Messiah (Matthew 4:1), while Christ himself 'was led by the spirit into the wilderness to be tempted by the devil' (Matthew 4:1; Mark 1:12ff.). It was through the environment of evil and hardship, characteristic of the dominant Judaeo-Christian perception of the wilderness, that spiritual catharsis could occur, a sentiment that exists through to this day (Graber 1978). (See Chapter 6 on the role of natural areas in rural tourism.)

The example of the prophets venturing into the wilderness was followed by early Christian ascetics (Williams 1962). Hermits and monks established themselves in wilderness surroundings in order to avoid the temptations of earthly wealth and pleasure and to find a solitude conducive to spiritual ideals. As Tuan (1974) recorded:

The monastic community in the wilderness was a model of paradise set in an unredeemed world. Wilderness was often perceived as the haunt of demons but in the neighbourhood of the monastery it could acquire some of the harmony of redeemed nature and the animals in it, like their human suzerains in the monastery, lived in peace.

(Tuan 1974: 148)

The desert ascetics drew on an appreciation of nature that sprang from the Bible itself. As Glacken (1967: 151) observed, 'The intense otherworldliness and rejection of the beauties of nature because they turn men away from the contemplation of God are elaborated upon far more in theological writings than in the Bible itself'. The desert monks lived in the solitude of the wilderness to remove themselves from other humans, not from nature. Psalm 104 provides one of the clearest statements of the existence of a sympathetic attitude in Christianity towards nature, noting that everything in nature has its place in a divine order: 'the high mountains are for the wild goats; the rocks are a refuge for the badgers' (Psalm 104:18). 'O Lord, how manifold are thy works! In wisdom hast thou made them all' (Psalm 104:24). As Glacken (1967) noted:

It is not to be wondered at that Psalm 104 has been quoted so often by thinkers sympathetic to the design argument and the physico-theological proof for the existence of God. The life, beauty, activity, order, and reasonableness in nature are described without mysteries, joyously – even triumphantly. God is separate from nature but he may be understood in part from it.

(Glacken 1967: 157)

The theme of the wisdom of the Lord being shown in the order of nature was similarly indicated elsewhere in the Bible. The psalmist in Psalm 8:1 exclaimed: 'O Lord, our Lord, how majestic is thy name in all the earth!' The notion that 'The heavens are telling the glory of God; and the firmament proclaims his handiwork' (Psalm 19:1) proved to be influential throughout Christendom in the Dark and Middle Ages, although by no means enabling a universally sympathetic attitude towards nature. Nature came to be regarded as a book which could reveal the works of the Lord in a manner similar to the Scriptures. In the early exegetical writings, God was regarded as being made manifest in his works:

> There is a book of nature which when read along with the book of God, allows men to know and understand Him and his creation; not only man but nature suffered from the curse after the Fall; one may admire and love the beauty of the earth if this love and admiration is associated with the love of God.
>
> (Glacken 1967: 203)

This view of nature played an important role in establishing a favourable attitude towards wild country. St Augustine (in Glacken 1967: 204) wrote, 'Some people in order to discover God, read books. But there is a great book: the very appearance of created things.' Pulpit eloquence was 'adopted by medieval mystico-philosophical speculation, and finally passed into common usage' (Curtius 1953: 321, in Glacken 1967: 104).

Reading the book of nature for the word of God was eventually to lead to the reading of nature itself, but the notion of nature as a book was also to prepare the way for the development of a natural theology in the writings of St Francis of Assisi, St Bonaventura and Ramon Sibiude. To St Francis, living creatures were not only symbols, but also 'placed on earth for God's own purposes (not for man's), and they, like man, praise God' (Glacken 1967: 216). St Francis' theology represented a revolutionary change in Christian attitudes towards nature because of the distinct break they make from the anthropocentric nature of earlier theology (L. White 1967). Upon the foundation built by the natural theologians and their intellectual heirs, such as John Ray and Gilbert White, came to be built the framework for the discovery of nature by the Romantic movement. Nevertheless, despite a continuing appreciation of nature as part of God's divine presence by some theologians, the dominant attitude in the Judaeo-Christian tradition until the seventeenth century was that true appreciation of God could be gained only by looking inwards, not out at nature. Nature was provided for humans to utilise. Wilderness and wild lands were to be tamed

and cultivated to display the divine order as interpreted by humankind. However, while in the minority within Christian attitudes towards nature, the environmental theology of St Francis remains a significant theme within Christian thought not only because of attitudes towards wild nature but also in the development of a broader understanding of humankind's responsibilities for environmental stewardship.

The dominant Judaeo-Christian view of wilderness may be contrasted with that of eastern religions. In eastern thought, wilderness 'did not have an unholy or evil connotation but was venerated as the symbol and even the very essence of the deity' (Nash 1967: 20). The aesthetic appreciation of wild land began to change far earlier in the Orient than in the West. By the fourth century AD, for instance, large numbers of people in China had begun to find an aesthetic appeal in mountains, whereas they were still seen as objects of fear in Europe (Nicholson 1962; Tuan 1974). Eastern faiths such as Shinto and Taoism 'fostered love of wilderness rather than hatred' (Nash 1982: 21). Shinto deified nature in favour of pastoral scenes. The polarity that existed between city and wilderness in the Judaeo-Christian experience did not exist outside European cultural traditions (Callicott 1982). In contrast, western civilisation has tended to dominate, rather than adapt, to its surrounding landscape whereas traditional eastern and non-European cultures have tended to attempt to blend into their surroundings. As Tuan (1974: 148) noted, 'In the traditions of Taoist China and pre-Dorian Greece, nature imparted virtue or power. In the Christian tradition sanctifying power is invested in man, God's vice regent, rather than nature.' However, it should be emphasised that Oriental civilisations, such as those of China, India and Japan, have also had highly destructive impacts on the environment despite arguably a more sympathetic cultural attitude towards nature and will continue to do so as production and consumption imperatives prevail in contemporary policy settings.

The attitude of different cultures to nature and, hence, wilderness is important (Tuan 1971, 1979; Saarinen 1998). As Eidsvik (1980, 1985) has recognised, wilderness has only recently taken on global meaning with the increasing dominance of western culture throughout the world and with respect to the governance and regulation of the environment and natural heritage in particular. The perception of wilderness as an alien landscape of fear is derived from the northern European set of attitudes towards nature, where the Judaeo-Christian perception of nature became combined with the Teutonic fear of the vast northern forests. It is perhaps of no coincidence therefore that the creation of designated wilderness areas began in lands occupied by peoples who have inherited European cultural attitudes. However, despite retaining something of its original attributes the meaning of wilderness has changed substantially over time and now incorporates wider scientific and conservation values. Table 7.1 portrays the development of the wilderness concept in the United States, Canada, New Zealand and Australia: those countries within which the idea of wilderness has been most influential in outdoor recreation and tourism policy and in the production and consumption of tourism experiences.

The classic example of changing popular attitudes towards wilderness in western culture is witnessed in the history of the evolution of the wilderness concept in the United States (Table 7.1). The founding fathers of the American colonies saw the wild lands before them in classical biblical terms, and although attitudes towards wilderness did change gradually through the seventeenth and eighteenth centuries it was not until the late eighteenth century that positive appreciation of American nature began to emerge. The political independence of the American nation found cultural expression in the extolment of the virtues of American natural scenery. However, a similar cultural expression was not to be found in colonial Canada where untamed nature still assumed the guise of a landscape of fear (Kline 1970). Nevertheless, America's cultural independence from the Old World produced a desire to laud the moral purity of the wild forests and mountains of the New World, untainted as they were by the domination of things European, a cultural movement

which, perhaps somewhat ironically, sprang from the Romantic movement then sweeping Europe.

The American Romantic movement laid the groundwork upon which a popular appreciation of the value of wild land would come to be based. Artistic, literary and political perceptions of the importance of contact with wild nature provided the stimulus for the creation of positive cultural attitudes towards the American wilderness. Once positive attitudes towards primitive, unordered nature had developed then the emergence of individuals and societies dedicated to the preservation of wilderness values was only a short step away. However, an appreciation of the aesthetic values of wild land was countered by the utilitarian ethic that dominated American society.

The majority of Americans saw the land as an object to be conquered and made productive. The first reservations for the preservation of scenery therefore tended to be established in areas that were judged to be wastelands that had no economic value in terms of agriculture, grazing, lumbering or mining. The aesthetic value of wilderness was upheld by national parks and reserves which were intended to protect national scenic monuments that expressed the cultural independence of America in addition to providing for the development of the area through the tourist dollar. Monumentalism was characterised by the belief that natural sites, such as Niagara Falls or the Rockies, were grand, noble and elevated in idea and had something of the enduring, stable and timeless nature of the great architecture of Europe, and proved a significant theme in the establishment of American parks (Runte 1979).

Although the national parks in Australia, Canada and New Zealand did not assume the same importance as national monuments, their development nevertheless parallels that of the American park system. The themes of aesthetic romanticism, recreation and the development of 'worthless' or 'waste' lands through tourism characterised the creation of the first national parks in Australia, Canada and New Zealand. Banff National Park in Canada was developed by the Canadian Pacific Railroad as a tourist spa (Marsh 1985). New

Table 7.1: The development of the wilderness concept in the United States, Canada, New Zealand and Australia

Date	United States	Canada	New Zealand	Australia
Pre-1860	Major romantic influence on American art and literature			A 'New Britannia'
1832	Joseph Catlin calls for the creation of a 'nation's Park'			Aesthetic and utilitarian visions of the Australian landscape
1832	Arkansas Hot Springs reserved			
1851	Transcendentalism – Thoreau's Walking proclaims that 'in Wildness is the preservation of the World'	Development of a romantic perception of the Canadian landscape		Rapid clearfelling of land for agriculture and mining
1860	Romantic Monumentalism			
1864	George Perkins Marsh's Man and Nature is published, heralds the start of 'economic conservation'; Yosemite State Park established			Marsh's book well received in Australia
				1866 Jenolan Caves reserved
1870	Wilderness perceived as 'worthless land'			The need to conserve forests argued by Clarke, Goyder and von Mueller 'Scientific Vision'
1872	Yellowstone National Park established; John Muir begins writing and campaigning for wilderness preservation			1879 Royal National Park established in New South Wales
			1878 T. Potts publishes National Domains	
			1881 Thermal Springs Districts Act	
1880	Rise of 'Progressive Conservation' led by Gifford Pinchot	1885 Banff Hot Springs Reserve declared	1887 Tongariro deeded to the New Zealand government	Rise of the 'Bush Idyll' National Parks associated with recreation and tourism 'Sydney or the Bush'
				1891 National Park Act (S.A.)
				1892 Tower Hill National Park Act (Vic.)
1890	F.J. Turner declares the end of the American frontier; Yosemite National Park created with help of railroads; Forests Reserves Act 1891	Strengthening of a romantic vision of nature in Canada and rise of progressive conservation		
1891	Cult of the Wilderness	1894 Algonquin Park established		
1900	Tourism a major motive for the establishment of parks in all four countries		1892 J. Matson calls for Australasian Indigenous Parks	
1905	US Forest Service created			1905 State Forests and National Parks Act (Queensland)
1910		1911 Dominion Forest Reserves and Parks Act		
1913	Preservationists lose battle to prevent Hetch Hetchy being dammed			1915 Scenery Preservation Act (Tas.)
1916	US National Park Service created			Growth of the 'Bushwalking Movement' under Myles Dunphy in NSW
1920	Rise of Ecological Perspectives Forest Service areas retained as 'primitive lands'		Negative reaction to introduced animals in National Parks begins	

Year				
1927				Formation of the National Parks and Primitive Areas Council
1928	Forest Service Regulation L-20			
1930	National Parks Act			
1934	Everglades National Park established			Greater Blue Mountains National Park Scheme
1937	Formation of the Wilderness Society			
1939	Forest Service 'U' Regulations			Development of Snowy-Indi Proposal (NSW)
1940				
1944				Kosciusko State Park Act
1949	Keyser Report			
1950	Dinosaur National Monument Campaign			
1952			National Parks Act	
1955		Wilderness Areas Act (Ontario)	Reserves and Domains Act	
1956	First Wilderness Bill			
1957				Victorian National Park Authority created
1960	ORCC Report			
1962	Wilderness Act becomes law; Agencies begin implementation			
1963				Kosciusko Primitive Area established (NSW)
1964	RARE I commences			
1967				NSW National Parks and Wildlife Service created. Wilderness becomes a major policy issue: Little Desert, Great Barrier Reef, Fraser Island and Lake Pedder
1969			Study tour of National Parks Director to North America	
1970	Mounting pressure from tourists and commercial interests in national parks in all countries			
1974	Eastern Wilderness Act; RARE II commences; Bureau of Land Management commences inventory; 'Sagebrush Rebellion'; Provision for wilderness in Alaska			
1975				National Parks and Wildlife Service (Commonwealth) created
1977			Reserves Act	
1980		Major conflicts over wilderness preservation	National Parks Act	
1981			Wilderness Advisory Group established	
1982				National Conservation Strategy
1983				Franklin Dam Case
1984		South Moresby Island campaign	New wilderness areas established	Calls for establishment of National Wilderness System
1985				CONCOM discussion paper
1986			World Heritage listing for South Westland Park	
1987			Creation of Department of Conservation	Federal government acts to preserve the Wet Tropics, Kakadu, and the Lemonthyme and Southern Forests; NSW Wilderness Act passed
1990	Increased attention given to concept of ecotourism and sustainable tourism by governments and industry bodies; Renewed threats to explore for oil in the Alaskan wildlife reserve during Bush presidency			
2000		Continued debate over timber cutting in British Columbia, Ontario and Newfoundland	Labour government restricts cutting of native forest on government land	Continuing concern over vegetation clearance and soil and river salination
2004			renewed focus on public access rights to crown land and reserves	

Zealand's first parks had lodges and hostels established within them that matched the tourist developments in the North American parks. Australia's first parks, particularly those of Queensland and Tasmania, were also marked by the influence of the desire of government to boost tourism. However, the Australian parks were also noted for their establishment, in unison with railway development, as areas where city-dwellers could find mental restoration in recreation and communion with nature (Hall 1985, 1992a).

With the closing of the American frontier at the end of the nineteenth century the preservation of America's remaining wilderness received new impetus. A massive but unsuccessful public campaign by wilderness preservationists led by John Muir to protect Hetch Hetchy Valley in Yosemite National Park from a dam scheme, a conservation-minded President (Theodore Roosevelt) in the White House, and the emergence of economically oriented 'progressive conservation' under the leadership of Gifford Pinchot all led to wilderness preservation becoming a matter of public importance in the United States.

The United States Forest Service and National Park Service responded to pressures from recreationists for the creation of designated wilderness areas. Contemporaneously, the development of the science of ecology led to a recognition of the scientific importance of preserving wilderness. The various elements of wilderness preservation blended together in the inter-war years to lay a framework for the establishment of legally protected wilderness areas.

Economic conservation and the development of a scientific perception of wilderness was also influential in Australia, Canada and New Zealand. In Australia, the publication of George Perkins Marsh's (1864 (1965)) book *Man and Nature* stimulated the colonial governments into establishing forest reserves. In addition, significant scientists such as Baron von Mueller, and bodies such as the Australasian Association for the Advancement of Science argued for the preservation of native flora and fauna in both Australia and New Zealand. However, the first national parks in Australia were created for reasons of aesthetics, tourism and recreation with science gaining little recognition (Hall 1992a).

In Canada, progressive conservation proved influential in the creation of forest reserves, and it is significant to note that many of the early Canadian parks were established under forestry legislation. However, the preservation of wilderness lagged behind the efforts of the United States (Nicol 1969).

The declaration of the Wilderness Act in 1964 marked the beginning of the current legislative era of wilderness preservation in the United States. Under the Wilderness Act wilderness is defined as 'an area where the earth and its community of life are untrammelled by man, where man himself is the visitor that does not remain'. The four defining qualities of wilderness areas protected under the Act are that such areas

- generally appear to be affected by the forces of nature, with the imprint of man substantially unnoticeable
- have outstanding opportunities for solitude or a primitive and unconfined type of recreation
- have at least 5000 acres or be of sufficient size as to make practical its preservation and use in an unimpaired condition
- may also contain ecological, geological or features of scientific, educational, scenic or historical value.

The protection of wilderness through legal means gave new impetus to the task of improving the process of defining and compiling a wilderness inventory as well as providing for its management, a process that is still continuing at the present time in North America as well as in countries such as Australia, which have tended to follow the American model for wilderness and national park protection. Although wilderness in New Zealand is given administrative protection under a variety of acts, there is no specific legislation for the preservation of wilderness (Hall and Higham 2000). Similarly, until late 1987 with the passing of the New South Wales Wilderness Act, no wilderness legislation had been enacted in Australia (Hall 1992a). In Canada, wilderness areas have received a degree of protection under provincial legislation. However, as in Australia and New Zealand, there is no national wilderness Act. Yet, in recent years increasing attention has been given to the implications of international heritage agreements, such as the World Heritage Convention, as a mechanism for the preservation of wilderness and other natural areas of international significance (Hall 1992a).

INSIGHT: What is the effect of World Heritage listing?

World Heritage properties are areas or sites of outstanding universal value recognised under the Convention for the Protection of the World's Cultural and Natural Heritage (the World Heritage Convention (WHC)), adopted by a Unesco Conference on 16 November 1972. The Convention is usually regarded as one of the pinnacles of international conservation.

> The philosophy behind the Convention is straight-forward: there are some parts of the world's natural and cultural heritage which are so unique and scientifically important to the world as a whole that their conservation and protection for present and future generations is not only a matter of concern for individual nations but for the international community as a whole.
>
> (Slatyer 1983: 138)

Such is the significance of World Heritage Status (WHS) that World Heritage sites have been described as 'magnets for visitors' and World Heritage designation 'virtually a guarantee that visitor numbers will increase' (Shackley 1998, preface). Indeed, it is often suggested that WHS increases the popularity of a location or destination with visitors (e.g. Ashworth and Tunbridge 1990; Unesco 1995; Drost 1996; Pocock 1997; Shackley 1998; J. Carter et al. 2001; Thorsell and Sigaty 2001). However, many of the assertions regarding the tourist attractiveness of World Heritage sites and, similarly, the attractiveness of newly designated national parks is often based on extremely weak empirical evidence that does not consider locations within the context of historical visitation trends; other factors influencing visitation may have very little to do with designation. This does not mean that locations may be unattractive to visitation, rather that attraction is primarily derived from other attributes. For example, Hall and Piggin (2001) reported on a 1999 survey sent to forty-four World Heritage managers in OECD countries. Over two-thirds of sites reported an increase in visitor numbers since gaining WHS, the majority of them natural sites. Most of the sites reported an average increase of 1–5 per cent per annum since designation. However, significantly, the rate of increase or decline in visitation since designation as World Heritage was little different from overall trends with respect to tourism visitation. Indeed, less than half of respondents reported that the sites they managed had specific areas for the explanation of the World Heritage Convention and why the sites were granted WHS, even though almost two-thirds of sites used such status in order to attract international and domestic visitors. Nevertheless, over half of the sites considered the effect of WHS on tourism at the sites to have been either 'positive' or 'extremely positive', eighteen site managers were neutral about the relationship between tourism and WHS, and only one site manager reported that WHS had been 'extremely negative' for tourism.

An interesting study of the effects of World Heritage designation was that of S. Wall (2004), who examined the Laponian World Heritage site in north-western Sweden which was declared a World Heritage site in 1996. The site includes four national parks established under the provisions of the Nature Protection Act 1909: Sarek National Park and Stora Sjöfallet National Park (1909), Muddus National Park (1941) and Padjelanta National Park (1962), and two nature reserves established under the provisions of the Nature Conservation Act 1964: Sjaunja (1986) and Stubba (1988). In total, 95 per cent of the site is protected as national park or nature reserve. The World Heritage site has a total area of approximately 9400 square kilometres. According to Wall (2004) only 3.7 per cent of her respondents (primarily Swedish and German tourists) stated that the visit would never have occurred or would have had different travel plans if it had not been a World Heritage site. Nevertheless, 64 per cent of her respondents agreed either completely or in part that World Heritage designation had value for the surroundings, while 51 per cent agreed either completely or in part that WHS also had value for visitors. As Wall (2004) noted, redesignation from national park to World Heritage Status may have long-term effects on perceptions of a location as a destination; however, such influences required longitudinal analysis in order to be better understood. Indeed, acquisition of WHS may have more impact in a developing country context rather than in the industrialised nations because of development of infrastructure and improved accessibility that designation may make possible.

ENVIRONMENTAL HISTORY OF NATIONAL PARKS AND WILDERNESS AREAS

Environmental history is a field concerned with the role and place of nature in human life (Worster 1977, 1988). Research and scholarship on the environmental history of national parks and wilderness lies at the intersection of a number of fields of geographic and academic endeavour. Within geography, as with history, the increased awareness of the environment as a social, economic and political issue has led to geographers and historians attempting to chart the history of land use of a given region or site in order to increase understanding of its significance, values and present-day use (I.G. Simmons 1993; Dovers 1994, 2000a, 2000b; Crosby 1995; Russell 1997; Hays 1998; Pawson and Brooking 2002). Such research is not just an academic exercise. As well as assisting in understanding how current natural resource management problems or user conflicts have developed, such research can also be used to develop interpretive material for visitors as part of a programme of heritage management, an area in which geographers are becoming increasingly involved (e.g. Ashworth and Tunbridge 1990; Tunbridge and Ashworth 1996; Hall and McArthur 1996, 1998). Cronan (1990) asserts that good work in environmental history incorporates three levels of analysis. These are the dynamics of natural ecosystems in time (ecology), the political economies that people erect within these systems (economy) and the cognitive lenses through which people perceive those systems (the history of ideas). Geographers, with their integrative approach to environment, cultural landscapes and land use, would therefore seem to be ideally poised to work in this area. As Mark (1996: 153) observed, 'Widening the scope of historical narrative has frequently resulted in more complex interpretation of the past and should point the way toward greater understanding of the past in heritage management.'

National parks are a major focus of heritage management but have been a relatively quiet backwater in traditional historical narrative, including historical geography. Environmental history, however, can place them within the larger context of interaction between nature and culture (Griffiths 1991; Mark 1996). For example, a number of extremely valuable park histories which highlight the role of tourism and outdoor recreation in park development have been written on the Yellowstone (Haines 1977), Grand Canyon (J.D. Hughes 1978), Rocky Mountain (Buchholtz 1983), Olympic (Twight 1983), Sequoia and Kings Canyon (Dilsaver and Tweed 1990) and Yosemite (Runte 1990) national parks in the United States; the Albertan (Bella 1987) and the Ontario (Killan 1993) national park systems in Canada, and with useful national overviews being provided by Nelson (1970), Hall (1992a) and Dearden and Rollins (1993).

Substantial methodological research is called for when undertaking research on environmental and park histories. In the New Worlds of North America and the Antipodes, travel accounts written during the period of initial European settlement have been utilised by scholars interested in historic environments (Powell 1978). They often hope to establish a pre-European settlement landscape as a baseline from which to assess subsequent environmental change. One difficulty with using travel accounts, however, is that they are often written in places where the journalist is not actually travelling; instead the diarist is summarising past events at a convenient place (Mark 1996). Another problem is how to tie the usually limited detail (little of which could be utilised quantitatively) to specific localities. The paucity of locality information is often present in even the best accounts, such as those left by collectors of natural history specimens.

The only site-specific records available in many areas about presettlement landscapes are land survey notes. These have been helpful in establishing an historic condition of some forests, riparian habitats and grasslands. Their reliability varies, however, because there can be limitations associated with insufficient description, bias in recording data, contract fraud and land use prior to survey (Galatowitsch 1990). Another technique which is useful for developing an historical record of land use change or for reconstructing past environments or heritage sites is repeat photography (Rogers et al. 1984). However, while such techniques may be useful for specific sites or attractions the photographic record of 'ordinary' landscapes, i.e. those which were not subject to the interest of visitors as a view or panorama, is more difficult to construct because of incomplete records. Indeed, the lack of longitudinal data on visitors to national parks and particular environments is a major problem in determining impacts of visitation and changing perceptions of the environment.

Cultural landscape documentation is somewhat narrower in scope than environmental history because the question of nature's character is not so central (Mark 1996). Nevertheless, it emphasises change over time and represents a way of integrating nature with culture. In a park setting, its emphasis becomes one of design, material, change, function and use, with one of its main effects on heritage management being the broadening of the focus of historic preservation beyond buildings to the associated landscape and environmental context (Mark 1991).

THE VALUE OF WILDERNESS

Decisions affecting environmental policies grow out of a political process (Henning 1971, 1974), in which 'value choice, implicit and explicit . . . orders the priorities of government and determines the commitment of resources within the public jurisdiction' (R. Simmons et al. 1974: 457). Therefore, in order to consider the means by which wilderness is utilised, it is essential to understand what the values of wilderness are. As Henning (1987: 293) observed: 'In the end, the survival of the wilderness will depend upon values being a respected factor in the political and governmental process.'

The value of wilderness is not static. The value of a resource alters over time in accordance with changes in the needs and attitudes of society. As noted above, ideas of the values of primitive and wild land have shifted in relation to the changing perceptions of western culture. Nevertheless, the dynamic nature of the wilderness resource does not prevent an assessment of its values as they are seen in present-day society. Indeed, such an evaluation is essential to arguments as to why wilderness should be conserved.

Broadly defined, the values of wilderness may be classified as being either anthropocentric or biocentric in nature. The principal emphasis of the anthropocentric approach is that the value of wilderness emerges in its potential for direct human use. In contrast, 'the biocentric perspective places primary emphasis on the preservation of the natural order'. The former approach places societal above ecological values and emphasises recreational and aesthetic rather than environmental qualities. Both perspectives focus on human benefits. However, 'the important distinction between them is the extent to which these benefits are viewed as being independent of the naturalness of wilderness ecosystems' (Hendee et al. 1978: 18).

A more radical, and increasingly popular, interpretation of the notion of the value of wilderness has been provided by what is often termed a deep ecology perspective (Godfrey-Smith 1979, 1980; R. Nash 1990; Oelschlaeger 1991). Deep ecologists argue that wilderness should be held as valuable not just because it satisfies a human need (instrumental value) but as an end in itself (intrinsically valuable). Instrumental anthropocentric values, derived from a Cartesian conception of nature, are regarded as being opposed to a holistic or systematic view 'in which we come to appreciate the symbiotic interdependencies of the natural world' (Godfrey-Smith 1979: 316). The holistic view broadly corresponds with the ecological conception of wilderness (Worster 1977; R. Nash 1990; Oelschlaeger 1991). However, it goes further by arguing that 'the philosophical task is to try and provide adequate justification . . . for a scheme of values according to which concern and sympathy for our environment is immediate and natural, and the desirability of protecting and preserving wilderness self-evident' (Godfrey-Smith 1979: 316), rather than justified purely according to human needs.

We can, however, provide – and it is important that we do so – an answer to the question: 'What is the use of wilderness?' We certainly ought to preserve and protect wilderness areas as gymnasiums, as laboratories, as stockpiles of genetic diversity and as cathedrals. Each of these reasons provides a powerful and sufficient instrumental justification for their preservation. But note how the very posing of this question about the utility of wilderness reflects an anthropocentric system of values. From a genuinely ecocentric point of view the question, 'What is the use of wilderness?' would be as absurd as the question, 'What is the use of happiness?' (Godfrey-Smith 1979: 319).

Hendee et al. (1978) identified three consistent themes in the values associated with wilderness: experiential, mental and moral restorational, and scientific. Experiential values highlight the importance of the 'wilderness experience' for recreationists and tourists (Scott 1974; Hamilton-Smith 1980; McKenry 1980). Several themes emerge in an examination of the wilderness experience including the aesthetic, the spiritual and the escapist (Table 7.2). Given its essentially personal nature, the wilderness experience is extremely difficult to define (Scott 1974). Nevertheless, the values recorded from writings on wilderness listed in Table 7.2 do point to the various aspects of the wilderness experience that are realised in human contact with wild and primitive lands.

Associated with the values of the wilderness experience is the idea that wilderness can provide mental and moral restoration for the individual in the face of modern civilisation (Carhart 1920; Boyden and Harris 1978). This values wilderness as a 'reservoir for renewal of mind and spirit' and in some cases offers 'an important sanctuary into which one can withdraw, either temporarily or permanently, to find respite' (Hendee et al. 1978: 12). This harks back to the biblical role of wilderness as a place of spiritual renewal (Funk 1959) and the simple life of Thoreau's Walden Pond (Thoreau 1854 (1968)). The encounter with wilderness is regarded as forcing the individual to rise to the physical challenge of wilderness with corresponding improvements in feelings of self-reliance and self-worth. As Ovington and Fox (1980) wrote: 'In the extreme', wilderness

> generates a feeling of absolute aloneness, a feeling of sole dependence on one's own capacities as new sights, smells and tastes are encountered. . . . The challenge and the refreshing and recreating power of the unknown are provided by unadulterated natural wilderness large enough in space for us to get 'lost' in. Here it is possible once again to depend upon our own personal faculties and to hone our bodies and spirits.
>
> (Ovington and Fox 1980: 3)

The third major theme in the values associated with wilderness is that of the scientific values of

Table 7.2: Components of the wilderness experience

Component	Nature of experience	Examples
Aesthetic appreciation	Appreciation of wild nature	Leopold 1921, 1925; Marshall 1930; McKenry 1972a; Smith 1977; Hamilton-Smith 1980; Alexander 1984; R. Nash 1990
Religious	The experience of God in the wilderness	McKenry 1972a; Hendee et al. 1978; Wright 1980; Hamilton-Smith 1980; R. Nash 1990
Escapist	Finding freedom away from the constraints of city living	McKenry 1972a; Smith 1977; Hendee et al. 1978; Hamilton-Smith 1980; Hawes 1981
Challenge	The satisfaction that occurs in overcoming dangerous situations and fully utilising physical skills	McKenry 1972a; Smith 1977; Gardner 1978; Hamilton-Smith 1980
Historic/romantic	The opportunity to relive or imagine the experiences of pioneers of the 'frontier' that formed national culture	Leopold 1925; Smith 1977; Hamilton-Smith 1980; Ride 1980; Alexander 1984; S. Johnston 1985
Solitude	The pleasure of being alone in a wild setting	Lee 1977; Smith 1977; Hamilton-Smith 1980; Hawes 1981; Sinclair 1986
Companionship	Paradoxically, in relation to the previous category, the desire to share the setting with companions	Lee 1977; Smith 1977; Hamilton-Smith 1980
Discovery/learning	The thrill of discovering or learning about nature in a natural setting	Smith 1977; Gardner 1978; Hamilton-Smith 1980
Vicarious appreciation	The pleasure of knowing that wilderness exists without actually ever having seen it	McKenry 1977; Smith 1977; Hawes 1981; S. Johnston 1985
Technology	Influence of technological change on outdoor activities	Marsh and Wall 1982

wilderness. Table 7.3 identifies the various ways in which wilderness is of importance to science.

The preservation of wilderness is regarded as an essential component in the scientific study of the environment and human impact on the environment. Furthermore, wilderness has increasingly come to assume tremendous economic importance because of the value of the genetic material that it contains. However, the multidimensional nature of the wilderness resource may lead to value conflicts over the use of wilderness areas.

A fourth theme which is inherent in the values of wilderness is that of economic worth. In addition to the economic significance of genetic resources, wilderness has importance as a tourist and recreation attraction. Indeed, the economic valuation of wilderness and natural areas has now become a critical factor in their designation (Hall 1992a), although it should be noted that the economic value of tourism has long been used to justify national park creation in areas that would otherwise be deemed worthless (Runte 1972a, 1972b, 1973, 1974a, 1974b, 1977, 1979, 2002). Such a value may also be enhanced through international recognition such as that achieved through listing as a World Heritage site (Mosley 1983).

McKenry (1977) has provided an analysis of the degree to which the values of wilderness are disrupted by activities such as forestry, mining, grazing and road construction. Table 7.4, based on

Table 7.3: The scientific values of wilderness

Value	Description
Genetic resources/biodiversity	Large natural communities such as those provided for in wilderness areas can serve as sources of genetic materials which are potentially useful to humans. As more of the world's natural ecosystems are removed or simplified, the remaining natural areas will assume even greater importance as storehouses of genetic material.
Ecological research and biological monitoring	Wilderness areas provide protection for large natural ecosystems. Within these areas a variety of research on ecological processes can occur. Research may consist of ecosystem dynamics, comparative ecology, ethology, surveys of fauna and flora, and the relationship of base ecological data to environmental change.
Environmental baselines	Wilderness areas, representative of particular biomes, can be used as reference areas in the monitoring of environmental change both within the biome and on a global scale.
The evolutionary continuum	Wilderness areas provide the conditions in which the evolutionary continuum of adaptation, extinction and speciation can occur without the direct interference of humans.
Long term	Wilderness areas provide conditions in which flora and fauna conservation can occur, particularly for those species which require large territories to reproduce and be preserved.

Sources: P.E. Smith (1977); Frankel (1978); Hendee et al. (1978); Hall (1992a)

Table 7.4: Interactions between values associated with wilderness and common disruptive activities

Common disruptive activities	Water resources	Traditional aboriginal habitat	Wildlife resources and habitat	Plant resources and habitat	Research and education	Wilderness recreation resources	Vicarious appreciation of wilderness	Reserve resource pool
Hydro	1–2	5	3–4	3–4	4–5	4–5	4–5	4–5
Forestry	3–4	5	3–4	3–4	3–4	4–5	4–5	2–3
Mining	3–4	5	3–4	3–4	3–4	4–5	5	4–5
Agriculture	3–4	5	3–4	4–5	3–4	5	5	4–5
Grazing	3–4	4–5	2–3	3–4	2–3	3–4	3–4	2–3
Road	2–3	4–5	2–3	2–3	2–3	4–5	4–5	2–3
Tourism	3–4	5	3–4	2–3	2–3	4–5	4–5	2–3
Off-road	2–3	4–5	2–3	2–3	2–3	4–5	2–3	1–2

Scale of disruption to wilderness values
1 No incompatible interaction (i.e. mutually compatible)
2 Slightly incompatible
3 Substantial incompatibility
4 Slight compatibility only
5 Totally incompatible (i.e. mutually exclusive)
Source: adapted from McKenry (1977: 209)

McKenry's research, records the level of compatibility between wilderness values and common disruptive activities. The significant factor which emerges from Table 7.4 is that because of the intrinsic characteristics of wilderness as primitive and remote land the range of uses that can occur within wilderness areas without diminishing the values of wilderness is extremely limited and will require careful management. As soon as the characteristics of the wilderness resource are infringed through the activities of western humans then wilderness values are reduced. Emphasis is placed upon the impacts of western society, rather than those of technologically underdeveloped peoples, because as the following discussion will illustrate, the present-day concept of wilderness is a product of western thought. Indeed, geographers such as Nelson (1982, 1986) have argued for the adoption of a human–ecological approach to wilderness and park management which sees the incorporation of the attitudes and practices of indigenous peoples as being an essential part of a contemporary perspective on the notion of wilderness.

INSIGHT: National parks and indigenous peoples

National parks are a western concept (R. Nash 1967, 1982). National parks have their origins in the New World desire to conserve nature and appropriately aesthetic landscapes for economic development through tourism (Hall 1992a, 2000b). Until recently, the creation of national parks was marked by the exclusion of aboriginal populations as undesirable elements in the 'natural' landscape. The drawing of boundaries between the natural parks and the rural human landscape available for agriculture, forestry, mining and/or grazing reflecting the Cartesian divide of western society has long sought to separate 'civilisation' and 'wilderness'. However, since the late 1960s, the separation between natural and cultural heritage has come to be seen as increasingly artificial (Mels 1999). In part, this has been due to the renaissance of aboriginal and indigenous cultures in the New Worlds of North America and Australasia as well as greater assertion of native cultural values in post-colonial societies (Butler and Hinch 1996; Ryan and Huyton 2002; Hall and Tucker 2004). In addition, there has been an increased realisation by ecologists and natural resource managers that many ecological relationships in so-called natural landscapes are actually the result of a complex set of interrelations between the use of the land by native peoples and the creation of habitat. For example, through burning regimes (e.g. Aagesen 2004), or through grazing in relation to transhumance (e.g. Bunce et al. 2004), as in the case of the Sami in the Nordic countries. Such developments have had enormous influence not only on the ways in which parks are managed but also on how they are established and re-created for tourist consumption (Cohen 1993; Pedersen and Viken 1996; Hinch 1998; Waitt 1999; Pettersson 2004).

The influence of the Romantic movement on the establishment of national parks was extremely significant (Hall 1992a). For example, the first call for the establishment of national parks in the United States came in 1832 from an artist, George Catlin, who on seeing the slaughter of buffalo on the Great Plains described the waste of animals and humankind to be a 'melancholy contemplation', but he found it 'splendid' when he imagined that there might be in the future '(by some great protecting policy of government) . . . a magnificent park', which preserved the Animal and the North American Indian 'in their pristine beauty and wildness'. 'What a beautiful and thrilling specimen for America to preserve and hold up to the view of her refined citizens and the world, in future ages! A nation's Park, containing man and beast, in all the wild and freshness of their nature's beauty!' Catlin's seminal call for 'a nation's park' highlighted the new mood in America towards wilderness. Almost exactly forty years after Catlin's journal entry, President Ulysses S. Grant signed an Act establishing Yellowstone Park, creating the institution of which Catlin desired 'the reputation of having been the founder' (Catlin 1968: 8, 9).

Similarly, John Matson (1892) compared the efforts made in New Zealand to protect wildlife

268 THE GEOGRAPHY OF TOURISM AND RECREATION

with the absence of such attempts in the Australian colonies and appealed for the creation of 'indigenous parks' in order to preserve the animal and bird life of Australasia. Significantly, Matson quoted a New Zealand 'poet', George Phipps Williams, to conclude his case for the preservation of wildlife and their habitat, in a manner which is reminiscent of Catlin:

> Out in the wilderness is there no desolate space,
> Which you may spare to the brutes of indigenous race?
> Grant us the shelter we need from the pitiless chase.
> Gone are the stateliest forms of the apteryx kind,
> Short is the space that the kiwi is lagging behind;
> Soon you shall painfully seek what you never shall find.
>
> (George Phipps Williams, *A Plea of Despair*, in Matson 1892: 359)

Williams' comments, along with those of Catlin, may seem ill at ease with political and cultural sensibilities at the beginning of the twenty-first century. However, in the late nineteenth century such sentiments were commonplace. Maori, along with other aboriginal peoples, were seen as the remnant of a dying race and placing them in parks and reserves, so long as the land was not required for other economic purposes, was often seen as the most appropriate course of action. Despite the initial Romantic sentiments which helped create the momentum for the establishment of parks, humans, including the aboriginal peoples who had often created the park landscapes through their hunting and food-gathering practices, were excluded from the parks through loss of ownership and access rights, management and regulatory actions and policing strategies. Such measures were the result of ecological and cultural blindness at best, and outright racism and cultural imperialism at worst, with park boundaries serving as the demarcation between the natural and the cultural in European eyes.

Although the political status of aboriginal peoples is still a highly contested issue in many societies, substantial shifts have occurred in management practices with respect to aboriginal peoples and their role in national parks since the 1890s. A number of broad social and political factors in relation to the overall rights of aboriginal peoples have contributed to these changes, including

- a renaissance of aboriginal culture in a number of western countries which has led to renewed pride in traditional cultural practices
- the withdrawal of colonial powers in African and Asian states and the development of new modes of administration and management
- the assertion of ownership of and/or access to natural resources through treaty settlements and other legal channels
- changed government policies with respect to native peoples which has led to greater economic and political self-determination
- greater political influence of aboriginal peoples.

The management of national parks has been substantially affected and a number of changes have occurred at the micro level in parallel to the shifts which have occurred at the macro-political level. This has occurred in a number of different locations and jurisdictions but aboriginal peoples have gradually had a greater involvement in national park management in Australia, Canada, New Zealand, South Africa and the United States. Hall (2000c) identified several factors in influencing these processes:

- A recognition that many supposedly 'natural' landscapes are the product of a long period of aboriginal occupancy which has created a series of ecological conditions and relationships which are dependent on certain types of human behaviour. This means that the traditional knowledge of native peoples becomes a vital ingredient in effective ecosystem management.
- Growth of the tourist appeal of some indigenous cultural attractions.
- Greater emphasis by park management authorities on the role of various stakeholder

be added and current data modified. Indeed, in Australia,

> information about access and landuse is often poorly recorded and lacking in currency. Even the most recently available information may be inaccurate and out of date. This makes the compilation of a reliable database difficult, particularly because of the necessary dependence on published sources for much of the required information.
>
> (Lesslie et al. 1991b: 13)

Second, the process is spatially flexible, enabling scale to be matched to purpose. Furthermore, maps showing the distribution of wilderness identified in the inventory can be generated rapidly and efficiently in order to assist decision-making (Lesslie et al. 1993, 1995).

FROM IDENTIFICATION TO PRESERVATION

The purpose of wilderness inventory in Australia has, on the whole, been to identify areas of wilderness quality for the possible enactment of conservation measures by government. Inventories provide a systematic means of ensuring the designation areas of high environmental quality. 'Recognition of wilderness is the necessary first step towards protecting, appreciating and managing wilderness areas' (Manidis Roberts Consultants 1991: 2). However, identifying an area as wilderness does not, by itself, ensure that its wilderness qualities can be maintained; this may only be done through the appropriate legislation and management. 'Decisions of this kind are inevitably judgemental, requiring comparative assessments of the social worth of alternative and often conflicting landuse opportunities' (Lesslie et al. 1988a: v). Nevertheless, from a management perspective:

> The delimitation of wilderness management boundaries for any particular location is a separate question. The major point to be made here is that the commonly accepted practice of placing a wilderness management boundary around a location of high wilderness quality, and ensuring no wilderness degrading activities take place within, will not ensure the retention of high wilderness quality. For instance, a development in lesser quality wilderness on the margin of an area of higher quality wilderness will reduce wilderness quality within the higher quality area.
>
> The lesson to be drawn from this is that areas of lower quality wilderness which fringe areas of high quality are important in maintaining these quality areas. In order to ensure protection of wilderness quality, a wilderness management area therefore must include all marginal areas.
>
> (Lesslie et al. 1991b: 20)

CONCOM (1986: 8) proposed that the following key criteria be used to identify and evaluate land which has potential as a wilderness area:

- *Remoteness and size*: a large area, preferably in excess of 25,000 hectares, where visitors may experience remoteness from roads and other facilities.
- *Evidence of people*: an area with minimal evidence of alteration by modern technology.

However, CONCOM (1985) was not sure that these criteria would reflect differences in landscape and ecological diversity across Australia. The CONCOM criteria may be contrasted with the United States wilderness legislation which suggests as a guideline for minimum wilderness size an area of 5000 acres (2023 ha), and where impacted ecosystems may be included if they contribute to the viability and integrity of the wilderness area. One of the ironies of the criteria for wilderness identification chosen by CONCOM is that they exclude many of the wilderness areas that have already been established under state legislation! According to CONCOM (1986: 4), 'Wilderness areas are established to provide opportunities for the visitor to enjoy solitude, inspiration and empathy with his or her natural surroundings'. The CONCOM position is to preserve the 'wilderness experience', not necessarily the intrinsic qualities of wilderness. However, to preserve wilderness mainly for recreation values is to ignore the significant range of other values of a wilderness area (see above).

Unlike the United States government, the Australian government does not have vast areas of federal land upon which wilderness legislation would be readily enforceable. State governments, which under the Australian constitution have primary control over land use, regard the reservation of wilderness areas under appropriate legislation as being a state responsibility. This situation therefore means that unless the Federal government exercises its constitutional powers in relation to the environment, any national wilderness system may be achieved only through consensus between the Commonwealth and the various state and Territory governments. More recently the Australian Federal government has renamed the NWI as a disturbance database, with disturbance referring to that resulting from post-European technological and population impacts. Arguably, the change of name may not be as politically charged as wilderness given

the contestation over environmental conservation in Australia since the 1960s (Dovers 2000a). Nevertheless, the NWI still serves as a valuable management tool by which to evaluate the potential loss of wilderness quality which new developments might bring and the potential corresponding loss of visitor satisfaction.

SUMMARY POINTS

- Identification of high value natural resources may not necessarily lead to subsequent action for conservation within the policy and planning process.
- Remoteness and primitiveness are the two essential attributes of wilderness.
- GIS is an extremely valuable tool with which to undertake natural resource inventories.

The Australian Land Disturbance Database can be viewed and downloaded at http://www.heritage.gov.au/anlr/code/ald.html

Plate 7.1: Arizona. Some national parks are often under enormous pressure in terms of visitor numbers. The Grand Canyon National Park, Arizona, receives over 5 million visitors a year.

TOURIST AND RECREATIONAL DEMAND FOR WILDERNESS, NATIONAL PARKS AND NATURAL AREAS

Many values are attached to wilderness in western society. Tourism and recreation has increasingly become significant as one of the main values attached to wilderness and its conservation with substantial increases in demands for access to wilderness in recent years. Demand for tourist or recreational experience of wild country or wilderness may be related to two major factors: first, changing attitudes towards the environment; second, access to natural areas.

As discussed above, there has been the development of a more favourable response to wild country in western society over the past 200 years. These positive responses have been reinforced in recent years by the overall development of a climate of environmental concern which has served to influence recreation and tourism patterns in natural areas. Going hand-in-hand with the increase in demand for personal contact with nature has been the production of natural areas for tourist consumption. While the setting of a boundary for a national park may be appropriate for assisting conservation management it can also serve as a marker for tourist space on which it is appropriate for the viewer to gaze. In the same way that notions of rurality are complex spaces of production and consumption (see Chapter 6), so it is that the ideas of wilderness and naturalness are bound up in the commodification of landscapes for tourist and recreational enjoyment (Olwig and Olwig 1979; Short 1991; Evernden 1992; Mels 1999, 2002; Saarinen 2001, 2005). For some, such a perspective is at odds with the mythology that national parks are ecological rather than cultural landscapes, but the cultural idea of wilderness is implicit in the very notion of wilderness itself. For example, R. Nash (1982: 1) noted that wilderness is 'heavily freighted with meaning of a personal, symbolic and changing kind'. Although the personal meaning of wilderness may not be of great value when it comes to the designation of wilderness areas from a biocentric perspective which concentrates on actual rather than perceived naturalness (see above), it is of value in terms of the recreation and tourism values of wilderness.

Since the early 1990s, there has been growing academic attention in the field of wilderness perception imagery (e.g. Kliskey and Kearsley 1993; Kliskey 1994; Higham 1997). Stankey and Schreyer (1987), for example, demonstrate that wilderness perceptions may be shaped by a wide range of influences. These include social attitudes, cultural influences, recreational experiences, expectation and personal cognition. It is apparent, therefore, that 'while wilderness environments have an objective physical reality, what makes that reality "wilderness" rests very much with personal cognition, emotion, values and experience' (Higham and Kearsley 1994: 508).

Kliskey (1994) argued that, while demand for access to wilderness increases, so too does the need to define the extent to which certain qualities of wilderness are sought. Kearsley (1990) illustrates this point with his proposal for a classification of natural areas based on degrees of naturalness, ease of access and the provision of facilities. Implementation of such a classification would facilitate the use of 'degrees of wilderness'. This would allow custodians of tourist facilities to provide for a wide range of wilderness preferences and utilise a wide range of natural settings. However, arguably such an approach had already been considered in the Australian wilderness inventory process.

The wider spatial distribution of recreationists based upon an appreciation of wilderness perceptions could contribute to the attainment of two fundamental goals: the maximising of visitor satisfaction and the mitigation of environmental impact at tourist sites. Kliskey and Kearsley (1993) also identified the need for a tourism development approach that does not impact upon the values sought by those who try to avoid the infrastructure of mass tourism, and to protect the social and environmental values that nature-based tourists, or ecotourists, seek. However, this demands that wilderness imagery assumes a role in the marketing and management of recreational and tourism resources in natural settings.

Higham (1997) examined the dimensions of wilderness imagery by international tourists in the South Island of New Zealand. This was done via a list of variables that may be considered appropriate or inappropriate to wilderness recreation and tourism. A five-point Likert scale allowed respondents to express the extent to which each variable was considered acceptable or unacceptable. Higham (1997) noted that in 'classic' (i.e. high quality in terms of absence of human impact) wilderness terms it should be expected that these variables would be considered to violate or compromise qualities of wilderness recreation. However, only seven of the twenty-two variables listed received a generally negative response (a mean value less than 3.0). Thirteen variables returned mean values exceeding 3.0 indicating a generally

Table 7.6: Responses to variables listed in question 'Indicate whether you feel that the following activities/ facilities are acceptable based on your perception of wilderness' (%)

Variable list	1	2	3	4	5	Mean
Search and rescue operations	4.0	3.1	16.6	21.2	49.1	4.3
Distant from towns and cities	4.0	6.7	19.8	22.6	45.1	4.0
Swing bridges/walkwires over rivers or streams	5.2	6.8	21.8	28.3	36.9	3.9
Restricted group size	10.5	9.5	16.6	24.9	33.5	3.8
Restricted access to prevent crowding	10.5	8.0	17.5	25.2	34.2	3.8
Big enough to take at least two days to walk across	8.9	6.8	18.8	24.3	39.4	3.8
Water provided in huts	14.3	7.9	17.7	22.3	36.9	3.6
Maintained huts and shelters	9.5	11.0	22.7	27.9	26.4	3.6
Toilet facilities	14.0	8.5	18.6	22.9	34.5	3.6
Exotic plants/trees (pines, thistles and foxgloves)	11.2	11.6	20.4	20.7	33.4	3.6
Signposts/information	7.0	12.8	24.8	24.5	29.4	3.6
Road access to the start of track	12.5	11.6	27.1	22.0	25.0	3.4
Maintained tracks (e.g. tracks cleared of fallen trees)	13.1	18.3	21.7	27.2	18.0	3.2
Developed camping sites	20.2	14.4	25.2	24.2	14.1	3.0
Grazing of stock (cattle, sheep)	31.2	15.9	25.7	11.9	11.3	2.7
Gas provided in huts for cooking	33.7	16.7	21.3	10.3	16.7	2.6
Stocking of animals and fish not native to NZ	40.1	20.7	21.0	4.6	7.7	2.4
Hunting/trapping	38.6	18.8	21.9	9.3	8.0	2.4
Motorised transport (powered vehicles, boats)	44.9	22.5	15.7	6.2	8.3	2.2
Plantation logging/mining/hydro development	52.8	18.1	16.6	4.3	4.0	2.0
Commercial recreation (e.g. guided tours)	52.7	20.1	13.1	5.5	6.4	2.0

Non-essential/unacceptable 1–2–3–4–5 Essential/acceptable
Where percentage figures do not total 100, the difference is explained by non-response to variables.

Source: Higham (1997: 82)

favourable disposition within the sample frame (Table 7.6).

In Higham's (1997) study, 'distance from civilisation' (mean = 4.0) is clearly an important aspect of wilderness recreation to most inbound tourists. The desire for remoteness is reinforced in the similar high regard for the scale of the location ('big enough to take at least two days to walk across' mean = 3.8). However, there is also a desire for the provision of safeguard mechanisms to reduce risk, with the provision of search and rescue operations receiving the highest mean score (4.3) of all listed variables. The desire for swing bridges and walkwires over watercourses, signposting and well-marked and maintained tracks confirm the widely held desire for wilderness recreation in a natural but relatively safe and humanised environment.

Furthermore, the placement of restrictions upon access and group size, again inconsistent with the notion of wilderness as free from human influences, was widely considered acceptable by inbound visitors. The variables 'restricted access' and 'restricted group size' share a mean of 3.8, placing them favourably on Table 7.6. As Higham (1997: 83) observed, 'It is quite possible that positive disposition toward these variables derives from trampers visiting high profile tracks on which social carrying capacities are being approached and, at times, exceeded.'

Only seven listed variables returned a mean response which indicated a generally negative disposition (Table 7.6). Six of these seven variables described activities that were likely to present associated social or physical impacts. These included commercial recreation and motorised transport, and grazing of stock and hunting/trapping and plantation logging, respectively. The seventh such variable, 'gas provided in huts for cooking', is exceptional in that it described the provision of a facility that may ease the passage of visitors in back-country locations. This was the only such variable that was generally rejected by inbound tourists, all other visitor provisions and facilities (huts, shelters, the provision of water and toilet facilities) being considered generally acceptable or compatible with wilderness recreation and tourism.

Higham's (1997) research raises important questions about the role of accessibility to wilderness areas. Indeed, issues of access are now presenting major management problems in wilderness and national parks. For many years access to wilderness was restricted by both the nature of the terrain and the capacity of individuals to travel there. Up until the Second World War the main means of access to most national parks was by train, with many of the national parks in the New World actually being developed in association with the railroads (Runte 1974a, 1974b, 1979; Hall 1992a). However, in the post-war period there was a substantial increase in the proportion of personal car ownership, thereby increasing accessibility to parks. National park management agencies also promoted themselves to the public through 'parks for the people campaigns'. Herein though lies the critical situation in which many parks and wilderness managers now find themselves. National parks were originally established to provide both recreational enjoyment and conservation (Hall 1992a). The founders of the park movement, though, such as John Muir, could never have imagined the almost continuous growth in demand for park access from tourists and recreationists seeking to escape the urban environment. The situation now sees traffic jams occurring in some parks, congestion on walking tracks, displacement of local users by tourists, increased pollution and other adverse environmental impacts, and reduced visitor satisfaction (e.g. Hall and McArthur 1996, 1998; Higham 1997; Kearsley 1997). Within this context, therefore, park and wilderness managers are now seeking both a better understanding of their visitors and how they may be satisfied, and strategies to find a better match between visitor needs and the capacities of the resource to be used, yet to retain the values that attract people in the first place (Hall and McArthur 1998).

Historically, tourist profiles have been generated to assist in the planning and management of visitor demand at a particular destination, attraction or site. Analysing tourist demand has traditionally been based on one of two main approaches: a socio-economic approach and a psychological or psychographic approach (see Chapter 2). The socio-economic approach attempts to establish a correlation between a visitor's actions at a particular destination and their social position (Lowyck et al. 1992). Mathieson and Wall (1982) argue that visitor attitudes, perceptions and motivations at a destination are influenced by socio-economic characteristics such as age, education, income, residence and family situation. Representative of this form of research is Blamey's (1995) study of international ecotourists to Australia, a country which has paid particular attention to promoting its natural features to tourists in recent years (Hall 1995).

According to Blamey (1995), Japanese and other Asian tourists are the most common inbound visitors to national parks on an absolute basis (21 and 19 per cent respectively of all such visitors), although they have the lowest propensities to do so on a per visit basis. Visitors from Switzerland have the highest propensity to visit natural areas (74 per cent) followed by Germany, Canada, Scandinavia and other European countries (all above 65 per cent). In addition, the economic expenditure of nature-based tourists may be substantial. Blamey (1995) reported that the average expenditure per trip for international visitors undertaking bushwalks during their stay was Aus.\$2824 in 1993, or 58 per cent above the average expenditure of all inbound visitors (Aus.\$1788).

Psychographic or psychological approaches classify people into groups according to their lifestyles, including values, motivations and expectations (Blamey and Braithwaite 1997). Lifestyles are distinctions in people's behaviour which are identified and categorised to distinguish different types of respondents. In a comparative study of Canadian tourists, ecotourists were found to be more motivated by features such as wilderness and parks than the rest of the Canadian population in choosing a destination (Kretchmann and Eagles 1990; Eagles 1992).

Higham (1997) investigated a variety of wilderness motivations in an attempt to identify qualities of back-country recreation that motivate tourists to visit tracks in the New Zealand conservation estate. Eighteen wilderness motivation variables were drawn from a review of the wilderness literature. The degree to which variables were supported or refuted by sample units is illustrated in Table 7.7. Motivation variables are listed on this table in order of mean response. Perhaps not surprisingly, natural beauty and outstanding scenery are primary motivations as identified by international visitors. Indeed, Higham (1997: 80) argued that this is a result that explains and entrenches the overwhelming popularity of the high-status Great Walks (of New Zealand). The reputations of the Milford, Routeburn and Kepler tracks are, in large part, explained by outstanding oppor-

tunities to experience alpine scenery. While these tracks remain those of unequalled scenic repute it is likely that inbound tourist interest in them will remain high.

The eighteen variables listed appeared in random order in Higham's (1997) original questionnaire. It is thus interesting to note the order in which variables appear in Table 7.7 when listed by mean response. When paired sequentially, the first ten listed variables demonstrate consistency in terms of both motivation and mean response. Table 7.7 presents a clear impression of the motivations that attracted inbound tourists to visit the walking tracks. These, in decreasing strength of motivation, were as follows:

1 To experience natural beauty and outstanding scenery.
2 To experience remote and relatively untouched nature.
3 To experience New Zealand's distinctive flora, fauna and natural systems.

Table 7.7: Responses to variables listed in question 'Motivations for coming to this location' (%)

Variable list	1	2	3	4	5	Mean
To appreciate the beauty of nature	85.6	11.4	1.8	0.3	0.6	1.2
Scenic beauty/naturalness	84.1	11.4	3.3	0.6	0.6	1.2
To encounter wilderness/untouched nature	61.6	25.5	7.2	3.6	1.2	1.6
To experience remoteness, peace and quiet	46.2	31.2	13.5	4.8	3.3	1.9
To see New Zealand's native birds and animals	38.9	30.7	18.8	8.5	2.1	2.1
To learn about NZ's flora/fauna/natural systems	28.3	32.5	21.7	12.3	4.8	2.3
For a totally new and different experience	30.9	21.6	23.7	14.4	9.0	2.5
To get away from life's pressures	34.2	22.8	16.2	9.6	15.3	2.5
To face the challenges of nature	24.9	24.9	21.6	13.8	12.6	2.7
To undertake strenuous physical exercise	22.8	23.7	23.4	15.6	12.0	2.8
To experience solitude	20.9	19.7	21.8	17.6	13.6	3.0
To meet people and make friends	12.9	18.0	30.2	21.6	16.8	3.1
Relax with family, friends or partner	23.1	17.4	17.1	10.5	30.3	3.1
Self-awareness/contemplation	14.2	21.1	25.1	18.1	15.7	3.2
To feel rejuvenated	18.8	14.8	21.2	11.8	24.8	3.3
To learn more about conservation/management issues	5.4	7.2	28.7	26.9	29.9	3.7
To confront hazards and take risks	5.7	8.7	21.0	24.6	37.5	3.9
To test mental skills (direction, mapping)	6.0	9.0	17.5	27.7	38.6	3.9

Strong motivation 1–2–3–4–5 No motivation
Where percentage figures do not total 100, the difference is explained by non-response to variables.

Source: Higham (1997: 81)

4 To escape civilisation and engage in something completely new and different.
5 To engage in the physical challenge that natural areas present.

The desire to experience solitude, one of the classic principles of wilderness recreation (see above), represents the eleventh variable listed in Table 7.7. This variable receives a mean score of 3.0. The last seven listed variables returned mean scores that described a negative rather than positive disposition. The last two relate to the physical and mental challenges that classic wilderness recreation offers, yet these receive distinctly low levels of endorsement by tourists. Such a situation therefore raises fundamental questions about the benefits which people are seeking when they visit wilderness areas and the extent to which agencies should seek to supply such benefits.

Another major issue in terms of tourism and recreation in national parks and wilderness areas is the extent to which tourism economically benefits such peripheral areas. Researchers disagree on the economic impact of nature tourists on local communities (Crabtree et al. 1994; Hull 1998; Weaver 1998; Walpole and Goodwin 2000; Hall and Boyd 2005). On the one hand, there is the argument that since these visitors spend most of their time out on the land or in the wilderness their economic impacts on local communities are minimal (e.g. Rudkin and Hall 1996). On the other, environmentalists have promoted tourism as a non-consumptive use of nature and a win–win development strategy for underdeveloped rural areas. As an influential World Wildlife Fund publication on ecotourism states:

> One alternative proposed as a means to link economic incentives with natural resources preservation is the promotion of nature tourism. With increased tourism to parks and reserves, which are often located in rural areas, the populations surrounding the protected areas can find employment through small-scale tourism enterprises. Greater levels of nature tourism can also have a substantial economic multiplier effect for the rest of the country. Therefore, tourism to protected areas demonstrates the value of natural resources to tourists, rural populations, park managers, government officials and tour operators.
>
> (Boo 1990: 3)

Indeed, Boo (1990) found that nature-oriented tourists had higher daily expenditures than those tourists who were not nature oriented. Grekin and Milne (1996) also argued that ecotourism is an industry where the physical isolation of a destination may work to its economic advantage by providing a taste of the unknown and the untouched. Similarly, Stoffle et al. (1979) in a study on indigenous tourism in the south-western United States also found that tourists who felt positive about residents at a particular destination were likely to purchase items to remember their experience. Hull (1998), in examining the average daily expenditure patterns of ecotourists on the North Shore of Quebec, found that package ecotourists had a substantially higher average daily expenditure than did independent tourists. Accommodation was the area of largest expenditure with package tourists spending on average Can.$42.04 and independent tourists spending Can.$11.76. For package tourists, accommodation costs represented 59.6 per cent of their average daily expenditure while for independent tourists accommodation costs represent only 23.8 per cent. Package tourists' second largest expenditure category was transportation at 22.2 per cent while for independent tourists meals were the second largest category at approximately 17.8 per cent (Hull 1998). Expenditure patterns show that over 75 per cent of the package tourists' costs are restricted to accommodation and transportation while independent tourists, even though they spend less overall, are spending more money in different sectors of the local economy and contributing more to the sustainability of the industry. Hull's findings are supported by those of Place (1998), who also noted that

> ecotourism can provide an economic base, but it does not happen automatically, or without social and environmental impacts. If it is to be sustainable, local populations must be allowed to capture a significant amount of the economic multipliers generated by tourism. Successful reduction of multiplier leakage requires local participation in development planning and outside assistance with the provision of necessary infrastructure, training and credit.
>
> (Place 1998: 117)

Tourism and recreation in natural environments can undoubtedly bring economic benefits to both communities on the periphery and to the wholesalers and suppliers of such experience if managed appropriately, and it is for this reason that increasing attention is being given to the supply of the experience of wild nature (Fennell 1999). However, a number of issues are starting to emerge with the potential impact of visitors not just on the landscape but also on individual species (MacLellan 1999; Woods 2000; Orams 2002; Hall and Boyd 2005).

SUPPLYING THE WILDERNESS AND OUTDOOR RECREATION EXPERIENCE

In many ways the idea that one can 'supply' a wilderness or outdoor recreation experience seems at odds with the implied freedom of wilderness. However, the tourism industry is in the business of producing such experiences, while national parks and wilderness areas, by virtue of their formal designation, are places which have been defined as places where such experiences may be found. One of the most important transformations in the production of leisure on the periphery has been the way in which the initial construction of national parks as places of spectacular scenery and national monuments for the few were transformed into places of mass recreation in the 1950s and 1960s and to places of tourist commodification in the 1980s and 1990s, particularly through the notion of ecotourism.

A number of different meanings applied to the concept of 'ecotourism' (P. Valentine 1992; Hall 1995; Weaver 1998, 2001; Fennell 2001; Higham and Lück 2002) which range from 'shallow' to 'deeper' statements of the tourism environment relationship:

- ecotourism as any form of tourism development which is regarded as environmentally friendly and has the capacity to act as a branding mechanism for some forms of tourist products

- ecotourism as 'green' or 'nature-based' tourism which is essentially a form of special interest tourism and refers to a specific market segment and the products generated for that segment
- ecotourism as a form of nature-based tourism that involves education and interpretation of the natural environment and is managed to be ecologically and culturally sustainable.

The Office of National Tourism (1997) in Australia, for example, defined ecotourism as 'nature-based tourism that involves interpretation of the natural and cultural environment and ecologically sustainable management of natural areas'.

> Ecotourism is seen as ecologically and socially responsible, and as fostering environmental appreciation and awareness. It is based on the enjoyment of nature with minimal environmental impact. The educational element of ecotourism, which enhances understanding of natural environments and ecological processes, distinguishes it from adventure travel and sightseeing.
> (Office of National Tourism 1997)

Many countries and regions around the world are now focusing on the supply of an ecotourism product as a means of tourism development (Fennell 1999; Garrod and Wilson 2003). Unfortunately, much of the ecotourism promotion best fits into the shallow end of the ecotourism spectrum, in that much of it revolves around the branding of a product or destination rather than seeking to ensure sustainability. Indeed, one of the greatest problems of ecotourism is the extent to which such experiences can be supplied without a limit on the number of people who visit natural areas, as visitation may lead not only to environmental damage, but also to perceptions of crowding thereby reducing the quality of the experience. As Kearsley et al. (1997: 71) noted, 'From the viewpoint of tourism . . . it is the impact of tourists upon tourists that has increasingly led to concern. Issues of crowding, displacement and host community dissatisfaction have risen to prominence.'

Crowding is a logical consequence of rising participation in outdoor recreation and nature-based tourism activities (Gramann 1982). It should therefore be of no great surprise that crowding is the most frequently studied aspect of wilderness recreation (Shelby et al. 1989). Indeed, many issues in wilderness management and outdoor recreation, such as satisfaction, desired experiences, carrying capacity and displacement are all related to the primary issue of crowding. Furthermore, social carrying capacity is increasingly being recognised as the most critical of all types of carrying capacity, since ecological impacts can often be controlled by management actions other than limiting use levels; for example, facilities may be extended and made more effective, and physical capacities are usually high (Shelby and Heberlein 1984).

Importantly, crowding should not be confused with density. Density refers to the number of individuals in a given area while crowding refers to the evaluation of a certain density (Graefe et al. 1984a, 1984b). In a review of thirty-five studies of crowding, Shelby et al. (1989) identified four sources of variation in perceptions of crowding:

- *Temporal variation* either in terms of time or season within which outdoor recreation activities are taking place. For example, weekends and public holidays are likely to experience higher than average use densities thereby resulting in inflated perceptions of crowding.
- *Resource availability* variation of resource availability (e.g. the opening and closing of tracks in alpine areas) may act to alter the presence of people at recreational sites.
- *Accessibility* distance (expressed in terms of time, cost, spatial or perceived distance) will affect crowding and densities, particularly if there is little or no recreation resource substitution.
- *Management strategies* management can intervene directly (e.g. use restrictions), or indirectly (e.g. de-marketing) to reduce visitor numbers at recreation sites.

Shelby et al. (1989) also investigated the hypothesis that crowding perceptions would vary according to the type of recreational use, although they were not able to resolve this hypothesis. However, research by Higham (1996) indicates that recreational use history is a substantial factor in influencing perceptions of crowding.

Concerns over crowding are closely related to issues of social carrying capacity in wilderness and outdoor recreation areas. Social carrying capacity in recreation areas 'has typically been defined as a use level beyond which some measure of experiential quality becomes impaired' (Graefe et al. 1984b: 500). However, as Chapter 6 noted, there is no 'absolute value' of social carrying capacity, there is no single response to specific levels of use in a particular area. Instead, indicators of social or behavioural capacity will be dependent on the management objectives for a given recreation site (Graefe et al. 1984a). Shelby and Heberlein (1986: 21) therefore refined this definition to read: 'Social carrying capacity is the level of use beyond which social impacts exceed acceptable levels specified by evaluative standards.'

Several factors have been identified as influencing crowding norms, with a number of variables contributing to the interpretation of increasing recreational use density as perceived crowding (Manning 1985):

- visitor characteristics: motivations, preferences and expectations, previous use experiences, visitors' attitudes towards wilderness
- characteristics of those encountered: type and size of groups encountered, behaviour of those encountered, perceptions of alikeness
- situational variables: type of area and location within an area.

Manning (1985) concluded that crowding norms are extremely diverse, yet the significance of visitor characteristics as a factor and the psychographic variables which comprise this factor indicate the possibility of a high degree of agreement being reached on crowding norms within particular subsets of the recreational population. This latter possibility highlights the importance of managers having a good understanding of the psychographic and demographic profiles of their visitor base in order to optimise levels of visitor satisfaction and attainment of management objectives (Hall and McArthur 1998).

Density alone provides no measure of visitor satisfaction. Satisfaction will be determined by expectations, prior experiences and commitment to the recreational activity. Perceptions of crowding are therefore influenced by use densities, but this relationship is mediated by a range of other factors and variables (Graefe et al. 1984a). Indeed, a range of reactions or coping strategies are possible in recreationalist response to decreased recreational satisfaction, which may result not only from crowding, but also from such factors as littering, noise and worn out camp sites (e.g. Anderson and Brown 1984). Such reactions include

- modifying behavioural patterns (e.g. by camping rather than using developed facilities)

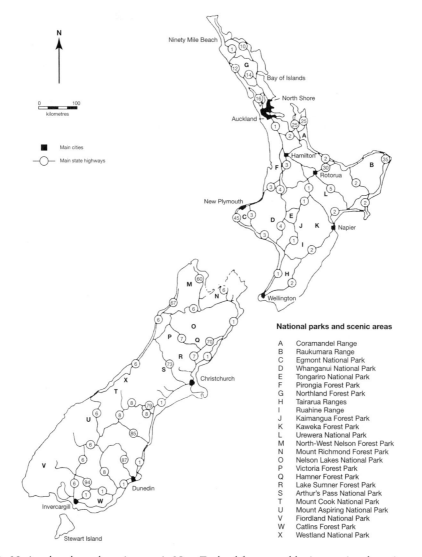

National parks and scenic areas

A	Coramandel Range
B	Raukumara Range
C	Egmont National Park
D	Whanganui National Park
E	Tongariro National Park
F	Pirongia Forest Park
G	Northland Forest Park
H	Tairarua Ranges
I	Ruahine Range
J	Kaimangua Forest Park
K	Kaweka Forest Park
L	Urewera National Park
M	North-West Nelson Forest Park
N	Mount Richmond Forest Park
O	Nelson Lakes National Park
P	Victoria Forest Park
Q	Hamner Forest Park
R	Lake Sumner Forest Park
S	Arthur's Pass National Park
T	Mount Cook National Park
U	Mount Aspiring National Park
V	Fiordland National Park
W	Catlins Forest Park
X	Westland National Park

Figure 7.2: National parks and scenic areas in New Zealand frequented by international tourists

- changing time of visit or use (e.g. visiting in shoulder or off-peak periods in order to avoid conflicts with other users)
- changing perceptions, expectations and recreation priorities (also referred to as product shift (Shelby et al. 1988), e.g. developing a new set of expectations about a recreational setting in order to maintain satisfaction)
- recreational displacement, where those who are most sensitive to recreational conflicts seek alternative sites to achieve desired outcomes.

Of the above strategies, recreational displacement is probably the most serious from the manager's perspective as displacement appears to be a reality of wilderness use regardless of the level of recreational experience (Becker 1981; Anderson and Brown 1984). Therefore, increases in numbers of visitors to wilderness and other natural areas, particularly at a time when such areas have to cope with their promotion as places for ecotourism experiences as well as the pressures of traditional recreation users, may lead to a decline in wilderness qualities as users are displaced from site to site. For example, in the case of major walking tracks in the South Island of New Zealand, Kearsley (1997) observes:

Plate 7.2: Waitakere Regional Park, Auckland, New Zealand. In order to minimise erosion caused by large visitor numbers in natural areas, substantial site and trail hardening may have to be undertaken, as here. However, what effect does such work have on the visitor experience and does the increased ease of access actually encourage more visitation?

> In a context where there is a clear hierarchy of sites, as in Southern New Zealand, displacement down the hierarchy is an all-too-likely possibility . . . the very large increase in overseas users of the Routeburn has displaced some domestic recreationists (and perhaps some tourists) to second tier tracks such as the Hollyford or Dart-Rees, or, indeed, out of tramping altogether. Similarly, their arrival might displace others yet further down the hierarchy to even less well known places, and there is a danger that trampers might be forced into wild and remote environments that are beyond their safe capacity.
>
> One consequence of this, if it is happening, is increased visitor pressure on more remote locations and displacement of moderate wilderness purists to a limited reservoir of pristine sites . . . with obvious physical impacts. A second consequence is the effect upon host community satisfaction, as domestic recreationists are displaced by overseas visitors [Figure 7.2]. Both of these consequences have serious implications for the sustainability of tourism.
>
> (Kearsley 1997: 95)

The case of crowding and other variables which influence visitor satisfaction and behaviour, including displacement, highlights the significance of understanding the factors of supply and demand of the recreation and tourist experience (see Chapters 2 and 3). Just as importantly they indicate the need for sound planning and management practice in trying to achieve a balance between the production and consumption of tourism and recreation, particularly in environmentally sensitive areas.

Plate 7.3: Northern Sweden. Wild rivers may provide options for jetboating, but the noise of such river use may disturb other recreationists.

INSIGHT: Peripheral areas, wilderness and global environmental change

Although human impacts have long been recognized as a threat to the integrity of wilderness area they have usually been seen in terms of immediate or relatively short-term impacts in the form of erosion, changed species behaviour, or reduction of naturalness. Arguably, a far more serious long-term impact that is also wider in scale is that of global environmental change (Gössling and Hall 2005; Hall and Higham 2005). Many alpine environments have already begun to be affected by climate change (Beniston 2003). For example, since 1850 the glaciers of the European Alps have lost about 30 to 40 per cent of their surface area and about half of their volume (Haeberli and Beniston 1998). Glaciers in the Southern Alps of New Zealand have lost 25 per cent of their area over the last 100 years (Chinn 1996). Glacial retreat is also prevalent in the US Pacific Northwest (Beniston 2003) and the higher elevations of the tropics, with Mt Kenya and Mt Kilimanjaro having lost over 60 per cent of their ice cover during the twentieth century (Hastenrath and Greischar 1997).

Climate change is regarded as being potentially extremely damaging to Southern Hemisphere ski tourism operations (Hall and Higham 2005). Whetton et al. (1996) write of the total loss of the Australian skiing industry by 2020 in a worst case scenario. Similarly, Perry and Illgner (2000) argue that skiing in the Drakensberg Mountains of South Africa will cease to be viable by 2050 if the current rate of temperature increase continues.

In their study of the Swiss ski industry Abegg and Froesch (1994) demonstrated that if temperatures were to rise by about 2–3°C by the year 2050, the low to medium elevation resorts located below 1200–1500 m above sea level would be substantially affected. Warmer winters bring less snow at these elevations, and the probability of snow lying on the ground at peak vacation periods (Christmas, February and Easter) would be reduced (Beniston 2003). Using a general rule for the viability of the ski season in Europe of a continuous snow cover of over 30 cm depth for at least 100 days, Koenig and Abegg (1997) indicated that whereas in the 1980s and 1990s, 85 per cent of ski resorts have had reliable amounts of snow for skiing, a 2°C warming would bring this figure down to 63 per cent. Hantel et al. (2000) predict that a temperature increase of only 1°C would reduce the snow season in Austria by 73 days over winter and spring. The reduction in the economic viability of low-altitude ski resorts has already led to increased user conflict in high-altitude areas in Europe, many of which are nature reserves and national parks, where some developers want to establish new resorts or enlarge existing ones so as to maintain a winter ski season. For example, McKie (2004: 3) reporting that a half of all resorts in Europe may have to close by 2050 with 'Politicians throughout the Alps are now being pressed by business to relax environmental regulations that might block new developments. This applies in particular to the higher, colder, parts of the Alps'.

However, alpine areas are not the only peripheral areas to be potentially impacted by climate change. According to Arctic Climate Impact Assessment (ACIA) (2004) the Arctic is warming much more rapidly than previously known, at nearly twice the rate of the rest of the globe, and increasing greenhouse gases from human activities are projected to make it even warmer. At least half of the summer sea ice in the Arctic is projected to melt by the end of this century, along with a significant portion of the Greenland Ice Sheet, as the region is projected to warm an additional 7–13°F (4–7°C) by 2100. According to ACIA (2004) these changes will have major global impacts, such as contributing to global sea-level rise and intensifying global warming. Key findings of ACIA (2004) included:

- In Alaska, Western Canada, and Eastern Russia average winter temperatures have increased as much as 3–4°C (4–7°F) since the mid-1950s and are projected to rise 4–7°C (7–13°F) over the next 100 years. The potential impact of climate change on some fish species such as lake trout, salmon, Arctic char and cod may also have significant repercussions for fishing tourism which is an important activity in the Nordic countries and Canada (Ivanov 1999; Mariussen and Heen 1999; Eide and Heen 2002).
- Arctic sea ice during the summer is projected to decline by at least 50 per cent by the end of the twenty-first century with some models showing near-complete disappearance of summer sea ice. This is very likely to have devastating consequences for some Arctic animal species such as ice-living seals and for local people for whom these animals are a primary food source (Thompson et al. 2001; Van Parijs et al. 2004). At the same time, reduced sea ice extent is likely to increase marine access to some of the region's resources (Callaghan et al. 1999; Ivanov 1999).
- Warming over Greenland will lead to substantial melting of the Greenland Ice Sheet, contributing to global sea-level rise at increasing rates. Over the long term, Greenland contains enough melt water to eventually raise sea level by about 7 metres (about 23 feet).
- In the United States, low-lying coastal states like Florida and Louisiana are particularly susceptible to rising sea levels as a result of the melting of the polar ice cap.
- Should the Arctic Ocean become ice-free in summer, it is likely that charismatic megafauna such as polar bears and some seal species, which are significant nature-based tourism resources, would be driven toward extinction.
- Arctic climate changes present serious challenges to the health and food security of some indigenous peoples, challenging the survival of some cultures if they are to attempt to try and maintain traditional foodways and life strategies.
- Over the next 100 years, climate change is expected to accelerate, contributing to major physical, ecological, social and economic changes, and the Assessment has documented that many of these changes have already begun.

CONCLUSION

This chapter has highlighted a number of areas in which geographers have contributed to research and scholarship in the tourism and recreation periphery. From the topophilia of Tuan (1974), the sacred space of Graber (1978) and the breathtaking historical analysis of Glacken (1967), geographers have been at the forefront of understanding the human relationship not only to the natural environment and wild lands in particular, but also to the behaviours of tourists and recreationists in the wilderness. In addition, geographers have assisted in developing techniques to identify wilderness areas, undertake environmental histories and to cast light on their values. More recently, geographies have been at the forefront of understanding the development and management of nature-based tourism development (P. Valentine 1992; Fennell 1999, 2001; Weaver 2001), including the impact of human visitation on wildlife (MacLellan 1999; Orams 2002, 2005).

As a resource analyst, the geographer therefore 'seeks to understand the fundamental characteristics of natural resources and the processes through which they are allocated and utilised' (Mitchell 1979: 3). The geographer's task is also relayed by Coppock (1970: 25), who has made remarks of direct relevance to a better understanding of the relationship between tourism, recreation and wilderness conservation: 'A concern with problem solving and with the processes of human interaction with resources, particularly in respect of decision making, will powerfully assist a more effective geographical contribution to conservation.'

QUESTIONS

- Is wilderness only a concept of the New World or does the concept also have relevance to western Europe?
- Is the methodology of Australia's national wilderness inventory easily transferable to other countries?
- What are the main factors which influence crowding norms?

READING

On wilderness see

Nash, R. (1982) *Wilderness and the American Mind*, 3rd edn, New Haven, CT: Yale University Press.
Oelschlaeger, M. (1991) *The Idea of Wilderness: From Prehistory to the Age of Ecology*, New Haven, CT: Yale University Press.
Hall, C.M. (1992a) *Wasteland to World Heritage: Preserving Australia's Wilderness*, Carlton, Vic.: Melbourne University Press.

On wilderness inventories in Europe see Fritz et al. (2000) and for the UK in particular see

Carver, S., Evans, A. and Fritz, S. (2002) 'Wilderness attribute mapping in the United Kingdom', *International Journal of Wilderness*, 8(1): 24–9 (this article provides an interesting modification of the Australian national wilderness inventory discussed in the case study above).

For an excellent overview on national parks and tourism around the world see

Butler, R. and Boyd, S. (eds) (2000) *Tourism and National Parks*, Chichester: Wiley.

On ecotourism and nature-based tourism see

Fennell, D. (1999) *Ecotourism: An Introduction*, London: Routledge.
Fennell, D. (2001) 'A content analysis of ecotourism definitions', *Current Issues in Tourism*, 4(5): 403–21.
Weaver, D. (ed.) (2001) *The Encyclopedia of Ecotourism*, Wallingford: CAB International.
Hall, C.M. and Boyd, S. (eds) (2005) *Tourism and Nature-based Tourism in Peripheral Areas: Development or Disaster*, Clevedon: Channel View.

For an excellent introduction to some of the problems encountered in the management of natural areas see

Newsome, D., Moore, S. and Dowling, R. (2002) *Natural Area Tourism: Ecology, Impacts and Management*, Clevedon: Channel View.

8

COASTAL AND MARINE
RECREATION AND TOURISM

The coastal environment is a magnet for tourists and recreationists although its role in leisure activities has changed in time and space, as coastal destinations have developed, waned, been re-imaged and redeveloped in the twentieth century. The coastal environment is a complex system which is utilised by the recreationist for day trips, while juxtaposed to these visits are those made by the domestic and international tourist. In an early attempt to identify the complexity of the coastline for tourism, D.G. Pearce and Kirk (1986) identified three elements to the coastal environment: the *hinterland* (where accommodation and services are provided); the *transit* zone (i.e. dunes) and the *recreational activity* zone (beach and sea). This model typifies much of the research by geographers prior to the 1990s: to observe, record, synthesise and model recreational and tourism phenomena in pursuit of an explanation of the spatial relationships and nature of the coast. In Lavery's (1971b) analysis of resorts, the distinction between recreation and tourism blurred but the coastal resort was a dominant element of the observed patterns and models of tourism activity. The pursuit of explanations of the spatial structure of coastal tourism and preoccupation with the resort morphology has led to the replication of a multiplicity of studies that look at the similarities and differences between resorts in different parts of the world. As D.G. Pearce (1988a) rightly concluded:

> In stressing the physical form tourism takes along the coast, geographers have largely neglected the way tourists actually use this space. The questions of where and how coastal tourists spend their time appear to have been taken for granted for they have rarely been addressed explicitly nor examined in any detail.
> (D.G. Pearce 1988a: 11)

This assessment may equally be applied to the recreational activities of visitors to the coastal environment since this neglect is not germane to tourism alone. This was confirmed by Patmore (1983: 209) since 'For such extensive resource, it has been little studied in any comprehensive fashion'.

Ocean and coastal tourism is widely regarded as one of the fastest growing areas of contemporary tourism (Pollard 1995; Kim and Kim 1996; Orams 1999). While tourism development has been spatially focused on the beach for much of the post-war years, as witnessed, for example, in the slogan of the four 'S's' of tourism – sun, sand, surf and sex – the coastal and the marine environment as a whole has become one of the new frontiers and fastest growing areas of the world's tourism industry (M.L. Miller and Auyong 1991). The exact numbers of marine tourists remain unknown. Nevertheless, the selling of 'sun, sand and surf experiences', the development of beach resorts and the increasing popularity of marine tourism (e.g. fishing, scuba diving, windsurfing and yachting) has all placed increased pressure on the coast, an area for which use may already be highly concentrated in terms of agriculture, human settlements, fishing and industrial location (M. Miller 1993; ESCAP 1995a, 1995b). However, because of the highly dynamic nature of the coastal environment any development which interferes with the natural coastal system may have severe consequences for the long-term stability of the environment (Cicin-Sain and Knecht 1998). Indeed, in the United States, the National Oceanic and Atmospheric Administration (NOAA) (1997) recognised that:

> Of all the activities that take place in coastal zones and the near-shore coastal ocean, none is increasing in both volume and diversity more than coastal tourism and recreation. Both the dynamic nature of this sector and its magnitude demand that it be actively taken into account in government plans, policies, and programs related to the coasts and ocean. Indeed, virtually all coastal and ocean issue areas affect coastal tourism and recreation either directly or indirectly. Clean water, healthy coastal habitats, and a safe, secure, and enjoyable environment are clearly fundamental to successful coastal tourism. Similarly, bountiful living marine resources (fish, shellfish, wetlands, coral reefs, etc.) are of critical importance to most recreational experiences. Security from risks associated with natural coastal hazards such as storms, hurricanes, tsunamis, and the like is a requisite for coastal tourism to be sustainable over the long term.

The concept of coastal tourism embraces the full range of tourism, leisure and recreationally oriented activities that take place in the coastal zone and the offshore coastal waters. These include coastal tourism development (accommodation, restaurants, food industry and second homes) and the infrastructure supporting coastal development (e.g. retail businesses, marinas and activity suppliers). Also included are tourism activities such as recreational boating, coast- and marine-based ecotourism, cruises, swimming, recreational fishing, snorkelling and diving (Miller and Auyong 1991; Miller 1993). Marine tourism is closely related to the concept of coastal tourism but also includes ocean-based tourism such as deep-sea fishing and yacht cruising. Orams (1999: 9) defines marine tourism as including 'those recreational activities that involve travel away from one's place of residence and which have as their host or focus the marine environment (where the marine environment is defined as those waters which are saline and tide-affected)'. Such a definition is significant, for as well as having a biological and recreational base it also emphasises that consideration of the elements

of marine and coastal tourism must include shore-based activities, such as land-based whale watching, reef walking, cruise ship supply and yachting events, within the overall ambit of marine tourism.

This chapter seeks to review the principal ways in which the geographer has approached the coastal and marine environment. In particular, it highlights the reluctance of geographers to adopt a holistic understanding, whereby recreation and tourism are analysed as competing and yet complementary activities using the same resource base. The chapter commences with a discussion of the way in which the coast, and the beach in particular, was created by recreationalists and tourists. Like wilderness areas, the comparatively recent discovery of the coast as a potential resource for leisure use illustrates that leisure resources are *created*: they exist in a latent form until their discovery, recognition and their development leads to their use. In most geographical analyses of the coastline as such a resource, the value of a historical approach is acknowledged in virtually every textbook on resorts. And yet the geographer has been largely remiss in addressing this vital theme – how the resource was discovered and developed. It developed in the human consciousness, supplanting perceptions of the coastal zone as a repulsive environment once the lure of the seaside marked a changing sensibility in society. For this reason, historical reconstructions of coastal environment need to recognise the way in which the resource was discovered, popularised and developed, and assumed a cultural significance in society.

COASTLINE AS A RECREATION AND TOURIST RESOURCE: ITS DISCOVERY AND RECOGNITION AS A LEISURE RESOURCE

According to Lenĉek and Bosker (1999):

> The beach as we know it is, historically speaking, a recent phenomenon. In fact, it took hundreds of years for the seashore to be colonised as the pre-eminent site for human recreation. . . . A proscenium for history, the beach has become a conspicuous

signpost against which Western culture has registered its economic, aesthetic, sexual, religious, and even technological milestones.

(Lenĉek and Bosker 1999: xx)

This illustrates the changing perception of a natural resource for leisure through history: the European acceptance of the beach embodied notions of utility which replaced a reverence for the sea and images of nature dominating human existence in the littoral zone. In the Romantic period the beach represented a site for pleasure, spiritual exercise and a positive experience. The symbolic value of the beach was also incorporated in poetry, landscape painting and created a new sensibility and practices. This brought new social, psychological, economic and spatial prestige to a landscape as a place of leisure and pleasure (see Lenĉek and Bosker's (1999) stimulating cultural history of the beach for more detail). In Corbin's (1995) *The Lure of the Sea: The Discovery of the Seaside 1750–1840*, the dramatic changes in western attitudes towards the sea, the seaside and the landscape are reviewed in a European context. As a French translation of the European literature, it provides a fascinating reconstruction of those elements in western society which contributed to the discovery of the coast as a leisure resource (i.e. Romanticism) and the impact on perceptions of the seaside. The publication of Jane Austen's *Sanditon* in 1817, heralded as the first 'seaside' novel, was a parody of coastal tourism as a fashion-driven experience with health and recuperative benefits. What is significant in Corbin's (1995) thesis is the discovery of the pleasure qualities of the coast and the transformation from 'the classical period [which] knew nothing of the attraction of seaside beaches, the emotion of a bather plunging into the waves, or the pleasures of a stay at the seaside. A veil of repulsive images prevented the seaside from exercising its appeal' (Corbin 1995: 1). What the period 1750 to 1840 witnessed was a fundamental reassessment of the ways in which leisure time and places were used with the evolution of the seaside holiday. Within that evolutionary process the beach was invented as part of a resort complex. The beach developed as the activity space for recreation and tourism,

with distinct cultural and social forms emerging in relation to fashions, tastes and innovations in resort form. The development of piers, jetties and promenades as formal spaces for organised recreational and tourism activities led to new ways of experiencing the sea. The coastal environment, resort and the beach have been an enduring resource for tourism and recreation since the 1750s in western consciousness, with its meaning, value to society and role in leisure time remaining a significant activity space.

Indeed, the beach 'invites watchers to unearth not only the dominant, culturally elite themes of a period, but its popular sensibilities: a blank piece of real estate on which each wave of colonizers puts up its own idea of paradise' (Lenĉek and Bosker 1999: xx): in short the coast represents a liminal landscape in which the juncture of pleasure, recreation and tourism are epitomised in the postmodern consumption of leisure places (Preston-Whyte 2002). However, as Preston-Whyte (2004) acknowledged, the discussion on beaches as liminal spaces needs to be deepened particularly the dominance of a western perspective that assumes liminality to be associated with heightened sensibilities associated with the temporary suspension of normal states, and a paucity of empirical exploration of the nature of the symbolism of these spaces. Preston-Whyte (2004) argued, two main issues need to be addressed. First, the human actors, with their cultural discourse and symbols to conceptualize and tame the beach, and the non-human actors that constitute the material conditions of the beach itself with its attractions and dangers, must be dealt with on equal terms. Second, dualisms such as nature/culture, that feature so strongly in sociospatial analysis (Murdock 1997; Watmore 1998, 2000), need to be addressed. In doing so, Preston-Whyte (2004) believed that researchers would then be in a better position to understand the cryptic comment made by Richard in Alex Garland's influential novel (and subsequent film) *The Beach*: 'It doesn't matter why I found it so easy to assimilate myself into beach life. The question is why the beach life found it so easy to assimilate me' (Garland 1997: 116, quoted in Preston-Whyte 2004: 357).

As Edgerton (1979) observed, for some Californian beaches in the 1970s, 400,000 visitors a day was not uncommon. Given the spatial distribution of beaches in California (Table 8.1; see also Figure 8.1), this is a dominant cultural element of the region's leisure culture. In fact in 2001, the visits to California's top three state beaches were: Santa Monica (7.8 million visits), Lighthouse Field (7.3 million visits) and Dockweiler (3.8 million visits). Beach visits generated US$75.4 million in travel and tourism expenditure for the Californian economy, supporting up to 1 million jobs and generating a further US$4.8 million in tax revenue. The scale of such visits also illustrates the evolution of California's beaches as a playground (Löfgren 2002), popularised in popular culture in the 1950s by the diffusion of surfing from Waikiki beach in Hawaii. In the 1960s, the evolution of a Californian beach music culture (e.g. the Beach Boys, named after the Waikiki beach surfers) generated a new

Table 8.1: California state beaches

Beach name	County	Acres	Beach name	County	Acres
Alamitos Beach	Orange	0.90	New Brighton	Santa Cruz	157.39
Asilomar	Monterey	106.97	Pacifica	San Mateo	20.73
Bean Hollow	San Matro	44	Pelican	Del Norte	5.15
Big Rock Beach	Los Angeles	0.43	Pescardo	San Mateo	699.75
Bolsa Chica	Orange	169.42	Pismo	San Luis Obispo	1,342.68
Cardiff	San Diego	507.12	Point Dume	Los Angeles	31.87
Carlsbad	San Diego	28.38	Point Sal	Santa Barbara	84.03
Carmel River	Monterey	296.69	Pomponio	San Mateo	2,420.64
Carpinteria	Santa Barbara/Ventura	62.29	Refugio	Santa Barbara	905.08
Caspar Headlands	Mendocino	2.95	Robert H. Meyer		
Cayucos	San Luis Ubispo	15.63	Memorial	Los Angeles	37.04
Corona Del Mar	Orange	29.57	Robert W. Crown		
Dockweiler	Los Angeles	91.40	Memorial	Alameda	132.22
Doheny	Orange	254.34	Salinas River	Monterey/Santa Cruz	281.84
El Capitan	Santa Barbara	133.98	San Buenaventura	Ventura	110.08
Emma Wood	Ventura	111.91	San Clemente	Orange	117.54
Gray Whale Cove	San Mateo	3.10	San Elijo	San Diego	587.62
Greenwood	Mendocino	47.22	San Gregorio	San Mateo	171.60
Half Moon Bay	San Mateo	180.93	San Onofre	San Diego	2,109.65
Huntington	Orange	121.13	Santa Monica	Los Angeles	48.48
Leucadia	San Diego	10.60	Schooner Gulch	Mendocino	53.62
Lighthouse Field	Santa Cruz	37.60	Seacliff	Santa Cruz	86.49
Little River	Humboldt	111.63	Silver Strand	San Diego	267.18
McGrath	Ventura	314.45	Sonoma Coast	Sonoma	5,427.38
Malibu Lagoon	Los Angeles	157.65	South Carlsbad	San Diego	118.46
Mandalay	Ventura	92.12	Sunset	Santa Cruz	302.11
Manhattan	Los Angeles	5.37	Thornton	San Mateo	58.0
Manresa	Santa Cruz	137.87	Torrey Pines	San Diego	61.36
Marinia	Monterey	170.71	Trinidad	Humboldt	158.76
Montava	San Mateo	780.27	Twin Lakes	Santa Cruz	95.36
Monterey	Monterey	100.21	Westport Union		
Moonlight	San Diego	12.73	Landing	Mendocino	57.03
Morro Strand	San Luis Obispo	160.19	Will Rogers	Los Angeles	82.14
Moss Landing	Monterey	60.37	William Randolph		
Natural Bridges	Santa Cruz	58.59	Hearst Memorial	San Luis Obispo	8.14

Source: modified and developed from Department of Parks and Recreation and State of California website

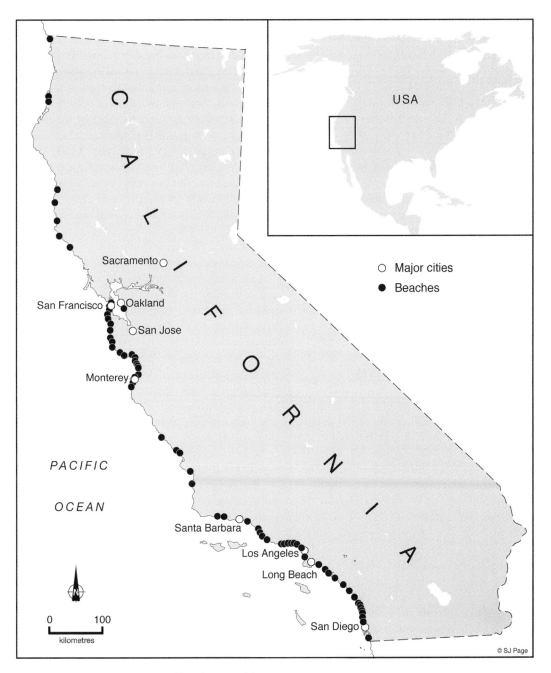

Figure 8.1: Spatial distribution of beaches in California

stimulus to beach use, especially with the rise of the beach party. The 1970s and 1980s have seen additional stimuli which have continued the beach culture, particularly the television series *Baywatch* (Löfgren 2002). As Braun and Soskin (2002) show in relation to Daytona Beach, Florida, day trippers to coastal areas can help stabilise seasonal fluctuations in demand. Yet conversely, they can also increase resource degradation due to volume of use, generate image problems and additional policing and maintenance costs.

The beach is an environment where hordes are prepared to tolerate overcrowding to experience the human–nature environmental landscape – being at one with nature so that the sun, sea and sand can be experienced in the tourist and recreationalist consciousness and pursuit of the liminal existence.

THE GEOGRAPHER'S CONTRIBUTION TO THE ANALYSIS OF COASTAL RECREATION AND TOURISM

The coast has emerged as one of the popular, yet hidden and underplayed elements in the geographer's application of the hallmark traits of spatial analysis, observation and explanation. From the early context for economics, such as Hötelling's (1929) model of ice-cream sellers on the beach to Weaver's (2000) model of resort scenarios, the coast has assumed a significance as a context for research, but not as a veritable resource for the legitimate analysis of tourism and recreation. This dependence on the coast as a laboratory for the analysis of spatial concepts, interdependencies and the application of geographical methodologies does not adequately reflect the cultural and leisure significance of the beach and coastline in recreational and tourism activity in time and space. To the contrary, locating a landmark study which embodies the coastline as one of the most significant resources for recreation and tourism is notoriously difficult. The literature is fragmented, with tourism and recreational geographers seemingly obdurate given their reluctance to move this theme higher

up the research agenda to fully appreciate its wider significance in modern-day patterns and consumption of day trips and holidaymaking. Despite the fact that the coast remains one of the most obvious contexts for tourism and recreation, it is poorly understood. Research is reliant on a host of very dated and highly disjointed studies of the coastal environment. Despite the publication of two important studies in the 1990s (Fabbri 1990; Wong 1993b), the area has barely moved forward in the mainstream tourism literature, with ad-hoc studies published in non-tourism sources. Even in D.G. Pearce's (1995a) review of coastal tourism, much of the emphasis was on spatial patterns, resort morphology, the significance of the seafront and planning issues.

This is extremely problematic for both tourism and recreation studies and geographers. The early interest in coastal tourism and recreation (e.g. E.W. Gilbert 1939; Patmore 1968; Lavery 1971b; Pearce and Kirk 1986) has not been accompanied by a sustained interest and, as a result, the research published has been highly specialised (see Table 8.2) and not been situated in a wider ecosystem/environmental context where the interconnections and sustainability of coastal environments can be understood in a holistic context.

Where research has been published, it has made significant contributions to advancing knowledge on the coastal–leisure interface, where physical processes are entwined with human action on a dynamic and volatile resource base. What Table 8.2 shows in this context is that the geographer has contributed to the historical analysis of resorts, in conjunction with seminal studies by social historians such as Walton (1983), and have formulated models to describe the process of development and change. The main dynamics of change, combined with temporal and spatial seasonality embodied in tourist and recreational travel to the coast, have remained an enduring theme in the geographer's analysis of this resource for leisure. The recreational and tourist behaviour which occurs in the coastal environment has also generated a number of seminal studies (i.e. Mercer 1972; Cooper 1981), while the physical geographers have made valid studies

Table 8.2: Illustrations of the geographer's contribution to the analysis of coastal recreation and tourism

Theme	Example(s)
Historical analysis of recreation and tourism in the coastal zone	E.W. Gilbert (1939), The development of coastal resorts
	Naylon (1967), The development of tourism in Spain
	Patmore (1968), Spa resorts in Britain
	H. Robinson (1976), Geography of tourism and resort development
	Barke and Towner (1996), The evolution of tourism in Spanish resorts
	Towner (1996), Synthesis of the process of development of resorts and patterns of tourism
Models of recreation and tourism	Stansfield and Rickert (1970), The recreational business district
	Miossec (1972), The process of resort development
	Pigram (1977), Analysis of beach resort morphology
	Britton (1982), Model of postcolonialist development of resort development
	Jeans (1990), Analysis of beach resort morphology in England and Australia
	Weaver (2000), Destination development scenarios
Tourist and recreationalist travel to the coast	Patmore (1971), Routeways and tourist/recreational travel
	Wall (1971, 1972), Patterns of travel by Hull car owners
	Mercer (1972), Recreational use of Melbourne beaches
Tourist and recreationalist behaviour	Coppock (1977a), Second home ownership
	Cooper (1981), The behaviour and activities of tourists in Jersey
	P.P. Wong (1990), Recreational activities in coastal areas of Singapore
	Walmsley and Jenkins (1994), Perception of coastal areas
	D.G. Pearce (1998), Tourist time budget study in Vanuatu
	Tunstall and Penning-Rowsell (1998), Beach user perceptions in England
Geomorphology of coasts and interrelationship with tourism/recreation	May (1993), Survey of South England
	Morris (1996), Environmental management in coastal Spain
Coastal processes and the relationship and impact on tourism/recreation activity	Burns et al. (1990), Analysis of coastal processes affecting the SW Cape coastline in South Africa
	Kirkby (1996), Recreation and the quality of coastal water in Spain
Resort development	D.G. Pearce (1978), The form and function of French resorts
	Carter (1982), Caravan site development in Ireland
	P.P. Wong (1986, 1993a), The development of island tourism in Peninsula Malaysia
	Morrison and Dickinson (1987), Costa Brava in Spain
	Kent et al. (2002), Water supply and coastal resorts in Mallorca
	McEwen et al. (2002), Flood warning and caravan parks
Conservation of coastal environment	A. White et al. (1997), Special Area Management and coastal tourism resources in Sri Lanka
	Leafe et al. (1998), Shoreline management
	Turner et al. (1998), Sustainable management of the coastline
	Barke and Towner (2003), Sustainable tourism in Andalucia
	Wong (2003), Coastal erosion in South East Asia
Human–environment interactions within coastal environments	Edwards (1987), Ecological impacts of tourism on heritage coasts in the UK
	R. Carter et al. (1990), Man's impact on the Irish coastline
	McDowell et al. (1990), Man's impact on the Costa del Sol
	Catto (2002), Anthropogenic pressure on coastal dunes
Management and planning of coastal areas for recreation and tourism	Pearce and Kirk (1986), Carrying capacity for coastal tourism
	R. Carter (1988), The coastline as an area to manage for recreation and tourism
	Ghelardoni (1990), Planning the Aquitaine coastline in France for tourism
	Nielsen (1990), Constructing a recreational beach in Denmark
	K. Nichols (1999), Integrated coastal management
Other contributions	Dumas (1982), The commercial structure of Benidorm
	Penning-Rowsell et al. (1992), Economics of coastal management
	Kim and Kim (1996), Overview of coastal and marine tourism in Korea

of the processes affecting vulnerable coastal environments. This has been complemented by studies of the pattern and impact of resort development which raises important conservation issues associated with the human–environment interactions in these environments. Finally, geographers have also made useful contributions to the policy, planning and management of coastal environments. But what marks this area out in the geography of recreation and tourism is the sparse nature of these studies within the mainstream literature, with the entire theme seeming almost unfashionable and knowledge often being based on findings from studies published in the 1960s, 1970s and 1980s, despite the significance of Fabbri's (1990) and Wong's (1993b) collection of papers on the topic by geographers and non-geographers. As a result, the following section examines the different contributions geographers have made and the significance to increasing our knowledge of the coast in the formation of distinct leisure and tourism geographies.

HISTORICAL ANALYSIS OF RECREATION AND TOURISM IN THE COASTAL ZONE

In many geographical analyses of recreation (e.g. Lavery 1971c; Patmore 1973, 1983) and tourism

(e.g. Towner 1996; S. Williams 1998), the English seaside resort is a popular topic for discussion. Indeed, A.M. Williams and Shaw's (1998) interesting analysis of the rise and fall of the English seaside or coastal resort examined two principal concerns of the historical geographer and contemporary tourism geographer: continuity and change in the development, organisation and prospects for the resort. Most analyses of the English seaside resort by geographers (e.g. Patmore 1968) refer to the seminal studies by E.W. Gilbert (1939, 1949) and the doctoral thesis by Barrett (1958). Despite these influential studies, the most notable contributions to the analysis of English resorts came from the social and economic historians, such as Walton (1983) and the geographical analysis by Towner (1996). What these studies emphasise are the role of historical sources, such as the census, development plans, advertising, photographic archives and other documentary sources in reconstructing the recreational and tourism environments in coastal areas in the Victorian, Edwardian and subsequent periods. Specific phenomena, such as the English holiday camp, examined by Ward and Hardy (1986), are also charted using similar sources. An illustration of the importance of examining the historical issues in the development of the coast as a tourism and leisure resource can be seen in the following Insight.

INSIGHT: Promotion of the seaside resort: place-promotion strategies

Following the promotion of spa resorts in the UK, with the royal patronage of individual sites such as by Queen Anne in 1702, the link with the coast was harnessed where spa resorts were located in seaside locations. For example, Walvin (1978) highlighted how many of the spa visitors also began to bathe in the sea and use the beach. 'By the 1730s Brighton and Margate, along with Scarborough, had distinct seabathing seasons' (Ward 1998: 31). But the rise of the coastal resorts did not simply mirror those of earlier spa resorts. The seaside with its beach and sea were not in

private ownership, providing opportunities for different social classes to partake in the pleasures of the coast. As Walton (1983: 190–1) argued, 'At the seaside rich and poor, respectable and ungodly, staid and rowdy, quiet and noisy not only rubbed shoulders . . . they also had to compete for access to, and use of, recreational space'.

This reflects the improved access. For example, in the 1820s, London Steamers to Thanet in Kent improved access as did the railway in the period after the 1840s, particularly initially as day excursionists then as holidaymakers.

To encourage visitors, resorts in the nineteenth century engaged in place-promotion strategies, building on the more crude methods which predate this period, such as guidebooks, limited newspaper advertising and editorials in popular national journals such as the *Gentleman's Magazine* (Brown 1988). One of the prime movers in place-promotion were the railway companies. While some resorts produced guidebooks to promote their wares, the railway companies used newspapers, posters and handbills to promote day excursions. This in turn also helped shape place-images and stereotypes of individual resorts, where hedonism and cheap excursions were popular (e.g. Blackpool). In contrast, private promoters of railway tours such as Thomas Cook adopted a more educative approach to tours, aiming the products to specific niches rather than the mass market.

Blackpool, among the UK resorts, entered the place promotion role after the Lancashire and Yorkshire Railway's fare policy threatened its excursion and holiday business from working-class areas. By an Act of 1879, the town council levied a local tax on the rates to undertake advertising at railway stations, attractions and amusements in the town. Not only did the town's Advertising Committee start with illustrated brochures aimed at the middle class market, but after 1881 Blackpool posters began to appear to publicise attractions, the Blackpool Tower, constructed in 1894 and the illuminations, introduced after 1912. In France, railway advertising on the Compagnie de l'Oust after 1886, saw colour posters introduced to advertise coastal destinations. Soon, individual resorts also used this method of place advertising, despite the expense and print runs of up to 6000. Due to the cost, many posters in France were displayed for up to three years and brochures would also have a similar life expectancy.

In the UK, the railway companies approached this method of promotion more cautiously according to Ward (2001). Although some companies produced posters for individual resorts

such as 'Skegness is so bracing' in 1908 by the Great Northern Railway, this was not the norm. Indeed, the Local Government Board in 1914 deemed municipal advertising on tourism inappropriate despite Blackpool's highly developed publicity programme on the rates.

Even so, a 'highly competitive resort selling game' (Ward 2001: 37) existed in the UK, and only limited powers were granted prior to 1914. After 1914, the UK saw a greater resort and railway company partnership in place-promotion, with the Health Resorts and Watering Places Act 1921 allowing resort municipalities the right to spend up to 1d rate on certain forms of advertising. After this point, cooperative railway–resort marketing emerged although the 1930s saw greater pressure for local authorities to increase their marketing and place promotion activities as the car and charabancs opened up new day trip markets. In the case of the most prolific railway advertiser, the Great Western Railway (GWR), A. Bennett (2002) acknowledged that

> The GWR's literary and visual representations drew heavily upon the concept of departure, that is, the qualitative distinction between daily or accepted routine and that of a special experience. Departure could assume an historical form, a particular location, an aesthetic appreciation or the sheer, exuberant pleasures of the seaside . . . GWR marketing also stressed the experience of the journey itself in its various forms, as a spectacle, an adventure and often as a unique and glamorous event . . . These were brought together in prestige advertising, a dimension of place marketing.
>
> (Bennett 2002: 3)

The iconography of railway poster advertising provides not only an expression of place marketing, but also a distinct style and mode of representing the imagery of the coast for potential visitors. As Bennett (2002) observed, the GWR view of the seaside had two key elements: that of a fashionable and exclusive 'watering place' for certain locations (e.g. Torquay) through to family-based resorts (e.g. Paignton and Porthcawl). GWR also took a lead role in the overseas marketing of

Britain, with its influential role in developing the Travel Association of Great Britain and Ireland, to promote the country overseas due to the economic benefits of inbound tourism.

Ward (2001) acknowledged that the 1920s were the heydays of railway company place-promotion and the 1930s saw municipalities increase their role. By 1939, Blackpool was producing 150 holiday guides to send to potential visitors, while resorts began a greater market segmentation, attracting conferences off-season.

Therefore what this Insight shows is that a number of agents and actors in coastal resorts (e.g. the railway companies and municipalities) devised a wide range of promotional tools to sell and advertise their localities. This in itself was highly controversial in the Victorian, Edwardian and inter-war periods and remains so even at the present day. It is also interesting to note that entrepreneurial and forward-looking companies like GWR created images and marketing strategies which saw a massive investment in tourism advertising. This was very influential in developing new and repeat business among the domestic and overseas markets, with carefully targeted market positioning of specific resorts to meet the expectations, desires and perception of prospective visitors.

In each of the studies of the English seaside resort, geographers have sought to map and analyse the changing dynamics of resort development. In these analyses, the preconditions for resort development (see Bescancenot et al. 1978), the role of stakeholders, developers and planners have been examined, and D.G. Pearce (1995a) reviews many of the French geographers' contributions to coastal tourism research. In the analysis of Spanish tourism by Barke et al. (1996), a number of useful historical reconstructions of coastal tourism exist (e.g. Barke and Towner 1996; Walton and Smith 1996), which review the emergence of coastal areas in the era during and after the Grand Tour. The late nineteenth and early twentieth century patterns of coastal tourism in Spain, and the dynamics of tourist circuits, were reconstructed from historical guidebooks. The relationship of tourist circuits, the evolution of the Spanish railway system and the development of tourist accommodation highlighted the consumption of leisure resources, particularly the evolution of seaside resorts. Walton and Smith (1996: 57) concluded that 'The importance of the quality of local government to resort success has been strongly apparent in studies of English resorts, but its role in San Sebastian was even more impressive'. Evaluations of coastal resources, such as the development of England and Wales Heritage Coastline (Romeril 1984, 1988), have emerged as a resource with a historical connotation. In other countries (e.g. the USA and Australia), historical studies of coastal tourism and recreation (see Pigram 1977; M. Miller 1987; Jeans 1990; Pigram and Jenkins 1999) have considered resorts, their life cycles and development in a longitudinal context. The historical geography of specific resorts has provided a focal point for research, where a range of factors explain why resorts developed where they did, why they developed and the pace and scale of change. This often remains a starting point for most analyses of the coast as an evolving resource for leisure use.

MODELS OF COASTAL RECREATION AND TOURISM

As already mentioned, model building is one of the hallmarks of the logical positivist traditions in human geography (see Johnston 1991). In the early studies of coastal recreation and tourism (e.g. E.W. Gilbert 1939), the major contribution to spatial knowledge was predicated on developing models which had a universal or more general application. By far the most extensive review of models of coastal recreation and tourism is D.G. Pearce (1995a).

D.G. Pearce (1995a) reviewed models of resort development, acknowledging the role of historical

Plate 8.1: Blackpool Pier, England. The Victorians built piers to enable promenading as well as to represent humans dominating and taming nature (i.e. the coast and sea).

antecedents (e.g. the role of developers in developing resorts for different social classes). Using the resort life cycle developed by Butler (1980), various factors were used to explain similarities and differences in development paths and the resulting morphological structure of the resort. D.G. Pearce (1995a) identified the problem of tourism functions being added to existing urban centres in coastal locations where a day trip market may also exist. What Pearce concluded was that 'a spectrum of coastal resorts exists, ranging from those with a wholly tourist function, notably the new planned resorts, to those where a significant amount of tourist activity occurs alongside a variety of other functions' (D.G. Pearce 1995a: 137). Interestingly, this reiterates the earlier typology developed by Lavery (1971c) in a recreational context, where a similar notion of a continuum was implicit but not explicitly developed. What Pearce (1995a) could have added is that the recreational market in many resorts will numerically outnumber the tourist market, though the behaviour of the former is very much climatically conditioned and opportunistic.

Among the most widely cited models of the resort is Stansfield and Rickert's (1970) discussion of the impact of consumption on resort morphology. Their resulting model, identified as the Recreational Business District (RBD), utilised earlier concepts from urban morphology models where central place functions of urban centres exist. The RBD, as distinct from the CBD, was viewed as the locale for recreational services and activities. Stansfield and Rickert (1970: 215) defined the RBD as 'the seasonally oriented linear aggregation of restaurants, various specialty food stands, candy stores and a varied array of novelty and souvenir shops which cater to visitors' leisurely shopping needs'. Although the model was based only on two New Jersey seaside resorts, the important distinction for current cultural interest in coastal recreation and tourism was that the RBD was not only an economic manifestation but also a social phenomenon. Similar relationships between the CBD, which is spatially detached from the RBD in resorts, was an important focus for research in the 1970s and 1980s. Had such models been developed in the 1990s, the research agenda and formulation of the model framework would have been very different. A greater emphasis would be placed upon the supply dynamics which created the RBD (i.e. the role of capital) (Judd and Fainstein 1999), the cultural and social meaning attached to the tourist, and recreationalists' experience of the RBD as a place in time and space (see Britton 1991 for a fuller discussion of these ideas). It would not be viewed in a static context, since the processes of change and evolution of the RBD to accommodate consumer tastes would also be emphasised.

In the emerging tourist destinations in South East Asia (see Hall and Page 2000), the RBD is a more complex phenomenon where the addition of hawker stalls, souvenir sellers and the informal economy combine to create a distinct entertainment district. D.G. Pearce (1995a) identified the addition of a night-life function in Patong, Phuket (Thailand) where the commodification of sex tourism is an additional function evident in the RBD (see Ryan and Hall 2001 for further discussion). Research by planners, most notably R.A. Smith (1991, 1992b), observed that in integrated resort development in South East Asia, the RBD function is incorporated as a key function. Land use zoning and the spatial separation of accommodation from the RBD to increase resort carrying capacity in locations such as Cancun (Gormsen 1982) highlighted the use of spatial concepts to manage tourist development. Pigram's (1977) influential study of morphological changes in Surfers Paradise (Queensland, Australia) between 1958 and 1975 recognised the spatial separation of the RBD and CBD. Yet relatively little interest has been shown in models of beach use, with a notable exception (Jeans 1990) where a semiotic model was developed. This model distinguished between the resort which represented culture and the sea which represented nature. What emerged was a transitional zone between culture and nature, a zone of 'ambiguity' – the beach. A second axis of meaning was also recognised, where the beach zone had a social periphery, where nonconformists (i.e. semi-nude and nude bathers and surfers) inhabited the area. This further refines D.G. Pearce and Kirk's (1986) model, though it was valuable in identifying the complexities of understanding the different types of carrying capacity of the resort and wider coastal zone.

TOURIST AND RECREATIONAL TRAVEL TO THE COAST

Within the tourism literature, the role of transport as a facilitating mechanism to explain tourist travel, patterns of tourism and development have only belatedly been acknowledged (Page 1994b, 1998, 1999). There are a number of seminal studies (e.g. Patmore 1968) in explaining the development of spas. Similarly, Pearson's (1968) study of the evolution of coastal resorts in East Lincolnshire illustrated the geographers' interest in the transport dimension. Patmore's (1971: 70) recognition that 'Deep-rooted in the very concept of outdoor recreation is the "journey to play", the fundamental movement linking residence or workplace to recreation resource. Such movement varies in scale, in duration and frequency'. A similar analogy may also be applied to tourism, and geographers have utilised a wide range of concepts from transport geography to analyse the patterns of travel for coastal activity by recreationalists and tourists. As Patmore (1971) recognised, it is the identification

of the routeways (the lines of movement) and the link to nodes of intensive leisure activity which have preoccupied geographers' analysis of tourism and recreational travel, seeking to model and understand this phenomenon (Mansfield 1969; Colenutt 1970). As Patmore (1971) argued:

> The crux of recreational planning is therefore the location, design and management of a relatively limited number of sites devoted wholly or partially to recreation, together with a concern for the routes which link them both to each other and to the residences of the users.
>
> (Patmore 1971: 72)

For the coastal environment, it has been the mobility afforded by the car (Wall 1971, 1972) which has posed many of the resulting pressures, planning problems and conflicts in environments that are constrained in the number of visitors they can absorb. Wall (1971) recognised that holidaymakers generate a considerable proportion of the road traffic in resorts. As Wall (1971) poignantly and ironically commented:

> One of the major advantages of automobile travel is that it appears to be quite cheap. The capital expenditure involved in the purchase of an automobile is likely to be large, but having incurred this outlay, the cost of additional increments of travel is comparatively small.
>
> (Wall 1971: 101)

The irony in 2005 is the £5 gallon of petrol in the UK, but this has not constrained the recreational or tourist use of the car for pleasure travel. The car remains convenient and flexible, and adds a degree of readily available mobility which is not constrained by public transport timetables. Probably the greatest constraint for the car is in accommodating the space demand in relation to recreational and tourist routeways in coastal environments (i.e. parking space). There is also growing evidence from the public sector of pressure in some coastal environments to exclude the car from certain areas. The car may reduce what the geographer terms 'the friction of distance', making coastal environments attractive and accessible to urban-dwellers.

However, one has to place the coastal environment in the wider recreational and tourist context of participation levels. Patmore (1971: 76–7) aptly summarised this issue where 'The nearest seaside or open moorland may lure people from conurbations six times a year, while the local park is used every day to exercise the dog'. This hierarchy of tourism and leisure resources can often be overlooked.

Access to the coastal environment is a key term, though as Patmore (1971) argued it was a relative term, since improvements in transport routes and technology may directly change the nature of the access. The historical geographer's emphasis on the role of railway companies in Victorian Britain has identified their function in developing major visitor hinterlands for specific coastal resorts. Even some 150 years later, coastal resorts still have a limited reliance upon the rail network as a source of visitors, although the car is by far the most important mode of travel for recreational trips. The coastal environment and the routeways developed along coastlines, with viewing areas and a network of attractions, may also be a major recreational resource. For example, on the upper North Island of New Zealand, the collaboration between regional tourism organisations (see Page et al. 1999) created the Pacific Coastal Highway scenic drive. Not only did this utilise coastal routeways that receive comparatively limited traffic outside of the main summer season, but also it reduced congestion on other routeways between Auckland and the Bay of Islands. Geographers have also examined one other contentious element of movement in coastal environments: the use of recreational footpaths (Huxley 1970). These are a major routeway resource, a linear recreational resource that often transects a variety of other leisure resources, from the coastline to the built environment through to the countryside. Many countries contain dense networks of footpaths, with Patmore (1971) referring to an estimated 120,000 miles in England and Wales. The issue is contentious, especially in coastal environments where the coastline is adjacent to privately owned land, and access is carefully guarded. In England and

Wales, the designation of Heritage Coasts (Romeril 1988) has improved access issues and provided an opportunity for management agreements to be developed between private landowners and planners. As Keirle (2002) has shown in relation to Wales, coastal land should be considered as open countryside so that the public have right of access.

TOURIST AND RECREATIONAL BEHAVIOUR: USE AND ACTIVITY PATTERNS IN COASTAL ENVIRONMENTS

Among the influential studies by geographers from the 1970s were the development of a behavioural geography and its application to recreation and tourism, especially in relation to coastal environments. Mercer (1971a: 51) summarised the significance of the behavioural perspective where 'The values and attributes of any outdoor recreation site, whether a local neighbourhood park or major wilderness area are perceived somewhat differently by numerous sub-groups within society'. Mercer (1971a) outlined the recreationalists' decision-making process (subsequently modified by Pigram 1983) and the meaning attached to tourism and recreational experiences. Mercer's (1970) analysis of recreational trips to beaches in Melbourne highlighted the urban resident's vague notion of the outdoor recreational opportunities open to them. The role of image in choosing beach environments is an important factor, and may override concerns of overcrowding and even pollution. Perceived distance and accessibility are also important factors affecting recreational search behaviour, and may account for why certain coastal environments attract large crowds and others do not. In England and Wales, the coast is no more than 120 km away for the most inland population, and, building on the model by Pearce and Kirk (1986), it is evident that the coast contains a variety of recreational environments: the shore, beach and the marine environment (Orams 1999). Each resource is perceived in a variety of ways by different individuals and groups, and the potential for resource conflict is high unless research can harmonise the needs and wishes of multiple resource users.

There is also a need to understand fundamental differences in the user's perception of the developed coastal resort and the nature of the natural environment, such as the beach, sea and coastline, because as Patmore (1983: 209) remarked, 'the coast is the epitome of the wider problems of recreational use' of resources. The behaviour and activities of coastal tourists and recreationalists are therefore vital to understanding the nature of the problems and impacts which occur. The use of coastal environments is very much temporarily contingent on the availability of leisure time as holidays and free time at weekends. This led Patmore (1983: 158) to argue that 'on a day-to-day basis, holidaymakers' patterns of activities within the holiday area differ, but little from the use of day visitors. . . . Little attention, however, has been given to the sequence of those activities as the holiday progresses'. One of the seminal studies which addressed this topic was Cooper's (1981) analysis of holidaymaker patterns of behaviour in Jersey. As a laboratory for tourism research, Jersey offers many attractions, for it is almost a closed system with a limited number of resorts, attractions and defined tourist itineraries.

What Cooper (1981) observed was a spatial and temporal pattern of tourist use of the coastal environment and non-coastal resources. For example, the holiday begins at the tourist's accommodation to maximise uncertainty in visiting unknown places. As a result, at St Heliers (the location of two-thirds of the island's accommodation stock), 75 per cent of tourists surveyed spent their first day in the town. After that point, a growing spatial awareness of coastal resources developed, and the two most popular beaches (St Brelade's Bay and Gorey) were visited on days two and three. The touring of the island to derive spatial familiarity with the tourist resources also occurred on days two and three. As spatial knowledge of the island developed, smaller and lesser known recreational sites were visited. What Cooper's (1981) research highlighted was a wave pattern in visitation, as visitors' use of

resources (especially the use of the coastal environment) moved down the hierarchy, spreading to a wider distribution of sites. This reveals a classic geographical diffusion process and offers a great deal of advice for planners and coastal management.

D.G. Pearce (1988a) continued the interest in tourist behaviour using a time budget methodology in 1985 in Vanuatu (South Pacific) to extend Cooper's (1981) research on the tourists filtering down the hierarchy of sites. This behavioural research had an explicit spatial focus – patterns of tourist circulation. The problem with Pearce's (1988a) island-based study was the geographically constrained activity patterns of visitors, with resort hotels at Vila dominating the activities.

Probably one of the most interesting studies published by geographers was Tunstall and Penning-Rowsell's (1998) review of the English beach. As they observed,

> England's beaches and coasts have a special place in the nation's consciousness. A day at the English beach is a particularly notable experience, full of rituals, symbolism, nostalgia and myths. The holiday at the coast, or the day visit, brings special activities, enjoyment and memories that virtually no other recreational experience provides. The English beach, with its particular characteristics and contexts, holds special meanings for those it attracts, and creates experiences which have life-long echoes.
>
> (Tunstall and Penning-Rowsell 1998: 319)

In their analysis of the beach, they precisely identify it as the inter-tidal zone, the area which occurs above the high-watermark where beach material exists (i.e. sand, shingle and mud). The significance of the coast is epitomised in the UK Day Visits Survey, with over 137 million visits a year in England to rural areas, seaside resorts and the coastline. Cultural geographies of the beach and coastal environment (e.g. Shields 1991) mark the change, continuity and endurance of the beach as a social construction. In the post-war period, the English coastline has attracted a growing retirement migration (for an early analysis of this trend in the UK, see Cosgrove and Jackson 1972), increasing the recreational appeal of these environments. This is complemented by the rise of second home ownership in coastal locations (Coppock 1977a). Some coastal resorts have also sought to diversify their appeal, with the development of conference and convention business (Shaw and Williams 1997). What Tunstall and Penning-Rowsell (1998) recognised was that the coastal resort, and particularly the beach/sea-wall/promenade which protects the RBD from nature, is a costly infrastructure that needs ongoing investment.

Tunstall and Penning-Rowsell used a longitudinal research technique, focused on fifteen beaches in England over a decade, examining preferences towards beaches and protection methods to consider the values attached to beaches. A model of beach users' attitudes and values was developed to explain the factors which contribute to the values attached to beaches. The role of recreational constraints (i.e. time and income), frequency of visitation, cost of visit, tastes and values (i.e. subjective enjoyment value) and the values assigned to specific resorts and beaches were incorporated into the model. A range of popular and less popular beaches were examined with commercial resort towns and smaller towns. Each location had the potential to experience beach erosion problems. Among the main factors motivating beach visits to popular recreational sites were the cleanliness of the site, type of beach material available, the natural setting and familiarity with the site. In the case of undeveloped coasts such as Spurn Head (Humberside), the quietness and natural setting were important attractions. The convenience of access and a number of other factors were important (albeit in varying degrees according to the place visited) as pull factors, including

- the town and its facilities
- quality of the seafront promenade
- characteristics of the beach
- the coastal scenery
- scenery and places to visit in the hinterland
- suitability of the sea for swimming and paddling
- convenience of the journey
- cost of the trip.

(modified from Tunstall and
Penning-Rowsell 1998)

What Tunstall and Penning-Rowsell's (1998) study confirm is Patmore's (1983) earlier assertion on the diversity of coastal resources and reasons for visiting them. The coast, the sea, the seashore and landscape are all integral elements associated with the social, aesthetic and cultural meaning attached to the coast. However, 'There is considerable diversity in what attracted visitors to particular places but it is clear that seafront elements were more important at almost all locations than other aspects of the resort' (Tunstall and Penning-Rowsell 1998: 323). What detracted from visitation at specific sites were sewage, cleanliness, litter and the water-bathing quality, though as R. Morgan (1999) found, even the visitors' perception of these issues was complex to deconstruct and explain, since perception and behaviour were not necessarily rational and predictable.

In temporal and spatial terms, Tunstall and Penning-Rowsell (1998) found that beach visits not only are experienced differently but also have different meanings. This varied according to residents, day visitors and tourists. For residents, the beach was a local leisure resource, a regular and routine element of their everyday lives (similar to parks for urban-dwellers). For the day visitor, the beach was construed as a special event, an occurrence perhaps experienced only a couple of times a year. For holidaymakers, it is a special experience, but one often repeated with tourists who return to the same location year on year. What is culturally significant with a beach visit is the way in which it can enable the visitor to recollect childhood memories and a process repeated through time by families. It also marks a social occasion, with large proportions arriving by car as groups of two to four. In the summer season, beach visits are interconnected with families and young children. Even so, the beach readily accommodates solitary visitors, and in some locations up to one-third of users were unaccompanied. In this respect, the beach can function like a park with its ability to accommodate a multitude of users.

The amount of time spent at the beach varied by resort, with the majority of people spending less than four hours on the beach. It was typically between two and four hours in duration. Beach activities included a diversity of marine activities (sailboarding, jetskiing for a minority) through to a common range of activities including

- sitting/sunbathing/picnicking on the beach
- sitting/sunbathing/picnicking on the promenade
- swimming/paddling
- walking/strolling on the promenade/cliffs
- long walks of 3 km or more
- informal games or sports
- walking the dog
- playing with sand, stones and shells.

(modified from Tunstall and
Penning-Rowsell 1998)

This shows that while activities are important, so are relaxing and passive pastimes. This seminal study by Tunstall and Penning-Rowsell (1998: 330) recognised not only that 'English beaches are important to the English' but also that environmental concerns for pollution and the quality of the resource are important to recreationalists, tourists and residents alike. The following assessment by Tunstall and Penning-Rowsell (1998: 331) really encapsulates the wider meaning, significance and value of the beach.

The English seaside and its beaches are special because they are special places to play, to relax, to exercise or to enjoy. They bring back memories – mainly of families and childhood. They are places of discovery and adventure, and contact with nature. Their meanings come from these imaginings and these activities, and from the repeated visits to the same familiar and reassuring locales. Their beaches have a coherence that derives from their enduring physical character – waves, tides, sand and noise and from the assemblage of features that keeps them there: the sea-wall, the promenade and the groynes. Each is understood and valued, for its timelessness and familiarity.

A number of novel studies of beach behaviour by non-geographers have also been undertaken (Carr 1999) which explore the youth market and their behaviour within resorts (e.g. Ford and Eiser 1996), particularly the meaning and significance of the

beach and liminality. What Carr (1999) emphasised was that there were comparatively few gendered differences in leisure and tourism activities among visitors aged 18 to 24 years of age. In fact, these results appear to confirm the findings of Tunstall and Penning-Rowsell (1998), in that the resort and beach are major attractions for coastal tourism. Other studies published in non-geographical journals (e.g. R. Morgan et al. 1993) have also examined issues of perception among beach users, but the literature is increasingly scattered across a wide range of coastal-related journals which are not necessarily tourism- or recreation-related. However, R. Morgan's (1999) examination of beach rating systems for tourist beaches highlighted the contribution which coastal researchers can make to understanding the perception of beach users. By using beach awards, such as the European Blue Flag (UNEP/WTO 1996; Mihalic 2002), the Seaside Award and Good Beach Guide (Marine Conservation Society 1998), there are indications of a growing interest in the promotion of beach tourism in relation to quality measures (A.M. Williams and Morgan 1995). Even so, poor public knowledge of these rating schemes and their significance, even though in the EU the number of Blue Flag beaches increased from 1454 in 1994 to 1927 in 19 countries in 1998. Morgan (1999)

Plate 8.2: Denarau Island, Fiji. Modifying a mangrove swamp to build a resort complex has meant that erosion measures are necessary now the ecosystem has been changed.

assessed 70 beaches in Wales and concluded that beaches are different, with users having different preferences in line with Tunstall and Penning-Rowsell's (1998) study. Many of these issues have also been examined in the context of Ireland and Portugal, where beaches were valued in different ways with cultural and climactic factors influential in attitudes to beach use (MacLeod et al. 2002).

ENVIRONMENTAL PERSPECTIVES ON COASTAL RECREATION AND TOURISM

The environment for coastal leisure pursuits has seen the geographer make a number of influential contributions from a range of perspectives. In the early analysis of the coastline for tourism and recreation, Cosgrove and Jackson (1972) identified the vital characteristic which makes the coast a major focal point for geographical analysis: it is a zonal resource, with activities concentrated at specific places, making management a key issue in time and space. Although the coast may have a number of different resource designations (e.g. Heritage Coastline and Area of Outstanding Natural Beauty in England and Wales), the impacts of tourism and recreation are multifaceted. In the wide-ranging study by the German Federal Agency for Nature Conservation (1997), the dominant coastline regions globally were the Mediterranean, the Caribbean, the Gulf of Mexico, the Indian Ocean islands, Australasia and the Pacific islands. In this context, the coastal resource is a global environmental issue which is complex, diverse and not simply reduced to beach resorts, as the discussion has alluded so far. (See Visser and Njunga's (1992) examination of the Kenyan coastline where the ecological diversity in the coastal environment comprises coral reefs, sea grass and seaweed beds, mangrove forests, sand-dunes and inland tropical forests.)

According to the German Federal Agency for Nature Conservation (1997), coastal tourism environments may be categorised as follows:

- oceanic islands
- coral reefs
- offshore waters
- mangroves
- near-coastal wetlands
- sandy beaches
- coastal dunes.

In terms of the environments under the greatest recreational and tourism pressure are sandy beaches followed by coastal dunes (see Nordstom et al. 2000 for a review of management practices to restore dunes). Within a European context, the principal erosion and sedimentation processes affecting coastal environments are related to natural processes including

- wave and tidal action
- geomorphological factors (e.g. rivers which impact upon the river mouth and deltas)
- meteorological factors (e.g. wind and storms)
- changes in sea-level
- geological processes (e.g. seismic and volcanic activity).

In addition, the European coastline is also subjected to a great number of environmental stresses, to the point where some researchers consider it to be under the greatest pressure of any coastal environment globally (German Federal Agency for Nature Conservation 1997). As a consequence, the pressures from the natural environment are being compounded by

- large-scale pollution by oil spills
- the development of harbours
- increasing shore erosion caused by sediment processes are interrupted by building on the coastline (Gössling 2001)
- high levels of freshwater removal which is causing salt-water to encroach upon the water-table
- increasing impacts from tourism and recreational activities: approximately 100 million tourists visit the European coastline annually, a figure which could rise to 230 million by 2030.

Some of the visible signs of environmental deterioration include water pollution and the rise of algal blooms. This problem is exacerbated by sewage pollutants (see Daby et al. 2002) where nutrient enrichment leads to algal blooms. In the Mediterranean between 1900 and 1990 there was a 75 per cent loss of sand dunes in France and Spain due to sand loss. As A.T. Williams et al. (2001) suggest, visitor pressure increases dune degradation and vulnerability highlighting the need for close monitoring of impacts and changes in dune morphology. This is a clear indication of the scale of the problem in relation to tourism which is sand and beach dependent. How has the geographer contributed to the wider understanding, analysis and debates associated with coastal environments for recreation and tourism?

The physical geographer (e.g. May 1993) has examined the geomorphological characteristics which underlie the creation of existing coastal environments. In the case of the Cape coastline in South Africa, Burns et al. (1990) indicated the need to develop tourism according to sound environmental principles. They argued that the physical characteristics of soft shorelines need to be recognised, and near-shore and aeolian sediment transport regimes must be understood and quantified. This highlighted the active nature of the littoral zone of coastlines, so that long-term shore erosion can be reduced to create recreational environments. What emerges from much of the literature on beach erosion, particularly dune erosion, is that intervention is a costly strategy. In the case of Florida, 'there has been a tendency to build so close to the shoreline as possible: Florida is no exception. Such actions have destroyed dunes, wetlands and beaches which formed protective barriers against storms and floods' (Carter 1990: 8). In an historical analysis of coastline destruction in Florida, Carter (1990) examined the speed of environmental degradation where

> The first shoreline buildings were beach houses in the dunes. Very often the seawardmost dunes were lowered or removed altogether to give a view of the sea. Very soon, house owners became aware of shoreline changes, especially natural erosion, and began to

protect against it. Much of this protection was unapproved, unsightly and ineffective. Along the east coast, bulkheads and groynes were common after 1925, yet by the mid 1930s, much of the duneline was destroyed. . . . It quickly became clear that such an approach was exacerbating erosion, and there was mounting pressure for official assistance . . . Florida became a natural laboratory for shore protection devices, including inlet bypassing and back-passing, beach nourishment and diverse species of revetments, breakwaters and groynes. . . . Not all were successful.
> (Carter 1990: 8–9)

What emerged from Carter's (1990) study was that by the 1980s, of the 870 km of Florida's coastline, 40 per cent of the coastline with sand dunes was under threat, which also affected roads, houses and other development. Much of the impact is recreation and tourism-related, since in areas where no recreation occurs, no erosion exists. In the case of Denmark, Nielsen (1990) examined the positive enhancement of the environment with the creation of Koege Bay Beach Park in 1980 to meet the recreational needs of the Greater Copenhagen area. Using land reclamation methods, including extensive beach nourishment, a new beach environment was created. Some 5 million cubic metres of sand were used, dredged from lagoon areas and a 20 m wide dyke was built of sand to a height of 3 m above sea-level. Various environmental management measures were needed, including sluices for the lagoon environment to prevent stagnant water. A programme of planting on the dunes was also implemented to stabilise the resource. By developing the beach park to fit the underlying geomorphology, it represents a good example of an attempt to develop a sustainable leisure resource although it is not without environmental effects. However, the time frame is too short at this stage to observe long-term consequences and impacts or to assess the extent to which it is a truly sustainable resource. What is clear is that where significant demand exists in close proximity to an urban population, the creation of a local resource may act as a honeypot and attract a significant number of visitors, taking pressure off other sites.

What Nielsen (1990) identified was the close involvement in physical geographers' monitoring and evaluation of coastal processes to understand how the coastal geomorphology will respond to such a radical change – the creation of a new recreational environment. In a detailed coastal geomorphological study of the German coastline, Kelletat (1993) documented the major beach nourishment needed for islands along the German North Sea coast. This was due to tourism, recreation and storms. However, in a study of Sylt Island, the growth of tourism has also provided the impetus and funding for coastal tourism on islands of the German North Sea coast (Kelletat 1993).

A range of other studies (e.g. D.G. Pearce 1988a; Carter et al. 1990; McDowell et al. 1990) have also documented the recreation, the production of coastal recreation strategies and coastal management plans to co-ordinate decision-making in the coastal zone. The diverse range of interest groups associated with coastal environments highlights the complexity of developing management plans where collaboration, communication and management solutions are introduced to control tourist and recreational use.

One related aspect of the geographers' interest in the coastal environment has been the development of resorts and planning measures to manage these physical impacts. In a conceptual context, the dynamics of resort development and change have hinged on the Butler (1980) model, and subsequent criticisms (e.g. Cooper and Jackson 1989; Cooper 1990) and concerns with the post-stagnation phase (Agarwal 1994; Priestley and Mundet 1998). This distinguishes between the land use and physical planning and management measures needed for the coastal environment and strategic planning measures needed to ensure the long-term prosperity, viability and development of the resort. The concern with land use and planning measures has been well documented in Inskeep (1994) and D.G. Pearce (1989, 1995b) with specific examples of planning measures implemented in resort development documented by Meyer-Arendt (1990) and P.P. Wong (1986, 1990). In a detailed study by Penning-Rowsell et al. (1992), the economic cost of coastal protection schemes for recreation and

Plate 8.3: Sidmouth, England. Beach erosion protection.

other purposes and various valuation techniques were reviewed.

A synthesis of coastal recreation management was produced by Goodhead and Johnson (1996) where the planning issues affecting recreation and tourism activity in the marine environment were reviewed in a UK context. One approach developed to approach the management of coastal areas is integrated coastal zone management (ICZM) (Johnson 2002).

INTEGRATED COASTAL ZONE MANAGEMENT

As the DoE (1996) explained, ICZM is 'the process which brings together all those involved in the development, management and use of the coast within a framework which facilitates the integration of their interests and responsibilities to achieve common objectives', a feature reiterated by the European Commission (1997). This reflects the increased demands placed on coastal resources for recreation and tourism use. ICZM is underpinned by the need for beach management, where a well-planned beach layout with effective spatial zoning and development can accommodate increased opportunities for recreation (see Micallel and Williams 2002). This can also lead to reduced maintenance costs, more clearly articulated strategies for coastal defence and conservation and improved bathing water quality.

In a more strategic context, ICZM is based upon the need to integrate environmental considerations with coastal tourism policies and plans. This can assist in integrating key decisions on the carrying capacity of specific beach sites, the necessary management plans for specific sites and zones as a means of integrating a diverse range of planning policies and stakeholder needs. It may also assist in achieving a sustainable balance between recreational use and nature conservation, so that conflicts associated with achieving a consensus on appropriate recreational uses (see Roe and Benson 2001 for the example of jetski use and conflict resolution in coastal areas) can be progresses. Here, core or activity centre locations for active water sports is one option in zoning informal and formal/active recreational activities. As Roe and Benson (2001) argue:

> zoning in time and space is a well-established method of recreational management. It has been recommended for coastal zone management . . . as has the reduction of the levels of activity in particular areas through the provision of alternative sites. It is, however, understood that by itself, zoning is unlikely to prevent the emergence of problems. Time zoning allows a particular activity access to a stretch of water between specified time limits on a voluntary basis.
>
> (Roe and Benson 2001: 32)

Yet such a system is often ineffective due to irregular loss of waterspace in tidal areas and ineffective sanctions for non-compliance. In some instances the use of by-laws may help in the enforcement of zoning strategies. This requires education strategies and cooperation with formal clubs (e.g. sport clubs).

One interesting development in Maine, USA was the introduction of a volunteer programme to help monitor the shoreline change with scientists from the University of Maine to understand the changes induced by anthropogenic effects, sea-level changes and changing mechanism of erosion (Hill et al. 2002). A series of articles published in 2003 in the *Journal of Sustainable Tourism* (vol. 11 (2/3): 95–294) also provides a range of examples of

progress towards sustainable coastal management for tourism and the need to involve the local community in ICZM (see Caffyn and Jobbins 2003). One immediate problem facing policy-makers and planners in relation to the implementation of ICZM is the challenge posed by climate change (Gössling 2002; WTO 2003; Gössling and Hall 2005; Hall and Higham 2005), particularly for small island states which have a dependence upon coastal locations for inbound tourism. However, the impacts of climate change are not necessarily negative for tourism in all coastal regions. For example, in a report on the implications of a warming Arctic, it was noted that because of the decline of sea ice, tourism related shipping through key marine routes, including the Northern Sea Route and the Northwest Passage, is likely to increase (Arctic Climate Impact Assessment 2004).

As Johnson (2002) has shown in the UK, there are a number of instances of urban coastal resorts pursuing regeneration projects, reflecting the fact that 'The UK coastline is an example of a natural resource that has been used and abused for many years' (Johnson 2002: 177). Much of the leadership is from the local government sector but sustainability ideas are the antithesis of the resort development models which many mass tourism destinations in the UK and Europe have promoted, often driven by private sector interests. Although not developed by geographers, ICZM offers a useful range of perspectives on the planning process for marine and coastal areas in relation to land use and the different needs of stakeholders. Yet one also has to be cognisant of the fact that the coast, the beach and the resort are major cultural icons in a postmodern society, retaining much of their value, meaning and significance from previous eras. In this context, the experience of the coast, the beach, the resort and of the place are socially and culturally conditioned. There is a continuity in the transmission and formation of values of the beach and coast which may help to explain the ongoing love affair the recreationalist and tourist has with such special 'places'. In historical terms, the resort morphology, rules, meanings and behaviour embodied in the coastal environment have changed in line with what society will tolerate, condone and legiti- mate. But these special, highly valued, natural and human-made environments remain central to the recreational and tourist experience of leisure places and space. For most social groups, the coastline is a social leveller, a free resource to be enjoyed and consumed according to the vagaries of the season and weather.

INSIGHT: Cruise tourism

Cruise tourism has become significant for a number of ports because cruise tourists are higher yield tourists, spending, on average, much higher amounts per day than other categories of inter- national tourists (Dwyer and Forsyth 1996, 1998; Ritter and Schafer 1999; Kester 2003). In 2000 worldwide cruise passenger volumes reached 10.4 million (up from 8.4 million in 1998) and in North America reached 6.9 million in 2000 up from 5.5 million in 1998 (Environmental Planning Group of Canada (EPGC) 2002; Economic Development and Tourism Department (EDTD) 2003). Interestingly, the North American cruise ship industry was not negatively affected by terrorism concerns, registering 7.2 per cent growth to 7.4 million passengers in 2002 (EDTD 2003). There is substantial competition for the cruise ship market in various parts of the world, particularly because it tends to be highly seasonal in nature. For example, in the summer of 2001 48 per cent of visitors to Alaska arrived by cruise ship (49 per cent by air). In comparison about 7 per cent of visitors to Newfoundland in 2001 were cruise visitors (EPGC 2002).

In a study of cruise tourism in Australia, Dwyer and Forsyth (1996) reported that home-porting cruise ships in Australia, with a marketing empha- sis on fly-cruise packages for inbound tourists, had the greatest potential for generating large expenditure inflows to Australia. In addition, they reported that because of leakages due to foreign ownership and foreign sourcing of inputs, the average expenditure per passenger per cruise injected into the Australian economy is twice as great for the coastal as opposed to the inter- national cruise.

Because of the overall growth in the cruise ship market, partly allied to ageing populations in developed countries, greater numbers of retirees and security concerns, a number of coastal destinations are aggressively competing for cruise ship visitation. For example, in the case of Newfoundland, 'Cruise was seen as having long-term growth potential, and is appealing since cruise visitors return for conventional vacations' (EPGC 2002: 49). However, in an evaluation of potential activity markets, 'The cruise potential rated lowest as it is the cruise lines, not the destination, that develops the market, although the cruise lines like to see marketing support for their efforts, particularly destination aware- ness marketing support' (EPGC 2002: 60). Nevertheless, the provincial capital, the City of St John's, has placed substantial emphasis on developing the cruise market and has developed a public–private partnership in order to attract more cruise ships. Traditionally, cruise lines utilised St John's as a stopover port of call for their small to mid-sized vessels. However, since the late 1990s the economic value of the cruise industry has been fuelled by both the increased efforts placed on home-porting vessels out of St John's and the widening of the navigation channel to St John's Harbour to accommodate the newer and larger vessels in the marketplace.

In a study of the economic impact of the cruise ship industry in St John's it was reported that the cruise market was the fastest growing sector of the St. John's tourism industry, growing an average of 38 per cent per year between 1995 and 2002. Over this time period the number of passengers has grown 868 per cent from 1259 in 1995 to 12,191 in 2002. The economic impact of the cruise sector increased 25 per cent to Can.$1.73 million in 2002; Can.$1,435,931 (83 per cent) of the industry expenditures was derived from the in-transit market while the remaining Can.$293,736 (17 per cent) was obtained through the turnaround/home-porting market. Although the in-transit market was the most lucrative market in terms of total visitors and total economic impacts, the economic benefit per passenger was much higher for the home-porting market (Can.$699.37) than it was for the in-transit market (Can.$123.60). The overall economic benefit per passenger for both markets combined was Can.$143.68 (EDTD 2003).

Nevertheless, there is significant debate over the impacts of cruise ships. Ritter and Schafer (1999), for example, argue that the ecological impact of cruises is low, spending by individual tourists high, and accultural processes minimal, and claim that although the number of jobs directly created as a result of cruises is low, it compares very favourably against most other forms of travel as a sustainable development option. In contrast, Marsh and Staple (1995) in a study of cruise tourism in the Canadian Arctic concluded that given the environmental fragility of much of the region and the vulnerability of

small, remote, largely aboriginal communities to impact, great care should be exercised in using the area for cruise tourism. Similarly, in examining some of the cultural dimensions of the cruise ship experience, Wood (2000) argued that the global nature of the cruise market has meant that cruise ships have become examples of 'globalisation at sea' with corresponding deterritorialisation, cultural theming and simulation. In addition, concern over the environmental impacts of cruise ships led the United States Environmental Protection Agency (EPA) to host a series of meetings in 2000 to solicit input from the public, the cruise ship industry and other stakeholders on the issue of discharges from cruise ships. These meetings were part of an information-gathering effort on the part of the agency to prepare an in-depth assessment of environmental impacts and existing and potential measures to abate impacts from these discharges. Cruise discharges are currently regulated through a combination of domestic and international pollution prevention laws and the EPA was assessing whether these laws adequately protect the environment and whether there are gaps in coverage or in application of these laws which may pose a risk to the environment (Rethinking Tourism Project 2000).

Plate 8.4: Victoria Harbour, British Columbia, Canada, serves as a base for marine tourism operations as well as private vessels, ferries, cruise ships and float planes.

CONCLUSION

The coastal environment has been neglected in one sense by the geographer, where recreational and tourism activity have not been understood in the wide context of the resource, its use, impacts and planning needs. The development of studies such as Tunstall and Penning-Rowsell (1998), has re-established geographers' major contributions to the analysis of coastal recreation and tourism, building on seminal studies by Fabbri (1990) and P.P. Wong (1993b). Yet even these are not cited as mainstream studies or recognised for their synthe-sising role in bringing together different disciplines to disseminate a diverse and rich range of experi-ence and knowledge of coastal processes, impacts, applied research and concerns about the leisure use of fragile coastal environments. The coastline needs to be moved higher up the geographer's research agenda in tourism and recreation, reiterating Patmore's (1983) criticism of the comparative neglect of this issue. Given the value and significance attached to the beach and coast observed by Tunstall and Penning-Rowsell (1998), it is evident that the coast is a major recreational environment. The association with resorts and the geographer's preoccupation with resort models and development should arguably be directed to a fuller understanding of the impact of human beings on the coastal environment, particularly the interference with coastal processes and the resulting measures needed to redress the consequences for the coastal environment.

There is no doubt that the coastal environment is facing a wide range of environmental pressures not least of which is the intensity of use. This, combined with environmental impacts from human activity, poses many severe planning problems for one simple reason: the scale and rate of change associated with coastal processes (e.g. erosion) are rapid, as the examples provided by R. Carter (1990) and Kelletat (1993) have shown. This requires costly remedial action, particularly in the case of beach nourishment and in coastal protection schemes where the natural environment is directly altered by tourist and recreational development.

Given the potential impacts of tourism on the coastal environment, it is therefore not surprising that organisations such as ESCAP (1995a, 1995b) have been trying to encourage sustainable forms of coastal development in Asia and the Pacific. Sustainable development of coastal tourism is recognised as being dependent on

- good coastal management practices (particularly regarding proper siting of tourism infrastructure and the provision of public access)
- clean water and air, and healthy coastal ecosystems
- maintaining a safe and secure recreational environment through the management of coastal

hazards (such as erosion, storms, floods) and the provision of adequate levels of safety for boaters, swimmers and other water users
- beach restoration efforts that maintain the recreational and amenity values of beaches
- sound policies for wildlife and habitat protection.

(NOAA 1997)

However, such a statement, while laudable, fails to reflect the complexities and difficulties of the management and regulation of tourism with respect to the physical environment. Unfortunately, there is usually little or no co-ordination between programmes that promote and market tourism and those that aim to manage coastal and marine areas (R.A. Smith 1994; B. Hudson 1996). Environmental or planning agencies often fail to understand tourism, while tourism promotion authorities tend not to be involved with the evaluation of its effects or its planning and management. This particularly appears to be the case with some species of charismatic marine fauna although significant advances have been made with respect to whale watching management in some countries. Nevertheless, for many peripheral coastal destinations marine ecotourism (Garrod and Wilson 2003, 2004) and commercial recreational fishing would appear to be an appropriate development mechanism if it can be managed appropriately. Implementation strategies often fail to recognise the interconnections that exist between agencies in trying to manage environmental issues, particularly when, as in the case of the relationship between tourism and the environment, responsibilities may cut across more traditional lines of authority. Therefore, one of the greatest challenges facing coastal managers is how to integrate tourism development within the ambit of coastal management, and thus increase the likelihood of long-term sustainability of the coast as a whole (A. White et al. 1997; Cicin-Sain and Knecht 1998). Nevertheless, solving such dilemmas will clearly be of importance to many countries in the region which has substantial emphasis on marine and coastal tourism, particularly when environmental quality becomes another means to achieve a competitive edge in the tourism marketplace.

The coastal environment has a great deal of potential for the cultural and social geographer to explore the value and role of tourism and recreation in these leisure places. There is also a role for applied geographers to combine their skills with planners, to understand, explain and develop planning measures to safeguard these threatened environments. The coastal environment is one of the best examples where geographers can harness their ability to construct a holistic understanding of the human and physical environment in a coastal context, where the interactions, impacts and measures needed to ameliorate negative effects can be addressed. The period since 1970 has not, with a few notable exceptions, seen the geographical fraternity rise to this challenge and lead the coastal research agenda in a tourism and recreational context. One would hope, indeed expect, geographers to engage their skills, building on a long tradition of the geographer's involvement with the recreational and tourism use of the coast.

QUESTIONS

- Why is the coastline such a popular area for recreationalists and tourists globally?
- What techniques have geographers used to examine tourist use of the coastline, and how effective are they in explaining the motivation for such activities?
- What are the environmental problems associated with the coastal environment as a recreational and tourist resource?

- What are the planning and management measures which have been successful in reconciling the use of coastal environments with the need for preservation and recuperation of the resource base?

READING

For general overviews of marine and ocean tourism see

Garrod, B. and Wilson, J.C. (eds) (2003) *Marine Ecotourism: Issues and Experiences*, Clevedon: Channel View.
Orams, M. (1999) *Marine Tourism*, London: Routledge.

In terms of the environmental impact of tourism and recreational activities in coastal environments, see

Baldwin, J. (2000) 'Tourism development, wetland degradation and beach erosion in Antigua, West Indies', *Tourism Geographies*, 2(2): 193–218.
Fabbri, P. (ed.) (1990) *Recreational Uses of Coastal Areas: A Research Project of the Commission on the Coastal Environment*, Dordrecht: Kluwer.
German Federal Agency for Nature Conservation (ed.) (1997) *Biodiversity and Tourism: Conflicts on the World's Seacoasts and Strategies for their Solution*, Berlin: Springer.
Wong, P.P. (1999) 'Adaptive use of a rock coast for tourism – Mactan Island, Philippines', *Tourism Geographies*, 1(2): 226–43.

9

TOURISM AND RECREATION PLANNING AND POLICY

Geographers have long been interested in planning. Indeed, a number of academic departments combine geography and planning, while many geography students have gone on to specialise in planning as a professional career. Planning and the associated area of policy analysis are therefore substantive areas of applied geographical research, particularly as geographers have sought to make their work more relevant to the society in which they work (Johnston 1991).

It should therefore come as no surprise that tourism and recreation planning and policy have long been major areas of interest for geographers (Hall and Jenkins 1995, 2004; J. Jenkins 2001; Bramwell 2004; Church 2004; Gill 2004). This chapter examines the nature of recreation and tourism planning and policy and then goes on to discuss the contributions that geographers have made in these fields, particularly with respect to the role of planning and policy at a regional or destination level. More specific applications in recreational and tourism planning have been introduced in earlier chapters and so this chapter discusses many of the principles, concepts and geographical contributions to the field as a whole.

RECREATION PLANNING POLICY

According to Henry and Spink (1990), the

> treatment of leisure planning in the literature can be described as unsystematic and fragmented. At the outset it is important to make the distinction between the organisational planning which commercial bodies

in leisure and recreation conduct, and statutory planning which the public sector undertake, where the public good is normally the underlying rationale (Jenkins 2000). The public sector is often charged with the management and maintenance of facilities, locational issues and wider strategic goals for the population.

> (Henry and Spink 1990: 33)

To understand the evolution of recreation planning and the role of public sector agencies, it is useful to briefly examine the historical context.

THE EVOLUTION OF LEISURE AND RECREATION PLANNING

In many industrialising nations, the nineteenth century saw the intervention by philanthropists and reformers to address the squalor and living conditions of the working population, embodied in government legislation. Environmental improvement was predicated on the notion that it had a positive effect on the human condition. This shaped government legislation where a wide range of utopian, humanitarian and determinist attitudes (see D. Taylor 1999) were reflected in the debates on improvement. In the UK, the Housing and Town Planning Act 1909 highlighted the need for government intervention to generate more socially appropriate forms of land use which market forces would not address (i.e. public open space). In the period after 1800, and the UK planning acts of 1909, 1919, 1932, 1947, 1968, 1980, 1986 shaped the subsequent role of the state in town and planning in relation to leisure, where political ideology shaped the nature of state intervention in the UK. In a rural context, the Countryside Act 1968 established a network of country parks, picnic sites, nature trails and bird sanctuaries. This was accompanied by the state's division of planning powers into two levels of local government: structure plans came under county and regional authorities, with a view to a ten- to twenty-year time frame and framework for local plans which were the responsibility of district authorities. Despite subsequent modifications in the 1980s and 1990s in the 'retreat from state planning', these two levels of planning remain. They can also be discerned in many other countries. Much of their concern has been with land use planning and site-specific planning for recreation, since this has been the public sector concern: the ordering of leisure space and provision through time.

RECREATION PLANNING: THE CONCERN WITH SPACE AND PLACE

According to Pigram and Jenkins (1999: 270), 'In the planning of recreation space, the aim should be to provide a range of functional and aesthetically pleasing environments for outdoor recreation, which avoid the friction of unplanned development, without lapsing into uniformity and predictability'. Since people decide on recreation participation as a discretionary use of time and on a voluntary basis, planning is beset by a wide range of factors that need to be considered. One of the most persuasive issues is the trends and tastes in leisure and outdoor recreation. Here the problem is in matching potential demand to the supply of recreation space, while a growing sophistication among recreation users means issues such as quality and satisfaction are also important in public sector provision.

There is also a temporal and cyclical factor which is often overlooked, namely that in times of economic downturn, recreation assumes a new dimension in the amelioration of hardship (Glyptis 1989b). At the same time, such economic stringen-

cies may also put the public sector under increased pressure in terms of its priorities for resource allocation (i.e. what is the opportunity cost of additional expenditure on leisure provision). At the local planning level, different local authorities will have varying levels of commitment to recreation provision, which will also vary according to the political persuasion of the elected politicians that varies in time and space.

Against this background, planners need to understand societal changes, namely demographic trends, lifestyle changes (see the early study by Havighurst and Feigenbaum 1959), social attitudes to recreation and the increasing demands of ethnic groups (Floyd 1998; Johnson et al. 1998), people with disabilities and other minority groups to achieve equity goals in local planning for leisure (Shinew and Arnold 1998). In many countries, notably the USA, Canada, New Zealand, Britain and Australia, issues of cultural pluralism and a multicultural population pose new challenges to conventional notions of recreation planning. Probably one of the greatest technological innovations that now exist to assist planners in integrating these new perspectives into social and land use planning is GIS. It enables planners to spatially integrate the demand and supply of recreation and to evaluate possible locational issues and outcomes. This is also invaluable in modelling resource degradation (see Bahaire and Elliott-White 1999 for more detail). In essence, GIS operates on spatial data which have a standard geographical frame of reference. It also utilises attribute data, which are statistical and non-locational. GIS allows planners to link planning goals to basic geographical issues such as location, trends through time, patterns at specific points in time and an ability to model issues such as recreational impacts (see Briggs and Tantrum (1997) for specific recreational applications and Kliskey and Kearsley (1993) for an application to wilderness perception mapping in New Zealand; also see the case study on wilderness inventories in Australia in Chapter 8).

Pigram and Jenkins (1999) argued that a more strategic approach to recreation planning is needed but much of the existing practice of planning is concerned with geographical issues of the availability of recreational opportunities, the location of services and facilities. Although recreation planning should be a complex process, its application in the public sector often remains a simplistic activity, focused on the provision of specific facilities rather than the wider context of recreation opportunity, desire and provision. According to G.M. Robinson (1999), eight approaches to planning for leisure may be discerned and a number of them utilise spatial principles (see Table 9.1). Even in seemingly advanced recreational contexts such as the Netherlands with an enviable reputation for recreation planning, Dietvorst (1993: 84) argued that 'During the 1980s it was realised that public tastes had changed and that the amenities for outdoor recreation in many ways no longer satisfied demand'. This reflected the changing policy framework which saw a convergence of interest towards recreation and tourism with common goals in terms of provision (Jansen-Verbeke and Dietvorst 1987). Indeed, Dietvorst (1993) criticised the strong normative planning framework prevailing in the Netherlands as not offering flexible and market-oriented forms of outdoor recreation. What is clear is that the state, its agencies (e.g. the newly amalgamated Countryside Agency in the UK) (see Coalter 1990 for more detail on agencies) have a wide remit for the management and planning of outdoor recreation resources given the diversity and extent of recreational environments (Figure 9.1), while the statutory planning framework is based on the twin goals of development plans and development control (Ravenscroft 1992). Even so, Ravenscroft (1992) concluded that

> the whole framework upon which planning has been predicated has, for the most part, tended to neglect recreation. By largely basing development plans on land use zoning, it has tended to subjugate multiple uses in favour of primary ones. . . . This means that

Table 9.1: Approaches to planning for leisure

Approach	Content
Standards	Planning based on per capita specifications of levels of provision laid down by some authoritative body. Usually based on demand estimates.
Gross demand	Estimation of broad demand levels based on existing national or regional participation surveys. This is the most basic of demand estimation approaches but can be varied to consider local socio-demographic conditions.
Spatial approaches	Localised demand estimation incorporating consideration of facility catchment areas. This extends the gross demand approach when considering the question of facility location.
Hierarchies of facilities	Recognises that different types and scales of facility have different catchment areas. Especially relevant for planning new communities and for facilities involving spectator audiences.
Grid or matrix approach	Examines impacts of all of an authority's leisure services on all social groups via impact evaluation.
Organic approach	Strategy development based on assessment of existing service provision and spatial gaps in demand. It is incremental rather than comprehensive and is common within the private sector.
Community development approach	Planning and policy development based on community consultation
Issues approach	Plans based on initial identification of 'key issues' rather than comprehensive needs/demand assessment. Corresponds to SWOT (strengths, weaknesses, opportunities, threats) analysis. Most common for ad-hoc, one-off projects.

Sources: based on Veal (1994: 92–3, in G. M. Robinson 1999: 260)

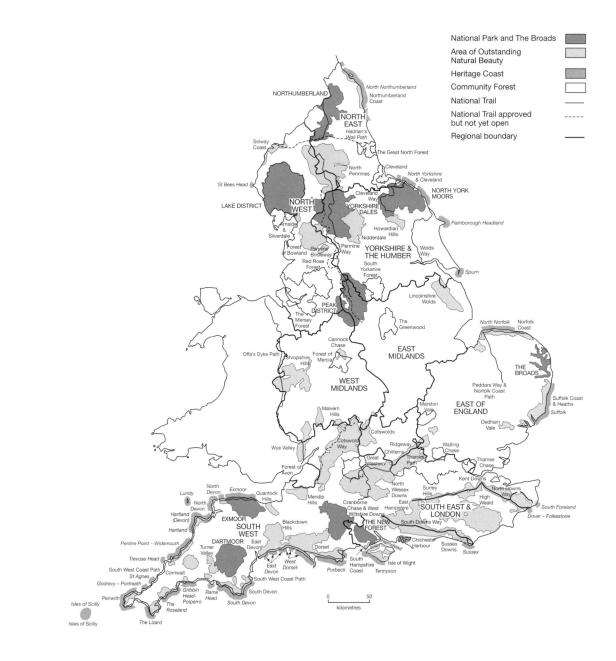

Figure 9.1: The Countryside Agency's designated and defined interests

in areas where provision for recreation is seen as important, such as National Parks, primary uses such as agriculture and forestry still dominate . . . [and] the reactive nature of the planning process means that opportunities to secure recreation provision are not taken up.

(Ravenscroft 1992: 135)

In fact, the political processes associated with local authority recreation planning and issues such as planning gain are increasingly being used by developers as betterment payments for the right to develop, making recreation and community benefit a tool to exercise leverage on planning applications.

TOURISM PLANNING AND POLICY

The partially industrialised nature of tourism means that tourism, like the environment, should be regarded as a meta-problem which represents highly interconnected planning and policy 'messes' (Ackoff 1974) which cut across fields of expertise and administrative boundaries and, seemingly, become connected with almost everything else. Tourism, therefore, 'is merely an acute instance of the central problem of society' (P. Hall 1992: 249) of creating a sense of the whole which can then be effectively planned and managed. Nevertheless, planning for tourism is still regarded as important because its effects are so substantial and potentially long-standing. Indeed, concern with making tourism, along with all development, sustainable has provided an even greater imperative for developing relevant tourism planning frameworks (C.M. Hall 2000a). Yet despite use by tourism researchers of the evolving network paradigm in management literature (e.g. Selin 1993, 1998; Selin and Chavez 1994; Jamal and Getz 1995; Buhalis and Cooper 1998) there has been, given the central role of government in tourism promotion and development, surprisingly little reference to the wider planning public policy literature which analyses what has been, until recently, a 'neglected' aspect of contemporary administration and policy-making (O'Toole 1997).

Planning for tourism has traditionally focused on land use zoning, site development, accommodation and building regulations, the density of tourist development, the presentation of cultural, historical and natural tourist features, and the provision of infrastructure including roads and sewage (Getz 1987). However, in recent years, tourism planning has adapted and expanded to include broader environmental and socio-cultural concerns, and the need to develop and promote economic development strategies at local, regional and national scales, particularly within an increasingly globalised tourism environment (Hall 2000a).

The diverse nature of recreation and tourism has meant that the industry is difficult for policy-makers and planners to define and grasp conceptually. This has meant that there have been substantial difficulties for policy-makers to develop appropriate policies, while the coordination of the various elements of the recreation and tourism product has been extremely difficult (Hall 1994; Hall and Jenkins 1995). Yet, somewhat paradoxically, it is the very nature of the industry, particularly the way in which local communities, their culture and lifestyles, and the environment are part of the broad leisure product which makes planning so important (Murphy 1985) and, perhaps, academically appealing (Hall et al. 1997).

Planning and policy-making are 'filtered through a complex institutional framework' (Brooks 1993: 79). However, the institutional arrangements for tourism have received little attention in the tourism literature (D.G. Pearce 1992b; Hall and Jenkins 1995; Hall 2000a). Institutions may be thought of as a set of rules which may be explicit and formalised (e.g. constitutions, statutes and regulations) or implicit and informal (e.g. organisational culture, rules governing personal networks and family relationships). Thus institutions are an entity devised to order interrelationships between individuals or groups of individuals by influencing their behaviour. As a concept and as an aspect of tourism policy-making, institutions cast a wide net; they are extensive and pervasive forces in the tourism policy system (J. Jenkins 2000). In a broad context, O'Riordan (1971) observed that:

One of the least touched upon, but possibly one of
the most fundamental, research needs in resource
management [and indeed, tourism management] is the
analysis of how institutional arrangements are formed,
and how they evolve in response to changing needs and
the existence of internal and external stress. There is
growing evidence to suggest that the form, structure
and operational guidelines by which resource management institutions are formed and evolve clearly affect
the implementation of resource policy, both as to the
range of choice adopted and the decision attitudes of
the personnel involved.

(O'Riordan 1971: 135)

Institutions therefore 'place constraints on decision-
makers and help shape outcomes . . . by making
some solutions harder, rather than by suggesting
positive alternatives' (Simeon 1976: 574). As the
number of checkpoints for policy increase, so too
does the potential for bargaining and negotiation.
In the longer term, 'institutional arrangements may
themselves be seen as policies which, by building
in to the decision process the need to consult
particular groups and follow particular procedures,
increase the likelihood of some kinds of decisions
and reduces that of others' (Simeon 1976: 575).
For example, new government departments may
be established as part of the growth in the activity
and influence of government, particularly as new
demands, such as environmental concerns, reach a
high priority on the political agenda.

The setting up of entirely new government departments, advisory bodies or sections within the existing
administration is a well established strategy on the part
of governments for demonstrating loudly and clearly
that 'something positive is being done' with respect to
a given problem. Moreover, because public service
bureaucracies are inherently conservative in terms of
their approach to problem delineation and favoured
mode of functioning . . . administrative restructuring,
together with the associated legislation, is almost
always a significant indicator of public pressure for
action and change.

(Mercer 1979b: 107)

The implications of the structure and nature of the
tourist industry are not merely academic as it is
difficult for government to develop policies and
design institutions for a policy area that is hard to

determine (J. Jenkins 1993; A.M. Williams and
Balaz 2000). Indeed, quality information concerning the tourist industry is relatively limited when
compared to the collection of information on other
industries and sectors of the economy. Hall and
Jenkins (1995) even hypothesise that there is an
element of inexperience in tourism policy formulation and implementation, as much government
activity in the tourist industry is relatively recent
when compared with other traditional concerns
of government, such as economics, manufacturing
and social welfare, and suggests that tourism public
policies are therefore likely to be ad hoc and incre-
mental. Indeed, Hall (2000a) in a review of the role
of government in New Zealand tourism identified
three government agencies with primary responsibilities with respect to tourism policy and over
thirty agencies with secondary responsibilities, with
there typically being very little formal tourism
policy co-ordination between the various agencies.
Such a situation though should not be surprising,
since the nature of tourism means that it cuts
across a range of government responsibilities
which make policy and planning co-ordination
inherently difficult unless a lead agency is clearly
identified.

WHAT IS TOURISM PLANNING?

What is planning? 'Planning is a process, a process
of human thought and action based upon that
thought – in point of fact, forethought, thought for
the future – nothing more or less than this is planning, which is a very general human activity' (G.
Chadwick 1971: 24). Similarly, according to P.
Hall (1982a: 303), planning 'should aim to provide
a resource for democratic and informed decision-
making. This is all planning can legitimately do,
and all it can pretend to do. Properly understood,
this is the real message of the systems revolution in
planning and its aftermath'. P. Hall's (1982a) observation reflects Johnston's (1991: 209) comment
that underlying the geographer's involvement in
planning and policy is 'the basic thesis that geographers should be much more involved in the

creation and monitoring and policies', yet, as he went on to note, 'what sort of involvement?', a point discussed in Chapter 1.

As a general field of research, tourism planning has mirrored broader trends within the urban and regional planning traditions (e.g. Getz 1986a, 1987; C.M. Hall 2000a) primarily because it has been focused on destination planning rather than individual tourism business planning. Moreover, planning for tourism tends to reflect the economic, environmental and social goals of government and, increasingly, industry interests, at whichever level the planning process is being carried out (C.M. Hall et al. 1997).

Planning for tourism occurs in a number of forms (development, infrastructure, promotion and marketing), structures (different government and non-government organisations), scales (international, national, regional, local and sectoral) and times (different time scales for development, implementation and evaluation). However, planning is rarely exclusively devoted to tourism per se. Instead, planning for tourism tends to be 'an amalgam of economic, social and environmental considerations' which reflect the diversity of the factors which influence tourism development (Heeley 1981: 61). In contrast, recreational planning has assumed a more integrated form, being an integral part of most public sector planning schemes alongside other fundamental themes such as housing. As Chapter 5 demonstrates this is very evident in urban areas. In this respect, recreation is often a local need-based activity or a regional planning function to deal with the impacts, needs and effects of visitors on the host community. The contribution of recreation to quality of life issues in the local and visitor population, particularly in park, national park and natural areas, remains a well-developed planning activity as described by Patmore (1983) and contributions in Lavery (1971c) (also see Chapters 4 and 8 which note the contribution of geographers to natural area and wilderness planning activities). Therefore, recreational activity has emerged as largely a public sector exercise where geographers have not made major contributions to the methodology, activities

and actions associated with this concept. Where geographers have made major contributions, they have been in the area of policy in the 1970s (e.g. Coppock 1976; Patmore 1973) advising government on sport and recreation policy. For this reason, this chapter focuses on tourism, since recreational planning is more accepted as a public sector activity and geographers have made fewer lasting methodological or critical contributions to recreational planning and policy in the 1980s and 1990s. Furthermore, much of what is considered as tourism outside urban areas also subsumes recreational activity in natural and wilderness areas (see Chapter 7).

Tourism planning does not just refer specifically to tourism development and promotion, although these are certainly important. The focus and methods of tourism planning have evolved to meet the demands which been placed on government with respect to tourism. For example, international tourism policies among the developed nations may be divided into four distinct phases (Table 9.2). Of particular importance has been the increased direct involvement of government in regional development, environmental regulation and the marketing of tourism, although more recently there has been reduced direct government involvement in the supply of tourism infrastructure, greater emphasis on the development of public–private partnerships and industry self-regulation.

The attention of government to the potential economic benefits of tourism and recreation has provided the main driving force for tourism planning (Richards 1995; Charlton and Essex 1996). The result has often been 'top-down planning and promotion that leaves destination communities with little input or control over their own destinies' (Murphy 1985: 153). However, attention is gradually becoming focused on the need to integrate social and environmental concerns into the economic thrust of much tourism development (D.G. Pearce 1989; Timothy 2002). Tourism must be integrated within the wider planning processes in order to promote certain goals of economic, social and environmental enhancement or maximisation that may be achieved through appropriate tourism

Table 9.2: International tourism policies, 1945 to the present

Phase	Characteristics
1945–55	Dismantling and streamlining of the police, customs, currency and health regulations that had been put into place following the Second World War
1955–70	Greater government involvement in tourism marketing in order to increase tourism earning potential
1970–85	Government involvement in the supply of tourism infrastructure and in the use of tourism as a tool of regional development.
1985–2000	Continued use of tourism as a tool for regional development, increased focus on environmental issues, reduced direct government involvement in the supply of tourism infrastructure, greater emphasis on the development of public–private partnerships and industry self-regulation, and the development of tourism business networks to meet policy goals
2000 to present	Same as 1985–2000 but increasing growth of tourism as an intermistic political issue with focus by many subnational governments on place marketing and the creation of strategic sister-city linkages

Source: after Hall (1994, 2000a, 2005a)

development (Hall 1995). As Murphy (1985: 156) observed, 'planning is concerned with anticipating and regulating change in a system, to promote orderly development so as to increase the social, economic, and environmental benefits of the development process'. Therefore, tourism planning must be 'a process, based on research and evaluation, which seeks to optimize the potential contribution of tourism to human welfare and environmental quality' (Getz 1987: 3).

APPROACHES TO TOURISM PLANNING

Getz (1987) identified four broad traditions or approaches to tourism planning: 'boosterism', an economic, industry-oriented approach, a physical/spatial approach, and a community-oriented approach which emphasises the role the destination community plays in the tourism experience. As Getz (1987) noted:

> the four traditions are not mutually exclusive, nor are they necessarily sequential. Nevertheless, this categorisation is a convenient way to examine the different and sometimes overlapping ways in which tourism is planned, and the research and planning methods, problems and models associated with each.
>
> (Getz 1987: 5)

To these four approaches, Hall (1995) added a further approach, that of sustainable tourism plan-

ning. Table 9.3 provides a detailed overview of the components of each tourism planning approach. Different planning approaches, while not mutually exclusive, conceptualise tourism planning in distinct ways. Each perspective differs in its underlying assumptions about planning, problem definition, the appropriate level of analysis and research methods. Researchers therefore choose their perspective/s according to their profession, education, values, the organisational context within which they work, and the nature of the planning problem.

Boosterism is the simplistic attitude that tourism development is inherently good and of automatic benefit to the hosts. Residents of tourist destinations are not involved in the decision-making, planning and policy processes surrounding tourism development. According to Getz (1987):

> Boosterism is still practised, and always will be, by two groups of people: politicians who philosophically or pragmatically believe that economic growth is always to be promoted, and by others who will gain financially by tourism. They will go on promoting it until the evidence mounts that they have run out of resources to exploit, that the real or opportunity costs are too high, or that political opposition to growth can no longer be countered. By then the real damage has usually been done.
>
> (Getz 1987: 10)

In contrast, an economic planning approach towards tourism aims to promote growth and development in specific areas. The planning emphasis is on the

Table 9.3: Tourism planning approaches: assumptions, problem definition, methods and models

Planning tradition	Underlying assumptions and related attitudes	Definition of the tourism planning problem	Some examples of related methods	Some examples of related models
Boosterism	• tourism is inherently good • tourism should be developed • cultural and natural resources should be exploited • industry as expert • development defined in business/corporate terms	• how many tourists can be attracted and accommodated? • how can obstacles be overcome? • convincing hosts to be good to tourists	• promotion • public relations • advertising • growth targets	• demand forecasting models
Economic	• tourism equal to other industries • use tourism to create employment, earn foreign revenue and improve terms of trade, encourage regional development, overcome regional economic disparities • planner as expert • development defined in economic terms	• can tourism be used as a growth pole? • maximisation of income and employment multipliers • influencing consumer choice • providing economic values for externalities • providing economic values for conservation purposes	• supply–demand analysis • benefit–cost analysis • product–market matching • development incentives • market segmentation	• management processes • tourism master plans • motivation • economic impact • economic multipliers • hedonistic pricing
Physical/spatial	• tourism as a resource user • ecological basis to development • tourism as a spatial and regional phenomenon • environmental conservation • development defined in environmental terms • preservation of genetic diversity	• physical carrying capacity • manipulating travel patterns and visitor flows • visitor management • concentration or dispersal of visitors • perceptions of natural environment • wilderness and national park management • designation of environmentally sensitive areas	• ecological studies • environmental impact assessment • regional planning • perceptual studies	• spatial patterns and processes • physical impacts • resort morphology • LAC (limits of acceptable change) • ROS (recreational opportunity spectrum) • TOS (tourism opportunity spectrum) • destination life cycles

Table 9.3: continued

Planning tradition	Underlying assumptions and related attitudes	Definition of the tourism planning problem	Some examples of related methods	Some examples of related models
Community	• need for local control • search for balanced development • search for alternatives to mass tourism development • planner as facilitator rather than expert • development defined in socio-cultural terms	• how to foster community control? • understanding community attitudes towards tourism • understanding the impacts of tourism on a community • social impact	• community development • awareness and education • attitudinal surveys • social impact assessment	• ecological view of community • social/perceptual carrying capacity • attitudinal change • social multiplier
Sustainable	• integration of economic, environmental and socio-cultural values • tourism planning integrated with other planning processes • holistic planning • preservation of essential ecological processes • protection of human heritage and biodiversity • intergenerational and intra-generational equity • achievement of a better balance of fairness and opportunity between nations • planning and policy as argument • planning as process • planning and implementation as two sides of the same coin • recognition of political dimension of tourism	• understanding the tourism system • setting goals, objectives and priorities • achieving policy and administrative co-ordination in and between the public and private sectors • co-operative and integrated control systems • understanding the political dimensions of tourism • planning for tourism that meets local needs and trades successfully in a competitive marketplace	• strategic planning to supersede conventional approaches • raising producer awareness • raising consumer awareness • raising community awareness • stakeholder input • policy analysis • evaluative research • political economy • aspirations analysis • stakeholder audit • environmental analysis and audit • interpretation	• systems models • integrated models focused on places and links and relationships between such places • resources as culturally constituted • environmental perception • business ecology • learning organisations

Sources: after Getz (1987); Hall et al. (1997); Hall (1999)

economic impacts of tourism and its most efficient use to create income and employment benefits for regions or communities.

One of the main areas to which geographers have contributed is the physical/spatial approach under which tourism is regarded as having an ecological base with a resultant need for development to be based upon certain spatial patterns, capacities or thresholds that would minimise the negative impacts of tourism on the physical environment (Getz 1983, 1987). Indeed, much of the concern with the physical and behavioural carrying capacities of specific locations discussed in Chapter 8 falls into this particular approach. Research by Page and Thorn (1997) in New Zealand reviewed the impact of a market-led approach to tourism planning at the national level where a lack of rational national policy or planning advice has significant implications for local areas which are required to deal with the micro scale issues. The ability to incorporate sustainable planning principles and to manage visitors was also a notable problem for many public sector planning agencies highlighted by Page and Thorn (1997). A more preferable focus for local areas is the contribution which a community approach can make (Timothy 2002).

A community approach emphasises the social and political context within which tourism occurs and advocates greater local control over the development process. Geographers have also been active in this area, as it builds upon a strong urban and regional planning tradition that is concerned with being relevant to community needs. The best known exemplar of this approach is the work of Murphy (1985, 1988; Murphy and Murphy 2004), although a community development approach is also influential in developing country destinations as well as in the developed world (Singh et al. 2003).

A community approach to tourism planning is an attempt to formulate a bottom-up form of planning, which emphasises development *in* the community rather than development *of* the community. Under this approach, residents, not tourists, are regarded as the focal point of the tourism planning exercise, and the community, which is often equated with a region of local gov-

ernment, is usually used as the basic planning unit. Nevertheless, substantial difficulties will arise in attempting to implement the concept of community planning in tourist destinations. As Dowling (1993: 53) noted, 'research into community attitudes towards tourism is reasonably well developed, although incorporation of such views into the planning process is far less common'. For example, J. Jenkins (1993) identified seven impediments to incorporating public participation in tourism planning:

- the public generally has difficulty in comprehending complex and technical planning issues
- the public is not always aware of or understands the decision-making process
- the difficulty in attaining and maintaining representativeness in the decision-making process
- the apathy of citizens
- the increased costs in terms of staff and money
- the prolonging of the decision-making process
- adverse effects on the efficiency of decision-making.

One notable exception here is the research reported by Page and Lawton (1997) which sought to incorporate residents' views as part of the planning process for tourism in a local area.

As the above discussion indicates, one of the major difficulties in implementing a community approach to tourism planning is the political nature of the planning process. Community planning implies a high degree of public participation in the planning process. However, public participation implies that the local community will have a degree of control over the planning and decision-making process. Therefore, a community approach to tourism planning implies that there will be a need for partnership in, or community control of, the tourism development process.

Yet power is not evenly distributed within a community, and some groups and individuals will therefore have the ability to exert greater influence over the planning process than others (Hall and Jenkins 1995). Therefore, in some circumstances, the level of public involvement in tourism planning may be more accurately described as a form of tokenism in which decisions or the direction of decisions have already been prescribed by government. Communities rarely have the opportunity to say 'no' (Hall 1995). Nevertheless, as Murphy (1985: 153) argued: 'If tourism is to become the successful and self-perpetuating industry many have advocated, it needs to be planned and managed as a renewable resource industry, based on local capacities and community decision making', with an increased emphasis being given to the interrelated and evolutionary nature of tourist development.

Since the late 1990s, geographers have become concerned with the development of sustainable approaches towards tourism (Hall and Lew 1998). Sustainable tourism planning is therefore an integrative form of tourism planning, which bears much similarity to the many traditionally applied concerns of the geographer as resource manager (L.S. Mitchell 1979). Sustainable tourism planning seeks to provide lasting and secure livelihoods with minimal resource depletion, environmental degradation, cultural disruption and social instability. The approach therefore tends to integrate features of the economic, physical/spatial and community traditions.

The concern for equity, in terms of both intra- and intergenerational equity, in sustainable development means that we should be concerned with not only the maintenance of 'environmental capital' (M. Jacobs 1991) but also the maintenance and enhancement of social capital (Healey 1997), in terms of the rich set of social networks and relationships that exist in places, through appropriate policies and programmes of social equality and political participation (Blowers 1997). Such an approach has considerable implications for the structure of tourism planning and policy-making. To fulfil the sustainable goal of equity, decision-making processes will need to be more inclusive of the full range of values, opinions and interests that surround tourism developments and tourism's overall contribution to development, and provide a clearer space for public argument and debate (Smyth 1994). As B. Evans (1997: 8) argued, 'if environmental planning for sustainability . . . is to be anywhere near effective, the political processes of public debate and controversy, both formal and informal, will need to play a much more significant role than has hitherto been the case'.

Dutton and Hall (1989) identified five key elements of sustainable tourism planning: co-operative and integrated control systems, development of industry co-ordination mechanisms, raising consumer awareness, raising producer awareness, and strategic planning to supersede conventional approaches.

Plate 9.1/9.2: Cairndow/Loch Fyne, Scotland. Community based and owned tourism developments.

CO-OPERATIVE AND INTEGRATED CONTROL SYSTEMS

In a typical planning process, stakeholders are consulted minimally, near the end of the process, and often via formal public meetings. 'The plan that results under these conditions tends to be a prescriptive statement by the professionals rather than an agreement among the various parties'; by contrast, an interactive style 'assumes that better decisions result from open, participative processes' (Lang 1988, in Wight 1998: 87). An integrative planning approach to tourism planning and management at all levels (from the regional plan to individual resort projects) would assist in the distribution of the benefits and costs of tourism development more equitably, while focusing on improved relationships and understanding between stakeholders may also assist in agreement on planning directions and goals. However, co-operation alone will not foster commitment to sustainable development without the incentive of increased mutual benefits.

One of the most important aspects of co-operative and integrated control systems is the selection of indicators of sustainability. The role of an indicator is to make complex systems understandable. An effective indicator or set of indicators helps a destination, community or organisation determine where it is, where it is going and how far it is from chosen goals. Sustainability indicators provide a measure of the long-term viability of a destination or community based on the degree to which its economic, environmental and social systems are efficient and integrated (Gill and Williams 1994; Hall 1999). However, indicators are useful only in the context of appropriately framed questions (Hall and McArthur 1998). In choosing indicators, one must have a clear understanding of planning goals and objectives. For example, a typology of indicators might include

- economic, environmental and social indicators (measuring changes in the state of the economy, environment and society)
- sustainability indicators (measuring distance between that change and a sustainable state of the environment)
- sustainable development indicators (measuring progress to the broader goal of sustainable development in a national context).

There has been a tendency to pick indicators that are easiest to measure and reflect most visible change; therefore important concerns from a holistic perspective of tourism development, such as the social and cultural impacts of tourism, may be dropped. In addition, appropriate indicators may not be selected because organisations might not want to be held accountable for the results of evaluations (Hall and McArthur 1998). According to Wight (1998), indicators to reflect desired conditions and use should ideally

- be directly observable
- be relatively easy to measure
- reflect understanding that some change is normal, particularly in ecological systems, and be sensitive to changing use conditions
- reflect appropriate scales (spatial and temporal)
- have ecological, not just institutional or administrative boundaries
- encompass relevant structural, functional and compositional attributes of the ecosystem
- include social, cultural, economic and ecological components
- reflect understanding of indicator function/type (e.g. baseline/reference, stress, impact, management, system diagnostic)
- relate to the vision, goals and objectives for the destination region
- be amenable to management.

INSIGHT: The changing role of government and sustainability

Changes in government's role as interest protector has major implications for tourism and sustainability (Bianchi 2002; Mercer 2004; Weaver 2004). As Blowers (1997: 36) noted in the case of the United Kingdom, 'the long period of privatisation, deregulation, cuts in public expenditure and attacks on local government have resulted in a 'democratic deficit' – a dispersal of power to unelected quangos and business interests – and have led to unsustainable developments'. A critique also reflected in the comments of Haughton and Hunter (1994):

> The unregulated market approach, being relatively amoral, can allow individuals to be immoral. The ethical dimension is important since the market does not provide a sufficient basis for the resolution of the profound moral issues which face us every day; it can play a part in avoiding distorted decision making by individuals and organizations, but alone it cannot reconcile all of the environmental problems facing society.
>
> (Haughton and Hunter 1994: 272)

The above comments highlight the need to see partnership and collaboration between government and the private sector within the context of the public interest as opposed to the market interest. Incorporation of a wider range of inputs into the policy process would lead to the formation of issue networks as opposed to subgovernments. Issue networks are structures of interaction among participants in a policy area that are marked by their transience and the absence of established centres of control (Heclo 1978). According to Heclo (1978), the term 'issue network' describes

> a configuration of individuals concerned about a particular aspect of an issue and the term policy community is used more broadly to encompass the collection of issue networks within a jurisdiction. Both describe the voluntary and fluid configuration of people with varying degrees of commitment to a particular cause.
>
> (Heclo 1978: 102)

One of the great problems in examining the role of interest groups in the tourism policy-making process is deciding what the appropriate relationship between an interest group and government should be (Hall and Jenkins 1995; Bramwell 2004). At what point does tourism industry membership of government advisory committees or of a national, regional or local tourism agency represent a 'closing up' of the policy process to other interest groups rather than an exercise in consultation, co-ordination, partnership or collaboration? As Deutsch (1970) recognised:

> this co-operation between groups and bureaucrats can sometimes be a good thing. But it may sometimes be a very bad thing. These groups, used to each other's needs, may become increasingly preoccupied with each other, insensitive to the needs of outsiders, and impervious to new recruitment and to new ideas. Or the members of the various interest group elites may identify more and more with each other and less and less with the interests of the groups they represent.
>
> (Deutsch 1970: 56)

The relationship between the tourism industry and government tourism agencies clearly raises questions about the extent to which established policy processes lead to outcomes which are in the 'public interest' and which contribute to sustainability rather than meeting just narrow sectoral interests. Mucciaroni (1991: 474) noted that 'client politics is typical of policies with diffuse costs and concentrated benefits. An identifiable group benefits from a policy, but the costs are paid by everybody or at least a large part of society'. As Hall and Jenkins (1995) argued, tourism policy is one such area, particularly in terms of the costs of tourism promotion and marketing. However, the implications of this situation also affect the overall sustainability of tourism and of communities. In reviewing the tourism and collaboration literature Hall (1999) concluded that the present focus by government tourism agencies on partnership and collaboration is laudable.

> But the linguistic niceties of partnership and collaboration need to be challenged by focusing on who is involved in tourism planning and policy processes and who is left out. . . . Unless there are attempts to provide equity of access to all stakeholders than collaboration will be one more approach consigned to the lexicon of tourism planning clichés.
>
> (Hall 1999)

> Therefore, the policy arguments surrounding networks and collaboration need to be examined within broader ideas of the appropriate role of government and changing relationships and expectations between government and communities.

DEVELOPMENT OF INDUSTRY CO-ORDINATION MECHANISMS

While a range of formal and informal tourism industry bodies exist in almost every country in the world, few of these address such complex issues as sustainable development. The support by industry groups of environmental codes is perhaps indicative of possible directions if common needs can be agreed upon. However, for such guidelines to be effective, it must be ensured that they do not constitute a 'lowest common denominator' approach to development and implementation (Hall 1999). Therefore, government and public interest groups tend to use their influence to encourage greater industry co-ordination on planning issues by creating structures and processes which enable stakeholders to talk to each other and create effective relationships and partnerships. In many ways such measures are easier to achieve at a local level because the range of stakeholders which need to be incorporated into co-ordinating bodies will be narrower. In addition, contact at the local level provides a greater capacity for face-to-face contact to occur and therefore trust-building to develop (Hall 2000a; Bramwell 2004).

Co-ordination refers to formal institutionalised relationships among existing networks of organisations, interests and/or individuals, while co-operation is 'characterized by informal trade-offs and by attempts to establish reciprocity in the absence of rules' (Mulford and Rogers 1982: 13). Often, the problem of developing co-ordinated approaches towards tourism planning and policy problems, such as the meta-problem of sustainability, is identified in organisational terms (e.g. the creation of new organisations or the allocation of new responsibilities to existing ones). However, such a response does not by itself solve the problem of bringing various stakeholders and interests together which is an issue of establishing collaborative processes. Instead, by recognising the level of interdependence that exists within the tourism system (Hall 2000a), it may be possible for 'separate, partisan interests to discover a common or public interest' (Friedmann 1973: 350). For example, moves towards the implementation of an 'ecosystem management' approach among United States government natural resource management agencies has opened up new ways of thinking about heritage and natural area management (Hall and McArthur 1998). Notions of collaboration, co-ordination and partnership are separate, though closely related, ideas within the emerging network paradigm. Networks refer to the development of linkages between actors (organisations and individuals) where linkages become more formalised towards maintaining mutual interests. The nature of such linkages exists on a continuum ranging from 'loose' linkages to coalitions and more lasting structural arrangements and relationships. Mandell (1999) identifies a continuum of such collaborative efforts as follows:

- linkages or interactive contacts between two or more actors
- intermittent co-ordination or mutual adjustment of the policies and procedures of two or more actors to accomplish some objective
- ad hoc or temporary task force activity among actors to accomplish a purpose or purposes

- permanent and/or regular co-ordination between two or more actors through a formal arrangement (e.g. a council or partnership) to engage in limited activity to achieve a purpose or purposes
- a coalition where interdependent and strategic actions are taken, but where purposes are narrow in scope and all actions occur within the participant actors themselves or involve the mutually sequential or simultaneous activity of the participant actors
- a collective or network structure where there is a broad mission and joint and strategically inter-dependent action; such structural arrangements take on broad tasks that reach beyond the simultaneous actions of independently oper-ating actors.

However, as Mandell (1999) cautions:

> because we as professionals are eager to achieve results, we often look for prescriptions or answers as to how to solve ongoing dilemmas . . . it is tempting for both academics and practitioners to try to develop a model of success that will fit this complex world. In this regard, the concepts of networks and network struc-tures can easily become the next in line for those in the field to 'latch onto' and use wholesale. Although it may be tempting to do so, this 'one size fits all' type of modelling does not take into consideration the myriad of factors and events that must be understood before these concepts can be of much use in the 'real world'.
>
> (Mandell 1999: 8)

RAISING CONSUMER AWARENESS

One of the hallmarks of tourism, and other industries, in recent years has been the increased consumer demand for 'green' or 'environmentally friendly' products; such demand is often related to increased consumer awareness of environmental and social issues associated with trade and tourism. However, in many cases, the difference between a sustainable and non-sustainable tourism operation may be difficult for consumers to detect, partic-ularly if the greening of tourism is regarded more

as a branding device than a fundamental change in product development.

One development which is usually regarded as an indicator of increased consumer awareness is the development of tourist codes of behaviour in order to minimise the negative impacts of tourists on the social and physical environment (Hall and Lew 1998). For example, P. Valentine (1992) cites the example of the Audubon Society, one of the largest conservation groups in the United States, which has developed the Audubon Travel Ethic in order to draw attention to the appropriate behaviours and ethics to which individuals travelling with the society should follow:

1 The biota shall not be disturbed.
2 Audubon tours to natural areas will be sustain-able.
3 The sensibilities of other cultures will be respected.
4 Waste disposal shall have neither environmental nor aesthetic impacts.
5 The experience a tourist gains in travelling with Audubon will enrich his or her appreciation of nature, conservation and the environment.
6 The effect of an Audubon tour will be to strengthen the conservation effort and enhance the natural integrity of places visited.
7 Traffic in products that threaten wildlife and plant populations shall not occur.

However, while consumer awareness is impor-tant and may result in shifts in tourism product, particularly if one believes the old adage that the consumer is king, fundamental changes are also required on the supply side of the tourism equation.

RAISING PRODUCER AWARENESS

According to Hall (1995), greater attention has been given to meeting the demands of different consumer segments than the needs of the supplier of the tourist product. As with the raising of consumer awareness, much attention has been given to the production of environmental codes of conduct or practice for tourism associations (Hall and McArthur 1998). For example, extensive guidelines have been developed for tourism operators in the Antarctic (Hall and Johnston 1995). However, such guidelines, while undoubtedly influencing the actions of some tourism operators, may need to be backed up by government regulation and environmental planning legislation if they are to have any overall effect on development practices. For example, where such codes of conduct are voluntary, what practical measures exist to punish operators who do not subscribe to them?

INSIGHT: International Association of Antarctica Tour Operators (IAATO)

IAATO (http://www.iaato.org) was founded in August 1991 by seven charter members (Enzenbacher 1992) and now includes most of the main cruise lines which operate in the Antarctic. In 2001 IAATO had fourteen full members, six provisional members, one probational member, and fourteen associate members. IAATO members meet annually in conjunction with the National Science Foundation/Antarctic Tour Operators Meeting; attendance is compulsory as memberships, by-laws and other important issues are discussed. It is estimated that IAATO members carry approximately 70% of all Antarctic tourists (Enzenbacher 1995). As Claus (1990, quoted in Enzenbacher 1995) noted,

> Over the past few years we have been involved in Antarctic policy meetings, US Congressional hearings and scientific conferences, not only in the US but in Australia and New Zealand as well, where we have taken a leading role in the environmental protection of Antarctica.
> (Enzenbacher 1995: 188)

IAATO has two sets of guidelines, the first is addressed to Antarctica tour operators (IAATO 1993a), the second is directed at Antarctica visitors (IAATO 1993b). IAATO tour operator guidelines are intended for crew and staff members of Antarctic tour companies. The agreed principles contained within aim at increasing awareness and establishing a code of behaviour that minimises tourism impacts on the environment. The willingness of industry members to cooperate with Antarctic Treaty Parties in regulating tourism is crucial to the protection of the Antarctic environment given that the Antarctic is transnational space within which domestic laws are complicated in their application (Keage and Dingwall 1993; Hall and Johnston 1995). Tour operators maintain that current IAATO guidelines are adequate, noting that tourists often serve as effective guardians of the wildlife and environment. Yet, as Enzenbacher (1995: 188) noted, 'it is not clear that self-regulation sufficiently addresses all issues arising from tourist activity as no neutral regulatory authority currently exists to oversee all Antarctic operators'. Infractions of IAATO guidelines by members have been documented, but it is not known to what extent the environment was seriously affected by them (Enzenbacher 1992).

STRATEGIC PLANNING TO SUPERSEDE CONVENTIONAL APPROACHES

Strategic planning is becoming increasingly important in tourism (e.g. Dowling 1993). Strategic planning aims to be proactive, responsive to community needs, to incorporate implementation within a single planning process, and to be ongoing. A 'strategy' is a means to achieve a desired end. Strategic planning is the process by which an organisation effectively adapts to its management environment over time by integrating planning and management in a single process. The strategic plan is the document which is the output of a strategic planning process, it is the template by which progress is measured and which serves to guide future directions, activities, programmes and actions. The outcome of the strategic planning process is the impact the process has on the organisation and its activities. Such impacts are then monitored and evaluated through the selection of appropriate indicators as part of the ongoing revision and readjustment of the organisation to its environment. Strategic planning therefore emphasises the process of continuous improvement as a cornerstone of organisational activity in which strategic planning is linked to management and operational decision-making. According to Hall and McArthur (1998) there are three key mechanisms to achieving strategic planning which differentiate it from conventional planning approaches:

- a planning framework which extends beyond organisational boundaries and focuses on strategic decisions concerning stakeholders and resources
- a planning process that stimulates entrepreneurial and innovative thinking
- an organisational values system that reinforces managers and staff commitment to the organisational strategy.

Effective strategic planning for sustainable tourism recognises the importance of factors that affect the broad framework within which strategies are generated, such as institutional arrangements, institutional culture and stakeholder values and attitudes. These factors are significant because it is important to recognise that strategic plans will be in line with the legislative powers and organisational structures of the implementing organisation(s) and the political goals of government. However, it may also be the case that once the strategic planning process is underway, goals and objectives formulated and the process evaluated, the institutional arrangements may be recognised as being inadequate for the successful

achievement of sustainable goals and objectives. In addition, it must be recognised that in order to be effective, the strategic planning process needs to be integrated with the development of appropriate organisational values (see Hall and Jenkins 1995 on the role of values in planning and policy). Indeed, with respect to the significance of values it may be noted that the strategic planning process is as important as its output, i.e. a plan. By having an inclusive planning process by which those responsible for implementing the plan are also those who helped formulate it, the likelihood of 'ownership' of the plan and, hence, effective implementation will be dramatically increased (Heath and Wall 1992; Hall and McArthur 1996).

A strategic planning process may be initiated for a number of reasons (Hall and McArthur 1998):

- *Stakeholder demands* Demand for the undertaking of a strategic plan may come from the pressure of stakeholders (e.g. environmental conservation groups or government).
- *Perceived need* The lack of appropriate information by which to make decisions or an appropriate framework with which to implement legislative requirements may give rise to a perception that new management and planning approaches are required.
- *Response to crisis* The undertaking of strategic planning exercises is often the result of a crisis in the sense that the management and planning system has failed to adapt to aspects of the management environment (e.g. failure to conserve the values of an environmentally significant site from visitor pressures).
- *Best practice* Visitor managers can be proactive with respect to the adoption of new ideas and techniques. Therefore, a strategic planning process can become a way of doing things better.
- *Adaptation, innovation and the diffusion of ideas* Individuals within an organisation can encourage strategic planning processes as part of the diffusion of ideas within and between responsible management agencies.

tourism and regional development has been added which returns to the earlier economic concerns (e.g. D.G. Pearce 1992a). This is the perception of rural tourism as a major mechanism for arresting the decline of agricultural employment and therefore as a mechanism for agricultural diversification (Rural Development Commission 1991a, 1991b). In the case of Europe, for example, we see the identification of specific rural development areas (Pearce 1992a; Jenkins et al. 1998). Rural tourism has also been given substantial emphasis in Australia, New Zealand and North America because of its development potential (Butler et al. 1998). For example, in Australia, as the Commonwealth Department of Tourism (1993) noted:

> Diversification of traditional rural enterprises into tourism would provide considerable benefits to local rural economies including:
>
> - wider employment opportunities;
> - diversifying the income base of farmers and rural towns;
> - additional justification for the development of infrastructure;
> - a broader base for the establishment, maintenance and/or expansion of local services;
> - scope for the integration of regional development strategies; an enhanced quality of life through extended leisure and cultural opportunities.
> (Commonwealth Department of Tourism 1993: 24)

Yet despite government enthusiasm for tourism as a mechanism to counter problems arising out of rural restructuring and depopulation, the success of these policies has been only marginally successful, with the greatest growth from tourism- and recreation-related industries occurring in the larger rural service centres and the rural–urban fringe, arguably those areas which least need the benefits that tourism can bring (Butler et al. 1998; Jenkins et al.1998). Why has this occurred?

To a great extent it relates to a failure by government to understand the nature of tourism and its relationship with other sectors of the economy and the policy and planning process itself. First, all the dimensions of development need to

be considered. Second, it implies the need for us to be aware of the various linkages that exist between the elements of development. Third, it also implies that 'successful' regional development will require co-ordination and, at times, intervention, in order to achieve desired outcomes. Fourth, it also means that tourism should not be seen as the be-all and end-all of regional development, but instead should be utilised as an appropriate response to the real needs of regions. Furthermore, the role of growth coalitions and the distribution of power in a community has enormous implications for the tourism policy and planning process and its outcomes (Logan et al. 1997; Meethan 1998; Judd and Fainstein 1999; N.J. Morgan and Pritchard 1999; Church and Reid 2000; Judd 2000; P.E. Long 2000; Schollmann et al. 2001; Hall 2005a). As Getz (1987: 3–4) stated, tourism 'can be a tool in regional development or an agent of disruption or destruction'. Or, to put it another way, to quote an article from British Columbia in Canada: 'Those who think a bit of Victorian architecture and an overpriced cappuccino bar are going to turn their community into a gold mine are in for a disappointment' (Threndyle 1994). However, the problems of rural tourism and recreation development have long been recognised. For example, as Baum and More (1966) stated with respect to the American experience in the early 1960s:

> there are and there will be increasing opportunities for [tourism] development, but this industry should not be considered to be a panacea for the longstanding problems of substantial and persistent unemployment and underemployment besetting low-income rural areas. . . . The successful development of a particular [tourism] enterprise or complex of enterprises requires the same economic considerations as the planning and development of economic activities in other sectors.
> (Baum and More 1966: 5)

The starting point with respect to determining successful regional tourism development is deciding in the first place what the objectives should be and how a community is going to get there. Such a decision should not be made by the tourism industry alone As P.T. Long and Nuckolls (1994) noted:

Pro-active, community-driven planning, that goes beyond developing and promoting the static supply side of tourism, is essential for successful development of a sustainable tourism industry. Furthermore, tourism plans must be integrated into broader strategies for community, economic and regional development and management. Communities that fail to organise resources and strategically plan for tourism will likely be faced with short term, haphazard development, resulting in long term, negative economic, social and environmental impacts.

(P.T. Long and Nuckolls 1994: 19)

An understanding of tourism policy processes therefore lies at the heart of broader goals of rural and regional development. Yet, as Hall and Jenkins (1998) argued, the formulation and implementation of rural tourism and recreation public policies present several conundrums. Unrealistic expectations of tourism's potential are unfortunately combined with ignorance or wilful neglect by decision-makers of the potentially adverse economic, environmental and social consequences of tourist development that threaten to curtail its benefits (Bachvarov 1999; Boyd 2000; Cater 2000; Bianchi 2002; Ribeiro and Marques 2002; Turnock 2002). Yet, as Duffield and Long (1981: 409) observed, 'Ironically, the very consequences of lack of development, the unspoilt character of the landscape and distinctive local cultures, become positive resources as far as tourism is concerned.' Government involvement in tourism development is therefore often quite unsuccessful:

Management decisions for the allocation of related outdoor recreation resources are seldom guided by strategic policy frameworks. Decisions are typically made in a reactive manner in response to various pressures from groups competing for the same resource or lobbying for different management of a particular resource. . . . Even in Europe, where rural tourism has been increasingly promoted over the last decade as an important mechanism for regional economic development and European integration, substantial problems have emerged with respect to policy formulation and implementation.

(Hall and Jenkins 1998: 28)

The reason for such failures lies in a lack of understanding of policy processes (Hall and Jenkins 1995; J. Jenkins 2001; Michael 2001), while the goals of 'tourism development are fairly clear at the regional level, little research has been conducted on the most appropriate policy mix to achieve such objectives and there is often minimal monitoring and evaluation of policy measures' (Hall and Jenkins 1998). Therefore, for each location within which regional development objectives are being sought through the development of tourism, there are a range of policy measures available (Table 9.4). Five different measures were identified:

- *regulatory instruments*: regulations, permits and licences that have a legal basis and which require monitoring and enforcement
- *voluntary instruments*: actions or mechanisms that do not require expenditure
- *expenditure*: direct government expenditure to achieve policy outcomes
- *financial incentives*: including taxes, subsidies, grants and loans, which are incentives to undertake certain activities or behaviours and which tend to require minimal enforcement
- *non-intervention*: where government deliberately avoids intervention in order to achieve its policy objectives.

The selection of the most appropriate measure or, more likely, a range of measures, is dependent on the particular circumstances of each region. There is no universal 'best way'; each region or locale needs to select the appropriate policy mix for its own development requirements (Sharpley and Telfer 2002). However, this does not mean that the policy and planning process occurs in a vacuum. Rather the attention to policy and planning processes has the intent of making such processes as overt as possible, so that the values, influence and interests of various stakeholders are relatively transparent. There is no perfect planning or policy process, yet we can, through the geographer's contribution, help make it more relevant to the people who are affected by tourism development and continually strive for improvement.

Table 9.4: Rural tourism development policy instruments

Categories	Instruments	Examples
Regulatory instruments	• Laws	Planning laws can give considerable power to government to encourage particular types of rural tourism development through, for example, land use zoning
	• Licences, permits and standards	Regulatory instruments can be used for a wide variety of purposes at local government level, e.g. they may set materials standards for tourism developments, or they can be used to set architectural standards for heritage streetscapes or properties
	• Tradeable permits	Permits are often used in the United States to limit resource use or pollution; however, the instrument requires effective monitoring for it to work
	• Quid pro quos	Government may require businesses to do something in exchange for certain rights, e.g. land may be given to a developer below market rates, or a development is of a particular type or design
Voluntary instruments	• Information	Expenditure on educating the local public, businesses or tourists to achieve specific goals, e.g. appropriate recreational behaviour
	• Volunteer associations and non-governmental organisations	Government support of community tourism organisations is very common in tourism. Support may come from direct grants and/or by provision of office facilities. Examples of this type of development include local or regional tourist organisations, heritage conservation groups, mainstreet groups, tour guide programmes, or helping to establish a local farmstay or homestay association
	• Technical assistance	Government can provide technical assistance and information to businesses with regard to planning and development requirements
Expenditure	• Expenditure and contracting	This is a common method for government to achieve policy objectives as government can spend money directly on specific activities. This may include the development of infrastructure, such as roads, or it may include mainstreet beautification programmes. Contracting can be used as a means of supporting existing local businesses or encouraging new ones
	• Investment or procurement	Investment may be directed into specific businesses or projects, while procurement can be used to help provide businesses with a secure customer for their products
	• Public enterprise	When the market fails to provide desired outcomes, governments may operate their own businesses, e.g. rural or regional development corporations or enterprise boards. If successful, such businesses may then be sold off to the private sector
	• Public–private partnerships	Government may enter into partnership with the private sector in order to develop certain products or regions; these may take the form of a corporation which has a specific mandate to attract business to a certain region, for example
	• Monitoring and evaluation	Government may allocate financial resources to monitor rural economic, environmental and socio-economic indicators. Such measures not only may be valuable to government to evaluate the effectiveness and efficiency of rural tourism development objectives but also can be a valuable source of information to the private sector as well
	• Promotion	Government may spend money on promoting a region to visitors either with or without financial input from the private sector. Such promotional activities may allow individual businesses to reallocate their own budgets, reducing planned expenditure on promotion

Table 9.4: (continued)

Categories	Instruments	Examples
Financial incentives	• Pricing	Pricing measures may be used to encourage appropriate behaviour or to stimulate demand, e.g. use of particular walking trails, lower camping or permit costs
	• Taxes and charges	Governments may use these to encourage appropriate behaviours by both individuals and businesses, i.e. pollution charges. Taxes and charges may also be used to help fund infrastructure development, e.g. regional airports
	• Grants and loans	Seeding money may be provided to businesses to encourage product development or to encourage the retention of heritage and landscape features
	• Subsidies and tax incentives	Although subsidies are often regarded as creating inefficiencies in markets they may also be used to encourage certain types of behaviour with respect to social and environmental externalities, e.g. heritage and landscape conservation, that are not taken into account by conventional economics
	• Rebates, rewards and surety bonds	Rebates and rewards are a form of financial incentive to encourage individuals and businesses to act in certain ways. Similarly, surety bonds can be used to ensure that businesses act in agreed ways, if they don't then the government will spend the money for the same purpose
	• Vouchers	Vouchers are a mechanism to affect consumer behaviour by providing a discount on a specific product or activity, e.g. to shop in a rural centre
Non-intervention	• Non-intervention (deliberate)	Government deciding not to directly intervene in sectoral or regional development is also a policy instrument, in that public policy is what government decides to do and not do. In some cases the situation may be such that government may decide that policy objectives are being met so that their intervention may not add any net value to the rural development process and that resources could be better spent elsewhere

Source: after Hall and Jenkins (1998: 29–32)

CONCLUSION

This chapter has provided a broad overview of the tourism and recreation planning and policy process. It has noted the various strands of tourism planning, and emphasised the particular contribution of geographers to the physical/spatial, community and sustainable approaches to tourism planning.

The reasons for focusing on tourism which is not as well developed or articulated in local, regional and national development plans beyond statements and broad objectives contrasts with recreational planning which has a much longer history of development and application. In fact if the experience of urban areas is considered, one can see the emergence of recreational planning in the nineteenth century in the UK with the role of the public

sector in park development, the provision of libraries and other items to meet the wider public good. What geographers have contributed to recreational planning is the synthesis and analysis of good practice, rather than being actively involved as academics, beyond a research role, to assist public and private sector bodies in locational analysis and land use planning. This chapter has therefore placed a great deal of emphasis on the importance of policy analysis, especially from a descriptive approach. This does not mean that prescription is without value, rather it argues that prescription must be seen in context, with particular reference to those who are in any way affected by policy statements.

In looking at the application of policy analysis to tourism issues we have therefore almost come full circle. The interests which have long concerned tourism and recreation geographers that are applied and relevant to the needs of the subjects of our research remain, and it is to these issues that we will return in the final chapter.

QUESTIONS

- Is there anything that makes planning for tourism distinct from other forms of planning?
- Why is recreation planning such an integral component of resource management?
- What are the institutional arrangements for tourism and recreation in your country? Describe them and their interrelationships between the national, regional and local level.
- What is the appropriate relationship between government and the tourism industry in the formulation of tourism policy?

READING

There are several classic works that relate to tourism planning. In particular see Gunn (2002) and Murphy (1985, 1988). For a traditional approach to resort and tourism planning see

Inskeep, E. (1991) *Tourism Planning: An Integrated and Sustainable Development Approach*, New York: Van Nostrand Reinhold.

Hall (2000a) is a theoretically informed work which attempts to integrate planning and policy concerns at different scales of analysis. More practical guides to tourism planning and dealing with stakeholders include

Hall, C.M. and McArthur, S. (1998) *Integrated Heritage Management*, London: The Stationery Office.

Murphy, P.E. and Murphy, A.E. (2004) *Strategic Management for Tourism Communities: Bridging the Gaps*, Clevedon: Channel View.

On community development see

Singh, S., Timothy, D. and Dowling, R. (eds) (2003) *Tourism in Destination Communities*, Wallingford: CAB International.

There is relatively little useful work on international dimension of tourism policy, although the aftermath of 9/11 has meant a focus on issues of security in particular. See

Hall, C.M. (2000a) 'Travel safety, terrorism and the media: The significance of the issue-attention cycle', *Current Issues in Tourism*, 5(5): 458–66.

Hall, C.M., Timothy, D. and Duval, D. (2003) 'Security and tourism: Towards a new understanding?', *Journal of Travel and Tourism Marketing*, 15(2–3): 1–18.

Hall, C.M., Duval, D. and Timothy, D. (eds) (2004) *Safety and Security in Tourism: Relationships, Management and Marketing*, New York: Haworth Press.

Timothy, D.J. (2001) *Tourism and Political Boundaries*, London: Routledge.

Timothy, D.J. (2004) 'Political boundaries and regional cooperation in tourism', in A. Lew, C.M. Hall and A. Williams (eds) *Companion to Tourism*, Oxford: Blackwell, pp. 584–95.

A useful work on British tourism policy is

Church, A., Ball, R., Bull, C. and Tyler, D. (2000) 'Public policy engagement with British tourism: The national, local and the European Union', *Tourism Geographies*, 2(3): 312–36.

Other works with more of a recreational planning emphasis include

Cope, A., Doxford, D. and Probert, C. (2000) 'Monitoring visitors to UK countryside resources: The approaches of land and recreation resource management organisations to visitor monitoring', *Land Use Policy*, 17: 59–66.

Ferreira, S. and Harmse, A. (1999) 'The social carrying capacity of Kruger National Park, South Africa: Policy and practice', *Tourism Geographies*, 1(3): 325–42.

Wezenaar, H. (1999) 'Leisure land-use planning and sustainability in the new town of Almere, The Netherlands', *Tourism Geographies*, 1(4): 460–76.

10

THE FUTURE

Speaking only as one individual, I feel strongly that I should not go into research unless it promises results that would advance the aims of the people affected and unless I am prepared to take all practicable steps to help translate the results into action.

(G. White 1972: 102)

If geographical research is to maintain its own distinctiveness, which it surely has to do for the sake of its own survival and respect, it needs to make explicit its sense of what is important. The sheer number of people, the economic value and the significance to people's lives of leisure, recreation and tourism will eventually make even the most doubting sceptic accept that these topics are worthy of study and that battle for acceptance of [leisure, recreation and tourism] as valid areas of research will be won. It would be depressing if geography was not there to claim its unique place and interests.

(Butler 2004: 156)

As the various chapters in this book have indicated, geographers have made substantial contributions to the understanding of tourism and recreation. However, as noted in Chapter 1, the geographers who are working in the field are, increasingly, not based in geography departments but instead are located in departments of tourism and recreation or leisure, environmental studies or business. Indeed, the authors, while still regarding themselves as geographers, were working in faculties of business as this book was being completed.

Such a situation is a reflection of several things: the growth of tourism and recreation as a separate, legitimate area of academic endeavour, the poor standing in which studies of tourism and recreation have generally been held within academic geography, and the applied nature of much work in tourism and recreation geography, which has meant a professional career in the public and private sectors for many geography graduates in the field. Such a situation clearly raises substantial questions about what the future of the subdiscipline will be. As Johnston (1991: 2) recognised: 'It is the advancement of knowledge – through the conduct of fundamental research and the publication of its original findings – which identifies an academic discipline; the nature of its teaching follows from the nature of its research.' But geography has also undergone many profound transformations. As L. Murphy and Le Heron (1999) explain, since 1900, a number of different schools of geographical thought have evolved from the regional geographies in the late nineteenth century, through to the 1960s, to quantitative geography in the 1960s and 1970s, humanistic geographies in the 1970s and 1980s, to GIS, political economy geographies, feminist geographies, new regional geographies and postmodern geographies in the period since the 1980s. What is apparent is the plurality of these diverse approaches now available to geographers which has characterised many of the approaches embodied in this book. These new approaches have spawned new research agendas, critical debate, often opposing philosophical and methodological positions as each perspective has been informed by the multiplicity of knowledge from each platform of research. Yet critics of this growing diversity of geographical research agendas in human geography have also become alarmed at the lack of coherence and focus in the discipline of geography as the seemingly fragmented range of geographies have been discovered, reinvented, reimaged and given new life within new research agendas. If one of the core strengths of geography is its ability to offer synthesis and a conceptual underpinning based on notions of space, place, people and environment, the geographer faces a growing challenge: synthesising an exponential growth in 'geographies of leisure, recreation and tourism' within the context of an exponential growth in human knowledge from both academic and the public/private sector, made available by the electronic age.

This final chapter will briefly revisit the place of tourism and recreation geography in the applied geography tradition. It will then discuss the contributions that geography can bring to the study of tourism and recreation and highlight a possible future for the field.

GEOGRAPHY – THE DISCIPLINE: DIRECTION AND PROGRESS

According to R.J. Johnston (1985b: 326), 'geographers, especially but not only human geographers, have become parochial and myopic in recent decades' and have been accompanied by a disengagement from close field contact and a global concern with human phenomena. The disengagement from the region has been seen as a mechanism to synthesise systematic investigations. In seeking to advance the discipline, Johnston (1985b) argued that geographers need both a theoretical appreciation of the general processes of the capitalist mode of production and an empirical appreciation of the social formations that result. The discipline versus detachment from the skills of fieldwork, observation and description continue to remain fundamental weaknesses, and in many respects the 'core' elements of a geographical education at university level now reflect the often fragmented specialisation that characterises many geography curricula. In fact, geography is a subject in retreat in many contexts, particularly in Australia where the specialisation function has now led to the dissipation of geography departments and the

emergence of more multidisciplinary groupings focused on environmental science, for example. In the UK, the declining enrolments being experienced by many geography departments has been attributed to the rapid growth in tourism and recreation studies with the focus on business, management and vocationalism and a declining interest at the post-16 level in schools and colleges. Geography is perceived as having failed to move with the times to integrate a greater vocationalism and applied focus, and in many cases to offer students a practical, real-world engagement with society. Even though the rise of GIS and its application to planning and problem-solving has assisted in real-world problem-solving, the main body of the discipline has often not engaged students in fundamental elements of the real world through fieldwork and practical knowledge.

In the United States the position of geography may be slightly more positive thanks in great part to the growth of government and industry awareness of the value of GIS; nevertheless, as the President of the Association of American Geographers noted, there is only a very limited presence of geography in the elite universities and institutions (Cutter 2000). While the authors may agree with Cutter's remarks that 'The lack of formal geography (courses, an undergraduate minor, major, or graduate study) in many of the most prestigious universities in the nation is a missed opportunity for these elite institutions of higher education' (Cutter 2000: 3), such a comment also reflects the failings of geography and geographers to effectively communicate their interests and contributions in a wide range of contemporary issues and subjects, including tourism and recreation, as well as the vagaries of academic conflict for resources.

Although the new synthesis of applied geography (Pacione 1999b) outlines the way in which some geographers perceive themselves and their contribution to research, this is not being adequately communicated to students, particularly in the marginalisation of applied geography as a hybrid according to concerns purists and qualitative researchers have about social and cultural theory as their analytical framework. Nevertheless, it is important to revisit applied geography and to provide some illustrations of how tourism and recreational geographers make contributions to 'problem-solving', 'policy-analysis' and the wider public good. Pacione (1999b) in his protocol for applied geographical analysis (Figure 10.1) outlines the DEEP process, Description, Explanation, Evaluation and Prescription, which may be followed by Implementation and Monitoring.

REVISITING APPLIED GEOGRAPHY

Within the literature on the geography of recreation and tourism there have been comparatively few studies which have emphasised how the tourism and recreation geographer has made a valuable contribution to the wider development of 'applied geography'. According to Sant (1982), the scope of applied geography comprises a concern with

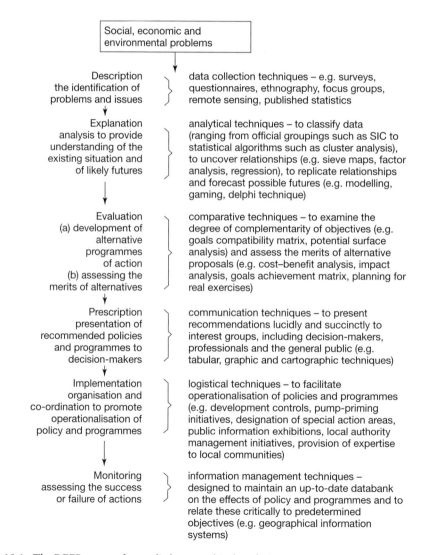

Figure 10.1: The DEEP process for applied geographical analysis
Source: Pacione (1999b)

policy-making and the monitoring of problems. More specifically it focuses on 'the sense of the problem, the contribution to decision making and policy, the monitoring of actions and the evaluation of plans. But these are common to all applied social sciences' (Sant 1982: 3) and so the geographer must ensure that he or she can make a distinctive contribution through the use of approaches, tools, techniques or skills which other social scientists, consultants and policy-makers do not possess, if it is regarded as important that a geographical approach survives.

Pacione (1999b:1) argued that 'Applied geography is concerned with the application of geographical knowledge and skills to the resolution of real-world social, economic and environmental problems' such as those associated with recreation and tourism. Pacione also developed the argument of 'useful knowledge' which also raises the inevitable criticisms of what might be non-useful geographical knowledge and useful for whom? As Frazier (1982: 17) observed, 'applied geography uses the principles and methods of pure geography but is different in that it analyses and evaluates real-world action and planning and seeks to implement and manipulate environmental and spatial realities'. Indeed Sant (1982) viewed theory as crucial to applied geography in providing a framework for analysis and a context by which moral goals could be judged. These arguments were developed by Palm and Brazel (1992: 342) as 'applied research in any discipline is best understood in contrast with basic or pure research'. In geography, basic research aims to develop new theory and methods that help explain the processes through which the spatial organisation of physical or human environments evolves. In contrast, applied research uses existing geographic theory or techniques to understand and solve specific empirical problems'. In practice, a dichotomy between pure and applied knowledge has been laboured, particularly to question the academic value of applied research, even though it has often had policy or decision-making outcomes that esoteric and seemingly inward-looking pure research can rarely contribute. To the contrary, as Harvey (1984: 7) commented, 'geography is far too

important to be left to generals, politicians and corporate chiefs. Notions of applied and relevant geography pose questions of objectives and interests served . . . there is more to geography than the production of knowledge'. By engaging with people external to the university applied geography has a contribution to make to society, even if there are questions about the values and objectives of applied research and its potential uses. Critics of publicly commissioned research may point to the role of studies in validating perspectives on the agenda of the commissioning agency, not seeking critical debate in extreme cases. But any applied geographical researcher with the skills and experience to engage with agencies and to recognise the constraints and limits imposed by the private and public may be outweighed by the wider benefits to society. Moreover, applied research need not be research undertaken for development agencies or industry and can also include community-based research or research undertaken for non-government organisations. For example, Croy and Hall (2003) described how student research undertaken as part of their degree programme could be used to transfer intellectual capital to rural communities that otherwise did not have the resources to either afford or undertake such research. Such an activity directly connects with the issue of the relevance of research, and as Hall (2004) commented in writing on the issue of reflexivity in qualitative tourism research:

> I have great frustration with much of the research and scholarship undertaken in tourism. Often competently done, but without reflexion and thought as to whose interests are being served – which is normally those from business and government with access to power. For all the talk of sustainable and alternative tourism, few alternatives have really shown up which explore the potential for other spaces and places which reflexivity may provide. In my more sanguine moments I believe that this is because researchers often take the easier path in tourism research because within current academic structures that is what provides the rewards.
> (Hall 2004a: 151)

In this bean-counting society where academics are now driven by academic outputs (see Page 2003b), applied research has often been downgraded or dismissed where academic publications cannot be obtained from commissioned research. Yet this in itself is self-defeating and inward-looking, missing the wider community service and social benefits of the knowledge economy associated with universities and its main clients – the population. These debates have also been aired in the Spanish geographical community (e.g. Segrelles-Serrano 2002) and the lack of social awareness in the training and education of geography graduates for professional careers (Naranjo 2001). Indeed, while there is much discussion about knowledge management in tourism, it often tends to be seen just in terms of transferring knowledge to industry rather than all those for whom knowledge, in its various forms, may be relevant.

All too often the application of geographical skills outside the academy in commercial and non-commercial contexts has been poorly developed. There are notable exceptions in the history of geographical thought where the skills of spatial analysis have been used for practical and commercial purposes, particularly in colonial times where the pursuit of resource inventories and mapping assisted in imperialist expansion in new territories (see Johnston 1991). In the post-war period some aspects of geography clearly dissipated to new disciplines such as town planning while the greater social science involvement and expansion of geographical subject matter saw geographers lose some of their competitive edge which had been gained in the pre-war and inter-war years. In recent times, some geographers have made transitions into the public and private sector where their skills have been in high demand (e.g. GIS) and some have made major contributions to public policy formulation and analysis in recreation and tourism (e.g. Patmore 1983). There has been the development of new specialisms which have emerged from a geographical tradition with an explicit public and commercial dimension. Recreation and tourism are two examples which have furnished many opportunities for geographers to apply their skills in a wider context than academia, although

this has not always meant that they have been particularly successful in capitalising on such opportunities.

While geographers still make a substantial contribution to planning, this contribution is perhaps not widely acknowledged by society at large. Similarly, GIS is increasingly being usurped by marketers, while the contribution of geographers to tourism and recreation is now adding far more of an academic base for the field of tourism and recreation studies than it is for geography. Should we care? The answer we believe is 'yes'. As Harvey (2000) commented:

> In facing up to a world of uncertainty and risk, the possibility of being quite undone by the consequences of our own actions weighs heavily upon us, often making us prefer 'those ills we have than flying to others that we know nor of'. But Hamlet, beset by angst and doubt and unable to act, brought diaster upon himself and upon his land by the mere fact of his inaction.
>
> (Harvey 2000: 254)

As the book stated at the outset by imitating the title of Massey and Allen's (1984) work, *Geography Matters!*, the geography of tourism and recreation also matters. One of the problems however is that we are often not very good at convincing other people that we do, as geography does not have a long history of engagement with the public and private sector. In fact declining enrolments in geography at university level in the UK have been attributed to the growth of interest in cognate subjects like tourism and recreation, though this is part of a growing interest in vocational subjects such as business studies as previously mentioned. Given increasing demands for the development of sustainable forms of tourism on the one hand and a relevant academic geography on the other, geography and geographers have an important role to play. In some senses those geographers who have moved to business schools to pursue their interest in tourism and recreation have at least managed to retain a spatial component to such curricula.

CONTRIBUTIONS

According to Stamp (1960: 9), 'the unique contribution of the geographer is the holistic approach in which he sees the relationship between man and his [*sic*] environment'. This statement is just as relevant to the application of geography to problem-solving today as it was when originally written. Indeed, perhaps more so given the size of the environmental, social and economic problems we face. Doornkamp (1982) posed a range of questions related to the role of applied geography, and two of these are of significance to tourism and recreation:

- Is the geographical contribution sufficiently unique to make it worth pursuing?
- How, in the commercial world, can the work of the applied geographer be sold?

These two questions highlight the need for geographers to assess what inherent skills they have which may be of value in an applied context. While accepting that the nature of geographical training

in the 1990s may be somewhat different from that in the 1970s and 1980s, Table 10.1 does still provide a useful assessment of how the geographer can contribute to problem-solving. While skills are important in addressing problems, Doornkamp (1982) and Dawson and Doornkamp's (1973) research in applied geography provides many key pointers to the value of a spatial approach. Doornkamp highlights the need to separate knowledge from the ability to use skills. During a geographical education, exposure to the systematic elements of the discipline in human and physical geography combines with practical and fieldwork in spatial techniques, which, together with regional studies, is where many of the former elements can be synthesised. This continues to provide the core of knowledge for the geographer and more advanced training then focuses on a specialised study in a particular subdiscipline of geography. It is often at this point that the cross-over between geography and other social science disciplines occurs when the knowledge base becomes shared. The problem within business schools is that the spatial component is often watered down to an

Table 10.1: The skills of a geographer

- To think in spatial terms.
- To be able to assess the implications of the distribution of any one 'landscape' characteristic.
- To be able to think about more than one distribution at a time – and to perceive from this any likely generic links between the items under study.
- To be able to change the scale of thinking according to the needs of the phenomena or problems being analysed.
- To be able to add the dimension of time as appropriate.
- To be able to place phenomena within a 'model' or 'systems' framework.
- To be able to comprehend and initiate thinking that links the human and physical systems operating in the landscape.
- To 'read' and 'understand' landscape.
- To be able to use certain techniques, for example:
  - to acquire information through fieldwork, map analysis or from remote sensing sources – with an emphasis on spatial distributions and relationships
  - to be able to handle and analyse large data sets, incomplete data sets, spatial data or time-based data, through quantitative methods using computer technology
  - to be equally at home in a literary search among archives and historical records
  - to be able to monitor landscape components, and to be able to submit them to further analyses as appropriate
  - to present information with clarity, and especially in map form
  - to utilise technological developments such as GIS to assist in gaining a holistic view of the problem in hand.
- To be able to provide a statement of one's findings which integrates one's own knowledge with that of allied disciplines.

Source: after Doornkamp (1982: 7)

extremely basic conceptualisation of place, space and environment. At the same time, the inquisitive nature of geographical research, particularly the interest in human–environment relationships at a variety of spatial scales, often means that the geographer pursues a holistic perspective not often found in other disciplines. Yet conveying this to the new generation of students interested in the business applications of recreation and tourism requires the geographer not only to sell the value of a synthesising holistic approach, but also to move forward to meet the new challenge for applied geography in a new millennium.

Equally, the geographer also has a formidable challenge in convincing colleagues and researchers in mainstream geography of the validity and intellectual rigour associated with research in recreation and tourism.

But harnessing this training and the range of skills acquired in order to apply them in a problem-solving context requires one important prerequisite. According to Doornkamp (1982: 9), this is an ability to see the problem from the point of view of the person who needs a solution. Having convinced this person of their ability to conceptualise the problem in their terms, in order to provide a solution three principal factors need to be considered:

- The research must be framed and reported in a manner which the client requires: it needs to be as concise and as thorough as possible. It is not to be a thesis or academic research paper, otherwise the client will simply not recommend or use the organisation again. This is a principal failing for many academics who are unable to bridge the industry–academic interface.
- Personal relationships of trust and respect need to be built up in a commercial environment, often framed around numerous meetings and regular interfacing, and the work must be professionally presented, being easy to read, targeted at the audience intending to read it, and precise and unambiguous.
- Even where the client is a non-paying customer (i.e. if the research is undertaken as a

contribution to the local community), such criteria are equally important. Otherwise, the outside world's image of the geographer will remain one of the ivory tower academic perceived as being distant from the real world and problem-solving contributions they can make. Likewise, academics need to be willing to incorporate changes on drafts and to recognise that in this environment their view is not necessarily without reproach. This is nowhere more the case than in recreation and tourism where an explicit business dimension is incorporated into such research.

It is fair to agree with Doornkamp's (1982: 26) analogy that practising geographers left the discipline in the immediate post-war period and joined the commercial world, calling themselves planners. A similar move may be occurring in recreation and tourism, with the movement of staff to business schools and specialist tourism and/or recreation departments either from academic positions in departments of geography or after completion of their graduate studies. The 'professional practice' side of the discipline of geography has continued to lose out to other disciplines even when its skills are more relevant and analytical. Interfacing with the real world has meant that a small proportion of recreation and tourism geographers have made a steady transition to professional practice without compromising their academic integrity and reputation. While payment for their services may have filled some of their peers and contemporaries with horror, recreation and tourism are commercial activities. In some cases, not using the label 'geographer' can have a great deal of benefit when interfacing with recreation and tourism businesses, since the public perception of geographers is not of practitioners making commercial or social contributions to society. So in summary, it is clear that applied geography problem-solving in recreation and tourism contexts can enhance the geographer's skills and relationship with society. In the longer term, it may help address the public image of the discipline as one of major value to research in applied fields such as tourism.

But ultimately the main barrier to geographers using their skills for an applied purpose is their own willingness and ability to interface in commercial and public contexts where they can be heard, listened to, taken seriously and their skills harnessed. In many cases, there is often a belated recognition of the value of such skills when a client uses such a person. Therefore, the public face of geography can be enhanced only if it embraces recreation and tourism as legitimate subdisciplines of a post-industrial society/geography that can have a major contribution to make in various applied contexts.

THE ROLE OF GIS AND TOURISM: A TOOL FOR APPLIED GEOGRAPHIC RESEARCH

GIS, developed by advances in computer hardware and software (such as ArcInfo), incorporates more sophisticated systems to search, query, present and analyse data in a spatial context. Table 10.2 outlines the capabilities of a GIS and its role in enabling geographers to assist decision-makers in making planning decisions. In fact, Butler (1992) outlined some of the possible problem-solving roles of GIS in tourism as shown in Table 10.3. What is evident from Table 10.3 is the application of GIS

to tourism planning, particularly in tourism and recreational resource management, as well as in tourism marketing (Elliott-White and Finn 1998; Farsari and Prastacos 2004). The ability to incorporate the dynamics of tourism and recreational activity and its effect on tourism and recreational resources has a major role to play. As Boyd and Butler (1996) observed, GIS can be used to identify suitable areas for ecotourism in Northern Ontario. The process of employing a GIS involved the inventory mapping, buffering (which is the identification of areas of human intrusion) with overlaps to map the appropriate areas for ecotourism. A very early application of GIS in the UK by Duffield and Coppock (1975) was associated with the development of the Tourism and Recreation Information Package (TRIP) to assist with tourism planning in Scotland. What the use of GIS highlights is which agency is the most appropriate framework for tourism and recreation planning, as outlined in Chapter 9, given the decline in strategic planning in the 1980s and 1990s. What Bahaire and Elliott-White's (1999) review of GIS and its use in tourism reveals is a passivity in geographers' impact and influence. The problem is that the technique is valuable, but few geographers are making the fundamental linkage with public sector planning agencies, political decision-makers and policy-

Table 10.2: Capabilities of a Geographical Information System

Examples of functional capabilities of a GIS	Examples of basic questions that can be investigated using a GIS (after Rhind 1990)		Examples of tourism applications
Data entry, storage and manipulation	Location	What is at?	Tourism resource inventories
Map production	Condition	Where is it?	Identifying most suitable locations for development
Database integration	Trend	What has changed?	Measuring tourism impacts
Data queries and searches	Routing	Which is the best route?	Visitor management/flows
Spatial analysis	Pattern	What is the pattern?	Analysing relationships associated with resource use
Spatial modelling	Modelling	What if . . .?	Assessing potential impacts of tourism development

Source: Bahaire and Elliott-White (1999: 161)

Table 10.3: Problems of tourism and the potential of Geographical Information Systems (based on Butler 1992: 33)

Problems of tourism	Nature of problem	GIS application
Ignorance	• Of dimensions, nature, power of tourism, i.e. by key decision-makers and communities	A key point is that stakeholders do not have the types of information needed to assert their point of view. Using GIS for the *systematic inventory* of tourism resources and analysis of *trends* can help ameliorate this problem
	• To determine levels of sustainable tourism development given the fuzziness of the concept	GIS can be used to monitor and control tourism activities once levels of development deemed appropriate and acceptable by stakeholders have been determined. By integrating tourism, environmental, socio-cultural and economic data GIS facilitates the identification and monitoring of indicators of sustainable development
Lack of ability	• To manage and control development – associated with uses, capabilities, capacities	GIS can be used to identify suitable locations for tourism development, identify zones of conflict/complementarity
Lack of appreciation	• That tourism is an industry and causes impacts which cannot be easily reversed	GIS can be used to *stimulate* and *model* spatial outcomes of proposed developments. To sensitise stakeholders to externalities associated with their actions, e.g. visibility analysis, network analysis, gravity models
	• That tourism is dynamic and causes change as well as responding to change, i.e. tourism is just a part of a wider development process which can produce intra- and inter-industry conflict which may destroy the tourism resource	GIS enables the *integration* of datasets representing socio-economic development and environmental capital within a given spatial setting. GIS sits comfortably on top of integrated and strategic spatial planning
Lack of agreement	• Over levels of appropriate development, control and direction	GIS functions as a decision support system – to produce more informed arguments and (hopefully) facilitate compromise and resolution. However, this presupposes the existence of a coherent planning and development control framework

Source: Bahaire and Elliott-White (1999: 162)

makers (see Page et al. 1999 for a discussion of this issue in relation to Maori tourism in New Zealand). For example, in the case of Scotland's first national park, the Loch Lomond and Trossachs National Park, it has embraced the use of GIS as a tool to help develop the planning framework for identifying the zoning and management of visitor areas and destinations as a basis for the development of spatial policies and actions to manage visitor activity. This highlights how a range of geographical skills are being harnessed to shape public policy through a partnership of public sector and university researchers to provide a series of outcomes which are in the wider public interest. While critics of such applied research might suggest that this is both theoretically devoid and imbued with the values of the agencies concerned, university input was selected for its impartial perspective and also due to the understanding of the complex theoretical and methodological issues associated with developing such a framework. Indeed without that geographical training, knowledge of theory and practice, then such inputs to the planning and policy forming process could not occur. The role of theory and synthesis in the management of tourism and recreation phenomena in a spatial context is critical in informing the way forward, based on best practice and robust methodological development to model the situation so that the wider public and policy-makers can understand some of the spatial dynamics of visitor activity and impacts within the new national park. The 1970s and early 1980s saw recreational and tourism geographers (e.g. Coppock, Patmore and Glyptis in the UK) play a vital role in advancing the geographer's role in policy-making and planning at all levels in the public sector. Yet in the 1990s and the new millennium, this lead has not been carried out in such a high profile manner by the new generation of geographers although notable examples of university and public/private sector partnerships do exist to develop solutions to applied geographical problems within the wider domain of leisure. While there are exceptions to the rule, the discipline and subdiscipline of tourism and recreation have not made a major impact with political decision-makers and this remains a key area of concern, given the role of spatial analysis in understanding the effects and management needs of tourism and recreation.

THE ROLE OF THE GEOGRAPHER IN THE NEW MILLENNIUM: WHITHER TOURISM AND RECREATION?

The perceived domain of the geographer – the quest for investigations associated with environment, humans, place and space – is not necessarily viewed by other social scientists and non-academics in the same way. Indeed, a multidisciplinary approach to problems underpinned and informed by a spatial analytical approach often provides an understanding beyond that achieved by the geographer working in isolation. One consequence of building multidisciplinary research teams peopled by non-geographers is a growing disciplinary

marginalisation by other geographers and the stated 'gatekeepers' within the subdiscipline. This can impair the wider assimilation of the research area within the subdiscipline and within the wider context of geography as a discipline. This is somewhat ironic at a time when tourism and recreation have experienced rapid growth as activities within global, national and local space economies. Further, with tourism and recreation comprising major components of the service economies of many countries and regions, it is somewhat surprising that the contribution of geographers to understanding this phenomenon is still constrained by perceptions within the discipline of what is appropriate to study and research as serious topics of geographical investigation.

Both authors of this book are probably viewed as 'outsiders' in the wider geographical domain of consciousness that now besets the discipline, even though there is a growing strength of interest in tourism and recreation. (If some of Butler's (2004) comments regarding the relatively peripheral role of geography in tourism studies generally holds true then they may also be seen as outsiders in that disciplinary context as well.) The major 'internal' problem facing the discipline of geography is related to the tension between positivism and humanism/the new cultural geography and the army of geographers turned social theorists. This fragmentation or internal realignment to develop careers related to the latest bandwagon (a theme the authors were frequently confronted with in the 1980s and early 1990s in relation to tourism and recreation) have certainly made a geographical education a less unified and structured process. Disciplinary fragmentation and communication within the wider domain of geography creates barriers and constraints to the wider integration of this exciting, dynamic and fast-changing area of research. The fundamental difference between the authors as 'outsiders' and the new social theorists is that the authors utilise applied geographical concepts and analysis to study tourism and recreation. One of the central messages implicit in this book is that it is inappropriate to simply decry previous paradigms as redundant and analytically bankrupt:

within tourism and recreation geography, the early studies established many of the central tenets and building blocks of the subdiscipline and, in fact, lay much of the intellectual foundation for current interests in themes such as mobility, the body, performity and place (Hall 2005a). Indeed, as Livingstone (1992) commented,

> Fragmentation of knowledge, social differentiation, and the questioning of scientific rationality have all coalesced to reaffirm the importance of the particular, the specific, the local. And in this social and cognitive environment a geography stressing the salience of place is seen as having great potential.
>
> (Livingstone 1992: 358)

The importance of place and the application of geographical knowledge is reflected in the richness of the literature reviewed throughout the book, and the value it has added to spatial analysis of tourism. The discontinuities between positivism, humanism, critical social theory and Marxism may enrich a geographical awareness of how to interpret the real world, but it does not produce a skill set among graduates which can broadly be termed spatial analysis. Indeed the emergence of GIS as the new 'saviour' of the discipline, in terms of relevance, practical application and as a recruiter of students in the information age (see Forer 1999) certainly gave the discipline a new lease of life at the end of the twentieth century. The effect has also been to create a new specialisation that is not a core element of the discipline, since it is the 'applied' domain and not the theoretically derived core of the purists.

These constant revolutions in geographical knowledge and thinking pose a central question for the student of tourism and recreation. What is the role of the geographer? Is there a role? How is that role mediated, nurtured and negotiated within the discipline, outside the discipline and how does the geographer engage political influence to ensure the profile, relevance and continued survival of the subject? One way of engaging in this debate is through introspection and reflexivity – or through a refocusing of attention on the possible contribution which specific approaches to geography may make to problem-solving (i.e. the applied perspective).

These questions and issues are a useful starting point, to assess the role of the geographer beyond the synthesising role and integrating ability to harmonise a wide range of social science perspectives. R. Bennett (1985) warned of the dangers of such an approach since it may contribute to a loss of identity among geographical contributions, as other disciplines and their methodologies overtake the spatial focus. What is clear is that the quest for relevance, understanding and explanation cannot solely be achieved from the logical positivist approach to research. It can be as blind as it is revealing: it can obscure understanding and explanation – it is only a partial focus on a problem and its solution. Thus, the non-positivist or humanist perspective needs to be used as a counterweight to expand, develop, question and reinterpret the positivist paradigm. In this context, Powell (1985) re-examined the four main concerns of the geographer which remain as relevant two decades later. These are:

- *Space:* what is the human meaning and experience of space?
- *Place:* as a centre of action and intention in relation to human activity, where perception, human activity and changes in the life course of individuals and groups occur.
- *Time:* how it is fundamental to human activity, action and the interaction with humans and their environment, in terms of resource conflict in outdoor recreation and their use of leisure time.
- *People:* as the fundamental focus in a relevant 'human geography'.

These four central themes characterise the geographer's focus and, even though it is specific to the way the humanist views the world, place, space and time which is different from the positivist, they are key elements in establishing research questions and a particular view of the world. Therefore, in the new millennium, tourism and recreational geographers are increasingly being divided into the positivist–humanistic camps, with the ongoing quest for relevance, explanation and recognition of their respective contributions to a spatially relevant subject. At a personal level, the authors recognise the criticisms of applied geography as critiqued and debated by Pacione (1999a, 1999b) and would proffer the following role for the geographer in a wider leisure context: to utilise an applied analytical science with its focus on space, place, time and people with a view to problem-solving, understanding and explanation. One important qualification needs to be added, however: to adopt a radical critique, such as Peet (1977a, 1977b), will likely not contribute to a wider public policy debate for geographers and an ability to improve the human condition, albeit from within the capitalist system. This is not to say that the authors are not empathetic with such a perspective – far from it. However, we would argue that to actually improve the human condition (and we remain such unreconstructed children of the Enlightenment that we still see this as a goal of geography and ourselves as academics), one needs to engage and communicate with stakeholders, most especially the wider public and those who are affected by our work, in a language which is broadly understandable and not the domain of arcane, inward-looking academic subcommunities.

This does not mean that we seek the corporatisation of the university nor that we wish just to talk the language of industry – it means we need to argue and communicate in a manner which can be understood in the public sphere. As one of the author's experience of working on the education–industry interface, being funded by an enterprise company, suggests, geographers and other academics who engage with the wider world need to be able to 'talk the talk' of industry and other groups when required to engage them effectively rather than remain marginalised on the periphery looking in. It is that marginalisation that has continued to dominate the discipline's relationships with the outside world. Being able to engage effectively requires not only a specific skill set to understand the needs and values of such bodies, but also a direct, focused and concise manner of communication. In very simple terms, industry poses a problem to solve and it wants a

credible, robust and methodologically sound solution, although people in industry may not want to engage with all the complexities of how you arrived at such a solution. They just need to know it has integrity and will stand up to scrutiny. What industry does not want to know is the ephemeral and somewhat indulgent rhetoric that surrounds many academics when they engage with outside bodies on what they have published recently and how influential it is. External agencies and companies frequently return to a set series of questions:

- Do you have the right skill set for the job?
- Do you have relevant experience and expertise supported by track records in similar activities (i.e. commercial reports and consultancies rather than academic publications on the topic)?
- Can you deliver a solution on time? (This is where most academics fall down as they overrun, cannot manage time well and so provide a bad image for others.)
- Is the solution cost-effective and value for money?
- Will the outcomes be capable of being used and solutions implemented in a direct and effective manner?

If the answer is *yes* to these questions, then it is apparent that individual geographers or groups of geographers rather than geography per se can be relevant to society, to the needs of policy-makers, planners, communities, individuals and to the future of the planet. In the tourism–recreation context, the skills of the geographers are increasingly being harnessed, recognised and utilised within academia, frequently in the field of market surveys, position papers and data analysis rather than in the more skilled area of feasibility studies, though examples of the latter do exist. Ironically, it is often when geographers drop the label of 'geography' and move to an applied academic environment such as a business school or planning department, that their skills gain a greater acceptance, legitimacy and validity with political decision-makers. Introspection, the idiosyncratic nature of much of the cultural turn in recent human geography and much of the discipline's detachment from the real world of politics, decision-making and problem-solving to improve the human condition has not gained the subject widespread societal support.

To the discipline's ideologues, the gatekeepers of knowledge, its leaders and scholars, tourism and recreation will continue to remain a fringe activity – amorphous and seemingly didactic in its conception of space, place and environment. Yet in a changing postmodern society where consumption is a basic element associated with the growth of tourism, leisure and recreation, a discipline which does not embrace this new domain of study is regulating itself to a 'non-relevant', esoteric and increasingly distant position. Recreational activity and tourism per se are now culturally embedded in the lifestyles of much of the world's population. This may be a function of globalisation, westernisation or other socially contingent processes; if they wish to pursue them it is a reality. It exists – and poses new research agendas and

opportunities for a generation of geographers. The area is exciting, ever-changing, socially, economically, politically and environmentally challenging. Understanding the dynamics, processes, elements of change (e.g. see the Insight below) and wider meaning and value of recreation and tourism in society has opened so many avenues for spatial and multidisciplinary research. For the main discipline, these opportunities should be fostered, nurtured and encouraged since the area has the potential to engage not only students, but the wider public decision-makers and politicians. Geographers can make a difference, even if it is in a neo-liberal market-driven economy, making gradual changes to the status quo. Geography is relevant, intellectually challenging and capable of developing the wider context of leisure studies, so that recreation and tourism are respectable areas of study within the discipline, and increasingly outside of the discipline, with geographers working in business schools, public and private sector contexts in the development of this area of study.

INSIGHT: The future – the ageing population

At the end of the twentieth century, 11 per cent of the world's population was aged 60 and above. By 2050, one in five will be 60 years or older, and by 2150, one in three will be 60 years or older. However, the older population itself is ageing. The health revolution, which has given millions of elderly persons relatively good health well into their eighties, has also helped drive tourism's growth in general and health-related travel in particular. The population of 45 to 64 year olds will grow nearly five times faster than the total population between 2000 and 2010; between 2010 and 2030, the population over 65 will grow eight times faster than the total population (Tarlow and Muehsam 1992). The increase in the number of very old people (aged 80+ years) between 1950 and 2050 is projected to grow by a factor of from eight to ten times on the global scale. On current trends, by 2150,

about one-third of the older population will be 80 years or older. As well as a general ageing of the world's population there are also substantial regional differences in the aged population. For example, currently one in five Europeans is 60 years or older, but one in twenty Africans is 60 years or older. In some developed countries, the proportion of older persons is close to one in five. According to the United Nations, during the first half of the twenty-first century that proportion will reach one in four and, in some countries, one in two (United Nations, Division for Social Policy and Development 1998). Given that the vast majority of the world's tourists come from the developed countries, such a demographic shift will clearly have substantial implications for the international health tourism industry. Not only may particular types of tourism continue to grow in popularity, such as cruising, but also second homes and retirement homes and the provision of health facilities for retired people may become increasingly important in destination development strategies. For example, areas of the European Mediterranean, the Iberian Peninsula and the south-west United States and Florida are already subject to substantial seasonal (e.g. Hall and Müller 2004) and permanent retirement migration (e.g. A.M. Williams et al. 1997; King et al. 1998, 2000) that is designed to further healthy retirement lifestyles.

In the United States the number of persons aged 65 and above has grown faster than the general population. The Travel Industry Association of America estimated that by the year 2000, elderly people would comprise approximately one-quarter of the nation's population (Tarlow and Muehsam 1992). With people living longer following retirement, the lifestyles of the mature traveller will have a substantial influence on the development and supply of tourism infrastructure. For example, *Modern Maturity*, a North American lifestyles journal for the over-fifties, surveyed its subscribers about their travel habits and preferences. Over 37 per cent travelled three to five times a year, 46 per cent preferred car travel over any other type of transportation, 42 per cent indicated that the purpose of their trip was to relax, 39 per cent preferred just their partner as a travelling companion, 46 per cent preferred to go to museums over any other tourist attraction, and 67 per cent stayed in hotels (Modern Maturity 1999: 12). This group not only will have the most available free time of any segment of the population, but also will have the greatest amount of disposable income. Already, travellers over age 60 make up well over 30 per cent of all room nights sold within the American lodging industry. Older travellers spend more nights away from home (8.2) than do travellers under age 50 (4.8), according to the American Association of Retired Persons (AARP). Financially and physically able elderly people will significantly increase the demand for leisure travel, with health-related tourism being a significant component of growth in the retired travel market (Tarlow and Muehsam 1992). Nevertheless, a critical factor in the tourism, leisure and second home patterns of retirees is not only their time budget but also their level of income. Growth of retirement tourism therefore requires continued economic growth in order to maintain pension and superannuation packages. Yet in many western countries the retirement age is now being increased by government (e.g. New Zealand) or such increase are being debated (e.g. Germany and the United Kingdom) because of concerns over the affordability of pensions. In addition, many retirees are continuing to work either out of choice or of necessity because of the inadequacy of retirement savings (Hall 2005d). Indeed, a further influential factor with respect to demographic change and tourism is that it is estimated that among the major industrialised countries only the United States is estimated to have significant population growth by 2050 (Population Reference Bureau 2004).

TRANSFORMATIONS?

As this book has indicated, the geography of tourism and recreation, as with the discipline as a whole, has undergone considerable change since it began in the 1930s. This is to be expected, since geography, as with any discipline, adapts and reacts in relation to the society and culture within which it operates (see Chapter 1). The case for understanding the changing nature of tourism and recreation 'contextually closely parallels the case made by realists for appreciating all human activity; the operation of human agency must be analysed within the constraining and enabling conditions provided by its environment' (Johnston 1991: 280). In this sense the environment for the study of tourism and recreation must be positive given the growth of international tourism and the role it now plays within government policy-making. Given the significance of globalisation, mobility, postmodernism, post-Fordism and localisation to contemporary social theory, it should also be no surprise that many human geographers and other social scientists are now discovering tourism and recreation as having some significance for social change. Indeed, the emerging paradigm of mobility which is acting to link research in tourism geography with that of migration, and is also connecting geographers, sociologists and demographers, appears to be a research direction potentially rich in possibilities (see e.g. Urry 2000; A.M. Williams and Hall 2000; Hall and Williams 2002; Coles et al. 2004). However, previous work in the area is often ignored while many authors discussing contemporary tourism phenomena, particularly in an urban or rural setting, seem to think that all tourists and tourism are the same and fail to perceive the complexity of the phenomena they are investigating.

It would also be true to note that many tourism and recreation geographers find the discovery of 'their' field by social theory and cultural studies somewhat amusing given that they have been ignored for so long. Others will also find it threatening given that their own work bears all the hallmarks of traditional spatial science, excellent maps, flows and patterns but a limited role for more critical examination of tourism phenomena.

The geography of tourism and recreation therefore bears the hallmarks of much Anglo-North American geography in terms of the tensions that exist between the different approaches within the discipline. Such tensions, if well managed, can be extremely healthy in terms of the debate they generate and the 'freshness' of the subject matter. However, if not well managed and if external influences become too attractive, splits will occur. Research and scholarship in the geography of tourism and recreation are now at this stage. Unless greater links are built between the subdiscipline and the discipline as a whole then, potentially, much of the field will be swallowed up by the rapidly expanding field of tourism studies which bears many of the hallmarks of being a discipline

in its own right (Hall 2005a). Even if only in terms of student numbers, such a shift would have substantial implications for geography as already mentioned above.

The geography of tourism and recreation is at a crossroads. It is to be hoped that a situation will not develop where those concerned with social theory will stay in geography and those who do not will go to the business and tourism schools. An understanding of social theory by itself will not provide geography graduates or tourism graduates with a career. Of course it should never be just about jobs; we hope it is also about the joy of gaining knowledge for its own sake. However, the integration of some of the central concerns of social theory, and the central concerns of the geographer – sites, places, landscapes, regions and national configurations, and the spatial arrangements and relationships that interconnect them – with the subject of tourism and recreation will lead to the development of a more relevant applied area of geography that can better contribute to all its stakeholders, including its students who are then exposed to the right range of traditions that have contributed to geographical knowledge and its application. To this end we can only reiterate the words of Gilbert White as a guiding light for a relevant tourism and recreation geography:

> Speaking only as one individual, I feel strongly that I should not go into research unless it promises results that would advance the aims of the people affected and unless I am prepared to take all practicable steps to help translate the results into action.
> (G. White 1972: 102)

QUESTIONS

- Is geography a relevant subject to study in the twenty-first century as a basis for understanding tourism and recreational phenomena?
- What is applied geography and how does it relate to tourism and recreation?
- How has the geographer contributed to the wider public policy and problem-solving approach to tourism and recreation research?

Has this been at the expense of academic credibility within the discipline?

• What is the role of GIS in tourism and recreational research?

READING

For a critical review of the role of geography as a discipline see

Johnston, R.J. (1985) 'Introduction: Exploring the future of geography', in R.J. Johnston (ed.) *The Future of Geography*, London: Methuen, pp. 3–26.

Meyer-Arendt, K. (2000) 'Commentary: Tourism geography as the subject of North American doctoral dissertations and masters theses, 1951–98', *Tourism Geographies*, 2(2): 140–57.

On the role of applied geography and the scope/extent of the geographer's engagement with 'real-world problems' and the wider public policy arena see

Pacione, M. (ed.) (1999) *Applied Geography: Principles and Practice*, London: Routledge (a very good comprehensive overview of the geographer's attempts to engage with research issues outside of academia).

For more applied examples, see journals such as *Tourism Geographies*, *Tourism Management*, *Journal of Sustainable Tourism*, *Journal of Ecotourism* and *Current Issues in Tourism*, which contain articles where similar applied research has been conducted within a spatially analytical framework.

On the use of GIS in tourism and recreational research see

Farsari, Y. and Prastacos, P. (2004) 'GIS applications in the planning and management of tourism', in A. Lew, C.M. Hall and A. Williams (eds) *Companion to Tourism*, Oxford: Blackwell, pp. 596–607.

Tarrant, M. and Cordell, H. (1999) 'Environmental justice and the spatial distribution of outdoor recreation sites: An application of geographic information systems', *Journal of Leisure Research*, 31(1): 18–34.

Van der Knaap, W. (1999) 'Research report: GIS-oriented analysis of tourist time–space patterns to support sustainable tourism development', *Tourism Geographies*, 1(1): 56–69.

BIBLIOGRAPHY

Aagesen, D. (2004) 'Burning monkey-puzzle: Native fire ecology and forest management in northern Patagonia', *Agriculture and Human Values*, 21(2–3): 233–42.

Aaker, D. and Day, G. (1986) *Marketing Research*, New York: Wiley.

Abegg, B. and Froesch, R. (1994) 'Climate change and winter tourism: Impact on transport companies in the Swiss Canton of Graubünden', in M. Beniston (ed.) *Mountain Environments in Changing Climates*, London: Routledge, pp. 328–40.

Abercrombie, P. (1938) 'Geography, the basis of planning', *Geography*, 20(3): 196–200.

Ackerman, E.A. (1963) 'Where is a research frontier?', *Annals of the Association of American Geographers*, 53: 429–40.

Ackoff, R.L. (1974) *Redesigning the Future*, New York: Wiley.

Adams, D.L. (1973) 'Uncertainty in nature: Weather forecasts and New England beach trip decision', *Economic Geographer*, 49: 287–97.

Adler, S. and Brenner, J. (1992) 'Gender and space: Lesbians and gay men in the city', *International Journal of Urban and Regional Research*, l6: 24–34.

Agarwal, S. (1994) 'The resort cycle revisited: Implications for resorts', in C. Cooper and A. Lockwood (eds) *Progress in Tourism, Recreation and Hospitality Management Volume 5*, London: Belhaven Press, pp. 194–208.

Agarwal, S., Ball, R., Shaw, G. and Williams, A. (2000) 'The geography of tourism production: Uneven disciplinary development', *Tourism Geographies*, 2(3): 241–63.

Agnew, M. and Viner, D. (2001) 'Potential impact of climate change on international tourism', *Tourism and Hospitality Research*, 3: 37–60.

Aitchison, C. (1997) 'A decade of compulsory competitive tendering in the UK sport and leisure services: Some feminist perspectives', *Leisure Studies*, 16: 85–105.

Aitchison, C. (1999) 'New cultural geographies: The spatiality of leisure, gender and sexuality', *Leisure Studies*, 18: 19–39.

Aitchison, C., Macleod, N. and Shaw, S. (2000) *Leisure and Tourism Landscapes: Social and Cultural Geographies*, London: Routledge.

Aldskogius, H. (1968) 'Modeling the evolution of settlement patterns: Two case studies of vacation house settlement', *Geografiska regionstudie*, 6, Uppsala, Sweden: Geografiske institutionen.

Aldskogius, H. (1977) 'A conceptual framework and a Swedish case study of recreational behaviour and environmental cognition', *Economic Geography*, 53: 163–83.

Alexander, K. (1984) 'In search of the spirit of wilderness', *Habitat*, 12(5): 3–5.

Allen, L.R., Long, P.T., Perdue, R.R. and Kieselbach, S. (1988) 'The impact of tourism development on residents' perceptions of community life', *Journal of Travel Research*, 27(1): 16–21.

Allix, A. (1922) 'The geography of fairs: Illustrated by old-world examples', *Geographical Review*, 12: 532–69.

Amin, A. (2002) 'Spatialities of globalisation', *Environment and Planning A*, 34: 385–99.

Amin, N., Shah, A.H. and Ahmad, F. (2001) 'Use and management of public parks in newly developed housing: Hayatabad, Peshawar', *Sarhad Journal of Agriculture*, 17(2): 183–7.

Anderson, D.H. and Brown, P.J. (1984) 'The displacement process in recreation', *Journal of Leisure Research*, 16(1): 61–73.

Anderson, J. (1971) 'Space-time budgets and activity studies in urban geography and planning', *Environment and Planning*, 3(4): 353–68.

Anderson, S., Smith, C., Kinsey, R. and Wood, J. (1990) *The Edinburgh Crime Survey: First Report*, Edinburgh: Scottish Office.

Anon. (1994) Sustainable Rural Tourism Development (special issue), *Trends*, 31(1).

Appleton, I. (1974) *Leisure Research and Policy*, Edinburgh: Scottish Academic Press.

Arbel, A. and Pizam, A. (1977) 'Some determinants of hotel location: The tourists' inclination', *Journal of Travel Research*, 15 (winter): 18–22.

Archer, B. (1973) *The Impact of Domestic Tourism*, Cardiff: University of Wales Press.

Archer, B.H. (1976) 'Uses and abuses of multipliers', in W.W. Swart and T. Var (eds) *Planning for Tourism Development: Quantitative Approaches*, New York: Praeger, pp. 115–32.

Archer, B.H. (1977a) 'The economic costs and benefits of tourism', in B.S. Duffield (ed.) *Tourism a Tool for Regional Development*, Leisure Studies Association Conference, Edinburgh, 1977, Edinburgh: Tourism and Recreation Research Unit, University of Edinburgh, pp. 5.1–5.11.

Archer, B.H. (1977b) *Tourism Multipliers: The State of the Art*, Occasional Papers in Economics No. 11, Bangor: University of Wales Press.

Archer, B.H. (1978) 'Tourism as a development factor', *Annals of Tourism Research*, 5: 126–41.

Archer, B.H. (1982) 'The value of multipliers and their policy implications', *Tourism Management*, 3: 236–41.

Archer, B.H. (1984) 'Economic impact: Misleading multiplier', *Annals of Tourism Research*, 11: 517–18.

Archer, J. and Yarman, I. (1991) *Nature Conservation in Newham*, Ecology Handbook 17, London: London Ecology Unit.

Arctic Climate Impact Assessment (ACIA) (2004) *Impacts of a Warming Arctic*, Cambridge: Cambridge University Press.

Argyle, M. (1996) *The Social Psychology of Leisure*, London: Penguin.

Aronsson, L. (2000) *The Development of Sustainable Tourism*, London: Continuum.

Ashworth, G. (2003) 'Urban tourism: Still an imbalance in attention', in C. Cooper (ed) *Classic Reviews in Tourism*, Channel View: Clevedon, 143–63.

Ashworth, G.J. (1989) 'Urban tourism: An imbalance in attention', in C.P. Cooper (ed.) *Progress in Tourism, Recreation and Hospitality Management*, Vol. 1, London: Belhaven Press, pp. 33–54.

Ashworth, G.J. (1992a) 'Is there an urban tourism?', *Tourism Recreation Research*, 17(2): 3–8.

Ashworth, G.J. (1992b) 'Planning for sustainable tourism: A review article', *Town and Planning Review*, 63(3): 325–9.

Ashworth, G.J. (1999) 'Heritage tourism: A review', *Tourism Recreation Research*, 25(1): 19–29.

Ashworth, G.J. and Dietvorst, A. (eds) (1995) *Tourism and Spatial Transformations*, Wallingford: CAB International.

Ashworth, G.J. and Ennen, E. (1998) 'City centre management: Dutch and British experiences', *European Spatial Research and Policy*, 5(1): 1–15.

Ashworth, G.J. and de Haan, T.Z. (1986) 'Uses and users of the tourist–historic city', *Field Studies*, 10, Groningen: Faculty of Spatial Sciences.

Ashworth, G.J. and Tunbridge, J.E. (1990) *The Tourist-Historic City*, London: Belhaven Press.

Ashworth, G.J. and Tunbridge, J.E. (1996) *Dissonant Heritage*, Chichester: Wiley.

Ashworth, G.J. and Voogd, H. (1988) 'Marketing the city: Concepts, processes and Dutch applications', *Town Planning Review*, 59(1): 65–80.

Ashworth, G.J. and Voogd, H. (1990a) *Selling the City*, London: Belhaven Press.

Ashworth, G.J. and Voogd, H. (1990b) 'Can places be sold for tourism?', in G.J. Ashworth and B. Goodall (eds) *Marketing Tourism Places*, London: Routledge, pp. 1–16.

Ashworth, G.J. and Voogd, H. (1994) 'Marketing of tourism places: What are we doing?', in M. Uysal (ed.) *Global Tourist Behaviour*, New York: International Press, pp. 5–20.

Ashworth, G.J., White, P.E. and Winchester, H.P. (1988) 'The red light district in the West-European City: A neglected aspect of the urban landscape', *Geoforum*, 19(2): 201–12.

Ateljevic, I. and Doorne, S. (2000) '"Staying within the fence": Lifestyle entrepreneurship in tourism', *Journal of Sustainable Tourism*, 8(5): 378–92.

Attfield, R. (1983) *The Ethics of Environmental Concern*, Oxford: Blackwell.

Atwood, W.W. (1931) 'What are National Parks?', *American Forests*, 37(September): 540–3.

Audit Commission (1993) *Realising the Benefits of Competition: The Client for Contracted Services*, London: HMSO.

Audit Commission (2003) *Leisure Services: Walsall Metropolitan Borough Council Inspection Report*, Leicester: Audit Commission.

Austin, M. (1974) 'The evaluation of urban public facility location: An alternative to cost–benefit analysis', *Geographical Analysis*, 6: 135–46.

Bachvarov, M. (1999) 'Troubled sustainability: Bulgarian seaside resorts', *Tourism Geographies*, 1(2): 192–203.

Bagnall, U., Gillmore, D. and Phipps, J. (1978) 'The recreational use of forest land', *Irish Forestry*, 35: 19–34.

Bahaire, T. and Elliott-White, M. (1999) 'The application of geographical information systems (GIS) in sustainable tourism planning', *Journal of Sustainable Tourism*, 7(2): 159–74.

Bailey, M. (1989) 'Leisure, culture and the historian: Reviewing the first generation of leisure historiography in Britain', *Leisure Studies*, 8: 107–27.

Bailie, J.G. (1980) 'Recent international travel trends in Canada', *Canadian Geographer*, 24(1): 13–21.

Baines, G.B.K. (1987) 'Manipulation of islands and men: Sand-cay tourism in the South Pacific', in S. Britton and W.C. Clarke (eds) *Ambiguous Alternative: Tourism in Small Developing Countries*, Suva: University of the South Pacific, pp. 16–24.

Baird, I.A. and Mitchell, J.M. (2001) '"Telling it how it is": Balancing user expectations and open space management resources in Canberra's "Garden City"', *Australian Parks and Leisure*, 4(3): 29–33.

Baker, A. and Genty, A. (1998) 'Environmental pressures on conserving cave speleothems: effects of changing surface land use and increased cave tourism', *Journal of Environmental Management*, 53: 165–75.

Baldridge, J.V. and Burnham, R.A. (1975) 'Organizational innovation: Individual, organizational, and environmental impacts', *Administrative Science Quarterly*, 20: 165–76.

Ball, R.M. (1989) 'Some aspects of tourism, seasonality and local labour markets', *Area*, 21: 35–45.

Balmer, K. (1971) 'Urban open space and outdoor recreation', in P. Lavery (ed.) *Recreation Geography*, Newton Abbot: David and Charles, pp. 112–26.

Balmer, K. (1973) *Open Space in Liverpool*, Liverpool: Liverpool Corporation.

Bandura, A. (1977) 'Self-efficacy: Toward a unifying theory of behavioural change', *Psychological Review*, 84: 191–215.

Bannan, M., Adams, C. and Pirie, D. (2000) 'Hydrocarbon emissions from boat engines: Evidence of recreational boating impact on Loch Lomond', *Scottish Geographical Journal*, 116(3): 245–56.

Bao, J. (2002) 'Tourism geography as the subject of doctoral dissertations in China 1989–2000', *Tourism Geographies*, 4(2): 148–52.

Barbaza, Y. (1966) *Le Paysage humain de la Costa Brava*, Paris: A. Colin.

Barber, A. (1991) *Guide to Management Plans for Parks and Open Spaces*, Reading: Institute of Leisure and Amenity Management.

Barbier, B. and Pearce, D.G. (1984) 'The geography of tourism in France: Definition, scope and themes', *GeoJournal*, 9(1): 47–53.

Bardwell, S. (1974) 'The National Park movement in Victoria', unpublished PhD thesis, Mebourne: Department of Geography, Monash University.

Bardwell, S. (1979) 'National parks for all: A New South Wales interlude', *Parkwatch*, 118: 16–20.

Bardwell, S. (1982) '100 years of national parks in Victoria: Themes and trends', *Parkwatch*, 129(winter): 4–11.

Baretje, R. (1982) 'Tourism's external account and the balance of payments', *Annals of Tourism Research*, 9(1): 57–67.

Barke, M. and Towner, J. (1996) 'Exploring the history of leisure and tourism in Spain', in M. Barke, J. Towner and M. Newton (eds) *Tourism in Spain: Critical Issues*, Wallingford: CAB International, pp. 189–212.

Barke, M. and Towner, J. (2003) 'Learning from experience? Progress towards a sustainable future for tourism in the Central and Eastern Andalucian littoral', *Journal of Sustainable Tourism*, 11(2–3): 162–80.

Barke, M., Towner, J. and Newton, M. (eds) (1996) *Tourism in Spain: Critical Issues*, Wallingford: CAB International.

Barnes, B. (1982) *T.S. Kuhn and Social Science*, London: Macmillan.

Barnes, M. and Wells, G. (1985) 'Myles Dunphy father of conservation dies', *National Parks Journal*, 29(1): 7.

BarOn, R. (1984) 'Tourism terminology and standard definitions', *Tourist Review*, 39(1): 2–4.

BarOn, R. (1989) *Travel and Tourism Data: A Comprehensive Research Handbook on the World Travel Industry*, London: Euromonitor.

Baron-Yellés, N. (1999) *Le Tourisme en France: Territoires et stratégies*, Paris: A. Colin.

Barrett, J. (1958) 'The seaside resort towns of England and Wales', unpublished PhD thesis, London: University of London.

Barry, F. (1991) 'Industrialisation strategies for developing countries: Lessons from the Irish experience', *Development Policy Review*, 9: 85–98.

Barry, K. (1984) *Female Sexual Slavery*, New York: New York University Press.

Baudrillard, J. (1981) *For a Critique of the Economy of the Sign*, St Louis, MO: Telos Press.

Baum, E.L. and Moore, E.J. (1966) 'Some economic opportunities and limitations of outdoor recreation enterprises', in G.W. Cornwall and C.J. Holcomb (eds) *Guidelines to the Planning, Developing, and Managing of Rural Recreation Enterprises*, Bulletin 301, Blacksburg, VA: Cooperative Extension Service, Virginia Polytechnic Institute, pp. 52–64.

Baum, T. (ed.) (1993) *Human Resource Issues in International Tourism*, Oxford: Butterworth-Heinemann.

Baxter, M.J. (1979) 'The interpretation of the distance and attractiveness components in models of recreational trips', *Geographical Analysis*, 11(3): 311–15.

Bayliss, D. (2003) 'Building better communities: Social life on London's cottage council estates, 1919–1939', *Journal of Historical Geography*, 29(3): 376–95.

Becker, R.H. (1981) 'Displacement of recreational users between the Lower St. Croix and Upper Mississippi Rivers', *Journal of Environmental Management*, 13(3): 259–67.

Belford, S. (1983) 'Rural tourism', *Architects Journal*, 178: 59–71.

Bell, D. and Valentine, G. (eds) (1997) *Consuming Geographies; We Are Where We Eat*, London: Routledge.

Bell, M. (1977) 'The spatial distribution of second homes: A modified gravity model', *Journal of Leisure Research*, 9(3): 225–32.

Bell, M. and Ward, G. (2000) 'Comparing temporary mobility with permanent migration', *Tourism Geographies*, 2(1), 87–107.

Bell, P.J.P. (2000) 'Contesting rural recreation: The battle over access to Windermere', *Land Use Policy*, 17(4): 295–303.

Bella, L. (1987) *Parks for Profit*, Montreal: Harvest House.

Benington, J. and White, J. (eds) (1988) *The Future of Leisure Services*, Harlow: Longman.

Beniston, M. (2003) 'Climate change in mountain regions: a review of possible impacts', *Climatic Change*, 59: 5–31.

Benko, G. and Strohmmayer, U. (1997) *Space and Social Theory: Interpreting Modernity and Postmodernity*, Oxford: Blackwell.

Bennett, A. (2002) *Great Western Lines and Landscapes*, Cheltenham: Runpast.

Bennett, R. (1985) 'Quantification and relevance?', in R. Johnston (ed.) *The Future of Geography*, London: Methuen, pp. 211–24.

Bennett, R. (1991) 'Rethinking London government', in K. Hoggart and D. Green (eds) *London: A New Metropolitan Geography*, London: Edward Arnold.

Bentley, T. and Page, S.J. (2001) 'Scoping the extent of tourist accidents in New Zealand', *Annals of Tourism Research*, 28(3): 705–26.

Bentley, T., Page, S.J. and Laird, I. (2000) 'Safety in New Zealand's adventure tourism industry: The client accident experience of adventure tourism operators', *Journal of Travel Medicine*, 7(5): 239–45.

Bentley, T., Page, S.J., Meyer, D. and Chalmers, D. (2001) 'The role of adventure tourism recreation injuries among visitors to New Zealand: An exploratory analysis using hospital discharge data', *Tourism Management*, 22(4): 373–81.

Bescancenot, J., Mounier, J. and Laverne, F. (1978) 'Climatological conditions for coastal tourism: A comprehensive research method', *Morois*, 99: 357–82.

Bevins, M., Brown, T., Cole, G., Hock, K. and LaPage, W. (1974) *Analysis of the Campground Market in the Northeast*, USDA, Forest Service Bulletin 679, Burlington, VT: University of Vermont Agricultural Experimental Station.

Bianchi, R. (2002) 'Towards a new political economy of global tourism', in R. Sharpley and D.J. Telfer (eds) *Tourism and Development: Concepts and Issues*, Clevedon: Channel View, pp. 265–99.

Billinge, M. (1996) 'A time and place for everything: An essay on recreation, re-creation and the Victorians', *Journal of Historical Geography*, 22(4): 443–59.

Bishop, R. and Robinson, L.S. (1998) *Night Market: Sexual Cultures and the Thai Economic Miracle*, London and New York: Routledge.

Bisset, N., Grant, A. and Adams, C. (2000) 'Long term changes in recreational craft utilisation on Loch Lomond', *Scottish Geographical Journal*, 116(3): 257–66.

Bitner, M.J. (1992) 'Servicescapes: The impact of physical surroundings on customers and employees', *Journal of Marketing*, 56(2): 57–71.

Bitner, M.J., Booms, B.H. and Tetreault, M.S. (1990) 'The service encounter: Diagnosing favourable and unfavourable incidents', *Journal of Marketing*, 54(2): 71–84.

Bittman, M. (2002) 'Social participation and family welfare: The money and time costs of leisure in Australia', *Social Policy and Administration*, 36(4): 408–25.

Blackwell, J. (1970) 'Tourist traffic and the demand for accommodation: Some projections', *Economic and Social Review*, 1: 323–43.

Blake, A. and Sinclair, M.T. (2003) 'Quantifying the effects of foot and mouth disease on tourism and UK economy', *Tourism Economics*, 9(4): 449–65.

Blake, J. (1996) 'Resolving conflict? The rural white paper, sustainability and countryside policy', *Local Environment*, 1(2): 211–18.

Blamey, R.K. (1995) *The Nature of Ecotourism*, Occasional Paper No. 21, Canberra: Bureau of Tourism Research.

Blamey, R.K. and Braithwaite, V.A. (1997) 'A social values segmentation of the potential ecotourism market', *Journal of Sustainable Tourism*, 5(1): 29–45.

Blank, U. and Petkovich, M. (1980) 'The metropolitan area: A multifaceted travel destination complex', in D. Hawkins, E. Shafer and J. Ravelstad (eds) *Tourism Planning and Development*, Washington, DC: George Washington University Press, pp. 393–405.

Blom, T. (2000) 'Morbid tourism: A postmodern market niche with an example from Althorp', *Norsk Geografisk Tidsskrift*, 54(1): 29–36.

Blowers, A. (1997) 'Environmental planning for sustainable development: The international context', in A. Blowers and B. Evans (eds) *Town Planning into the 21st Century*, London: Routledge, pp. 34–53.

Board, C., Brunsden, D., Gerrard, J., Morgan, B.S., Morley, C.D. and Thornes, J.B. (1978) 'Leisure and the countryside: The example of the Dartmoor National Park', in J. Blunden, P. Haggett, C. Hamnett and P. Sarre (eds) *Fundamentals of Human Geography: A Reader*, London: Harper & Row, pp. 44–52.

Bodewes, T. (1981) 'Development of advanced tourism studies in Holland', *Annals of Tourism Research*, 8(1): 35–51.

Bodlender, J.A. and Davies, E.J.G. (1985) *A Profile of Government Financial Grant Aid to Tourism*, Madrid: World Tourism Organization/Horwath and Horwath International.

Boo, E. (1990) *Ecotourism: The Potentials and Pitfalls*, 2 vols, Washington, DC: World Wildlife Fund.

Boschken, H. (1975) 'Second home subdivision: Market suitability for recreational and pastoral use', *Journal of Leisure Research*, 7(1): 63–72.

Bote Gomez, V. (1996) La investigacion turistica espanola en economia y geografia (special issue), *Estudios Turisticos*.

Bouquet, M. and Winter, M. (eds) (1987a) *Who from their Labours Rests? Conflict and Practice in Rural Tourism*, Aldershot: Avebury.

Bouquet, M. and Winter, M. (1987b) 'Introduction: Tourism, politics and practice', in M. Bouquet and M. Winter (eds) *Who from their Labours Rests? Conflict and Practice in Rural Tourism*, Aldershot: Avebury, pp. 1–8.

Bowler, I. and Strachan, A. (1976) *Parks and Gardens in Leicester*, Leicester: Recreation and Cultural Services Department, Leicester City Council.

Boyd, S.W. (2000) '"Heritage" tourism in Northern Ireland: Opportunity under peace', *Current Issues in Tourism*, 3(2): 150–74.

Boyd, S. and Butler, R. (1996) 'Seeing the forest through the trees: Using GIS to identify potential ecotourism sites in Northern Ontario', in L. Harrison and W. Husbands (eds) *Practising Responsible Tourism: International Case Studies in Tourism Planning, Policy and Development*, Chichester: Wiley, pp. 380–403.

Boyden, S.V. and Harris, J.A. (1978) 'Contribution of the wilderness to health and wellbeing', in G. Mosley (ed.) *Australia's Wilderness: Conservation Progress and Plans, Proceedings of the First National Wilderness Conference*, Australian Academy of Science, Canberra, 21–23 October 1977, Hawthorn, Vic.: Australian Conservation Foundation, pp. 34–7.

Boyer, M. (1996) *L'Invention du tourisme*, Paris: Le Seuil.

Bracey, H. (1970) *People and the Countryside*, London: Routledge & Kegan Paul.

Bradshaw, J. (1972) 'The concept of social need', *New Society*, 30(3): 640–3.

Brady Shipman Martin (1991) *Wicklow Mountain's National Park Visitor Centre Environmental Impact Statement*, Dublin: Brady Shipman Martin.

Brady Shipman Martin and Hyde, N. (1972–73) *National Coastline Study*, Dublin: Bord Fáilte and Foras Forbartha.

Brainard, J., Bateman, I. and Lovett, A. (2001) 'Modelling demand for recreation in English woodlands', *Forestry* 74(5): 423–38.

Bramham, P. and Henry, I. (1985) 'Political ideology and leisure policy in the United Kingdom', *Leisure Studies*, 4: 1–19.

Bramwell, B. (1991) 'Sustainability and rural tourism policy in Britain', *Tourism Recreation Research*, 16(2): 49–51.

Bramwell, B. (1993) *Tourism Strategies and Rural Development*, Paris: OECD.

Bramwell, B. (1994) 'Rural tourism and sustainable rural tourism', *Journal of Sustainable Tourism*, 2: 1–6.

Bramwell, B. (2004) 'Partnerships, participation, and social science research in tourism planning', in A. Lew,

C.M. Hall and A. Williams (eds) *Companion to Tourism*, Oxford: Blackwell, pp. 541–54.

Bramwell, B. and Lane, B. (1993) 'Sustainable tourism: An evolving global approach', *Journal of Sustainable Tourism*, 1(1): 6–16.

Bramwell, B. and Lane, B. (eds) (2000) *Tourism Collaboration and Partnerships: Politics, Practice and Sustainability*, Clevedon: Channel View.

Bramwell, B. and Rawding, L. (1996) 'Tourism marketing images of industrial cities', *Annals of Tourism Research*, 23(2): 201–21.

Braun, B. and Soskin, M. (2002) 'The impact of day trips to Daytona Beach', *Tourism Economics*, 8(3): 289–301.

Brennan, E. (ed.) (1990) *Heritage: A Visitor's Guide*, Dublin: Stationery Office.

Briassoulis, H. and van der Straaten, J. (1999) 'Tourism and the environment: An overview', in H. Briassoulis and J. van der Straaten (eds) *Tourism and the Environment*, 2nd edn, Dordrecht: Kluwer, pp. 1–20.

Briggs, A. (1969) *Victorian Cities*, Harmondsworth: Penguin.

Briggs, D. and Tantrum, D. (1997) *Using GIS for Countryside Management: The Experience of National Parks*, Cheltenham: Countryside Commission.

Bristow, R., Leiber, S. and Fesenmaier, D. (1995) 'The compatibility of recreation activities in Illinois', *Geografiska Annaler B*, 77(1): 3–15.

British Tourist Authority (1993) *Guidelines for Tourism to Britain 1993–97*, London: British Tourist Authority.

British Travel Association and University of Keele (1967 and 1969) *Pilot National Recreation Survey*, Keele: University of Keele.

Britton, S.G. (1980a) 'A conceptual model of tourism in a peripheral economy', in *South Pacific: The Contribution of Research to Development and Planning*, NZ MAB Report No. 6, Christchurch, NZ: NZ National Commission for Unesco/Department of Geography, pp. 1–12.

Britton, S.G. (1980b) 'The spatial organisation of tourism in a neo-colonial economy: A Fiji case study', *Pacific Viewpoint*, 21: 144–65.

Britton, S.G. (1982) 'The political economy of tourism in the Third World', *Annals of Tourism Research*, 9(3): 331–58.

Britton, S.G. (1991) 'Tourism, capital and place: Towards a critical geography of tourism', *Environment and Planning D: Society and Space*, 9: 451–78.

Brocx, M. (1994) *Visitor Perceptions and Satisfaction Study Winter 1993*, Auckland: Tourism Auckland.

Brooks, S. (1993) *Public Policy in Canada*, Toronto: McClelland and Stewart.

Brougham, J.E. and Butler, R.W. (1981) 'A segmentation analysis of resident attitudes to the social impacts of tourism', *Annals of Tourism Research*, 8: 569–90.

Brown, B. (1988) 'Developments in the promotion of major seaside resorts: How to effect a transition by really making an effort', in B. Goodall and G. Ashworth (eds) *Marketing in the Tourism Industry*, London: Routledge, pp. 176–86.

Brown, R.M. (1935) 'The business of recreation', *Geographical Review*, 25: 467–75.

Bryant, C. (1989) 'Entrepreneurs in the rural environment', *Journal of Rural Studies*, 5(4): 337–48.

Buchholtz, C.W. (1983) *Rocky Mountain National Park: A History*, Boulder, CO: Colorado Associated University Press.

Buhalis, D. and Cooper, C. (1998) 'Competition or co-operation? Small and medium sized tourism enterprises at the destination', in E. Laws, B. Faulkner and G. Moscardo (eds) *Embracing and Managing Change in Tourism: International Case Studies*, London: Routledge, pp. 324–46.

Bull, A. (1991) *The Economics of Travel and Tourism*, London: Pitman.

Bull, C. and Wibberley, G. (1976) *Farm Based Recreation in South-East England: Studies in Rural Land Use Report 12*, London: Wye College, University of London.

Bull, P. and Church, A. (1994) 'The hotel and catering industry of Great Britain during the 1980s: Sub-regional employment change, specialisation and dominance', in C.P. Cooper and A. Lockwood (eds) *Progress in Tourism, Recreation and Hospitality Management*, Vol. 5, Chichester: Wiley, pp. 248–69.

Buller, H. amd Hoggart, K. (1994) *International Counterurbanization: British Migrants in Rural France*, Aldershot: Avebury.

Bunce, R.G.H., Pérez Soba, M., Jongman, R.H.G., Gómez Sal, A., Herzog, F. and Austad, I. (eds) (2004) *Transhumance and Biodiversity in European Mountains*, IALE Publication 2004:1, International Association for Landscape Ecology.

Bureau of Industry Economics (BIE) (1991a) *Networks: A Third Form of Organisation*, Discussion Paper 14, Canberra: BIE.

Bureau of Industry Economics (1991b) 'Networks: A third form of organisation', *Bulletin of Industry Economics*, 10: 5–9.

Bureau of Land Management (1978) *Wilderness Inventory Handbook: Policy, Direction, Procedures, and Evidence for Conducting Wilderness Inventory on the Public Lands*, Washington, DC: Bureau of Land Management, Department of the Interior.

Burgess, E. (1925) 'The growth of the city' in R. Park and E. Burgess (eds) *The City*, Chicago, IL: University of Chicago Press, 47–62.

Burgess, J., Harrison, C. and Limb, M. (1988a) 'People, parks and the urban green: A study of popular meanings and values for open spaces in the city', *Urban Studies*, 26: 455–73.

Burgess, J., Harrison, C. and Limb, M. (1988b) 'Exploring environmental values through the medium of small groups. Part one: Theory and practice', *Environmental and Planning A*, 20: 309–26.

Burgess, J., Harrison, C. and Limb, M. (1988c) 'Exploring environmental values through the medium of small groups. Part two: Illustrations of a group at work', *Environment and Planning A*, 20: 457–76.

Burkart, A. and Medlik, S. (1974) *Tourism, Past, Present and Future*, Oxford: Heinemann.

Burkart, A. and Medlik, S. (1981) *Tourism, Past Present and Future*, 2nd edn, London: Heinemann.

Burnet, L. (1963) *Villégiature et tourisme sue les côtes de France*, Paris: Hachette.

Burns, J.P.A. and Mules, T.L. (1986) 'A framework for the analysis of major special events', in J.P.A. Burns, J.H. Hatch and T.L. Mules (eds) *The Adelaide Grand Prix: The Impact of a Special Event*, Adelaide: Centre for South Australian Economic Studies, pp. 5–38.

Burns, M., Barwell, L. and Heinecken, T. (1990) 'Analysis of critical coastal processes affecting recreation and tourism development opportunities along South-Western Cape coastline', in P. Wong (ed.) *Tourism vs Environment: The Case for Coastal Areas*, Dordrecht: Kluwer, pp. 19–32.

Burtenshaw, D., Bateman, M. and Ashworth, G.J. (1991) *The City in West Europe*, 2nd edn, Chichester: Wiley.

Burton, R. (1974) *The Recreational Carrying Capacity of the Countryside*, Occasional Publication No. 11, Keele: Keele University Library.

Burton, T. (1966) 'A day in the country: A survey of leisure activity at Box Hill in Surrey', *Chartered Surveyor*, 98(7): 378–80.

Burton, T. (1971) *Experiments in Recreation Research*, London: Allen & Unwin.

Burton, T.L. (1982) 'A framework for leisure policy research', *Leisure Studies*, 1: 323–35.

Butler, R.W. (1974) 'The social implications of tourist developments', *Annals of Tourism Research*, 2: 100–11.

Butler, R.W. (1975) 'Tourism as an agent of social change', in F. Helleiner (ed.) *Tourism as a Factor in National and Regional Development*, Occasional Papers in Geography No. 4, Peterborough: Trent University, pp. 89–50.

Butler, R.W. (1980) 'The concept of a tourist area cycle of evolution: Implications for management of resources', *Canadian Geographer*, 24(1): 5–12.

Butler, R.W. (1990) 'Alternative tourism: Pious hope or Trojan horse', *Journal of Travel Research*, 28(3): 40–5.

Butler, R.W. (1991) 'Tourism, environment, and sustainable development', *Environmental Conservation*, 18(3): 201–9.

Butler, R.W. (1992) 'Alternative tourism: The thin edge of the wedge', in V.L. Smith and W.R. Eadington (eds) *Tourism Alternatives: Potentials and Problems in the Development of Tourism*, Philadelphia, PA: University of Pennsylvania Press, pp. 31–46.

Butler, R.W. (1998) 'Sustainable tourism – looking backwards in order to progress?', in C.M. Hall and A. Lew (eds) *Sustainable Tourism Development: A Geographical Perspective*, London: Addison Wesley Longman, pp. 25–34.

Butler, R.W. (2000) 'Tourism and the environment: A geographical perspective', *Tourism Geographies*, 2(3): 337–58.

Butler, R.W. (2004) 'Geographical research on tourism, recreation and leisure: Origins, eras and directions', *Tourism Geographies*, 6(2): 143–62.

Butler, R.W. (ed.) (2005) *The Tourism Life Cycle: Conceptual and Theoretical Issues*, 2 vols, Clevedon: Channel View.

Butler, R.W. and Clark, G. (1992) 'Tourism in rural areas: Canada and the UK', in I. Bowler, C. Bryant and M. Nellis (eds) *Contemporary Rural Systems in Transition*, Volume 2: *Economy and Society*, Wallingford: CAB International, pp. 166–86.

Butler, R.W. and Hall, C.M. (1998) 'Conclusion: The sustainability of tourism and recreation in rural areas', in R. Butler, C.M. Hall and J. Jenkins (eds) *Tourism and Recreation in Rural Areas*, Chichester: Wiley, pp. 249–58.

Butler, R.W. and Hinch, T. (eds) (1996) *Tourism and Indigenous Peoples*, London: International Thomson.

Butler, R.W. and Wall, G. (1985) 'Themes in research on the evolution of tourism', *Annals of Tourism Research*, 12: 287–96.

Butler, R.W., Hall, C.M. and Jenkins, J. (eds) (1998) *Tourism and Recreation in Rural Areas*, Chichester: Wiley.

Button, M. (2003) 'Private security and the policing of quasi-public space', *International Journal of the Sociology of Law*, 31: 227–37.

Byrne, A., Edmondson, R. and Fahy, K. (1993) 'Rural tourism and cultural identity in the West of Ireland', in B. O'Connor and M. Cronin (eds) *Tourism in Ireland: A Critical Analysis*, Cork: Cork University Press, pp. 233–57.

Byrne, D. (1999) *Social Exclusion*, Buckingham: Open University Press.

Caffyn, A. and Jobbins, G. (2003) 'Governance capacity and stakeholder interactions in the development and management of coastal tourism: Examples from Morocco and Tunisia', *Journal of Sustainable Tourism*, 11(2–3): 224–45.

Caffyn, A. and Lutz, J. (1999) 'Developing the heritage tourism product in multi-ethnic cities', *Tourism Management*, 20(2): 213–21.

Calais, S.S. and Kirkpatrick, J.B. (1986) 'The impact of trampling on the natural ecosystems of the Cradle Mt. Lake St. Claire National Park', *Australian Geographer*, 17: 6–15.

Callaghan, T.V., Körner, C., Heal, O.W., Lee, S.E. and Cornelissen, J.H.C. (1999) 'Global change in Europe's cold regions: Scenarios for ecosystem responses to global change', in M.A. Lange, B. Bartling and K. Grosfeld (eds) *Global Changes and the Barents Sea Region*, Proceedings of the First International BASIS Research Conference St Petersburg, Russia, 22–25 February 1998, Münster: Institute for Geophysics, University of Münster, pp. 17–50.

Callicott, J.B. (1982) 'Traditional American Indian and Western European attitudes toward nature: An overview', *Environmental Ethics*, 4: 293–318.

Campbell, C.K. (1966) *An Approach to Recreational Geography*, BC Occasional Papers No. 7.

Canadian Council on Rural Development (1975) *Economic Significance of Tourism and Outdoor Recreation for Rural Development*, Working Paper, Ottawa: Canadian Council on Rural Development.

Cannon, J. (1987) 'Issues in sampling and sample design – a managerial perspective', in J.B. Ritchie and C. Goeldner (eds) *Travel, Tourism and Hospitality Research: A Handbook for Managers and Researchers*, New York: Wiley, pp. 101–16.

Carhart, A.H. (1920) 'Recreation in the forests', *American Forests*, 26: 268–72.

Carlson, A.S. (1938) 'Recreation industry of New Hampshire', *Economic Geography*, 14: 255–70.

Carlson, A.W. (1978) 'The spatial behaviour involved in honeymoons: The case of two areas in Wisconsin and North Dakota', *Journal of Popular Culture*, 11: 977–88.

Carr, N. (1999) 'A study of gender differences: Young tourist behaviour in a UK coastal resort', *Tourism Management*, 20: 223–28.

Carter, J., Jollife, L. and Baum, T. (2001) 'Heritage tourism and World Heritage sites: The case of Newfoundland', *Tourism Recreation Research*, 26(1): 113–16.

Carter, R. (1982) 'Coastal caravan sites in Northern Ireland 1960–1980', *Irish Geography*, 15: 123–6.

Carter, R. (1988) *Coastal Environments*, London: Academic Press.

Carter, R. (1990) 'Recreational use and abuse of the coastline of Florida', in P. Fabbri (ed.) *Recreational Uses of Coastal Areas*, Dordrecht: Kluwer, pp. 3–18.

Carter, R. and Parker, A. (1989) 'Resources and management of Irish coastal waters and adjacent coasts', in R. Carter and A. Parker (eds) *Ireland: Contemporary Perspectives on a Land and its People*, London: Routledge, pp. 393–420.

Carter, R., Eastwood, D. and Pollard, J. (1990) 'Man's impact on the coast of Ireland', in P. Wong (ed.) *Tourism vs Environment: The Case for Coastal Areas*, Dordrecht: Kluwer, pp. 211–25.

Carver, S. (2000) 'Wilderness and landscape', Wilderness Britain? Social and Environmental Perspectives on Recreation and Conservation, Newsletter No. 4, Mapping the Wild: Spatial Patterns and Landscape Character.

Carver, S., Evans, A. and Fritz, S. (2002) 'Wilderness attribute mapping in the United Kingdom', *International Journal of Wilderness*, 8(1): 24–9.

Cater, E.A. (1987) 'Tourism in the least developed countries', *Annals of Tourism Research*, 14: 202–26.

Cater, E.A. (1993) 'Ecotourism in the third world: Problems for sustainable development', *Tourism Management*, 14(2): 85–90.

Cater, E.A. (2000) 'Tourism in the Yunnan Great Rivers National Parks System Project: Prospects for sustainability', *Tourism Geographies*, 2(4): 472–89.

Cater, E.A. and Lowman, G. (eds) (1994) *Ecotourism: A Sustainable Option?*, Chichester: Wiley.

Catlin, G. (1968) 'An artist proposes a National Park', in R. Nash (ed.) *The American Environment: Readings in the History of Conservation*, Reading, MA: Addison-Wesley, pp. 5–9.

Catto, N. (2002) 'Anthropogenic pressures on coastal dunes, Southwestern Newfoundland, *Canadian Geographer* 46(1): 17–32.

Ceballos-Lascuarain, H. (1996) *Tourism, Ecotourism and Protected Areas: The State of Nature Based Tourism around the World and Guidelines for its Development*, Gland, Switzerland: IUCN.

Chadwick, G. (1971) *A Systems View of Planning*, Oxford: Pergamon.

Chadwick, R. (1987) 'Concepts, definitions and measures used in travel and tourism research', in J.R. Brent Ritchie and C. Goeldner (eds) *Travel, Tourism and Hospitality Research: A Handbook for Managers and Researchers*, New York: Wiley, pp. 47–62.

Chadwick, R. (1994) 'Concepts, definitions and measures used in travel and tourism research', in J.R. Brent Ritchie and C. Goeldner (eds) *Travel, Tourism and Hospitality Research: A Handbook for Managers and Researchers*, 2nd edn, New York: Wiley, pp. 65–80.

Champeaux, J.P. (1987) 'Le marché du tourisme social en Europe', *Espaces*, 86: 17–20.

Champion, A.G. (1998) 'Studying counter-urbanisation and the rural population turnaround', in P. Boyle and K. Halfacree (eds) *Migration into Rural Areas: Theories and Issues*. Chichester: Wiley, pp. 21–40.

Chang, T.C. (1998) 'Regionalism and tourism: Exploring integral links in Singapore', *Asia Pacific Viewpoint*, 39(1): 73–94.

Chang, T.C. (2000) 'Singapore's Little India: A tourist attraction in a contested landscape', *Urban Studies*, 37(2): 343–66.

Chang, T.C. and Yeoh, B.S.A. (1999) 'New Asia-Singapore: Communicating local cultures through global tourism', *Geoforum*, 30(2): 101–15.

Chang, T.C., Milne, S., Fallon, D. and Pohlmann, C. (1996) 'Urban heritage tourism: The global–local nexus', *Annals of Tourism Research*, 23: 1–19.

Chapin, F. (1974) *Human Activity Patterns in the City*, New York: Wiley.

Chapman, H.H. (1938) 'National parks, national forests and wilderness areas', *Journal of Forestry*, 36(5): 469–474.

Charlton, C. and Essex, S. (1996) 'The involvement of District Councils in tourism in England and Wales', *Geoforum*, 27(2): 175–92.

Chartered Institute of Public Finance and Accountancy (CIPFA) (1990) *Leisure and Recreation Statistics 1990–91 Estimates*, London: CIPFA.

Chavas, J.P., Stoll, J. and Sellar, C. (1989) 'On the commodity value of travel time in recreational activities', *Applied Economics*, 21: 711–22.

Chinn, T. (1996) 'New Zealand glacier responses to climate change of the past century', *New Zealand Journal of Geology and Geophysics*, 39: 415–28.

Christaller, W. (1933) *Die Zentralen Orte in Süddeutschland*, Jena, Germany: Gustav Fischer.

Christaller, W. (1963) 'Some considerations of tourism location in Europe: The peripheral regions – under-developed countries – recreation areas', *Regional Science Association Papers*, 12: 95–105.

Chubb, M. and Chubb, H. (1981) *One Third of our Time? An Introduction to Recreation Behaviour and Resources*, New York: Wiley.

Church, A. (1988) 'Urban regeneration in London's Docklands: A five year policy review', *Environment and Planning C: Government and Policy*, 6: 187–208.

Church, A. (1990) 'Transport and urban regeneration in London Docklands', *Cities: The International Journal of Urban Policy and Planning*, 7(4): 289–303.

Church, A. (2004) 'Local and regional tourism policy and power', in A. Lew, C.M. Hall and A. Williams (eds) *Companion to Tourism*, Oxford: Blackwell, pp. 541–55.

Church, A. and Reid, P. (2000) 'Urban power, international networks, and competition: the example of cross-border co-operation', *Urban Studies*, 33(8): 1297–318.

Church, A., Ball, R., Bull, C. and Tyler, D. (2000) 'Public policy engagement with British tourism: The national, local and the European Union', *Tourism Geographies*, 2(3): 312–36.

Cichetti, C. (1971) 'Some economic issues in planning urban recreation facilities', *Land Economics*, 47: 14–23.

Cicin-Sain, B. and Knecht, R.W. (1998) *Integrated Coastal and Ocean Management: Concepts and Experiences*, Washington, DC: Island Press.

Clark, G., Gertler, M. and Feldman, M. (eds) (2000) *Handbook of Economic Geography*, Oxford: Oxford University Press.

Clark, J. and Crichter, C. (1985) *The Devil Makes Work: Leisure in Capitalist Britain*, London: Macmillan.

Clark, R.N. and Stankey, G.H. (1979) *The Recreation Opportunity Spectrum: A Framework for Planning, Management and Research*, USDA Forest Service, General Technical Report PNW-98.

Clarke, P. (ed.) (1981) *Country Towns in Pre-industrial England*, Leicester: Leicester University Press.

Clarke, W.C. (1991) 'Time and tourism: An ecological perspective', in M.L. Miller and J. Auyong (eds) *Proceedings of the 1990 Congress on Coastal and Marine Tourism*, Honolulu: National Coastal Research and Development Institute, pp. 387–93.

Clary, D. (1984a) 'Coastal tourism: Research methods', *Revue de Geographie de Lyon*, 59(1–2): 63–72.

Clary, D. (1984b) 'The impact of social change on a leisure region, 1960–1982: A study of Nord Pays D'Auge', in J. Long and R. Hecock (eds) *Leisure, Tourism and Social Change*, Dunfermline: Centre for Leisure Research, Dunfermline College of Physical Education, pp. 51–6.

Clary, D. (1993) *Le Tourisme dans l'espace français*, Paris: Editions du CRNS.

Claus, J.E. (1990) *Promotional Letter to Antarctic Tour Members from the Chief Operating Officer, Society Expeditions*, Seattle, WA: Society Expeditions.

Clawson, M. (1958) *Statistics on Outdoor Recreation*, Washington, DC: Resources for the Future.

Clawson, M. and Knetsch, J. (1966) *The Economics of Outdoor Recreation*, Baltimore, MD: Johns Hopkins University Press.

Clawson, M. and Knetsch, J. (1968) *The Economics of Outdoor Recreation*, Baltimore, MD: Johns Hopkins University Press.

Clawson, M., Held, R. and Stoddart, C. (1960) *Land for the Future*, Baltimore, MD: Johns Hopkins University Press.

Cleveland, T., Jr. (1910) 'National forests as recreation grounds', *Annals of the American Academy of Political and Social Science*, 35(March): 25–31.

Clewer, A., Pack, A. and Sinclair, M.T. (1992) 'Price competitiveness and inclusive tour holidays', in P. Johnson and B. Thomas (eds) *Choice and Demand in Tourism*, London: Mansell, pp. 123–44.

Clift, S. and Page, S.J. (eds) (1996) *Health and the International Tourist*, London: Routledge.

Cloke, P. (1992) 'The countryside', in P. Cloke (ed.) *Policy and Change in Thatcher's Britain*, Oxford: Pergamon, pp. 269–96.

Cloke, P. and Perkins, H. (1999) 'Cracking the canyon with the awesome foursome: Representation of adventure tourism in New Zealand', *Environment and Planning D: Society and Space*, 16: 185–218.

Clout, H.D. (1987) 'Western Europe in context', in H.D. Clout (ed.) *Regional Development in Western Europe*, 3rd edn, London: David Fulton, pp. 3–18.

Coalter, F. (1990) 'The "mixed economy" of leisure: The historical background to the development of the commercial, voluntary and public sectors of the leisure industries', in I. Henry (ed.) *Management and Planning in the Leisure Industries*, London: Macmillan, pp. 3–32.

Coalter, F. (1993) 'Sports participation: Price or priorities?', *Leisure Studies*, 12: 171–82.

Coalter, F. (1998) 'Leisure studies, leisure policy and social citizenship: The failure of welfare or the limits of welfare?', *Leisure Studies*, 17: 21–36.

Cockerell, N. (1997) 'Urban tourism in Europe', *Travel and Tourism Analyst*, 6: 44–67.

Coccossis, H. (2004) *Tourism and Carrying Capacity*, London: Continuum.

Cohen, E. (1972) 'Towards a sociology of international tourism', *Social Research*, 39: 164–82.

Cohen, E. (1974) 'Who is a tourist? A conceptual clarification', *Sociological Review*, 22: 527–55.

Cohen, E. (1979a) 'Rethinking the sociology of tourism', *Annals of Tourism Research*, 6: 18–35.

Cohen, E. (1979b) 'A phenomenology of tourist experiences', *Sociology*, 13: 179–201.

Cohen, E. (1983) 'Thai girls and farang men', *Annals of Tourism Research*, 9: 403–8.

Cohen, E. (1993) 'The study of touristic images of native people: Mitigating the stereotype of a stereotype', in D.G. Pearce and R.W. Butler (eds) *Tourism Research: Critiques and Challenges*, London: Routledge, pp. 36–69.

Cole, D.N., Petersen, M.E. and Lucas, R.C. (1987) *Managing Wilderness Recreation Use: Common Problems and Potential Solutions*, USDA Forest Service General Technical Report, INT–230, Ogden, UT: Intermountain Forest and Range Experiment Station.

Colenutt, R. (1970) 'An investigation into the factors affecting the pattern of trip generation and route of choice of day visitors to the countryside', unpublished PhD thesis, Bristol: University of Bristol.

Coles, T.E. (2003) 'A local reading of a global disaster: Some lessons on tourism management from an Annus Horribilis in Southwest England', *Journal of Travel and Tourism Marketing*, 15(2–3): 143–62.

Coles, T.E. and Timothy, D.J. (eds) (2004) *Tourism, Diasporas and Space*, London: Routledge.

Coles, T., Duval, D. and Hall, C.M. (2004) 'Tourism, mobility and global communities: New approaches to theorising tourism and tourist spaces', in W. Theobold (ed.) *Global Tourism*, 3rd edn, Oxford: Heinemann, pp. 463–81.

Colley, A. (1984) 'The Greater Blue Mountains National Park', *National Parks Journal*, 28(4): 29–31.

Colwell, P., Dehring, C. and Turnbull, G. (2002) 'Recreation demand and residential location', *Journal of Urban Economics*, 51: 418–28.

Commission of the European Community (1991) *Fourth Periodic Report on the Social and Economic Situation and Development of the Regions of the*

Community, Luxembourg: Commission of the European Community.

Committee of the Federal Republic of Germany for the IGU (ed.) (2000) *German Geographical Research 1996–1999: Bibliography of Publications in Geographical Series*, Trier, Germany: Dokumentationszentrum für deutsche Landeskunde, Universität Trier.

Commonwealth Department of Tourism (1993) *Rural Tourism*, Tourism Discussion Paper No. 1, Canberra: Commonwealth Department of Tourism.

Conforti, J. (1996) 'Ghettos as tourism attractions', *Annals of Tourism Research*, 23(4): 830–42.

Connell, J. (1988) *Sovereignty and Survival: Island Microstates in the Third World*, Research Monograph No. 3, Sydney: Department of Geography, University of Sydney.

Connell, J. (2005) 'Managing gardens for visitors: A story of continuity and change', *Tourism Management*, 26(2): 185–201.

Connell, J. and Page, S.J. (2005) 'Evaluating the economic and spatial effects of an event: The case of the World Medical and Health Games, *Tourism Geographies*, 7(1): 63–85.

Conway, H. (1991) *People's Parks: The Design and Development of Victorian Parks in Britain*, Cambridge: Cambridge University Press.

Cooke, K. (1982) 'Guidelines for socially appropriate tourism development in British Columbia', *Journal of Travel Research*, 21(1): 22–8.

Cooke, P. (ed.) (1986) *Global Restructuring, Local Responses*, London: Economic and Social Research Council.

Cooke, P. (1989) *Localities: The Changing Face of Urban Britain*, London: Unwin Hyman.

Cooper, C.E. (1947) 'Tourism', *Journal of Geography*, 46: 115–20.

Cooper, C.P. (1981) 'Spatial and temporal patterns of tourist behaviour', *Regional Studies*, 15: 359–71.

Cooper, C.P. (1987) 'The changing administration of tourism in Britain', *Area*, 19(3): 249–53.

Cooper, C.P. (1990) 'Resorts in decline: The management response', *Tourism Management*, 11: 63–7.

Cooper, C.P. (1992) 'The life cycle concept and tourism', in P. Johnson and B. Thomas (eds) *Choice and Demand in Tourism*, London: Mansell, pp. 145–60.

Cooper, C.P. (1994) 'Product lifecycle', in S.F. Witt and L. Moutinho (eds) *Tourism Marketing and Management Handbook*, Englewood Cliffs, NJ: Prentice Hall, pp. 145–60.

Cooper, C.P. and Jackson, S. (1989) 'Destination life cycle: The Island of Man case study', *Annals of Tourism Research*, 16(3): 377–98.

Cooper, C.P., Fletcher, J., Gilbert, D.G. and Wanhill, S. (1993) *Tourism: Principles and Practice*, London: Pitman.

Cooper, M.J. and Pigram, J.J. (1984) 'Tourism and the Australian economy', *Tourism Management*, 5(1): 2–12.

Cope, A., Doxford, D. and Probert, C. (2000). 'Monitoring visitors to UK countryside resources: The approaches of land and recreation resource management organisations to visitor monitoring', *Land Use Policy*, 17: 59–66

Coppock, J.T. (1966) 'The recreational use of land and water in rural Britain', *Tidschrift voor Economische en Sociale Geografie*, 57: 81–96.

Coppock, J.T. (1970) 'Geographers and conservation', *Area*, 2: 24–26.

Coppock, J.T. (1974) 'Geography and public policy: Challenges, opportunities and implications', *Transactions of the Institute of British Geographers*, 63: 1–16.

Coppock, J.T. (1976) 'Geography and public policy: Challenge, opportunities and implications', in J.T. Coppock and W. Sewell (eds) *Spatial Dimensions of Public Policy*, Oxford: Pergamon.

Coppock, J.T. (ed.) (1977a) *Second Homes: Curse or Blessing?*, Oxford: Pergamon.

Coppock, J.T. (1977b) 'Tourism as a tool for regional development', in B.S. Duffield (ed.) *Tourism: A Tool for Regional Development*, Edinburgh: Tourism and Recreation Research Unit, University of Edinburgh, pp. 1.1–1.5.

Coppock, J.T. (1980) 'The geography of leisure and recreation', in E.H. Brown (ed.) *Geography Yesterday and Tomorrow*, London: Royal Geographical Society, pp. 243–79.

Coppock, J.T. (1982) 'Geographical contributions to the study of leisure', *Leisure Studies*, 1: 1–27.

Coppock, J.T. and Duffield, B. (1975) *Outdoor Recreation in the Countryside: A Spatial Analysis*, London: Macmillan.

Coppock, J.T. and Sewell, W. (1976) *Spatial Dimensions of Public Policy*, Oxford: Pergamon.

Corbin, A. (1995) *The Lure of the Sea: The Discovery of the Seaside 1750–1840*, London: Penguin.

Cordell, H., Betz, C. and Green, G. (2002) 'Recreation and the environment as cultural dimensions in contemporary American society', *Leisure Sciences* 24: 13–41.

Corner, J. and Harvey, S. (eds) (1991) *Enterprise and Heritage: Crosscurrents of National Culture*, London and New York: Routledge.

Cornish, V. (1930) 'The claim of the coast', *Geography*, 15(5): 384–7.

Cornish, V. (1934) 'A national park at the Lands End', *Geography*, 19(4): 288–91.

Cornwall, G.W. and Holcomb, C.J. (eds) (1966) *Guidelines to the Planning, Developing, and Managing of Rural Recreation Enterprises*, Bulletin 301, Blacksburg, VA: Cooperative Extension Service, Virginia Polytechnic Institute.

Corsi, T.M. and Harvey, M.E. (1979) 'Changes in vacation travel in response to motor fuel shortages and higher prices', *Journal of Travel Research*, 17(4): 6–11.

Cosgrove, I. and Jackson, R. (1972) *The Geography of Recreation and Leisure*, London: Hutchinson.

Council of Nature Conservation Ministers (CONCOM) Working Group on Management of National Parks (1985) *Identification and Management of Wilderness Areas in Australia*, Discussion Paper, Canberra: CONCOM.

Council of Nature Conservation Ministers (CONCOM) Working Group on Management of National Parks (1986) *Guidelines for Reservation and Management of Wilderness Areas in Australia*, Canberra: CONCOM.

Countryside Agency (2000) *The State of the Countryside 1999*, Cheltenham: Countryside Agency.

Countryside Agency (2003) *Living Landscapes*, Cheltenham: Countryside Agency, http://www.countryside.gov.uk.

Countryside Commission (1970) *Countryside Recreation Glossary*, London: Countryside Commission.

Countryside Commission (1974) *Advice Note on Country Parks*, Cheltenham: Countryside Commission.

Countryside Commission (1983) *A Management Plan for the Green Belt Area in Barnet and South Havering*, CCP 147, Cheltenham: Countryside Commission.

Countryside Commission (1987) *Visitors to the countryside*, Countryside Commission: Cheltenham.

Countryside Commission (1988) *Countryside Management in the Urban Fringe*, CCP 136, Cheltenham: Countryside Commission.

Countryside Commission (1992) *Enjoying the Countryside – Policies for People*, CCP 371, Cheltenham: Countryside Commission.

Coventry, N. (1998) 'December dive', *Inside Tourism*, March: 1.

Cowie, I. (1985) 'Housing policy options in relation to the America's Cup', *Urban Policy and Research*, 3: 40–1.

Crabtree, R., Leat, P.M., Santarossa, J. and Thompson, K.J. (1994) 'The economic impact of wildlife sites in Scotland', *Journal of Rural Studies*, 10(1): 61–72.

Crandall, R. (1980) 'Motivations for leisure', *Journal of Leisure Research*, 12: 45–54.

Crang, M. and Travelou, S. (2001) 'The city and topology of memory', *Environment and Planning D*, 19(2): 161–77.

Crawford, D. and Godbey, G. (1987) 'Reconceptualising barriers to family leisure', *Leisure Sciences*, 9: 119–27.

Crawford, D., Jackson, E. and Godbey, G. (1991) 'A hierarchical model of leisure constraints', *Leisure Sciences*, 13: 309–20.

Crisler, R.M. and Hunt, M.S. (1952) 'Recreation regions in Missouri', *Journal of Geography*, 51(1): 30–9.

Crompton, J.L. (1979) 'An assessment of the image of Mexico as a vacation destination', *Journal of Travel Research*, 17(fall): 18–23.

Crompton, J.L. and Richardson, S.L. (1986) 'The tourism connection where public and private leisure services merge', *Parks and Recreation*, October: 38–44, 67.

Crompton, J.L. and Van Doren, C. (1976) 'Amusement parks, theme parks, and municipal leisure services: Contrasts in adaption to cultural change', *Journal of Physical Education and Recreation*, 47: 18–22.

Cronan, W. (1990) 'Modes of prophecy and production: Placing nature in history', *Journal of American History*, 76(4): 1122–31.

Crosby, A.W. (1995) 'The past and present of environmental history', *American Historical Review*, 100(4): 1177–90.

Crotty, R. (1979) 'Capitalist colonialism and peripheralisation: The Irish case', in D. Seers, B. Schaffer and M.L. Kiljunen (eds) *Under-developed Europe: Studies in Core–Periphery Relations*, Totowa, NJ: Humanities Press, pp. 225–35.

Crouch, D. (1989a) 'Patterns of cooperation in the cultures of outdoor leisure – the case of allotments', *Leisure Studies*, 8(2): 189–99.

Crouch, D. (1989b) 'The allotment, landscape and locality', *Area*, 21(3): 261–7.

Crouch, D. (1994) 'Home, escape and identity: Rural identities and sustainable tourism', *Journal of Sustainable Tourism*, 2(1/2): 93–101.

Crouch, D. (1999a) 'Introduction: Encounters in leisure/tourism', in D. Crouch (ed.) *Leisure/Tourism Geographies: Practices and Geographical Knowledge*, London: Routledge, pp. 1–16.

Crouch, D. (ed.) (1999b) *Leisure/Tourism Geographies: Practices and Geographical Knowledge*, London: Routledge.

Crouch, D. (2000) 'Places around us: Embodied lay geographies in leisure and tourism', *Leisure Studies*, 19(2): 63–76.

Crouch, D. and Lübbren, N. (eds) (2003) *Visual Culture and Tourism*, Oxford: Berg.

Crouch, G. (1994) 'The study of tourism demand: A review of findings', *Journal of Travel Research*, 33(1): 2–21.

Croy, G. and Hall, C.M. (2003) 'Developing a tourism knowledge: Educating the student, developing the rural area', *Journal of Teaching in Travel and Tourism*, 3(1): 3–24.

Csikszentmihalyi, M. (1975) *Beyond Boredom and Anxiety*, San Francisco, CA: Jossey Bass.

Curiel, J. and Radvansky, G. (2002) 'Mental maps in memory retrieval and comprehension', *Memory*, 10(2): 113–26.

Curry, N. (1992) 'Recreation, access, amenity and conservation in the United Kingdom: The failure of integration', in I.R. Bowler, C.R. Bryant and M.D. Nellis (eds) *Contemporary Rural Systems in Transition*, Vol. 2, Wallingford: CAB International, pp. 141–54.

Curry, N. (1994) *Countryside Recreation: Access and Land Use Planning*, London: E&FN Spon.

Curry, N. (2000) 'Community participation in outdoor recreation and the development of Millennium Greens in England', *Leisure Studies*, 19(1): 17–35.

Curry, N. and Ravenscroft, N. (2001) 'Countryside recreation provision in England: Exploring a demand-led approach', *Land Use Policy* 18(3): 281–91.

Cushman, G., Veal, A. and Zuzanek, J. (eds) (1996a) *World Leisure Participation: Free Time in the Global Village*, Wallingford: CAB International.

Cushman, G., Veal, A. and Zuzanek, J. (eds) (1996b) 'National participation surveys: An overview', in G. Cushman, A. Veal and J. Zuzanek (eds.) *World Leisure Participation: Free Time in the Global Village*, Wallingford: CAB International, pp. 1–15.

Cutter, S. (2000) 'President's column: Bring geography back to Harvard and Yale and . . .', *AAG Newsletter*, 35(10): 2–3.

Cybriwsky, R. (1999) 'Changing patterns of urban public space: Observations and assessments from the Tokyo and New York metropolitan areas', *Cities: The International Journal of Urban Policy and Planning*, 4: 223–31.

Daby, D., Turner, J. and Jago, C. (2002) 'Microbial and nutrient pollution of coastal bathing waters in Mauritius', *Environmental International*, 27(7): 555–66.

Dagenais, M. (2002) 'Inscribing municipal power in urban space: The formation of a network of parks at Montreal and Toronto, 1880–1940', *Canadian Geographer*, 46(4): 347–64.

Dahles, H. (1998) 'Redefining Amsterdam as a tourism destination', *Annals of Tourism Research*, 25: 55–69.

Damette, F. (1980) 'The regional framework of monopoly exploitation: new problems and trends', in J. Carney, R. Hudson and J.R. Lewis (eds) *Regions in Crisis*, London: Croom Helm, pp. 76–92.

Dann, G. (1981) 'Tourist motivation: An appraisal', *Annals of Tourism Research*, 8 (2): 187–219.

Dann, G. (1993) 'Limitations in the use of nationality and country of residence variable', in D. Pearce and R. Butler (eds) *Tourism Research: Critique and Challenges*, London: Routledge, pp. 88–112.

DART (1974) *Farm Recreation and Tourism in England and Wales*, Report to the Countryside Commission, English Tourist Board and Wales Tourist Board, Publication No. 14, CCP 83, Cheltenham: Countryside Commission.

Dasmann, R.F. (1973) *Classification and Use of Protected Natural and Cultural Areas*, IUCN Occasional Paper No. 4, Morges, Switzerland: International Union for the Conservation of Nature and Natural Resources.

Davidson, R. and Maitland, R. (1997) *Tourism Destinations*, London: Hodder & Stoughton.

Davies, E. (1971) *Farm Tourism in Cornwall and Devon: Some Economic and Physical Considerations*, Report No. 184, Exeter: Agricultural Economics Unit, University of Exeter.

Davies, E. (1987) 'Planning in the New Zealand National Parks', *New Zealand Geographer*, 43(2): 73–8.

Davis, B. (1981) 'Characteristics and influence of the Australian conservation movement', unpublished PhD thesis, Hobart: University of Tasmania.

Dawson, J. and Doornkamp, J. (eds) (1973) *Evaluating the Human Environment: Essays in Applied Geography*, London: Edward Arnold.

Dear, M. (1994) 'Postmodern human geography: A preliminary assessment', *Erdkunde*, 48(1): 2–13.

Dear, M. (1999) 'The relevance of post modernism', *Scottish Geographical Magazine*, 115(2): 143–50.

Dear, M. and Flusty, S. (1998) 'Postmodern urbanism', *Annals of the Association of American Geographers*, 88(1): 50–72.

Dear, M. and Flusty, S. (1999) 'Engaging postmodern urbanism', *Urban Geography*, 20(5): 412–16.

Dearden, P. (1993) 'Cultural aspects of tourism and sustainable development: Tourism and the hill-tribes of Northern Thailand', in J.G. Nelson, R. Butler and G. Wall (eds) *Tourism and Sustainable Development: Monitoring, Planning and Managing*, Waterloo, Ont.: Department of Geography, University of Waterloo.

Dearden, P. and Rollins, R. (eds) (1993) *Parks and Protected Areas in Canada: Planning and Management*, Toronto: Oxford University Press.

Deasy, G.F. (1949) 'The tourist industry in a north woods county', *Economic Geography*, 25(2): 240–59.

Deasy, G.F. and Griess, P.R. (1966) 'Impact of a tourist facility on its hinterland', *Annals of the Association of American Geographers*, 56(2): 290–306.

Debarbieux, B. (1995) *Tourisme et montagne*, Paris: Economica.

Debbage, K.G. (1990) 'Oligopoly and the resort cycle in the Bahamas', *Annals of Tourism Research*, 18(2): 251–68.

Debbage, K.G. (1991) 'Spatial behaviour in a Bahamian resort', *Annals of Tourism Research*, 18(2): 251–68.

Debbage, K.G. and Ioannides, D. (eds) (1998) *The Economic Geography of the Tourism Industry*, London: Routledge.

Debbage, K.G. and Ioannides, D. (2004) 'The cultural turn? Towards a more critical economic geography of tourism', in A. Lew, C.M. Hall and A. Williams (eds) *Companion to Tourism*, Oxford: Blackwell, pp. 99–109.

Deblock, A. (1986) 'Le tourisme pêche en France', *Espaces*, 82: 22–5.

de Botton, A. (2003) *The Art of Travel*, London: Penguin.

Deegan, J. and Dineen, D. (1996) *Tourism Policy and Performance*, London: International Thomson.

Deem, R. (1986) *All Work and No Play? The Sociology of Women and Leisure*, Milton Keynes: Open University Press.

de Freitas, C.R. (1990) 'Recreation climate assessment', *International Journal of Climatology*, 10: 89–103.

de Freitas, C.R. (2003) 'Tourism climatology: Evaluating environmental information for decision making and business planning in the recreation and tourism sector', *International Journal of Biometeorology*, 47(4): 190–208.

De Kadt, E. (ed.) (1979) *Tourism – Passport to Development?*, Oxford: Oxford University Press.

Del Casino, V. and Hanna, S. (2000) 'Representations and identities in tourism map spaces', *Progress in Human Geography*, 24(1): 23–46.

Deller, S.C., Marcouiller, D.W and Green, G.P. (1997) 'Recreational housing and local government finance', *Annals of Tourism Research*, 24(3): 687–705.

Denman, R. (1978) *Recreation and Tourism in Farms, Crofts and Estates*, Report to the Highlands and Islands Development Board and the Scottish Tourist Board, Edinburgh.

Department for Culture, Media and Sport (1999) *Policy Action Team 10: Report on Social Exclusion*, London: Department for Culture, Media and Sport.

Department of Regional Economic Expansion (1972) *The Canada Land Inventory: Land Capability Classification for Outdoor Recreation*, Report No. 6, Ottawa: Queen's Printer for Canada.

Department of the Environment (DoE) (1990) *Tourism and the Inner City*, London: HMSO.

Department of the Environment (1996) *Coastal Zone Management: Towards Best Practice*, London: DoE.

Department of the Environment and Ministry of Agriculture, Fisheries and Food (DoE/MAFF) (1995) *Rural England: A Nation Committed to a Living Countryside*, London: HMSO.

Department of the Environment, Transport and the Regions (DETR) (2000) *Our Countryside: The Future. A Fair Deal for Rural England* (Rural White Paper), London: HMSO.

Department of Tourism and Transport (1989) *Improving the Performance of Irish Tourism: A Summary Report*, Dublin: Stationery Office.

Deprest, F. (1997) *Enquête sur le tourisme de masse: l'écologie face au territoire*, Paris: Belin.

Dernoi, L.A. (1983) 'Farm tourism in Europe', *Tourism Management*, 4(3): 155–66.

Deutsch, K. (1970) *Politics and Government: How People Decide their Fate*. Boston, MA: Houghton Mifflin.

Dewailly, J. and Flament, E. (eds) (1993) *Géographie du tourisme et des loisirs*, Paris: SEDES.

d'Hautesserre, A. (1996) 'A response to Dimitri Ioannides, "Strengthening the ties between tourism and economic geography: A theoretical agenda"', *Professional Geographer*, 48(2): 218–19.

Dickinson, G. (2000) 'The use of Loch Lomond area for recreation', *Scottish Geographical Journal*, 116(3): 231–44.

Dietvorst, A. (1993) 'Planning for outdoor recreation and tourism in the Netherlands', in H. van Lier and

P. Taylor (eds) *New Challenges in Recreation and Tourism Planning*, Amsterdam: Elsevier Science, pp. 69–86.

Dietz, T. and Kwaad, F. (2000) *Dutch Geography 1996–2000*, Utrecht, Netherlands: International Geographical Union.

Dilley, R.S. (1986) 'Tourist brochures and tourist images', *Canadian Geographer*, 30(1): 59–65.

Dilsaver, L.M. and Tweed, W.C. (1990) *Challenge of the Big Trees: A Resource History of Sequoia and Kings Canyon National Parks*, Three Rivers, Quebec: Sequoia Natural History Association.

Ding, P. and Pigram, J. (1995) 'Environmental audits: An emerging concept for sustainable tourism development', *Journal of Tourism Studies*, 2: 2–10.

Dingsdale, A. (1986) 'Ideology and leisure under socialism: The geography of second homes in Hungary', *Leisure Studies*, 5: 35–55.

Doering, T.R. (1976) 'A reexamination of the relative importance of tourism to state economies', *Journal of Travel Research*, 15(1): 13–17.

Domestic Tourism Statistics, WTO: Madrid.

Donajgrodski, A. (ed.) (1978) *Social Control in Nineteenth Century Britain*, London: Croom Helm.

Doorne, S. (1998) 'The last resort: a study of power and participation on the Wellington waterfront', unpublished PhD thesis, Wellington, NZ: Department of Tourism and Services Management, Victoria University of Wellington.

Doornkamp, J. (1982) *Applied Geography*, Nottingham Monographs in Applied Geography No. 1, Nottingham: Department of Geography, University of Nottingham.

Doren, C., Priddle, G. and Lewis, J. (1979) *Land and Leisure: Concepts and Methods in Outdoor Recreation*, London: Methuen.

Douglas, N. and Douglas, N. (1996) 'Tourism in the Pacific: Historical factors', in C.M. Hall and S.J. Page (eds) *Tourism in the Pacific: Issues and Cases*, London: International Thomson Business Press, pp. 19–35.

Dovers, S. (ed.) (1994) *Australian Environmental History: Essays and Cases*, Melbourne: Oxford University Press.

Dovers, S. (ed.) (2000a) *Environmental History and policy: Still Settling Australia*, Melbourne: Oxford University Press.

Dovers, S. (2000b) 'On the contribution of environmental history to current debate and policy', *Environment and History*, 6: 131–50.

Dower, M. (1965) *The Challenge of Leisure*, London: Civic Trust.

Dower, M. (1977) 'Planning aspects of second homes', in J.T. Coppock (ed.) *Second Homes: Curse or Blessing*, Oxford: Pergamon.

Dower, M. and McCarthy, P. (1967) 'Planning for conservation and development', *Journal of the Royal Town Planning Institute*, 53(1): 99–105.

Dowling, R.K. (1993) 'Tourism planning, people and the environment in Western Australia', *Journal of Travel Research*, 31(4): 52–8.

Dowling, R.K. (1997) 'Plans for the development of regional ecotourism: Theory and practice', in C.M. Hall, J. Jenkins and G. Kearsley (eds) *Tourism Planning and Policy in Australia and New Zealand: Cases, Issues and Practice*, Sydney: Irwin, pp. 110–26.

Downs, R.M. (1970) 'Geographic space perception: Past approaches and future prospects', *Progress in Geography*, 2: 65–108.

Downs, R.M. and Stea, D. (1973) *Image and Environment*, New York: Aldine.

Downs, R.M. and Stea, D. (1977) *Maps in Minds: Reflections on Cognitive Mapping*, New York: Harper & Row.

Doxey, G.V. (1975) 'A causation theory of visitor–resident irritants: Methodology and research inferences', in *Proceedings of the Travel Research Association sixth Annual Conference*, San Diego, CA: Travel Research Association, pp. 195–8.

Driver, B.L. (1989) 'Recreation Opportunity Spectrum: A framework for planning, management and research', in *Proceedings of a North American Workshop on Visitor Management in Parks and Protected Areas*, Waterloo, Ont.: Tourism Research and Education Centre, University of Waterloo and Environment, Canada Park Service, pp. 127–58.

Drost, A. (1996) 'Developing sustainable tourism for World Heritage sites', *Annals of Tourism Research*, 23(2): 479–92.

Drummond, L. (2000) 'Street scenes: Practices of public and private space in urban Vietnam', *Urban Studies* 37(12): 2377–2391.

Dubaniewicz, H. (1976) 'An appraisal of the natural environment of the Ködz Region for the needs of economic development and recreation', *Geographica Polonica*, 34: 265–71.

Dubé, P. and Gordon, G. (2000) 'Capital cities: Perspectives and convergence', *Plan Canada*, 40(3): 6–7.

Duffield, B. (1984) 'The study of tourism in Britain: A geographical perspective', *GeoJournal*, 9(1): 27–35.

Duffield, B. and Coppock, J. (1975) 'The delineation of

recreational landscapes: The role of computer-based information systems', *Transactions of the Institute of British Geographers*, 66(2): 141–8.

Duffield, B. and Long, J. (1981) 'Tourism in the Highlands and Islands of Scotland: Rewards and conflicts', *Annals of Tourism Research*, 8(3): 403–31.

Duffield, B. and Owen, M. (1970) *Leisure + Countryside = A Geographical Appraisal of Countryside Recreation in Lanarkshire*, Edinburgh: University of Edinburgh.

Duffield, B. and Walker, S. (1983) *Urban Parks and Open Spaces: A Review*, Edinburgh: Tourism and Recreation Research Unit.

Dumas, D. (1982) 'Le commerce de detail dans une grande station touristique balneaire espagnole: Benidorm', *Annales de Géographie*, 506: 486–9.

Dunning, J. and McQueen, M. (1982) *Transnational Corporations in International Tourism*, New York: United Nations.

Dunphy, M.J. (1973) 'How the Sydney Bushwalkers began' (Compiled from the Minutes Book of the Mountain Trails Club, September, 1948), *The Sydney Bushwalker*, October: 3–5, 7.

Dunphy, M.J. (1979a) *The Incidence of Major Parklands in New South Wales*, Book 1, unpublished manuscript held by the New South Wales National Park and Wildlife Service Library, Sydney.

Dunphy, M.J. (1979b) 'The bushwalking conservation movement, 1914–1965', *Parks and Wildlife*, 2(3–4): 54–64.

Durbarry, R. and Sinclair, M.T. (2003) 'Market shares analysis: The case of French tourism demand', *Annals of Tourism Research*, 30(4): 927–41.

Durie, A. (2003) *Scotland for the Holidays: Tourism in Scotland 1780–1939*, East Linton: Tuckwell.

Dutton, I. and Hall, C.M. (1989) 'Making tourism sustainable: The policy/practice conundrum', in *Proceedings of the Environment Institute of Australia Second National Conference*, Melbourne: Environment Institute of Australia, pp. 196–296.

Duval, D.T. (2003) 'When hosts become guests: Return visits and diasporic identities in a Commonwealth Eastern Caribbean community', *Current Issues in Tourism*, 6(4): 267–308.

Duval, D.T. (ed.) (2004) *Tourism in the Caribbean*, London: Routledge.

Dwyer, L. and Forsyth, P. (1996) 'Economic impacts of cruise tourism in Australia', *Journal of Tourism Studies*, 7(2): 36–43.

Dwyer, L. and Forsyth, P. (1998) 'Economic significance of cruise tourism', *Annals of Tourism Research*, 25(2): 393–415.

Dye, T. (1992) *Understanding Public Policy*, 7th edn, Englewood Cliffs, NJ: Prentice Hall.

Eagles, P. (1992) 'The travel motivations of Canadian ecotourists', *Journal of Travel Research*, 31(2): 3–7.

Eaton, B. and Holding, D. (1996) 'The evaluation of public transport alternatives to the car in British National Parks', *Journal of Transport Geography*, 4(1): 55–65.

Economic Development and Tourism Department (EDTD) (2003) *Cruise Ship Impacts City of St. John's – 2002*, St John's, Nfld: Economic Development and Tourism Department, City of St John's.

Edensor, T. (2000) 'Staging tourism: Tourists as performers', *Annals of Tourism Research*, 27: 322–44.

Edgerton, R. (1979) *Alone Together: Social Order on an Urban Beach*, Berkeley, CA: University of California Press.

Edington, J.M. and Edington, M.A. (1986) *Ecology, Recreation and Tourism*, Cambridge: Cambridge University Press.

Edwards, J. (1987) 'The UK heritage coasts: An assessment of the ecological impacts', *Annals of Tourism Research*, 14: 71–87.

Edwards, J. (1991) 'Guest–host perceptions of rural tourism in England and Portugal', in M.T. Sinclair and M.J. Stabler (eds) *The Tourism Industry: An International Analysis*, Wallingford: CAB International, pp. 143–64.

Egner, H. (2002) 'Freizeit als "Individualisierungs-plattform": Entwicklung und Ausdifferenzierung sportorientierter Freizeitaktivitaten aus systemtheoretischer Perspektive' (Leisure as a platform for individualization: A systems theory approach to the evolution and diversification of sports oriented leisure activities), *Geographische-Zeitschrift*, 90(2): 89–102.

Eide, A. and Heen, K. (2002) 'Economic impacts of global warming: A study of the fishing industry in North Norway', *Fisheries Research*, 56(3): 261–74.

Eidsvik, H.K. (1980) 'National parks and other protected areas: Some reflections on the past and prescriptions for the future', *Environmental Conservation*, 7(3): 185–90.

Eidsvik, H.K. (1985) 'Wilderness policy – an international perspective', paper presented at the National Wilderness Resources Conference, Fort Collins, Colorado, July.

Eidsvik, H.K. (1987) *Categories Revision – A Review*

and a Proposal, Commission on National Parks and Protected Areas, Morges, Switzerland: International Union for the Conservation of Nature and Natural Resources.

Eiselen, E. (1945) 'The tourist industry of a modern highway, US16 in South Dakota', Economic Geography, 21: 221–30.

Ellerbrook, M.J. and Hite, J.C. (1980) 'Factors affecting regional employment in tourism in the United States', Journal of Travel Research, 18(3): 26–32.

Elliott-White, M. and Finn, M. (1998) 'Growing in sophistication: The application of GIS in post-modern marketing', Journal of Travel and Tourism Marketing, 7(1): 65–84.

Elson, M. (1977) A Review and Evaluation of Countryside Recreation Site Surveys, Cheltenham: Countryside Commission.

Elson, M. (1979) The Leisure Use of Green Belts and Urban Fringes, London: Sports Council and Social Science Research Council.

Elson, M. (1986) Green Belts: Conflict Mediation in the Urban Fringe, London: Heinemann.

Elson, M. (1993) 'Sport and recreation in the green belt countryside', in S. Glyptis (ed.) Leisure and the Environment: Essays in Honour of Professor J.A. Patmore, London: Belhaven Press, pp. 131–7.

English Historic Towns Forum (1992) Retailing in Historic Towns: Research Study 1992, London: Donaldsons.

English Tourist Board/Employment Department (1991) Tourism and the Environment: Maintaining the Balance, London: English Tourist Board.

Environmental Impact Services Limited (1991) Great Blasket Island National Park Visitor Centre, Dun Chaoirsn, Co. Kerry, Dublin: Environmental Impact Services Limited.

Environmental Planning Group of Canada [EPGC] (2002) Newfoundland and Labrador Tourism Marketing Strategy Review. Final Report, Halifax: Environmental Planning Group of Canada.

Enzenbacher, D.J. (1992) 'Antarctic tourism and environmental concerns', Marine Pollution Bulletin, 25(9–12): 258–65.

Enzenbacher, D.J. (1995) 'The regulation of Antarctic tourism', in C.M. Hall and M. Johnston (eds) Polar Tourism: Tourism in the Arctic and Antarctic Regions, Chichester: Wiley, pp. 179–216.

Erkip, F. (1997) 'The distribution of urban public services: The case of parks and recreational services in Ankara', Cities: The International Journal of Urban Policy and Planning, 14(6): 353–61.

ESCAP (1995a) Guidelines on Environmentally Sound Development of Coastal Tourism, ST/ESCAP/1371, Bangkok: ESCAP.

ESCAP (1995b) Planning Guidelines on Coastal Environmental Management, ST/ESCAP/1316, Bangkok: ESCAP.

Escourrou, P. (1993) Tourisme et environnement, Paris: SEDES.

Esser, J. and Hirsch, J. (1989) 'The crisis of fordism and the dimensions of a "post-fordist" regional and urban structure', International Journal of Urban and Regional Research, 13: 417–37.

Ettema, D.F. and Timmermans, H.J.P. (1997) Activity-based Approaches to Travel Analysis, Oxford: Pergamon.

Euromonitor (1992) European Tourism Report, London: Euromonitor.

European Commission (1997) Better Management of Coastal Resources – A European Programme for Integrated Coastal Zone Management, Luxembourg: Official Publication of the European Communities.

Evans, B. (1997) 'From town planning to environmental planning', in A. Blowers and B. Evans (eds) Town Planning into the 21st Century, London and New York: Routledge, pp. 1–14.

Evans, G. (1998) 'Urban leisure: Edge city and the new leisure periphery', in M. Collins and I. Cooper (eds) Leisure Management: Issues and Applications, Wallingford: CAB International, pp. 113–38.

Evans, N.J. (1992a) 'Advertising and farm-based accommodation: A British case study', Tourism Management, 13(4): 415–22.

Evans, N.J. (1992b) 'The distribution of farm-based accommodation in England and Wales', Journal of the Royal Agricultural Society of England, 153: 67–80.

Evans, N.J. (1992c) 'Towards an understanding of farm-based tourism in Britain', in A.W. Gilg (ed.) Progress in Rural Policy and Planning, Vol. 2, London: Belhaven Press.

Evans, N.J. and Ilbery, B.W. (1989) 'A conceptual framework for investigating farm-based accommodation and tourism in Britain', Journal of Rural Studies, 5(3): 257–66.

Evernden, N. (1992) The Social Creation of Nature, Baltimore, MD: Johns Hopkins University Press.

Ewert, A. and Hollenhurst, S. (1989) 'Testing the adventure model: Empirical support for a model of risk recreational participation', *Journal of Leisure Research*, 21: 124–9.

Fabbri, P. (ed.) (1990) *Recreational Use of Coastal Areas: A Research Project of the Commission on the Coastal Environment*, International Geographical Union, Dordrecht: Kluwer.

Fagence, M. (1990) 'Geographically-referenced planning strategies', *Journal of Environmental Management*, 3(1): 1–18.

Fagence, M. (1991) 'Geographic referencing of public policies in tourism', *Revue de Tourisme*, 3(3): 8–19.

Farmers Markets Ontario (2001) History http://www.fmo.reach.net/history.html

Farrell, B.H. (ed.) (1978) *The Social and Economic Impact of Tourism on Pacific Communities*, Santa Cruz, CA: Centre for South Pacific Studies, University of California.

Farrell, B.H. and McLellan, R.W. (1987) 'Tourism and physical environment research', *Annals of Tourism Research*, 14: 1–16.

Farrell, B.H. and Runyan, D. (1991) 'Ecology and tourism', *Annals of Tourism Research*, 18: 26–40.

Farrell, T.A. and Marion, J.L. (2001) 'Identifying and assessing ecotourism visitor impacts in eight protected areas in Costa Rica and Belize', *Environmental Conservation*, 28: 215–25.

Farsari, Y. and Prastacos, P. (2004) 'GIS applications in the planning and management of tourism', in A. Lew, C.M. Hall and A. Williams (eds) *Companion to Tourism Communities*, Clevedon: Channel View, pp. 596–607.

Faulkner, B. and Tideswell, C. (1996) 'Gold Coast resident attitudes toward tourism: The influence of involvement in tourism, residential proximity, and period of residence', in G. Prosser (ed.) *Tourism and Hospitality Research: Australian and International Perspectives*, Canberra: Bureau of Tourism Research, pp. 19–36.

Featherstone, M. (1987) 'Leisure, symbolic power and the life course', in J. Horne, D. Jary and A. Tomlinson (eds) *Sport, Leisure and Social Relations*, London: Routledge & Kegan Paul, pp. 113–38.

Fedler, A. (1987) 'Introduction: Are leisure, recreation and tourism interrelated?', *Annals of Tourism Research*, 14(3): 311–13.

Feehan, J. (ed.) (1992) *Tourism on the Farm*, Dublin: Environmental Institute, University College.

Feller, M., Hooley, D., Dreher, T., East, I. and Jung, R. (1979) *Wilderness in Victoria: An Inventory*, Monash Publications in Geography No. 21, Clayton, Vic.: Department of Geography, Monash University.

Fennell, D. (1999) *Ecotourism: An Introduction*, London: Routledge.

Fennell, D. (2001) 'A content analysis of ecotourism definitions', *Current Issues in Tourism*, 4(5): 403–21.

Ferguson, M. and Munton, R. (1978) *Informal Recreation in the Urban Fringe: Provision and Management of Sites in London's Green Belt*, Working Paper No. 2, Land for Informal Recreation, London: Department of Geography, University College.

Ferguson, M. and Munton, R. (1979) 'Informal recreation sites in London's green belt', *Area*, 11: 196–205.

Ferrario, F.F. (1979a) 'The evaluation of tourist resources: An applied methodology part I', *Journal of Travel Research*, 17(3): 18–22.

Ferrario, F.F. (1979b) 'The evaluation of tourist resources: An applied methodology part II', *Journal of Travel Research*, 17(4): 24–9.

Fesenmaier, D.R. and Lieber, S.R. (1987) 'Outdoor recreation expenditure and the effects of spatial structure', *Leisure Sciences*, 9(1): 27–40.

Fianna Fail (1987) *Putting Growth Back into Tourism*, Dublin: Fianna Fail.

Filoppovich, L. (1979) 'Mapping of recreational development around a large city', *Soviet Geography*, 20: 361–9.

Fines, K. (1968) 'Landscape evaluation: A research project in East Sussex', *Regional Studies*, 2(1): 41–5.

Finn, A. and Erden, T. (1995) 'The economic impact of a mega-multi mall: Estimation issues in the case of West Edmonton Mall', *Tourism Management*, 16(5): 367–73.

Finnveden, B. (1960) 'Den dubbla bosattingen och sommermigrationen: Exempel från Hallandskustens fritidsbebyggelse', *Svensk Geografisk årsbok*, 36: 58–84.

Fisher, D., Lewis, J. and Priddle, G. (eds) (1974) *Land and Leisure: Concepts and Methods in Outdoor Recreation*, Chicago: Maaroufa Press.

Fitton, M. (1976) 'The urban fringe and the less privileged', *Countryside Recreation Review*, 1: 25–34.

Fitton, M. (1979) 'Countryside recreation: The problems of opportunity', *Local Government Studies*, 5: 57–90.

Fitzpatrick, J. and Montague, M. (1989) 'Irish Republic outbound', *Travel and Tourism Analyst*, 6: 40–55.

Fleischer, A. and Tsur, Y. (2003) 'Measuring the recreational value of open space', *Journal of Agricultural Economics* 54(2): 262–83.

Fletcher, J. and Snee, H.R. (1989) 'Tourism multiplier

efforts', in S.F. Witt and L. Moutinho (eds) *Tourism Marketing and Management Handbook*, Hemel Hempstead: Prentice Hall, pp. 529–31.

Flognfeldt, T. (1998) 'A spectator's view of the results of the development of an Olympic host town, before and after the games', *Festival Management and Event Tourism*, 5: 93–4.

Flognfeldt, T. (2002) 'Second home ownership: A sustainable semi-migration', in C.M. Hall and A.M. Williams (eds) *Tourism and Migration: New Relationships between Production and Consumption*, Dordrecht: Kluwer, pp. 187–203.

Floor, H. (1990) *Aktiviteten Systemen en Bereikboaheid*, Amsterdam: Siswo.

Floyd, M. (1998) 'Getting beyond marginality and ethnicity: The challenge for race and ethnic studies in leisure research', *Journal of Leisure Research*, 30(1): 3–22.

Floyd, M. and Johnson, C. (2002) 'Coming to terms with environmental justice in outdoor recreation: A conceptual discussion with research implications', *Leisure Sciences*, 24(1): 59–77

Ford, N. and Eiser, J. (1996) 'Risk and liminality: The HIV-related socio–sexual interaction of young tourists', in S. Clift and S.J. Page (eds) *Health and the International Tourist*, London: Routledge, pp. 152–78.

Forer, P. (1999) 'Fabricating space', in R. Le Heron, L. Murphy, P. Forer and M. Goldstone (eds) *Explorations in Human Geography: Encountering Place*, Auckland: Oxford University Press, pp. 85–117.

Forer, P. and Pearce, D.G. (1984) 'Spatial patterns of package tourism in New Zealand', *New Zealand Geographer*, 40: 34–42.

Forster, J. (1964) 'The sociological consequences of tourism', *International Journal of Comparative Sociology*, 5: 217–27.

Forsyte Research (2000) 'Topline results of the 1999 Domestic Travel Study', paper presented at the NZTIA Conference, Wellington, 11 August.

Fountain, J. and Hall, C.M. (2002) 'The impact of lifestyle migration on rural communities: A case study of Akaroa, New Zealand', in C.M. Hall and A.M. Williams (eds) *Tourism and Migration: New Relationships between Production and Consumption*, Dordrecht: Kluwer, pp. 153–68.

Fowler, J. (1991) 'Farm house holidays in Ireland', *Tourism Recreation Research*, 16: 72–5.

Frändberg, L. and Vilhelmson, B. (2003) 'Personal mobility – a corporeal dimension of transnationalisa-tion: The case of long-distance travel from Sweden', *Environment and Planning A*, 35(10): 1751–68.

Frankel, O.H. (1978) 'The value of wilderness to science', in G. Mosley (ed.) *Australia's Wilderness: Conservation Progress and Plans, Proceedings of the First National Wilderness Conference, Australian Academy of Science, Canberra, 21–23 October, 1977*, Hawthorn, Vic.: Australian Conservation Foundation, pp. 101–5.

Frater, J. (1982) *Farm Tourism in England and Overseas*, Research Memorandum No. 93, Birmingham: Centre for Urban and Regional Studies, University of Birmingham.

Frater, J. (1983) 'Farm tourism in England', *Tourism Management*, 4(3): 167–79.

Frazier, J. (1982) *Applied Geography: Selected Perspectives*, Englewood Cliffs, NJ: Prentice Hall.

Freathy, P. (2004) 'The changing airport environment: Past, present and future imperfect?', in L. Lumsdon and S.J. Page (eds) *Tourism and Transport: Issues and Agendas for the New Millennium*, Oxford: Elsevier, pp. 105–16.

Frechtling, D.C. (1976a) 'Proposed standard definitions and classifications for travel research', *Marketing Travel and Tourism, Seventh Annual Conference Proceedings*, Boca Raton, FL: Travel Research Association, pp. 59–74.

Frechtling, D.C. (1976b) 'Travel as an employer in the state economy', *Journal of Travel Research*, 15(4): 8–12.

Frechtling, D.C. (1987) 'Assessing the impacts of travel and tourism: Introduction to travel impact estimation', in J.R.B. Ritchie and C.R. Goeldner (eds) *Travel, Tourism and Hospitality Research: A Handbook for Managers and Researchers*, New York: Wiley, pp. 325–31.

Frechtling, D.C. (1996) *Practical Tourism Forecasting*, Oxford: Butterworth-Heinemann.

Freeman, T.W. (1961) *A Hundred Years of Geography*, London: Gerald Duckworth.

Fretter, A.D. (1993) 'Place marketing: A local authority perspective', in G. Kearns and C. Philo (eds) *Selling Places: The City as Cultural Capital, Past and Present*, Oxford: Pergamon, pp. 163–74.

Friedmann, J. (1966) *Regional Development Policy: A Case Study of Venezuela*, Boston, MA: MIT Press.

Friedmann, J. (1973) 'A conceptual model for the analysis of planning behaviour', in A. Faludi (ed.) *A Reader in Planning Theory*, Oxford: Pergamon, pp. 344–70.

Fritz, R. (1982) 'Tourism, vacation home development

and residential tax burden: A case of the local finances of 240 Vermont towns', *American Journal of Economics and Sociology*, 41(4): 375–85.

Fritz, S., Carver, S. and See, L. (2000) 'New GIS approaches to wild land mapping in Europe', in S.F. McCool, D.N. Cole, W.T. Borrie and J. O'Loughlin, *Wilderness Science in a Time of Change Conference, Volume 2: Wilderness within the Context of Larger Systems*, Missoula, 23–7 May 1999, Proceedings RMRS-P-15-VOL-2, Ogden, UT: US Department of Agriculture, Forest Service, Rocky Mountain Research Station.

Fukaz, G. (1989) 'Hungary: More work, less leisure', in A. Olszewska and K. Roberts (eds) *Leisure and Lifestyle: A Comparative Analysis of Free Time*, London: Sage, pp. 39–46.

Funk, R.W. (1959) 'The wilderness', *Journal of Biblical Literature*, 78: 205–14.

Furmidge, J. (1969) 'Planning for recreation in the countryside', *Journal of the Royal Town Planning Institute*, 55(2): 62–7.

Furnham, A. (1984) 'Tourism and culture shock', *Annals of Tourism Research*, 11: 41–58.

Fyfe, N. and Banister, J. (1996) 'City watching: Closed circuit television surveillance in public spaces', *Area*, 28(1): 37–46.

Galatowitsch, S.M. (1990) 'Using the original land survey notes to reconstruct presettlement landscapes of the American West', *Great Basin Naturalist*, 50(2): 181–91.

Gale, F. and Jacobs, J.M. (1987) *Tourists and the National Estate Procedures to Protect Australia's Heritage*, Australian Heritage Commission Special Australian Heritage Publication Series No. 6, Canberra: Australian Government Publishing Service.

Gallent, N. (1997) 'Improvement grants, second homes and planning control in England and Wales: A policy review', *Planning Practice and Research*, 12(4): 401–10.

Gallent, N. and Tewdwr-Jones, M. (2000) *Rural Second Homes in Europe: Examining Housing Supply and Planning Control*, Aldershot: Ashgate.

Gannon, J. and Johnston, K. (1995) 'The global hotel industry: The emergence of continental hotel companies', *Progress in Tourism and Hospitality Research*, 1: 31–42.

Gardner, J.S. (1978) 'The meaning of wilderness: A problem of definition', *Contact – Journal of Urban and Environmental Affairs*, 10(1): 7–33.

Garland, A. (1997) *The Beach*, London: Penguin.

Garner, C. (1996) 'Park life is given £50 million injection', *The Independent*, 29 January.

Garreau, J. (1991) *Edge City: Life on the New Frontier*, New York: Doubleday.

Garrod, B. and Wilson, J.C. (eds) (2003) *Marine Ecotourism: Issues and Experiences*, Clevedon: Channel View.

Garrod, B. and Wilson, J.C. (2004) 'Nature on the edge? Marine ecotourism in peripheral coastal areas', *Journal of Sustainable Tourism*, 12(2): 95–120.

Gartner, W.C. (1986) 'Temporal influences on image change', *Annals of Tourism Research*, 13: 635–44.

Gartner, W.C. (1987) 'Environmental impacts of recreational home developments', *Annals of Tourism Research*, 14(1): 38–57.

Gaviria, M. (1975) *Turismo de Playa en Espana*, Madrid: Edicione S. Turner.

German Federal Agency for Nature Conservation (ed.) (1997) *Biodiversity and Tourism: Conflicts on the World's Seacoasts and Strategies for their Solution*, Berlin: Springer.

Getz, D. (1977) 'The impact of tourism on host communities: A research approach', in B.S. Duffield (ed.) *Tourism: A Tool for Regional Development*, Edinburgh: Tourism and Recreation Research Unit, University of Edinburgh, pp. 9.1–9.13.

Getz, D. (1981) 'Tourism and rural settlement policy', *Scottish Geographical Magazine*, 97 (December): 158–68.

Getz, D. (1983) 'Capacity to absorb tourism: Concepts and implications for strategic planning', *Annals of Tourism Research*, 10: 239–63.

Getz, D. (1984) 'Tourism, community organisation and the social multiplier', in J. Long and R. Hecock (eds) *Leisure, Tourism and Social Change*, Dunfermline: Centre for Leisure Research, Dunfermline College of Physical Education, pp. 85–100.

Getz, D. (1986a) 'Models in tourism planning towards integration of theory and practice', *Tourism Management*, 7(1): 21–32.

Getz, D. (1986b) 'Tourism and population change: Long term impacts of tourism in the Badenoch–Strathspey District of the Scottish Highlands', *Scottish Geographical Magazine*, 102(2): 113–26.

Getz, D. (1987) 'Tourism planning and research: Traditions, models and futures', paper presented at the *Australian Travel Research Workshop*, Bunbury, Western Australia, 5–6 November.

Getz, D. (1991a) *Festivals, Special Events, and Tourism*, New York: Van Nostrand Reinhold.

Getz, D. (1991b) 'Assessing the economic impacts of festivals and events: Research issues', *Journal of Applied Recreation Research*, 16(1): 61–77.

Getz, D. (1992) 'Tourism planning and destination life cycle', *Annals of Tourism Research*, 19: 752–70.

Getz, D. (1993a) 'Planning for tourism business districts', *Annals of Tourism Research*, 20: 583–600.

Getz, D. (1993b) 'Tourist shopping villages: Development and planning strategies', *Tourism Management*, 14(1): 15–26.

Getz, D. (1993c) 'Impacts of tourism on residents' leisure: Concepts, and a longitudinal case study of Spey Valley, Scotland', *Journal of Tourism Studies*, 4(2): 33–44.

Getz, D. (1994a) 'Students' work experiences, perceptions and attitudes towards careers in hospitality and tourism: A longitudinal case study in Spey Valley, Scotland', *International Journal of Hospitality Management*, 13(1): 25–37.

Getz, D. (1994b) 'Residents' attitudes towards tourism: A longitudinal study in Spey Valley, Scotland', *Tourism Management*, 15(4): 247–58.

Getz, D. (1997) *Event Management and Tourism*, New York: Cognizant.

Getz, D. and Carlsen, J. (2000) 'Characteristics and goals of family and owner-operated businesses in the rural tourism and hospitality sectors', *Tourism Management*, 21: 547–60.

Getz, D., Carlsen, J. and Morrison, A. (2004) *The Family Business in Tourism and Hospitality*, Wallingford: CAB International.

Ghelardoni, P. (1990) 'Tourist planning along the coast of Aquitane, France', in P. Fabbri (ed.) *Recreational Use of Coastal Areas*, Dordrecht: Kluwer, pp. 191–8.

Gibson-Graham, J.K. (1996) *The End of Capitalism (as we knew it): A Feminist Critique of Political Economy*, Oxford: Blackwell.

Giddens, A. (1984) *The Constitution of Society: Outline of the Theory of Structuration*, Cambridge: Polity Press.

Giddens, A. (1990) 'Modernity and utopia', *New Statesmen and Society*, 2 November, pp. 20–2.

Gilbert, D. and Clark, M. (1997) 'An exploratory examination of urban tourism impact with reference to residents' attitudes in the cities of Canterbury and Guildford', *Cities: The International Journal of Urban Policy and Planning*, 14(6): 343–52.

Gilbert, D. and Joshi, I. (1992) 'Quality management and the tourism and hospitality industry', in C. Cooper and A. Lockwood (eds) *Progress in Tourism, Recreation and Hospitality Management*, Vol. 4, London: Belhaven Press, pp. 149–68.

Gilbert, E.W. (1939) 'The growth of inland and seaside health resorts in England', *Scottish Geographical Magazine*, 55: 16–35.

Gilbert, E.W. (1949) 'The growth of Brighton', *Geographical Journal*, 114: 30–52.

Gilbert, E.W. (1951) 'Geography and regionalism', in G. Taylor (ed.) *Geography in the Twentieth Century*, London: Methuen.

Gilbert, E.W. (1954) *Brighton: Old Ocean's Bauble*, London: Methuen.

Gilg, A. (1985) *An Introduction to Rural Geography*, London: Edward Arnold.

Gill, A. (2004) 'Tourism communities and growth management', in A. Lew, C.M. Hall and A. Williams (eds) *Companion to Tourism*, Oxford: Blackwell, pp. 569–84.

Gill, A. and Williams, P.W. (1994) 'Managing growth in mountain tourism communities', *Tourism Management*, 15(3): 212–20.

Girard, T.C. and Gartner, W.C. (1993) 'Second home second view: Host community perceptions', *Annals of Tourism Research*, 20(4): 685–700.

Glacken, C. (1967) *Traces on the Rhodian Shore, Nature and Culture in Western Thought from Ancient Times to the End of the Eighteenth Century*, Berkeley, CA: University of California Press.

Glasson, J., Godfrey, K. and Goodey, B. with Absalom, H. and Van Der Borg, J. (1995) *Towards Visitor Impact Management: Visitor Impacts, Carrying Capacity and Management Responses in Europe's Historic Towns and Cities*, Aldershot: Avebury.

Glyptis, S. (1979) 'Countryside visitors: Site use and leisure lifestyles', unpublished PhD thesis, Hull: University of Hull.

Glyptis, S. (1981a) 'Leisure life-styles', *Regional Studies*, 15: 311–26.

Glyptis, S. (1981b) 'People at play in the countryside', *Geography*, 66(4): 277–85.

Glyptis, S. (1981c) 'Room to relax in the countryside', *The Planner*, 67(5): 120–2.

Glyptis, S. (1989a) 'Recreational resource management', in C. Cooper (ed.) *Progress in Tourism, Recreation and Hospitality Management*, Vol. 1, London: Belhaven Press, pp. 135–53.

Glyptis, S. (1989b) *Leisure and Unemployment*, Milton Keynes: Open University Press.

Glyptis, S. (1991) *Countryside Recreation*, Harlow: Longman.

Glyptis, S. (1993) 'Leisure and the environment', in S. Glyptis (ed.) *Essays in Honour of Professor J.A. Patmore*, London: Belhaven Press, pp. 3–12.

Glyptis, S. and Chambers, D. (1982) 'No place like home', *Leisure Studies*, 1(3): 247–62.

Go, F. (1991) *Competitive Strategies for the International Hotel Industry*, Economist Intelligence Unit (EIU) Special Report, London: EIU.

Go, F. and Pine, R. (1995) *Globalization Strategy in the Hotel Industry*, London: Routledge.

Gobster, P. (2002) 'Managing urban parks for a racially and ethnically diverse clientele', *Leisure Sciences*, 24(2): 143–59.

Godbey, G. (1976) *Recreation and Park Planning: The Exercise of Values*, Waterloo, Ont.: University of Waterloo.

Godfrey-Smith, W. (1979) 'The value of wilderness', *Environmental Ethics*, 1: 309–19.

Godfrey-Smith, W. (1980) 'The value of wilderness: A philosophical approach', in R.W. Robertson, P. Helman and A. Davey (eds) *Wilderness Management in Australia, Proceedings of a Symposium Held at the Canberra College of Advanced Education 19–23 July 1978*, Canberra: School of Applied Science, Canberra College of Advanced Education, pp. 56–71.

Gold, J. (1980) *An Introduction to Behavioural Geography*, Oxford: Oxford University Press.

Gold, J. and Gold, M. (1995) *Imaging Scotland: Tradition, Representation and Promotion in Scottish Tourism since 1750*, Aldershot: Ashgate.

Gold, J. and Ward, S. (eds) (1994) *Place Promotion: The Use of Publicity and Public Relations to Sell Places*, London: Belhaven Press.

Gold, S. (1973) *Urban Recreation Planning*, Philadelphia, PA: Lea & Febiger.

Gold, S. (1980) *Recreation Planning and Design*, New York: McGraw Hill.

Goodall, B. (ed.) (1989) Tourism Accommodation (special issue), *Built Environment*, 15(2).

Goodall, B. (1990) 'The dynamics of tourism place marketing', in G.J. Ashworth and B. Goodall (eds) *Marketing Tourism Places*, London: Routledge, pp. 259–79.

Goodall, B. and Whittow, J. (1975) *Recreation Requirements and Forest Opportunities*, Geographical Paper No. 378, Reading: Department of Geography, University of Reading.

Goodenough, R. and Page, S.J. (1994) 'Evaluating the environmental impact of a major transport infra-structure project: The Channel Tunnel high speed rail link', *Applied Geography*, 14(1): 26–50.

Goodhead, T. and Johnson, D. (eds) (1996) *Coastal Recreation Management: The Sustainable Development of Maritime Leisure*, London: E&FN Spon.

Goodwin, M. (1993) 'The city as commodity: The contested spaces of urban development', in G. Kearns and C. Philo (eds) *Selling Places: The City as Cultural Capital, Past and Present*, Oxford: Pergamon, pp. 145–62.

Gormsen, E. (1982) 'Tourism as a development factor in tropical countries: A case study of Cancun, Mexico', *Applied Geography and Development*, 19: 46–63.

Gössling, S. (2001) 'The consequences of tourism for sustainable water use on a tropical island: Zanzibar, Tanzania', *Journal of Environmental Management*, 61: 179–91.

Gössling, S. (2002) 'Global environmental consequences of tourism', *Global Environmental Change*, 12(4): 283–302.

Gössling, S. (2003) *Tourism and Development in Tropical Islands: Political Ecology Perspectives*, Aldershot: Edward Elgar.

Gössling, S. and Hall, C.M. (eds) (2005) *Tourism and Global Environmental Change*, London: Routledge.

Gössling, S., Borgström-Hansson, C., Hörstmeier, O. and Saggel, S. (2002) 'Ecological footprint analysis as a tool to assess tourism sustainability', *Ecological Economics*, 43(2–3): 199–211.

Gottmann, J. (1983) 'Capital cities', *Ekistics*, 50: 88–93.

Graber, K. (1997) 'Cities and the destination life cycle', in J.A. Mazanec (ed.) *International City Tourism: Analysis and Strategy*, London: Pinter, pp. 39–53.

Graber, L.H. (1978) *Wilderness as Sacred Space*, Monograph No. 8, Washington, DC: Association of American Geographers.

Graburn, N.H.H. (1983) 'The anthropology of tourism', *Annals of Tourism Research*, 10: 9–33.

Graefe, A.R. (1989) 'Visitor management in Canada's national parks', in *Towards Serving Visitors and Managing our Resources, Proceedings of a North American Workshop on Visitor Management in Parks and Protected Areas*, Waterloo, Ont.: Tourism Research and Education Centre, University of Waterloo and Canada Parks Service.

Graefe, A.R. (1991) 'Visitor impact management: An integrated approach to assessing the impacts of tourism in national parks and protected areas', in A.J. Veal, P. Jonson and G. Cushman (eds) *Leisure and Tourism: Social and Environmental Change, Papers* from the World Leisure and Recreation Association Congress, Sydney, Sydney: University of Technology, pp. 74–83.

Graefe, A.R. and Vaske, J.J. (1987) 'A framework for managing quality in the tourist experience', Annals of Tourism Research, 14: 389–404.

Graefe, A.R., Vaske, J.J. and Kuss, F.R. (1984a) 'Social carrying capacity: An integration and synthesis of twenty years of research', Leisure Sciences, 6(4): 395–431.

Graefe, A.R., Vaske, J.J. and Kuss, F.R. (1984b) 'Resolving issues and remaining questions about social carrying capacity', Leisure Sciences, 6(4): 497–507.

Graham, B. (1995) Geography and Air Transport, Chichester: Wiley.

Graham, B. (1998) 'Liberalisation, regional economic development and the geography of demand for air transport in the European Union', Journal of Transport Geography 6(2): 87–104.

Graham, B., Ashworth, G.J. and Tunbridge, J.E. (2000) A Geography of Heritage, London: Arnold.

Grahn, P. (1991) 'Landscaped in our minds: People's choice of recreative places in towns', Landscape Research, 16: 11–19.

Gramann, J.H. (1982) 'Toward a behavioural theory of crowding in outdoor recreation: An evaluation and synthesis of research', Leisure Sciences, 5(2): 109–26.

Grano, O. (1981) 'External influence and internal change in the development of geography', in D.R. Stoddart (ed.) Geography, Ideology and Social Concern, Oxford: Blackwell, pp. 17–36.

Gratton, C. and Richards, G. (1997) 'Structural change in the European package tour industry – UK and German comparisons', Tourism Economics, 3(3): 213–26.

Graves, H.S. (1920) 'A crisis in national recreation', American Forestry, 26(July): 391–400.

Greater London Council (GLC) (1968) Surveys of the Use of Open Space, Vol. 1, GLC Research Paper No. 3, London: GLC.

Greater London Council (GLC) (1969) Greater London Development Plan, London: GLC.

Greater London Council (1975) Greater London Recreation Study, London: GLC.

Greater London Council (1976) Greater London Recreation Study: Part 1, Demand, London: GLC.

Green, B. (1990) Countryside Conservation, London: Unwin Hyman.

Green, E., Hebron, S. and Woodward, D. (1987) Leisure and Gender: A Study of Sheffield Women's Leisure Experiences, Sheffield: Sports Council/Economic and Social Research Council.

Green, E., Hebron, S. and Woodward, D. (1990) Women's Leisure, What Leisure?, London: Macmillan.

Green, G., Marcouiller, D., Deller, S., Erkkil, D. and Sumathi, N. (1996) 'Local dependency, land use attitudes, and economic development: Comparisons between seasonal and permanent residents', Rural Sociology, 61(3): 427–45.

Greenhut, M. (1956) Plant Location in Theory and Practice, Chapel Hill, NC: University of North Carolina Press.

Greer, T. and Wall, G. (1979) 'Recreational hinterlands: A theoretical and empirical analysis', in G. Wall (ed.) Recreational Land Use in Southern Ontario, Department of Geography Publication Series No. 14, Waterloo, Ont.: University of Waterloo, pp. 227–46.

Gregory, J. (1988) Perceptions of Open Space: A Report on Research Undertaken by the Urban Wildlife Group, Birmingham: Urban Wildlife Trust.

Grekin, J. and Milne, S. (1996) 'Toward sustainable tourism development: The case of Pond Inlet, NWT', in R.W. Butler and T. Hinch (eds) Tourism and Indigenous Peoples, London: International Thomson Business, pp. 76–106.

Griffin, K. (1999) 'The inter-organisational relationships in Irish tourism', Irish Geography, 32(1): 57–72.

Griffith, D. and Elliot, D. (1988) Sampling Errors on the IPS, London: OPCS New Methodology Series.

Griffiths, T. (1991) 'History and natural history: Conservation movements in conflict', in D.J. Mulvaney (ed.) The Humanities and the Australian Environment, Canberra: Australian Academy of the Humanities, pp. 87–109.

Griffiths, T. and Libby, R. (eds) (1997) Ecology and Empire: Environmental History of Settler Societies, Edinburgh: Keele University Press.

Grinstein, A. (1955) 'Vacations: A psycho-analytic study', International Journal of Psycho-Analysis, 36: 177–86.

Grocott, A. (1990) 'Parks for people', Leisure Management, 8: 31–2.

Groome, D. and Tarrant, C. (1984) 'Countryside recreation: Achieving access for all?', Countryside Planning Yearbook 1984: 77–98.

Groundwork Foundation (1986) Putting Wasteland to Good Use, Birmingham: Groundwork Foundation.

Gunn, A. (2002) Tourism Planning: Basics, Concepts, Cases, 4th edn, London: Routledge.

Gunn, C. (1972) Vacationscape: Designing Tourist Regions, Austin, Tx: University of Texas.

Gunn, C. (1988) *Tourism Planning*, 2nd edn, London: Taylor & Francis.

Guo, L., Wu, B., Liu, F. and Fau, Y. (2000) 'Study on the tourist resources classification system and types evaluation in China', *Acta Geographica Sinica*, 55(3): 294–301.

Gustafson, P. (2002a) Place, place attachment and mobility: Three sociological studies. Göteborg Studies in Sociology No. 6, Göteborg: Department of Sociology, Göteborg University.

Gustafson, P. (2002b) 'Tourism and seasonal retirement migration', *Annals of Tourism Research*, 29(4): 899–918.

Guthrie, H.W. (1961) 'Demand for goods and services in a world market', *Regional Science Association Papers*, 7: 159–75.

Guy, B.S. and Curtis, W.W. (1986) 'Consumer learning or retail environment: A tourism and travel approach', paper presented at the American Academy of Marketing Conference, Tourism Services Marketing: Advances in Theory and Practice, Cleveland, OH: American Academy of Marketing Conference, Cleveland University.

Gvozdeva, G. (1999) 'Time balance changes and women's use of their right to rest', *Loisir et Société*, 22(1): 127–44.

Haeberli, W. and Beniston, M. (1998) 'Climate change and its impacts on glaciers and permafrost in the Alps', *Ambio*, 27: 258–65.

Hägerstrand, T. (1970) 'What about people in Regional Science?', *Papers of the Regional Science Association*, 24: 7–21.

Hägerstrand, T. (1984) 'Escapes from the cage of routines: Observations of human paths, projects and personal scripts', in J. Long and R. Hecock (eds) *Leisure, Tourism and Social Change*, Dunfermline: Dunfermline College of Physical Education, pp. 7–19.

Haggett, P. (1979) *Geography: A Modern Synthesis*, New York: Harper & Row.

Haggett, P. (1986) 'Geography', in R.J. Johnston, D. Gregory and D.M. Smith (eds) *The Dictionary of Human Geography*, Oxford: Blackwell, pp. 175–8.

Haines, A.L. (1977) *The Yellowstone Story*, 2 vols, Yellowstone National Park, WY: Yellowstone Library and Museum Association, and Niwot, CO: University Press of Colorado.

Haley, A. (1979) 'Municipal recreation and park standards in the United States: Central cities and suburbs', *Leisure Sciences*, 2: 277–91.

Halkett, I. (1978) 'The recreational use of private gardens', *Journal of Leisure Research*, 10(1): 13–20.

Hall, C.M. (1985) 'Outdoor recreation and national identity: A comparative study of Australia and Canada', *Journal of Canadian Culture*, 2(2): 25–39.

Hall, C.M. (1987) 'Wilderness inventories in Australia', in A. Conacher (ed.) *Readings in Australian Geography, Proceedings of the Twenty-first Institute of Australian Geographers' Conference*, Perth, 10–18 May 1986, Nedlands, WA: Department of Geography, University of Western Australia, pp. 466–76.

Hall, C.M. (1988) 'The geography of hope', PhD thesis, Nedlands, WA: Department of Geography, University of Western Australia.

Hall, C.M. (1989) 'The definition and analysis of hallmark tourist events', *GeoJournal*, 19(3): 263–8.

Hall, C.M. (1990) 'From cottage to condominium: Recreation, tourism and regional development in northern New South Wales', in D.J. Walmesley (ed.) *Change and Adjustment in Northern New South Wales*, Armidale, NSW: Department of Geography and Planning, University of New England, pp. 85–99.

Hall, C.M. (1992a) *Wasteland to World Heritage: Preserving Australia's Wilderness*, Carlton, Vic.: Melbourne University Press.

Hall, C.M. (1992b) *Hallmark Events: Impacts, Management and Planning*, London: Belhaven Press.

Hall, C.M. (1994) *Tourism and Politics: Policy, Power and Place*, Chichester: Wiley.

Hall, C.M. (1995) *Introduction to Tourism in Australia*, 2nd edn, Melbourne: Longman Australia.

Hall, C.M. (1996a) 'Tourism and the Maori of Aoteroa/New Zealand', in R.W. Butler and T. Hinch (eds) *Tourism and Indigenous Peoples*, London: International Thomson Business, pp. 155–70.

Hall, C.M. (1996b) 'Wine tourism in New Zealand', in *Proceedings of Tourism Down Under II: A Tourism Research Conference*, Dunedin, NZ: University of Otago, pp. 109–19.

Hall, C.M. (1997a) *Tourism in the Pacific: Development, Impacts and Markets*, 2nd edn, Melbourne: Addison Wesley Longman.

Hall, C.M. (1997b) 'Geography, marketing and the selling of places', *Journal of Travel and Tourism Marketing*, 6(3–4): 61–84.

Hall, C.M. (1998) *Introduction to Tourism: Development, Dimensions and Issues*, 3rd edn, Melbourne: Addison Wesley Longman.

Hall, C.M. (1999) 'Rethinking collaboration and

partnership: A public policy perspective', *Journal of Sustainable Tourism*, 7(3–4): 274–89.

Hall, C.M. (2000a) *Tourism Planning: Policies, Processes and Relationships*, Harlow: Prentice Hall.

Hall, C.M. (2000b) 'Tourism and the establishment of national parks in Australia', in R. Butler and S. Boyd (eds) *Tourism and National Parks*, Chichester: Wiley, pp. 29–38.

Hall, C.M. (2000c) 'Tourism, national parks and aboriginal populations', in R. Butler and S. Boyd (eds) *Tourism and National Parks*, Chichester: Wiley, pp. 57–71.

Hall, C.M. (2001a) 'Territorial economic integration and globalisation', in C. Cooper and S. Wahab (eds) *Tourism in the Age of Globalisation*, London: Routledge, pp. 22–44.

Hall, C.M. (2001b) 'Imaging, tourism and sports event fever: The Sydney Olympics and the need for a social charter for mega-events', in C. Gratton and I.P. Henry (eds) *Sport in the City: The Role of Sport in Economic and Social Regeneration*, London: Routledge, pp. 166–83.

Hall, C.M. (2002a) 'Travel safety, terrorism and the media: The significance of the issue–attention cycle', *Current Issues in Tourism*, 5(5): 458–66.

Hall, C.M. (2002b) 'Tourism in capital cities', *Tourism: An International Interdisciplinary Journal*, 50(3): 235–48.

Hall, C.M. (2003a) *Introduction to Tourism in Australia*, 4th edn, Melbourne: Hospitality Press.

Hall, C.M. (2003b) 'Wine and food tourism networks: A comparative study', in K. Pavlovich and M. Akoorie (eds) *Strategic Alliances and Collaborative Partnerships: A Case Book*, Palmerston North, NZ: Dunmore Press, pp. 262–8.

Hall, C.M. (2003c) 'Biosecurity and wine tourism: Is a vineyard a farm?', *Journal of Wine Research*, 14(2–3): 121–6.

Hall, C.M. (2004a) 'Reflexivity and tourism research: Situating myself and/with others', in J. Phillimore and L. Goodson (eds) *Qualitative Research in Tourism: Ontologies, Epistemologies and Methodologies*, London: Routledge, pp. 137–55.

Hall, C.M. (2004b) 'Small firms and wine and food tourism in New Zealand: Issues of collaboration, clusters and lifestyles', in R. Thomas (ed.) *Small Firms in Tourism: International Perspectives*, Oxford: Elsevier, pp. 167–81.

Hall, C.M. (2005a) *Tourism: Rethinking the Social Science of Mobility*, Harlow: Prentice Hall.

Hall, C.M. (2005b) 'Reconsidering the geography of tourism and contemporary mobility', *Australian Geographical Research*, 43: 125–39.

Hall, C.M. (2005c) 'Space-time accessibility and the tourist area cycle of evolution: The role of geographies of spatial interaction and mobility in contributing to an improved understanding of tourism', in R. Butler (ed.) *The Tourism Life Cycle: Conceptual and Theoretical Issues*, Vol. 2, Clevedon: Channel View.

Hall, C.M. (2005d) 'Demography', in D. Buhalis and C. Costa (eds) *Tourism Dynamics: Present and Future Issues*, Oxford: Butterworth-Heinemann, pp. 9–18.

Hall, C.M. (2005e) 'Biosecurity and wine tourism', *Tourism Management*, in press.

Hall, C.M. and Boyd, S. (eds) (2005) *Tourism and Nature-based Tourism in Peripheral Areas: Development or Disaster*, Clevedon: Channel View.

Hall, C.M. and Härkönen, T. (2006) 'Lake tourism: An introduction to lacustrine tourism systems', in C.M. Hall and T. Härkönen (eds) *Lake Tourism: An Integrated Approach to Lacustrine Tourism Systems*, Clevedon: Channel View.

Hall, C. M. and Higham, J.E.S. (2000) 'Wilderness management in the forests of New Zealand: Historical development and contemporary issues in environmental management', in X. Font and J. Tribe (eds) *Forest Tourism and Recreation: Case Studies in Environmental Management*, Wallingford: CAB International, pp. 143–60.

Hall, C.M. and Higham, J. (eds) (2005) *Tourism, Recreation and Climate Change*, Clevedon: Channel View.

Hall, C.M. and Hodges, J. (1996) 'The party's great, but what about the hangover? The housing and social impacts of mega-events with special reference to the Sydney 2000 Olympics', *Festival Management and Event Tourism*, 4(1–2): 13–20.

Hall, C.M. and Jenkins, J. (1995) *Tourism and Public Policy*, London: Routledge.

Hall, C.M. and Jenkins, J. (1998) 'The policy dimensions of rural tourism and recreation', in R. Butler, C.M. Hall and J. Jenkins (eds) *Tourism and Recreation in Rural Areas*, Chichester: Wiley, pp. 19–42.

Hall, C.M. and Jenkins, J. (2004) 'Tourism and public policy', in A. Lew, C.M. Hall and A. Williams (eds) *Companion to Tourism*, Oxford: Blackwell, pp. 525–40.

Hall, C.M. and Johnston, M.E. (eds) (1995) *Polar Tourism: Tourism in the Arctic and Antarctic Regions*, Chichester: Wiley.

Hall, C.M. and Kearsley, G.W. (2001) *Tourism in New Zealand: An Introduction*, Melbourne: Oxford University Press.

Hall, C.M. and Lew, A.A. (eds) (1998) *Sustainable Tourism Development: Geographical Perspectives*, Harlow: Addison Wesley Longman.

Hall, C.M. and McArthur, S. (1994) 'Commercial whitewater rafting in Australia', in D. Mercer (ed.) *New Viewpoints in Australian Outdoor Recreation Research and Planning*, Melbourne: Hepper Marriott, pp. 109–18.

Hall, C.M. and McArthur, S. (eds) (1996) *Heritage Management in Australia and New Zealand: The Human Dimension*, Sydney: Oxford University Press.

Hall, C.M. and McArthur, S. (1998) *Integrated Heritage Management*, London: The Stationery Office.

Hall, C.M. and Macionis, N. (1998) Wine tourism in Australia and New Zealand', in R.W. Butler, C.M. Hall and J.M. Jenkins (eds) *Tourism and Recreation in Rural Areas*, Chichester: Wiley, pp. 267–98.

Hall, C.M. and Mark, S.R. (1985) *Saving All the Pieces: Wilderness and Inventory and Prospect in Western Australia, A Working Paper*, Nedlands, WA: Department of Geography, University of Western Australia.

Hall, C.M. and Mitchell, R. (2002) 'The changing nature of the relationship between cuisine and tourism in Australia and New Zealand: From fusion cuisine to food networks', in A-M. Hjalager and G. Richards (eds) *Tourism and Gastronomy*, London: Routledge.

Hall, C.M. and Müller, D. (eds) (2004) *Tourism, Mobility and Second Homes: Between Elite Landscape and Common Ground*, Clevedon: Channel View.

Hall, C.M. and Page, S.J. (eds) (1996) *Tourism in the Pacific: Cases and Issues*, London: International Thomson Business.

Hall, C.M. and Page, S.J. (eds) (2000) *Tourism in South and South-East Asia: Cases and Issues*, Oxford: Butterworth-Heinemann.

Hall, C.M. and Page, S.J. (2002) *Geography of Tourism and Recreation: Environment, Place and Space*, 2nd edn, London: Routledge.

Hall, C.M. and Piggin, R. (2001) 'Tourism and World Heritage in OECD countries', *Tourism Recreation Research*, 26(1): 103–5.

Hall, C.M. and Rusher, K. (2004) 'Risky lifestyles? Entrepreneurial characteristics of the New Zealand bed and breakfast sector', in R. Thomas (ed.) *Small Firms in Tourism: International Perspectives*, Oxford: Elsevier, pp. 83–97.

Hall, C.M. and Selwood, H.J. (1987) 'Cup gained, paradise lost? A case study of the 1987 America's Cup as a hallmark event', in *Proceedings of the New Zealand Geography Society Conference*, Palmerston North, NZ: Department of Geography, Massey University, pp. 267–74.

Hall, C.M. and Tucker, H. (eds) (2004) *Tourism and Postcolonialism*, London: Routledge.

Hall, C.M. and Williams, A.M. (eds) (2001) *Tourism and Migration*, Dordrecht: Kluwer.

Hall, C.M. and Williams, A.M. (eds) (2002) *Tourism and Migration: New Relationships between Consumption and Production*, Dordrecht: Kluwer.

Hall, C.M., Selwood, H.J. and McKewon, E. (1995) 'Hedonists, ladies and larrikins: Crime, prostitution and the 1987 America's Cup', *Visions in Leisure and Business*, 14(3): 28–51.

Hall, C.M., Jenkins, J.M. and Kearsley, G. (eds) (1997) *Tourism Planning and Policy in Australia and New Zealand: Cases and Issues*, Sydney: Irwin.

Hall, C.M., Cambourne, B., Macionis, N. and Johnson, G. (1997–8) 'Wine tourism and network development in Australia and New Zealand: Review, establishment and prospects', *International Journal of Wine Marketing*, 9(2–3): 5–31.

Hall, C.M., Johnson, G. and Mitchell, R. (2000a) 'Wine tourism and regional development', in C.M. Hall, E. Sharples, B. Cambourne and N. Macionis (eds) *Wine Tourism around the World: Development, Management and Markets*, Oxford: Butterworth-Heinemann, pp. 169–225.

Hall, C.M., Sharples, E., Cambourne, B. and Macionis, N. (eds) (2000b) *Wine Tourism around the World: Development, Management and Markets*, Oxford: Butterworth-Heinemann.

Hall, C.M., Mitchell, R. and Sharples, E. (2003a) 'Consuming places: the role of food, wine and tourism in regional development', in C.M. Hall, E. Sharples, R. Mitchell, B. Cambourne and N. Macionis (eds) *Food Tourism around the World: Development, Management and Markets*, Oxford: Butterworth-Heinemann, pp. 25–59.

Hall, C.M., Timothy, D. and Duval, D. (2003b) 'Security and tourism: Towards a new understanding?, *Journal of Travel and Tourism Marketing*, 15(2–3): 1–18.

Hall, C.M., Duval, D. and Timothy, D. (eds) (2004a) *Safety and Security in Tourism: Relationships, Management and Marketing*, New York: Haworth Press.

Hall, C.M., Williams, A.M. and Lew, A. (2004b) 'Tourism: Conceptualisations, institutions and issues', in A. Lew, C.M. Hall, C.M. and A.M. Williams (eds) *Companion to Tourism*, Oxford: Blackwell, pp. 3–21.

Hall, D.R. (ed.) (1991) *Tourism and Economic Development in Eastern Europe and the Soviet Union*, London: Belhaven Press.

Hall, D.R. and O'Hanlon, L. (eds) (1998) *Rural Tourism Management: Sustainable Options, Proceedings of an International Conference*, Scottish Agricultural College Auchincruive, Ayr, 9–12 September.

Hall, J.M. (1972) 'Leisure motoring in Great Britain: Patterns and policies', *Geographica Polonica*, 24: 211–25.

Hall, J.M. (1974) 'The capacity to absorb tourists', *Built Environment*, 3: 392–7.

Hall, P. (1982a) *Urban and Regional Planning*, 2nd edn, Harmondsworth: Penguin.

Hall, P. (1982b) *Great Planning Disasters*, Harmondsworth: Penguin.

Hall, P. (1992) *Urban and Regional Planning*, 3rd edn, London: Routledge.

Hall, P. (2000) 'The changing role of capital cities', *Plan Canada*, 40(3): 8–12.

Halseth, G. (1998) *Cottage Country in Transition: A Social Geography of Change and Contention in the Rural-Recreational Countryside*, Montreal: McGills-Queen's University Press.

Halseth, G. and Rosenberg, M.W. (1995) 'Cottagers in the urban field', *Professional Geographer*, 47: 148–59.

Hamilton, L.M. (2002) 'The American farmers market', *Gastronomica*, 2(3): 73–7.

Hamilton-Smith, E. (1980) 'Wilderness: Experience or land use', in R.W. Robertson, P. Helman and A. Davey (eds) *Wilderness Management in Australia, Proceedings of a Symposium Held at the Canberra College of Advanced Education 19–23 July 1978*, Canberra: School of Applied Science, Canberra College of Advanced Education, pp. 72–81.

Hammitt, W.E. and Cole, D.N. (1998) *Wildland Recreation*, 2nd edn, Chichester: Wiley.

Hannigan, J. (1998) *Fantasy City: Pleasure and Profit in the Postmodern Metropolis*, London: Routledge.

Hantel, M., Ehrendorfer, M. and Haslinger, A. (2000) 'Climate sensitivity of snow cover duration in Austria', *International Journal of Climatology*, 20: 615–40.

Harmston, F.K. (1980) 'A case study of secondary impacts comparing through and vacationing travelers', *Journal of Travel Research*, 18(3): 33–6.

Harris, C.C., McLaughlin, W.J. and Ham, S.H. (1987) 'Integration of recreation and tourism in Idaho', *Annals of Tourism Research*, 14(3): 405–19.

Harrison, C. (1980–1) 'Recovery of lowland grassland and heathland in Southern England from disturbance by trampling', *Biological Conservation*, 19: 119–30.

Harrison, C. (1981) *Preliminary Results of a Survey of Site Use in the South London Green Belt*, Working Paper No. 9, Land for Informal Recreation, London: Department of Geography, University College.

Harrison, C. (1983) 'Countryside recreation and London's urban fringe', *Transactions of the Institute of British Geographers*, 8: 295–313.

Harrison, C. (1991) *Countryside Recreation in a Changing Society*, London: TML Partnership.

Harrop, A. and Palmer, G. (2002) *Indicators of Poverty and Social Exclusion in Rural England: 2002*, London: New Policy Institute.

Hart, W. (1966) *A Systems Approach to Park Planning*, Morges, Switzerland: International Union for the Conservation of Nature.

Hartmann, R. (1984) 'Tourism, seasonality and social change', in J. Long and R. Hecock (eds) *Leisure, Tourism and Social Change*, Dunfermline: Centre for Leisure Research, Dunfermline College of Physical Education, pp. 101–12.

Harvey, D. (1974) 'What kind of geography, for what kind of public policy', *Transactions of the Institute of British Geographers*, 63: 18–24.

Harvey, D. (1984) 'On the historical and present condition of geography: An historical materialist manifesto', *Professional Geographer*, 36: 1–11.

Harvey, D. (1987) 'Flexible accumulation through urbanisation', *Antipode*, 19: 260–86.

Harvey, D. (1988) 'Voodoo cities', *New Statesman and Society*, 30 September, pp. 33–5.

Harvey, D. (1989a) 'From managerialism to entrepreneurialism: The transformation in urban governance in late capitalism', *Geografiska Annaler*, 71B: 3–17.

Harvey, D. (1989b) *The Condition of Postmodernity: An Enquiry into the Origins of Cultural Change*, Oxford: Blackwell.

Harvey, D. (1990) 'Between space and time: Reflection on the geographic information', *Annals of the Association of American Geographers*, 80: 418–34.

Harvey, D. (1993) 'From space to place and back again: Reflections on the condition of postmodernity', in J. Bird, B. Curtis, T. Putnam, G. Robertson and L. Tickner (eds) *Mapping the Futures: Local Cultures, Global Change*, London: Routledge, pp. 3–29.

Harvey, D. (2000) *Spaces of Hope*, Berkeley, CA: University of California Press.

Harwood, C. and Kirkpatrick, J.B. (1980) *Forestry and Wilderness in the South West*, rev. edn, Hobart: Tasmanian Conservation Trust.

Hastenrath, S. and Greischar, L. (1997) 'Glacier recession on Kilimanjaro, East Africa, 1912–89', *Journal of Glaciology*, 43: 455–59.

Haughton, G. and Hunter, C. (1994) *Sustainable Cities*, London: Jessica Kingsley.

Havighurst, R. and Feigenbaum, K. (1959) 'Leisure and lifestyle', *American Journal of Sociology*, 64: 396–405.

Hawes, M. (1981) 'In search of wilderness that speaks to the heart', *Habitat*, 9(6): 3.

Hawes, M. and Heatley, D. (1985) *Wilderness Assessment and Management, A Discussion Paper*, Hobart: The Wilderness Society.

Hawkins, J.P. and Roberts, C.M. (1994) 'The growth of coastal tourism in the Red Sea: Present and future effects on coral reefs', *Ambio*, 23(8): 503–8.

Haynes, R. (1980) *Geographical Images and Mental Maps*, London: Macmillan.

Hays, S.P. (1998) *Explorations in Environmental History*, Pittsburgh, PA: University of Pittsburgh Press.

Haywood, K.M. (1986) 'Can the resort–area life cycle be made operational?', *Tourism Management*, 7: 154–67.

Haywood, K.M. and Muller, T.E. (1988) 'The urban tourist experience: Evaluating satisfaction', *Hospitality Education and Research Journal*, 12: 453–9.

Healey, P. (1997) *Collaborative Planning: Shaping Places in Fragmented Societies*, London: Macmillan.

Heath, E. and Wall, G. (1992) *Marketing Tourism Destinations: A Strategic Planning Approach*, Chichester: Wiley.

Heclo, H. (1978) 'Issue networks and the executive establishment', in A. King (ed.) *Annual Review of Energy*, Vol. 4, Palo Alto, CA: Annual Reviews.

Heeley, J. (1981) 'Planning for tourism in Britain', *Town Planning Review*, 52: 61–79.

Helber, L.E. (1988) 'The roles of government in planning in tourism with special regard for the cultural and environmental impact of tourism', in D. McSwan (ed.) *The Roles of Government in the Development of Tourism as an Economic Resource*, Seminar Series No. 1, Townsville, Qld: Centre for Studies in Travel and Tourism, James Cook University, pp. 17–23.

Helburn, N. (1977) 'The wilderness continuum', *Professional Geographer*, 29: 337–47.

Helman, P.H. (1979) *Wild and Scenic Rivers: A Preliminary Study of New South Wales*, Occasional Paper No. 2, Sydney: New South Wales National Parks and Wildlife Service.

Helman, P.H., Jones, A.D., Pigram, J.J.J. and Smith, J.M.B. (1976) *Wilderness in Australia: Eastern New South Wales and South-East Queensland*, Armidale, NSW: Department of Geography, University of New England.

Hendee, J.C., Stankey, G.H. and Lucas, R.C. (1978) *Wilderness Management*, Miscellaneous Publication No. 1365, Washington, DC: US Department of Agriculture, Forest Service.

Henderson, K. (1997) 'A critique of constraints theory: A response', *Journal of Leisure Research*, 29(4): 453–7.

Hendry, L., Shucksmith, J., Love, J. and Glendinning, A. (1993) *Young People's Leisure and Lifestyles*, London: Routledge.

Heneghan, P. (1976) 'The changing role of Bord Fáilte 1960–1975', *Administration*, 24: 394–406.

Henning, D.H. (1971) 'The ecology of the political/ administrative process for wilderness classification', *Natural Resources Journal*, 11: 69–75.

Henning, D.H. (1974) *Environmental Policy and Administration*, New York: Elsevier.

Henning, D.H. (1987) 'Wilderness politics: Public participation and values', *Environmental Management*, 11(3): 283–93.

Henry, I. (1988) 'Alternative futures for the public leisure service', in J. Benington and J. White (eds) *The Future of Leisure Services*, Harlow: Longman, pp. 207–44.

Henry, I. (ed.) (1990) *Management and Planning in the Leisure Industries*, London: Macmillan.

Henry, I. and Spink, J. (1990) 'Planning for leisure: The commercial and public sectors', in I. Henry (ed.) *Management and Planning in the Leisure Industries*, London: Macmillan, pp. 33–69.

Herbert, D.T. (1987) 'Exploring the work–leisure relationship: An empirical study of South Wales', *Leisure Studies*, 6: 147–65.

Herbert, D.T. (1988) 'Work and leisure: Exploring a relationship', *Area*, 20(3): 241–52.

Herbertson, A.J. (1905) 'The major natural regions', *Geographical Journal*, 25: 300–10.

Higgott, R. (1999) 'The political economy of globalisation in East Asia: The salience of "region building"', in K. Olds, P. Dicken, P.F. Kelly, L. Kong and H.W. Yeung (eds) *Globalisation and the Asia-Pacific: Contested Territories*, Warwickshire Studies in Globalisation Series, London: Routledge, pp. 91–106.

Higham, J.E.S. (1996) 'Wilderness perceptions of

international visitors to New Zealand: The perceptual approach to the management of international tourists visiting wilderness areas within New Zealand's Conservation Estate', unpublished PhD thesis, Dunedin, NZ: Centre for Tourism, University of Otago.

Higham, J.E.S. (1997) 'Visitors to New Zealand's backcountry conservation estate', in C.M. Hall, J. Jenkins and G. Kearsley (eds) *Tourism Planning and Policy in Australia and New Zealand*, Sydney: Irwin, pp. 75–86.

Higham, J.E.S. (1998) 'Tourists and albatrosses: The dynamics of tourism at the Northern Royal Albatross Colony, Taiaroa Head, New Zealand', *Tourism Management*, 19: 521–31.

Higham, J.E.S. and Kearsley, G.W. (1994) 'Wilderness perception and its implications for the management of the impacts of international tourism on natural areas in New Zealand', in C. Ryan (ed.) *Tourism Down-under: A Tourism Research Conference*, 6–9 December, Palmerston North, NZ: Department of Management Systems, Massey University, pp. 505–29.

Higham, J.E.S. and Lück, M. (2002) 'Urban ecotourism: A contradiction in terms?', *Journal of Ecotourism*, 1(1): 36–51.

Hill, H., Kelley, J., Belknap, D. and Dickson, S. (2002) 'Co-measurement of beaches in Maine, USA: Volunteer profiling of beaches and Annual meetings', *Journal of Coastal Research*, 36: 374–80.

Hillman, M. and Whalley, A. (1977) *Fair Play for All: A Study of Access to Sport and Informed Recreation*, Political and Economic Planning Broadsheet No. 571, London.

Hilton Group plc (2002) *Annual Report 2001*, Watford: Hilton Group plc.

Hinch, T.D. (1990) 'A spatial analysis of tourist accommodation in Ontario: 1974–1988', *Journal of Applied Recreation Research*, 15(4): 239–64.

Hinch, T.D. (1996) 'Urban tourism: Perspectives on sustainability', *Journal of Sustainable Tourism*, 4(2): 95–110.

Hinch, T.D. (1998) 'Ecotourists and indigenous hosts: Diverging views on their relationship with nature', *Current Issues in Tourism*, 1: 120–4.

Hinch, T. and Higham, J. (2003) *Sport Tourism Development*, Clevedon: Channel View.

Hitunen, M.J. and Pitkänen, K. (2004) 'Second housing in Finland: Perspective of mobility', paper presented at the Thirteenth Nordic Symposium on Tourism and Hospitality, Aalborg, Denmark, November.

Hobson, J.P. (2000) 'Tourist shopping in transit: The case of BAA plc', *Journal of Vacation Marketing*, 6(2): 170–83.

Hockin, R., Goodall, B. and Whitlow, J. (1978) *The Site Requirements and Planning of Outdoor Recreation Activities*, Geographical Paper No. 54, Reading: University of Reading.

Hoggart, K. (1988) 'Not a definition of rural', *Area*, 20: 35–40.

Hoggart, K. (1990) 'Let's do away with rural', *Journal of Rural Studies*, 6: 245–57.

Hoggart, K. and Green D. (eds) (1991) *London: A New Metropolitan Geography*, London: Edward Arnold.

Holden, A. (2000) *Environment and Tourism*, London: Routledge.

Hollis, G.E. and Burgess, J.A. (1977) 'Personal London: Students perceive the urban scene', *Geographical Magazine*, 50(3): 155–61.

Hooper-Greenhill, E. (1992) *Museums and the Shaping of Knowledge*, London: Routledge.

Hopley, D., van Woesik, R., Hoyal, D.C.J.D., Rasmussen, C.E. and Steven, A.D.L. (1993) *Sedimentation Resulting from Road Development, Cape Tribulation Area*, Great Barrier Reef Marine Park Authority Technical Memorandum No. 24, Townsville, Qld: Great Barrier Reef Marine Park Authority.

Horne, J. (1998) 'Understanding leisure time and leisure space in contemporary Japanese society', *Leisure Studies*, 17: 37–52.

Horwath and Horwath (1986) *London's Tourism Accommodation in the 1990s*, London: Horwath and Horwath.

Hötelling, H. (1929) 'Stability in competition', *Economic Journal*, 39: 41–57.

Houghton Evans, W. and Miles, J. (1970) 'Environmental capacity in rural recreation areas', *Journal of the Royal Town Planning Institute*, 56(10): 423–7.

Houinen, G. (1995) 'Heritage issues in urban tourism: An assessment of new trends in Lancaster County', *Tourism Management*, 16(5): 381–8.

Howell, S. and McNamee, M. (2003) 'Local justice and public sector leisure policy', *Leisure Studies*, 22(1): 17–35.

Hoyle, B. (2001) 'Lamu: Waterfront revitalization in an East African port-city', *Cities*, 18(5): 297–313.

Hoyle, B.S. and Pinder, D. (eds) (1992) *European Port Cities in Transition*, London: Belhaven Press.

Hoyles, M. (1994) *Lost Connections and New Directions*, Working Paper No. 6, London: Comedia & Demos.

Hudman, L. (1978) 'Tourist impacts: The need for

regional planning', *Annals of Tourism Research*, 9: 563–83.

Hudson, B. (1996) 'Paradise lost: A planner's view of Jamaican tourist development', *Caribbean Quarterly*, 42(4): 22–31.

Hudson, K. (1987) *Museums of Influence*, Cambridge: Cambridge University Press.

Hudson, P. (1990a) 'Stresses in small towns in north-western Australia: The impact of tourism and development', paper presented at the Twenty-fourth Institute of Australian Geographers Conference, University of New England, Armidale, NSW, September.

Hudson, P. (1990b) 'Structural changes in three small north-western Australian communities: The relationship between development and local quality of life', paper presented at the Annual Conference of Regional Science Association, Australian and New Zealand section, Perth, December.

Hudson, R. (2000) *Production, Places and the Environment: Changing Perspectives in Economic Geography*, Harlow: Prentice Hall, Pearson Education.

Hudson, R. and Townsend, A. (1992) 'Tourism employment and policy choices for local government', in P. Johnson and B. Thomas (eds) *Perspectives on Tourism Policy*, London: Mansell, pp. 49–68.

Huggins, M. (2000) 'More sinful pleasures? Leisure, respectability and the male middle classes in Victorian England', *Journal of Social History* 33(3): 585–600.

Hughes, G. (2004) 'Tourism, sustainability and social theory', in A. Lew, C.M. Hall and A. Williams (eds) *Companion to Tourism*, Oxford: Blackwell, pp. 498–509.

Hughes, H.L. (1984) 'Government support for tourism in the UK: A different perspective', *Tourism Management*, 5(1): 13–19.

Hughes, J.D. (1978) *In the House of Stone and Light: A Human History of the Grand Canyon*, Grand Canyon, AZ: Grand Canyon Natural History Association.

Hull, J. (1998) 'How sustainable is ecotourism in Costa Rica?', in C.M. Hall and A.A. Lew (eds) *Sustainable Tourism Development: Geographical Perspectives*, Harlow: Addison Wesley Longman, pp. 107–18.

Human Rights Watch (1999) *Trafficking*, http://www.hrw.org/about/projects/traffcamp/intro.html

Hummelbrunner, R. and Miglbauer, E. (1994) 'Tourism promotion and potential in peripheral areas: The Austrian case', *Journal of Sustainable Tourism*, 2: 41–50.

Hunter, C. and Green, H. (1995) *Tourism and the Environment*, London: Routledge.

Hurst, F. (1987) 'Enroute surveys', in J.B. Ritchie and C. Goeldner (eds) *Travel Tourism and Hospitality Research: A Handbook for Managers and Researchers*, 1st edn, New York: Wiley, pp. 401–16.

Hutchinson, B. (2004) 'Vancouver adores its stinking herons', *National Post*, 12 May: A1, A6

Huxley, T. (1970) *Footpaths in the Countryside*, Edinburgh: Countryside Commission for Scotland.

Iazzarotti, O. (1995) *Les Loisirs à la conquête des espaces périurbains*, Paris: L'Harmattan.

Iazzarotti, O. (2002) 'French tourism geographies: A review', *Tourism Geographies*, 4(2): 135–47.

Ilbery, B. (1991) 'Farm diversification as an adjustment strategy on the urban fringe of the West Midlands', *Journal of Rural Studies*, 7(3): 2–18.

Ilbery, B. and Kneafsey, M. (2000a) 'Registering regional specialty food and drink products in the United Kingdom: The case of PDOs and PGIs', *Area*, 32(3): 317–25.

Ilbery, B. and Kneafsey, M. (2000b) 'Producer constructions of quality in regional speciality food production: A case study from South West England', *Journal of Rural Studies*, 16: 217–30.

Ilbery, B., Bowler, I., Clark, G., Crockett, A. and Shaw, A. (1998) 'Farm-based tourism as an alternative farm enterprise: A case study from the Northern Pennines, England', *Regional Studies*, 32(4): 355–64.

Industry Commission (1995) *Tourism Accommodation and Training*, Melbourne: Industry Commission.

Inskeep, E. (1991) *Tourism Planning: An Integrated and Sustainable Development Approach*, New York: Van Nostrand Reinhold.

Inskeep, E. (1994) *National and Regional Tourism Planning*, London: Routledge.

International Association of Antarctica Tour Operators (1993a) *Guidelines of Conduct for Antarctica Tour Operators as of November 1993*, Kent: IAATO.

International Association of Antarctica Tour Operators (IAATO) (1993b) *Guidelines of Conduct for Antarctica Visitors as of November 1993*, Kent: IAATO.

International Union for the Conservation of Nature and Natural Resources (IUCN) (1978) *Categories, Objectives and Criteria for Protected Areas: A Final Report Prepared by Committee on Criteria and Nomenclature Commission on National Parks and Protected Areas* (CNPPA), Morges, Switzerland: IUCN.

International Union of Tourism Organisations (IUOTO) (1974) 'The role of the state in tourism', *Annals of Tourism Research*, 1(3): 66–72.

Ioannides, D. (1992) 'Tourism development agents: The

Cypriot resort cycle', *Annals of Tourism Research*, 19: 711–31.

Ioannides, D. (1995) 'Strengthening the ties between tourism and economic geography: A theoretical agenda', *Professional Geographer*, 47(1): 49–60.

Ioannides, D. (1996) 'Tourism and economic geography nexus: A response to Anne-Marie d'Hauteserre', *Professional Geographer*, 48(2): 219–21.

Ioannides, D. (1998) 'Tour operators: The gatekeepers of tourism', in D. Ioannides and K. Debbage (eds) *The Economic Geography of the Tourist Industry: A Supply-side Analysis*, London: Routledge, pp. 139–58.

Ioannides, D. and Debbage, K. (eds) (1998) *The Economic Geography of the Tourist Industry: A Supply-side Analysis*, London: Routledge.

Ioffe, G. and Nefedova, T. (2001) 'Land use changes in the environs of Moscow', *Area*, 33(3): 273–86.

Isard, W. (1956) *Location and Space Economy*, Cambridge, MA: MIT Press.

Iso-Ahola, S. (1980) *The Social Psychology of Leisure and Recreation*, Springfield, IL: C. Thomas.

Ivanov, V.V. (1999) 'Effects of global changes on the hydrological regime, surface water (freshwater) and estuarian ecology of the Barnets Sea: Consequences for water resources and environmental threats', in M.A. Lange, B. Bartling, and K. Grosfeld (eds) *Global Changes and the Barents Sea Region*, Proceedings of the First International BASIS Research Conference St Petersburg, Russia, 22–25 February 1998, Münster: Institute for Geophysics, University of Münster, pp. 63–90.

Ivy, R. (2001) 'Geographical variations in alternative tourism and recreation establishments', *Tourism Geographies*, 3(3): 338–55.

Jaakson, R. (1986) 'Second-home domestic tourism', *Annals of Tourism Research*, 13: 367–91.

Jackson, E. (1988) 'Leisure constraints: A survey of past research', *Leisure Sciences*, 10: 203–15.

Jackson, E. (1990) 'Variations in the desire to begin a leisure activity: Evidence of antecedent constraints', *Journal of Leisure Research*, 22: 55–70.

Jackson, E. (1994) 'Geographical aspects of constraints on leisure', *Canadian Geographer*, 38: 110–21.

Jackson, E., Crawford, D. and Godbey, G. (1993) 'Negotiation of leisure constraints', *Leisure Sciences*, 15(1): 1–11.

Jackson, P. (1985) 'Urban ethnography', *Progress in Human Geography*, 9: 157–76.

Jackson, P. and Smith, S.J. (1984) *Exploring Social Geography*, London: Allen & Unwin.

Jacob, G. and Schreyer, R. (1980) 'Conflict in outdoor recreation: A theoretical perspective', *Journal of Leisure Research*, 12(4): 368–80.

Jacobs, C. (1973) *Farms and Tourism in Upland Denbighshire*, Tourism and Recreation Report No. 4, Denbigh: Denbighshire County Council.

Jacobs, M. (1991) *The Green Economy*, London: Pluto Press.

Jafari, J. and Aaser, D. (1988) 'Tourism as the subject of doctoral dissertations', *Annals of Tourism Research*, 15: 407–29.

Jamal, T.B. and Getz, D. (1995) 'Collaboration theory and community tourism planning', *Annals of Tourism Reseach*, 22: 186–204.

James, P.E. (1972) *All Possible Worlds: A History Of Geographical Ideas*, 1st edn, Indianapolis, IN: Odyssey Press.

Janiskee, R. and Mitchell, L. (1989) 'Applied recreation geography', in M. Kenzer (ed.) *Applied Geography Issues, Questions and Concerns*, Dordrecht: Kluwer, pp. 151–64.

Jansen-Verbeke, M. (1986) 'Inner-city tourism: Resources, tourists and promoters', *Annals of Tourism Research*, 13(1): 79–100.

Jansen-Verbeke, M. (1988) *Leisure, Recreation and Tourism in Inner Cities. Explorative Case Studies*, Netherlands Geographical Studies 58, Amsterdam: Koninklijk Nederlands Aardrijk skundig Genootschap.

Jansen-Verbeke, M. (1989) 'Inner cities and urban tourism in the Netherlands: New challenges for local authorities', in P. Bramham, I. Henry, H. Mommass and H. van der Poel (eds) *Leisure and Urban Processes: Critical Studies of Leisure Policy in Western European Cities*, London: Routledge, pp. 233–53.

Jansen-Verbeke, M. (1990) 'Leisure and shopping: Tourism product mix', in G.J. Ashworth and B. Goodall (eds) *Marketing Tourism Places*, London: Routledge, pp. 128–37.

Jansen-Verbeke, M. (1991) 'Leisure shopping: A magic concept for the tourism industry', *Tourism Management*, 12(1): 9–14.

Jansen-Verbeke, M. (1992) 'Urban recreation and tourism: Physical planning issues', *Tourism Recreation Research*, 17(2): 33–45.

Jansen-Verbeke, M. (1995) 'Urban tourism and city trips', *Annals of Tourism Research*, 22(3): 699–700.

Jansen-Verbeke, M. and Ashworth, G.J. (1990) 'Environmental integration of recreation and tourism', *Annals of Tourism Research*, 17(4): 618–22.

Jansen-Verbeke, M. and Dietvorst, A. (1987)

'Leisure, recreation and tourism: A geographic view on integration', *Annals of Tourism Research*, 14: 361–75.

Jansen-Verbeke, M. and Rekom, J. (1996) 'Scanning museum visitors: Urban tourism marketing', *Annals of Tourism Research*, 23(2): 364–75.

Jansson, B. and Müller, D.K. (2003) *Fritidsboende i Kvarken*, Umeå, Sweden: Kvarkenrådet.

Jeans, D. (1990) 'Beach resort morphology in England and Australia: A review and extension', in P. Fabbri (ed.) *Recreational Use of Coastal Areas*, Dordrecht: Kluwer, pp. 277–85.

Jenkins, C. and Henry, B. (1982) 'Government involvement in tourism in developing countries', *Annals of Tourism Research*, 9(4): 499–521.

Jenkins, J. (1993) 'Tourism policy in rural New South Wales: Policy and research priorities', *GeoJournal*, 29(3): 281–90.

Jenkins, J. (1997) 'The role of the Commonwealth Government in rural tourism and regional development in Australia', in C.M. Hall, J. Jenkins and G. Kearsley (eds) *Tourism Planning and Policy in Australia and New Zealand: Cases, Issues and Practice*, Sydney: Irwin, pp. 181–91.

Jenkins, J. (2000) 'The dynamics of regional tourism organisations in New South Wales, Australia: History, structures and operations', *Current Issues in Tourism*, 3(3): 175–203.

Jenkins, J. (2001) 'Editorial: Special issue tourism policy', *Current Issues in Tourism*, 4(2/3/4): 69–77.

Jenkins, J. and Pigram, J. (1994) 'Rural recreation and tourism: Policy and planning', in D. Mercer (ed.) *New Viewpoints in Australian Outdoor Recreation Research and Planning*, Melbourne: Hepper Marriott, pp. 119–28.

Jenkins, J. and Prin, E. (1998) 'Rural landholder attitudes: The case of public recreational access to "private" lands', in R. Butler, C.M. Hall and J. Jenkins (eds) *Tourism and Recreation in Rural Areas*, Chichester: Wiley, pp. 179–96.

Jenkins, J. and Walmesley, D.J. (1993) 'Mental maps of tourists: A study of Coffs Harbour, New South Wales', *GeoJournal*, 29(3): 233–41.

Jenkins, J., Hall, C.M. and Troughton, M. (1998) 'The restructuring of rural economies: Rural tourism and recreation as a government response', in R. Butler, C.M. Hall and J. Jenkins (eds) *Tourism and Recreation in Rural Areas*, Chichester: Wiley, pp. 43–68.

Jenkins, R.L. (1978) 'Family vacation decision-making', *Journal of Travel Research*, 16(spring): 2–7.

Jenkins, W.I. (1978) *Policy Analysis: A Political and Organizational Perspective*, New York: St Martin's Press.

Jessop, B. (1999) 'Reflections on globalisation and its (il)logic(s)', in K. Olds, P. Dicken, P.F. Kelly, L. Kong and H.W. Yeung (eds) *Globalisation and the Asia-Pacific: Contested Territories*, Warwickshire Studies in Globalisation Series, London: Routledge, pp. 19–38.

Johnson, C., Bowker, J., English, D. and Worthen, D. (1998) 'Wildland recreation in the rural South: An examination of marginality and ethnic theory', *Journal of Leisure Research*, 30(1): 101–20.

Johnson, D. (2002) 'Towards sustainability: Examples from the UK coast', in R. Harris, T. Griffin and P. Williams (eds) *Sustainable Tourism: A Global Perspective*, Oxford: Butterworth-Heinemann, pp. 167–79.

Johnson, D., Snepenger, J. and Akis, S. (1994) 'Residents' perceptions of tourism development', *Annals of Tourism Research*, 21(3): 629–42.

Johnston, R.J. (1983a) 'On geography and the history of geography', *History of Geography Newsletter*, 3: 1–7.

Johnston, R.J. (1983b) 'Resource analysis, resource management and the integration of human and physical geography', *Progress in Physical Geography*, 7: 127–46.

Johnston, R.J. (1985a) 'Introduction: Exploring the future of geography', in R.J. Johnston (ed.) *The Future of Geography*, London: Methuen, pp. 3–26.

Johnston, R.J. (1985b) 'To the ends of the earth', in R. Johnston (ed.) *The Future of Geography*, London: Methuen, pp. 326–38.

Johnston, R.J. (1986) 'Applied geography', in R.J. Johnston, D. Gregory and D.M. Smith (eds) *The Dictionary of Human Geography*, Oxford: Blackwell, pp. 17–20.

Johnston, R.J. (1991) *Geography and Geographers: Anglo-American Human Geography since 1945*, 4th edn, London: Edward Arnold.

Johnston, R.J., Gregory, D. and Smith, D.M. (eds) (1986) *The Dictionary of Human Geography*, 2nd edn, Oxford: Blackwell.

Johnston, R.J., Gregory, D. and Smith, D.M. (eds) (1994) *The Dictionary of Human Geography*, 4th edn, Oxford: Blackwell.

Johnston, S. (1985) 'The beauty and significance of wild places', *Habitat*, 13(1): 27–8.

Jones Lang Wooten (1989) *Retail, Leisure and Tourism*, London: English Tourist Board.

Jones, A.D. (1978) 'Measuring our wilderness', *Habitat*, 6(2): 16–19.

Jones, D.R.W. (1986) 'Prostitution and tourism', in J.S. Marsh (ed.) *Canadian Studies of Parks, Recreation and Tourism in Foreign Lands*, Occasional Paper No. 11, Peterborough: Department of Geography, Trent University, pp. 241–8.

Jones, S.B. (1933) 'Mining tourist towns in the Canadian Rockies', *Economic Geography*, 9: 368–78.

Jones, T. (1994) 'Theme park development in Japan', in C. Cooper and A. Lockwood (eds) *Progress in Tourism, Recreation and Hospitality Management*, Vol. 6, Chichester: Wiley, pp. 111–25.

Jordan, J.W. (1980) 'The summer people and the natives: Some effects of tourism in a Vermont vacation village', *Annals of Tourism Research*, 7(1): 34–55.

Jordison, S. and Kieran, D. (2003) *Crap Towns: The 50 Worst Places to Live in the UK*, London: Boxtree.

Judd, D. (1995) 'Promoting tourism in US cities', *Tourism Management*, 16(3): 175–87.

Judd, D. (2000) 'Strong leadership', *Urban Studies*, 37(5–6): 951–61.

Judd, D. and Fainstein, S. (1999) *The Tourist City*, New Haven, CT: Yale University Press.

Jung, B. (1994) 'For what leisure? The role of culture and recreation in post-communist Poland', *Leisure Studies*, 13(4): 262–76.

Jung, B. (1996) 'Poland', in G. Cushman, A. Veal and J. Zuzanek (eds) *World Leisure Participation Free Time in the Global Village*, Wallingford: CAB International, pp. 183–99.

Kabanoff, B. (1982) 'Occupational and sex differences in leisure needs and leisure satisfaction', *Journal of Occupational Behaviour*, 3: 233–45.

Kaltenborn, B.P. (1997a) 'Recreation homes in natural settings: Factors affecting place attachment', *Norsk Geografisk Tidsskrift*, 51: 187–98.

Kaltenborn, B.P. (1997b) 'Nature of place attachment: A study among recreation homeowners in southern Norway', *Leisure Sciences*, 19: 175–89.

Kaltenborn, B.P. (1998) 'The alternate home: Models of recreation home use', *Norsk Geografisk Tidsskrift*, 52: 121–34.

Kassem, M. (1987) 'Marketing of tourism: An investigation of the application of marketing concepts and practices in promoting Egypt as a tourist destination in Britain and Ireland', unpublished PhD thesis, Glasgow: University of Strathclyde.

Kay, R. and Alder, J. (1999) *Coastal Planning and Management*, London: E&FN Spon.

Kay, T. and Jackson, G. (1991) 'Leisure despite constraint: The impact of leisure constraints on leisure participation', *Journal of Leisure Research*, 23: 301–13.

Keage, P.L. and Dingwall, P.R. (1993) 'A conservation strategy for the Australian Antarctic Territory', *Polar Record*, 29(170): 242–4.

Keane, M.J. and Quinn, J. (1990) *Rural Development and Rural Tourism*, Galway: SSRC, University College.

Keane, M.J., Briassoulis, H. and van der Stratten, J. (1992) 'Rural tourism and rural development', in H. Briassoulis and J. van der Stratten (eds) *Tourism and the Environment: Regional, Economic and Policy Issues, Environment and Assessment*, Vol. 2, Dordrecht: Kluwer, pp. 43–56.

Kearns, G. and Philo, C. (eds) (1993) *Selling Places: The City as Cultural Capital, Past and Present*, Oxford: Pergamon.

Kearsley, G.W. (1990) 'Tourism development and the user's perceptions of wilderness in Southern New Zealand', *Australian Geographer*, 21(2): 127–40.

Kearsley, G.W. (1997) 'Managing the consequences of over-use by tourists of New Zealand's conservation estate', in C.M. Hall, J. Jenkins and G. Kearsley (eds) *Tourism Planning and Policy in Australia and New Zealand*, Sydney: Irwin, pp. 87–98.

Kearsley, G.W., Hall, C.M. and Jenkins, J. (1997) 'Tourism planning and policy in natural areas: Introductory comments', in C.M. Hall, J. Jenkins and G. Kearsley (eds) *Tourism Planning and Policy in Australia and New Zealand*, Sydney: Irwin, pp. 66–86.

Keeble, D., Owens, P. and Thompson, C. (1982) 'Regional accessibility and economic potential in the European Community', *Regional Studies*, 16: 419–32.

Keen, D. and Hall, C.M. (2004) 'Second homes in New Zealand', in C.M. Hall and D. Müller (eds) *Tourism, Mobility and Second Homes: Elite Landscapes or Common Ground*, Clevedon: Channel View.

Keirle, I. (2002) 'Should access to the coastal lands of Wales be developed through a voluntary or statutory approach? A discussion', *Land Use Policy*, 19(2): 177–85.

Keller, C.P. (1984) 'Centre–periphery tourism development and control', in J. Long and R. Hecock (eds) *Leisure, Tourism and Social Change*, Dunfermline: Centre for Leisure Research, Dunfermline College of Physical Education, pp. 77–84.

Kelletat, D. (1993) 'Coastal geomorphology and tourism on the German North Sea coast', in P. Wong (ed.)

Tourism vs Environment: The Case for Coastal Areas, Dordrecht: Kluwer, pp. 139–66.

Kelly, J. (1982) *Leisure*, Englewood Cliffs, NJ: Prentice Hall.

Kelly, P.F. and Olds, K. (1999) 'Questions in a crisis: The contested meanings of globalisation in the Asia-Pacific', in K. Olds, P. Dicken, P.F. Kelly, L. Kong and H.W. Yeung (eds) *Globalisation and the Asia-Pacific: Contested Territories*, Warwickshire Studies in Globalisation Series, London: Routledge, pp. 1–15.

Ken, S. and Rapoport, R. (1975) 'Beyond palpable mass demand – Leisure provision and human demands: The life cycle approach, paper presented to Planning and Transport Research and Computation (International) Company Ltd, Summer Annual Meeting.

Kent, M., Newham, R. and Essex, S. (2002) 'Tourism and sustainable water supply in Mallorca: A geographical analysis', *Applied Geography*, 22(3): 351–74.

Kent, W.E., Meyer, R.A. and Reddam, T.M. (1987) 'Reassessing wholesaler marketing strategies: The role of travel research', *Journal of Travel Research*, 25(3): 31–3.

Kenzer, M. (ed.) (1989) *Applied Geography Issues, Questions and Concerns*, Dordrecht: Kluwer.

Keogh, B. (1984) 'The measurement of spatial variations in tourist activity', *Annals of Tourism Research*, 11: 267–82.

Keown, C. (1989) 'A model of tourists' propensity to buy: The case of Japanese visitors to Hawaii', *Journal of Travel Research*, winter: 31–4.

Kerr, W. (2003) *Tourism Public Policy in Scotland: The Strategic Management of Failure*, Oxford: Pergamon.

Kester, J.G.C. (2003) 'Cruise tourism', *Tourism Economics*, 9(3): 337–50.

Khan, N. (1997) 'Leisure and recreation among women of selected hill-farming families in Bangladesh', *Journal of Leisure Research*, 29(1): 5–20.

Killan, G. (1993) *Protected Places: A History of Ontario's Provincial Parks System*, Toronto: Dundurn Press.

Kim, K. (2000) 'Topics of human geography', in W. Yu and I. Son (eds) *Korean Geography and Geographers*, Seoul: Hanul, pp.195–265.

Kim, S. and Kim, J. (1996) 'Overview of coastal and marine tourism in Korea', *Journal of Tourism Studies*, 7(2): 46–53.

King, R. (1995) 'Tourism, labour and international migration', in A. Montanari and A.M. Williams (eds) *European Tourism: Regions, Spaces and Restructuring*, Chichester: Wiley, pp. 177–90.

King, R., Warnes, A.M. and Williams A.M. (1998) 'International retirement migration in Europe', *International Journal of Population Geography*, 4(2): 91–112.

King, R., Warnes, A.M. and Williams, A.M. (2000) *Sunset Lives: British Retirement to the Mediterranean*, Oxford: Berg.

Kinnaird, V. and Hall, D. (eds) (1994) *Tourism: A Gender Analysis*, Chichester: Wiley.

Kirkby, S. (1996) 'Recreation and the quality of Spanish coastal waters', in M. Barke, J. Towner and M. Newton (eds) *Tourism in Spain: Critical Issues*, Wallingford: CAB International, pp. 189–212.

Kirkpatrick, J.B. (1980) 'Hydro-electric development and wilderness: Report to the Department of the Environment', attachment to *Department of the Environment (Tas.), Assessment of the HEC Report on the Lower Gordon River Development Stage Two*, Hobart: Department of the Environment.

Kirkpatrick, J.B. and Haney, R.A. (1980) 'The quantification of developmental wilderness loss: The case of forestry in Tasmania', *Search*, 11(10): 331–5.

Kissling, C. (1989) 'International tourism and civil aviation in the South Pacific: Issues and innovations', *GeoJournal*, 19(3): 309–16.

Kline, M.B. (1970) *Beyond the Land Itself: Views of Nature in Canada and the United States*, Cambridge, MA: Harvard University Press.

Kliskey, A.D. (1994) 'A comparative analysis of approaches to wilderness perception mapping', *Journal of Environmental Management*, 41: 199–236.

Kliskey, A.D. and Kearsley, G.W. (1993) 'Mapping multiple perceptions of wilderness in southern New Zealand', *Applied Geography*, 13: 203–23.

Knafou, R. (1978) *Les Stations de sports d'hiver des Alpes françaises: L'améagement de la montagne à la françaises*, Paris: Masson.

Knafou, R. (2000) 'Tourismes en France: Vivre de la diversité', in Union Géographique Internationale Comité National Français de Géographie, *Historiens & géographes: Vivre en France dans la diversité*, Paris: Union Géographique Internationale Comité National Français de Géographie, pp. 367–84.

Knafou, R., Bruston, M., Deprest, F., Duhamel, P., Gay, J. and Sacareau, I. (1997) 'Une approache géographique du tourisme', *L'Espace géographique*, 3: 193–204.

Kneafsey, M. (1998) 'Tourism and place identity: A case study in rural Ireland', *Irish Geography*, 31(2): 111–23.

Knetsch, J. (1969) 'Assessing the demand for outdoor recreation', *Journal of Leisure Research*, 1(2): 85.

Koenig, U. and Abegg, B. (1997) 'Impacts of climate change on winter tourism in the Swiss Alps', *Journal of Sustainable Tourism*, 5: 46–57.

Konrad, V.A. (1982) 'Historical artifacts as recreational resources', in G. Wall and J. Marsh (eds) *Recreational Land Use*, Ottawa: Carleton University Press, pp. 393–416.

Koskela, H. and Pain, R. (2000) 'Revisiting fear and place: Women's fear of attack and the built environment', *Geoforum*, 31: 269–80.

Kosters, M.J. (1984) 'The deficiencies of tourism social science without political science: Comment on Richter', *Annals of Tourism Research*, 11: 609–13.

Kraas, F. and Taubmann, W. (eds) (2000) *German Geographical Research on East and Southeast Asia*, Sankt Augustin, Germany: Asgard-Verlag.

Kreisel, W. (2004) 'Geography of leisure and tourism research in the German-speaking world: Three pillars of progress', *Tourism Geographies*, 6(2): 163–85.

Kretchmann, J. and Eagles, P. (1990) 'An analysis of the motives of ecotourists in comparison to the general Canadian population', *Society and Leisure*, 13(2): 499–507.

Kreutzwiser, R. (1989) 'Supply', in G. Wall (ed.) *Outdoor Recreation in Canada*, Toronto: Wiley, pp. 21–41.

Kruzhalin, K. (2002) 'Economic geographical trends in the formation of the tourism market in Russia', *Vestnik-Moskovskogo-Universiteta-Seriya-5:-Geografiya*, 5: 72–7.

Kuhn, T. (1969) *The Structure of Scientific Revolutions*, 2nd edn, Chicago: University of Chicago Press.

Kuji, T. (1991) 'The political economy of golf', *AMPO, Japan-Asia Quarterly Review*, 22(4): 47–54.

Kwiatkowska, A. (1999) 'Nomadic-symbolic and settle-consumer leisure practices in Poland', in D. Crouch (ed.) *Leisure/Tourism Geographies: Practices and Geographical Knowledge*, London: Routledge, pp. 126–36.

Lane, B. (1994) 'What is rural tourism?', *Journal of Sustainable Tourism*, 2: 7–21.

Lang, R. (1988) 'Planning for integrated development', in F.W. Dykeman (ed.) *Integrated Rural Planning and Development*, Sackville, NB: Mount Allison University, pp. 81–104.

Lashley, C. (2000) 'Towards theoretical understanding', in C. Lashley and A. Morrison (eds) *In Search of Hospitality: Theoretical Perspectives and Debates*, Oxford: Butterworth-Heinemann, pp. 1–17.

Latham, J. (1989) 'The statistical measurement of tourism', in C.P. Cooper (ed.) *Progress in Tourism,*

Recreation and Hospitality Management, Vol. 1, London: Belhaven Press, pp. 57–76.

Latham, J. (1998) 'Patterns of international tourism', *Progress in Tourism and Hospitality Research* 4(1): 45–52.

Latham, J. and Edwards, C. (2003) 'The statistical measurement of tourism' in C. Cooper (ed) *Classic Reviews in Tourism*, Channel View, Clevedon, 55–76.

Lavery, P. (1971a) 'The demand for recreation', in P. Lavery (ed.) *Recreational Geography*, Newton Abbot: David and Charles, pp. 21–50.

Lavery, P. (1971b) 'Resorts and recreation', in P. Lavery (ed.) *Recreational Geography*, Newton Abbot: David and Charles, pp. 167–98.

Lavery, P. (ed.) (1971c) *Recreational Geography*, Newton Abbott: David and Charles.

Lavery, P. (1975) 'The demand for leisure: A review of studies', *Town Planning Review*, 46: 185–200.

Law, C.M. (1988) 'Conference and exhibition tourism', *Built Environment*, 13(2): 85–92.

Law, C.M. (1992) 'Urban tourism and its contribution to economic regeneration', *Urban Studies*, 29(3–4): 599–618.

Law, C.M. (1993) *Urban Tourism: Attracting Visitors to Large Cities*, London: Mansell.

Law, C.M. (ed.) (1996) *Tourism in Major Cities*, London: International Thomson Business.

Law, C.M. and Warnes, A.M. (1973) 'The movement of retired people to seaside resorts', *Town Planning Review*, 44: 373–90.

Law, S. (1967) 'Planning for outdoor recreation', *Journal of the Town Planning Institute*, 53: 383–6.

Lawrence, D., Kenchington, R. and Woodley, S. (2002) *The Great Barrier Reef: Finding the Right Balance*, Melbourne: Melbourne University Press.

Lawton, G. and Page, S.J. (1997a) 'Evaluating travel agents' provision of health advice to tourists', *Tourism Management*, 18(2): 89–104.

Lawton, G. and Page, S.J. (1997b) 'Health advice to the travellers to the Pacific Islands: Whose responsibility?', in M. Oppermann (ed.) *Pacific Rim Tourism*, Wallingford: CAB International, pp. 184–95.

Lawton, G., Page, S. and Hall, C.M. (1996) 'The provision of health advice to tourists', paper presented at the International Geographical Union Conference, The Hague, August.

Lawton, R. (1978) 'Population and society 1730–1900', in R. Dodgson and R. Butlin (eds) *An Historical Geography of England and Wales*, London: Academic Press, pp. 291–366.

Lea, J. (1988) *Tourism and Development in the Third World*, London: Routledge.

Leafe, R., Pethich, J. and Townsend, I. (1998) 'Realising the benefits of shoreline management', *Geographical Journal*, 164(3): 282–90.

Lee, H. (2000) 'Applied geography', in W. Yu and I. Son (eds) *Korean Geography and Geographers*, Seoul: Hanul, pp. 340–82.

Lee, I., Floyd, M. and Shinew, K. (2002) 'The relationship between information use and park awareness: A study of urban park users', *Journal of Park and Recreation Administration* 20(1):22–41.

Lee, R.G. (1977) 'Alone with others: The paradox of privacy in the wilderness', *Leisure Services*, 1: 3–19.

Leiper, N. (1984) 'Tourism and leisure: The significance of tourism in the leisure spectrum', *Proceedings of the Twelfth New Zealand Geography Conference*, Christchurch, NZ: New Zealand Geographical Society, pp. 249–53.

Leiper, N. (1989) *Tourism and Tourism Systems*, Occasional Paper No. 1, Palmerston North, NZ: Department of Management Systems, Massey University.

Leiper, N. (1990) *Tourism Systems: An Interdisciplinary Perspective*, Occasional Paper No. 2, Palmerston North, NZ: Department of Management Systems, Massey University.

Lenĉek, L. and Bosker, G. (1999) *The Beach: The History of Paradise on Earth*, London: Pimlico.

Lennon, J. (ed.) (2003) *Tourism Statistics: International Perspectives and Current Issues*, London: Continuum.

Leopold, A. (1921) 'The wilderness and its place in forest recreational policy', *Journal of Forestry*, 19(7): 718–21.

Leopold, A. (1925) 'Wilderness as a form of land use', *Journal of Land and Public Utility Economics*, 1(4): 398–404.

Lesslie, R.G. (1991) 'Wilderness survey and evaluation in Australia', *Australian Geographer*, 22: 35–43.

Lesslie, R.G. and Taylor, S.G. (1983) *Wilderness in South Australia*, Occasional Paper No. 1, Adelaide: Centre for Environmental Studies, University of Adelaide.

Lesslie, R.G. and Taylor, S.G. (1985) 'The wilderness continuum concept and its implications for Australian wilderness preservation policy', *Biological Conservation*, 32: 309–33.

Lesslie, R.G., Mackey, B.G. and Preece, K.M. (1987) *National Wilderness Inventory: A Computer Based Methodology for the Survey of Wilderness in Australia*,

prepared for the Australian Heritage Commission, Canberra: Australian Heritage Commission.

Lesslie, R.G., Mackey, B.G. and Shulmeister, J. (1988a) *Wilderness Quality in Tasmania, National Wilderness Inventory: Stage II*, report to the Australian Heritage Commission, Canberra: Australian Heritage Commission.

Lesslie, R.G., Mackey, B.G. and Preece, K.M. (1988b) 'A computer-based method for the evaluation of wilderness', *Environmental Conservation*, 15(3): 225–32.

Lesslie, R.G., Abrahams, H. and Maslen, M. (1991a) *Wilderness Quality on Cape York Peninsula, National Wilderness Inventory: Stage III*, Canberra: Australian Heritage Commission.

Lesslie, R.G., Maslen, M., Canty, D., Goodwins, D. and Shields, R. (1991b) *Wilderness on Kangaroo Island, National Wilderness Inventory: South Australia*, Canberra: Australian Heritage Commission.

Lesslie, R., Taylor, D. and Maslen, M. (1993) *National Wilderness Inventory: Handbook of Principles, Procedures and Usage*, Canberra: Australian Heritage Commission.

Lesslie, R., Taylor, D. and Maslen, M. (1995) *National Wilderness Inventory: Handbook of Principles, Procedures and Usage*, 2nd edn, Canberra: Australian Heritage Commission.

Lew, A.A. (1985) 'Bringing tourists to town', *Small Town*, 16: 4–10.

Lew, A.A. (1987) 'A framework for tourist attraction research', *Annals of Tourism Research*, 14(4): 553–75.

Lew, A.A. (1989) 'Authenticity and sense of place in the tourism development experience of older retail districts', *Journal of Travel Research*, 27(4): 15–22.

Lew, A.A. (2001) 'Defining a geography of tourism', *Tourism Geographies*, 3(1): 105–14.

Lew, A.A. and van Otten, G.A. (eds) (1997) *Tourism on American Indian Lands*, New York: Cognizant Communications Corporation.

Lew, A.A. and Wu, L. (eds) (1995) *Tourism in China: Geographic, Political and Economic Perspectives*, Boulder, CO: Westview Press.

Lew, A.A., Hall, C.M. and Williams, A. (eds) (2004) *Companion to Tourism*, Oxford: Blackwell.

Ley, D. and Olds, K. (1988) 'Landscape as spectacle: World's Fairs and the culture of heroic consumption', *Environment and Planning D*, 6: 191–212.

Li, Y. (2000) 'Geographical consciousness and tourism experience', *Annals of Tourism Research*, 27(4): 863–83.

Liddle, M. (1997) *Recreation Ecology*, London: Chapman and Hall.

Limb, M. (1986) 'Community involvement in the management of open space for recreation in the urban fringe, unpublished PhD thesis, London: University of London.

Lindberg, K. and McKercher, B. (1997) 'Ecotourism: A critical overview', *Pacific Tourism Review*, 1: 65–79.

Linton, D. (1968) 'The assessment of scenery as a recreation resource', *Scottish Geographical Magazine*, 84(3): 219–38.

Lipscombe, N. (1993) 'Recreation planning: Where have all the frameworks gone?', in *Track to the Future, Managing Change in Parks and Recreation*, Cairns, Qld: Royal Australian Institute of Parks and Recreation.

Livingstone, D.N. (1992) *The Geographical Tradition: Episodes in the History of a Contested Enterprise*. Oxford: Blackwell.

Llewelyn-Davis Planning/Leisureworks (1987) *Tourism Development in London Docklands: Themes and Facts*, London: London Docklands Development Corporation.

Lloyd, P. and Dicken, P. (1987) *Location in Space: A Theoretical Approach to Human Geography*, 2nd edn, London: Harper & Row.

Locke, S. (1985) *Country Park Visitor Surveys: Lessons from a Study at Sherwood Forest and Rufford Country Parks, Nottinghamshire*, CCP 180, Cheltenham: Countryside Commission.

Löfgren, O. (2002) *On Holiday: A History of Vacationing*, Berkeley, CA: University of California Press.

Logan, J.R., Whaley, R.B. and Crowder, K. (1997) 'The character and consequences of the growth regimes: An assessment of 20 years of research', *Urban Affairs Review*, 32(May): 603–30.

London Borough of Newham (1993) *Newham's Unitary Development Plan: Written Statement Parts One and Two*, London: London Borough of Newham.

London Tourist Board (1987) *The Tourism Strategy for London*, London: London Tourist Board.

London Tourist Board (1988) *London Tourism Statistics*, London: London Tourist Board.

Long, J.A. (1984) 'Introduction – tourism and social change', in J. Long and R. Hecock (eds) *Leisure, Tourism and Social Change*, Dunfermline: Centre for Leisure Research, Dunfermline College of Physical Education, pp. 69–76.

Long, J.A (1987) 'Continuity as a basis for change: Leisure and male retirement', *Leisure Studies*, 6: 55–70.

Long, J.A. (2002) *Count Me In: The Dimensions of Social Inclusion through Culture, Media and Sport*, Leeds: Leeds Metropolitan University.

Long, P.E. (2000) 'Tourism development regimes in the inner city fringe: The case of Discover Islington, London', in B. Bramwell and B. Lane (eds) *Tourism Collaboration and Partnerships: Politics, Practice and Sustainability*, Clevedon: Channel View, pp. 183–99.

Long, P.T. and Nuckolls, J.S. (1994) 'Organising resources for rural tourism development: The importance of leadership, planning and technical assistance', *Tourism Recreation Research*, 19(2): 19–34.

Long, P. and Perdue, R. (1990) 'The economic impact of rural festivals and special events: Assessing the spatial distribution of expenditures', *Journal of Travel Research*, 28(4): 10–14.

Long, P.T., Perdue, R.R. and Allen, L. (1990) 'Rural residents' perception and attitudes by community level of tourism', *Journal of Travel Research*, 29: 3–9.

Lösch, A. (1944) *Die Raümliche Ordnung der Wirtschaft*, Jena, Germany: Gustav Fischer.

Lovingwood, P. and Mitchell, L. (1978) 'The structure of public and private recreational systems: Columbia, South Carolina', *Journal of Leisure Research*, 10: 21–36.

Lowenthal, D. (1975) 'Past time, present place: Landscape and memory', *Geographical Review*, 65: 1–36.

Lowenthal, D. (1985) *The Past is a Foreign Country*, Cambridge: Cambridge University Press.

Lowyck, E., Van Langenhove, L. and Bollaert, L. (1992) 'Typologies of tourist roles', in P. Johnson and T. Barry (eds) *Tourism Policy*, London: Mansell, pp. 13–32.

Lozato, J. (1985) *Géographie du tourisme*, Paris: Masson.

Lucas, P. (1986) 'Fishy business', *Leisure Manager*, 4: 18–19.

Lucas, R. (1964) 'Wilderness perception and use: The example of the Boundary Waters Canoe Area', *Natural Resources Journal*, 3(1): 394–411.

Lumsdon, L. and Page, S.J. (eds) (2004) *Tourism and Transport: Issues and Agendas for the New Millennium*, Oxford: Pergamon.

Lundgren, J.O. (1984) 'Geographic concepts and the development of tourism research in Canada', *GeoJournal*, 9: 17–25.

Lundmark, L. and Marjavaara, R. (2004) 'Second home localization in the Swedish mountain range', paper presented at the Thirteenth Nordic Symposium on Tourism and Hospitality, Aalborg, Denmark, November.

Lutz, R.J. and Ryan, C. (1997) 'The impact inner city tourism projects: The case of the International Convention Centre, Birmingham, UK', in P. Murphy (ed.) *Quality Management in Urban Tourism*, Chichester: Wiley, pp. 41–53.

Lynch, K. (1960) *The Image of the City*, Cambridge, MA: MIT Press.

Lynch, K. (1984) 'Reconsidering the image of the city', in L. Rodwin and R. Hollister (eds) *Cities of the Mind*, New York: Plenum Press, pp. 151–61.

McAlvoy, L. (1977) 'Needs and the elderly: An overview', *Parks and Recreation*, 12(3): 31–5.

McArthur, S. (1996) 'Beyond the limits of acceptable change: Developing a model to monitor and manage tourism in remote areas', in *Tourism Down Under: 1996 Tourism Conference Proceedings*, Dunedin, NZ: Centre for Tourism, University of Otago.

McArthur, S. (2000a) 'Visitor management in action: An analysis of the development and implementation of visitor management models at Jenolan Caves and Kangaroo Island', unpublished PhD thesis, Belconnen, ACT: University of Canberra.

McArthur, S. (2000b) 'Beyond carrying capacity: Introducing a model to monitor and manage visitor activity in forests', in X. Font and J. Tribe (eds) *Forest Tourism and Recreation: Case Studies in Environmental Management*, Wallingford: CAB International, pp. 259–78.

McAvoy, L. (2002) 'American Indians, place meanings and the old/new west', *Journal of Leisure-Research*, 34(4): 383–396.

MacCannell, D. (1973) 'Staged authenticity: Arrangements of social space in tourist settings', *American Journal of Sociology*, 69: 578–603.

MacCannell, D. (1976) *The Tourist: A New Theory of the Leisure Class*, London: Macmillan.

McCool, S. (1978) 'Recreation use limits: Issues for the tourism industry', *Journal of Travel Research*, 17(2): 2–7.

McCool, S. and Cole, D. (1997) *Proceedings – Limits of Acceptable Change and related Planning Processes: Progress and Future Directions*, INT-GTR-371, Missoula, MT: USDA, Forest Service, Rocky Mountain Research Station.

McDermott, D. and Horner, A. (1978) 'Aspects of rural renewal in Western Connemara', *Irish Geography*, 11: 176–9.

McDowell, A., Carter, R. and Pollard, J. (1990) 'The impact of man on the shoreline environment of the Costa del Sol, Southern Spain', in P. Wong (ed.) *Tourism vs Environment: The Case for Coastal Areas*, Dordrecht: Kluwer, pp. 189–210.

McEwen, L., Hall, T., Hunt, J., Dempsey, M. and Harrison, M. (2002) 'Flood warning, warning response and planning control issues associated with caravan parks: The April 1998 floods on the lower Avon floodplain, Midlands region, UK'. *Applied Geography* 22(3): 271–305.

McGibbon, J. (2000) *The Business of Alpine Tourism in a Globalising World: An Anthropological Study of International Tourism in the Village of St. Anton am Arlberg in the Tirolean Alps*, Rosenheim, Germany: Vetterling Druck.

McGrath, F. (1989) 'Characteristics of pilgrims to Lough Derg', *Irish Geography*, 22: 44–7.

McIntosh, R.W. and Goeldner, C. (1990) *Tourism: Principles, Practices and Philosophies*, New York: Wiley.

McKenry, K. (1972a) *Value Analysis of Wilderness Areas*, Combined Universities Recreation Research Group, Monograph 2, Clayton, Vic.: Monash University.

McKenry, K. (1972b) 'A history and critical analysis of the controversy concerning the Gordon River Power Scheme', in Australian Conservation Foundation, *Pedder Papers Anatomy of a Decision*, Parkville, Vic.: Australian Conservation Foundation, Parkville, pp. 9–30.

McKenry, K. (1977) 'Value analysis of wilderness areas', in D. Mercer (ed.) *Leisure and Recreation in Australia*, Malvern, Vic.: Sorrett, pp. 209–21.

McKenry, K. (1980) 'The beneficiaries of wilderness', in R.W. Robertson, P. Helman and A. Davey (eds) *Wilderness Management in Australia, Proceedings of a Symposium Held at the Canberra College of Advanced Education 19–23 July 1978*, Canberra: School of Applied Science, Canberra College of Advanced Education, pp. 82–91.

McKercher, B. (1993a) 'Some fundamental truths about tourism: Understanding tourism's social and environmental impacts', *Journal of Sustainable Tourism*, 1(1): 6–16.

McKercher, B. (1993b) 'The unrecognized threat to tourism: Can tourism survive sustainability', *Tourism Management*, 14(2): 131–6.

McKercher, B. (1993c) 'Australian conservation organisations' perspectives on tourism in National Parks: A critique', *GeoJournal*, 29(3): 307–13.

McKercher, B. (1997) 'Benefits and costs of tourism in Victoria's Alpine National Park: Comparing attitudes of tour operators, management staff and public interest group leaders', in C.M. Hall, J. Jenkins and G. Kearsley (eds) *Tourism Planning and Policy in Australia and New Zealand: Cases, Issues and Practice*, Sydney: Irwin, pp. 99–109.

McKie, R. (2004) 'Fight to the last resort as Alpine crisis looms', *Observer*, 19 September, News: 3.

MacLellan, L.R. (1999) 'An examination of wildlife tourism as a sustainable form of tourism development in North West Scotland', *International Journal of Tourism Research*, 1(5): 375–87.

MacLeod, M., Silva, C. and Cooper, J. (2002) 'A comparative study of the perception and value of beaches in rural Ireland and Portugal: Implications for coastal zone management', *Journal of Coastal Research*, 18(1): 14–24.

McMillan, S. (1997) 'Balancing the books: Economic returns and corporate citizenship', mimeo of a paper presented at Business With Style: Adapting Heritage Buildings for Commercial Use, New South Wales Government, Heritage Office, Sydney.

McMurray, K.C. (1930) 'The use of land for recreation', *Annals of the Association of American Geographers*, 20: 7–20.

McMurray, K.C. (1954) 'Recreational geography', in P.E. James and C.F. Jones (eds) *American Geography: Inventory and Prospect*, Syracruse, NY: Syracruse University Press, pp. 251–7.

McVey, M. (1986) 'International hotel chains in Europe: Survey of expansion plans as Europe is rediscovered', *Travel and Tourism Analyst*, September: 3–23.

Madge, C. (1997) 'Public parks and the geography of fear', *Tijdschrift Voor Economische en Sociale Geografie*, 88: 237–50.

Madsen, H. (1992) 'Place-marketing in Liverpool: A review', *International Journal of Urban and Regional Research*, 16(4): 633–40.

Maitland, D. (1992) 'Space, vulnerability and dangers', *Operational Geographer*, 9: 28–9.

Malamud, B. (1973) 'Gravity model calibration of tourist travel to Las Vegas', *Journal of Leisure Research*, 5(1): 13–33.

Mandell, M.P. (1999) 'The impact of collaborative efforts: Changing the face of public policy through networks and network structures', *Policy Studies Review*, 16(1): 4–17.

Manidis Roberts Consultants (1991) *National Estate NSW Wilderness Review*, Sydney: National Estate Grants Program, Department of Planning.

Manidis Roberts Consultants (1996) *Tourism Optimisation Management Model for Kangaroo Island*, Adelaide: South Australian Tourism Commission.

Manning, R.E. (1984) 'Man and mountains meet: Journal of the Appalachian Mountains Club, 1876–1984', *Journal of Forest History*, 28(1): 24–33.

Manning, R.E. (1985) 'Crowding norms in backcountry settings: A review and synthesis', *Journal of Leisure Research*, 17(2): 75–89.

Mansfeld, Y. (1992) 'Industrial landscapes as positive settings for tourism development in declining industrial cities: The case of Haifa, Israel', *GeoJournal*, 28(4): 457–63.

Mansfield, N. (1969) 'Recreational trip generation', *Journal of Transport Economics and Public Policy*, 3(2): 152–64.

Marcouiller, D.W., Green, G.P, Deller, S.C., Sumathi, N.R and Erikkila, D.C (1998) *Recreational Homes and Regional Development: A Case Study from the Upper Great Lakes States*, Madison, WI: Cooperative Extension Publications.

Marine Conservation Society (1998) *Readers Digest Good Beach Guide*, Newton Abbot: David and Charles.

Mariussen, A. and Heen, K. (1999) 'Dependence, uncertainty and climatic change: The case of fishing', in M.A. Lange, B. Bartling and K. Grosfeld (eds) *Global Changes and the Barents Sea Region*, Proceedings of the First International BASIS Research Conference St Petersburg, Russia, 22–25 February 1998, Münster: Institute for Geophysics, University of Münster, pp. 91–104.

Mark, S. (1984) 'Wilderness review in the East Mojave National Scenic Area, California', unpublished MSc thesis, Ashland, OR: South Oregon State College.

Mark, S. (1985) 'Wilderness inventory of Western Australia', *Environment W.A.*, 7(3): 30–2.

Mark, S. (1991) 'Planning and development at Rim Village', in *Administrative History, Crater Lake National Park, Oregon*, Seattle, WA: US Department of the Interior, National Park Service.

Mark, S. (1996) 'Writing environmental and park histories', in C.M. Hall and S. McArthur (eds) *Heritage Management in Australia and New Zealand: The Human Dimension*, Melbourne: Oxford University Press, pp. 153–9.

Marketpower (1991) *A Report on the Structure of the UK Catering Industry*, London: Market Power.

Markusen, A. (1985) *Profit Cycles, Oligopoly and Regional Development*, Cambridge, MA: MIT Press.

Marne, P. (2001) 'Whose public space is it anyway? Class,

gender and ethnicity in the creation of the Sefton and Stanley Parks, Liverpool: 1858–72', *Social and Cultural Geography* 2(4):421–44.

Marsh, G.P. (1864 (1965)) *Man and Nature; Or, Physical Geography as Modified by Human Action*, ed. D. Lowenthal, Cambridge, MA: Belknap Press of Harvard University Press.

Marsh, J.G. (1983) 'Canada's parks and tourism: A problematic relationship', in P.E. Murphy (ed.) *Tourism in Canada: Selected Issues and Options*, Western Geographical Series, Vol. 21, Victoria, BC: Department of Geography, University of Victoria, pp. 271–307.

Marsh, J.G. (1985) 'The Rocky and Selkirk Mountains and the Swiss connection 1885–1914', *Annals of Tourism Research*, 12: 417–33.

Marsh, J.G. and Staple, S. (1995) 'Cruise tourism in the Canadian Arctic and its implications', in C.M.Hall and M.E. Johnston (eds) *Polar Tourism: Tourism in the Arctic and Antarctic Regions*, Chichester: Wiley, pp. 63–72.

Marsh, J.G. and Wall, G. (1982) 'Themes in the investigation of the evolution of outdoor recreation', in G. Wall and J. Marsh (eds) *Recreational Land Use, Perspectives on its Evolution in Canada*, Ottawa: Carleton University Press, pp. 1–12.

Marshall, R. (1930) 'The problem of the wilderness', *Scientific Monthly*, 30: 141–8.

Martin, R.L. (1999) 'The new "geographical turn" in economics: Some critical reflections', *Cambridge Journal of Economics*, 23: 65–91.

Martin, W. and Mason, S. (1979) *Broad Patterns of Leisure Expenditure*, London: Sports Council and Social Science Research Council.

Maslow, A. (1954) *Motivation and Personality*, New York: Harper & Row.

Mason, P. (2003) *Tourism Impacts, Planning and Management*, Oxford: Butterworth-Heinemann.

Masser, I. (1966–7) 'The use of outdoor recreational facilities', *Town Planning Review*, 37(1): 41–53.

Massey, D. and Allen, J. (eds) (1984) *Geography Matters! A Reader*, Cambridge: Cambridge University Press.

Mather, A. (2003) 'Access rights and rural sustainability in Britain', paper presented at the International Geographical Commission on Sustainable Rural Systems, Rio de Janeiro.

Mathieson, A. and Wall, G. (1982) *Tourism: Economic, Physical and Social Impacts*, London: Longman.

Matley, I.M. (1976) *The Geography of International Tourism*, Resource Paper No. 76–1, Washington, DC: Association of American Geographers.

Matson, J. (1892) 'The Australasian indigenous park', *New Zealand Country Journal*, 16(4): 356–60.

Matsui, Y. (1999) *Women in the New Asia*, London: Zed Books.

Matthews, H.G. (1983) 'Editor's page: On tourism and political science', *Annals of Tourism Research*, 10(4): 303–6.

Maude, A.J.S. and van Rest, D. J. (1985) 'The social and economic effects of farm tourism in the United Kingdom', *Agricultural Administration*, 20: 85–99.

Maver, I. (1998) 'Glasgow's public parks and the community 1850–1914', *Urban History*, 25(3): 323–47.

Mawhinney, K.A. (1979) 'Recreation', in D.A. Gilmore (ed.) *Irish Resources and Land Use*, Dublin: Institute of Public Administration.

Mawhinney, K.A. and Bagnall, G. (1976) 'The integrated social economic and environmental planning of tourism', *Administration*, 24: 383–93.

May, V. (1993) 'Coastal tourism, geomorphology and geological conservation: The example of South Central England', in P. Wong (ed.) *Tourism vs Environment: The Case for Coastal Areas*, Dordrecht: Kluwer, pp. 3–10.

Mazanec, J. (ed.) (1997) *International City Tourism: Analysis and Strategy*, London: Pinter.

Medlik, S. (1993) *Dictionary of Travel, Tourism and Hospitality*, Oxford: Butterworth-Heinemann.

Meethan, K. (1996) 'Consumed (in) in civilised city', *Annals of Tourism Research*, 32(2): 322–40.

Meethan, K. (1997) 'York: Managing the tourist city', *Cities: The International Journal of Urban Policy and Planning*, 14(6): 333–42.

Meethan, K. (1998) 'New tourism for old? Policy developments in Cornwall and Devon', *Tourism Management*, 19(6): 583–93.

Meethan, K. (2004) 'Transnational corporations, globalization and tourism', in A. Lew, C.M. Hall and A. Williams (eds) *Companion to Tourism*, Oxford: Blackwell, pp. 110–21.

Meinecke, E.P. (1929) *The Effect of Excessive Tourist Travel on California Redwood Parks*, Sacramento, CA: California State Printing Office.

Melbourne Parks (1983) *A Survey of the Use of Selected Sites*, Melbourne: Melbourne and Metropolitan Board.

Meleghy, T., Preglau, M. and Tafertsofer, A. (1985) 'Tourism development and value change', *Annals of Tourism Research*, 12: 201–19.

Mels, T. (1999) *Wild Landscapes: The Cultural Nature*

of *Swedish National Parks*, Lund, Sweden: Lund University Press.

Mels, T. (2002) 'Nature, home, and scenery: The official spatialities of Swedish national parks', *Environment and Planning D: Society and Space*, 20: 135–54.

Mercer, D. (1970) 'The geography of leisure: A contemporary growth point', *Geography*, 55(3): 261–73.

Mercer, D. (1971a) 'Perception in outdoor recreation', in P. Lavery (ed.) *Recreational Geography*, Newton Abbot: David and Charles, pp. 51–69.

Mercer, D. (1971b) 'Discretionary travel behaviour and the urban mental map', *Australian Geographical Studies*, 9: 133–43.

Mercer, D. (1972) 'Beach usage in the Melbourne region', *Australian Geographer*, 12(2): 123–9.

Mercer, D. (1973) 'The concept of recreational need', *Journal of Leisure Research*, 5: 37–50.

Mercer, D. (1979a) 'Outdoor recreation: Contemporary research and policy issues', in T. O'Riordan and R.D. Arge (eds) *Progress in Resource Management and Environmental Planning*, Vol. 1, New York: Wiley, pp. 87–142.

Mercer, D. (1979b) 'Victoria's land conservation council and the alpine region', *Australian Geographical Studies*, 17(1): 107–30.

Mercer, D. (1994) 'Native peoples and tourism: Conflict and compromise', in W.F. Theobald (ed.) *Global Tourism: The Next Decade*, Boston, MA: Butterworth-Heinemann, pp. 124–45.

Mercer, D. (2000) *A Question of Balance: Natural Resources Conflict Issues in Australia*, 3rd edn, Leichhardt, NSW: Federation Press.

Mercer, D. (2004) 'Tourism and resource management', in A. Lew, C.M. Hall and A. Williams (eds) *Companion to Tourism*, Oxford: Blackwell, pp. 462–73.

Meyer-Arendt, K. (1990) 'Recreational Business Districts in Gulf of Mexico seaside resorts', *Journal of Cultural Geography*, 11: 39–55.

Meyer-Arendt, K. (1993) 'Geomorphic impacts of resort evolution along the Gulf of Mexico coast: Applicability of resort cycle models', in P.P. Wong (ed.) *Tourism vs. Environment: The Case for Coastal Areas*, Dordrecht: Kluwer, pp. 125–38.

Meyer-Arendt, K. (2000) 'Commentary: Tourism geography as the subject of North American doctoral dissertations and masters theses, 1951–98', *Tourism Geographies*, 2(2): 140–57.

Meyer-Arendt, K. and Lew, A. (1999) 'A decade of American RTS geography', *Tourism Geographies*, 1(4): 477–87.

Micallel, A. and Williams, A. (2002) 'Theoretical strategy considerations for beach management', *Ocean and Coastal Management*, 45: 261–75.

Mieczkowski, Z. (1985) 'The tourism climatic index: A method of evaluating world climates for tourism', *Canadian Geographer*, 29(3): 220–33.

Michael, E. (2001) 'Public choice and tourism analysis', *Current Issues in Tourism*, 4(2): 308–30.

Michaud, J. (1983) *Le Tourisme face à l'environnement*, Paris: PUF.

Michaud, J. (ed.) (1992) *Tourismes: Chance pour l'économie, risque pour les sociétés?*, Paris: PUF.

Middleton, V. (1988) *Marketing in Travel and Tourism*, Oxford: Butterworth-Heinemann.

Mihalic, T. (2002) 'The European Blue Flag campaign for beaches in Slovenia: A programme for raising environmental awareness', in R. Harris, T. Griffin and P. Williams (eds) *Sustainable Tourism: A Global Perspective*, Oxford: Butterworth-Heinemann, pp. 89–102.

Miller, G. and Kirk, E. (2002) 'The Disability Discrimination Act: Time for the stick?', *Journal of Sustainable Tourism*, 10(1): 82–8.

Miller, G.A. and Ritchie, B.W. (2003) 'A farming crisis or a tourism disaster? An analysis of the Foot and Mouth disease in the UK', *Current Issues in Tourism*, 6(2): 150–71.

Miller, M. (1987) 'Tourism in Washington's coastal zone', *Annals of Tourism Research*, 14(1): 58–70.

Miller, M. (1993) 'The rise of coastal and marine tourism', *Ocean and Coastal Management*, 21(1–3): 183–99.

Miller, M.L. and Auyong, J. (1991) 'Coastal zone tourism: A potent force affecting environment and society', *Marine Policy*, 15(2): 75–99.

Milne, S. (1990) 'The impact of tourism development in small Pacific Island states', *New Zealand Journal of Geography*, 89: 16–21.

Milne, S. (1998) 'Tourism and sustainable development: The global–local nexus', in C.M. Hall and A.A. Lew (eds) *Sustainable Tourism Development: Geographical Perspectives*, Harlow: Addison Wesley Longman, pp. 35–48.

Milton Keynes Development Corporation (1988) *Study of the Use and Perception of Parks in Milton Keynes*, Milton Keynes: Milton Keynes Recreation Unit Study 18.

Milton Keynes Development Corporation (1989) *Parks Visitor Survey*, Milton Keynes: Milton Keynes Recreation Unit Study 18.

Milward, H.B. (1996) 'Symposium on the hollow state: Capacity, control and performance in interorganizational settings', *Journal of Public Administration Research and Theory*, 6(2): 193–5.

Minerbi, L. (1992) *Impacts of Tourism Development in Pacific Islands*, San Francisco, CA: Greenpeace Pacific Campaign.

Mings, R.C. (1978) 'The importance of more research on the impacts of tourism', *Annals of Tourism Research*, July/September: 340–4.

Ministry of Housing and Local Government (1955) *Green Belts*, Circular 42/55, London: HMSO.

Mitchell, B. (1989) *Geography and Resource Analysis*, 2nd edn, Harlow: Longman.

Mitchell, C.J.A. (2004a) 'Making sense of counterurbanization', *Journal of Rural Studies*, 20(1): 15–34.

Mitchell, C.J.A. (2004b) 'Visual artists: Counterurbanites in the Canadian countryside', *Canadian Geographer*, 48(2): 152–67.

Mitchell, L.S. (1969a) 'Recreational geography: Evolution and research needs', *Professional Geographer*, 21(2): 117–19.

Mitchell, L.S. (1969b) 'Towards a theory of public urban recreation', *Proceedings of the Association of American Geographers*, 1: 103–8.

Mitchell, L.S. (1979) 'The geography of tourism: An introduction', *Annals of Tourism Research*, 6: 235–44.

Mitchell, L.S. (1984) 'Tourism research in the United States: A geographical perspective', *GeoJournal*, 9: 5–15.

Mitchell, L.S. (1991) *A Conceptual Matrix for the Study of Tourism*, Les Cahiers du Tourisme, Aix en Provence, France: Centre des Haute Etudes Touristiques.

Mitchell, L.S. (1997) 'Rediscovering geography (i.e. RTS)', personal communication to Michael Hall, 13 June.

Mitchell, L.S. and Lovingwood, P. (1976) 'Public urban recreation: An investigation of spatial relationships', *Journal of Leisure Research*, 8: 6–20.

Mitchell, L.S. and Murphy, P.E. (1991) 'Geography and tourism', *Annals of Tourism Research*, 18(1): 57–70.

Mitchell, M. and Hall, D. (eds) (2005) *Rural Tourism and Sustainable Business*, Clevedon: Channel View.

Mitchell, N.C. (1970) 'Irish ports, recent developments', in N. Stephens and R. Glassock (eds) *Irish Geographical Studies in Honour of E. Estyn Evans*, Belfast: Queen's University of Belfast, pp. 325–41.

Mitchell, R. and Hall, C.M. (2001) 'The winery consumer: A New Zealand perspective', *Tourism Recreation Research*, 26(2): 63–75.

Mitchell, R. and Hall, C.M. (2003) 'Consuming tourists: Food tourism consumer behaviour', in C.M. Hall, E. Sharples, R. Mitchell, B. Cambourne and N. Macionis (eds) *Food Tourism Around the World: Development, Management and Markets*, Oxford: Butterworth-Heinemann, pp. 60–80.

Modern Maturity (1999) 'Results of travel survey', *Modern Maturity*, January: 12.

Montanari, A. and Williams, A.M. (eds) (1995) *European Tourism: Regions, Spaces and Restructuring*, Chichester: Wiley.

Moore, K., Cushman, G. and Simmons, D. (1995) 'Behavioural conceptualisation of tourism and leisure', *Annals of Tourism Research*, 22(1): 67–85.

Moran, W. (1993) 'Rural space as intellectual property', *Political Geography*, 12(3): 263–77.

Moran, W. (2000) 'Culture et nature dans la géographie de l'industrie vinicole néo-zélandaise', *Annales de Géographie*, 614–15: 525–51.

Moran, W. (2001) 'Terroir – the human factor', *Australian and New Zealand Wine Industry Journal of Oenology, Viticulture, Finance and Marketing*, 16(2): 32–51.

Morgan, C. and King, J. (1966) *Introduction to Psychology*, New York: McGraw-Hill.

Morgan, G. (1980) 'Wilderness areas in Queensland: The rake's approach', in R.W. Robertson, P. Helman and A. Davey (eds) *Wilderness Management in Australia, Proceedings of a Symposium held at the Canberra College of Advanced Education, 19–23 July 1978*, Natural Resources, School of Applied Science, Canberra College of Advanced Education, Canberra, pp. 103–7.

Morgan, G. (1991) *A Strategic Approach to the Planning and Management of Parks and Open Space*, Reading: Institute of Leisure and Amenity Management.

Morgan, N.J. and Pritchard, A. (1999) *Power and Politics at the Seaside*, Exeter: University of Exeter Press.

Morgan, R. (1999) 'A novel, user-based rating system for tourist beaches', *Tourism Management*, 20: 393–410.

Morgan, R., Jones, T. and Williams, A. (1993) 'Opinions and perceptions of England and Wales Heritage coast beach users: Some management implications from the Glamorgan Heritage Coast, Wales', *Journal of Coastal Research*, 9(4): 1083–93.

Mormont, M. (1987) 'Tourism and rural change', in M. Bouquet and M. Winter (eds) *Who from their Labours Rest? Conflict and Practice in Rural Tourism*, Aldershot: Avebury, pp. 35–44.

Mormont, M. (1990) 'Who is rural? Or how to be rural: Towards a sociology of the rural' in T. Marsden, P.

Lowe and S. Whatmore (eds) *Rural Restructuring*, London, David Fulton, 21–44.

Morris, A. (1996) 'Environmental management in coastal Spain', in M. Barke, J. Towner and M. Newton (eds) *Tourism in Spain: Critical Issues*, Wallingford: CAB International, pp. 213–28.

Morrison, A. and Dickinson, G. (1987) 'Tourist development in Spain: Growth versus conservation on the Costa Brava', *Geography*, 72: 16–25.

Mosley, J.G. (1983) 'Australia's World Heritage areas', *Habitat*, 11(1): 16–26.

Moutinho, L. (1987) 'Consumer behaviour in tourism', *European Journal of Marketing*, 21(10): 3–44.

Mowforth, M. and Munt, I. (1997) *Tourism and Sustainability: New Tourism in the Third World*, London: Routledge.

Mowforth, M. and Munt, I. (2003) *Tourism and Sustainability: New Tourism in the Third World*, 2nd edn, London: Routledge.

Mowl, G. and Turner, J. (1995) 'Women, gender leisure and place: Towards a more "humanistic" geography of women's leisure', *Leisure Studies*, 14: 102–16.

Mucciaroni, G. (1991) 'Unclogging the arteries: The defeat of client politics and the logic of collective action', *Policy Studies Journal*, 19(3–4): 474–94.

Mulford, C.L. and Rogers, D.L. (1982) 'Definitions and models', in D.L. Rogers and D.A. Whetten (eds) *Interorganizational Coordination: Theory, Research and Implementation*, Ames, IA: Iowa State University Press.

Müller, D.K. (1999) *German Second Home Owners in the Swedish Countryside: On the Internationalization of the Leisure Space*, Umeå, Sweden: Kulturgeografiska institutionen.

Müller, D.K. (2002a) 'German second home development in Sweden', in C.M. Hall and A.M. Williams (eds) *Tourism and Migration: New Relationships between Production and Consumption*, Dordrecht: Kluwer, pp. 169–86.

Müller, D.K. (2002b) 'Second home ownership and sustainable development in Northern Sweden', *Tourism and Hospitality Research*, 3: 343–55.

Müller, D.K. (2002c) 'German second home owners in Sweden: Some remarks on the tourism-migration nexus', *Revue Européenne des Migrations Internationales*, 18: 67–86.

Müller, D.K. (2002d) 'Reinventing the countryside: German second home owners in southern Sweden', *Current Issues in Tourism*, 5: 426–46.

Müller, D.K. (2004) 'Tourism, mobility and second homes', in A.A. Lew, C.M. Hall and A.M. William (eds) *A Companion to Tourism*, Oxford: Blackwell, pp. 387–98.

Müller, D.K. and Hall, C.M. (2003) 'Second homes and regional population distribution: On administrative practices and failures in Sweden', *Espace, populations, sociétés*, 2003(2): 251–61.

Mullins, G. and Heywood, J. (1984) *Unobtrusive Observation: A Visitor Survey Technique*, Columbus, OH: Ohio Agricultural Research Development Circular, Ohio Agricultural Development Centre No. 20.

Mullins, P. (1984) 'Hedonism and real estate: Resort tourism and Gold Coast development', in P. Williams (ed.) *Conflict and Development*, Sydney: Allen & Unwin.

Mullins, P. (1990) 'Tourist cities as new cities: Australia's Gold Coast and Sunshine Coast', *Australian Planner*, 28(3): 37–41.

Mullins, P. (1991) 'Tourism urbanization', *International Journal of Urban and Regional Research*, 15: 326–43.

Murdoch, J. (1993) 'Sustainable rural development: Towards a research agenda', *Geoforum*, 24(3): 225–41.

Murdock, J. (1997) 'Inhuman/nonhuman/human: Actor-network theory and prospects for a non-dualistic and symmetrical perspective on nature and society', *Environment and Planning D: Society and Space*, 15: 731–56.

Murphy, A. (2004) 'Geography and a liberal education', *AAG Newsletter*, 39(5): 3.

Murphy, L. and Le Heron, R. (1999) 'Encountering places, peoples and environments: Introducing human geography', in R. Le Heron, L. Murphy, P. Forer and M. Goldstone (eds) *Explorations in Human Geography: Encountering Place*, Auckland: Oxford University Press, pp. 1–23.

Murphy, P.E. (1982) 'Tourism planning in London: An exercise in spatial and seasonal management', *Tourist Review*, 37: 19–23.

Murphy, P.E. (1985) *Tourism: A Community Approach*, New York: Methuen.

Murphy, P.E. (1988) 'Community driven tourism planning', *Tourism Management*, 9(2): 96–104.

Murphy, P.E. (1994) 'Tourism and sustainable development', in W. Theobold (ed.) *Global Tourism: The Next Decade*, Oxford: Butterworth-Heinemann, pp. 274–90.

Murphy, P.E. (ed.) (1997) *Quality Management in Urban Tourism*, International Western Geographical Series, Chichester: Wiley.

Murphy, P.E. and Keller, C.P. (1990) 'Destination travel patterns: An examination and modelling of tourism patterns on Vancouver Island, British Columbia', *Leisure Sciences*, 12(1): 49–65.

Murphy, P.E. and Murphy, A.E. (2004) *Strategic Management for Tourism Communities: Bridging the Gaps*, Clevedon: Channel View.

Murphy, P.E. and Rosenblood, L. (1974) 'Tourism: An exercise in spatial search', *Canadian Geographer*, 18(3): 201–10.

Murphy, P.E. and Staples, W.A. (1979) 'A modernized family life cycle', *Journal of Consumer Research*, 6(1): 12–22.

Murphy, R.E. (1963) 'Geography and outdoor recreation: An opportunity and an obligation', *Professional Geographer*, 15(5): 33–4.

Murphy, W. and Gardiner, J.J. (1983) 'Forest recreating economics', *Irish Forestry*, 40: 12–19.

Naranjo, F. (2001) 'Relaciones entre formacion y dedicacion professional en la geografia espanola', *Documents d'Analisi Geografica*, 39: 37–56.

Nash, D. (1996) *The Anthropology of Tourism*, Oxford: Pergamon.

Nash, R. (1963) 'The American wilderness in historical perspective', *Journal of Forest History*, 6(4): 2–13.

Nash, R. (1967) *Wilderness and the American Mind*, New Haven, CT: Yale University Press.

Nash, R. (1982) *Wilderness and the American Mind*, 3rd edn, New Haven, CT: Yale University Press.

Nash, R. (1990) *The Rights of Nature: A History of Environmental Ethics*, Leichhardt, NSW: Primavera Press.

National Capital Commission (1991) *NCR Visitor Survey, Volume 1 – Analysis of Findings*, conducted for the National Capital Commission by Gallup Canada, Ottawa: National Capital Commission.

National Capital Commission (1998) *A Capital in the Making*, Ottawa: National Capital Commission.

National Capital Commission (1999) *Plan for Canada's Capital: A Second Century of Vision, Planning and Development*, Ottawa: National Capital Commission.

National Capital Commission (2000a) *Summary of the Corporate Plan 2000–2001 to 2004–2005*, Ottawa: National Capital Commission.

National Capital Commission (2000b) *Planning Canada's Capital Region*, Ottawa: National Capital Commission.

National Oceanic and Atmospheric Administration (NOAA) (1997) *1998 Year of the Ocean – Coastal Tourism and Recreation*, discussion paper, http://www.yoto98.noaa.gov/yoto/meeting/tour_rec_316.html

Naylon, J. (1967) 'Tourism – Spain's most important industry', *Geography*, 52: 23–40.

Nefedova, V. and Zemlianoi, O. (1997) 'Geographical forecast of recreation activity of development (the Moscow region case study)', *Vestnik-Moskovskogo-Universiteta-Seriya-Geografiya*, 4: 25–8.

Nelson, J.G. (ed.) (1970) *Canadian Parks in Perspective*, Montreal: Harvest House.

Nelson, J.G. (1973) 'Canada's national parks: Past, present and future', *Canadian Geographical Journal*, 86(3): 68–89.

Nelson, J.G. (1982) 'Canada's national parks: Past, present and future', in G. Wall and J.S. Marsh (eds) *Recreational Land Use Perspectives on its Evolution in Canada*, Carleton Library Series, Ottawa: Carleton University Press, pp. 41–61.

Nelson, J.G. (1986) *An External Perspective on Parks Canada Strategies*, Occasional Paper No. 2, Waterloo, Ont.: University of Waterloo Parks Canada Liaison Committee, University of Waterloo.

Neulinger, J. (1981) *The Psychology of Leisure*, Springfield, IL: C. Thomas.

New Zealand Tourism Board (1991a) *Tourism in the 90s*, Wellington: New Zealand Tourism Board.

New Zealand Tourism Board (1991b) *New Zealand Domestic Tourism Study*, Wellington: New Zealand Tourism Board.

New Zealand Tourism Board (1995) *New Zealand Tourism in the 90s*, Wellington: New Zealand Tourism Board.

New Zealand Travel and Publicity Department (1987) *The New Zealand Domestic Travel Study 1986–1987: General Report*, Wellington: New Zealand Travel and Publicity Department.

Newham Borough Council (1991a) *Newham's Policy for the Environment: A Consultation Document*, London: London Borough of Newham.

Newham Borough Council (1991b) *Shaped for Success: Leisure Development Strategy 1990–94*, London: London Borough of Newham.

Newsome, D., Moore, S. and Dowling, R. (2002) *Natural Area Tourism: Ecology, Impacts and Management*, Clevedon: Channel View.

Ngoh, T. (1985) 'Guidelines for the harmonisation of international tourism statistics among PATA member countries', in *The Battle for Market Share: Strategies in Research and Marketing*, Sixteenth Annual Conference Tourism and Travel Research Association, Salt

Lake City, UT: Graduate School of Business, University of Utah, pp. 291–306.

Nicholls, S. (2001) 'Measuring the accessibility and equity of public parks: A case study using GIS', *Managing Leisure*, 6(4): 201–19.

Nichols, K. (1999) 'Coming to terms with integrated coastal management', *Professional Geographer*, 51(3): 388–99.

Nichols, L.L. (1976) 'Tourism and crime', *Annals of Tourism Research*, 3: 176–81.

Nicholson, M.H. (1962) *Mountain Gloom and Mountain Glory*, New York: Norton.

Nicholson-Lord, D. (1994) 'Space for green reinvention', *The Independent*, 4 April.

Nickels, S., Milne, S. and Wenzel, G. (1991) 'Inuit perceptions of tourism development: The case of Clyde River, Baffin Island, NWT', *Etudes/Inuit/Studies*, 15(1): 157–69.

Nicol, J.I. (1969) 'The National Parks movement in Canada', in J.G. Nelson and R.C. Scace (eds) *The Canadian National Parks: Today and Tomorrow*, Vol. 1, Studies in Land Use History and Landscape Change National Park Series, Calgary, Alta: Department of Geography, University of Calgary, pp. 35–52.

Nielsen, N. (1990) ' Construction of a recreational beach using the original coastal morphology, Koege Bay, Denmark', in P. Fabbri (ed.) *Recreational Use of Coastal Areas*, Dordrecht: Kluwer, pp. 177–90.

Nordstrom, K., Lampe, R. and Vandemark, L. (2000) 'Reestablishing naturally functioning dunes on developed coasts', *Environmental Management*, 25(1): 37–51.

Norkunas, M.K. (1993) *The Politics of Memory: Tourism, History, and Ethnicity in Monterey, California*, Albany, NY: State University of New York Press.

Observer (1944) 'Britain can fight for her beaches: Seaside slums must go', *Observer*, 11 June: 7.

Oc, T. and Tiesdell, S. (eds) (1997) *Safer City Centres: Reviving the Public Realm*, London: Chapman and Hall.

O'Dell, A. (1935) 'European air services, June 1934', *Geography*, 19(4): 288–91.

Oelschlaeger, M. (1991) *The Idea of Wilderness: From Prehistory to the Age of Ecology*, New Haven, CT: Yale University Press.

Office of the Deputy Prime Minister (ODPM) (2002) *Cleaner, Safer, Greener Public Space*, London: ODPM.

Office for National Statistics (ONS) (2000) *Social Trends 30*, London: The Stationery Office.

Office for National Statistics (2002) *Time Use Survey*, London: ONS.

Office for National Statistics (2003) *Social Trends 33*, London: ONS.

Office of National Tourism (1997) *Ecotourism*, Tourism Facts No. 16, May, http://www.tourism. gov.au/new/cfa/cfa_fs16.html (accessed 31 December).

Office of Population Censuses and Surveys (OPCS) (1992) *1991 Census: Inner London*, London: OPCS.

Oglethorpe, M. (1984) 'Tourism and development in the Maltese Islands', in J. Long and R. Hecock (eds) *Leisure, Tourism and Social Change*, Dunfermline: Centre for Leisure Research, Dunfermline College of Physical Education, pp. 121–34.

Oguz, D. (2000) 'User surveys of Ankara's urban parks', *Landscape and Urban Planning*, 52(2–3): 165–71.

O'Hagan, J. and Harrison, M. (1984a) 'UK and US visitor expenditure in Ireland: Some econometric findings', *Economic and Social Review*, 15: 195–207.

O'Hagan, J. and Harrison, M. (1984b) 'Market share of US tourist expenditure in Europe: An econometric analysis', *Applied Economics*, 16: 919–31.

O'Hagan, J. and Mooney, D. (1983) 'Input–output multipliers in a small open economy: An application to tourism', *Economic and Social Review*, 14: 273–9.

Ohmae, K. (1995) *The End of the Nation State: The Rise of Regional Economies*, New York: HarperCollins and The Free Press.

Olds, K. (1998) 'Urban mega-events, evictions and housing rights: The Canadian case', *Current Issues in Tourism*, 1(1): 2–46.

O'Leary, J.T. (1976) 'Land use definition and the rural community: Disruption of community leisure space', *Journal of Leisure Research*, 8: 263–74.

Olkusnik, M. (2001) 'Countryside holidays as a cultural and social phenomenon in Warsaw at the end of the nineteenth century', *Kwartalnik Historii Kultury Materialnej* 69 (4): 367–86.

Olszewska, A. (1989) 'Poland: The impact of the crisis on leisure patterns', in A. Olszewska and K. Roberts (eds) *Leisure and Lifestyle: A Comparative Analysis of Free Time*, London: Sage, pp. 17–38.

Olwig, K. and Olwig, K. (1979) 'Underdevelopment and the development of "natural" parks ideology', *Antipode*, 11(2): 16–25.

ONS (2003) *Focus on London*, HMSO: London

Open Spaces Society (1992) *Making Space: Protecting and Creating Open Space for Local Communities*, Henley-on-Thames: Open Spaces Society.

Oppermann, M. (1992) 'International tourist flows in Malaysia', *Annals of Tourism Research*, 19(3): 482–500.

Oppermann, M. (1993) 'German tourists in New Zealand', *New Zealand Geographer*, 49(1): 31–4.

Oppermann, M. (1994) 'Regional aspects of tourism in New Zealand', *Regional Studies*, 28: 155–67.

Oppermann, M. (1995) 'Holidays on the farm: A case study of German hosts and guests', *Journal of Travel Research*, 33: 57–61.

Oppermann, M. (1998a) 'What is new with the resort cycle?', *Tourism Management*, 19(2): 179–80.

Oppermann, M. (1998b) 'Farm tourism in New Zealand', in R. Butler, C.M. Hall and J. Jenkins (eds) *Tourism and Recreation in Rural Areas*, Chichester: Wiley, pp. 225–35.

Oppermann, M. and Chon, K. (1997) *Tourism in Developing Countries*, London: International Thomson Business.

Orams, M. (1999) *Marine Tourism*, London: Routledge.

Orams, M. (2002) 'Feeding wildlife as a tourism attraction: A review of issues and impacts', *Tourism Management*, 22(3): 281–93.

Orams, M. (2005) 'Dolphins, whales and ecotourism in New Zealand: What are the impacts and how should the industry be managed?', in C.M. Hall and S. Boyd (eds) *Nature-based Tourism in Peripheral Areas: Development or Disaster*, Clevedon: Channel View, pp. 231–45.

Organisation for Economic Co-operation and Development (OECD) (1980) *The Impact of Tourism on the Environment*, Paris: OECD.

O'Riordan, T. (1971) *Perspectives on Resource Management*, London: Pion Press.

O'Riordan, T. and Paget, G. (1978) *Sharing Rivers and Canals*, Study 16, London: Sports Council.

O'Riordan, T. and Turner, R.K. (eds) (1984) *An Annotated Reader in Environmental Planning and Management*, Oxford: Pergamon.

O'Toole, L. (1997) 'Treating networks seriously: Practical and research based agendas in public administration', *Public Administration Review*, 57(1): 45–52.

Outdoor Recreation Resources Review Commission (1962) *Outdoor Recreation for America*, Washington, DC: Government Printing Office.

Ovington, J.D. and Fox, A.M. (1980) 'Wilderness – a natural asset', *Parks*, 5(3): 1–4.

Owen, C. (1990) 'Tourism and urban regeneration', *Cities: The International Journal of Urban Policy and Planning*, 7: 194–201.

Owen, J.G. (2003) 'The stadium game: Cities versus teams', *Journal of Sports Economics*, 4: 183–202.

Owens, P. (1984) 'Rural leisure and recreation research: A retrospective evaluation', *Progress in Human Geography*, 8: 157–85.

Pacione, M. (1999a) 'Applied geography: In pursuit of useful knowledge', *Applied Geography*, 19: 1–12.

Pacione, M. (1999b) 'In pursuit of knowledge: The principles and practice of applied geography', in M. Pacione (ed.) *Applied Geography: Principles and Practice*, London: Routledge, pp. 3–18.

Pacione, M. (ed.) (1999c) *Applied Geography: Principles and Practice*, London: Routledge.

Pacione, M. (2005) *Urban Geography: A Global Perspective*, London: Routledge.

Page, S.J. (1988) 'Poverty in Leicester 1881–1911: A geographical perspective', unpublished PhD thesis, Leicester: Department of Geography, University of Leicester.

Page, S.J. (1989) 'Tourist development in London Docklands in the 1980s and 1990s', *GeoJournal*, 19(3): 291–5.

Page, S.J. (1992) 'Perspectives on the environmental impact of the Channel Tunnel on tourism', in C. Cooper and A. Lockwood (eds) *Progess in Tourism, Recreation and Hospitality Management*, Vol. 4, London: Belhaven Press, pp. 82–102.

Page, S.J. (1994a) 'European bus and coach travel', *Travel and Tourism Analyst*, 1: 19–39.

Page, S.J. (1994b) *Transport for Tourism*, London: Routledge.

Page, S.J. (1994c) 'Perspectives on tourism and peripherality: A review of tourism in the Republic of Ireland', in C. Cooper and A. Lockwood (eds) *Progress in Tourism, Recreation and Hospitality Management*, Vol. 5, Chichester: Wiley, pp. 26–53.

Page, S.J. (1994d) 'Developing heritage tourism in Ireland in the 1990s', *Tourism Recreation Research*, 19(2): 79–90.

Page, S.J. (1995a) *Urban Tourism*, London: Routledge.

Page, S.J. (1995b) 'Waterfront revitalisation in London: Market-led planning and tourism in London Docklands', in S. Craig-Smith and M. Fagence (eds) *Recreation and Tourism as a Catalyst for Urban Waterfront Development*, Westport, CT: Greenwood Publishing, pp. 53–70.

Page, S.J. (1997a) 'Urban tourism: Analysing and evaluating the tourist experience', in C. Ryan (ed.) *The Tourist Experience: A New Introduction*, London: Cassell, pp. 112–35.

Page, S.J. (1997b) *The Cost of Accidents in the Adventure Tourism Industry*, Consultant's Report for the Tourism Policy Group, Ministry of Commerce, Wellington, NZ.

Page, S.J. (1998) 'Transport for recreation and tourism', in B. Hoyle and R. Knowles (eds) *Modern Transport Geography*, 2nd edn, Chichester: Wiley, pp. 217–40.

Page, S.J. (1999) *Transport and Tourism*, London: Addison Wesley Longman 1st edition.

Page, S.J. (2000) 'Urban tourism', in C. Ryan and S.J. Page (eds) *Tourism Management: Towards the New Millennium*, Oxford: Pergamon, pp. 197–202.

Page, S.J. (2001) 'Hubs and gateways in South East Asia: Implications for tourism,' in P. Teo and T. Chang (eds) *Interconnected Worlds: South East Asian Tourism in the Twenty-First Century*, Oxford: Pergamon, pp. 81–96.

Page, S.J. (2002) 'European rail travel', *Travel and Tourism Analyst*, 4:1–49.

Page, S.J. (2003a) *Tourism Management: Managing for Change*, Oxford: Butterworth-Heinemann.

Page, S.J. (2003b) 'Evaluating research performance in tourism: The UK experience', *Tourism Management*, 24(6): 607–22.

Page, S.J. (2003c) 'European bus travel', *Travel and Tourism Analyst*, 4:1–48.

Page, S.J. (2005) Transport and Tourism, 2nd edition, Harlow: Pearson Education.

Page, S.J. and Connell, J. (2006) Tourism: A Modern Synthesis, 2nd edition, London: Thomson Learning.

Page, S.J. and Dowling, R. (2001) *Ecotourism*, Harlow: Pearson Education.

Page, S.J. and Getz, D. (eds) (1997) *The Business of Rural Tourism: International Perspectives*, London: International Thomson Business Press.

Page, S.J. and Hall, C.M. (2002) *Managing Urban Tourism*, Harlow: Pearson Education.

Page, S.J. and Hall, C.M. (2003) *Managing Urban Tourism*, Harlow: Prentice-Hall.

Page, S.J. and Hardyman, R. (1996) 'Place marketing and town centre management: A new tool for urban revitalisation', *Cities: The International Journal of Urban Policy and Planning*, 13(3): 153–64.

Page, S.J. and Lawton, G. (1997) 'The impact of urban tourism on destination communities: Implications for community tourism planning in Auckland', in C.M. Hall, J. Jenkins and G. Kearsley (eds) *Tourism Planning and Policy in Australia and New Zealand: Cases, Issues and Practice*, Sydney: Irwin, pp. 209–26.

Page, S.J. and Meyer, D. (1996) 'Tourist accidents: An exploratory analysis', *Annals of Tourism Research*, 23(3): 666–90.

Page, S.J. and Sinclair, M.T. (1989) 'Tourism accommodation in London: Alternative policies and the Docklands experience', *Built Environment*, 15(2): 125–37.

Page, S.J. and Thorn, K. (1997) 'Towards sustainable tourism planning in New Zealand: Public sector planning responses', *Journal of Sustainable Tourism*, 5(1): 59–78.

Page, S.J. and Thorn, K. (1998) 'Sustainable tourism development and local government in New Zealand', in C.M. Hall and A. Lew (eds) *The Geography of Sustainable Tourism: Approaches, Issues and Experiences*, Harlow: Addison Wesley Longman, pp. 173–84.

Page, S.J. and Thorn, K. (2002) 'Towards sustainable tourism development and planning in New Zealand: The public sector response revisited', *Journal of Sustainable Tourism*, 10(3): 222–39.

Page, S.J., Nielsen, K. and Goodenough, R. (1994) 'Managing urban parks: User perspectives and local leisure needs in the 1990s', *Service Industries Journal*, 14(2): 216–37.

Page, S.J., Forer, P. and Lawton, G. (1999) 'Tourism and small business development: Terra incognita', *Tourism Management*, 20(3): 435–59.

Page, S.J., Brunt, P., Busby, G. and Connell, J. (2001) *Tourism: A Modern Synthesis*, London: Thomson Learning.

Page, S.J., Bentley, T. and Walker, L. (2005) 'Scoping the nature and extent of adventure tourism operations in Scotland: How safe are they?', *Tourism Management*, 26(3): 381–97.

Pahl, R.E. (1975) *Whose City? And Further Essays in Urban Society*, Harmondsworth: Penguin.

Pain, R. (1997) 'Social geographies of women's fear of crime', *Transactions of the Institute of British Geographers*, 22: 231–44.

Palm, R. and Brazel, A. (1992) 'Applications of geographic concepts and methods', in R. Abler, M. Marcus and J. Olsson (eds) *Geography's Inner Worlds*, New Brunswick, NJ: Rutgers University Press, pp. 342–62.

Panchuk, S. and Yudina, Y. (1977) 'Cottage settlements and garden cooperatives in the Moscow area', *Soviet Geography*, 18: 329–38.

Papatheodorau, A. (2003) 'Corporate strategies of British tour operators in the Mediterranean region: An economic geography approach', *Tourism Geographies*, 5(3): 280–304.

Papson, S. (1981) 'Spuriousness and tourism: Politics of two Canadian provincial governments', *Annals of Tourism Research*, 8: 220–35.

Parasuraman, A., Zeithmal, V. and Berry, L. (1985) 'A conceptual model of service quality and its implications for future research', *Journal of Marketing*, 49(4): 41–50.

Park, R., Burgess, E. and McKenzie, R. (1925) *The City*, Chicago: University of Chicago Press.

Parker, S. (1999) *Leisure in Contemporary Society*, Wallingford: CAB International.

Parliamentary Commissioner for the Environment (1997) *Management of the Environmental Effects Associated with the Tourism Sector*, Wellington, NZ: Office of the Parliamentary Commissioner for the Environment.

Passmore, J. (1974) *Man's Responsibility for Nature*, London: Duckworth.

Patmore, J.A. (1968) 'The spa towns of Britain', in R. Beckinsale and J. Houston (eds) *Urbanization and its Problems*, Oxford: Blackwell, pp. 47–69.

Patmore, J.A. (1970) *Land and Leisure*, Newton Abbot: David and Charles.

Patmore, J.A. (1971) 'Routeways and recreation', in P. Lavery (ed.) *Recreational Geography*, Newton Abbot: David and Charles, pp. 70–96.

Patmore, J.A. (1973) 'Recreation', in J. Dawson and J. Doornkamp (eds) *Evaluating the Human Environment: Essays in Applied Geography*, London: Edward Arnold, pp. 224–48.

Patmore, J.A. (1977) 'Recreation and leisure', *Progress in Human Geography*, 1: 111–17.

Patmore, J.A. (1978) 'Recreation and leisure', *Progress in Human Geography*, 2: 142–7.

Patmore, J.A. (1979) 'Recreation and leisure', *Progress in Human Geography*, 3: 126–32.

Patmore, J.A. (1980) 'Recreation and leisure', *Progress in Human Geography*, 4: 91–8.

Patmore, J.A. (1983) *Recreation and Resources: Leisure Patterns and Leisure Places*, Oxford: Blackwell.

Patmore, J.A. and Collins, M. (1981) 'Recreation and leisure', *Progress in Human Geography*, 5(1): 87–92.

Patmore, J.A. and Rodgers, J. (eds) (1972) *Leisure in the North-West*, Salford: North-West Sports Council.

Paul, A.H. (1972) 'Weather and the daily use of outdoor recreation areas in Canada', in J.A. Taylor (ed.) *Weather Forecasting for Agriculture and Industry*, Newton Abbot: David and Charles, pp. 132–46.

Pawson, E. and Brooking, T. (eds) (2002) *Environmental Histories of New Zealand*, Melbourne: Oxford University Press.

Pearce, D.G. (1978) 'Form and function in French resorts', *Annals of Tourism Research*, 5(1): 142–56.

Pearce, D.G. (1979) 'Towards a geography of tourism', *Annals of Tourism Research*, 6: 245–72.

Pearce, D.G. (1981) *Tourist Development*, Harlow: Longman.

Pearce, D.G. (1986) 'The spatial structure of coastal tourism: A behavioural approach', paper presented at the International Geographical Union Commission on the Geography of Tourism and Leisure, Palma de Mallorca.

Pearce, D.G. (1987a) *Tourism Today: A Geographical Analysis*, Harlow: Longman.

Pearce, D.G. (1987b) 'Motel location and choice in Christchurch', *New Zealand Geographer*, 43(1): 10–17.

Pearce, D.G. (1987c) 'Tourist time-budgets', *Tourism Management* 25(2): 106–21.

Pearce, D.G. (1988a) 'The spatial structure of coastal tourism: A behavioural approach', *Tourism Recreation Research*, 13(2): 11–14.

Pearce, D.G. (1988b) 'Tourist time-budgets', *Annals of Tourism Research*, 15: 106–21.

Pearce, D.G. (1988c) 'Tourism and regional development in the European Community', *Tourism Management*, 9: 11–22.

Pearce, D.G. (1989) *Tourist Development*, 2nd edn, Harlow: Longman.

Pearce, D.G. (1990a) 'Tourism, the regions and restructuring in New Zealand', *Journal of Tourism Studies*, 1(2): 33–42.

Pearce, D.G. (1990b) 'Tourism in Ireland: Questions of scale and organisation', *Tourism Management*, 11: 133–51.

Pearce, D.G. (1992a) 'Tourism and the European regional development fund: The first fourteen years', *Journal of Travel Research*, 30: 44–51.

Pearce, D.G. (1992b) *Tourist Organizations*, Harlow: Longman.

Pearce, D.G. (1993a) 'Comparative studies in tourism research', in D. Pearce and R. Butler (eds) *Tourism Research: Critiques and Challenges*, London: Routledge, pp. 113–34.

Pearce, D.G. (1993b) 'Domestic tourist travel patterns in New Zealand', *GeoJournal*, 29(3): 225–32.

Pearce, D.G. (1995a) *Tourism Today: A Geographical Analysis*, 2nd edn, Harlow: Longman.

Pearce, D.G. (1995b) 'Planning for tourism in the 90s: An integrated, dynamic, multi-scale approach', in R.W. Butler and D.G. Pearce (eds) *Change in*

Tourism: People, Places, Processes, London: Routledge, pp. 229–44.

Pearce, D.G. (1998) 'Tourism development in Paris: Public intervention', *Annals of Tourism Research*, 25(2): 457–76.

Pearce, D.G. (1999a) 'Towards a geography of the geography of tourism: Issues and examples from New Zealand', *Tourism Geographies*, 1(4): 406–24.

Pearce, D.G. (1999b) 'Tourism districts in Paris: Structure and functions', *Tourism Management*, 19(1): 49–65.

Pearce, D.G. and Butler, R.W. (eds) (1993) *Tourism Research: Critiques and Challenges*, London: Routledge.

Pearce, D.G. and Kirk, D. (1986) 'Carrying capacities for coastal tourism', *Industry and Environment*, 9(1): 3–6.

Pearce, D.G. and Mings, R. (1984) 'Geography, tourism and recreation in the Antipodes', *GeoJournal*, 9(1): 91–5.

Pearce, J.A. (1980) 'Host community acceptance of foreign tourists: strategic considerations', *Annals of Tourism Research*, 7: 224–33.

Pearce, P.L. (1977) 'Mental souvenirs: A study of tourists and their city maps', *Australian Journal of Psychology*, 29: 203–10.

Pearce, P.L. (1981) 'Route maps: A study of travellers' perceptions of a section of countryside', *Journal of Environmental Psychology*, 1: 141–55.

Pearce, P.L. (1982) *The Social Psychology of Tourist Behaviour*, Oxford: Pergamon.

Pearce, P.L. (1984) 'Tourist guide interaction', *Annals of Tourism Research*, 11: 129–46.

Pearce, P.L. (1993) 'The fundamentals of tourist motivation', in D. Pearce and R. Butler (eds) *Tourism Research: Critique and Challenges*, London: Routledge.

Pearce, P.L. (2005) *Tourist Behaviour: Themes and Conceptual Issues*, Clevedon: Channel View.

Pearson, R. (1968) 'Railways in relation to resort development in East Lincolnshire', *East Midland Geographer*, 4: 281–95.

Pedersen, K. and Viken, A. (1996) 'From Sami nomadism to global tourism', in M.F. Price (ed.) *People and Tourism in Fragile Environments*, Chichester: Wiley, pp. 69–88.

Peet, R. (ed.) (1977a) *Radical Geography: Alternative Viewpoints on Contemporary Social Issues*, London: Methuen.

Peet, R. (1977b) 'The development of radical geography in the United States', *Progress in Human Geography*, 1: 240–63.

Penning-Rowsell, E. (1973) *Alternative Approaches to Landscape Appraisal and Evaluation*, Planning Research Group, Report No. 11, Enfield: Middlesex Polytechnic.

Penning-Rowsell, E. (1975) 'Constraints on the application of landscape evaluation', *Transactions of the Institute of British Geographers*, 66: 49–55.

Penning-Rowsell, E., Green, C., Thompson, P., Coker, A., Tunstall, S., Richards, C. and Parker, D. (1992) *The Economics of Coastal Management: A Manual of Benefit Assessment Techniques*, London: Belhaven Press.

Pentz, D. (2002) *Towards an Open Space Strategy for the Papakura District*, Briefing Paper, Auckland, NZ: Papakura District Council.

Pepper, D. (1984) *The Roots of Modern Environmentalism*, London: Croom Helm.

Perdue, R. (1985) 'The 1983 Nebraska Visitor Survey: Achieving a high response rate', *Journal of Travel Research*, 24(2): 23–6.

Perkins, H. (1993) 'Human geography, recreation and leisure', in H. Perkins and G. Cushman (eds) *Leisure, Recreation and Tourism*, Auckland: Longman Paul, pp. 116–29.

Perkins, H. and Gidlow, B. (1991) 'Leisure research in New Zealand: Patterns, problems and prospects', *Leisure Studies*, 10: 93–104.

Perry, A.H. and Illgner, P. (2000) 'Dimensions of winter severity in Southern Africa: Is a skiing industry in the Drakensberg Mountains viable?', *Journal of Meteorology*, 25: 226–30.

Pettersson, R. (2004) *Sami Tourism in Northern Sweden: Supply, Demand and Interaction*, ETOUR European Tourism Research Institute 2004: 14, Umeå, Sweden: Department of Social and Economic Geography, Umeå University.

Phelps, N. (1992) 'External economies, agglomeration and flexible accumulation', *Transactions of the Institute of British Geographers*, 17: 35–46.

Pigram, J.J. (1977) 'Beach resort morphology', *Habitat International*, 2(5–6): 525–41.

Pigram, J.J. (1980) 'Environmental implications of tourism development', *Annals of Tourism Research*, 7: 554–83.

Pigram, J.J. (1983) *Outdoor Recreation and Resource Management*, London: Croom Helm.

Pigram, J.J. (1985) *Outdoor Recreation and Resource Management*, 2nd edn, London: Croom Helm.

Pigram, J.J. (1987) *Tourism in Coffs Harbour: Attitudes, Perceptions and Implications*, Coffs Harbour, NSW: North Coast Regional Office, Department of Continuing Education, University of New England.

Pigram, J.J. (1990) 'Sustainable tourism: Policy considerations', *Journal of Tourism Studies*, 1(2): 2–9.

Pigram, J.J. and Jenkins, J. (1999) *Outdoor Recreation Management*, London: Routledge.

Pimlico Li, Y. (2000) 'Geographical consciousness and tourism experience', *Annals of Tourism Research*, 27(4): 863–83.

Piperoglou, J. (1966) 'Identification and definition of regions in Greek tourist planning', *Regional Science Association Papers*, pp. 169–76.

Piven, F. (1995) 'Is it global economics or neo-laissez-faire?' *New Left Review*, 213: 107–14.

Pizam, A. (1978) 'Tourism's impacts: The social costs to the destination community as perceived by its residents', *Journal of Travel Research*, 16(4): 8–12.

Place, S.E. (1998) 'How sustainable is ecotourism in Costa Rica?', in C.M. Hall and A.A. Lew (eds) *Sustainable Tourism Development: Geographical Perspectives*, Harlow: Addison Wesley Longman, pp. 107–18.

Plog, S. (1974) 'Why destination areas rise and fall in popularity', *Cornell Hotel and Restaurant Administration Quarterly*, 14(4): 55–8.

Plog, S. (1977) 'Why destination areas rise and fall in popularity', in E. Kelly (ed.) *Domestic and International Tourism*, Wellesey, MA: Institute of Certified Travel Agents.

Plog, S. (2001) 'Why destination areas rise and fall in popularity: An update of a Cornell Quarterly classic', *Cornell Hotel and Restaurant Administration Quarterly*, 42(3): 13–24.

Pocock, D. (1997) 'Some reflections on World Heritage', *Area*, 29(3): 260–8.

Pollard, D.A., Lincoln Smith, M.P. and Smith, A.K. (1996) 'The biology and conservation of the grey nurse shark (*Carcharias taurus*) in New South Wales, Australia', *Aquatic Conservation: Marine and Freshwater Ecosystems*, 6: 1–20.

Pollard, J. (1995) 'Tourism and the environment', in P. Breathnach (ed.) *Irish Tourism Development*, Maynooth: Geographical Society of Ireland, pp. 61–77.

Pompl, W. and Lavery, P. (eds) *Tourism in Europe: Structures and Development*, Wallingford: CAB International.

Poon, A. (1989) *Tourism, Technology and Competitive Strategies*, Wallingford: CAB International.

Population Reference Bureau (2004) *2004 World Population Data Sheet*, Washington, DC: Population Reference Bureau.

Poria, Y., Butler, R.W. and Airey, D. (2003) 'Revisiting Mieczkowski's conceptualisation of tourism', *Tourism Geographies*, 5(1): 26–38.

Porter, M. (1980) *Competition in Global Industries*, Boston, MA: Harvard Business School Press.

Potier, F. and Cazes, G. (1996) *Le Tourisme urbain*, Paris: PUF.

Potier, F. and Cazes, G. (1998) *Le Tourisme et la ville: Expériences européennes*, Paris: L'Harmattan.

Powell, J. (1985) 'Geography, culture and liberal education', in R. Johnston (ed.) *The Future of Geography*, London: Methuen, pp. 307–25.

Powell, J.M. (1978) *Mirrors of the New World: Images and Image – Makers in the Settlement Process*, Canberra: Australian National University Press.

Pratt, A. (1998) 'The cultural industries production system: A case study of employment change in Britain, 1984–91', *Environment and Planning A*, 29: 1953–74.

Pred, A. (1977) 'The choreography of existence: Comments on Hagerstrand's time-geography and its usefulness', *Economic Geography*, 53: 207–21.

Pred, A. (1981) 'Production, family and free-time projects: A time-geographic perspective on the individual and societal changes in nineteenth century US cities', *Journal of Historical Geography*, 7: 3–86.

Preece, K.M. and Lesslie, R.G. (1987) *A Survey of Wilderness Quality in Victoria*, Melbourne/Canberra: Ministry for Planning and Environment (Vic) and Australian Heritage Commission.

Preston-Whyte, R.A. (2002) 'Construction of surfing space at Durban, South Africa', *Tourism Geographies*, 4(3): 307–28.

Preston-Whyte, R.A. (2004) 'The beach as liminal space', in A. Lew, C.M. Hall and A. Williams (eds) *Companion to Tourism*, Oxford: Blackwell, pp. 349–59.

PriceWaterhouseCooper (1999) Landscape Heritage Trust Report, PWC: London.

Priestley, G. and Mundet, L. (1998) 'The post-stagnation phase of the resort cycle', *Annals of Tourism Research*, 25(1): 85–111.

Prineas, P. (1976–7) 'The story of the park proposal', *National Parks Journal*, December/January: 9–11.

Prineas, P. and Gold, H. (1983) *Wild Places: Wilderness in Eastern New South Wales*, Chatswood, NSW: Kalianna Press.

Pritchard, A. and Morgan, N. (2000) 'Privileging the male gaze: Gendered tourism landscapes', *Annals of Tourism Research*, 27(4): 884–905.

Pritchard, R. (1976) *Housing and the Spatial Structure of the City*, Cambridge: Cambridge University Press.

Pritchard, A., Morgan, N. and Sedgley, D. (2002) 'In search of lesbian space? The experience of Manchester's gay village', *Leisure Studies* 21(2): 105–23.

Prosser, G. (1986a) 'The limits of acceptable change: An introduction to a framework for natural area planning', *Australian Parks and Recreation*, autumn: 5–10.

Prosser, G. (1986b) 'Beyond carrying capacity: Establishing limits of acceptable change for park planning', in *Developing Communities into the 21st Century: Proceedings from the 59th National Conference of the Royal Australian Institute of Parks and Recreation*, Melbourne: Royal Australian Institute of Parks and Recreation, pp. 223–33.

Purvis, A. (2002) 'So what's your beef?', *Observer*, 14 April, http://www.observer.co.uk/foodmonthly/story/0,9950,681828,00.html

Queensland Department of Environment and Heritage (1993) *Green Island and Reef Management Plan*, Cairns, Qld: Department of Environment and Heritage.

Ragatz, R.L. (1977) 'Vacation homes in rural areas: Towards a model for predicting their distribution and occupancy patterns', in J.T. Coppock (ed.) *Second Homes: Curse or Blessing*, Oxford: Pergamon.

Ralph, E. (2000) 'Oppose the trafficking of women and children', Testimony before the Senate Committee on Foreign Relations Subcommittee on Near Eastern and South Asian Affairs by Regan E. Ralph, Executive Director, Women's Rights Division, Human Rights Watch, International Trafficking of Women and Children, 22 February.

Rapoport, R.N. and Rapoport, R. (1975) *Leisure and the Family Life Cycle*, London: Routledge & Kegan Paul.

Ravenscroft, N. (1992) *Recreation Planning and Development*, London: Macmillan.

Ravenscroft, N. and Markwell, S. (2000) 'Ethnicity and the integration and exclusion of young people through urban park and recreation provision', *Managing Leisure*, 5(3): 135–50.

Redclift, N. and Sinclair, M.T. (eds) (1991) *Working Women: International Perspectives on Labour and Gender Ideology*, London: Routledge.

Reeves, N. (2000) 'The condition of public urban parks and greenspace in Britain', *Water and Environmental Management*, 14(3): 157–63.

Reid, D.G. (2003) *Tourism, Globalization and Development: Responsible Tourism Planning*, London: Pluto Press.

Reilly, W. (1931) *The Law of Retail Gravitation*, New York: Putnam Press.

Reisel, W. (2004) 'Geography of leisure and tourism research in the German-speaking world: Three pillars to progress', *Tourism Geographies*, 6(2): 163–85.

Relph, E. (1976) *Place and Placelessness*, London: Pion.

Relph, E. (1981) *Rational Landscapes and Humanistic Geography*, London: Croom Helm.

Restaurant Brands (1997) *Restaurant Brands New Zealand Ltd. Prospectus 1997*, Auckland: F R Partners Limited and Merrill Lynch and Company.

Rethinking Tourism Project (2000) 'EPA solicits public input on cruise ship discharges', *EPA Water News, Electronic Newsletter*, 29 August.

Reynolds, P.C. (1993) 'Food and tourism: Towards an understanding of sustainable culture', *Journal of Sustainable Tourism*, 1(1): 48–54.

Rhind, D. (1990) 'Global databases and GIS', in M. Foster and P. Shands (eds). The Association for Geographic Information Yearbook 1990, Taylor & Francis: London 218–23.

Rhodes, R.A.W. (1997) 'From marketisation to diplomacy: It's the mix that matters', *Australian Journal of Public Administration*, 56(2): 40–53.

Ribeiro, M. and Marques, C. (2002) 'Rural tourism and the development of less favoured areas – between rhetoric and practice', *International Journal of Tourism Research*, 4(3): 211–20.

Richards, G. (1995) 'Politics of national tourism policy in Britain', *Leisure Studies*, 14(3): 153–73.

Ride, W.D.L. (1980) 'Wilderness: An Australian perspective', in R.W. Robertson, P. Helman and A. Davey (eds) *Wilderness Management in Australia, Proceedings of a Symposium Held at the Canberra College of Advanced Education 19–23 July 1978*, Occasional Papers in Recreational Planning, Natural Resources, School of Applied Science, Canberra: Canberra College of Advanced Education, pp. 35–45.

Rink, D.R. and Swan, J.E. (1979) 'Product life cycle research: Literature review', *Journal of Business Research*, 78: 219–42.

Riordan, J. (1982) 'Leisure: The state and the individual in the USSR', *Leisure Studies*, 1(l): 65–80.

Ritchie, J.R.B. (1975) 'Some critical aspects of measurement theory and practice in travel research', in R. McIntosh and C. Goeldner, *Tourism Principles, Practices and Philosophies*, New York: Wiley, pp. 437–51.

Ritchie, J.R.B. (1984) 'Assessing the impact of hallmark events: Conceptual and research issues', *Journal of Travel Research*, 23(1): 2–11.

Ritchie, J.R.B. and Aitken, C. (1984) 'Assessing the impacts of the 1988 Olympic Winter Games: The research program and initial results', *Journal of Travel Research*, 22(3): 17–25.

Ritchie, J.R.B. and Beliveau, D. (1974) 'Hallmark events: An evaluation of a strategic response to seasonality in the travel market', *Journal of Travel Research*, 14(fall): 14–20.

Ritchie, J.R.B. and Yangzhou, H. (1987) 'The role and impact of mega-events and attractions on national and regional tourism: A conceptual and methodological overview', Thirty-seventh Annual Congress of the International Association of Scientific Experts in Tourism (AIEST), Calgary, Alta: AIEST.

Ritter, W. and Schafer, C. (1999) 'Cruise-tourism: A chance of sustainability', *Tourism Recreation Research*, 23(1): 65–71.

Ritzer, G. (1993) *The McDonaldization of Society*, Thousand Oaks, CA: Pine Forge.

Roberts, K. (1999) *Leisure in Contemporary Society*, Wallingford: CAB International.

Roberts, K., Fagan, C., Bontenko, I. and Razlogov, K. (2001) 'Economic polarization, leisure practices and policies, and the quality of life: A study in post-communist Moscow', *Leisure Studies*, 20(3): 161–72.

Roberts, R. (1971) *The Classic Slum: Salford Life in the First Quarter of the Century*, Harmondsworth: Penguin.

Roberts, R. (1976) *A Ragged Schooling: Growing Up in the Classic Slum*, London: Fontana.

Robinson, D. (1991) 'Living with peripherality', *Transport*, November/December: 177–85.

Robinson, G.M. (1990) *Conflict and Change in the Countryside*, London: Belhaven Press.

Robinson, G.M. (1999) 'Countryside recreation management', in M. Pacione (ed.) *Applied Geography: Principles and Practice*, London: Routledge, pp. 257–73.

Robinson, G.W. (1972) 'The recreational geography of South Asia', *Geographical Review*, 62(4): 561–73.

Robinson, H. (1976) *A Geography of Tourism*, Harlow: Longman.

Robinson, R. (1973) *The Drift of Things: An Autobiography 1914–52*, Melbourne: Macmillan.

Roche, F.W. and Murray, J.A. (1978) *Tourism and Archaeology: A Study of Wood Quay*, Dublin: McIver.

Roche, M. (1992) 'Mega-events and micro-modernisation: On the sociology of the new urban tourism', *British Journal of Sociology*, 43(4): 563–600.

Roche, M. (2000) *Mega-Events and Modernity: Olympics and Expos in the Growth of Global Culture*, London: Routledge.

Rodgers, H. (1969) *British Pilot National Recreation Survey Report No. 1*, London: British Travel Association/University of Keele.

Rodgers, H. (1973) 'The demand for recreation', *Geographical Journal*, 13(9): 467–73.

Rodgers, H. (1977) 'The leisure future: Problems of prediction', in J. Settle (ed.) *Leisure in the North-West: A Tool for Forecasting*, Sports Council Study No. 11, Manchester: Sports Council.

Rodgers, H. (1993) 'Estimating local leisure demand in the context of a regional planning strategy', in S. Glyptis (ed.) *Leisure and the Environment: Essays in Honour of Professor J. A. Patmore*, London: Belhaven Press, pp. 116–30.

Rodgers, H. and Patmore, J.A. (eds) (1972) *Leisure in the North-West*, Manchester: North-West Sports Council.

Roe, M. and Benson, J. (2001) 'Planning for conflict resolution: Jet-ski use on the Northumberland coast', *Coastal Management*, 29(1): 19–39.

Rogers, G.F., Malde, H.E. and Turner, R.M. (1984) *Bibliography of Repeat Photography for Evaluating Landscape Change*, Salt Lake City, UT: University of Utah Press.

Rogerson, C.M. and Visser, G. (eds) (2004) *Tourism and Development Issues in Contemporary South Africa*, Pretoria, SA: Africa Institute of South Africa.

Romeril, M. (1984) 'Coastal tourism: The experience of Great Britain', *Industry and Environment*, 7(1): 4–7.

Romeril, M. (1988) 'Coastal tourism and the Heritage Coast programme in England and Wales', *Tourism Recreation Research*, 13(2): 15–19.

Rose, M. (ed.) (1985) *The Poor and the City: The English Poor Law in its Urban Context 1834–1914*, Leicester: Leicester University Press.

Rosemary, J. (1987) *Indigenous Enterprises in Kenya's Tourism Industry*, Geneva: Unesco.

Rosenfried, S. (1997) 'Global sex slavery', *San Francisco Examiner*, 6 April.

Rothman, R.A. (1978) 'Residents and transients: Community reaction to seasonal visitors', *Journal of Travel Research*, 16(3): 8–13.

Rothman, R.A., Donnelly, P.G. and Tower, J.K. (1979) 'Police departments in resort communities: Organizational adjustments to population undulation', *Leisure Sciences*, 2: 105–18.

Rowntree, S. and Lavers, G. (1951) *English Life and Leisure: A Social Study*, London: Longmans, Green.

Royer, L.E., McCool, S.F. and Hunt, J.D. (1974) 'The relative importance of tourism to state economies', *Journal of Travel Research*, 11(4): 13–16.

Rubio, F. (1998–9) 'La imagen geográphica del turismo en Espana (1962–1998): Creónica breve de una gran expansión', *Boletín de la Real Sociedad Geográfica*, 134–5: 67–103.

Rudkin, B. and Hall, C.M. (1996) 'Unable to see the forest for the trees: Ecotourism development in Solomon Islands', in R. Butler and T. Hinch (eds) *Tourism and Indigenous Peoples*, London: International Thomson Business, pp. 203–26.

Runte, A. (1972a) 'How Niagara Falls was saved: The beginning of aesthetic conservation in the United States', *The Conservationist*, 26(April–May): 32–5, 43.

Runte, A. (1972b) 'Yellowstone: It's useless, so why not a park', *National Parks and Conservation Magazine: The Environment Journal*, 46(March): 4–7.

Runte, A. (1973) '"Worthless" lands – our national parks: The enigmatic past and uncertain future of America's scenic wonderlands', *American West*, 10(May): 4–11.

Runte, A. (1974a) 'Pragmatic alliance: Western railroads and the national parks', *National Parks and Conservation Magazine: The Environmental Journal*, 48(April): 14–21.

Runte, A. (1974b) 'Yosemite Valley Railroad highway of history', *National Parks and Conservation Magazine: The Environmental Journal*, 48(December): 4–9.

Runte, A. (1977) 'The national park idea: Origins and paradox of the American experience', *Journal of Forest History*, 21(2): 64–75.

Runte, A. (1979) *National Parks The American Experience*, Lincoln, NE: University of Nebraska Press.

Runte, A. (1990) *Yosemite: The Embattled Wilderness*, Lincoln, NE: University of Nebraska Press.

Runte, A. (2002) 'Why national parks?', *The George Wright Forum*, 19(2): 67–71.

Runyan, D. and Wu, C. (1979) 'Assessing tourism's more complex consequences', *Annals of Tourism Research*, 6: 448–63.

Rural Development Commission (1991a) *Tourism in the Countryside: A Strategy for Rural England*, London: Rural Development Commission.

Rural Development Commission (1991b) *Meeting the Challenge of Rural Adjustment: A New Rural Development Commission Initiative*, London: Rural Development Commission.

Russell, E.W.B. (1997) *People and the Land through Time: Linking Ecology and History*, New Haven, CT: Yale University Press.

Russell, J.A., Matthews, J.H. and Jones, R. (1979) *Wilderness in Tasmania: A Report to the Australian Heritage Commission*, Occasional Paper No. 10, Hobart: Centre for Environmental Studies, University of Tasmania.

Ryan, C. (1991) *Recreational Tourism: A Social Science Perspective*, London: Routledge.

Ryan, C. (1995) *Researching Tourism Satisfaction: Issues, Concepts, Problems*, London: Routledge.

Ryan, C. (ed.) (1997) *The Tourist Experience: A New Introduction*, London: Cassell.

Ryan, C. and Hall, C.M. (2001) *Sex Tourism: Travels in Liminality*, London: Routledge.

Ryan, C. and Huyton, J. (2002) 'Tourists and aboriginal peoples', *Annals of Tourism Research*, 29: 631–47.

Saarinen, J. (1998) 'Cultural influence on response to wilderness encounters: A case study from Finland', *International Journal of Wilderness*, 4(1): 28–32.

Saarinen, J. (2001) 'The transformation of a tourist destination: Theory and case studies on the production of local geographies in tourism in Finnish Lapland', *Nordia Geographical Publications*, 30(1): 1–105.

Saarinen, J. (2003) 'Tourism and recreation as subjects of research in Finnish geographical journals', *Tourism Geographies*, 5(2): 220–7.

Saarinen, J. (2005) 'Tourism in the northern wildernesses: Wilderness discourses and the development of nature-based tourism in northern Finland', in C.M. Hall and S. Boyd (eds) *Nature-based Tourism in Peripheral Regions: Development or Disaster*, Clevedon: Channel View, pp. 36–49.

Saarinen, J. and Hall, C.M. (eds) (2004) *Nature-Based Tourism Research in Finland: Local Contexts, Global Issues*, Finnish Forest Research Institute, Research Paper No. 916, Rovaniemi, Finland: Rovaniemi Research Station.

Sadler, D. (1993) 'Place-marketing, competitive places and the construction of hegemony in Britain in the 1980s', in G. Kearns and C. Philo (eds) *Selling Places: The City as Cultural Capital, Past and Present*, Oxford: Pergamon, pp. 175–92.

Saeter, J.A. (1998) 'The significance of tourism and economic development in rural areas: A Norwegian case study', in R. Butler, C.M. Hall and J. Jenkins (eds) *Tourism and Recreation in Rural Areas*, Chichester: Wiley, pp. 237–47.

Samdahl, D. and Jekubovich, N. (1997) 'A critique of

leisure constraints: Comparative analyses and understandings', *Journal of Leisure Research*, 29(4): 430–52.

Sant, M. (1982) *Applied Geography*, Harlow: Longman.

Sawicki, D. (1989) 'The festival marketplace as public policy', *Journal of the American Planning Association*, 55 (summer): 347–61.

Schaer, U. (1978) 'Traffic problems in holiday resorts', *Tourist Review*, 33: 9–15.

Schafer, A. (2000) 'Regularities in travel demand: An international perspective', *Journal of Transportation and Statistics*, 3(3): 1–31.

Schafer, A. and Victor, D. (2000) 'The future mobility of the world population', *Transportation Research A*, 34(3): 171–205.

Scheyvens, R. (2002) *Tourism for Development*, Harlow: Prentice-Hall.

Schofield, P. (1996) 'Cinematographic images of a city: Alternative heritage tourism in Manchester', *Tourism Management*, 17(5): 333–40.

Schollmann, A., Perkins, H.C. and Moore, K. (2001) 'Rhetoric, claims making and conflict in touristic place promotion: The case of central Christchurch, New Zealand', *Tourism Geographies*, 3(3): 300–25.

Schwarz, C.F., Thor, E.C. and Elsner, G.H. (1976) *Wildland Planning Glossary*, Washington, DC: US Department of Agriculture, Forest Service.

Scott, N.R. (1974) 'Towards a psychology of the wilderness experience', *Natural Resource Journal*, 14: 231–7.

Scraton, S., Bramham, P. and Watson, B. (1998) 'Staying in and going out: Elderly women, leisure and the postmodern city', in S. Scraton (ed.) *Leisure, Time and Space: Meanings and Values in People's Lives*, 101–120, Leisure Studies Association, Eastbourne.

Seaton, A. and Bennett, M. (eds) (1996) *Marketing Tourism Products*, London: International Thomson Business.

Seeley, I. (1983) *Outdoor Recreation and the Urban Environment*, London: Macmillan.

Seers, D. and Ostrom, K. (eds) (1982) *The Crisis of the European Regions*, New York: St Martin's Press.

Seers, D., Schaffer, B. and Kiljunen, M. (eds) (1979) *Underdeveloped Europe: Studies in Core–Periphery Relations*, Hassocks, Sussex: Harvester Press.

Segrelles-Serrano, J. (2002) 'Luces y sombras de la geografia aplicada', *Documents d'Analisi Geografica*, 40: 153–72.

Selin, S. (1993) 'Collaborative alliances: New inter-organizational forms in tourism', *Journal of Travel and Tourism Marketing*, 2(2–3): 217–27.

Selin, S. (1998) 'The promise and pitfalls of collaborating', *Trends*, 35(1): 9–13.

Selin, S. and Chavez, D. (1994) 'Characteristics of successful tourism partnerships: A multiple case study design', *Journal of Park and Recreation Administration*, 12(2): 51–62.

Selke, A.C. (1936) 'Geographic aspects of the German tourist trade', *Economic Geography*, 12: 206–16.

Selwood, H.J. and Hall, C. (1986) 'The America's Cup: A hallmark tourist event', in J.S. Marsh (ed.) *Canadian Studies of Parks, Recreation and Tourism in Foreign Lands*, Occasional Paper No. 11, Peterborough: Department of Geography, Trent University.

Selwood, J. and May, A. (2001) 'Resolving contested notions of tourism sustainability on Western Australia's "Turquoise Coast": The squatter settlements', *Current Issues in Tourism*, 4: 381–91.

Selwood, J., Curry, G. and Koczberski, G. (1995) 'Structure and change in a local holiday resort: Peaceful Bay, on the southern coast of Western Australia', *Urban Policy and Research*, 13: 149–157.

Semple, E.C. (1891) *Influences of Geographic Environment*, New York: Henry Holt.

Sessa, A. (1993) *Elements of Tourism*, Rome: Catal.

Sewell, W.R.D. and Dearden, P. (1989) Wilderness: Past, Present and Future (special issue), *Natural Resources Journal*, 29: 1–222.

Shackleford, P. (1980) 'Keeping tabs on tourism: A manager's guide to tourism statistics', *International Journal of Tourism Management*, 1(3): 148–57.

Shackley, M. (ed) (1998) *Visitor Management: Case Studies from World Heritage Sites*, Oxford: Butterworth-Heinemann.

Share, B. (1992) *Shannon Departures: A Study in Regional Initiatives*, Dublin: Gill & Macmillan.

Sharpley, R. (1993) *Tourism and Leisure in the Countryside*, Managing Tourism Series No. 5, Huntingdon: Elm.

Sharpley, R. and Sharpley, J. (1997) *Rural Tourism*, London: International Thomson Business.

Sharpley, R. and Telfer, D. (eds) (2002) *Tourism and Development: Concepts and Issues*, Clevedon: Channel View.

Shaw, B.J. (1985) 'Fremantle and the America's Cup . . . the spectre of development?', *Urban Policy and Research*, 3: 38–40.

Shaw, B.J. (1986) *Fremantle W.A. and the America's Cup: The Impact of a Hallmark Event*, Working Paper No. 11, London: Australian Studies Centre,

Institute for Commonwealth Studies, University of London.

Shaw, D.J. (1979) 'Recreation and the socialist city', in R. French and F. Hamilton (eds) *The Socialist City: Spatial Structure and Urban Policy*, Chichester: Wiley, pp. 119–44.

Shaw, G. and Williams, A.M. (1990) 'Tourism, economic development and the role of entrepreneurial activity', in C. Cooper (ed.) *Progress in Tourism, Recreation and Hospitality Management*, Vol. 2, London: Belhaven Press, pp. 67–81.

Shaw, G. and Williams, A.M. (1994) *Critical Issues in Tourism: A Geographical Perspective*, Oxford: Blackwell.

Shaw, G. and Williams, A.M. (eds) (1997) *The Rise and Fall of British Coastal Resorts: Cultural and Economic Perspectives*, London: Mansell.

Shaw, G. and Williams, A.M. (2002) *Critical Issues in Tourism: A Geographical Perspective*, 2nd edn, Oxford: Blackwell.

Shaw, G. and Williams, A.M. (2004) *Tourism and Tourism Spaces*, Beverly Hills, CA: Sage.

Shaw, G., Agarwal, S. and Bull, P. (2000) 'Tourism consumption and tourist behaviour: A British perspective', *Tourism Geographies*, 2(3): 264–89.

Shaw, S., Bonen, A. and McCabe, J. (1991) 'Do more constraints mean less leisure? Examining the relationship between constraints and participation', *Journal of Leisure Research*, 23: 286–300.

Shelby, B. and Heberlein, T.A. (1984) 'A conceptual framework for carrying capacity', *Leisure Sciences*, 6: 433–51.

Shelby, B. and Heberlein, T.A. (1986) *Carrying Capacity in Recreation Settings*, Corvallis, OR: Oregon State University Press.

Shelby, B., Bregenzer, N.S. and Johnston, R. (1988) 'Displacement and product shift: Empirical evidence from Oregon Rivers', *Journal of Leisure Research*, 20(4): 274–88.

Shelby, B., Vaske, J.J. and Heberlein, T.A. (1989) 'Comparative analysis of crowding in multiple locations: Results from fifteen years of research', *Leisure Sciences*, 11(4): 269–91.

Shields, R. (1991) *Places on the Margin: Alternative Geographies of Modernity*, London: Routledge.

Shinew, K. and Arnold, M. (1998) 'Gender equity in the leisure services field', *Journal of Leisure, Research*, 30(2): 177–94.

Shoard, M. (1976) 'Fields which planners should conquer', *Forma*, 4: 128–35.

Short, J.R. (1991) *Imagined Country: Society, Culture and Environment*, London: Routledge.

Short, R. (2001) *Wanderlust: A History of Walking*, London: Verso.

Shucksmith, M. (1983) 'Second homes: A framework for policy', *Town Planning Review*, 54(2): 174–93.

Shurmer-Smith, P. and Hannam, K. (1994) *Worlds of Desire, Realms of Power: A Cultural Geography*, London: Arnold.

Sidaway, R. and Duffield, B. (1984) 'A new look at countryside recreation in the urban fringe', *Leisure Studies*, 3: 249–71.

Simeon, R. (1976) 'Studying public policy', *Canadian Journal of Political Science*, 9(4): 558–80.

Simmons, D.G. (1997) *National Profiles: Domestic Tourism Prototype Survey*, Lincoln: Lincoln University.

Simmons, I.G. (1974) *The Ecology of Natural Resources*, London: Edward Arnold.

Simmons, I.G. (1975) *Rural Recreation in the Industrial World*, London: Edward Arnold.

Simmons, I.G. (1993) *Environmental History: A Concise Introduction*, Cambridge: Blackwell.

Simmons, R., Davis, B.W., Chapman, R.J. and Sager, D.D. (1974) 'Policy flow analysis: A conceptual model for comparative public policy research', *Western Political Quarterly*, 27(3): 457–68.

Simpson Xavier Horwath (1990) *Irish Hotel Industry Review*, Dublin: Simpson Xavier Horwath.

Sinclair, J. (1986) 'Counting the loss of wilderness', *Habitat*, 14(3): 14–15.

Sinclair, M.T. (1991) 'The economics of tourism', in C. Cooper (ed.) *Progress in Tourism, Recreation and Hospitality Management*, Vol. 3, London: Belhaven Press, pp. 1–27.

Sinclair, M.T. (1998) 'Tourism and economic development: A survey', *Journal of Development Studies*, 34(5): 1–51.

Sinclair, M.T. and Stabler, M. (eds) (1992) *The Tourism Industry: An International Analysis*, Wallingford: CAB International.

Sinclair, M.T., Blake, A. and Sugiyarto, G. (2003) 'The economics of tourism', in C. Cooper (ed) *Classic Reviews of Tourism*, Clevedon: Channel View.

Singapore Tourism Board (STB) (1996) *Tourism 21: Vision of a Tourism Capital*, Singapore: STB.

Singh, S., Timothy, D. and Dowling, R. (eds) (2003) *Tourism in Destination Communities*, Wallingford: CAB International.

Siwiński, W. (1998) 'Leisure preferences of Polish students with disabilities', in S. Scraton (ed.) *Leisure,*

Time and Space: Meanings and Values in People's Lives, Brighton: Leisure Studies Association, pp. 193–8.

Slatyer, R. (1983) 'The origin and evolution of the World Heritage Convention', *Ambio*, 12(3–4): 138–45.

Slee, W. (1982) *An Evaluation of Country Park Policy*, Gloucestershire Papers in Local and Rural Planning No. 16, Cheltenham: GLOSCAT.

Slee, B. (2002) 'Social exclusion in the countryside', *Countryside Recreation*, 10(1): 2–7.

Smith, A. and Hall, C.M. (2003) 'Restaurants and local food in New Zealand', in C.M. Hall, E. Sharples, R. Mitchell, B. Cambourne and N. Macionis (eds) *Food Tourism around the World: Development, Management and Markets*, Oxford: Butterworth-Heinemann, pp. 248–68.

Smith, D.M. (1977) *Human Geography: A Welfare Approach*, London: Edward Arnold.

Smith, K. (1990) 'Tourism and climate change', *Land Use Policy*, April: 176–80.

Smith, M. and Turner, L. (1973) 'Some aspects of the sociology of tourism', *Society and Leisure*, 3: 55–71.

Smith, P.E. (1977) 'A value analysis of wilderness', *Search*, 8(9): 311–17.

Smith, R.A. (1991) 'Beach resorts: A model of development evolution', *Landscape and Urban Planning*, 21: 189–210.

Smith, R.A. (1992a) 'Beach resort evolution: Implications for planning', *Annals of Tourism Research*, 19: 304–22.

Smith, R.A. (1992b) 'Review of integrated beach resort development in South East Asia', *Land Use Policy*, 211–17.

Smith, R.A. (1994) 'Planning and management for coastal eco-tourism in Indonesia: A regional perspective', *Indonesian Quarterly*, 22(2): 148–57.

Smith, R.V. and Mitchell, L.S. (1990) 'Geography and tourism: A review of selected literature', in C. Cooper (ed.) *Progress in Tourism, Recreation and Hospitality Management*, Vol. 2, London: Belhaven Press, pp. 50–66.

Smith, S.J. (1987) 'Fear of crime: Beyond a geography of deviance', *Progress in Human Geography*, 11: 1–23.

Smith, S.L.J. (1982) 'Reflections on the development of geographic recreation in recreation: Hey, buddy, can you s'paradigm?', *Ontario Geography*, 19: 5–29.

Smith, S.L.J. (1983a) *Recreational Geography*, Harlow: Longman.

Smith, S.L.J. (1983b) 'Restaurants and dining out: Geography of a tourism business', *Annals of Tourism Research*, 10(4): 515–49.

Smith, S.L.J. (1987) 'Regional analysis of tourism resources', *Annals of Tourism Research*, 14: 253–73.

Smith, S.L.J. (1989) *Tourism Analysis*, Harlow: Longman.

Smith, S.L.J. (1990a) 'A test of Plog's allocentric/psychocentric model: Evidence from seven nations', *Journal of Travel Research*, 28(4): 40–2.

Smith, S.L.J. (1990b) 'Another look at the carpenter's tools: Reply to Plog', *Journal of Travel Research*, 29(2): 50–1.

Smith, S.L.J. (1994) 'The tourism product', *Annals of Tourism Research*, 21(3): 582–95.

Smith, S.L.J. (1995) *Tourism Analysis*, 2nd edn, Harlow: Longman.

Smith, S.L.J. (2000) 'New developments in measuring tourism as an area of economic activity', in W.C. Gartner and D.W. Lime (eds) *Trends in Outdoor Recreation, Leisure, and Tourism*, Wallingford: CAB International, pp. 225–34.

Smith, S.L.J. and Brown, B.A. (1981) 'Directional bias in vacation travel', *Annals of Tourism Research*, 8: 257–70.

Smith, S.L.J. and Wilton, D. (1997) 'TSAs and the WTTC/WEFA methodology: Different satellites or different planets?', *Tourism Economics*, 3: 249–64.

Smith, V.L. (ed.) (1977) *Hosts and Guests: The Anthropology of Tourism*, Philadelphia, PA: University of Pennsylvania Press.

Smith, V.L. (ed.) (1992) *Hosts and Guests: An Anthropology of Tourism*, 2nd edn, Philadelphia, PA: University of Pennsylvannia Press.

Smyth, H. (1994) *Marketing the City: The Role of Flagship Developments in Urban Regeneration*, London: E&FN Spon.

Snaith, T. and Haley, A. (1999) 'Resident opinions of tourism development in the historic city of York, England', *Tourism Management*, 20(5): 595–603.

Snepenger, D., Murphy, L., O'Connell, R. and Gregg, E. (2003) 'Tourists and residents use of a shopping space', *Annals of Tourism Research*, 30(3): 567–580.

Soja, E.W. (1989) *Postmodern Geographies: The Reassertion of Space in Critical Social Theory*, London: Verso.

Solecki, W. and Welch, J. (1995) 'Urban parks: Green spaces or green walls?', *Landscape and Urban Planning*, 32: 93–106.

Sopher, D. (1968) 'Pilgrim circulation in Gujarat', *Geographical Review*, 58: 392–45.

Spencer, J. and Thomas, W. (1948) 'The hill stations and summer resorts of the Orient', *Geographical Review*, 38: 637–51.

Spink, J. (1994) *Leisure and the Environment*, Oxford: Butterworth- Heinemann.

Squire, S.J. (1993) 'Valuing countryside: Reflections on Beatrix Potter tourism', *Area*, 25(1): 5–10.

Squire, S.J. (1994) 'Accounting for cultural meanings: The interface between geography and tourism studies revisited', *Progress in Human Geography*, 18: 1–16.

Stabler, M. (1990) 'The concept of opportunity sets as a methodological framework for the analysis of selling tourism places: The industry view', in G.J. Ashworth and B. Goodall (eds) *Marketing Tourism Places*, London: Routledge, pp. 23–41.

Stamp, D. (1948) *The Land of Britain: Its Use and Misuse*, Harlow: Longman.

Stamp, D. (1960) *Applied Geography*, London: Penguin.

Stankey, G.H. (1973) *Visitor Perception of Wilderness Carrying Capacity*, USDA, Forest Service Research Paper, INT–42, Ogden, UT: Intermountain Forest and Range Experiment Station.

Stankey, G.H. (1989) 'Beyond the campfire's light: Historical roots of the wilderness concept', *Natural Resources Journal*, 29: 9–24.

Stankey, G.H. and McCool, S.F. (1984) 'Carrying capacity in recreational settings: Evolution, appraisal, and application', *Leisure Sciences*, 6(4): 453–73.

Stankey, G.H. and Schreyer, R. (1987) 'Attitudes toward wilderness and factors affecting visitor behaviour: A state of knowledge review', in *Proceedings – National Wilderness Research Conference: Issues, State of Knowledge and Future Directions*, General Technical Report INT–220, Ogden, UT: Intermountain Research Station, pp. 246–93.

Stankey, G.H., Cole, D.N., Lucas, R.C., Petersen, M.E. and Frissell, S. (1985) *The Limits of Acceptable Change System for Wilderness Planning*, USDA, Forest Service Research Paper, INT–176, Ogden, UT: Intermountain Forest and Range Experiment Station.

Stansfield, C.A. (1972) 'The development of modern seaside resorts', *Parks and Recreation*, 5(10): 14–46.

Stansfield, C.A. (1978) 'Atlantic City and the resort cycle: Background to the legalization of gambling', *Annals of Tourism Research*, 5(2): 238–51.

Stansfield, C.A. and Rickert, J.E. (1970) 'The recreational business district', *Journal of Leisure Research*, 2(4): 213–25.

Stanton, J.P. and Morgan, M.G. (1977) *Project 'RAKES' – A Rapid Appraisal of Key and Endangered Sites, Report No. 1: The Queensland Case Study*, report to the Department of Environment, Housing and Community Development, Armidale, NSW: School of Natural Resources, University of New England.

Stea, R. and Downs, R. (1970) 'From the outside looking in at the inside looking out', *Environment and Behaviour*, 2: 3–12.

Stebbins, R.A. (1979) *Amateurs: On the Margin between Work and Leisure*, Beverly Hills, CA: Sage.

Stebbins, R.A. (1982) 'Serious leisure: A conceptual statement', *Pacific Sociological Review*, 25: 251–72.

Steffen, R., deBarnardis, C. and Banos, A. (2003) 'Travel epidemiology – a global perspective', *International Journal of Antimicrobial Agents*, 21(2): 89–95.

Stevens, T. (1987) 'Going underground', *Leisure Management*, 7: 48–50.

Stevens, T. (1991) 'Irish eyes are smiling', *Leisure Management*, 11: 46–8.

Stockdale, J.E. (1985) *What is Leisure? An Empirical Analysis of the Concept of Leisure and the Role of Leisure in People's Lives*, London: Sports Council.

Stoddart, D.R. (1981) 'Ideas and interpretation in the history of geography', in D.R. Stoddart (ed.) *Geography, Ideology and Social Concern*, Oxford: Blackwell, pp. 1–7.

Stodolska, M. (2000) 'Changes in leisure participation patterns after immigration', *Leisure Sciences*, 22(1): 39–63.

Stoffle, R.W., Last, C. and Evans, M. (1979) 'Reservation-based tourism: Implications of tourist attitudes for Native American economic development', *Human Organization*, 38(3): 300–6.

Stokowski, P. (2002) 'Languages of place and discourses of power: Constructing new senses of place', *Journal of Leisure Research*, 34(4): 368–82.

Stone, G. and Taves, M. (1957) 'Research into the human element in wilderness use', *Proceedings of the 1956 Meeting of the Society of American Foresters*, Memphis, TN, pp. 26–32.

Strachan, A. and Bowler, I. (1976) 'The development of public parks in the City of Leicester', *East Midland Geographer*, 6: 275–83.

Stringer, P. (1984) 'Studies in the socio-environmental psychology of tourism', *Annals of Tourism Research*, 11: 147–66.

Stringer, P. and Pearce, P.L. (1984) 'Towards a symbiosis of social psychology and tourism studies', *Annals of Tourism Research*, 11: 5–18.

Strong, R. (1997) 'External factors: State and local government controls; community expectations', mimeo of paper presented at Business With Style: Adapting

Heritage Buildings for Commercial Use, New South Wales Government, Heritage Office, Sydney.

Sun, D. and Walsh, D. (1998) 'Review of studies on environmental impacts of recreation and tourism in Australia', *Journal of Environmental Management*, 53: 323–38.

Survey Research Associates (1991) *London Docklands Visitor Survey: Summary of Findings*, London: London Docklands Development Corporation.

Svenson, S. (2004) 'The cottage and the city: An interpretation of the Canadian second home experience', in C.M. Hall and D. Müller (eds) *Tourism, Mobility and Second Homes: Between Elite Landscape and Common Ground*, Clevedon: Channel View, pp. 55–74.

Swaffield, S. and Fairweather, J. (1998) 'In search of arcadia: The persistence of the rural idyll in New Zealand rural sub-divisions', *Journal of Environmental Planning and Management*, 4(1): 111–27.

Szulczewska, B. and Kaliskuk, E. (2003) 'Challenges in the planning and management of green structure in Warsaw, Poland', *Built Environment*, 29(2): 144–56.

Takeuchi, K. (1984) 'Some remarks on the geography of tourism in Japan', *GeoJournal*, 9(1): 85–90.

Talbot, M. (1979) *Women and Leisure*, London: Sports Council/Social Science Research Council Joint Panel on Leisure and Recreation Research.

Tanner, M. (1971) 'The planning and management of water recreation areas', in P. Lavery (ed.) *Recreational Geography*, Newton Abbot: David and Charles, pp. 197–214.

Tanner, M. (1973) 'The recreational use of inland waters', *Geographical Journal*, 139: 486–91.

Tanner, M. (1977) *Recreational Use of Water Supply Reservoirs in England and Wales*, Research Report No. 3, London: Waterspace Amenity Commission.

Tarlow, P.E. and Muehsam, M.J. (1992) 'Wide horizons: Travel and tourism in the coming decades', *The Futurist*, 26(5): 28–33.

Tarrant, M. and Cordell, H. (1999) 'Environmental justice and the spatial distribution of outdoor recreation sites: An application of geographic information systems', *Journal of Leisure Research*, 31(1): 18–34.

Taylor, D. (1999) 'Central Park as a model for social control: Urban parks, social class and leisure behaviour in nineteenth century America', *Journal of Leisure Research*, 31(4): 426–77.

Taylor, G. (ed.) (1951) *Geography in the Twentieth Century*, London: Methuen.

Taylor, J., Legellé, J.G. and Andrew, C. (eds) (1993) *Capital Cities: International Perspectives/Les Capitales: Perspectives internationales*, Ottawa: Carleton University Press.

Taylor, P.J. (1985) 'The value of a geographical perspective', in R.J. Johnston (ed.) *The Future of Geography*, London: Methuen, pp. 92–110.

Taylor, R., Shumaker, S. and Gottfredson, S. (1985) 'Neighbourhood-level links between physical features and local sentiments: Deterioration, fear of crime and confidence', *Journal of Architectural and Planning Research*, 2: 261–75.

Taylor, S.G. (1990) 'Naturalness: The concept and its application to Australian ecosystems', *Proceedings of the Ecological Society of Australia*, 16: 411–18.

Tchistiakova, E. and Pabane, C. (1997) 'Urban tourism and rural tourism in Russia', *Norois* 176: 571–83.

Teisl, M. and Reiling, S. (1992) 'Measuring tourism impacts at the community level: The impact of tourism on local government public service expenditures', www.msue.edu/msue/imp/modtd/33519758.htr

Telfer, D.J. (2000a) 'The Northeast Wine Route: Wine tourism in Ontario, Canada and New York State', in C.M. Hall, E. Sharples, B. Cambourne and N. Macionis (eds) *Wine Tourism around the World: Development, Management and Markets*, Oxford: Butterworth-Heinemann, pp. 253–71.

Telfer, D.J. (2000b) 'Tastes of Niagara: Building strategic alliances between tourism and agriculture', *International Journal of Hospitality and Tourism Administration*, 1: 71–88.

Telfer, D.J. (2001) 'Strategic alliances along the Niagara Wine Route', *Tourism Management*, 22: 21–30.

Telfer, D.J. and Wall, G. (1996) 'Linkages between tourism and food production', *Annals of Tourism Research*, 23(3): 635–53.

Teo, P. and Chang, T.C. (2000) 'Singapore: Tourism development in a planned context', in C.M. Hall and S.J. Page (eds) *Tourism in South and South-East Asia: Cases and Issues*, Oxford: Butterworth-Heinemann, pp. 117–28.

Terkenli, T. (2002) 'Landscapes of tourism: Towards a global cultural economy of space?', *Tourism Geographies*, 4(3): 227–54.

Therborn, G. (1996) *Monumental Europe: The National Years of the Iconography of European Capital Cities*, Gothenberg: University of Gothenberg.

Thomas, R. (ed.) (2003) *Tourism and Small Firms*, Oxford: Pergamon.

Thompson, P. (1985) 'Dunphy and Muir: Two mountain men', *Habitat*, 13(2): 26–7.

Thompson, P. (1986) *Myles Dunphy: Selected Writings*, Sydney: Ballagirin.

Thompson, P.M., Van Parijs, S.M. and Kovacs, K.M. (2001) 'Local declines in the abundance of harbour seal, implications for the designation and monitoring of protected areas', *Journal of Applied Ecology*, 38: 117–25.

Thoreau, H.D. (1854 (1968)) *Walden*, Everyman's Library, London: Dent.

Thorpe, H. (1970) 'A new deal for allotments: Solutions to a pressing land use problem', *Area*, 3: 1–8.

Thorsell, J. and Sigaty, T. (2001) 'Human use in World Heritage natural sites: A global inventory', *Tourism Recreation Research*, 26(1): 85–101.

Thorsen, E.O. and Hall, C.M. (2001) 'What's on the wine list? Wine policies in the New Zealand restaurant industry', *International Journal of Wine Marketing*, 13(3): 94–102.

Threndyle, S. (1994) 'Towns in transition: Careful tourism-planning can soften the blows of changing times in resource-based economies, but there's no panacea', *Georgia Straight*, 22–29 July.

Thrift, N. (1977) *An Introduction to Time Geography*, Norwich: Catmog 13.

Thurot, J.M. and Thurot, G. (1983) 'The ideology of class and tourism confronting the discourse of advertising', *Annals of Tourism Research*, 10: 173–89.

Tillman, A. (1974) *The Program Book for Recreation Professionals*, Palo Alto, CA: National Press Books.

Timmermans, H.J.P. and Morgansky, M. (eds) (1999) Direct Marketing: Where the Old Meets the New (special issue), *Journal of Business Research*, 45: 247–304.

Timothy, D.J. (2002) 'Tourism and community development issues', in R. Sharpley and D.J. Telford (eds) *Tourism and Development: Concepts and Issues*, Clevedon: Channel View. pp. 149–64.

Timothy, D.J. (2004) 'Political boundaries and regional cooperation in tourism', in A. Lew, C.M. Hall and A. Williams (eds) *Companion to Tourism*, Oxford: Blackwell, pp. 584–95.

Tinsley, H.E.A., Tinsley, D.J. and Croskeys, C.E. (2002) 'Park usage, social milieu, and psychosocial benefits of park use reported by older urban park users from four ethnic groups', *Leisure Sciences*, 24(2): 199–218.

Tissot, L. (2000) *Naissance d'une industrie touristique: Les Anglais et la Suisse au XIXe siècle*, Lausanne: Editions Payot.

Tombaugh, L.W (1970) 'Factors influencing home location', *Journal of Leisure Research*, 2(1): 54–63.

Torkildsen, G. (1983) *Leisure and Recreation Management*, London: E&FN Spon.

Torkildsen, G. (1992) *Leisure and Recreation Management*, 3rd edn, London: E&FN Spon.

Tourism Council of the South Pacific (1988) *Nature Legislation and Nature Conservation as a Part of Tourism Development in the Island Pacific: A Report Covering Cook Islands, Fiji, Kiribati, Niue, Papua New Guinea, Solomon Islands, Tonga, Tuvulu, Vanuatu and Western Samoa*, Suva: Tourism Council of the South Pacific.

Towner, J. (1985) 'The Grand Tour: A key phase in the history of tourism', *Annals of Tourism Research*, 12(3): 297–333.

Towner, J. (1996) *An Historical Geography of Recreation and Tourism in the Western World 1540–1940*, Chichester: Wiley.

Townsend, A. (1991) 'Services and local economic development', *Area*, 23: 309–17.

Townsend, P. (1979) *Poverty in the UK: A Survey of Household Resources and Standards of Living*, Harmondsworth: Penguin.

Tress, G. (2002) 'Development of second-home tourism in Denmark', *Scandinavian Journal of Hospitality and Tourism*, 2: 109–22.

Tuan, Yi-Fu (1971) *Man and Nature*, Washington, DC: Commission on College Geography, Association of American Geographers.

Tuan, Yi-Fu (1974) *Topophilia: A Study of Environmental Perception, Attitudes, and Values*, Englewood Cliffs, NJ: Prentice Hall.

Tuan, Yi-Fu (1979) *Landscapes of Fear*, New York: Pantheon.

Tubridy, M. (ed.) (1987) *Heritage Zones: The Co-existence of Agriculture, Nature Conservation and Tourism: The Clonmacnoise Example*, Environmental Science Unit Occasional Publication, Dublin: Trinity College.

Tunbridge, J.E. (1998) 'Tourism management in Ottawa, Canada: Nurturing in a fragile environment', in D. Tyler, Y. Guerrier and M. Robertson (eds) *Managing Tourism in Cities: Policy, Process and Practice*, London: Wiley, pp. 91–108.

Tunbridge, J.E. (2000) 'Heritage momentum or maelstrom? The case of Ottawa's Byward Market', *International Journal of Heritage Studies*, 6(3): 269–91.

Tunbridge, J.E. and Ashworth, G.J. (1996) *Dissonant Heritage: The Management of the Past as a Resource in Conflict*, Chichester: Wiley.

Tunstall, S. and Penning-Rowsell, E. (1998) 'The English

beach: Experience and values', *Geographical Journal*, 164(3): 319–32.

Turner, R., Lorenzon, I., Beaumont, N., Bateman, J., Langford, I. and McDonald, A. (1998) 'Coastal management for sustainable development: Analysing environmental and socio-economic changes', *Geographical Journal*, 164(3): 269–81.

Turnock, D. (2002) 'Prospects for sustainable rural cultural tourism in Maramure, Romania', *Tourism Geographies*, 4(1): 62–94.

Twight, B. (1983) *Organizational Values and Political Power: The Forest Service Versus the Olympic National Park*, University Park, PA: Pennsylvania State University Press.

Tyler, D., Guerrier, Y. and Robertson, M. (eds) (1998) *Managing Tourism in Cities: Policy, Process and Practice*, Chichester: Wiley.

Ullman, E.L. (1954) 'Amenities as a factor in regional growth', *Geographical Review*, 54: 119–32.

Ullman, E.L. and Volk, D.J. (1961) 'An operational model for predicting reservoir attendance and benefits: Implications of a location approach to water recreation', *Papers of the Michigan Academy of Science, Arts and Letters*, 47: 473–84.

UNEP/WTO (1996) *Awards for Improving the Coastal Environment: The Example of the Blue Flag*, Paris: UNEP/WTO.

Unesco (United Nations Educational, Scientific and Cultural Organisation) (1976) 'The effects of tourism on socio-cultural values', *Annals of Tourism Research*, November/December: 74–105.

Unesco (1995) 'Tourism and World Heritage', *The World Heritage Newsletter*, 8, http://www.unesco.orgLwhc/news/8newseng.htm, accessed 1 April 2001.

United Nations (UN) (1994) *Recommendations on Tourism Statistics*, New York: UN.

United Nations, Division for Social Policy and Development (1998) *The Ageing of the World's Population*, New York: UN, http://www.un.org/esa/socdev/agewpop.htm

United States Department of the Interior (1978) *National Urban Recreation Study*, Washington, DC: Department of the Interior.

Unwin, K. (1976) 'The relationship of observer and landscape in landscape evaluation', *Transactions of the Institute of British Geographers*, 66: 130–4.

Urry, J. (1987) 'Some social and spatial aspects of services', *Society and Space*, 5: 5–26.

Urry, J. (1988) 'Cultural change and contemporary holidaymaking', *Theory, Culture and Society*, 5: 35–55.

Urry, J. (1990) *The Tourist Gaze: Leisure and Travel in Contemporary Societies*, London: Sage.

Urry, J. (1991) 'The sociology of tourism', in C.P. Cooper (ed.) *Progress in Tourism, Recreation and Hospitality Management*, Vol. 3, London: Belhaven Press, pp. 48–57.

Urry, J. (1995) *Consuming Places*, London: Routledge.

Urry, J. (2000) *Sociology Beyond Societies: Mobilities for the Twenty-First Century*, London: Routledge.

Urry, J. (2004) 'Small worlds and the new "social physics"', *Global Networks*, 4(2): 109–30.

Uysal, M. (1998) 'The determinants of tourism demand: A theoretical perspective', in D. Ioannides and K. Debbage (eds) *The Economic Geography of the Tourist Industry: A Supply-side Analysis*, London: Routledge, pp. 79–95.

Uysal, M. and Crompton, J.L. (1985) 'An overview of approaches to forecasting tourist demand', *Journal of Travel Research*, 23(4): 7–15.

Uzzell, D. (1984) 'An alternative structuralist approach to the psychology of tourism marketing', *Annals of Tourism Research*, 11: 79–100.

Uzzell, D. (1995) 'The myth of the indoor city', *Journal of Environmental Psychology*, 15: 299–310.

Valentine, G. (1989) 'The geography of woman's fear', *Area*, 21(4): 385–90.

Valentine, G. (1990) 'Women's fear and the design of public space', *Built Environment*, 16(4): 288–303.

Valentine, P. (1980) 'Tropical rainforest and the wilderness experience', in V. Martin (ed.) *Wilderness*, Moray, Scotland: Findhorn Press, pp. 123–32.

Valentine, P. (1984) 'Wildlife and tourism: Some ideas on potential and conflict', in B. O'Rourke (ed.) *Contemporary Issues in Australian Tourism, 19th Institute of Australian Geographer's Conference and International Geographical Union Sub-Commission on Tourism in the South West Pacific*, Sydney: Department of Geography, University of Sydney, pp. 29–54.

Valentine, P. (1992) 'Review: Nature-based tourism', in B. Weiler and C.M. Hall (eds) *Special Interest Tourism*, London: Belhaven Press.

Van der Knaap, W. (1999) 'Research report: GIS-oriented analysis of tourist time–space patterns to support sustainable tourism development', *Tourism Geographies*, 1(1): 56–69.

Van Parijs, S., Van Parijs, S.M. and Lydersen, C. (2004) 'The effects of ice cover on the behaviour of aquatic mating male bearded seals', *Animal Behaviour*, 68: 89–96.

Van Raaij, W.F. (1986) 'Consumer research on tourism:

Mental and behavioural constructs', *Annals of Tourism Research*, 13: 1–10.

Van Raaij, W.F. and Francken, D.A. (1984) 'Vacation decisions, activities, and satisfactions', *Annals of Tourism Research*, 11: 101–13.

Van Westering, J. (1999) 'Heritage and gastronomy: The pursuits of the "new" tourist', *International Journal of Heritage Studies*, 5(2): 75–81.

Vaughan, D.R. (1977) 'Opportunity cost and the assessment and development of regional tourism', in B.S. Duffield (ed.) *Tourism: A Tool for Regional Development*, Edinburgh: Tourism and Recreation Research Unit, University of Edinburgh, pp. 8.1–8.9.

Vaughan, D.R., Farr, H. and Slee, W. (2000) 'Estimating and interpreting the local economic benefits of visitor spending', *Leisure Studies*, 19(2): 95–118.

Veal, A.J. (1987) *Leisure and the Future*, London: Unwin & Hyman.

Veal, A.J. (1992) *Research Methods for Leisure and Tourism: A Practical Guide*, Harlow: Longman.

Veal, A.J. (1994) *Leisure Policy and Planning*, London: Pitman.

Veal, A. (2001) 'Using Sydney's Parks', *Australian Parks and Leisure* 4(3):21–23.

Veal, A. and Travis, T. (1979) 'Local authority leisure services – the state of play', *Local Government Studies*, 5: 5–16.

Vendenin, Y. (1978) 'Evolution of the recreational functions of a territory', *Soviet Geography*, 19: 646–59.

Vetter, F. (ed.) (1985) *Big City Tourism*, Berlin: Dietrich Verlag.

Vickerman, R. (1975) *The Economics of Leisure and Recreation*, London: Macmillan.

Vidal, J. (1994) 'Parks: Who needs them?', *Guardian*, 21 July.

Virden, R. and Walker, G. (1999) 'Ethnic/racial and gender variations among meanings given to, and preferences for, the natural environment', *Leisure Sciences*, 21(3): 219–39.

Visser, G. (2004) 'Second homes and local development: Issues arising from Cape Town's De Waterkant', *GeoJournal*, 60(3): 259–71.

Visser, G. and Rogerson, C. (eds) (2004) Tourism and Development Issues in South Africa (special issue), *GeoJournal*, 60(3).

Visser, N. and Njunga, S. (1992) 'Environmental impacts of tourism on the Kenya coast', *Industry and Environment*, 15(3–4): 42–52.

Vogeler, I. (1977) 'Farm and ranch vacationing', *Journal of Leisure Research*, 9: 291–300.

Wagar, J.A. (1964) *The Carrying Capacity of Wildlands for Recreation*, Forest Service Monograph No. 7, Washington, DC: Society of American Foresters.

Wager, J. (1995) 'Developing a strategy for the Angkor World Heritage site', *Tourism Management*, 16(7): 515–23.

Waitt, G. (1997) 'Selling paradise and adventure: Representations of landscape in the tourist advertising of Australia', *Australian Geographical Studies*, 35(1): 47–60.

Waitt, G. (1999) 'Naturalizing the "primitive" a critique of marketing Australia's indigenous peoples as "hunter-gatherers"', *Tourism Geographies*, 1(2): 142–63.

Waitt, G. and McGuirk, P.M. (1997) 'Marking time: Tourism and heritage representation at Millers Point, Sydney', *Australian Geographer*, 27(1): 11–29.

Walker, L. and Page, S. J. (2003) 'Risk, rights and responsibilities in tourist well-being: Who should manage visitor well-being at the destination?', in J. Wilks and S.J. Page (eds) *Managing Tourist Health and Safety in the New Millennium*, Oxford: Pergamon, pp. 215–36.

Wall, G. (1971) 'Car-owners and holiday activities', in P. Lavery (ed.) *Recreational Geography*, Newton Abbot: David and Charles, pp. 97–111.

Wall, G. (1972) 'Socio-economic variations in pleasure trip patterns: The case of Hull car-owners', *Transactions of the Institute of British Geographers*, 57: 45–58.

Wall, G. (1983a) 'Atlantic City tourism and social change', *Annals of Tourism Research*, 10: 555–6.

Wall, G. (1983b) 'Cycles and capacity: A contradiction in terms?', *Annals of Tourism Research*, 10: 268–70.

Wall, G. (ed.) (1989) *Outdoor Recreation in Canada*, Toronto: Wiley.

Wall, G. and Badke, C. (1994) 'Tourism and climate change: an international perspective', *Journal of Sustainable Tourism*, 2(4): 193–203.

Wall, G. and Marsh, J. (eds) (1982) *Recreational Land Use: Perspectives on its Evolution in Canada*, Ottawa: Carleton University Press.

Wall, G. and Wright, C. (1977) *The Environmental Impacts of Outdoor Recreation*, Publication Series No. 11, Waterloo, Ont.: Department of Geography, University of Waterloo.

Wall, G., Dudycha, D. and Hutchinson, J. (1985) 'Point pattern analysis of accommodation in Toronto', *Annals of Tourism Research*, 12(4): 603–18.

Wall, G., Harrison, R., Kinnaird, V., McBoyle, G. and Quinlan, C. (1986) 'The implications of climatic change for camping in Ontario', *Recreation Research Review*, 13(1): 50–60.

Wall, S. (2004) 'Protected areas as tourist attractions', paper presented at *Tourism Crossroads – Global Influences, Local Responses*, Thirteenth Nordic Symposium in Tourism and Hospitality Research, Aalborg, Denmark, 4–7 November.

Walle, A. (1997) 'Quantitative versus qualitative tourism research', *Annals of Tourism Research*, 24(3): 524–36.

Walmesley, D.J. and Jenkins, J. (1992) 'Tourism cognitive mapping of unfamiliar environments', *Annals of Tourism Research*, 19(3): 268–86.

Walmesley, D.J. and Jenkins, J. (1994) 'Evaluations of recreation opportunities: Tourist impacts of the New South Wales North Coast', in D. Mercer (ed.) *New Viewpoints in Australian Outdoor Recreation Research and Planning*, Melbourne: Hepper Marriott, pp. 89–98.

Walmesley, D.J. and Lewis, G.J. (1993) *People and Environment: Behavioural Approaches in Human Geography*, 2nd edn, Harlow: Longman.

Walmesley, D.J., Boskovic, R.M. and Pigram, J.J. (1981) *Tourism and Crime*, Armidale, NSW: Department of Geography, University of New England.

Walmesley, D.J., Boskovic, R.M. and Pigram, J.J. (1983) 'Tourism and crime: An Australian perspective', *Journal of Leisure Research*, 15: 136–55.

Walpole, M. and Goodwin, H. (2000) 'Local economic impacts of dragon tourism in Indonesia', *Annals of Tourism Research*, 27(3): 559–76.

Walsh, K. (1988) 'The consequences of competition', in J. Bennington and J. White (eds) *The Future of Leisure Services*, Harlow: Longman, pp. 37–56.

Walter, R.D. (1975) *The Impact of Tourism on the Environment*, Australian Recreation Research Association (ARRA) Monograph No. 7, Melbourne: ARRA.

Walton, J. (1983) *The English Seaside Resort: A Social History 1750–1914*, Leicester: Leicester University Press.

Walton, J. (2000) 'The hospitality trades: A social history', in C. Lashley and A. Morrison (eds) *In Search of Hospitality: Theoretical Perspectives and Debates*, Oxford: Butterworth-Heinemann, pp. 56–76.

Walton, J. and Smith, J. (1996) 'The first century of beach tourism in Spain: San Sebastian and the Playas del Norte from the 1830s to the 1930s', in M. Barke, J. Towner and M. Newton (eds) *Tourism in Spain: Critical Issues*, Wallingford: CAB International, pp. 189–212.

Walvin, J. (1978) 'Beside the Seaside: A Popular History of the Seaside Holiday', Allen Lane: London.

Ward, C. and Hardy, D. (1986) *Goodnight Campers: The History of the British Holiday Camp*, London: Mansell.

Ward, S. (1998). *Selling Places: The Marketing and Promotion of Towns and Cities 1850–2000*, London: E&FN Spon.

Ward, S. (2001) *Selling Places: The Marketing and Promotion of Towns and Cities 1850–2000*, London: E&FN Spon.

Warnes, A.M. (1992) 'Migration and the lifecourse', in A.G. Champion and A. Fielding (eds) *Migration Processes and Patterns*, Volume 1: *Research Progress and Prospects*, London: Belhaven Press, pp. 175–87.

Warnes, A.M. (2001) 'The international dispersal of pensioners from affluent countries', *International Journal of Population Geography*, 7(6): 373–88.

Warnes, T. (1994) 'Permanent and seasonal international retirement prospects for Europe', *Nederlandse Geografische Studies*, 173: 69–79.

Warnken, J. and Buckley, R. (2000) 'Monitoring diffuse impacts: Australian tourism developments', *Environmental Management*, 25: 453–61.

Warr, M. (1985) 'Fear of rape among urban women', *Social Problems*, 32: 238–50.

Watmore, S. (1998) 'Wild(er)ness: Reconfiguring the geographies of wildlife', *Transactions, Institute of British Geographers*, NS23: 435–54.

Watmore, S. (2000) 'Elephants on the move: Spatial formations of wildlife exchange', *Environment and Planning D: Society and Space*, 18: 185–203.

Wayens, B. and Grimmeau, J.P. (2003) 'L'influence du tourisme sur le géographie du commerce de détail en Belgique', *Belgeo*, 3: 289–302.

Weaver, D. (1998) *Ecotourism in the Less Developed World*, Wallingford: CAB International.

Weaver, D. (2000) 'A broad context model of destination development scenarios', *Tourism Management*, 21: 217–34.

Weaver, D. (ed.) (2001) *The Encyclopedia of Ecotourism*, Wallingford: CAB International.

Weaver, D. (2004) 'Tourism and the elusive paradigm of sustainable development', in A. Lew, C.M. Hall and A. Williams (eds) *Companion to Tourism*, Oxford: Blackwell, pp. 510–20.

Weightman, B. (1981) 'Towards a geography of the gay community', *Journal of Cultural Geography*, 1: 106–12.

Weiler, B. (1991) *Ecotourism: Conference Proceedings*, Canberra: Bureau of Tourism Research.

Weiler, B. and Hall, C.M. (1991) 'Meeting the needs of the recreation and tourism partnership: A comparative study of tertiary education programmes in Australia and Canada', *Leisure Options: Australian Journal of Leisure and Recreation*, 1(2): 7–14.

Weiler, B. and Hall, C.M. (eds) (1992) *Special Interest Tourism*, London: Belhaven Press.

Welch, D. (1991) *The Management of Urban Parks*, Harlow: Longman.

Westover, T. (1985) 'Perceptions of crime and safety in three midwestern parks', *Professional Geographer*, 37: 410–20.

Whatmore, S. (1993) 'Sustainable rural geographies', *Progress in Human Geography*, 17(4): 538–47.

Whetton, P.H., Haylock, M.R. and Galloway, R. (1996) 'Climate change and snow cover duration in the Australian Alps', *Climatic Change*, 32: 447–79.

Whitbeck, R.H. (1920) 'The influence of Lake Michigan upon its opposite shores, with comments on the declining use of the lake as a waterway', *Annals of the Association of American Geographers*, 10: 41–55.

White, A., Barker, V. and Tantrigama, G. (1997) 'Using integrated coastal management and economics to conserve coastal tourism resources in Sri Lanka', *Ambio*, 26(6): 335–44.

White, G. (1972) 'Geography and public policy', *Professional Geographer*, 24: 101–4.

White, K. and Walker, M. (1982) 'Trouble in the travel account', *Annals of Tourism Research*, 9(1): 37–56.

White, L., Jr (1967) 'The historical roots of our ecological crisis', *Science*, 155(10 March): 1203–7.

Whitehead, J.W.R. (1993) *The Making of the Urban Landscape*, Oxford: Blackwell.

Whyte, D. (1978) 'Have second homes gone into hibernation?', *New Society*, 45: 286–8.

Wight, P.A. (1993) 'Sustainable ecotourism: Balancing economic, environmental and social goals within an ethical framework', *Journal of Tourism Studies*, 4(2): 54–66.

Wight, P.A. (1995) 'Sustainable ecotourism: Balancing economic, environmental and social goals within an ethical framework', *Tourism Recreation Research*, 20(1): 5–13.

Wight, P.A. (1998) 'Tools for sustainability analysis in planning and managing tourism and recreation in the destination', in C.M. Hall and A.A. Lew (eds) *Sustainable Tourism Development: A Geographical Perspective*, Harlow: Addison Wesley Longman, pp. 75–91.

Wilks, J. and Page, S.J. (eds) (2003) *Managing Tourist Health and Safety in the New Millennium*, Oxford: Elsevier.

Williams, A. (2000) 'Consuming hospitality: Learning from post-modernism?', in C. Lashley and A. Morrison (eds) *In Search of Hospitality: Theoretical Perspectives and Debates*, Oxford: Butterworth-Heinemann, pp. 217–32.

Williams, A. and Zelinsky, W. (1970) 'On some patterns of international tourism flows', *Economic Geography*, 46(4): 549–67.

Williams, A.M. (2004) 'Toward a political economy of tourism', in A. Lew, C.M. Hall and A.M. Williams (eds) *Companion to Tourism*, Oxford: Blackwell, pp. 61–73.

Williams, A.M. and Balaz, V. (2000) *Tourism in Transition Economic Change in Central Europe*, London: I.B. Tauris.

Williams, A.M. and Hall, C.M. (2000) 'Tourism and migration: New relationships between production and consumption', *Tourism Geographies*, 2(1): 5–27.

Williams, A.M. and Hall, C.M. (2002) 'Tourism, migration, circulation and mobility: The contingencies of time and place', in C.M. Hall and A.M. Williams (eds) *Tourism and Migration*, Dordrecht: Kluwer.

Williams, A.M. and Morgan, R. (1995) 'Beach awards and rating systems', *Shore and Beach*, 63(4): 29–33.

Williams, A.M. and Shaw, G. (eds) (1988) *Tourism and Economic Development: Western European Experiences*, London: Belhaven Press.

Williams, A.M. and Shaw, G. (eds) (1991) *Tourism and Economic Development: Western European Experiences*, 2nd edn, London: Belhaven Press.

Williams, A.M. and Shaw, G. (1998) 'Tourism and the environment: Sustainability and economic restructuring', in C.M. Hall and A.A. Lew (eds) *Sustainable Tourism Development: Geographical Perspectives*, Harlow: Addison Wesley Longman, pp. 49–59.

Williams, A.M., King, R. and Warnes, A.M. (1997) 'A place in the sun: International retirement migration from Northern to Southern Europe', *European Urban and Regional Studies*, 4: 15–34.

Williams, A.T., Alveirinho-Dias, J., Garcia Novo, F., Garcia-Mora, M., Curr, R. and Pereira, A. (2001) 'Integrated coastal dune management: Checklists', *Continental Shelf Research*, 21: 1937–60.

Williams, C.H. (1985) *Language Planning, Marginality and Regional Development in the Irish Gaeltacht*, Discussion Paper in Geolinguistics No. 10, Stoke-on-

Trent: Department of Geography and Recreation Studies, North Staffordshire Polytechnic.

Williams, D. and Kaltenborn, B. (1999) 'Leisure places and modernity: The use and meaning of recreational cottages in Norway and the USA', in D. Cronin (ed.) *Leisure/Tourism Geographies: Practices and Geographical Knowledge*, London: Routledge, pp. 214–31.

Williams, G.H. (1962) *Wilderness and Paradise in Christian Thought*, New York: Harper & Brothers.

Williams, P. (1978) 'Building societies and the inner city', *Transactions of the Institute of British Geographers*, 3(1): 23–49.

Williams, R. (1976) *Keywords*, London: Fontana.

Williams, S. (1995) *Recreation in the Urban Environment*, London: Routledge.

Williams, S. (1998) *Tourism Geography*, London: Routledge.

Williams, W.M. (1979) 'Some applications in social geography', in P. Whiteley (ed.) *Geography*, London: Sussex Books, pp. 115–26.

Willis, A. (1992) *Women and Crime. Key Findings from the Report on Crime Prevention in the Leicester City Challenge Area*, Leicester: School of Social Work, Leicester University.

Winsberg, M.P. (1966) 'Overseas travel by American civilians since World War II', *Journal of Geography*, 65: 73–9.

Winter, M. (1987) 'Farm-based tourism and conservation in the uplands', *Ecos: A Review of Conservation*, 5(3): 10–15.

Winterbottom, D. (1967) 'How much urban space do we need', *Journal of the Royal Town Planning Institute*, 53: 144–7.

Wirth, L. (1938) 'Urbanism as a way of life', *American Journal of Sociology*, 44: 1–24

Withington, W. (1961) 'Upland resorts and tourism in Indonesia: Some recent trends', *Geographical Review*, 51: 418–23.

Withyman, W. (1985) 'The ins and outs of international travel and tourism data', *International Tourism Quarterly*, Special Report No. 55.

Witt, S. and Martin, C. (1989) 'Demand forecasting in tourism and recreation', in C.P. Cooper (ed.) *Progress in Tourism, Recreation and Hospitality Management*, Vol. 1, London: Belhaven Press, pp. 4–32.

Witt, S. and Martin, C. (1992) *Modelling and Forecasting Demand in Tourism*, London: Academic Press.

Witt, S., Brooke, M. and Buckley, P. (1991) *The Management of International Tourism*, London: Routledge.

Wolfe, R.J. (1951) 'Summer cottages in Ontario', *Economic Geography*, 27(1): 10–32.

Wolfe, R.J. (1952) 'Wasage Beach: The divorce from the geographic environment', *Canadian Geographer*, 1(2): 57–65.

Wolfe, R.J. (1964) 'Perspectives on outdoor recreation: A bibliographical survey', *Geographical Review*, 54(2): 203–38.

Wolfe, R.J. (1966) 'Recreational travel: The new migration', *Canadian Geographer*, 10: 1–14.

Wolfe, R.J. (1967) 'Recreational travel: The new migration', *Geographical Bulletin*, 9: 73–9.

Wolfe, R.J. (1970) 'Discussion of vacation homes, environmental preferences and spatial behaviour', *Journal of Leisure Research*, 2(1): 85–7.

Women's Equality Unit (1993) *Women and Safety Project*, Leicester: Leicester City Council.

Wong, J. and Law, R. (2003) 'Difference in shopping satisfaction levels: a study of tourists in Hong Kong', *Tourism Management*, 24(4): 401–10.

Wong, P.P. (1986) 'Tourism development and resorts on the east coast of Peninsula Malaysia'. *Singapore Journal of Tropical Geography*, 7(2): 152–62.

Wong, P.P. (1990) 'Recreation in the coastal areas of Singapore', in P. Fabbri (ed.) *Recreational Use of Coastal Areas*, Dordrecht: Kluwer, pp. 53–62.

Wong, P.P. (1993a) 'Island tourism development in Peninsula Malaysia: Environmental perspective', in P. Wong (ed.) *Tourism vs Environment: The Case for Coastal Areas*, Dordrecht: Kluwer, pp. 83–98.

Wong, P.P. (ed.) (1993b) *Tourism vs Environment: The Case for Coastal Areas*, Dordrecht: Kluwer.

Wong, P. (2003) 'Where have al the beaches gone? Coastal erosion in the tropics', Singapore *Journal of Tropical Geography* 24(1)111–32.

Wong, P.P. (2004) 'Environmental impacts of tourism', in A. Lew, C.M. Hall and A. Williams (eds) *Companion to Tourism*, Oxford: Blackwell, pp. 450–61.

Woo, Kyung-Sik (1996) 'Korean tourists' urban activity patterns in New Zealand', unpublished research report, Master of Business Studies, Massey University at Albany, Auckland, NZ.

Wood, R.E. (2000) 'Caribbean cruise tourism: Globalization at sea', *Annals of Tourism Research*, 27(2): 345–70.

Woods, B. (2000) 'Beauty and the beast: Preferences for animals in Australia', *Journal of Tourism Studies*, 11(2): 25–35.

Woolley, H. and Noor-Ul-Amin (1999) 'Pakistani

teenagers' use of public open space in Sheffield', *Managing Leisure*, 4(3): 156–67.

World Tourism Organisation (WTO) (1981) *Guidelines for the Collection and Presentation of Domestic and International Tourism Statistics*, Madrid: WTO.

World Tourism Organisation (1983) *Definitions Concerning Tourism Statistics*, Madrid: WTO.

World Tourism Organisation (1985) *The Role of Transnational Tourism Enterprises in the Development of Tourism*, Madrid: WTO.

World Tourism Organisation (1991a) *Guidelines for the Collection and Presentation of Domestic and International Tourism Statistics*, Madrid: WTO.

World Tourism Organisation (1991b) *Resolutions of International Conference on Travel and Tourism, Ottawa, Canada*, Madrid: WTO.

World Tourism Organisation (1996) *International Tourism Statistics*, Madrid: WTO.

World Tourism Organisation (1998) 'WTO revises forecasts for Asian tourism', Press Release, 27 January, Madrid: WTO.

World Tourism Organization (1999) *Tourism Satellite Account: The Conceptual Framework*, Madrid: WTO.

World Tourism Organisation (2001) 'Millennium tourism boom in 2001', Press Release, 31 January, Madrid: WTO.

World Tourism Organisation (2003) *Climate Change and Tourism*, Madrid: WTO.

World Tourism Organisation (2004a) 'Global troubles took toll on tourism in 2003, growth to resume in 2004', WTO New Release, 27 January, Madrid: WTO.

World Tourism Organisation (2004b) 'Spectacular rebound of international tourism in 2004', WTO New Release, 27 October, Madrid: WTO.

World Travel and Tourism Council (WTTC) (2000) 'Tourism satellite accounting confirms travel and tourism as world's foremost economic activity', WTTC Press Release, 11 May.

World Travel and Tourism Council (2001a) 'World Travel and Tourism Council forecast places tourism among leading economic and employment generators', WTTC Press Release, 8 May.

World Travel and Tourism Council (2001b) 'Demographic trends and economic research lead international tourism conferences', WTTC Press Release, 7 May.

Worster, D. (1977) *Nature's Economy: A History of Ecological Ideas*, Cambridge: Cambridge University Press.

Worster, D. (ed.) (1988) *The Ends of the Earth: Perspectives on Modern Environmental History*, Cambridge: Cambridge University Press.

Wrathall, J.E. (1980) 'Farm-based holidays', *Town and Country Planning*, 49(6): 194–5.

Wright, D. (trans.) (1957) *Beowulf*, Harmondsworth: Penguin.

Wright, J. (1980) 'Wilderness, waste and history', *Habitat*, 8(1): 27–31.

Wrigley, G.M. (1919) 'Fairs of the Central Andes', *Geographical Review*, 2: 65–80.

Wu, C-T. (1982) 'Issues of tourism and socioeconomic development', *Annals of Tourism Research*, 9: 317–30.

Yilmaz, S. and Zengin, M. (2003) 'User surveys of Erzincan's urban parks', *Pakistan Journal of Applied Sciences*, 3(1): 47–51.

Young, G. (1973) *Tourism: Blessing or Blight*, Harmondsworth: Penguin.

Young, M. and Wilmott, P. (1973) *The Symmetrical Family*, London: Routledge & Kegan Paul.

Young, T. (1996) 'Modern urban parks', *Geographical Review*, 85(4): 535–51.

Yüksel, A. (2004) 'Shopping experience evaluation: A case of domestic and international visitors', *Tourism Management*, in press.

Zetter, F. (1971) *The Evolution of Country Park Policy*, Cheltenham: Countryside Commission.

Zhang, H.Q., Chong, K. and Ap, J. (1999) 'An analysis of tourism policy development in modern China', *Tourism Management*, 20: 471–85.

Zurick, D.N. (1992) 'Adventure travel and sustainable tourism in the peripheral economy of Nepal', *Annals of the Association of American Geographers*, 82: 608–28.

Zuzanek, J., Beckers, T. and Peters, P. (1998) 'The "harried leisure class" revisited: Dutch and Canadian trends in the use of time from the 1970s to the 1990s', *Leisure Studies*, 17(1): 1–20.

INDEX

accessibility 103, 114, 186
accommodation 132–5
Africa 1
Agarwal, S. 110
Aitchison, C. 47
Alpine areas 288–9
Antarctic 332, 332
applied geography 18–9, 20–4, 345–6
Arctic 289
Arctic Climate Impact Assessment (ACIA) 289
Asia 301
Argyle, M. 43, 45
Ashworth, G.J. 198, 213
Asia 1
Association of American Geographers 1
Australia 23, 54–8, 246, 247, 257–9, 269–78, 281, 311
    New South Wales 54–8, 211
        Armidale 211
    Queensland
        Gold Coast 156
        Sunshine Coast 156
    South Australia
        Kangaroo Island 153, 154
aviation 111–2

Bailie, J.G. 162
Barnes, B. 25
barriers, see constraints
Baum, E.L. 338
behavioural geography 18, 159
Bennett, A. 299
Benson, J. 310
Board, C 10
Boo, E. 283
boosterism 323
Bramwell, B. 229
brands 245
Britain, see United Kingdom
Britton, S.G. 28, 114, 120, 121
Brown, R.M. 9

Bureau of Industry Economics 247
Burkart, A. 76
bushwalking 54–8
Butler, R.W. 112–3, 223, 227, 229, 242, 250, 251, 343

Canada 238, 249, 257–9, 283, 311
    Alberta
        Edmonton 139
    British Columbia
        Vancouver 173
    Newfoundland
        St John's 311
    Ontario 249
        Niagara 249
        Ottawa 203–4
    Quebec 283
        Montreal 176
Canada Land Inventory 98
capital cities 203–4
Caribbean 1
carrying capacity 147–9, 235–6
Carter, R. 308
Carver, S. 253
catering facilities 135–7
Ceballos-Lacuarain, H. 149
central place theory 99–100
Champion, A.G. 251
city as theme park 200
Clark, G. 229, 242
Clark, J. 177
Clawson, M. 94
climate change 288–9
Cloke, P. 225,
coastal environment 168–70, 291–6
coastal and marine tourism and recreation 291–314
cognitive mapping 208–13
Cohen, E. 71
Commission for Architecture and the Built Environment (CABE) 179
community-based tourism 326

Computer Reservation Systems (CRS) 115
constraints 41–53, 186–7
Cooper, C.P. 69
Coppock, J.T. 35, 37, 58, 156, 173, 223, 239
Cosgrove, I. 6
coral reef 168, 169
Council of Nature Conservation Ministers
        (CONCOM) 269, 277
country parks 106–8
Countryside Agency 98, 107, 180, 319
countryside recreation and tourism, see rural recreation
        and tourism
Crap Towns 213
Crichter, C. 177
critical geography 114–8
crowding 284–6
cruise tourism 311–2
cultural geography 8, 46–7, 141
cultures of heteropolis 200

Dann, G. 71
demand 33–91, 278–84
demographic change 355–6
Denmark 238, 308
Department of Tourism (Australia) 338
dependency theory 121–2
destination life-cycle 112–4
Deutsch, K. 329
developing countries 120
distance-decay 52, 113, 302
Doornkamp, J. 348
Duffield, B. 35, 37, 58
Dunphy, M. 54–7

economic impacts of tourism and recreation 1–2,
        154–8, 242–3
    employment 1–2
ecotourism 173, 283–4
Edmonton Mall 139
Edwards, J. 83
empiricism 7–8
enclave model 121
English Historic Towns Forum 138, 140,
environmental determinism and possibilism 14
environmental history 262–3
environmental impacts of tourism and recreation
        165–70, 240, 307–9, 312
    research problems 165–6
    in coastal environment 168–70, 307–9, 312
    in urban environment 167
    in rural environment 240, 244
environmentalism 165, 179
Enzenbacher, D. 332
Europe 1, 45
events 157, 158

excursionist 6
exploration and geography 14

fantasy city 200, 201
farm tourism 243–4, see also rural tourism
farmers' markets 247
Featherstone, M. 4
Finland 238
food tourism 244–9
fortified city 200
Fox, A.M. 264
Freeman, T.W. 12, 14

gender 45–7
Geographical Information Systems (GIS) 22, 276,
        350–2
Geography
    disciplinary characteristics 11–6, 343–7, 352–5
    skills 348–50
geography of fear 46–50
geography of tourism and recreation
    development of 2–3, 8–11, 28–30, 96
    position within Geography 2–3, 10, 25–6, 352–5,
        356–7
    sociology of knowledge of 7–8, 10–30
Germany 309
Getz, D. 128, 323
Giddens, A. 7
Glacken, C. 255, 256
Glasson, J. 213
Global Distribution Systems 115
global environmental change 288–9
globalisation 118–9
Glyptis, S. 94
Grano, O. 12
Great Western Railway (GWR) 299
green belts 105–8, see also open space, urban parks
Greenland 289

Hall, C.M. 7, 13, 114, 250, 251, 329, 339, 346
Hall, P. 321
Harrison, C. 107,
Harvey, D. 125, 347
Haughton, G. 329
Hägerstrand, T. 7
health 162
Heclo, H. 329
Henry, I. 315
Herbert, D.T. 3
heritage 162, 213–5
hierarchy of needs 37–40, 70
Higham, J.E.S. 279–80, 282
historical geography 33–4, 298
hospitality 135–8
hotel chains 119–22

Hudson, R. 156
humanistic geography 8, 18
Hunter, C. 329

identity 8
indicators 328
indigenous peoples 162, 267–9
Institutional arrangements 320–1
interdictory space 200
International Association of Antarctic Tour Operators
    (IAATO) 332
International Geographical Union 23, 27
international tourism arrivals 1
integrated coastal zone management 309–11

Jackson, R. 6
Janiskee, R. 24
Jansen-Verbeke, M. 208
Jenkins, J. 36, 92, 339
Jenkins, W.I. 337
Johnston, R. 11, 16, 21, 25, 27, 344
journey to play 302

Kearsley, G.W. 287
Knetsch, J. 94

landscape 47, 97–9
Law, C.M. 111, 207
Leiper, N. 71, 130, 131
Leisure
    definition of 3–7
    needs 39
    participation 41, 50–2
    policy 101, 315–20
    product 122–3
    relationship to tourism and recreation 3–7,
        122–3
    services 96
    time-budget 58
leisure ladder 73
Lesslie, R. 270, 276, 277
Lew, A.A. 13, 130
Lewis, G.J. 209
life-cycle 40
Limits of Acceptable Change (LAC) 150–1
Livingstone, D. 353
local government 95–6, 176
locales 229
location 97–102
Long, P.T. 338
low-cost carriers 111–2
Lynch, K. 210–1

Madge, C. 49
Mandell, M.P. 331

Marsh, G.P. 260
Martin, W. 44
Mason, S. 44
Maslow, A. 37–40, 70
Medlik, S. 76,
Meethan, K. 201
Mercer, D. 321
Middle East 1
migration 117–8, 240
Millennium Green (MG) 180
Minerbi, L. 169
Mitchell, L.S. 2, 13, 24, 26
mobility 6–7
Moore, E.J. 338
Moran, W. 245
Mullins, P. 156
multiplier 155–5
Murphy, A. 1
Murphy, P.E. 13

Nash, R. 254
National Capital Commission (Ottawa) 203, 204
national parks 55–7, 147, 253–87
National Oceanic and Atmospheric Administration
    (NOAA) 292, 313
Netherlands 207–8
New Labour 179
New Zealand 23, 86–9, 166, 238, 257–9, 267–8,
    279–80, 282, 286, 287, 303
    Auckland 190
Norkunas, M. 214
North America 1
Nuckolls, J.S. 338

O'Riordan, T. 165, 320
Office of National Tourism 284
open space 179–80, 181–5, 191, 192–6 see also green
    belt, national parks, urban parks
Ovington, J.D. 264
Owens, P. 228, 233, 235, 238

Pacific 168
Pacione, M. 21, 24, 345
Page, S.J. 172
Parker, S. 4
parks, see national parks, urban parks
passive recreation 37
Patmore, J. 43, 44, 57, 174, 188, 234, 302
Pearce, D.G. 13, 87, 123, 127, 291
Pearce, P.L. 71
Penning-Rowsell, E. 304
Perkins, H. 227, 228
Pigram, J.J. 6, 36, 92, 223
place 46, 209
place promotion 298–300

Place, S.E. 283
Plog, S. 71, 72
Poland 63–4
    Warsaw 189–90
policy, see leisure policy, tourism policy
postmodern city 200–1
Powell, J.M. 353
privatopia 200

radical geographies 19
railways 299–300
Ravenscroft, N. 318
recreation
    accessibility 44–5, 186
constraints and opportunities 41–53
    decision-making 36
    definition of, 3–7
    demand 35–7, 45, 57–67, 233–6
    environments 97–8
    facilities 101, 190
    motivation 40
    participation 41, 44, 50–2
    planning 144–54, 188–96, 315–20
    resources 93–7, 103, 104–5, 144, 187, 292–4
    supply 92–109, 236–7
Recreational Business District, see Tourism Business
        District
Recreation Opportunity Spectrum (ROS) 150
recreation resource typology 187, 188
recreational conflict 109
regeneration 140, 197
regional geography 15–16
resort development 6, 176, 298–300, 301
Rights-of-way 44–5
Robinson, G.M. 224, 234
Roe, M. 310
Royal Geographical Society 14
rural recreation and tourism 94, 223–252
    definitional issues 224–6
    demand 233–6
    development of 232–3, 340–1
    impact 237–8, 240–4
    supply 236–7
rurality, concept of 224–30
Russia 35

Sadler, D. 125
sand cays 168
Sant, M. 22,
scale 7–8
seasonality 43–4
second homes 52, 238–40
service quality 216–7
sex tourism 162, 163–4, 301
Shaw, G. 110, 123, 157

Short, R. 53
Shucksmith, M. 238
Sinclair, M.T. 109
Singapore 334–5
site studies 234
site surveys 65–7
Slatyer, R. 261
Smith, R.V. 10, 13
Smith, S.L.J. 35, 95
social exclusion 50–2
social impacts of tourism and recreation 159–64, 240
    community attitudes 161
    crime 162
South Africa 213
South America 1
South Asia 1
space 47
spatial analysis 18
spatial fixity 110
Spink, J. 315
Stabler, M. 109
Stamp, D.H. 348
Stansfield, C. 113
Stebbins, R.A. 4,
sustainable tourism 250–1, 327–4
Sweden 52, 238, 239–40, 261–2

territorial justice 102
Thailand 164
time-budget 7, 58–60
tourism
    attractions 130–2
    definition 3–7, 75–8, 205–6
    demand 67–75, 233–6
    development 121, 123–7, 161, 240
    domestic 79–80, 86–9
    experiences 201–3
    facilities 127–30, 132–8
    industry 110
    international 1, 81–6, 119–22, 322
    and leisure product 122–3
    marketing 204
    motivation 68–73
    planning 188–96, 217–9, 320–35, 339–42
    policy 124, 126–7, 335–42
    production 114–8
    statistics 73–84
    supply 109–42, 284–7
    time budget 58–69
    workforce 116–8
Tourism Business District 127–30, 301–2
Tourism Geographies 26
Tourism Optimisation Management Model 151–4
tourism satellite account 1
tourism transaction chains 115

tourist
  behaviour 303–7
  perception and cognition 208–13
  shopping 138–41
Towner, J. 232
Townsend, A. 156
trafficking 163–4
transport 111–2
Tuan, Y-F. 255
Tunbridge, J.E. 204, 213
Tunstall, S. 304
Turkey 101
  Ankara 101–2
Turner, R.K. 165

United Kingdom 44, 47–50, 59–62, 174–5, 177–9,
    232, 243, 304, 305
  Jersey 304
  Leicester 47–50, 181–5
  Loch Lomond 147
  London 64–5, 105, 107–8, 133–5, 192–6
United States of America 62–3, 164, 239, 257–9, 267,
    289
  Atlantic City 113
  California 294–6
  San Francisco 176
urban fringe 104–5
urban parks 47–50, 100, 173 see also green belts, open
    space
urban recreation and tourism 122–3, 127–30, 132–8,
    167, 172–222
  analysis of 172–3, 185–8, 198–201
  behavioural issues 201–3, 206–8, 208–13
  evolution of 174–5, 177–9, 197–8
  planning of 188–96, 217–9
Urry, J. 110, 226

Vaske, J.J.
visitor management 217–9
visual culture 141

walking 53–4, 54–8
Wall, G. 302
Walmesley, D.J. 209
welfare geography 102
White, G. 343
wilderness 253–90
  demand 278–84
  inventory 269–78
  meaning of 253–61
  supply 284–7
  values 263–7, 279
Williams, A. 10
Williams, A.M. 110, 123, 157
Williams, S. 174
wine tourism 244–9
Withyman, W. 81
World Heritage Convention 261–2
World Tourism Organisation (WTO) 1, 76–7, 79, 80,
    86
World Travel and Tourism Council (WTTC) 1

Zelinsky, W. 10